DUMBARTON OAKS STUDIES

❧ I ❧

JUSTIN
THE FIRST

JUSTIN
THE FIRST

An Introduction to the Epoch of

Justinian the Great

by

A. A. VASILIEV

HARVARD UNIVERSITY PRESS

Cambridge, Massachusetts

1950

Preface

For several years I have been planning to write a monograph on the reign of Justin I (518–527) as an introduction to the epoch of his brilliant nephew Justinian, whose spectacular era quite overshadowed the nine years of the reign of his elderly uncle. I thought that a detailed monograph on Justin might serve as an essential basis for a better understanding and a more profound interpretation of the epoch of Justinian whose rule, behind the throne, of course, started, in my opinion, from the moment of Justin's elevation. Such a monograph might stimulate some scholars to embark on a new study of Justinian's period, a work which is urgently needed, even though we have studies by Charles Diehl, J. B. Bury, W. G. Holmes and others. This task, it is true, will require quite a few years of assiduous and hard work which should deal not only with the external affairs or the problems of Byzantine art, which we know rather well, but also with the social-economic conditions of the empire, with the growing feudalizing processes within it, with the complicated theological situation in the country in which the emperor himself was an accomplished theologian, with his colossal legislative production, and finally, with the general cultural environment which was an extremely complicated conglomeration of diverse elements going back to classical times, to the oriental influences, and to the various irreconcilable theological problems.

As I have pointed out in my book (pp. 6–7), there is no special study on Justin's reign, and the general histories of the Byzantine Empire devote just a few pages to his period. My book of more than four hundred pages on the nine years of Justin's reign may seem to be too lengthy. But my aim has not been to compile mere *Jahrbücher*. In order to render comprehensible the full significance of his reign, I have been compelled at many points to turn back to previous times and also to look ahead to events which took place after Justin's death.

I think I have used all the primary sources on the subject, with perhaps a few omissions; but as to secondary works, I am sure that I have missed several new publications, because of the unavailability of European books immediately after the war, and only lately have I become acquainted with recent works; therefore some books and articles have almost certainly escaped my attention.

I have also indicated in my study (p. 7) that the second volume of Ernst Stein's work *Geschichte des spätrömischen Reiches* is soon to be published, and that this book would certainly contain a chapter devoted to the reign of Justin I. Now I have been informed that this volume, written in French and entitled *L'histoire du Bas-Empire*, has appeared in Belgium. Unfortunately I have not yet seen it, but I may hope that the chapter on Justin I in Stein's book will not render my researches absolutely useless; especially because I am aware of his general estimate of Justin's reign as it is revealed in his very substantial article, in fact brief monograph, "Justinus," compiled by him for Pauly-Wissowa-Kroll, *Real-Encyclopädie der classischen Altertumswissenschaft*, X (1919), 1314–1329.

I tender my warmest thanks to Mrs. Ednah Shepard Thomas, my faithful collaborator and friend of many years, who, with remarkable conscientiousness, has revised my manuscript and corrected the inadequacies of my English.

My grateful acknowledgments are also due the Dumbarton Oaks Research Library and Collection of Harvard University which accepted this book as the first item in the series entitled *Dumbarton Oaks Studies*.

A. A. VASILIEV

Dumbarton Oaks,
Harvard University
December, 1949

CONTENTS

CONTENTS

JUSTIN THE FIRST

Historical Background

The Roman Empire in 518, when Justin started his reign, did not differ in extent from the Roman Empire at the close of the fifth century, under his predecessor Anastasius I. All western European provinces were occupied by the Germanic tribes of the Franks, Burgundians, and Visigoths; the western coastline of North Africa was in the hands of the Vandals; the Appenine Peninsula, with the regions lying along the upper course of the Danube and the northern section of the eastern littoral of the Adriatic Sea, belonged to the Ostrogoths. The islands in the western Mediterranean, Sicily, Sardinia, Corsica, the Balearic Isles, were also under Germanic domination. In reality, the Roman Empire in 518 consisted only of the eastern fraction of the territory known by that name. But this fraction, comprising the Balkans, Greece, the islands of the Aegean Sea, the Crimean Peninsula in the northern basin of the Black Sea, some regions in Transcaucasia, for instance a part of Armenia, the whole of Asia Minor, Syria with a section of Mesopotamia, Palestine, and Egypt, composed a vast area involved in various important political, economic, and religious problems, which during Justin's rule became increasingly difficult.

No special monograph on Justin's period has yet been published. In studies on Justinian the Great and in the general histories of Byzantium, Justin's reign has always been briefly sketched as an introduction to the brilliant epoch of his nephew and immediate successor, Justinian, who "already seemed to be the soul of Justin's rule." Justin has been considered merely a prologue to Justinian, his rule but "the preface to a great reign," his period only one of anticipation, "un règne d'attente." [1]

Of course Justin's rule was unquestionably an introduction to that of Justinian; but it was an introduction of vital importance. It cleared the ground and laid a firm foundation for Justin's successor, and we should remember that Justinian's influence behind the throne was predominant from the opening years of Justin's reign, so that when

[1] L. Ranke, *Weltgeschichte*, IV, 2 (Leipzig, 1888), 12. J. Calmette, *Le monde féodal* (Paris, 1933), p. 62. N. Iorga, "La littérature byzantine," *Revue historique du sud-est européen*, II (1925), 391. A. Bailly, *Byzance* (Paris, 1939), p. 61.

Justinian wore the purple alone he was continuing policies already inaugurated. In 518 when Justin was chosen emperor, Justinian (born in 482) was already a mature man of about thirty-six. He had been thoroughly trained in the fields of theology and jurisprudence, and he had already formed high political ambitions. His strong personality must have played an extremely important part during the nine years of Justin's reign. This unquestionable influence on Justin's period, however, has not yet been adequately appreciated or emphasized, and the whole period deserves a special study.

With Justin's accession in 518 the government abandoned the monophysite policy of his predecessors and began a new Roman policy. During Justin's reign the monophysite elements in the east underwent severe persecution which undermined the political and economic foundation of the Empire in Syria and Palestine, those two very essential provinces of the Empire, although Egypt, as granary for the capital, was spared and was not disturbed. A man without theological education and without interest in the complicated subtleties of the religious problems of his time, Justin naturally left the religious policy of his administration, which was indissolubly connected with political interests, to his nephew, who at the time was already an accomplished theologian. Justinian's objective at the moment was the reëstablishment of normal relations with the Papacy. This not only showed a new religious orientation of Justin's government but also was a most important foundation for Justinian's future vast plans for the reconquest of the West, which, though they were never to be realized, were already forming in his mind during the preparatory period of his uncle's reign.

During Justin's rule a new page opened in the history of the Balkans. It was the beginning of the dense penetration and permanent settlements of the Slavs south of the Danube; from this time on, according to Uspensky, "the southern Slavs are entitled to begin their national history." [2] The Slavonic problem in the Balkans, which became firmly established during Justin's rule, was destined to have a further striking development under Justinian and his successors.

[2] Théodore Uspensky, *A History of the Byzantine Empire* (St. Petersburg, 1914), p. 464.

Justin's relations with the far south, with monophysite Abyssinia, where he appeared not as the defender of the official Chalcedonian credo which was energetically imposed within the boundaries of his empire but as the protector of Christianity in general, have left a deep impress upon Abyssinian historical tradition. At one of the most important periods in the national history of Ethiopia, when the so-called Solomonian dynasty ascended the throne in the thirteenth century, Abyssinian writers turned to the origin of the political power of their country, and emphatically stated that the political power of Abyssinia originated from the division of the earth between Justin I and their king, Kaleb. This story as it is given in *Kebra Nagast* (*The Glory of the Kings*), one of the most important works of Ethiopian literature, is of course merely a legend; but the legend goes back to the historical fact of the political, religious, and economic relations of Justin with Abyssinia. These will be discussed in detail below.

In spite of some rather tense relations with Sassanian Persia, the permanent foe and rival of the Byzantine Empire, Justin, during most of his rule, had no serious difficulty in maintaining the peace. Only at the very end of his reign did trouble break out.

The new dynasty represented by Justin I, his nephew Justinian, and Justinian's nephew Justin II (518–578), was of western origin, since its founder Justin originated from the province of Dardania in the West Balkans. He was, in other words, of barbarian origin, and belonged to a humble class, being probably a herdsman. The new dynasty had no connection with the East, and this fact was extremely important for Justin's rule. But in this respect the new dynasty was not unusual, because no emperor since Diocletian had been of eastern origin, with the single exception of Zeno the Isaurian, and many emperors had belonged to the lower classes. The new democratic dynasty inaugurated by the former herdsman occupied the throne sixty years, and its last representative, Justin II, secured the throne in 565 without a struggle.

There is no clear evidence that during Justin's rule there was any serious clash between him and the nobility represented by high-ranking officials and larger landowners, although, as one writer says, they always hated the upstart house of Justin.[3] A class struggle manifested itself later, between Justin's successor Justinian and the great landed proprietors, and this class struggle was one of the characteristic features of the social problems of Justinian's time.

In our sources Justin I is sometimes called Ἰουστῖνος ὁ μέγας, Justin the Great or Justin the Elder, while Justin II is named Ἰουστῖνος ὁ μικρός, that is, Justin the Younger.

Justin I was not a strong personality capable of conceiving vast horizons and broad plans. At his accession he was already an old man, sixty-six or sixty-eight years of age. His previous career had passed in military service, which had made him a good soldier, an efficient commander, but not a great statesman. From the opening years of his rule, therefore, he was dominated by the influence of his nephew Justinian, and the nine years of his reign were in reality nine years of unofficial rule by Justinian. By giving this book the subtitle *An Introduction to the Epoch of Justinian the Great*, I have wished to emphasize that the rule of Justinian really began behind the throne in 518, and that the reign of Justin I is to be regarded as the unofficial reign of Justinian. During this time all Justinian's principal ideas, his ambitious political plans of reconquest, his conception of a colossal legislative work, his building activities, especially the fortifications for the protection of his future empire, and his new religious orientation as one of the foundations for his future western campaigns — all these were definitely formulated. The nine years of Justin's rule are of utmost value for our better understanding of the manifold activities of his brilliant nephew. By studying the time of Justin we lay a foundation for our comprehension of the time of Justinian.

As I have noted above, there is no special monograph study on Justin's reign. The most detailed description of his rule, based on pri-

---

[3] H. Moss, *The Birth of the Middle Ages 395-814* (London, 1935), p. 84. A rather unusual interpretation of Justin's accession, which may be mentioned here as a curiosity, is presented by Rev. W. A. Wigram, who writes: "The accession of Justin and the Dacian dynasty makes a change in the foreign and ecclesiastical politics of the Empire that can only be compared to a change of trumps at whist. All the old figures remain, but their values and relations to one another have undergone a radical change, and the change has lasting results on the subject of this history." Rev. W. A. Wigram, *The Separation of the Monophysites* (London, 1923), p. 65.

mary sources and still useful, is found in the old French work of Lebeau, *Histoire du Bas-Empire*, new edition by M. de Saint Martin, VIII (Paris, 1827), 6–85. Among recent publications there is a very substantial article, in fact a brief monograph, "Justinus," compiled by Ernst Stein for Pauly-Wissowa-Kroll *Real-Encyclopädie der classischen Altertumswiessenschaft*, X (1919), coll. 1314–1329. Useful chapters are to be found in W. G. Holmes, *The Age of Justinian and Theodora*, 2nd ed., I (London, 1912), 299–320, and in J. Kulakovsky, *History of Byzantium*, II (Kiev, 1912), 1–36 (in Russian). Very brief sketches of no particular importance can be read in Charles Diehl, *Justinian et la civilisation byzantine au VIe siècle* (Paris, 1901), pp. 5–8; J. B. Bury, *History of the Later Roman Empire*, II (London, 1923), 16–23; Théodore Uspensky, *A History of the Byzantine Empire*, I (St. Petersburg, 1914), 410–412 (in Russian). In the most recent general history of the Byzantine Empire, L. Bréhier devotes to Justin's reign hardly a page: *Vie et mort de Byzance* (Paris, 1947), pp. 21–22. Of course occasional references to Justin's reign are to be found throughout these works.

It was known among scholars that the very eminent German historian Ernst Stein had for some time been working on the second volume of his history of the Byzantine Empire. The first volume, already published (*Geschichte des spätrömischen Reiches*, I, Vienna, 1928), covers the period from 284 to 476, that is, to the so-called fall of the Western Roman Empire. Without doubt the second volume includes Justin's period. To our great regret Stein died in Switzerland on February 25, 1945. But we have now the very encouraging news that he completed the second volume before his death. It is written in French (*Histoire de l'empire byzantin*) and is soon to be published under the editorship of M. Palanque.[4] It is my personal hope that the chapter devoted to the reign of Justin in Stein's forthcoming work will not render absolutely useless my own present study.

[4] See *Études byzantines*, III (Bucarest, 1945), 275.

CHAPTER ONE

Survey of the Sources

Greek Sources

The reign of Justin I had a contemporary historian, Hesychius of Miletus surnamed *Illustris*, who wrote a history of the reign of Justin and of the early years of Justinian. Unfortunately this work is completely lost, although in the ninth century the patriarch Photius, who had read it, kept it in his own library. All that we know about Hesychius comes to us from Photius and Suidas. Photius in his valuable work *Myriobiblon sive Bibliotheca* reports that Hesychius, son of Hesychius and Philosophia (Sophia), was the author of two important works: A *Compendium of Universal History* in six books from the time of ancient Assyria to the death in 518 of the Emperor Anastasius, whom Justin succeeded; and the *History* of Justin and the early years of Justinian, mentioned above.[1] The lexicographer of the tenth century, Suidas, mentions a third work, A *Biographical Dictionary* ('Ονοματο-λόγος or Πίναξ) *of Learned Men*, which he largely incorporated in his *Lexicon*.[2] A considerable fragment has been preserved from the sixth book of Hesychius' *Universal History* entitled Πάτρια Κωνσταντινουπό-λεως.[3] But the *History* of Justine is completely lost, and this is particularly regrettable because Photius not only praises Hesychius' style but also credits him with historical veracity.[4] Photius ends his comment on Hesychius with the statement that the death of his son John deeply

---

[1] Photius, *Bibliotheca*, cod. 69, ed. I. Bekker (Berlin, 1824), p. 34; Migne, *PG*, CIII, 165–168.

[2] Suidas, *Lexicon*, 'Ησύχιος Μιλήσιος; ed. Ada Adler, II (Leipzig, 1931), 594. Suidas briefly describes Hesychius' *Universal History* but fails to mention his book on the reign of Justin.

[3] See T. Preger, *Scriptores originum Constantinopolitanarum*, I (Leipzig, 1901), 1–18; see preface, pp. iii–viii.

[4] ὑπισχνεῖται δὲ καὶ ἀληθείας εἶναι φροντιστής.

9

affected Hesychius and prevented him from doing any further writing.[5]

The special contemporary historian of the epoch of Justinian was Procopius of Caesarea, who died about 562, and whose works have survived. He must be regarded also as a contemporary historian of Justin I, and his works give us much interesting material for Justin's period. In the eight books of his history of Justinian's wars with the Persians, Vandals, and Goths, the first four, which deal with the Persians and Vandals, are very important for the period of Justin. They give information about Justin's military career before his elevation, his attitude towards the Persian king, Cawades, his military campaigns and diplomatic activities, Justinian's elevation to the imperial power, and Justin's death. The last four books, which deal with the Goths, do not mention Justin. Procopius' work *On the Buildings*, which is a panegyric of Justinian and was probably written at his special order, contains some mention of buildings erected during Justin's reign. But Procopius' most important work for Justin's period is his famous *Secret History* or *Anecdota*, which differs strikingly from the two other works because it is a scandalous pamphlet directed against Justinian, his wife Theodora, their entourage, and Justinian's despotic government in general. The thesis of the *Secret History*, Bury says, was "that in all acts of his public policy Justinian was actuated by two motives, rapacity and an inhuman delight in evil-doing and destruction," and Runciman calls the book "an embittered conglomeration of gossip." [6] But if we allow for the bias of the *Secret History* and use it cautiously, this work is to be regarded as one of the most substantial sources for the sixth century. Procopius' hatred of Justinian does not dispose him to benevolence towards Justin either, who is portrayed as an entirely uneducated man, "a stupid donkey," who signs decrees with a stencil, and whose wife, his former concubine

---

[5] See Krumbacher. *Geschichte der byzantinischen Litteratur von Justinian bis zum Ende des Oströmischen Reiches*, 527–1453 (München, 1891), pp. 323–325. Montelatici, *Storia della letteratura bizantina* (Milan, 1916), pp. 63–64. A. Vasiliev, *Histoire de l'Empire Byzantin*, I (Paris, 1932), 240; Spanish edition, I (Barcelona, 1946), 228.

[6] Bury, *History of the Later Roman Empire*, II, 423. S. Runciman, *Byzantine Civilization* (London, 1933), p. 243.

Lupicina, was elderly and without capacity for rising to the demands of her high position. This work contains a particularly enjoyable description of Justin's first journey to Byzantium, where he was destined to become emperor, a record of his death, and some other details of his reign, which I shall discuss below. The *Secret History* clearly shows that Justin during all his reign was completely overshadowed by Justinian, and accordingly supplies us with a very solid foundation for our thesis that Justinian's rule unofficially started in 518 when Justin was elected, and not in 527 when Justinian officially became sole emperor.[7]

Another contemporary author who is very important for Justin's period is Peter the Patrician, diplomat and Master of Offices. He composed a *History of the Roman Empire from Augustus to Julian*, of which some fragments have survived. This book has no concern with Justin. But another work, the ceremonial book *Katastasis* (Κατάστασις), which consists of official documents which have been preserved in Constantine Porphyrogenitus' *De cerimoniis*, is extremely interesting for our purpose. One of those official documents, taken from the *Katastasis* of Peter the Patrician and preserved in the *Ceremonies* of Constantine Porphyrogenitus, contains the most detailed description extant of the elevation of Justin to the imperial throne.[8]

Theodore Lector or Anagnostes, a reader (lector) in the Church of St. Sophia in Constantinople, who lived in the first half of the sixth century, composed his *Ecclesiastical History* from 323 to 527, in other words, down to the death of Justin I. His work consists of two very different parts: the first part (four books) is a word-for-word extract from the works of the church historians Socrates, Sozomenos, and Theodoret (the so-called *Historia tripartita*), and the second part (two books) is his own continuation down to 527. The second part, then, and especially the second book of this part, is of great value for the reign of Justin as an independent contemporary source. This work unfortunately has been preserved only in fragments. Fragments from

---

[7] The best edition of Procopius is that in three volumes by J. Haury (Leipzig, 1905–1913). Haury's text, with a very fine English translation, is reproduced in seven volumes by H. B. Dewing (London-Cambridge, Massachusetts, 1914–1940). Volume VII, *Buildings*, is published with the collaboration of Glanville Downey.

[8] *De cerimoniis* I, 93, CSHB (Bonn, 1828–1897), pp. 426–430.

the second part, which is particularly important to us, have survived partly in manuscripts (especially Cod. Barocc. 142) and partly in the works of later Byzantine historians, for instance the church historian of the fourteenth century, Nicephorus Callistus Xanthopulos.

The fragments which concern Justin's period are very scanty; they mention only his political career, his origin, the name of his wife, Lupicina, later Euphemia, Justinian's coöption as Augustus, and Justin's death.[9]

Evagrius Scholasticus of Syria, who died at the close of the sixth century, composed his *Ecclesiastical History* in six books, which narrates events from the Council of Ephesus in 431 to 593. In addition to ecclesiastical history, Evagrius was also interested in the general history of his period. The first nine chapters of the fourth book of his *History* briefly describe Justin's period, mentioning the return of the men who had been exiled by his predecessor Anastasius, listing some natural phenomena such as earthquakes, fires, and floods in various regions of the empire, telling edifying stories about two Palestinian hermits, Zosimas and Johannes Khuzibites, and closing with the coöption of Justinian as Justin's colleague and with Justin's death. Evagrius gives a very useful addition to and confirmation of the facts told by other writers.[10]

Among chroniclers, John Malalas of Antioch, who compiled his chronicle perhaps about 550, is of great value for our study. His chronicle was written in the vulgar tongue with mass appeal; it hit the general taste and became very popular not only in Syria but all over the empire and even beyond its confines, especially in Slavic countries,

[9] Theodore Lector (or Anagnostes), *Ecclesiastical History* in J. A. Cramer, *Anecdota Graeca e codd. manuscriptis Bibliothecae Regiae Parisiensis*, II (Oxford, 1839), 108–109. Migne, *PG*, LXXXI, 1, col. 204 (Lib. II, 37). E. Miller, "Fragments inédits de Théodore le Lecteur et de Jean d'Égée," *Revue archéologique*, XXVI (1873), 400. On Theodore Lector see W. von Christ's *Geschichte der griechischen Litteratur*, umarbeitet von W. Schmid und O. Stählin, 6th ed., second part, *Die nachklassische Periode der griechischen Litteratur*, second half, "von 100 bis 530 nach Christus" (München, 1924), p. 1483 (§ 1086). This book fails to mention the publications of Cramer and Miller.

[10] Evagrius has been best edited by J. Bidez and L. Parmentier (London, 1898); section on Justin, pp. 153–160. The text and a Latin translation are found also in Migne, *PG*, LXXXVI, 2 (unsatisfactory Greek text). On the earlier editions of Evagrius see Bidez and Parmentier, introduction, pp. IX–XII.

where it was widely translated. Malalas' chronicle contains the history of the world from the creation to the close of Justinian's reign. The published text of the chronicle consists of eighteen books; book seventeen is devoted to the period of Justin. It deals with all the significant events of his reign, narrating with special detail natural phenomena such as earthquakes, floods, fires, and celestial signs; but it also includes Justin's relations with Lazica and Persia, and gives a very interesting record of the demes and circus factions in the empire.[11]

The chronicler of the seventh century, John of Antioch, who wrote a general history from Adam to the death of the Emperor Phocas in 610, and whose work has survived only in fragments, may be listed here as mentioning the place of John's birth; this, however, is known from other sources.[12]

The anonymous Easter Chronicle (*Chronicon Paschale*) of the seventh century relates events from Adam to 629 A.D. It fails to give new data on Justin's period but confirms those which we have from other sources. The events of Justin's time are told in chronological order, year after year; the dates are indicated, as usual in this chronicle, by Olympiads, indictions, the years of Justin's reign, and consulships. Of the nine years of his rule, three years only are marked by events; the other six are merely dates.[13]

Later chroniclers have no great significance, merely copying,

---

[11] John Malalas, *Chronographia*, liber XVII, *CSHB* pp. 410–424. Some important new fragments of Malalas' chronicle, from a manuscript of Escurial, in Spain, were published by Theodore Mommsen, "Bruchstücke des Johannes von Antioch und des Johannes Malalas," *Hermes*, VI (1872), 366–383 (Malalas); for Justin, p. 375; republished by Carl de Boor, *Excerpta historica iussu Imp. Constantini Porphyrogeniti*, III, *Excerpta de insidiis* (Berlin, 1905), pp. 151–176; on Justin, pp. 170–171 (fragment 43). Slavonic version of Book XVII in V. M. Istrin, "The Chronicle of John Malalas in the Slavonic Version," *Sbornik Otdeleniya russkago yazika i slovesnosti*, XCI, 2 (Petrograd, 1914), 17–25. An English translation of the Slavonic version of Book XVII by M. Spinka, in collaboration with Glanville Downey, *Chronicle of John Malalas*, books VIII–XVIII (Chicago, 1940), pp. 120–133.

[12] C. Müller, *Fragmenta Historicorum Graecorum*, V, 1 (Paris, 1870), 31 (fr. 214b). Theodore Mommsen, "Bruchstücke des Johannes von Antiochia," *Hermes*, VI, p. 339; reprinted in *Gesammelte Schriften von Th. Mommsen*, VII (Berlin, 1909), 726. On the complicated problem of John of Antioch, see Krumbacher, pp. 334–337; brief treatment by Vasiliev, *Histoire de l'Empire Byzantin*, I, 305 (Spanish edition, I, 290).

[13] *Chronicon Paschale*, *CSHB* I, 611–617.

abridging, or paraphrasing earlier sources. The chronicler Theophanes of the ninth century in his section on Justin I depended on Theodore Lector and even more on John Malalas.[14] To the ninth century also belongs the chronicler George the Monk, surnamed Hamartolus (Georgius Monachus Hamartolus), who compiled a chronicle covering the time from the creation to the death of the Emperor Theophilus in 842. Only one page is dedicated to Justin, and it contains nothing but a list of natural phenomena, such as earthquakes and other disasters.[15]

The tenth century gives us a group of chroniclers represented by four names: Leo the Grammarian; Theodosius of Melitene; the anonymous Continuator of George Hamartolus; and Symeon Magister and Logothete, the so-called Pseudo-Symeon Magister. But they are not original writers; they are all copyists, abbreviators, or revisers of the *Chronicle* of Symeon Logothete, of the tenth century, whose complete original Greek text has not yet been published, though it is fairly well known from many printed excerpts. In addition, this unpublished *Chronicle* has survived in an Old Slavonic version which was published by V. Sreznevsky in 1905. Two of the texts listed above, those of the anonymous Continuator of George Hamartolus and the so-called Pseudo-Symeon Magister, do not concern us because their printed texts begin with the reign of Leo V the Armenian (813–820). The unpublished Greek text of Symeon Logothete, so far as we can judge from its Slavonic version, is best reproduced by Leo the Grammarian, but he fails to supply us with new data. The text of Theodosius of Melitene is nothing but an abbreviation of that of Leo the Grammarian and of the original text of Symeon Logothete in its Slavonic version.[16]

[14] Theophanes, *Chronographia*, ed. Carl de Boor, I, 164–173. In his Latin translation of Theophanes' *Chronicle*, Anastasius Bibliothecarius abridges the Greek text, ed. de Boor (Leipzig, 1885), pp. 130–133.

[15] George the Monk, *Chronicon*, ed. Carl de Boor, II (Leipzig, 1904), 626. The old edition by E. Muralt, *Georgii Monachi dicti Hamartoli Chronicon* (St. Petersburg, 1859), pp. 524–525. Slavonic version of the Chronicle, ed. by V. M. Istrin, *The Chronicle of George Hamartolus in An Old Slavo-Russian Version*, I (Petrograd, 1920), 411.

[16] Leo Grammaticus, *Chronographia*, CSHB pp. 122–125. *Theodosii Meliteni qui fertur Chronographia*, ed. T. L. F. Tafel (München, 1859), pp. 86–87. *Monumenta Saecularia*, III. Slavonic version: *Simeona Metafrasta i Logotheta Spisanie mira ot bytiya i Letovnik*, ed. V. Sreznevsky (St. Petersburg, 1905), pp. 55–56.

The chroniclers of the twelfth century, George Cedrenus and Johannes Zonaras, in dealing with Justin's rule depend entirely on previous sources which are known to us.[17]

A late historian who lived in the fourteenth century, Nicephorus Callistus Xanthopulus (Νικηφόρος Κάλλιστος ὁ Ξανθόπουλος) wrote a *Church History*, of which eighteen books have come down to us, narrating events down to the death of the Emperor Phocas in 610. The first seven chapters of Book XVII deal with the period of Justin. Of course this narrative of Justin's epoch is not an original source; it is based on earlier writers, and, in this particular section, mainly on the history of Evagrius. Chapter VI of this book gives a detailed story of the martyr Arethas and his companions, who were massacred in South Arabia.[18]

Some hagiographic texts are also to be mentioned. The most important text is the *Life* of the founder of the Great Laura in Palestine, Sabas, one of the most famous Palestinian ascetics. In Saint Sabas' *Life*, written by Cyril of Scythopolis in the sixth century, we find interesting data of the reaction in Palestine, especially among the monks, to the new religious policy of Justin. Saint Sabas himself and his coreligionists were enthusiastic supporters of the new trend.[19]

The second hagiographic text which is important for our study is the Martyrology of Arethas and his companions (*Martyrium Arethae et sociorum*), which has come down to us in Greek. The author of the original Syriac text was, it has been conjectured by Duchesne, Sergius, Bishop of Rosapha, who, as we shall see later, was sent by Justin to

---

[17] George Cedrenus, *CSHB* I, 636–642. Johannes Zonaras, XIV, 5; ed. L. Dindorf, III (Leipzig, 1868–1875), 265–270, *CSHB* III, 144–151.

[18] Nicephorus Callistus Xanthopulus, *Nicephori Callisti Xanthopuli Ecclesiastica Historia* XVII, I–VII; Migne, *PG*, CXLVII, 220–236. On the writer himself, see Krumbacher, pp. 291–293.

[19] The *Life of St. Sabas* was first published by J. B. Cotelier, *Ecclesiae graecae monumenta*, III (Paris, 1686), 220–376; on Justin see pp. 305, 326–327, 336–337. J. Pomialovsky (St. Petersburg, 1890), published an old Russian version, pp. 294, 356–360, 386–388. A recent edition by Eduard Schwartz, *Kyrillos von Skythopolis* (Leipzig, 1939), pp. 85–200; on Justin, see pp. 146, 162, 170; see index. *Texte und Untersuchungen zur Geschichte der altchristlichen Literatur*, XLIX, 2. A sketch of Sabas' life and activities by Schwartz, *op. cit.*, p. 379ff. On Cyril of Skythopolis, *ibidem*, pp. 405–408.

the Arab chief (phylarchos) al-Mundhir. Arethas (the Arabic form of his name was Harith) and about two hundred and eighty other Christians were massacred in 523 in the fortified town of Nedjran (Nagran) in South Arabia by a Himyarite leader, Dhu Novas, of the Jewish faith. As a piece of hagiographic literature, the text is not devoid of the element of legend. But at the same time it contains valuable historical information about the Ethiopic-Himyarite war in Justin's period and his participation in it, supplies us with exact chronological dates, and gives interesting information on Byzantine ships trading in the Red Sea.[20]

Of much less importance for our study is the *Life* of Saint Gregentius, bishop of the Homerites (Himyarites) in South Arabia. Gregentius has long been known as the author of his public disputation with a learned Jew on the merits of Judaism and Christianity and as the compiler of a code of laws for Abram, King of the Himyarites; both texts have survived. So far as I know, the entire text of his *Life* has not yet been published. In 1907, however, I published from a manuscript of the Library of the Monastery of St. Catherine of Sinai all the historically and topographically interesting parts of his *Life*.[21] Our information on Gregentius is so scanty that some scholars are inclined to deny even his existence; and many assert that the *Life* has no historical significance. In 1925 Duchesne called it a novel, and in 1930 H. Grégoire "a fabrication of later epoch, a fiction which is con-

[20] *Martyrium Sancti Arethae et Sociorum, Acta Sanctorum* (Antwerp, 1643-1937), October, X, under October 24, 721–759. *Symeonis Metaphrastae Martyrium S. Arethae*, Migne, PG, CXV, 1249–1290. *The Armenian Version of the Life of Arethas: Le Synaxaire arménien de Ter Israel*, transl. by G. Bayan, *Patrologia Orientalis*, by Graffin and Nau, XV (Paris, 1927), 343 (407)–348 (412); under October 20. On the supposed author see L. Duchesne, *Eglises séparées* (Paris, 1896), p. 325; in English, *The Churches Separated from Rome* (London, 1907), p. 204. *Idem, L'Eglise au VIème siècle* (Paris, 1925), p. 289, n.1. On the original Syriac text of the *Martyrium*, see I. Guidi, *La lettera di Simeone vescovo di Bêth-Ăršâm sopra i martiri omeriti pubblicata e tradotta*, Atti della R. Accademia dei Lincei, 3rd series 278 (1880–81), *Memorie della classe di scienze e morali storiche e filologiche*, VII (Rome, 1881), 500. On the Arab versions of the *Martyrium* of Arethas see G. Graf, *Geschichte der christlichen arabischen Literatur*, I (Città del Vaticano, 1944), 516 (*Studi e testi*, 118).

[21] A. Vasiliev, "The Life of St. Gregentius, Homerite Bishop," *Viz. Vremennik*, XIV (1907), 23–67: Greek text, Russian translation, and commentary (in Russian). In 1925 L. Duchesne, who did not know my study, wrote that the beginning of the *Life* had not been published. L. Duchesne, *L'église au VIe siècle*, p. 289, n. 1.

demned without appeal." [22] But in spite of these drastic criticisms, some very eminent historians continue to use the *Life* of Gregentius as an historical source.[23] I believe that in spite of its length and verbosity, the *Life* of Gregentius contains historical foundation; the text is very close to the famous Syriac *Letter* of Symeon of Beth-Arsham, which is to be discussed below among Syriac sources, and to the Greek text of the *Life* of Saint Arethas mentioned previously.

The *Life* of Gregentius contains the well known story of the Martyrs of Nagran in South Arabia, and mentions the name of Justin and the latter's participation in the Ethiopian-Himyaritc war. This story fails to give any new data; but the material it gives on Gregentius' activities in South Arabia after the war, his participation in the crowning of the new king in Arabia, the latter's death, and the death of Gregentius himself should not be neglected.[24]

To the epoch of Justin and Justinian belongs a most remarkable writer, Cosmas Indicopleustes, "sailor to India" or "sailor of the Indian Sea," who compiled a book entitled *Christian Topography*. A native of Egypt, probably of Alexandria, and in early life a merchant, hc traveled far and wide, visiting Ceylon, the Persian Gulf, the Sinaitic Peninsula, and, in the time of Justin, Ethiopia. Later in life he settled in Alexandria and probably became a monk. Cosmas' work is extremely important and fascinating for our study since it gives a picture of trade activities of Byzantium in the far south in the sixth century, and of

---

[22] L. Duchesne, *loc. cit.*: "le roman connu sous le nom de *Vita Gregentii*." H. Grégoire, "Mahomet et le Monophysisme," *Mélanges Charles Diehl*, I (Paris, 1930), 115: "fabrication d'époque relativement tardive, une fiction qui est condamnée sans appel." Here Grégoire refers to the criticism of P. Peeters, in his review of my article on St. Gregentius, *Analecta Bollandiana*, XXXI (1912), 109 (à la condamner sans appel). See also O. Bardenhewer, *Geschichte der alt-kirchlichen Literatur*, V (Freiburg im Breisgau, 1932), 25 (he fails to mention the *Life* of Gregentius). Georg Graf, *Geschichte der christlichen arabischen Literatur*, I, Die Uebersetzungen, pp. 22–23; 370 (written with a knowledge of my edition of the *Life* of Gregentius), *Studi e testi*, 118.

[23] See, for instance, J. B. Bury, *History of the Later Roman Empire*, II, p. 327 and n. 1. G. Moravcsik, *Byzantinoturcica*, I (Budapest, 1942), p. 355.

[24] See a brief and rather confusing note on Gregentius in F. G. Holweck, *A Biographical Dictionary of the Saints* (St. Louis and London, 1924), p. 445. According to this note, Gregentius died in 552. Holweck's sources are not indicated.

Justin's participation in the war between Ethiopia and the Himyarites.[25] Cosmas' work was widely known outside the confines of the empire, especially in ancient Russia, where a great number of Russian versions have survived, some with miniatures. Cosmas' *Topography* and its significance for the history of Justin's period will be discussed later.

Suidas' *Lexicon*, which was compiled in the tenth century, contains two brief articles: Justin ('Ιουστῖνος) and his wife Euphemia (Εὐφημία). They supply us with no new data.

In the reign of Justin lived the greatest of the Greek hymn writers, Romanus Melodus. Arriving at Constantinople from Syria, where he had been deacon of a church in Beirut, in the time of Justin's predecessor Anastasius (491–518), according to the *Menaeon* for October 1 he miraculously received the gift of composition of church songs (*kontakia*), of which he composed about one thousand. The admirers of Greek hymnography call him the "Pindar of rhythmic poetry." His hymns, which unfortunately have still been only partially published, frequently mention natural phenomena such as earthquakes, floods, and shooting stars as well as human dangers such as the invasions of the Ismaelites (Arabs) and Assyrians (Persians). In 1901 I attributed some of his passages to the time of Anastasius.[26] But his brilliant productive period without doubt belonged to the time of Justin and Justinian. When his writings have been published in their entirety, we shall probably discover more historical data attributable to the period of Justin and Justinian. But for the time being we must confine ourselves to the statement that the most brilliant of the Byzantine liturgical poets arrived at Constantinople in the time of Anastasius but flourished under Justin and Justinian.[27]

[25] The best edition of Cosmas' work is that by E. O. Winstedt, *The Christian Topography of Cosmas Indicopleustes* (Cambridge, 1909); see also Migne, *PG*, LXXXVIII. A fine English translation of the *Topography* by McCrindle, Hakluyt Society Publications, no. 98 (London, 1897).

[26] A. Vasiliev, "The Time of the Life of Romanus Melodus," *Viz. Vremennik*, VIII (1901), 435–478 (in Russian). A study almost unknown outside Russia. In 1937, E. Mioni attributed this study to Vasilievsky, *Romano il Melode; Saggio critico e dieci inni inediti* (Turin, 1937), p. 228.

[27] The theory that Romanus lived in the eighth century in the time of Anastasius II (713–716) must now be absolutely dismissed. There is a very vast literature on Romanus Melodus. In addition to Krumbacher (pp. 663–671), some recent bibliography in the Greek study of Sophronius Eustratiades, "'Ρωμανὸς ὁ

SURVEY OF THE SOURCES

LATIN SOURCES

Among Latin chroniclers, the most important is Marcellinus Comes, who lived and wrote in Constantinople under Justinian. Illyrian by origin, he was Justinian's chief secretary (*egisse cancellos*) before the latter became emperor and maintained close relations with him after his elevation. He is a contemporary and very well informed source for Justin's period. His chronicle, a continuation of the chronicle of Eusebius-Hieronymus, which goes up to the year 378 A.D., covers the time from 379 to 534. Marcellinus narrates events chronologically according to the consulships. Up to Justin's period, Marcellinus records something under each consulship, except for the year 522 when he merely gives the names of the consuls, Symmachus and Boethius. He deals briefly with the events which took place in Constantinople, describes the Pope's visit to the capital, and pays much attention to natural phenomena, especially to earthquakes. Although he fails to supply us with much new data, Marcellinus is a valuable source because of his chronological sequence. For Justin's period at least, he makes no mention of war.[28] Marcellinus gives his own work the epithet "rustic." [29]

Victor Tonnennensis (Tunnunensis), a contemporary of Justinian, was bishop of a north African city, the name of which cannot be identified. Taking sides against Justinian in the controversy of the Three Chapters, he was sent into exile; about 564 or 565 he was allowed to return to Constantinople, but because he was unwilling to adopt the imperial point of view he was confined to a monastery there, where he died. He wrote his chronicle, which covers the period from 444 to 566, during his exile. Like Marcellinus Comes, Victor lists

---

Μελωδός," in Ἐπετηρὶς Ἑταιρείας Βυζαντινῶν Σπουδῶν, XV (1939), 184. The study itself is not of great importance. L. Bréhier, in *Histoire de l'Eglise*, ed. Fliche and Martin, IV (1937), 549 and n. 4.

[28] The best edition is *Marcellini Comitis Chronicon*, ed. Theodore Mommsen, *Chronica Minora*, II (Berlin, 1894), 101–102, *MGH*, Auctorum antiquissimorum tomus XI. Also in Migne, *PL*, LI. On Marcellinus himself see Mommsen's Introduction. Also *Geschichte der römischen Litteratur*, IV, 2, by M. Schanz, C. Hosius, and G. Krüger (München, 1920), pp. 110–112 (No. 1056).

[29] *Marcellini Praefatio*: id sunt simul anni centum quinquaginta sex, et meum rusticum opus subposui.

his brief entries under the names of the consuls; he deals mostly with events in Constantinople, adding some brief notes on church affairs in the empire in general, and on the death of the Vandal king Trasamund. The historical significance of Victor's chronicle for Justin's period is not great, and his chronology is often incorrect.[30]

Flavius Magnus Aurelius Cassiodorus Senator, who was born about 485 (479 or 480) and died a nonagenarian about 580 (575; 583), is extremely important for this study concerning the Italo-Byzantine relations between Justin and the Ostrogothic king Theodoric. As *magister officiorum* at the court of Theodoric, he was very well informed on state affairs under this eminent ruler. Among Cassiodorus' numerous works the most important for this study is the collection of the edicts of Theodoric, which vividly describes the active relations between the two monarchs, edicts which were drawn up by Cassiodorus himself. He died in his native place in Bruttium, South Italy, in the monastery Vivarium, which he had founded. The collection of edicts in twelve books, containing 468 items, came out in 537, and is known as *Variae*, i.e. *Variae epistolae*, a title which Cassiodorus himself gave to his work.[31]

The so-called *Collectio Avellana* contains a precious mine of information on the relations between Constantinople and Rome during Justin's period. But unfortunately this rich selection from papal records breaks off in the year 521, so that we have no letters for the last two years of the pontificate of Pope Hormisdas (514–523). But although this collection supplies us with information only for the four opening

---

[30] The best edition is *Victoris Tonnennensis episcopi Chronica*, ed. Theodore Mommsen, *Chronica Minora*, II (Berlin, 1894), 196–197, *MGH*, Auctorum antiquissimorum tomus XI. Also Migne, *PL*, LXVIII. On the author himself, in addition to his own information in his chronicle under the years 555, 556, 565, see Mommsen, Introduction to Victor's edition; also M. Schanz, *Geschichte der römischen Litteratur*, IV, 2, by M. Schanz, C. Hosius and G. Krüger (München, 1920), 112–113.

[31] The best edition is Theodore Mommsen, *Cassiodori Variae*, *MGH*, Auctorum antiquissimorum tomus XII (1894). Also Migne, *PL*, LXIX. A condensed English translation exists of Cassiodorus' letters. *The Letters of Cassiodorus, Being A Condensed Translation of the Variae Epistolae of Magnus Aurelius Cassiodorus Senator*, with an Introduction by Thomas Hodgkin (London, 1886). On Cassiodorus himself, among other works see M. Schanz, *Geschichte der römischen Litteratur*, IV, 2, 92–109. O. Bardenhewer, *Geschichte der altkirchlichen Literatur*, V (Freiburg im Breisgau, 1932), 264–278.

years of Justin's reign (518–521), the information is exceptionally varied and rich. The collection contains a large number of the letters of Hormisdas himself to Constantinople, to his envoys at the capital, to Justin, to Justinian, to the patriarch of Constantinople, and to many other Byzantines of various classes, as well as letters written from Constantinople back to Rome. From these papal records we may understand better the general trend of the religious policy of Justin, which was directed by his nephew Justinian.[32]

The historical narrative or series of papal biographies, the so-called *Liber Pontificalis*, is also of value for this study. According to modern scholars, the first series of papal biographies, which starts with Saint Peter, was compiled in the sixth or seventh century and is based on previous material of differing value. In a later time, every pope had his own official annalist. The lives of the three popes who belong to Justin's period, Hormisdas (514–523), John I (523–526), and Felix IV (526–530), are narrated in the *Liber Pontificalis*. Hormisdas' biography contains a detailed story of the papal embassy to Constaninople and gives the list of imperial presents sent by Justin to Rome. The biography of John I is almost entirely devoted to the description of his voyage to Constantinople, on which he was sent by King Theodoric. The very brief biography of Felix IV, whose pontificate for the greater part belongs to the time of Justinian, gives nothing for the period of Justin.[33]

The *Breviarium* of the Carthaginian deacon Liberatus, which was compiled between 560 and 566, covers the period from 428 to the time of its compilation. The author was one of the passionate defenders

[32] The best edition is *Epistulae imperatorum pontificum aliorum Avellana quae dicitur Collectio*, ed. Otto Günther, I–II (Vienna, 1895–1898); *Corpus scriptorum ecclesiasticorum latinorum*, vol. XXXV. Another edition by A. Thiel, *Epistolae romanorum pontificum genuinae et quae ad eos scriptae sunt*, I (Brunsbergae, 1868). But Thiel's text must always be verified by Günther's edition. These documents were also published in older collections, such as Mansi, *Conciliorum Collectio*, VIII; Migne, *PL*, LXIII; Baronius, Annales Ecclesiastici (Lucca, 1747–1756) under the years 518–521.

[33] Editions: *Le Liber Pontificalis*, text, introduction and commentary by Abbé L. Duchesne, I (Paris, 1886), 269–280; ed. Theodore Mommsen, MGH, *Gesta pontificum*, I (Berlin, 1898), 126–138. English translation, *The Book of the Popes* (Liber Pontificalis), I: To the pontificate of Gregory I, translated with an introduction by L. R. Loomis (New York, 1916), 124–139; a very useful introduction, pp. IX–XXII.

of the Three Chapters. His brief chronicle is regarded as one of the very important sources for the history of the church controversies of the fifth and sixth century. For Justin's period, Liberatus gives some data, also known from other sources, on Severus of Antioch and on some controversies in the religious life of Alexandria.[34]

The famous *Justiniani Vita* was supposedly written by Justinian's *preceptor* Theophilus-Bogomil, and on the basis of this scholars have claimed the Slavic origin of the family of Justin and Justinian. J. Bryce's study, however, has now established the fact that this is to be discarded as an historical source, since it is but a recent fabrication of the sixteenth or seventeenth century.[35]

SYRIAC SOURCES

Syriac sources are very important for Justin's period; some of them are original Syriac sources and some are based on Greek originals which have not come down to us.

Among the Syrian historians of first importance who lived in the sixth century was John, Bishop of Asia or Ephesus. He was born early in the sixth century and died about 586, when he was around eighty years of age. A convinced monophysite, he was very favorably received in Constantinople by Justinian, who appointed him as his missionary bishop of Ephesus to root out heathenism in Asia Minor. Under Justinian's successor, Justin II, his monophysitism brought him imprisonment. His greatest work is his *Ecclesiastical History* in three parts, the first two of which embraced the period from Julius Caesar to the seventh year of Justin II, while the third carried on the tale to the end of the author's life. The first part is almost entirely lost. Of the second, which dealt with the period of Justin I, we have copious excerpts in the so-called *Chronicle* of Dionysius of Tell-Mahre, who

---

[34] *Liberati Diaconi Breviarium*, Migne, *PL*, LXVIII, chapter XIX, 1033–1034. On the author, see Schanz, *Geschichte der römischen Litteratur*, IV, 2, 583 (no. 1236).

[35] J. Bryce, "Life of Justinian by Theophilus," *The English Historical Review*, II (1887), 657–684. *Idem*, in *Archivio della Reale Società Romana di Storia Patria*, X, I–II (Rome, 1887), 137–171. See A. Vasiliev, "The Problem of Justinian's Origin," *Vizantisky Vremennik*, I (1894), 469–492 (in Russian). Also J. B. Bury, Introduction to his edition of Gibbon, *Decline and fall of the Roman Empire*, I (New York, 1914), LIX–LX. This question is to be discussed below.

lived in the ninth century. The excerpts from the second part which have been preserved give us a detailed but highly colored story of the monophysite persecutions under Justin I and devote a great deal of attention to natural phenomena, especially earthquakes.[36] Of scarcely less value for the history of his time is another work of John of Ephesus entitled *Lives of the Eastern Saints*, including both men and women. Among many biographies, often full of legendary stories, some deal with the monophysite persecutions under Justin I and may serve as an addition to the data supplied by John's *Ecclesiastical History*.[37]

Simeon, Bishop of Beth-Arsham near Seleucia on the Tigris, also a monophysite and commonly called "the Persian disputant," lived at the end of the fifth and in the first half of the sixth century; his death must have taken place before 548, in which year Theodora died, because he came to Constantinople to see her. Among his very few writings, of great value for our study is his letter addressed to Simeon, Abbot of Gabbula, in which he treats of the persecution of the Christians at Nagran in South Arabia by the Jewish king, Dhu Nuwas. The letter, which with other scholars I consider genuine, is an authen-

[36] Our best information on the second part of the *History* of John of Ephesus is in F. Nau, "Analyse de la seconde partie inédite de l'Histoire Ecclésiastique de Jean d'Asie, patriarche jacobite de Constantinople (+ 585)," *Revue de l'Orient Chrétien*, II (1897), 455–493; on Justin I, pp. 467–474 (as usual in Syriac and Arab sources, Justin is called *Justinian* the Elder). Before Nau's publication, three fragments from the second part had been published in a Latin translation by W. J. van Douwen and J. P. N. Land, "Joannis episcopi Ephesi Syri Monophysitae Commentarii de beatis orientalibus et Historiae Ecclesiasticae Fragmenta," *Verhandelingen der Koninklijke Akademie van Wetenschappen*, Afdeeling Letterkunde, XVIII (Amsterdam, 1889), 216–249. The Syriac text only of fragments of the second part was published by E. W. Brooks, *Johannis Ephesini Historiae Ecclesiasticae Fragmenta*, CSCO, Scriptores Syri, text, 3rd series, II (Paris, 1933), 401–420.

[37] The Syriac text with an English translation was published by E. W. Brooks, *John of Ephesus, Lives of the Eastern Saints, Patrologia Orientalis*, XVII (1923), XVIII (1924), XIX (1925). Before Brooks' edition, the *Lives* had been published in a Latin translation by W. J. van Douwen and J. P. N. Land (see preceding note). The best fundamental monograph on John of Ephesus is the Russian work by A. Diakonov, *John of Ephesus and his Historico-Ecclesiastical Works* (St. Petersburg, 1908). See E. W. Brooks' appreciation of this book in *Patrologia Orientalis*, XVII (1923), III. General information on John of Ephesus in any history of Syriac literature, for instance those by W. Wright, R. Duval, A. Baumstark, J.-B. Chabot. Recently a substantial chapter on John of Ephesus appeared by N. Pigulevskaya, *The Syriac Sources for the History of the Peoples of the USSR* (Moscow-Leningrad, 1941), pp. 15–28 (in Russian).

tic and important contemporary source on the Himyaro-Ethiopic war and on Justin's participation in it. The letter is dated 524, in which year the author was himself at Ramla and al-Hirah with the Saracen chief al-Mundhir.[38]

The *Ecclesiastical History* of Zachariah of Mitylene, or better Pseudo-Zachariah, was completed about 569. Zacharias Rhetor or Scholasticus, Bishop of Mitylene in Lesbos, was a Greek writer, and his *Ecclesiastical History*, which he seems to have ended about the year 518, has not come down to us in its original Greek; but it became part of a compilation by an anonymous Syrian monophysite writer, who, as has been noted above, continued and completed his writing in twelve books about 569. The basis of Books three to six was the Greek history of Zacharias Rhetor, while Books one to two and seven to twelve were gathered from other sources. Since the name of this Syrian writer is unknown, all his work, rather inaccurately, is called the *Ecclesiastical History of Pseudo-Zachariah*. Book eight deals with Justin's period. A few words about his accession to the throne also appear in Book seven, chapter XIV, and a reference to his death occurs in Book nine, introduction and chapter I. In Book eight we have the story of Justin's accession and that of Vitalian; the author also gives detailed stories of the martyrs of Nagran and of the fighting with the Saracens of al-Mundhir, and accounts of floods, earthquakes, and fire. For our study this contemporary source is of great value.[39]

---

[38] The original text and its Italian translation were published by I. Guidi, *La lettera di Simeono vescovo di Bêth Arsâm sopra i martiri omeriti, Atti della R. Accademia dei Lincei,* CCLXXVIII (1880–1881), 3rd series, VII (Rome, 1881), 471–515 (study, pp. 471–480; Italian translation, pp. 480–495; some additions, pp. 495–500; Syriac text, pp. 501–515). This letter has been more or less fully reproduced by several Syriac historians, such as Pseudo-Zachariah, Dionysius of Tell-Mahre, Michael the Syrian. In 1889, J. Halévy denied the authenticity of the letter. J. Halévy, "Examen critique des sources relatives à la persécution des chrétiens de Nedjran par le roi juif des Himyarites," *Revue des études juives,* XVIII (1889), 16–42; 161–178; especially 26–42; 178.

[39] An English translation of the Syriac text by F. J. Hamilton and E. W. Brooks, *The Syriac Chronicle Known as That of Zachariah of Mitylene* (London, 1899). On Justin, pp. 187–221. A German translation by K. Ahrens and G. Krüger, *Die sogenannte Kirchengeschichte des Zacharias Rhetor* (Leipzig, 1899); on Justin, pp. 138–168. The Syriac text alone by J. P. N. Land, *Zachariae Episcopi Mitylenes aliorumque scripta historica. Anecdota Syriaca,* III (Leyden, 1870); a more recent edition by E. W. Brooks, *Historia ecclesiastica Zachariae Rhetori vulgo adscripta,* CSCO, Scriptores syri, 3rd series (Paris, 1925). On the *Chronicle*

SURVEY OF THE SOURCES

The anonymous *Chronicle of Edessa* (*Chronicon Edessenum*), which must have been compiled about 540, is another contemporary source. The author, an Orthodox with Nestorian sympathies whose native town was Edessa, made use of the archives of this city as well as of some other sources. His interest is concentrated on events which took place at Edessa or were connected with it. His brief entries referring to Justin's period deal mostly with church affairs and natural phenomena, like floods, earthquakes, and fires. His exact chronological data are very valuable.[40]

Jacob of Sarug, one of the most celebrated writers of the Syrian Church, "the flute of the Holy Spirit and the harp of the believing church," who died in 521, may be mentioned here as the author of a letter to the Himyarite Christians. The letter, which may have been written in 520, offered comfort and consolation to the Himyarite Christians who were persecuted by Dhu Nuwas. The letter may be regarded as an introductory source for the Himyaro-Abyssinian war in which Justin took part.[41]

---

itself and its author, see introductions to the above translations; also M.-A. Kugener, "La compilation historique de Pseudo-Zacharie le Rhéteur," *Revue de l'Orient Chrétien*, V (1900), 201–214; 416–480 (referring to the translations of Hamilton and Brooks, and Ahrens and Krüger). General information may be found in any history of Syriac Literature (see note to John of Ephesus). A very accurate chapter on Zacharias Rhetor recently came out in Russian. N. Pigulevskaya, *The Syriac Sources for the History of the Peoples of the USSR*, pp. 9–14. On the lost Greek text of Zacharias, see W. von Christ, *Geschichte der griechischen Litteratur*, II, 2 (Munich, 1924), 1484 (no. 1086).

[40] An old English translation of the *Chronicle* by B. Harris Cowper, "The Chronicle of Edessa," *The Chronicle of Sacred Literature and Biblical Record*, V, I, new series (London, 1864); on Justin, pp. 36–37. A German translation by L. Hallier, *Untersuchungen über die Edessenische Chronik mit dem syrischen Text und einer Uebersetzung, Texte und Untersuchungen zur Geschichte der altchristlichen Litteratur*, IX, 1 (Leipzig, 1893); on Justin, pp. 124–135. A Latin translation by I. Guidi, *CSCO*, Scriptores syri, Transl. 3rd series, vol. IV, *Chronica Minora*, 1st part (Paris, 1903); on Justin, pp. 9–10; in the same collection I. Guidi published the Syriac text of the *Chronicle*. The most recent study on the time of the compilation of the *Chronicle*, F. Haase, "Die Abfassungszeit der Edessenischen Chronik," *Oriens Christianus*, new series, VII–VIII (1918), 88–96; the *Chronicle* was written in 540 (p. 96). Hallier's dating — he asserted that the *Chronicle* could hardly have been compiled before 600, (*op. cit.*, p. 65) — is to be rejected.

[41] See R. Schröter, "Trostschreiben Jacob's von Sarug an die himjaritischen Christen," *Zeitschrift der Morgenländischen Gesellschaft*, XXXI (1877), 360–368; the Syriac text, pp. 369–385; German translation, pp. 385–395. On Jacob's literary

The most famous name among monophysite scholars of the seventh century is that of Jacob of Edessa, who died at the very beginning of the eighth century. "He appears before us as theologian, historian, philosopher, and grammarian, as a translator of various Greek works, and as the indefatigable correspondent of many students who sought his advice and assistance from far and near." [42] For this study Jacob of Edessa must be included as the author of a brief chronicle in which he mentions Justin's decree requiring that all imperial soldiers accept the Chalcedonian credo.[43]

A brief anonymous chronicle which carries events down to the year 819 A.D. and is known as *Chronicon Anonymum ad A.D. 819*, was compiled in the ninth century. Its manuscript, executed in the middle of that century, was found and copied in 1911 by a monk, Aphram Barsaum, who later became the Jacobite Patriarch of Antioch. The author is unknown, but apparently he was a monk in an oriental monastery (*in monasterio Cartaminensi*). He deals very briefly with the period from the birth of Jesus Christ to his own day. For Justin's time the *Chronicle* gives some fragmentary notes. As usual in Syriac chronicles, Justin is called Justinian. The opening lines dealing with his reign have been preserved in a very deteriorated text with many lacunae so that some statements are not clear. We read for instance, "Justin succeeded Anastasius" (one word is lacking) "and took his wife." The *Chronicle* treats particularly of the monophysite persecution, mentions the martyrdom of the Homerites, tells of the disastrous earthquake at Antioch, and closes with the account of the appearance

---

activities in general, especially his vast number of metrical compositions, see A. Baumstark, *Geschichte der syrischen Literatur* (Bonn, 1922), pp. 148–158. Also W. Wright, *A Short History of Syriac Literature* (London, 1894), pp. 67–72. P. Martin, "Un évêque poète au Ve et au VIe siècles ou Jacques de Saroug, sa vie, son temps, ses oeuvres, ses croyances," *Revue des sciences ecclésiastiques*, series IV, IV (1876), 309–352; 385–419. A very fine article by E. Tisserant in *Dictionnaire de théologie catholique*, VIII (Paris, 1924), 300–305; on the letter to the Himyarite Christians, col. 304. Now see P. Peeters, "Jacques de Saroug appartient-il à la secte monophysite?" *Analecta Bollandiana*, LXVI (1948), 134–198; esp. p. 195; Jacob of Sarug was orthodox, pp. 194–198.

[42] W. Wright, *A Short History of Syriac Literature*, p. 143.

[43] *Iacobi Edesseni Chronicon*, Transl. E. W. Brooks, *CSCO*, Scriptores syri, Transl., 3rd series, vol. IV, *Chronica Minora* (Paris, 1903), pp. 197–257; on Justin, pp. 239–240. On Jacob of Edessa in general, see W. Wright, *op. cit.*, pp. 141–154. Baumstark, *op. cit.*, pp. 248–256; on the *Chronicle*, p. 254.

of a comet. The *Chronicle* fails to supply us with new data, but indicates chronological dates.[44]

Another brief anonymous chronicle which carries events to the year 846 A.D. and is known as *Chronicon ad annum domini 846 pertinens*, was compiled in the ninth century. The anonymous author was a monophysite monk (*monachum Qartaminensem fuisse*). The *Chronicle*, which has been preserved in Cod. Mus. Brit. Add. 14642, begins with biblical times, and includes no new data on Justin's period. The author's interest is concentrated on Justin's new religious policy, which is of course estimated from the monophysite standpoint.[45] Chabot remarks that the author of this *Chronicle* copied almost word for word the *Chronicle* of A.D., 819,[46] but I am unable to confirm this from the brief notes the author devotes to Justin's reign.

One of the most important Syriac sources for our study is the *Chronicle* of Michael the Syrian or the Elder, who was Jacobite Patriarch from 1166 to 1199. Although of a later date, his vast *Chronicle*, the range of which extends from the Creation to the author's own day, is valuable because it preserves texts of previous sources which have not come down to us. The section dealing with Justin's period covers all aspects of his reign; but of course the presentation is highly colored because it is given from the strictly monophysite point of view which is utterly hostile to Justin's new religious orientation. Michael ironically remarks: "Justin imagines that if all countries accept the Synod (of Chalcedon) there will be but one empire." It is especially important to note that among other sources Michael has used and reproduced many passages from the second book of John of Ephesus, which deals with the events of Justin's period, and which, as we know, has not been preserved in its entirety.[47]

[44] *Chronicon Anonymum ad A. D. 819*, Transl. I.-B. Chabot, CSCO, Scriptores syri, 3rd series, vol. XIV (Louvain, 1937), pp. 1–16; on Justin, pp. 4–5. On the edition of the *Chronicle* and its anonymous author see *praefatio*, p. i.

[45] *Chronicon ad annum Domini 846 pertinens*, ed. E. W. Brooks. Transl. I.-B. Chabot, CSCO, Scriptores syri, versio, series tertia, tomus IV, Chronica Minora, pars secunda (Paris, 1903), pp. 121–180; on Justin, p. 169. On the *Chronicle* itself and bibliography, pp. 121–122.

[46] Chabot, *Chronicon Anonymum ad A. D. 819*, CSCO, Scriptores syri, 3rd series, vol. XIV, Trans. (Louvain, 1937), p. 1.

[47] A French translation of Michael's *Chronicle* by J.-B. Chabot, *Chronique de Michel le Syrien*, II (Paris, 1901); on Justin, pp. 169–190. On Michael's biography

Before the edition and translation of the *Chronicle* of Michael by Chabot (1900–1910), this work was already known in an Armenian version. This version was thought to be nothing but an abridged translation of the Syriac original, which became worthless after Chabot's work. But a more critical study of the Armenian version has shown that it is not a translation but an adaptation. The Armenian adaptors have treated the original text very freely, adding and subtracting at their pleasure in order to make their work more suitable for Armenian readers. Many additions contain valuable historical data, so that the Armenian *Chronicle* is important as an historical source even after the publication of the Syriac original. The Armenian version of Michael's *Chronicle*, according to a recent special study of this question, is an original work of Armenian redactors. But for Justin's period, the Armenian version fails to supply us with new data to the extent that the Syriac text does. The Armenian version calls Justin "a wicked and ignorant old man who accumulated upon his head many maledictions." [48]

A very little known Syriac anonymous chronicle, which carries events from the creation down to 1234 A.D., is known as *Chronicon anonymum ad annum Christi 1234 pertinens*. The *Chronicle* was compiled before the middle of the thirteenth century. The author's native country and name are unknown, but according to his own statement, he was with Saladin when the latter captured Jerusalem in 1187. He seems to have been a monk in the famous monastery of Barsuma near Melitene. The *Chronicle* has survived in a single manuscript which is not autograph but was probably executed at the end of the fourteenth

---

and works see any history of Syriac Literature. W. Wright's *Short History of Syriac Literature* is rather out of date; in 1894 the Syriac text of the *Chronicle* had not yet been published (pp. 250–253). Baumstark, *op. cit.*, pp. 298–300. The best article on Michael is that by E. Tisserant, "Michel le Syrien," *Dictionnaire de théologie catholique*, X, 2 (Paris, 1929), col. 1711–1719. The original Syriac text has also been reproduced by Chabot.

[48] *Chronique de Michel le Grand traduite pour la première fois sus la version arménienne du prêtre Ischôk*, by Victor Langlois (Venice-Paris, 1868); on Justin, pp. 175–187. An older French translation by Dulaurier, *Journal Asiatique*, XII (1848), 281–334; XIII (1849), 315–376. The most important study on the Armenian version is that of Felix Haase, "Die armenische Rezension der syrischen Chronik Michaels des Grossen," *Oriens Christianus*, new series, V (1915), 60–82; 271–284; especially p. 82; 284. In his article Tisserant (see preceding note) has utilized the results of Haase's study.

century. It is to be found in Istanbul, in the private possession of M. Peter Fehim. Like other brief anonymous Syriac chronicles, this monophysite chronicle of 1234 A.D. fails to supply us with new data. The author says that Justin, whom he calls Justinian, was a handsome old man from a fort of Myrina (*e castro Myrina*), in which we recognize a distorted name of Bederiana; he records Justin's new religious policy, the flood at Edessa, the fire and earthquake at Antioch, and the death of Justin without issue.[49] Michael the Syrian was the most important source of this chronicle.

One of the most learned and versatile men that Syria ever produced was Gregory Abul Faraj (1226–1286), commonly known as Bar Hebraeus, that is, "the Son of the Jew," because his father was a distinguished physician of Hebrew descent. His amazingly numerous works cover nearly every branch of science in vogue at his time. His historical works should be mentioned for our study. He wrote a *Universal History* in three parts, Part I containing the political *History of the World* from the creation down to the conquests of the Mongols which were taking place in his own time. One of his basic sources which covered the end of the twelfth century was the *Chronicle* of Michael the Syrian so that for Justin's period Abul Faraj's very brief narrative is entirely dependent on Michael.[50] In the last years of his life, at the request of some Muslim friends, he undertook to make a recension in Arabic of this part of his political history, but the Arabic version fails to add anything to his Syriac original.[51] Parts II and III

[49] *Chronicon Anonymum ad annum Christi 1234 pertinens*, I, interpretatus est I.-B. Chabot, CSCO, Scriptores syri, 3rd series, vol. XIV, Transl. (Louvain, 1937), pp. 150–151 (ch. LIII). On the *Chronicle* and its author, see praefatio, pp. i–ii. A. Baumstark, *Geschichte der syrischen Literatur*, p. 302 (bibliography). Baumstark says that the author was from Edessa. N. Pigulevskaya, *Byzantium and Iran on the Threshold of the Sixth and Seventh Centuries* (Moscow-Leningrad, 1946), pp. 48–49 (in Russian).

[50] The Syriac text and Latin translation, *Gregorii Abulpharagii sive Bar Hebraei Chronicon Syriacum*, ed. P. I. Bruns and G. G. Kirsch, II (Leipzig, 1789); on Justin, pp. 80–81 (translation). Recently, in English, *The Chronography of Gregory Abul Faraj . . . Commonly Known as Bar Hebraeus*, by E. A. Wallis Budge, I (London, 1932), 73. The Syriac text only was also published by Bedjan at Paris in 1890. On Bar Hebraeus, in addition to various histories of Syriac literature, see detailed information in Budge's Introduction, pp. xv–lxiii.

[51] *Gregorii Abulpharagii historia dynastiarum*, ed. E. Pocockio (Oxford, 1663); on Justin, p. 149 (Arabic text); pp. 93–94 (Latin translation). The Arabic text only edited by Salhani (Beirut, 1892); on Justin, pp. 147–148.

of Bar Hebraeus' *Universal History* are the history of the church from Aaron to the year 1285, especially in the East. For Justin's period he gives a brief record of religious persecutions, of course from the monophysite point of view, and refers to John of Ephesus (John of Amida) as one of his sources. He gives no new data.[52]

Among Syriac sources may be mentioned John Psaltes, archimandrite of Beith Aphthonia, Justin's contemporary, who composed a hymn on the Holy Himyarite (Homerite) martyrs, "who were martyred in the city of Nigran in the southern territories of the Saracens, in the days of Justin, king of the Romans, when the Christians were there persecuted by Masruk, king of the Arabs, who was a Jew by religion and forced to deny Christ." This document refers to the Abyssinian-Himyarite war in which Justin took part.[53]

In 1924 Axel Moberg published a previously unknown Syriac text which he entitled *The Book of the Himyarites*, dealing with the Abyssinian-Himyarite war during Justin's period.[54] Profesor H. Grégoire flatly proclaimed at once that the new text was a "patent falsification" (*le faux patent*),[55] but without any justification for his statement. Since I am inclined to use the text as an historical source, I

---

[52] *Gregorii Barhebraei Chronicon Ecclesiasticum*, ed. and transl. by J. B. Abbeloos and T. J. Lamy, I (Louvain, 1872), 194–204 (Latin translation).

[53] The Syriac text and English translation of James (Jacob) of Edessa's version of this hymn by E. W. Brooks, *James of Edessa: The Hymns of Severus of Antioch and Others, Patrologia Orientalis*, VII (1911), 613 (201)–614 (202). Another edition with a German translation by R. Schröter, "Hymne des Iohannes Psaltes auf die himjaritischen Märtyrer," *Zeitschrift der Morgenländischen Gesellschaft*, XXXI (1877), 400–405. I shall put aside the confusing possibility of two or more persons bearing the name of Iohannes who lived and wrote at the same time. See Brooks, *op. cit.*, p. 799; 801. M.-A. Kugener, in his review of Brooks' edition, *Byz. Zeitschrift*, XXI (1912), 263–264. Cf. F. Nau, "Histoire de Jean Bar Aphtonia," *Revue de l'Orient Chrétien*, VII (1902), 100; 132–133. Some confusion in W. Wright, *op. cit.*, pp. 84–85. A few lines in A. Baumstark, *op. cit.*, p. 185.

[54] Axel Moberg, *The Book of the Himyarites: Fragments of a Hitherto Unknown Syriac Work* (Lund, 1924).

[55] H. Grégoire, "Mahohet et le Monophysisme, *Mélanges Charles Diehl*, I, 115–116. See Henri Charles, *Le christianisme des Arabes nomades sur le limes et dans le desert syro-mésopotamien aux alentours de l'hégire* (Paris, 1936), p. 20; the author hesitates to use Moberg's text on account of serious objections made by P. Peeters in "La Passion de S. Michel le Sabaïte," *Analecta Bollandiana*, XLVIII (1930), 93. Here Peeters mentions "the conferences of the problematic S. Gregentius, bishop of Taphar in South Arabia, with the Jew Herban, in the epoch of Justinian." In this particular study Peeters fails to mention Moberg's text.

wish to say a few words about it. According to the editor, the *Book of the Himyarites* serves as fresh evidence and, as is often the case with new documents, it presents the solution of some old problems and the introduction of some new ones (pp. xxiv–xxv). *The Book of the Himyarites* is closely akin to the narratives which are told in the *Letter* of Simeon of Beth-Arsham and in the *Acta* of Arethas. The new text is by far the broadest and most detailed account of the incidents in question that is known to us, and it preserves the dates of events by the days of the week (pp. lvii–lviii). The *Book* claims to have been written shortly after the events described and on the basis mainly of oral records of eyewitnesses. The author is unknown. The editor says: "If the *Letter* of Beth-Arsham is genuine, then there is but little doubt that the *Book* also is what it claims to be. The discovery of the *Book* has furnished a fresh and, in my opinion, decisive argument for the authenticity of the *Letter*. As to the *Book*, it shows in itself, in style, in its inner coherence, in nearly every detail in its narrative, the marks of its own authenticity" (p. lxviii). The chief historical features of the narrative do not differ very much from those given in the *Acta* of Arethas. The name of Justin is not mentioned in the *Book*.

Since it has not yet been proved that the text published by Axel Moberg is a falsification,[56] and since the text does not contradict at all our other information on the Abyssinian-Himyarite war, I am using it in this study in the same way as the *Letter* of Beth-Arsham or the *Acta* of S. Arethas.

Among individual monophysite biographies, we may mention that of John (Ioannes) of Tella, which was compiled by a certain Elias, John's disciple, about 542, when the Persians took possession of Callinicum. The biography contains the story of John's persecution as a monophysite during the reign of Justin. He was exiled by Justin in 519 and died in 537.[57]

---

[56] See E. A. Wallis Budge, *A History of Ethiopia, Nubia and Abyssinia*, I (London, 1928), 263: "More light on the period of the introduction of Christianity into Yaman is afforded by the Syriac work *Kethabha dhe Himyaraye* which has been edited by Axel Moberg of Lund."

[57] The Syriac original with Dutch translation, H. G. Kleyn, *Het Leven van Iohannes van Tella door Elias* (Leiden, 1882): text, pp. 1–83; translation, pp. XIX–

The name of Dionysius of Tell-Mahre, who was raised to the Jacobite patriarchate in 818 and died in 845, is to be mentioned here because it has long been connected with the great work of the *Annals* (Chronicle), which covers the whole period of the world's history from the creation to his own time. It has now been proved that he did not write this work; its author is unknown, and this anonymous chronicle is accordingly often called the *Chronicle of Pseudo-Dionysius*. It has been supposed that the author was a monk or cleric from the monastery of Zuquin, near Amid. The chronicle consists of four parts. The first, dealing with the pre-Constantinian period, is based mostly on the *Chronicle* of Eusebius of Caesarea; the second covers the time from Constantine to Theodosius II; the third, which describes events from 444 to 578, deals with Justin's period; the fourth covers the time from 578 down to 774–775. The third part is important for us since it contains the second part of the history of John of Ephesus, which has not come to us in its entirety and which has not only been freely used by the anonymous author but in some cases even copied word for word.[58]

ETHIOPIC SOURCES

Among the sources which have come down to us in an Ethiopic version, the *Chronicle* of John, Bishop of Nikiu in Lower Egypt, is to be mentioned. The author, a monophysite who lived in the seventh century, compiled a summary of general history from the creation to

LXXXVIII; sketch of Iohannes' life and his works, pp. I–XVIII. A Latin translation by E. W. Brooks, *Vita Johannis Episcopi Tellae auctore Elia*, CSCO, Scriptores syri, Transl., 3rd series, vol. XXV, *Vitae virorum apud Monophysitas celeberrimorum* (Paris, 1907), 21–60; on Justin's time, pp. 33–57; on his death, p. 59. A few words in A. Baumstark, *op. cit.*, p. 180.

[58] See F. Nau, "Analyse de la seconde partie inédite de l'histoire Ecclésiastique de Jean d'Asie," *Revue de l'Orient Chrétien*, II, 455–493; on Justin, pp. 467–474. Also Introduction to *Dionysius I of Tell-Mahre*, Part IV, pub. and transl. by J.-B. Chabot (Paris, 1895), pp. IX–XXXIV. In the introduction to this fourth part, p. 18 the anonymous author writes: "from Theodosius to the Emperor Justinian (to read: Justin II), i.e. to the year 885 of the Greeks (i.e. 573–4), we have had as our guide John, bishop of Asia," (i.e. John of Ephesus). The Syriac text only of the fragments of the second part of the History of John of Ephesus: *Iohannis Ephesini Historiae Ecclesiasticae Fragmenta*, ed. E. W. Brooks, CSCO (1933), pp. 403–415. The most recent study by F. Haase, "Untersuchungen zur Chronik des Pseudo-Dionysios von Tell-Mahre," *Oriens Christianus*, VI (1916), 65–90; 240–270. Baumstark, *op. cit.*, p. 275.

640 A.D. Written originally in Greek, the *Chronicle* was translated into Arabic, and in 1601–1602 from Arabic into Ethiopic. Only the Ethiopic version has survived. Surprisingly, it has never been mentioned in Byzantine literature. The most important part of the *Chronicle* is the last part, dealing with the time of the Arab conquest of Egypt, when the author was a contemporary of the events described. The *Chronicle* contains a long chapter, XC, which is especially devoted to Justin's period and gives a general sketch of his reign. John's narrative is mostly based on the *Chronicle* of John Malalas; but in addition it furnishes some details which have as yet not been identified in other Greek sources. John of Nikiu is not a contemporary, but he is a useful source for Justin's time, although it is not to be forgotten that the original Greek, after passing from an Arabic to an Ethiopic version, may have undergone some alterations and distortions.[59]

In Ethiopia, probably at the end of the thirteenth century, when the new so-called Solomonian dynasty ascended the throne, a special book was composed to glorify the new dynasty, *Kebra Nagast* (*The Glory of the Kings*), one of the most important works of Ethiopian literature. Among many legends included in this book, one is of extreme importance for us. It proclaims that the two kings, Justinus the King of Rome and Kaleb the King of Ethiopia, met together in Jerusalem and divided the earth between them "from the half of Jerusalem." This legend will be discussed later.[60]

[59] Ethiopic text and French translation by H. Zotenberg, in the *Notices et extraits des manuscrits de la Bibliothèque Nationale*, XXIV, 1 (Paris, 1883), 125–605; on Justin, pp. 501–508. English translation by R. H. Charles, *The Chronicle of John, Bishop of Nikiu, translated from Zotenberg's Ethiopic Text* (London, 1916), pp. 132–138 (Ch. XC, 1–48). On John of Nikiu, Krumbacher, *op. cit.*, pp. 403–404. Introduction to Charles' translation. E. A. Wallis Budge, *A History of Ethiopia*, II, 567. The author of this book is incorrect in stating that Zotenberg's text and translation came out in 1876 (really 1883), and that the original text of John of Nikiu was Arabic (really Greek). John of Nikiu is not mentioned by Ignazio Guidi, *Storia della letteratura etiopica* (Rome, 1932). Georg Graf, *Geschichte der christlichen arabischen Literatur*, I, Die Uebersetzungen, pp. 470–472 (*Studi e testi*, 118): "the Greek original and the Arab version must, for the time being (vorläufig), be considered lost."

[60] There are two complete translations of the *Kebra Nagast*, in German and in English. Carl Bezold, *Kebra Nagast: Die Herrlichkeit der Könige*, Abh. der philos.-philol. Klasse der Bayerischen Akademie der Wissenschaften, XXIII (München, 1905), I, I–LXII (introduction), 170 and 160 (Ethiopic text and German translation); on the division of the earth, p. 136 (§ 117). E. A. Wallis Budge, *The Queen*

ARAB SOURCES

Arab sources which deal with Justin's period are of less importance than Syriac. They belong to later times and are mostly based on sources which are not contemporary with the sixth century. The interest of Arab writers for Justin's time is chiefly concentrated on the Nagran massacre and the Himyaro-Abyssinian war. I wish to mention four Arab historians: Tabari; Abu-l-Faradj al-Ispahani; Agapius or in Arabic Mahbub; and the anonymous writer of the so-called *Chronicle of Seert.*

Abu-Djafar-Muhammed-ibn-Djarir-ibn-Yazid-ibn-Kadir-ibn-Khalid-al-Tabari was born in 839 in the province of Tabaristan, not far off the Caspian Sea, whence he received his surname of Tabari, by which he is generally known. He died in 923 in Bagdad. His most important work is his colossal history of the world. He was the first among Arab writers to compile a *corpus* of all historical information which existed among the Arabs and to write a general history from the creation to his own day.

For Justin's period, Tabari gives a detailed report of the Himyaro-Ethiopian war, of the massacre of Nagran, of relations between the South-Arabian Christians and the Byzantine emperor, that is Justin, of Justin's vessels sent to support the Ethiopian king, and of the final victory of the Christians over Judaism. Tabari's source for Justin's period was Ibn-Ishak, an Arab author and authority on tradition, who died about 767. But Tabari used him not directly but through another Arab writer, Ibn-Hisham, who largely employed Ibn-Ishak's work and who died in Egypt in 834.[61]

---

of Sheba and Her Only Son Menyelek, English translation from Ethiopic MSS. in the British Museum (London, 1922), pp. 225-226. On the time of the compilation, Conti Rossini, "Aetiopica," second series, *Rivista degli studi orientali,* X (Rome, 1923-1925), 508, feels it was probably definitely compiled between 1314 and 1322. I. Guidi, *Storia della letteratura etiopica* p. 45, places it in the second half of the thirteenth century.

[61] Tabari's text covering the period of the Sassanian Empire has been translated into German with very good comments by T. Nöldeke, *Geschichte der Perser und Araber zur Zeit der Sasaniden* (Leyden, 1879), pp. 185-194. The Arab text only, *Annales quos scripsit Abu Djafar Mohammed ibn Djarir at-Tabari cum aliis,* ed. M. J. de Goeje, I, 2 (Leyden, 1881-1882), 926-928. On Tabari himself, in addition to general histories of Arabic literature, see A. Vasiliev, *Byzance et les*

In 963 the minister of the Samanide prince Balami (Belami) composed the famous Persian translation of Tabari's *History*, the oldest historical work in modern Persian. Before the publication of Tabari's Arab original, Balami's version had always been used as a substitute, and it made its way rapidly in various oriental countries. Later it was translated into Turkish, and even, curiously enough, into Arabic, gradually replacing Tabari's voluminous and diffuse original. For Justin's period Balami's text fully reproduces the Arab original.[62]

Agapius (in Arabic, Mahbub) the Greek, son of Constantine, Bishop of Menbidj (Hierapolis) in Syria, lived in the tenth century and was the first Arab-Christian historian. He wrote a general history from the creation to his own time; unfortunately the manuscript which contains the second part of Agapius' history, telling the events of the eighth century, breaks off in the middle of a phrase. But the section dealing with the rule of Justin, whom Agapius, like the Syrian writers, calls Justinian, has been preserved; it contains some brief statements referring to various aspects of Justin's reign, especially to natural phenomena, but fails to furnish any new data.[63]

Arabes, I, *La dynastie d'Amorium* (Bruxelles, 1935), pp. 278–279. *The Encyclopaedia of Islam*, IV (Leyden, 1908–36), 578–579. Brockelmann, *Geschichte der arabischen Literatur*, I (Weimar, 1898), 142–143; new edition (Leiden, 1945), pp. 148–149. On Ibn-Ishak, *Encyclopaedia of Islam*, II, 389–390. On Ibn-Hisham, *ibidem*, II, 387.

[62] *Chronique de Tabari traduite sur la version persane d'Abou-Ali Mohammed Belami* by Hermann Zotenberg, II (Paris, 1869), 181–184. On Balami see Zotenberg's introduction to the first volume of his translation. A. Vasiliev, *op. cit.*, p. 286. *Encyclopaedia of Islam*, I, 614 (article signed by W. Barthold). A few words in Edward G. Browne, *A Literary History of Persia*, I (Cambridge, 1929), 11, 356, 477. Browne erroneously refers Balami's death to the year 996 (see *Enc. of Islam*, I, 614).

[63] The Arab text with a French translation by A. Vasiliev, *Agapius (Mahbouh) de Menbidj. Kitab al-Unvan. Histoire universelle*, II, 2, *Patrologia Orientalis*, VIII (1912), 425 (165)–426 (166). The Arab text only, L. Cheikho, *Agapius episcopus Mabbugensis, Historia universalis* (Beirut, 1912); on Justin, p. 318–319, CSCO, Scriptores arabici, text, 3rd series, vol. V. On Agapius of Menbidj himself, Baron V. Rosen, "Notes on the Chronicle of Agapius of Menbidj," *Journal of the Ministry of Public Instruction* (January, 1884), pp. 47–75 (in Russian). A. Vasiliev, "Agapius of Menbidj, a Christian Arab Historian of the Tenth Century," *Viz. Vremennik*, XI (1904), 574–587 (in Russian). *Idem*, communication on Agapius at the International Congress of Orientalists at Algiers, *Revue Africaine* (1905), nos. 258–259, pp. 337–338. *Idem*, advertissement, in *Patrologia Orientalis*, V (1909), 561 (5)–564 (8). Both in French. A few lines from Vasiliev's Russian article by C. Brockelmann, "Die christlich-arabische Literatur," in the series of Ahmelang,

Abu-l-Faradj Ali ibn al Husain ibn Muhammed ibn Ahmed al-Korashi al-Isbahani (or al-Isfagani), an Arabian historian, was born in 897 and died in 967. His chief work, which alone has been preserved, is the great *Kitab al-Aghani* (Book of Songs); in this he collected the songs which were popular in his time, adding accounts of their authors. The book is our most important authority not only for the history of Arab literature but also for the history of Arab civilization. For Justin's period, Abu-l-Faradj gives the same detailed account of the Himyaro-Ethiopian-Byzantine relations which we have in Tabari's *Chronicle*.[64]

The so-called *Nestorian History* or the *Chronicle of Seert* consists of two parts. The first part, which has been preserved in one manuscript of the Library of the Chaldean Patriarchate in Mosul, and which contains the events of the first centuries of Christianity, does not concern us. But the second part, which was discovered in a manuscript in the Library of Seert, in Kurdistan, deals with the years 484 to 650. The author is unknown. The *Chronicle* itself was compiled soon after the year 1036. Several pages of the *Chronicle* are devoted to the period of Justin; they deal with Justin's new religious policy, mention the convocation of the Councils of Jerusalem and Tyre, natural phenomena, and persecutions, and describe the relations of Justin with the king of the Arabs, Mundhir. The anonymous author gives the name of the Jewish king of Nedjran, Masruq. His data are not new and his sources have not yet been identified.[65]

Die Litteraturen des Ostens in Einzeldarstellungen (1907). G. Graf, *Geschichte der christlichen arabischen Literatur*, II (Vatican City, 1947), 39–41, Studi e testi, 133.

[64] *Kitab al-Aghani* was published in twenty volumes in Bulak, in 1868 (1285 of the hegira), XVI, 71–72 (the Arab text only). A new edition, in twenty-one volumes, appeared in Cairo in 1905–1906. I am using the first edition. There is no translation into any European language. The story told in *Kitab al-Aghani* corresponds to Tabari-Nöldeke, pp. 189–191, to Tabari ed. de Goeje, I, 2, 926–928, and to the Persian version of Balami, II, 181–184. Very valuable for our orientation in this enormous work are *Tables alphabétiques du Kitab al-Aghani* by I. Guidi, I–II (Leiden, 1895–1900). On the author himself, see C. Brockelmann, *op. cit.*, I, 146; Erster Supplementband (Leiden, 1937), pp. 225–226 (many bibliographical additions); new edition, I (Leiden, 1945), 152–153. *Encyclopaedia of Islam*, I, 85 (article signed by Brockelmann).

[65] The Arab text and French translation, *Histoire nestorienne (Chronique de Seert)*, second part (1) by Addai Scher, Chaldean Archbishop of Seert (Kurdistan). *Patrologia Orientalis*, VII (1911); on Justin, pp. 138 (46)–145 (53); on the conversion of the inhabitants of Nedjran and on the Jewish king Masruq, *Patr.*

SURVEY OF THE SOURCES

Russian Sources

The name of Justin and some brief records of his reign occur in the Russian annals (letopisi). Since they merely reproduce, in one or another form, the Greek sources which are known to us, these records have no historical value; but they have a certain interest in indicating what Byzantine sources were known and used in Old Russia. Two of them were particularly popular: the chronicles of John Malalas and Georgius Hamartolus. Data from the history of Byzantium appear in the later compilations of the Russian annals at the point where the latter become a digest of earlier Greek chronographies and Russian chronicles. The *Nikonovsky Chronicle*, which is sometimes also called the *Patriarchal Chronicle*, compiled in the middle of the sixteenth century, simply mentions, with reference to Nicephorus, Patriarch of Tsargrad (Constantinople), "Justin the Hairy (Volosaty) who reigned nine years and twenty-three days," and in another place "Justin the Thrax (Thracian), from the city of Thakyya, a heretic, who ruled nine years and twenty-three days." [66]

In the items included at the beginning of the manuscript which contains the so-called *Chronicle of Lvov* (*Lvovskaya Letopis*), there are two brief notes on Justin. In the first note he is called Ustiyan the Thracian, under whom occurred the appearance of a comet and several violent earthquakes. In the second note he is called "Ustiyan Venderitin the Thracian who reigned 9 years and 22 days. He was of

Or., V (1910), pp. 330 (218)–331 (219). On the manuscripts and authorship see the introduction of Addai Scher to the first part of the *Chronicle*. *Patr. Orientalis*, IV (1908), pp. 215 (5)–218 (8). Addai Scher thought that the author might have lived in the first half of the thirteenth century. But in 1912 C. F. Seybold definitely proved that the *Chronicle* was compiled in the eleventh century soon after 1036, the year in which the Fatimid calif Zahir died. See Seybold's review of the first part of the *Chronicle* in *Zeitschrift der deutschen morgenländischen Gesellschaft*, LXVI (1912), 743. Seybold's conclusion has now been generally accepted. See A. Baumstark, *op. cit.*, p. 5. E. Amann, "L'église nestorienne," *Dictionnaire de théologie catholique*, XI, 1 (1931), col. 158.

[66] *Complete Collection of Russian Annals*, or in Russian, *Polnoe Sobranie Russkikh Letopisey*, to which I shall refer as *PSRL*. *PSRL*, IX (St. Petersburg, 1862), XIX and XX. "Justin the Hairy" goes back to the Greek words Ἰουστῖνος . . . πολιὸς μετὰ οὐλότητος καὶ δασείας κόμης. Leo Grammaticus, *CSHB*, p. 122, 20–21. "Thakyya" may be the name of Dacia. In the second statement Justin is called a heretic, showing that its author was a monophysite.

37

medium size, a good warrior, and he died at the age of seventy-seven. During his reign Nememtiyan was martyred." I am unable at present to identify this martyr.[67]

A brief general sketch of Justin's reign is given in two Russian *Chronographs*: the *Chronograph* of the redaction of the year 1512, and the *Chronograph* of West-Russian redaction which was compiled approximately at the beginning of the second half of the sixteenth century. The texts of both *Chronographs* are identical; the second *Chronograph* adds to the narrative a brief note on Justin's elevation and the coronation of Justinian. The two *Chronographs* tell of Justin's election and mention his persecution of Manichaeans and Nestorians as well as some earthquakes, especially those which took place at Antioch and Pompioupolis (*Pompiysky grad*). The additional note of the West-Russian *Chronograph* runs as follows: "During (the reign of) Justin his nephew Justinian the Great became Emperor; he was elevated and crowned by his uncle Justin. Justin died at the age of seventy-seven, after reigning with his nephew four months. From Adam down to the death of Justin passed 6032 years." [68]

Finally, in the *Stepennaya Kniga Tsarskago Rodosloviya* (*Book of Steps of the Imperial Genealogy*), the final redaction of which was made in 1563, there is a brief tale of the martyrs of Nagran and the final victory of the Ethiopian king Elizvan over the Jew Dunas (Dunas y *gidovin*.)[69]

I have dwelt on the Russian Annals at perhaps excessive length, especially since they fail to furnish us any new material. But I have done so because the Russian sources referring to Justin's period have never previously been indicated.

ARMENIAN SOURCES

Armenian historians have no value for Justin's period. As monophysites they are hostile to him on account of his Chalcedonian policy; from their point of view he is "a wicked and impious" man. Some of them mention his religious persecutions. As a whole, they fail to show any special interest in his other activities.

[67] *PSRL*, XX (1910), 9 and 32.
[68] *PSRL*, XXII, 1 (1911), 292–293 (ch. 136); XXII, 2 (1914), 108.
[69] *PSRL*, XXI (1908), 399–400.

If I am not mistaken, the first Armenian historian who devoted some attention to Justin's reign was the Armenian Patriarch John, the so-called John Catholicos, who died in 925. In chapter IX of his *History of Armenia* he writes: "The true doctrine had subsisted for thirty-five years. The impious Justin [70] reigned after Anastasius; he was a wicked man, who wished to destroy everything, to change everything, and to restore the heresy of the Council of Chalcedon; he crushed with griefs, pains, and horrible torments all holy men and all those who adhered to the true doctrine; and he plunged the Holy Church into an abyss of blood." [71]

An historian of the eleventh century, Stephen Asoghig of Taron (Daron), simply remarks in passing that after Anastasius, who had agreed with Zeno concerning Orthodoxy, Justin ruled nine years. "He accepted the Council of Chalcedon." [72]

An Armenian historian, Kiracos of Gantzac, who lived in the thirteenth century, wrote: "Anastasius was replaced by Justin the Old — an ignorant and merciless man — who inundated the earth with the blood of the Orthodox, because he put the Chalcedon in the first place and expelled those who recognized in the incarnated Word only one nature. . . . After Justin the crown passed to another Justin." [73] Another historian of the same century, Vardan (Vertan), wrote: "Yustianos (ruled) nine years. He restored the heresy of the Council (of Chalcedon)." [74]

---

[70] As in Syriac and Arabic tradition, the names of Justin and Justinian are also written identically in Armenian, *Hustianus*.

[71] *Histoire d'Arménie par le patriarche Jean VI dit Jean Catholicos*, Transl. by M. J. Saint-Martin (Paris, 1841), p. 53. On his life and work see Saint-Martin's introduction, pp. iii–xlviii. Now at length by Manook Abegyan, *History of Ancient Armenian Literature*, I (Erevan, 1948), 369–380 (in Russian).

[72] In French: Etienne Açoghig de Daron, *Histoire universelle traduite de l'arménien et annotée par E. Dulaurier*, part one (Paris, 1883), p. 168. In German: Stephanos von Taron, *Armenische Geschichte aus dem altarmenischen übersetzt von H. Gelzer und A. Burckhardt* (Leipzig, 1907), p. 104. There is a Russian translation by N. Emin (Moscow, 1864). On his life and work, Manook Abegyan, *op. cit.*, pp. 437–442.

[73] In French: Kiracos de Gantzac, *Histoire d'Arménie, traduite par M. Brosset*, I (St. Petersburg, 1870), 19–20. On Kiracos' life and works, see M. Brosset, *op. cit.*, II (St. Petersburg, 1871), II–VII. Armenian text (Venise, 1865), p. 22. As has been noted, *Justin* and *Justinian* are the same word in the Armenian sources.

[74] Armenian text of Vardapet Vardan (Venise, 1862), p. 83 (bottom of the page). I am greatly indebted to Miss S. Der Nersessian for indicating this passage

JUSTIN THE FIRST

LEGISLATIVE TEXTS

For the legislative activities of Justin's period the Justinian Code is of utmost importance because almost all his laws, most of them in Latin but some also in Greek, have been preserved here. Some novels and a passage from Justinian's *Institutes* (II, 7, 3) are of value.[75]

INSCRIPTIONS

The most important bilingual (Greek and Latin) inscription for Justin's period is the rescript issued by the joint emperors, Justin and Justinian, in 527, discovered in Asia Minor and published with comments by Charles Diehl. The rescript is addressed to Archelaus, who in 527 was the Praetorian Prefect of the Orient, and gives an interesting picture of the abuses in a rather remote corner of Asia Minor by

---

to me. On Vardan (Vartan) himself and his work *A General History*, which begins with the creation and ends with the year 1269, see the old French study of E. Dulaurier, "Les Mongols d'après les historiens arméniens: Extrait de l'Histoire Universelle de Vartan," *Journal Asiatique* (1860), 2, pp. 273–276. A complete Russian translation of Vardan's *History* exists. *Vardan the Great, General History*, transl. by N. Emin, with notes and additions (Moscow, 1881).

[75] I am using the *Codex Iustinianus* in the stereotyped edition by Paul Krueger (Berlin, 1887); the *Novellae*, that by R. Schoell and W. Kroll (Berlin, 1895); the *Institutiones*, by Paul Krueger (Berlin, 1867). A complete English translation of the *Code* and Justinian's *Novels* by S. P. Scott, M.A., is published in a seventeen volume set under the following lengthy title: *The Civil Law including the Twelve Tables, the Institutes of Gaius, the Rules of Ulpian, The Opinions of Paulus, The Enactments of Justinian and the Constitutions of Leo, translated from the original Latin, edited, and compared with all accessible systems of jurisprudence ancient and modern* (Cincinnati, 1932). Volumes XII–XV contain the *Code* (the laws issued in Greek have not been translated), and volumes XVI–XVII, the *Novels*. If it is used, this translation must be carefully compared with the original texts. The first translation of the Code in French: P.-A. Tissot, *Code et Novelles de Justinien; novelles de l'empereur Léon*, I–IV (Metz and Paris, 1806–1810). An old German translation in seven volumes exists: *Das Corpus Juris Civilis ins deutsche übersetzt von einem Vereine rechtsgelehrter und herausgegeben von Dr. Carl Eduard Otto, Dr. Bruns Schilling und Dr. Carl Friedrich Ferdinand Sintenis* (Leipzig, 1831–1839). Italian translation of the Code: *Corpo del Diritto* corredato dell note di Dionisio Gotofredo, e di C. E. Freiesleben altrimenti Ferromontano . . . per cura del consigliere Giovanni Vignali, I–II (Naples, 1860–1861). Text and translation. There is also a more recent Spanish edition: *Cuerpo del derecho civil romano a doble texto, traducido al castellano del latino, publicado por los hermanos Kriegel, Hermann y Osenbrüggen*, I–II (Barcelona, 1892–1895), in six volumes. There is a fine English translation of the *Institutes* by Thomas Collett Sandars, *The Institutes of Justinian with English introduction, translation, and notes* (London, New York, 1922).

imperial officers, passing soldiers, police agents, and troops stationed there.[76]

There are several other inscriptions, mostly casual and fragmentary, which deal largely with the erection of various structures, and which will be discussed in detail below. They are as follows: (1) an inscription discovered in 1927 in Syria, which mentions "an encampment (μῆτατον) of Saints Longinus, Theodore, and Georges," and is tentatively dated 524–525 (Syria, IX, 1928, 167): (2) a very interesting inscription from Egypt, dealing with the "kinglet" (βασιλίσκος) of the Nubians, Silko, which is important for the history of the relations of Byzantium with the African peoples of Blemyes and Nobadae (Nubians) in the sixth century; [77] (3) the Latin inscription which indicates that the consulship of Eutharic in 519 was not accepted in Burgundy (Corp. inscr. lat., XII, 1500); (4) an inscription indicating commercial relations between Palmyra with Egypt (Mélanges Franz Cumont, Bruxelles, 1936, p. 400); (5 and 6) two inscriptions from Palestine which mention that the town walls of the city of Bethsham-Scythopolis were repaired through a grant provided by Justin; [78] (7) another inscription of 522 A.D. discovered at Bethsham-Scythopolis, in Palestine, which deals with the construction of a monastery (Revue biblique, XLII, 1933, pp. 555–561. G. M. Fitzgerald, A Sixth Century Monastery at Beth-Shan (Scythopolis), Publications of the Palestine Section of the University Museum, University of Pennsylvania, IV (Philadelphia, 1939), 12 (no. 20); appendix, p. 19; see plate XXII). Several other secular inscriptions from Syria will be mentioned below. An interesting inscription of 524 from Syria records the political career of Euphraemius, one of the prominent collaborators of Justin, who ended his life as the patriarch of Antioch (Bulletin de correspondance hellénique, XXVI (1902), 166–167. Syria, XX (1939), 309–312).

[76] Charles Diehl, "Rescrit des empereurs Justin et Justinien en date du 1er juin 527," Bulletin de correspondance hellénique XVII (1893), 501–520.
[77] Corpus Inscriptionum Graecarum, ed. A. Boeckh, III, no. 5072, 2, p. 486. G. Lefebvre, Recueil des inscriptions grecques chrétiennes d'Egypte (Cairo, 1907), no. 628 (pp. 118–119).
[78] The most recent edition by J. Starr, American Journal of Philology, LVIII, 1 (1937), 83–84. More information below.

JUSTIN THE FIRST

PAPYRI

Comparatively little papyrologic evidence is to be indicated in reference to the period of Justin.

An heroic poem on a war with the Blemyes, the so-called *Blemyomachia*, which has been preserved on a papyrus, although attributed to the fifth century has some interest in connection with the "Blemyan danger" under Justin. Two papyri in the Museum of Cairo, dated about 522, mention Blemyan inroads upon Upper Egypt (Catalogue by Jean Maspero, I, Nos. 67004 and 67009). Another papyrus deals with the mediocre Egyptian poet of the sixth century, a Copt by birth, Dioscorus, son of Apollos, and with his poetry, which has some references to the Blemyes (J. Maspero, *Revue des études grecques*, XXIV, 1911, pp. 430–431). These examples show clearly that the Blemyan danger was of great importance in the life of Upper Egypt of the sixth century.

The Oxyrhynchus Papyri supply us with very interesting data about a wealthy Egyptian Apion family, whose members took part in imperial politics under Anastasius and Justin.

A number of papyrological items referring to the period of Justin in various European papyrological collections deal with the economic life of Byzantium Egypt; but these casual, brief, and fragmentary data may be fully appreciated and adequately employed only if they are included in the economic history of the sixth century as a whole.

CHAPTER TWO

From Swineherd to Emperor

Justin's Origin

Justin I presents an interesting phenomenon on the Byzantine throne from the point of view both of his racial origin and of his social standing as well. He was an Illyrian peasant, who, by his reign, by the reign of his famous nephew Justinian, and by the reign of Justinian's nephew Justin II, stands near the end of a long list of Roman emperors whom the Balkan Peninsula produced, and who, owing to their extraordinary energy, at the most crucial moments in her history were able to win back the peace and unity of the Roman Empire. In the anarchy and agony of the third century, the emperor Maximus (235–238) was the son of a Thracian peasant. Claudius Gothicus (268–270) belonged to the great soldiers of Illyricum. Aurelian (270–275), the "Restorer of the Empire" (*Restitutor orbis*), of humble birth, was probably a native of Sirmium (now Mitrovica) in Pannonia. Probus (276–282), an able Illyrian officer, was also born at Sirmium. Carus (282–283) was born in Illyria. Diocletian (284–305), an Illyrian soldier of humble origin, was a Dalmatian by birth. Constantine the Great (324–337), born at Naïssus (now Nish) in the province *Dacia mediterranea*, was the son of a Balkan peasant. In the fifth century and at the beginning of the sixth, Marcian (450–457) was a Thracian; Leo I (457–474) was a native of Dacia; and Anastasius I (491–518), Justin's predecessor, was a native of Dyrrhachium, in the province of New Epirus. Following the dynasty of Justin and Justinian, the emperors Tiberius (578–582) and Phocas (602–610) were Thracians. Only with the outset of the seventh century, when the long-lived dynasties made their appearance on the Byzantine throne, did new ethnic elements begin to play an important part in Byzantine history. The Heraclian dynasty (610–711) was of Armenian origin; the Isaurian or Syrian dynasty (717–802) was from the East; the Amorian or Phrygian dy-

43

nasty (820–867) came from Asia Minor; the Macedonian dynasty (867–1056) was of Armenian or Armeno-Slavic origin. The last four dynasties only, the Comneni, Angeli, Lascarids, and Palaeologi, were Greek.

Since Justin and his brilliant nephew Justinian were from the Balkan Peninsula, where at the end of the fifth century a new ethnic element, the Slavs, were not only entrenching themselves strongly but in all probability had already settled themselves permanently in various places, their names are closely connected with the problem of their Slavonic extraction, which has long been regarded by many scholars as an historical fact. This theory was based upon the *Life* of the emperor Justinian written in Latin by the abbot Theophilus (in Slavonic *Bogomil*), the supposed preceptor of Justinian, and published by the keeper of the Vatican Library, Nicholas Alemannus, in 1623, in his valuable commentary on his own edition of the *Anecdota* or *Secret History* (*Historia Arcana*), a work of the noted historian of the sixth century, Procopius of Caesarea. The *Justiniani Vita* of Bogomil introduces special names for Justinian and his relatives, names by which they were supposedly known in their native land, and which, in the opinion of many high authorities on Slavonic studies in the nineteenth century, were Slavonic names. For example, Justinian's father, whom Byzantine writers call Sabbatius, was named Istokus (Istok) according to the *Life*, an Illyrian word which means "the Orient"; the name of Justinian himself was Upravda, another Illyrian word, originating from *Pravda*, that is, *Justitia*; this name *Upravda* is given by Illyrian writers to Justinian and to both Justins (*uterque Justinus*). Although the origin of the *Iustiniani Vita* published by Alemannus remained rather vague and open to question, some of the best Slavonic authorities in the middle of the nineteenth century, such as Šafarik (Shafarik) and Hilferding, stated that Justinian was a Slav by origin, and that "in the sixth century a Slav, surrounded by his Slavonic family, was seated on the imperial throne in Byzantium." [1] In 1854, A. Kunik wrote that "Upravda-Justinian, in spite of his Slavonic origin, was so filled with

[1] Šafarik, *Slavonic Antiquities*, in Czech. Russian translation by Bodyansky, *Slovanské starožitnosti*, II part I, (Prague, 1837) 257ff.; sec. ed. in 1862–1863. A. Hilferding, *Works*, I (St. Petersburg, 1868), 7–8 (in Russian).

a sense of his dignity as successor of the Roman Caesars that he ordered his code to be compiled in the Latin vernacular and even called this language his paternal tongue (πάτριος φωνή)"; and at another point Kunik remarked that on the Byzantine throne were seated "hellenized Slavs." [2] In 1859 V. Lamansky wrote that in the sixth century "a Slav, son of Istok and Viglenitza, even reached the throne, upon which he was known by the name of Justinian I." [3] The Russian scholar M. Drinov, who in 1873 advanced his theory of the beginning of the Slavonic settlement in the Balkan Peninsula in the late second century A.D., saw in the Slavic names of Justinian and his relatives one of the most important bases for confirmation of his theory.[4]

When West European scholars unfamiliar with Slavic languages used the *Vita Theophili*, especially in the eighteenth century, they attempted to explain in their own way the strange names of Justinian's family. In 1731 a German writer Ludewig, in a Latin book on Justinian, Theodora, and Tribonian, attributed a barbarian origin to Justinian's family. Justinian, he said, was of foreign (*barbarus*) origin and one might call him Illyrian, or Macedonian, or Bulgarian. By his family he was called Upravda, which signifies (*barbaro significatu*) *uprait*, *ufrecht*, *erectus*, and *justus*. And a little later Ludewig concludes: "The Imperial family was foreign (*barbara*), id est Illyrian and Thracian." [5] Gibbon, who knew Ludewig's book, wrote that the names of these Dardanian peasants were Gothic, and almost English:

[2] A. Kunik, "Why Does Byzantium Remain Now A Riddle in Universal History?" *Uchenyja Zapiski* of the Imperial Academy of Sciences in St. Petersburg, first and third sections, II (1854), 430, n. 2; 435 (in Russian).

[3] V. Lamansky, *The Slavs in Asia Minor, Africa, and Spain* (St. Petersburg, 1859), p. 123. See also his "Historical Remarks on the Work *On the Slavs in Asia Minor, Africa, and Spain* (St. Petersburg, 1859), p. 2. Both works were published in the *Uchenyja Zapiski* of the second section of the Imperial Academy of Sciences, V (in Russian).

[4] M. Drinov, *The Slavic Occupation of the Balkan Peninsula* (Moscow, 1873), p. 48 (in Rusian). Reprinted in M. Drinov's *Works*, edited by V. N. Zlatarsky, I (Sofia, 1909), 139–364. In Soviet Russia several historians have gone back to Drinov's theory and have come to the conclusion that large Slavonic settlements in the Balkan Peninsula existed long before the sixth century. See *Twenty-five Years of Historical Studies in URSS* (Moscow-Leningrad, 1942), pp. 232–233 (in Russian). Some bibliography is given. I shall return to this question below, in the section on the Slavs.

[5] J. P. Ludewig, *Vita Iustiniani atquae Theodorae augustorum nec non Triboniani* (Halle, 1731), pp. 125, 127–129.

"Justinian is a translation of *upravda* (*upright*); his father Sabatius was styled in his village *istock* (*stock*)." [6]

The theory of the Slavonic origin of Justinian's family also took root among West European scholars in the nineteenth century. Lebeau, Finlay, and Paparrigopoulo accepted it. In 1870 a French historian, A. Rambaud, stated: "It seems there is no doubt of the origin of the dynasty of Justin I. The names of Istok, of Beglenica, of Upravda . . . provide a rather conclusive proof as to the origin of those peasants of Bederiana: let us not forget that, since the time of Constantine the Great, Slavonic colonies had been established in Thrace." [7] In 1886 James Muirhead, who was especially interested in Roman Law, wrote: "Justinian's family has been variously conjectured, on the strength of the proper names which its members are stated to have borne, to have been Teutonic or Slavonic. The latter seems the more probable view. His own name was originally Upravda." [8] In the same year (1886) H. J. Roby called Justinian "Uprauda the Slave or Goth reigning under the name of Justinian." [9] Muirhead's and Roby's mention of the Teutonic or Gothic origin of Justinian's family may be connected with the hypothesis of Gibbon indicated above.

But at the same time it is to be pointed out that some West European scholars expressed doubts concerning the authenticity of the information which we find in the *Iustiniani Vita*, especially from the philological point of view, in reference to the Slavonic origin of the proper names of Justinian's family; and in 1874 W. Tomaschek flatly asserted that the Slavonic origin of Justinian was idle talk (*das Geschwätz*).[10]

There was no corroborative evidence from any other source about the biographical notes which the *Justiniani Vita* contained, or about

[6] Gibbon, *The Decline and Fall of the Roman Empire*, chapter XL; ed. Bury, IV, 205, n. 2. See Bury's explanatory note for Gibbon's speculations in the same note; see also Bury's *Introduction* to I, pp. LIX–LX.

[7] A. Rambaud, *L'Empire grec au dixième siècle* (Paris, 1870), p. 535.

[8] J. Muirhead, *Historical Introduction to the Private Law of Rome*, third ed. revised and edited by Alexander Grant (London, 1916), p. 364. The first edition of this book came out in 1886, the second in 1898.

[9] H. J. Roby, *An Introduction to the Study of Justinian's Digest* (Cambridge, 1886), p. XV.

[10] W. Tomaschek, "Miscellen aus der alten Geographie," *Zeitschrift für die österreichischen Gymnasien*, XXV (1874), 658.

Justinian's *preceptor* Theophilus-Bogomil; nor had anyone since Alemannus seen the manuscript of the biography. The puzzle of Alemannus' source was solved by J. Bryce, who during his work at Rome in 1883 discovered in the library of the Barberini palace the original text from which Alemannus drew his information. It purported to be an extract from a work written in the Illyrian language (*litteris et characteribus Illyricis*) and composed by Bogomil, Abbot of the Monastery of St. Alexander in Dardania. The Illyrian language of the manuscript is obviously the same as Slavonic. This extract had been translated into Latin by Joannes Tomco Marnavich, Canon of Sebenico (1579–1639), afterwards Bishop of Bosnia, a friend of Alemannus. The result of Bryce's investigation was an important article, which came out in 1887.[11] In his study Bryce has clearly shown that this text is worthless as a historical document and that there is no reason to suppose that such a person as the Dardanian Bogomil ever existed. According to Bryce, the only result of the *Vita* is "to give us a glimpse into a sort of *cyclus* of Slavonic legends, attaching themselves to the great name of Justinian, as other Slavonic legends were connected with Alexander the Great." [12] V. Jagić says that all Slavonic names in the *Vita Theophili* are nothing but a quite recent fabrication of the sixteenth and seventeenth centuries, which came out of the pan-Slavonic school of the Ragusa-Dalmatian scholars of that time.[13] The theory of Justinian's Slavonic origin, then, must be discarded insofar as it is based upon the *Vita*.[14] In spite of this, in 1934 Voinovitch calls

[11] J. Bryce, "Life of Justinian by Theophilus," *The English Historical Review*, II, 657–684. This study was also printed in Italian in *Archivio della Reale Società Romana di Storia Patria*, X (Rome, 1887), 137–171 (La Vita Justiniani di Teofilo abate). The Italian edition does not contain the letter of Jireček and the opinion of Jagić which were added to the English edition.

[12] Bryce, *op. cit.*, p. 684. A detailed account of Bryce's discovery and study in A. Vasiliev, "The Problem of Justinian's Slavonic Origin," *Vizantiysky Vremennik*, I, 469–492 (in Russian). See also J. B. Bury, *Introduction* to his edition of Gibbon's work, I, pp. LIX–LX.

[13] V. Jagić, *Neuentdeckte Quelle der Fabel von Istok, Upravda u. a.*, Archiv für slavische Philologie, XI (1888), 302–303.

[14] In 1888 L. Ranke was inclined to accept Justinian's Slavonic origin. L. Ranke, *Weltgeschichte*, IV, 2, 8. But evidently in 1888, when his book came out, Ranke was not yet acquainted with Bryce's study which had appeared in 1887. In 1888, without mentioning Justinian's Slavonic origin, Knecht reproduced the Slavonic names of Justinian's father (Istock) and mother (Biglenitza). A. Knecht, *Die*

Justin and Justinian Slavo-Illyrians from Macedonia, and refers to the name *Upravda* "which means in Slavonic *Justitia*." [15]

Most sources, Greek, Oriental (Syriac, Arabian, Armenian), and Slavonic or Old Russian (the latter entirely dependent on their Greek originals) call Justin Thracian; some Greek sources and the Latin chronicle of Victor Tonnennensis call him Illyrian; and finally Procopius writes that the native country of Justinian, and by implication that of Justin as well, was Dardania.[16] In these three definitions of Justin's origin there is no contradiction. By his racial origin Justin, and consequently Justinian his nephew as well, might have belonged to the old warlike Thracian race, which in classical antiquity occupied the western part of the Balkan Peninsula.

It is an interesting question whether the Thracian language, or one of its dialects, was still spoken in the sixth century. In 1893 Tomaschek wrote that in the sixth century the Thracian language had been long extinct; but in the same study he mentioned that in the sixth century the language of one of the Thracian tribes, that of the Bessi, was still in use. In 1931 Skok stated that in the sixth century the Slavs were still encountering in the Balkans a Thracian population who spoke their own vernacular.[17] And it is true that the *lingua Bessorum* is well attested for that century. In this connection there is an extremely interesting record preserved in the *Life* of one of the Palestinian saints, Theodosius the Great, who died in 529 and whose *Life* was compiled by Theodore, Bishop of Petrae. The *Life* tells us that in a Palestinian

---

Religions-Politik Kaiser Justinians I (Würzburg, 1896), p. 6. In 1914 Uspensky wrote that the grounds were not sufficient either to assert or to deny the Slavonic origin of Justin and Justinian, because in the fifth and sixth centuries that region (North Macedonia) was already occupied by a Slavonic element, and the Slavonic origin of emigrants from North Macedonia was quite possible. Uspensky, *History of the Byzantine Empire*, I, 2, 410 (in Russian). Max Vasmer, "Die Slaven in Griechenland," *Abh. der Preussischen Akademie der Wissenschaften* (1941), Phil.-hist. Klasse, no. 12, p. 12 (discarded theory).

[15] L. de Voinovitch, *Histoire de Dalmatie*, I: *Des origines au marché infâme*, 1409 (Paris, 1934), p. 220.

[16] A list of the sources referring to Justin's origin is to be found in note 25 at the end of this section.

[17] W. Tomaschek, *Die alten Thraker: Eine ethnologische Untersuchung*, in *Sitzungsber. der phil.-hist. Classe der Akademie der Wiss. zu Wien*, LXXVIII (1893), 77. P. Skok, "Beiträge zur thrakisch-illyrischen Ortsnamenkunde," *Zeitschrift für Ortsnamenforschung*, VII (1931), 43.

monastery was a church where the Bessi, representatives of one of the old Thracian tribes, said prayers to God in their own language. Also in the sixth century a pilgrim to the Holy Places, Antoninus of Placentia, narrates that in the monastery of Sinai were three abbots as interpreters who knew the tongues of Greek, Latin, Syriac, Egyptian, and *Bessam*. These two independent and reliable records most probably refer not to the pure ancient Bessan, that is, the Thracian language which in the sixth century no longer existed, but to the new Bessan idiom probably consisting of old Thracian and Latin elements, which needed interpretation for those who spoke Latin or Greek.[18]

One proof more may be alleged for the Thracian origin of Justin and Justinian. According to R. Roesler, the name of Justinian's father and consequently of Justin's brother was Sabbatius, a pure Thracian name,[19] which undoubtedly goes back to Sabazius, the well known ancient mystical deity of the Thracians. We may conclude that Justin himself and his family were of Thracian origin; they were born and lived in Illyria, and they spoke Latin.

[18] See H. Usener, *Der heilige Theodosios*, in *Schriften des Theodoros und Kyrillos* (Leipzig, 1890), p. 45: ἑτέραν δὲ (ἐκκλησίαν) ἔνθα κατὰ τὴν οἰκείαν γλῶσσαν τὸ ἔνος Βεσσῶν τῷ ὑψίστῳ τὰς εὐχὰς ἀποδίδωσιν. Also *Symeonis Metaphrastae Vita S. Theodosii Coenobiarchae, Mensis Januarius*. Migne, *PG*, CXIV, col. 505. Antoninus Martyr, *De Locis Transmarinis, Itinera Hierosolymitana et Descriptiones Terrae Sanctae*, ed. T. Tobler and A. Molinier, *Latina lingua exarata*, I (Geneva, 1880), 377: In quo monasterio (on Mount Sinai) tres sunt abbates, scientes linguas Latinam, Graecam, Syram, Egyptiacam et Bessam; ed. J. Gildemeister (Berlin, 1880), cap. 37; *CSEL*, vol. 39, ed. P. Geyer (Vienna, 1898), p. 213, cap. 37. *Antonini Placentini Itinerarium saeculo sexti exeunte scriptum*, ed. J. Pomialovsky (St. Petersburg, 1895), cap. XXXVIII, p. 18; see note, p. 98 (*Pravoslavny Palestinsky Sbornik*, vol. 39). Latin text with a Russian translation. Pomialovsky gives other references on the Bessi in the sixth century. The *Bessa lingua* in this text is so unusual that some scholars have chosen to read *lingua Persa* instead. See *Antonini Placentini Itinerarium* in Migne, *PL*, LXXII, col. 912, cap. 37; also in an English translation: *Of the Holy Places Visited by Antoninus Martyr* (circa 560–570 A.D.) transl. by Aubrey Stewart (London, 1896), p. 29, cap. 37. See W. Tomaschek, *Die alten Thraker*, p. 77. Tomaschek writes that in the sixth century the Bessi already spoke the Romance tongue (in Romanian *die limba Rumanésca*). Under Anastasius, Justin's predecessor, the Goths, *Bessi and other Thracian peoples* are to be found in the army which was sent to fight the Persians. Theoph., ed. de Boor, p. 145. This passage is omitted in *Anastasii Chronographia Tripertita*, ed. de Boor, p. 120. Cf. L. Niederle, *Manuel de l'antiquité slave*, I (Paris, 1923), 70–71.

[19] R. Roesler, "Ueber den Zeitpunkt der slavischen Ansiedlung an der unteren Donau," *Sitzungsberichte der Akademie der Wissenchaften zu Wien*, philos.-histor. Classe, LXXIII (1873), pp. 115–116.

When I say that Justin and Justinian were of Thracian extraction, I do not mean that they were representatives of the pure Thracian race, which in the sixth century no longer existed in the Balkan Peninsula. Some other racial ingredients had penetrated into the veins of its heterogeneous population. The more we study the question of the Slavonic advance and settlements in the Peninsula, the more we are inclined to believe that the Slavs settled there in various places much earlier than the middle or the end of the sixth century. Therefore a certain admixture of Slavonic blood in the veins of Justin and Justinian's family is very possible. If this is so, the famous *Vita Iustiniani* of Theophilus-Bogomil, though devoid of historical value in itself, may be regarded as something more than a mere late fabrication of the Canon of Sebenico, Joannes Tomco Marnavich (+ 1639), with no historical background; it may vaguely reflect the old and popular local tradition which attributed Slavonic origin to Justinian, for Justin and Justinian's family may well have been of Thraco-Slavonic extraction.

At the beginning of the sixth century, the civil administration of the Balkan Peninsula belonged to two circumscriptions, or two prefectures, which had been established under praetorian prefects by Diocletian and Constantine the Great. In the sixth century the diocese of Thrace occupied the eastern region of the Peninsula extending north as far as the mouth of the Danube, and as an administrative unit it belonged to the prefecture of the East. Illyria, where the family of Justin and Justinian lived, is to be recognized as the *Praefectura praetorio per Illyricum*, the smallest of the prefectures, which at times had been united with the prefecture of Italy under one prefect. But from the end of the fourth century the Prefecture of Illyricum was organized as a separate circumspection composed of two dioceses: Dacia and Macedonia.[20] Thus when our sources write that Justin was an

---

[20] Scholars hold various opinions as to the exact dating of the final organization of the separate *Praefectura praetorio per Illyricum*. Mommsen gives the year 379; Seeck the years 395-397; Bury, 395; Stein, not before 395. Mommsen, *Die diocletianische Reichspraefectur: Historische Schriften*, III (Berlin, 1910), 291 (originally published in *Hermes*, XXXVI (1901), 201-217). O. Seeck, *Regesten der Kaiser und Päpste für die Jahre 311 bis 476 n. Chr.* (Stuttgart, 1919), p. 148. J. B. Bury, *History of the Later Roman Empire*, I, 26, n.1. E. Stein, *Untersuchungen zur spätrömischen Verwaltungsgeschichte*, Rheinisches Museum für Philologie, LXXIV (1925), 351.

Illyrian, they mean that he and his family were residents of the Prefecture of Illyricum; Agathias calls the native city of Justinian an Illyrian city.[21] And Procopius' statement that the place whence came the emperor Justinian, "the founder of the Roman world," was a city of the European Dardanians, who dwelt beyond the boundaries of the Epidamnians (*De aedificiis*, IV, 17), is to be understood as meaning that Justin and his family were born and lived in the province of Dardania which, with four others, belonged to the diocese of Dacia; and Dacia, as we have pointed out above, with the diocese of Macedonia, belonged to the prefecture of Illyricum.[22]

Historians of the twentieth century call Justin a Thracian or an Illyrian, and are inclined to ascribe to him an Illyrian origin.[23] Amantos calls Justin's dynasty the Illyrian or Thraco-illyrian dynasty; Wigram,

[21] Agathias, V, 21: πατρὶς δὲ ἦν αὐτῷ πόλις Ἰλλυρική. *CSHB* p. 324; ed. Dindorf, p. 384.

[22] E. Stein also thinks that Justin, by nationality a Thracian, was born in the prefecture of Illyricum. E. Stein, "Justinus I," *Real Encyklopädie*, X, col. 1314. Diehl also calls Justin a peasant from Illyricum, Charles Diehl and G. Marçais, *Le Monde oriental de 395 à 1081* (Paris, 1936), p. 47. C. Jireček wrote that Justin's family originated from Roman colonists in Dardania. "Die Romanen in den Städten Dalmatiens während des Mittelalters, I," *Denkschriften der Ak. der Wiss. zu Wien*, Philos.-hist. Classe, XLVIII (1902), 19.

[23] For Thracian origin: A. Diakonov, *John of Ephesus* (St. Petersburg, 1908), p. 24, n. 127 (in Russian). E. Stein; see preceding note. N. Iorga, *Histoire de la vie byzantine*, I (Bucarest, 1934), 36. E. Kornemann, *Römische Geschichte*, II (Stuttgart, 1939), 497 (Thracian-Macedonian). In 1885 A. J. Evans wrote, "Justin was of course of Thracian descent." Arthur John Evans, *Antiquarian Researches in Illyricum*, III and IV, *Archaeologia*, XLIX (London, 1885), 137. For Illyrian origin: A. P. Rudakov, *Outlines in Byzantine Culture Based on Data from Greek Hagiography* (Moscow, 1917), p. 186 and 268 (in Russian); F. Lot, *La Fin du monde antique et le début du moyen âge* (Paris, 1927), p. 298; S. Runciman, *Byzantine Civilization*, p. 35; N. Vulić, *L'origine ethnique de l'empereur Justinien; Actes du IVe Congrès international des études byzantines*, I (Sofia, 1934), 405: he feels that Justin was an Illyrian (*Bulletin de l'institut Archéologique Bulgare*, IX, 1935). M. Levchenko, *History of Byzantium* (Moscow-Leningrad, 1940), pp. 53-54 (in Russian). In 1928 and 1932 I wrote that Justin and Justinian might be considered as probably Illyrians, or perhaps Albanians, because according to some scholars the ancestors of the Albanians were the ancient Illyrians. A. Vasiliev, *History of the Byzantine Empire*, I (Madison, 1928), 162: II (Madison, 1929), 304-305 (French edition, I, 170; II, 294-295). See also Gerard, *Les Bulgares de la Volga et les Slaves du Danube* (Paris, 1939), p. 26: he feels that Justin was an Illyrian or Albanian peasant. But the more recent linguistic discoveries connect Albanians not with Illyrians but with Thracians. See A. Philippson, *Das byzantinische Reich als geographische Erscheinung* (Leiden, 1939), p. 113; some bibliography on pp. 118–120.

the Dacian dynasty. Several historians omit to deal with the question of Justin's racial origin,[24] especially since the sources are so complex and multifarious.[25]

JUSTIN'S BIRTHPLACE

The most important source for the birthplace of Justin and Justinian is the contemporary writer Procopius of Caesarea, who was closely

[24] C. Amantos, Ἱστορία τοῦ βυζαντινοῦ κράτους (Athens, 1939), 178. Rev. W. A. Wigram, *The Separation of the Monophysites*, p. 65. J. Popescu-Spineni, *Sur l'origine ethnique de Justinien*, IIIe Congrès International des études byzantines (Athens, 1930), Compte-rendu par A. C. Orlandos (Athens, 1932), p. 347. Popescu-Spineni remarks that the Slavonic origin of Justinian is a theory today *almost* entirely abandoned. He emphasizes the word almost, because some textbooks, namely those on Roman law, continue to speak of Justinian's Slavic origin, even in our day (p. 345). In this statement Popescu-Spineni refers to the book of James Muirhead mentioned above. In his article Popescu-Spineni erroneously calls the first editor and commentator of Procopius' *Secret History*, Alemannus, a German historian. Nicolas Alemanni (1583–1626) was a Greek scholar born in Italy (at Ancona). In 1896 Pančenko stated that the nationality of Justin and Justinian was unknown. "On Procopius' *Secret History*," *Viz. Vrem.*, III (1896), 99 (in Russian).

[25] The sources on Justin's origin, in order of nationality preferred, are as follows:

Justin a Thracian, Θρᾷξ or occasionally Θρᾷξ: Malalas, p. 410, 415. Evagrius, IV, 1; ed. Bidez and Parmentier, p. 153. *Chr. Paschale*, CSHB, p. 611. *Nicephori Archiepiscopi Constantinopolitani opuscula historica*, ed. C. de Boor, p. 231. *Georgii Monachi Chronicon*, ed. Muralt, p. 524; ed. de Boor, II, 626. Leo Grammaticus, CSHB, p. 122. *Scriptores originum constantinopolitanarum*, ed. Theodore Preger, II, 164, 237–238, 254, 273. Zonaras, XIV, 5, 1: CSHB, III, 144. Michael Glycas, p. 493. Joel, p. 44. Ephraemius, p. 53. Niceph. Callistus, XVII, 1; Migne, *PG*, CXLVII, col. 220: "Θράκην αὐχήσας πατρίδα." Georgius Codinus (Pseudo), *De annorum et imperatorum serie, Excerpta de antiquitatibus Constantinopolitanis*, CSHB, p. 151. *Eutychii Alexandrini patriarchae annales*, ed. L. Cheikho, I (Beyrouth, 1906), 198–199 (Arab text); Latin translation in Migne, *PG*, CXI, col. 1068 (in Arabic "from the city of Thrace"; in Latin "e provincia Thraciae oriundus"). Michel le Syrien, ed. Chabot, IX, 12; II, 169. Langlois, *Chronique de Michel le Grand*, p. 175. *Gregorii Barhebraei Chronicon Ecclesiasticum* (Louvain, 1872), 194. *Abulpharagii Gregorii sive Bar-Hebraei Chronicon Syriacum*, II, 80. Gregory Abûl Faraj commonly known as Bar Hebraeus, *The Chronography*, I, 73; Budge mistook the word Tarkî, *i.e.* Trace, for Turkey. Slavo-Russian sources: *Complete Collection of Russian Annals* (in Russian, *Polnoye Sobraniye Russkikh Letopisey* or *PSRL*). *The Patriarchal* or *Nikonov Chronicle* (*Patriarshaya* or *Nikonovskaya Letopis*), *PSRL*, IX (St. Petersburg, 1862), XX, no. 17: Justin Thrax (referring to the *Chronicle* of Nicephorus, Patriarch of Tsargrad; cf. ed. de Boor, p. 231. See above, in this note). *The Lvov Chronicle* (*Lvovskaya Letopis*), *PSRL*, XX (St. Petersburg, 1910), 9 (Ustiyan Thrakiyan); 32 (Ustiyan Thrax). "The Chronicle of John Malalas in a Slavonic Version, ed. V. M. Istrin, *Sbornik Otdeleniya Russkago Yazyka i Slovesnosti*, XCI, no. 2, (1914), 17; Iustin

connected with Justinian and very familiar with all the details of the personal life of the two emperors. In his work "On the Buildings" Procopius writes: "Among the Dardanians of Europe who live beyond the boundaries of the Epidamnians, very close to the fort which is called Bederiana, there was a place named Taurisium, whence sprang the Emperor Justinian, the founder of the Roman world. . . . And close by this place he built a very notable city which he named Justiniana Prima (this means *first* in the Latin tongue), thus paying a debt of gratitude to the home that fostered him." [26]

A little later in the same work Procopius reports: "[Justinian] also

---

Thrax. Chronicle of John Malalas, books VIII–XVIII, transl. M. Spinka, p. 120. *The Chronicle of George Hamartolus*, ed. V. M. Istrin, I, 411: "Iustin Thrakisanin."

Justin an Illyrian, 'Ιλλύριος: Procopius, *Anecdota*, VI, 2; ed. Haury, p. 38. Theodorus Lector, *Ecclesiasticae Historiae* Lib. II, 37; Migne, *PG*, LXXXI, col. 204; J. A. Cramer, *Anecdota Graeca*, II, 108; E. Miller, "Fragments inédits de Théodore le Lecteur et de Jean d'Égée, *Revue archéologique*, XXVI (1873), 400. Agathias, V, 21: πόλις 'Ιλλυρική, *CSHB*, p. 324; ed. Dindorf, p. 384. *Victoris Tonnennensis episcopi Chronica*, under the year 518: Illyricianus. *Chronica Minora*, ed. Mommsen, II, 196, *MGH*, *Auctorum antiquissimorum*, vol. XI. *Theophanis Chronographia*, ed. de Boor, p. 164. *Anastasii Bibliothecarii Historia Tripertita*, ed. de Boor, p. 130: Hillyrius genere. Cedrenus, *CSHB*, I, 636. Let me mention in passing that according to some scholars the Balkan Peninsula is to be regarded to some extent as the cradle of the Illyrians. H. Krahe, "Die Illyrier in ihren sprachlichen Beziehungen zu Italikern und Griechen, 2: Die Illyrier in der Balkanhalbinsel," *Die Welt als Geschichte*, III, 4 (Stuttgart, 1937), 284 (*Zeitschrift für universalgeschichtliche Forschung*).

Justin from Dardania: Procopius, *De aedificiis*, IV, 1, 17: (Justinian was born) ἐν Δαρδάνοις που τοῖς Εὐρωπαίοις, οἳ δὴ μετὰ τοὺς 'Επιδαμνίων ὄρους ᾤκηνται (ed. Haury, p. 104; ed. H. Dewing, 1940, p. 224). In 1874 W. Tomaschek asserted that Justinian's parents were romanized Dardanians. W. Tomaschek, *Miscellen aus der alten Geographie, Zeitschrift für die österreichischen Gymnasien*, XXV, 658. Tomaschek's opinion is to be understood as meaning that Justinian's parents were romanized residents in the province of Dardania.

I may mention that the Christian Arab historian of the tenth century, Agapius (Mahbûb) of Menbidj, writes that Justin (like most Oriental historians he calls him Justinian) was a Roman, or literally originated from Rome. Agapius, *Histoire universelle*, ed. and transl. into French by A. Vasiliev. *Patrologia Orientalis*, VIII, 425 (165). The same statement in Gregory Abul-Faraj, *Historia compendiosa dynastiarum*, p. 149 (93); Arab text only, ed. by Salhani, p. 147.

[26] Proc. *De aedificiis* IV, 1, 17, 19: 'Εν Δαρδάνοις που τοῖς Εὐρωπαίοις, οἳ δὴ μετὰ τοὺς 'Επιδαμνίων ὄρους ᾤκηνται, τοῦ φρουρίου ἄγχιστα ὅπερ Βεδερίανα ἐπικαλεῖται, χωρίον Ταυρίσιον ὄνομα ἦν, ἔνθεν 'Ιουστινιανὸς βασιλεὺς ὁ τῆς οἰκουμένης οἰκιστὴς ὥρμηται . . . (ed. Dewing, VII, 1940, p. 224). I have translated the word ἡ οἰκουμένη in its later sense "the Roman world." A. Stewart translates "the Founder of the Universe" (*Of the Buildings of Justinian by Procopius*. Transl. by Aubrey Stewart, London, 1896, p. 91); H. Dewing, "the founder of the civilised world" (p. 225).

rebuilt the entire fort of Bederiana and made it much stronger. And there was a certain city among the Dardanians, dating from ancient times, which was named Ulpiana (Οὐλπιᾶνα); he tore down most of its circuit-wall, for it was seriously damaged and altogether useless, and he added a very great number of improvements to the city, changing it to its present fair aspect; and he named it Justiniana Secunda (*secunda* is the Latin word for second). Near it he built another city which had not existed before, and which he called Justinopolis from his uncle's name." [27]

Procopius was thoroughly versed in classical literature and in his style and presentation frequently followed classical writers, especially Herodotus and Thucydides. His writing is not entirely free of artificiality and ostentation. For example, in the first excerpt quoted above, instead of saying that Taurision, Justinian's birthplace, was situated in the province of Dardania, he writes that this place was located "among the European Dardanians," apparently having in mind the ancient Trojans, who have often been called Dardanians, more specifically "Asiatic Dardanians." That Procopius in this text means the province Dardania is clear from the second quotation, where he says that the city Ulpiana was "among the Dardanians" (ἐν Δαρδάνοις). And we know that the province Dardania, which belonged to the diocese of Dacia, contained two towns: Scupi (Scupus) and Ulpiana.

It is not surprising that Justinian paid much attention to rebuilding Dardania. Apart from the fact that this province was his birthplace, during the last year of the reign of Anastasius, in 518, a violent earthquake had destroyed in Dardania twenty-four towns, and its metropolis Scupus (Scupi) was razed to the ground; fortunately the population had fled from the city because of a barbarian attack not long before the earthquake.[28]

These two texts of Procopius, then, supply us with precise and

[27] Procopius, *De aedif.* IV, 1, 28–30.

[28] Marcellinus Comes, Chronicon, *s. a.* 518: In provincia Dardania adsiduo terrae motu viginti quattuor castella uno momento conlapsa sunt. . . . Scupus namque metropolis, licet sine civium suorum hostem fugientium clade, funditus tamen corruit. Ed. Mommsen, *Chronica Minora*, II, 100. Some scholars believe that Procopius does not refer to the province of Dardania but to the country inhabited by the Dardanians. See, for example, J. Vulić, "Où était Justiniana Prima?" *Le Musée Belge*, XXXII (1928), 65.

absolutely reliable information that Justinian's birthplace was Taurisium (Taurision) in the province of Dardania.

For Justin's home most of our sources, both Greek and Syriac, agree that his birthplace was Bederiana, which is mentioned in both the quotations from Procopius given above, although it is not specified as his birthplace. But in his *Anecdota* Procopius says plainly that Justin was from Bederiana. Other Greek sources provide the same information. In a distorted form of the place of Justin's birth which has been preserved in Syriac sources, the name of Bederiana is easily discovered. Latin and Arab sources fail to mention Justin's birthplace. The Russian annals, based on Greek sources, reproduce their tradition and name Justin "Venderitan." [29]

From the sources indicated above we have seen that in the province of Dardania there were two important and probably fortified places, Scupus (Scupi) and Ulpiana, and two less important, the fort of Bederiana, the birthplace of Justin, and a hamlet Taurisium (Taurision), the birthplace of Justinian. According to the *Notitia Dignitatum*, Scupi and Ulpiana were the seats of the so-called *legiones pseudo-comitatenses: Scupenses* and *Ulpianenses*.[30] The name of Scupi survives

---

[29] Procopius, *Anecdota* VI, 2: Ἰουστῖνος ὁ ἐκ Βεδεριάνης. John of Antioch, C. Müller, FHG. V, 1, 31: ἐκ Βεδεριανῆς φρουρίου (fr. 214 b); ed. Mommsen, *Hermes*, VI (1872), 339: ἐκ Βεδεριανοῦ φρουρίου. Malalas, XVII, 410: ἀπὸ Βεδεριάνας; at the beginning of Book XVIII (p. 425) Malalas says that Justinian was also from Bederiana. Agathias, V, 21· πατρὶς δὲ ἦν αὐτῷ πόλις Ἰλλυρικὴ Βεδερίανα (*CSHB* p. 324; ed. Dindorf, p. 384). *Chr. Pasch. CSHB*, p. 611: ὁ Βενδαρίτης. In Syriac: *Zach. of Mit.*, VIII, 1; transl. by Hamilton and Brooks, p. 189: from the fortress of Mauriana in Illyricum; by Ahrens and Krüger, p. 140: *von Kastra Bederiana in Illyrikon.* Mich. le Syr., transl. by Chabot, IX, 12; II, 169: du village de B[e]drinos; in the Armenian version of the priest Ischôk, transl. by V. Langlois, p. 175: born in the village of Bedrine (Bederiana). *Gregorii Abulpharagii sive Bar Hebraei Chronicon Syriacum*, ed. Bruns and Kirsch, I, p. 80: Ex Thraciae oppido Cedreno. *Idem, The Chronography*, transl. by E. Wallis Budge, I, 73: from the village of Badrinos. *Chronicon Anonymum ad annum Christi 1234 pertinens*, transl. by Chabot, p. 150: e castro Myrina. In Old Slavonic: The *Lvov Chronicle*, *ГSRL*, XX, 32: Ustiyan Venderitin. Istrin, "The Chronicle of John Malalas in a Slavonic version," *Sbornik Otdeleniya Russkago Yazika i Slovesnosti*, XCI, no. 2, 17: Iustin Vendaritin. *Chronicle of John Malalas*, books VIII–XVIII, transl. by M. Spinka, p. 120.

[30] *Notitia Dignitatm et administrationum omnium tam civilium quam militarium in partibus Orientis et Occidentis*, ed. E. Böcking (Bonn, 1839–1853), I, 35; ed. O. Seeck (Berlin, 1876), nos. 43–44, p. 29. See very useful annotations by Böcking for Scupi and Ulpiana, pp. 229–230. Fluss, Scupi, *PW*, second series, II, col. 910.

in the name of the modern Serbian town of Skoplye, in Turkish Usküb, located on the upper course of the Axius (Vardar) River in so-called Old Serbia. The name of Ulpiana survives in the name of the Serbian town of Liplyan (in the later Middle Ages, Lipenium) north of Skoplye. All four places were disastrously affected by the earthquake of 518, which I have mentioned above. Justinian rebuilt his uncle's birthplace Bederiana and also built a new city near Ulpiana which he called Justinopolis in his honor. In my opinion, he built a new city in Dardania because the old city had been totally destroyed by the earthquake.

As we know, Scupi, according to the *Chronicle* of Marcellinus, had entirely disappeared — that is, was reduced to a heap of ruins. The new city erected by Justinian and called Justinopolis was situated near Scupi, not near Ulpiana. Justinian would not have called the new city Justinopolis had it not been situated close by Justin's birthplace. At Taurisium, his own birthplace, which evidently was also badly damaged by the earthquake, Justinian built a wall with four towers which he called Tetrapyrgia (Τετραπυργία. *De aedif*. IV, 1, 18). And in addition he built a new city close by which he named Justinian Prima. Then he restored and embellished the city of Ulpiana, which had also been seriously damaged, and named it Justiniana Secunda. Thus Dardania, which had given the empire two emperors, was distinguished by the erection of three cities, Justiniana Prima, Justiniana Secunda, and Justinopolis.

The names of Bederiana and Taurisium (Tauresium) have also survived in the names of two villages near Skoplye, Bader and Taor, which were identified in 1858 by an Austrian scholar and traveler, J. von Hahn. This identification was accepted in 1869 by an English scholar, H. F. Tozer; and both places were carefully explored in 1885 by a noted English archaeologist, A. J. Evans. Evans came to the conclusion that at Skoplye (he calls it Skopia) the hand of Justinian was still felt in what Evans did not scruple to call Justinian's native city. In addition to archaeological remains, he found very striking numismatic evidence attesting the importance of Skoplye in the fifth, sixth, and succeeding centuries, and he had no hesitation in identfying with Justiniana Prima the modern city of Scupi-Skoplye (Skopia)-

Usküb.[31] These conclusions of Evans, Tozer, and von Hahn seem to me to be decisive.

Evan's study was published in 1885. In 1931 his conclusions were once more confirmed and elaborated by P. Skok, who wrote: "Today we know quite exactly that the Roman-Dardanian Scupi, *i.e.* the city

[31] J. G. von Hahn, *Reise von Belgrad nach Salonik*, in *Denkschriften der Akademie der Wissensch. zu Wien*, Philos.-hist. Classe, XI (1861), 61. H. F. Tozer, *Researches in the Highlands of Turkey*, I (London, 1869), chapter XVI, "The city of Uskiub," pp. 366–370; Justinian's aqueduct, p. 369; II, Appendix E. The birthplace of Justinian, pp. 370–373; p. 372: it is Uskiub, the ancient Scupi, which alone fulfills all the conditions requisite to identify Justiniana Prima." Arthur John Evans, *Antiquarian Researches in Illyricum*, III and IV. *Archaeologia*, XLIX, 1–167; especially 133, 135–137, 141–142, 148–149. But the identification of Bederiana and Taurisium with Bader and Taor near Skoplye has not been universally accepted. See the indication of John of Antioch that the fort of Bederiana was situated near Naïssus (now Nish) in Illyria (ἐκ Βεδεριανῆς φρουρίου πλησιάζοντος Ναϊσσῷ τῇ Ἰλλυρίδι). *FHG*, V, 1, 31; *Hermes*, VI, 339. Mommsen, *Gesammelte Schriften*, VII, 726, W. Tomaschek wrote that Taurision, Bederiana, and Justiniana Prima are to be looked for farther north, in the region of Toplica, a tributary of the Bulgarian Morava. W. Tomaschek, "Miscellen aus der alten Geographie," *Zeitschrift für die österreichischen Gymnasien*, XXV, 658 (he says: "Die Sache ist entschieden"). But the assertion of John of Antioch, a chronicler who lived far from the Balkans, may be inaccurate. His statement that Bederiana was situated near Naïssus should not be taken literally but only approximately: "a distance not very far from Naïssus" would be admissable. See P. Skok, "Beiträge zur thrakisch illyrischen Ortsnamenkunde," *Zeitschrift für Ortsnamenforschung*, VII, 160. Honigmann follows John of Antioch and says that Justiniana Prima was situated in the environs of Naïssus. "Meridianus Episcopus," *Annuaire de l'Institut de philologie et d'histoire orientales et slaves*, VII (New York, 1939–1944), 146. In another study Tomaschek remarks that the similarity between the names Taor and Bader, and Taurisium and Bederiana may rest on mere chance, and he points out that near Agram is a place called Beder or Bedar and that Toarjan (Tauriana) exists in South Serbia. Tomaschek, "Bederiana," *PW*, III (1899), col. 184; in this article Tomaschek indicates that long before Evans, von Hahn discovered southeast of Skoplye two places, Taor (Tawor) and Bader, which he took for Tauresion and Bederiana. Scarcely any scholar now shares Tomaschek's opinion that Skupi (Scupi) is the Serbian city of Leskovac. W. Tomaschek, *Zur Kunde der Hämus-Halbinsel*, I: "Wo lag Skupi, die Metropolis von Dardania?" *Sitzungsber. der philos.-hist. Classe der Ak. der Wiss. zu Wien*, XCIX (1882), 437. See A. Philippson, *Das byzantinische Reich als geographische Erscheinung*, p. 100. Max Fluss, in his article "Taurisium" in *PW* (zweite Reihe, V, 1934, col. 14) says that this place was situated in Moesia Superior near Scupi, repeating what he found in the antiquated but still useful *Dictionary of Greek and Roman Geography* by W. Smith, II (Boston, 1857), 1309. Referring to Fluss' article, E. Honigmann is perfectly right in stating that in that particular region no province of Moesia Superior had existed since the epoch of the Emperor Aurelian. E. Honigmann, "Pour l'atlas byzantin," *Byzantion*, XI (1936), 559–560. See also Fluss, "Scupi," *PW*, 2nd series, II, col. 910. Uspensky remarks that the native city of Justin and Justinian is still a subject of dispute among scholars, who consider

which in 518 was destroyed by an earthquake, was situated between the villages Bardovci and Zlokućani, at a distance of about two kilometers from the Skoplye of today. Justinian did not restore these ruins; but he erected a new city near by, where lies the Skoplye of today. This is one thing. The other is that at a distance of twenty kilometers from there the village of Taor or Tavor is still to be found today, where Evans has identified some remains from Justinian's time. A connection between Taor and Taurision is therefore evident. Not far from this village, about ten kilometers as the crow flies, exactly according to Procopius' datum, on the river of Pčina lies another village, Bader, whose name clearly resembles in sound the name of Bederiana." [32] According to some scholars, however, the question of the exact location of Bederiana and Taurision, especially as they are mentioned in Justinian's *Novella XI, De privilegiis archiepiscopi Primae Iustinianae*, cannot be definitely settled, at least at present; some new archaeological evidence is particularly needed.[33] I myself share the

their fatherland either Northern Macedonia near the modern Bitoli, or the neighborhood of Usküb. Uspensky, *History of the Byzantine Empire*, I, 2, 410 (in Russian). A detailed discussion on Evans' opinion in J. Valić, "Où était Justiniana Prima?" *Le Musée Belge*, XXXII, 66–70. Evans' conclusions are supported by J. Zeiller, *Les origines chrétiennes dans les provinces danubiennes de l'Empire romain* (Paris, 1918), 385–393, and, with some modifications, by the same author in his article "Le site de Justiniana Prima," *Mélanges Charles Diehl*, I (Paris, 1930), 299–304. Recently the Serbian archaeologist, V. R. Petković, on the basis of excavations in 1936 and 1938 at Tsaritzin-Grad, in the region of Nish, has come to the conclusion that the site of Justiniana Prima is located there. It is true that the archaeological remains so far uncovered there correspond well with Procopius' description of Justiniana Prima. But of course final judgment will be possible only after further excavations. See V. R. Petković, "Excavations at Tsaritzin-Grad near Lebane," in the Serbian magazine *Starinar*, XII (1937), 81–92; XIII (1938), 179–198 (in Serbian). See also a brief note by D. Bošković, in *Byzantion*, XIV (1939), 446.

[32] P. Skok, "Beiträge zur thrakisch-illyrischen Ortsnamenkunde," *Zeitschrift für Ortsnamenforschung*, VII, 40. See also C. Jireček, *Geschichte der Serben*, I (Gotha, 1911), 53–54 (he identifies the destroyed Dardanian Scupi with the modern village Zlokućani). Honigmann is doubtful about identifying the hamlets Taor and Bedar with Tauresium and Bederiana merely "because of a slight resemblance in the names" ("Meridianus Episcopus," p. 143).

[33] See J. Vulić, "Où était Justiniana Prima?" Le Musée Belge, XXXII, 71. N. Vulić, "Le site de Justiniana Prima," Εἰς μνήμην Σπυρίδωνος Λάμπρου (Athens 1935), p. 338. On the uncertain location of Justiniana Prima see a detailed discussion in P. Leporsky, *History of the Exarchate of Thessalonica down to its Annexation to the Constantinopolitan Patriarchate* (St. Petersburg, 1901), pp. 188–190, note (in Russian). Also E. Honigmann, "Meridianus Episcopus," *Annuaire de*

conclusions of Evans supported by Skok, and I shall refrain in this study from any detailed discussion on the establishment of the arch-bishopric of Justiniana Prima by Justinian as a question which does not belong to the period of Justin's reign. Justin's birthplace is Bederiana, a name which has survived in the modern name of Bader, and Justinian's birthplace is Taurision (Taurisium), a name which has survived in the modern name of Taor.

Oriental (Syriac) sources relate a curious fable about the water of Bederiana. They say that the water at Bederiana was bad and turned to blood when it was boiled so that when Justinian built a great city there, he granted it privileges, stationed a military force, and had water brought from a distance because the local water was undrinkable.[34]

JUSTIN'S FAMILY

The names of Justin's parents have not come down to us. We know that he had a sister, Justinian's mother, but our sources fail to provide her name. The legendary *Vita Theophili*, which has been discussed above, is the only one to give her name, Bigleniza, which the canon of Sebenico, Marnavich, considers an Illyrian name, *ductum ab albe-dine*, that is, whiteness, and which is rendered in Latin as *albula* (whitish). The name of Bigleniza may represent the slavonized form of the Latin name of Vigilantia, which, as we shall see below, Justinian's sister bore. But according to so great an authority as C. Jireček, the name Bigleniza itself is not Slavonic. Since the *Vita Theophili* has no worth as an historical document, we cannot be certain that the name of Justinian's mother was Bigleniza.[35] Oriental sources, Syriac and

---

l'Institut de philologie et d'histoire, VII, 142–143. Apparently Honigmann does not know Leporsky's book.

[34] *Zach. of Mitylene*, VII, 14; IX, 1; transl. by Hamilton and Brooks, p. 187; 221; by Ahrens and Krüger, p. 138; 168. *Michel le Grand*, transl. by Chabot, II, 169; IX, 12; Armenian version of the priest Ischôk, by Langlois, p. 175.

[35] Proc., *Anecdota* VI, 19: ἀδελφιδοῦς δὲ αὐτῷ Ἰουστινιανός. Here of course the word ἀδελφιδοῦς may mean either a brother's or a sister's son. But see Marcellinus Comes, *Chronicon*, s. a. 527: Iustinus imperator Iustinianum ex sorore sua nepotem . . . (ed. Mommsen, *Chronica Minora*, II, 102). *Iordanis Romana*, ed. Mommsen, p. 47: Iustinus . . . Iustinianum ex sorore sua nepotem (*MGH Auctorum antiquissimorum* vol. V, 1st part). *Vita Theophili* in *Notae Alemanni in Historiam Arcanam*, Procopius, CSHB, III, 415. Bryce, *The English Historical Review*, II (1887), 661. In Russian, A. Vasiliev, *Viz. Vremennik*, I (1894), 475. C. Jireček, in his letter published in the *Eng. Hist. Rev.*, II 1887), 685.

Arabian, also state that Justinian's mother was Justin's sister.[36]

Although the name of Justinian's mother is unknown, the name of his father, the husband of Justin's sister, is well attested. It was Sabbatius, a name, as we have pointed out above, of Thracian origin. In his *Secret History* Procopius mentions this name and connects it with an imaginery story. He writes: "And they say that Justinian's mother stated to some of her intimates that he was not the son of her husband Sabbatius nor of any man. For when she was about to conceive him, a demon visited her; he was invisible but affected her with a certain impression that he was there with her as a man having intercourse with a woman and then disappeared as in a dream." [37] The chronicler of the ninth century Theophanes also mentions Sabbatius' name when he describes the frightful rising in Constantinople, the so-called Nika riot, which nearly deprived Justinian of the throne. The chronicle contains a remarkable record of a conversation between Justinian and the Green party in the Hippodrome. The Greens, obtaining no satisfaction for their complaints, became violently abusive and among many other outbursts of anger shouted: "Would that Sabbatius had never been born, to have a son who is a murderer!" [38]

We have some information about Justin's wife, whose original name was Lupicina. She was a slave, of barbarian origin, whom Justin had purchased and who was at first his concubine. Later he married

[36] Syriac sources: *Zachariah of Mitylene*, IX, 1; transl. by Hamilton and Brooks, p. 221; by Ahrens and Krüger, p. 168. *Chronicon anonymum ad annum p. Chr. 846 pertinens*, CSCO, p. 169. *Michel le Syrien*, ed. Chabot, IX, 20; II, 189. *Chronique de Michel le Grand*, p. 189. Gregory Abûl Faraj, *The Chronography*, transl. Budge, I, 73. Arabian sources: *Agapius. Patrologia Orientalis*, VIII, 426 (166). By an oversight, both in the Arabic text and in the French translation I have printed "the son of his brother"; this should be corrected to read "the son of his sister" (in Arabic the words *brother* and *sister* differ in diacritical dots only.) *Abul-Farajii Historia compendiosa dynastiarum*, ed. Pocockius, p. 149 (94); Arab text only, ed. by Salhani, p. 147.

[37] Proc., *Anecdota* XII, 18–19; ed. and transl. by H. B. Dewing, VI (1935), 148–151. I give here Dewing's translation.

[38] Theophanes, ed. de Boor, p. 183. An English translation of this curious scene by J. B. Bury in his *History of the Later Roman Empire*, II, 72–74. On Bury's doubts whether Theophanes' record is connected with the Nika riot see his book just mentioned, II, 40, n. 3; p. 72. Theophanes' Greek record with a Latin translation is also to be found in *Notae Alemanni in Historiam Arcanem*, Procopius, CSHB, III, 412–414; our passage, p. 414.

her; but according to Procopius, "she did not enter the Palace under her own name, thinking it to be ridiculous," so that she was crowned Augusta under the assumed and more decorous name of Euphemia, which was given her by the factions of the Blues and the Greens (οἱ δημῶται).[39] To her rather inconspicuous part in the government during the reign of her husband we shall return later.

Sabbatius and his wife had two children, Petrus Sabbatius and Vigilantia. The young man discarded the names Petrus Sabbatius and assumed the adoptive name of Justinian, by which he is always known. Justin adopted his nephew and brought him to Constantinople. Literary sources fail to mention Justinian's original name, and we should not know it at all had it not appeared in full on his consular diptych of 521: "Fl. Petr. Sabbat. Justinian. v. i., com. mag. eqq. et p. praes., et c. od.," meaning Flavius Petrus Sabbatius Iustinianus, vir illustris, comes, magister equitum et peditum praesentalium (praesentalis) et consul ordinarius."

A common type of consular diptych shows the consul seated in the *sella curulis* (magistrate's seat) holding a scepter in his left hand, and in his right the *mappa* or napkin which he is to throw down as the signal for the commencement of the games in the circus. In a lower zone are figures connected with the games, or men with sacks of coins, rep-

---

[39] Procopius, *Anecdota* VI, 17 (Λουππικίνη); IX, 49; ed. H. Dewing, VI, 72–73, 118–119. *Theod. Lector*, II, 37 (Λουπικία); Migne, *PG*, LXXXVI, 1, col. 204; J. A. Cramer, *Anecdota Graeca*, II 108 (Λουπίκινα); E. Miller, "Fragments inédits de Théodore le Lecteur," *Revue archéologique*, XXVI, 400 (Λουππίκινα). *Theoph.*, p. 165 (from Theod. Lector). Cedr. I, 637 (from Theophanes). *Victoris Tonn. Chronica*, s. a. 518 (Lupicina); *Chronica Minora*, ed. Mommsen, II, 196. In the *Vita Theophili*, for Lupicina, the name of Justin's wife is given as *Vukcizza*, and in his explanation about the *Vita* Marnavich writes that *Vukcizza* is an Illyrian name, *lupae proprium*; therefore the Latin and Greek authors call her *Lupicina*. Bryce, *The Eng. Hist. Rev.*, II, 664; but a little later Bryce writes: "Marnavich explains the name of Vukcizza as the Slavonic equivalent of Lupicina" (p. 665). See Vasiliev, *Viz. Vrem.*, I, 477, 479 (in Russian). Jireček says that the name of Vukcizza is of recent origin. His letter in *The Eng. Hist. Rev.*, II, 685. Jagić calls the name Vukcizza a very striking imitation of the Latin *Lupicina* (eine sehr auffallende Nachbildung). V. Jagić, *Neuentdeckte Quelle der Fabel von Istok, Upravda u. a. Archiv für slavische Philologie*, XI (1888), 302. The name Lupicina was probably the popular sobriquet for a prostitute, connected with *lupa*, a she-wolf, a prostitute; cf. *lupanar*. See W. G. Holmes, *The Age of Justinian and Theodora*, I (London, 1905), 304, n. 2. See also Alemannus, *Notae in Historiam Arcanam*, CSHB p. 384. Cf. *Anecdota* IX, 49: τῷ ὀνόματι τῷ αὐτῆς ἰδίῳ ἅτε καταγελάστῳ ὄντι.

resenting the newly made official's largess; sometimes other figures are represented. But the diptych of Justinian belongs to another type in which there are no figures; the middle is occupied by a dedication inscribed in a wreath of palmettes between four finely carved rosettes near the corners of each panel; the corners themselves hold lion heads.[40]

Vigilantia or Βιγλεντία, Justinian's sister, is well identified in the sources. Her husband was a certain Dulcidius, often called Dulcissimus, of whom we know nothing. Vigilantia and Dulcidius were the parents of the Emperor Justin II (565–578).[41]

[40] O. M. Dalton, *East Christian Art* (Oxford, 1925), p. 211. He says that there are two diptychs of Justinian, one in the Bibliothèque Nationale in Paris, and the other in the Metropolitan Museum in New York. L. Bréhier, *La sculpture et les arts mineurs byzantins* (Paris, 1936), p. 25. L. von Sybel, *Christliche Antike: Einführung in die altchristliche Kunst*, II (Marburg, 1909), 234. Sybel describes briefly these two diptychs and says that one was in Milan and the other in Le Puy (France). W. Meyer, "Zwei antike Elfenbeintafeln der K. Staats-Bibliothek in München," *Abh. der philos.-philolog. Classe der Bayerischen Akademie der Wissenschaften*, XV, 1 (1879), 58 and 70, nos. 23, 24, 25. Meyer mentions three diptychs with the name of Justinian: no. 23, in Milan; no. 24, in the Bibl. Nat. in Paris; and no. 25, in possession of Aymard in Le Puy (Haute Loire, France). A reproduction of Justinian's diptych, among others, is also to be found in E. Molinier, *Histoire générale des arts appliqués à l'industrie*, I: *Les ivoires* (Paris, 1896), no. 26 (pp. 28–29). Molinier describes three diptychs: Milan, Trivulzio Collection; Le Puy, Aymard Collection; and Bibl. Nat. of Paris. See also *Corpus inscriptionum latinarum*, V, 2, p. 1007, no. 8120, 3. By misprint, in reference to this edition, Bury (*op. cit.*, II, 19, n. 6) gives V, 8210, 3 for V, 2, 8120, 3. The most recent description of Justinian's three consular diptychs (1, Milan, Trivulzio; 2, Paris, Cabinet des médailles; 3, New York, Metropolitan Museum) and the best plates of them, in R. Delbrueck, *Die Consulardiptychen und verwandte Denkmäler*, text (Berlin-Leipzig, 1929), pp. 141–143 (nos. 26–28), and plates 26–28.

[41] Procopius, *De bello Vandalico*, II, 24, 3: "συνῆν δὲ τῷ Ἀρεοβίνδῳ ἥ τε ἀδελφὴ καὶ Πρεΐέκτα ἡ γυνὴ, Βιγλεντίας θυγάτηρ τῆς βασιλέως Ἰουστινιανοῦ ἀδελφῆς" (ed. Dewing, II, 416). *Vict. Tonn. Chronica*, ed. Mommsen, p. 206, 2, *s.a.* 567: Iustinus iunior Vigilantiae sororis Iustiniani Augusti filius, patre Dulcidio natus (*Chronica Minora*, II). Corippus, *In laudem Iustini Augusti Minoris libri IV*, ed. L. Partsch, praefatio, p. 115, 1. 21; 118, 11. 8–9; 119, 1. 55, *MGH, AA*, vol. III, 2. The correct name of Vigilantia's husband is Dulcidius. The form Dulcissimus which often occurs is due to defective manuscripts. Variants in *Chronica Minora*, II, 206. See E. Stein, *Studien zur Geschichte des byzantinischen Reiches vornehmlich unter den Kaisern Justinus II u. Tiberius Constantinus* (Stuttgart, 1919), p. 26. Cf. K. Groh, *Geschichte des oströmischen Kaisers Justin II* (Leipzig, 1889), p. 37: "his nephew Justin, the son of Dulcissimus and Vigilantia." Complete confusion as to Dulcissimus in N. Iorga, "Essai de synthèse de l'histoire de l'humanité," II, *Histoire du moyen âge* (Paris, 1927), 19, n. 3. Bury (II, 20, n. 1) uses the form *Dulcissimus*.

FROM SWINEHERD TO EMPEROR

A genealogical table follows of the members of Justin's family who have been discussed in this study.[42]

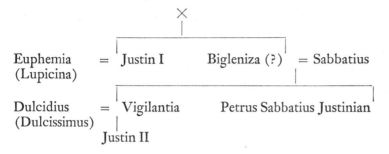

ARRIVAL IN CONSTANTINOPLE

Justin was born in 450 or 452 of an obscure and apparently very poor family; he was a peasant, or, according to Zonaras, a herdsman, a herder of cows and swine. Like hundreds of other country youths, Justin, who had to struggle continuously against poverty and misery at home, decided to quit his homeland and try to better his condition in the capital. At the end of the reign of Leo I (457–474), probably at the age of about twenty (about 470), Justin and two peasant compatriots, Zimarchus and Dityvistus (Ditybistus), all three Illyrians, set out for Constantinople. They made their way on foot, carrying on their shoulders rough cloaks (σισύρας) in which was wrapped only some toasted bread (διπύρους ἄρτους), with which they had provided themselves at home.[43]

---

[42] For much fuller genealogical tables of Justin's family, which are also carried to a later date than mine, see *Alemanni Notae in Historiam Arcanam*, Procopius, *CSHB* III, 417. Bury, *History of the Later Roman Empire*, II, p. IX. In this table Bury plainly calls Justinian's mother Vigilantia. The best collection of information on the members of Justin's family is still to be found in *Alemanni Notae*, pp. 418–420.

[43] Procopius, *Anecdota* VI, 2–3: γεωργοὶ νεανίαι τρεῖς. Zonaras, XIV, 5, 1: γονέων μὲν ἐκφὺς ἀσήμων καὶ ἀφανῶν, καὶ αὐτὸς τὸ πρότερον αὐτουργῶν ἢ βουκόλος τυγχάνων καὶ συφορβός (*CSHB* III, p. 144). The year of Justin's birth can be defined by his age at the time of his death; he died either at 75 (Malalas, 424) or 77 (*Chr. Pasch.*, 617). E. Stein accepts the year 450 and says that the information of the *Paschal Chronicle* is generally justly preferred to that of John Malalas. The Slavic version of John Malalas gives Justin's age at death as seventy-seven years, *Sbornik Otdeleniya Russkago Yazyka i Slovesnosti*, XCI, no. 2, 25. M. Spinka, *Chronicle of John Malalas*, books VIII–XVIII, p. 133: Justin died at the age of seventy-seven.

The cause of the emigration of these three youths as well as hundreds of other young men from their homeland may be explained by the devastation of their country at the hands of barbarian invaders in the middle of the fifth century. In 447 a Hunnic host crossed the Danube, descended the valley of the Axius (Vardas) River, and advanced, it is said, to Thermopylae. A hundred years later in one of his novels Justinian recalled how in the time of Attila Illyricum was devastated, and the Prefect Praetorio Apraemius forced to leave his residence at Sirmium on the Danube and flee to Thessalonica.[44] When the Emperor Leo I (457–474) refused to pay an annual sum of gold which his predecessor, Marcian, had granted the Ostrogoths, they ravaged the Illyrian provinces and seized Dyrrhachium. Peace was made in 461, and the money grant was continued. Economic and agricultural conditions in the provinces of Dardania and Dacia Mediterranea were therefore deplorable, and many of the residents, driven to despair by their misery and ruin, left their homes hoping to find something better in the capital.

Among these Fortune smiled on three poor youths, who after a long and exhausting journey on foot reached Constantinople. Just at that time the Emperor Leo formed a new body of palace guards with the title of excubitors as a counterbalance to the excessive influence of the Germans. The new corps was to be recruited from the residents of various regions of the empire, provided that they were stalwart and

---

Kulakovsky and some other historians erroneously call these three youths brothers; Kulakovsky comments that nothing is known as to how successful Justin's two brothers were in service. J. Kulakovsky, *History of Byzantium*, II, 1–2. See also R. Grosse, *Römische Militärgeschichte von Gallienus bis zum Beginn der byzantinischen Themenverfassung* (Berlin, 1920), p. 203, n. 2: The Emperor Justin and his brothers. Against this identification, W. Holmes, The Age of Justinian and Theodora, I, 300, n. 4.

[44] *Justiniani Novella* XI (a. 535), ed. R. Schoell, p. 94: omne fuerat Illyrici fastigium tam in civilibus quam in episcopalibus causis, postea autem Attilanis temporibus eiusdem locis devastatis Apraeemius praefectus praetorio de Sirmitana civitate in Thessalonicam profugus venerat. In the edition of this novel by Zachariae von Lingenthal (I, 131, no. XIX), the name of the prefect is Apenníus, with variants: Aperrius, Aprecinius, Apemius, Anthemius, Apenninus. In English by S. P. Scott, XVI, 68 (Appennius). I am not aware of the real name of this prefect. See O. Seeck, *Regesten der Kaiser und Päpste für die Jahre 311 bis 476 n. Chr.*, p. 474: Praefectus praetorio Italiae, Illyrici et Africae, Albinus, Aug. 17, 443–April, 449. Honigmann remarks: "Apraemius." According to him, the name is Syrian ("Meridianus Episcopus," p. 142).

brave. The number of the corps was three hundred.[45] Since the young newcomers were all three possessed of very fine physique, the emperor enrolled them in the ranks of his soldiers and designated them for his newly organized palace guards. Such was the beginning of the military career of the future emperor. We know nothing about his companions; "they are lost to our view forever afterwards in the obscurity of a private soldier's life." [46]

The case of Justin and his two fellow-countrymen was nothing unusual. Many other young peasants from everywhere in the empire came to Constantinople and were admitted into military service. In this connection the address of the Byzantine general Germanus, Justinian's cousin, to his soldiers in Africa in 537 is very interesting. Germanus called together the whole mutinous army and spoke as follows: "There is nothing, fellow soldiers, with which you can justly reproach the Emperor . . . for it was he who took you as you came from the fields with your wallets and one short frock apiece and brought you together in Byzantium and has caused you to be so powerful that the Roman state now depends upon you." [47] In the preface to his Novel LXXX in 539 Justinian announced: "We have found that the provinces

---

[45] Joannes Lydus, De magistratibus I, 16; ed. R. Wuensch (1903), p. 21: καὶ Λέων δὲ ὁ βασιλεὺς πρῶτος τοὺς λεγομένους ἐκσκουβίτορας τῶν παρεξόδων τοῦ παλατίου φύλακας ἐπινοησάμενος τριακοσίους μόνους ἐστράτευσε κατὰ τὴν ἀρχαιότητα. In spite of this text, which explicitly ascribes the formation of the excubitors to Leo I, historians usually write that this new corps was probably organized by him. See J. B. Bury, The Imperial Administrative System in the Ninth Century (London, 1911), p. 57. Idem, History of the Later Roman Empire, I, 318. (In this work Bury categorically states that we meet the excubitors for the first time in the reign of Leo). E. Stein, Geschichte des spätrömischen Reiches, I, 530 (vermutlich). See also Malalas, p. 371. It is true that we find a reference to an excubitor at an earlier period than that of Leo I, in a letter of St. Nilus the Ascetic, who lived in the first half of the fifth century and may have survived the Ecumenical Council of Ephesus in 431. S. Nili Epistolarum lib. II, ep. 322: Ἰσιδώρῳ Ἐξκουβίτορι. Migne, PG, LXXIX, col. 357. Very little is known, however, about St. Nilus' life and writings, and some of our information is very doubtful. The best account on St. Nilus in O. Bardenhewer, Geschichte der altkirchlichen Literatur, IV 161–178 (good bibliography). See also Histoire de l'eglise depuis les origines jusqu'à nos jours, ed. A. Fliche and V. Martin, IV (Paris, 1937), 151. On St. Nilus in Russian literature see Archbishop Sergius, The Complete Liturgical Calendar (Menologion) of the Orient, sec. ed. (Vladimir, 1901), II, 2, 467 (in Russian).

[46] Proc., Anecdota VI, 3: Κάλλιστα γὰρ ἅπαντες τὰ σώματα ἦσαν. The last statement from Holmes, op. cit., I, 300.

[47] Procopius, De bello Vandalico II, 16, 12–13 (ed. Haury, I, p. 499; ed. Dewing, II, 358): ὑμᾶς ἐξ ἀγροῦ ἥκοντας ξύν τε τῇ πήρᾳ καὶ χιτωνίσκῳ ἑνὶ ξυναγαγὼν ἐς Βυζάντιον

are gradually being deprived of their inhabitants; and that, on the other hand, this our great city is becoming much more populous on account of the arrival of various men, and above all of farmers, who abandon their homes and crops." [48]

JUSTIN'S EARLY CAREER

We know that on their arrival in Constantinople, at the end of the reign of Leo I about 470, Justin and his two fellow countrymen were enrolled in the palace guards. Though the subsequent destiny of the other two is unknown, some fragmentary information of Justin's career before he became emperor has survived. Nothing has come down to us about his activities during the reign of Zeno (474–491). Although an uneducated farmer, Justin evidently became a very good and effective soldier, successfully advancing in his military career so that under Zeno's successor, Anastasius I (491–518), under the command of the chief general, John the Hunchback (ὁ κυρτός) Justin had attained the rank of lieutenant-general (ὑποστράτηγος, dux) and took part in the Isaurian War.

During this war an episode occurred, now transmitted in a legendary form, which might have cost Justin his life. For some offense the commander John arrested Justin, threw him into prison, and was on the point of sentencing him to death on the following day. But for one reason or another John failed to carry the sentence into effect and spared Justin's life. Procopius, who tells the story, explains John's change of mind by the interference of a supernatural power: "This John was on the point of removing Justin from the world on the following day, and would have done so had not a vivid dream come to him in the meantime and prevented him. For the general declared that in a dream a certain person came to him, a creature of enormous size and in other respects too mighty to resemble a man. And this

---

τηλικούσδε εἶναι πεποίηκεν ὥστε τὰ Ῥωμαίων πράγματα νῦν ἐφ'ὑμῖν κεῖσθαι. English version by Dewing, II, 359.

[48] *Nevella Iustiniani LXXX, praefatio,* ed. R. Schoell, p. 391: εὕρομεν γὰρ ὅτι κατὰ μικρὸν αἱ μὲν ἐπαρχίαι τῶν ἑαυτῶν οἰκητόρων γυμνοῦνται, ἡ μεγάλη δὲ αὕτη πόλις ἡμῶν διενοχλεῖται πληθούσα διαφόρων ἀνθρώπων, καὶ μάλιστα γεωργῶν, τάς τε οἰκείας πόλεις καὶ τὴν γεωργίαν ἀπολιμπανόντων. This novel was published in Greek and Latin. In English by S. P. Scott, XVI, 296.

vision enjoined upon him to release the man whom he had chanced to imprison on that day; and John said that upon arising from sleep he paid no heed to the vision of his dream. But when the next night came on, he seemed once more in sleep to hear the words which he had heard before; yet even so he was unwilling to carry out the order. And a third time the vision stood over him and threatened him with a terrible fate if he should fail to carry out the instruction, and added that when he in later times should become exceedingly angry, he would have need of this man and of his family. So at that time it came about that Justin was saved in this way."

A later tradition has changed the story and connected it with the Emperor Anastasius, who, "not long before his death, discovered a conspiracy against his life, and arrested and destroyed many; among the culprits were Justin and Justinian. When he was ready to put to death these two men, a terrible creature appeared to him in a dream and said: 'O Emperor, it has been permitted to you to have destroyed the rest of the conspirators, but harm in no way Justin and Justinian; because even if you wish you will be unable to do so.' When he said that they were guilty of high treason (*laesa majestas*), [the vision] told him: 'They are vessels of divine will and providence; in their times both of them will serve God.' And Anastasius released both of them of accusation of high treason. Everything came to pass as the vision had told; after Anastasius' death they both became emperors." This legend was created by the contemporary writer Procopius, and modified by a later literary tradition to explain the unexpected rise of Justin from the plough and herd to the imperial throne.

In addition to the Isaurian War, Justin also took part in the Persian war under Anastasius, when after the taking of Amida he invaded the land of the Persians with Celer's army (Proc., *B.P.* II, 15, 7) and played an important part at the end of the war and in the conclusion of peace. Later, towards the close of Anastasius' reign, Justin distinguished himself in the repulse of Vitalian, who had rebelled against the emperor.[49]

[49] Justin in the Isaurian War: Proc., *Anecdota* VI, 4–5. *Joannis Antiocheni Fragmenta*, C. Müller, *FHG*, V, 1, p. 31 (fr. 214, 8); Mommsen, "Bruchstücke des Johannes von Antiochia und des Johannes Malalas," *Hermes*, VI 339; Mommsen. *Gesammelte Schriften*, VII, 726. On ὑποστράτηγος — dux see R. Grosse,

In view of his successful military activities, especially if we take into account his rustic origin, Justin made a brilliant career under Anastasius. He rose to be count (*comes*) of the excubitors; in other words, he became head of the corps in which he had started his service as a mere private soldier. In addition he received senatorial rank. But apparently he had no qualifications for a responsible administrative post, far less for the rule of the empire. Fate intervened.[50]

JUSTIN'S ELECTION AND CORONATION

The emperor Anastasius died at the age of eighty on the night of July 8–9, 518. He survived his wife, the Empress Ariadne, who had died in 515, by three years. They had no children and Anastasius had

Römische Militärgeschichte, p. 296. On Justin's arrest and the vision, Proc., *op. cit.*, VI, 5–10. On the later tradition of this episode, Cedr., I, p. 635. Zonaras, XIV, 4, 20–21; *CSHB* III, 142–143 (very brief version). Justin in the Persian war: Proc., *BP* I, 8, 3; II, 15, 7. *Theoph.*, p. 146, 5. The *Chronicle of Joshua the Stylite*, § 81, transl. by W. Wright (Cambridge, 1882), p. 65; in 1940 a complete Russian translation of this *Chronicle*, from the Syriac original, by N. Pigulevskaya came out in her book *Mesopotamia on the Threshold of the Fifth-Sixth Century of Our Era* (Moscow-Leningrad, 1940), § 81 on p. 164; see also p. 125 (*Works of the Oriental Institute*, vol. XXXI). *Zachariah of Mitylene*, VII, 4 and 14; transl. by F. Hamilton and E. Brooks, p. 160; 187. *Die sogenannte Kirchengeschichte des Zacharias Rhetor*, by K. Ahrens and G. Krüger, p. 111; 138. Justin and Vitalian's rebellion: *Joannis Antiocheni Fragmenta*, C. Müller, *op. cit.*, V, 1, p. 34, col. 2; Mommsen, *op. cit.*, p. 348; *Gesammelte Schriften*, VII, 733. On the participation of Justin in the rebellion of Vitalian see Bury, *op. cit.*, I, 451, n. 4.

[50] *Comes Excubitorum*: Procop., *Anecd.* VI, 11. Evagrius, IV, 1; ed. J. Bidez and L. Parmentier, p. 153. *Chr. Pasch.*, *CSHB* p. 611. *Constantini Porphyrogeniti De Cerimoniis* I, 93 (vol. I, p. 426). *Anonymus Valesianus*, 76; ed. V. Gardthausen (Leipzig, 1875), p. 300 (in volume two of his edition of Ammianus Marcellinus); ed. Mommsen, p. 326 (*MGH Chronica Minora*, I, *AA*, vol. IX); ed. R. Cessi (Città di Castello, 1913), p. 18 (new ed. of Muratori, *Rerum Italicarum Scriptores*, XXIV, part IV). *Iordanis De summa temporum vel origine actibusque gentis Romanorum*, 360; ed. Mommsen, p. 47, *MGH*, *AA*, V, 1. This work is often quoted as *Romana*.

Senator: Theod. Lector, Cramer, *Anecdota Graeca*, II (Oxford, 1839), 108; E. Miller, "Fragments inédits de Théodore le Lecteur," *Revue archéologique*, XXVI, 400: καὶ μέχρις τῆς συγκλήτου προκόψας. In Migne (*PG* LXXXVI, 1, col. 204; Theod. Lect. II, 37) these words are lacking. Theoph., 164, 17–18 (*Anast. Biblioth.*, p. 130). Cedr., I, 636. For the time being, I am unable to verify E. Stein's statement (with reference to *Const. Porph. De cer.* I, 93) that Justin was made *patricius*. P.-Wiss., X (1919), col. 1315. On the basis of Evagrius' text (IV, 1) ὑπὸ τῶν βασιλικῶν σωματοφυλάκων ἀναρρηθεὶς ὧνπερ καὶ ἦρχεν ἡγεμὼν τῶν ἐν τῇ αὐλῇ τάξεων καθεστώς, one may believe, as Stein remarks, that Justin was *magister officiorum*, but this is inadmissible (col. 1315). Stein is of course right in rejecting the rank of *magister officiorum* for Justin. Evagrius' text, however, which reads ἡγεμών, etc may be understood to mean *comes excubitorum*.

made no provision for the succession. It is quite probable that he intended to designate as his successor one of his nephews, Probus, Pompeius, or Hypatius; but this is only a hypothesis. A question of such first importance as the election of a new emperor, then, was in fact intrusted to mere chance, and the contemporary official record of Justin's election states that "some confusion (ἀταξία) occurred." Therefore it is not surprising that events turned out in a way that no one could have foreseen.

Fortunately a contemporary document describing Justin's election and coronation is preserved in Constantine Porphyrogenitus' *De cerimoniis* (I, 93). There is almost no doubt that the text belongs to a contemporary of Justinian and Procopius, the historian Peter the Patrician, master of the offices (*magister officiorum*), a brilliant lawyer and diplomat. Among other works of historical character he compiled a treatise *On the State Constitution*, a sort of ceremonial book (Κατάστασις), part of which Constantine included in his famous work on court ceremonies. Peter's description may be regarded not only as a contemporary but also as an official document; even if his text as it has survived in Constantine's *Ceremonies* does not represent an absolutely exact copy of the official record, it follows the latter so closely that it can be considered official. Although written in the Greek language, Peter's descriptions of the election and coronation of the Byzantine emperors from Leo I to Justinian I bear obvious traces of their Latin originals.

The picture of the election and coronation of Justin I, according to Peter's *Ceremonial*, which clearly shows complete uncertainty and confusion at this critical moment, runs as follows: "Since there was neither Augusta nor Emperor to influence the election, and since almost no provision whatever had been made to meet the situation (ἀπρονοήτων σχεδὸν ὄντων τῶν πραγμάτων) a certain confusion took place" (p. 426, 3–6). We know that Anastasius died on the night of July 8–9. Immediately the silentiaries (*silentiarii*), personal attendants of the emperor of senatorial rank with the title *clarissimi*, sent word to Celer, the master of offices, and to Justin, who at that time was the commander of the excubitors, to come to the palace. Upon their arrival Celer summoned the candidates (*candidati*) and other scholarians, who were in a strict sense bodyguards of the imperial person and were under the control of the master of offices; and Justin called together the excubitors, soldiers, and ordinary officers as well as those of higher rank (τοῖς στρατιώταις καὶ τριβούνοις καὶ βικαρίοις καὶ τοὺς πρώτους τῶν ἐξκουβιτόρων), that is, the whole body of palace guards, who were under his command; and he said to them: "Our lord (δεσπότης) as man, has passed away. We must all deliberate together and elect [an emperor] pleasing to God and useful to the empire." In the same way Celer addressed the candidates and the chiefs of the scholarians.

In the morning (July 9) the high officials, some of them clad in mouse-colored garments, some in garments of other various colors, assembled. The demes (ὁ δῆμος) also gathered in the Hippodrome and acclaimed the Senate: "Long live the Senate! Senate of the Romans, tu vincas! [We demand] the emperor, given by God, for the army (τῷ ἐξερκίτῳ), [we demand] the emperor, given by God, to the world (τῇ οἰκουμένῃ)." After seats had been set in the portico of the great hall, the so-called Triklinos of the Nineteen Akkubita, all high officials and the Patriarch (ὁ ἀρχιεπίσκοπος) sat down, and began to argue sharply with each other about the new emperor and were unable to come to terms. As time was passing by, the Magister Celer said to them: "While it is still possible to us, let us decide and act. If we decide promptly on the name, all will follow us and keep silent. But if we fail to come promptly to a decision, then we shall have to follow others." Here the word "others" in Peter's record indicates the army and the demes who in case of hesitation and procrastination could wrest the initiative from the hands of the high officials. Since even after Celer's appeal the officials were unable to agree, the excubitors in the Hippodrome proclaimed emperor a certain officer (τριβοῦνον), Justin's friend, John, who afterwards became the bishop of Heraclea, and raised him on a shield.

But the Blues resented their decision; they threw stones and in the tumult some were killed. Next the scholarians put forward an unnamed patrician, the master of soldiers (στρατηλάτην), brought him to the hall of the palace, raised him upon a table, and intended to crown him. But the excubitors would not accept him; setting upon him they drew him down [from the table] and would have put him to death had not Justinian, then a candidate (*candidatus*), rescued him. Justinian managed to send him to the quarters of the excubitors to be kept in safety there. All the excubitors then urged Justinian himself to accept the crown, but he excused himself. As each of these persons had been proposed, their advocates knocked at the Ivory Gate, through which probably the shortest way led to the imperial personal quarters in the palace, and called upon the chamberlains to deliver the imperial robes. But on the announcement of the names of the proposed candidates, the chamberlains refused to do so.

Finally all the senators agreed upon Justin, and constrained him to accept the purple. Some of the scholarians resented this choice and rushed upon Justin, and in the heat of altercation one of them struck the future emperor a blow of the fist and split his lip. The decision of the senators, however, backed by the army and the demes (ἡ γνώμη πάντων, καὶ συγκλητικῶν καὶ στρατιωτῶν καὶ δημοτῶν) prevailed. Justin was brought to the Hippodrome; even the antagonistic factions of the Blues and the Greens agreed upon him; the chamberlains immediately sent him the imperial robes which, as we have noted above, they had refused to deliver to the supporters of other nominees. Justin entered the imperial box (κάθισμα) in the Hippodrome, accompanied by the Patriarch John and other high officials who usually entered the box, while the rest of the high officials stood downstairs. Standing on a shield Justin received a chain (τὸν μανιάκιν) which was placed upon his head by Godila (παρὰ Γώδιλα), the campiductor (army guide) of the legion of the Lancers (Lanciarii; τοῦ καμπιδούκτορος τῶν λαγκιαρίων). The military insignia, the labara and the standards, which lay on the ground, were immediately raised, as was customary on such proclamations. Justin did not enter the triklinos, the special hall of the Hippodrome, to change his garment. But the soldiers held their shields over his head (ἐποίησαν χελώνην; Latin *testudo*), and under this shelter he donned the imperial garb in the box (*kathisma*) itself. Then the Patriarch (ὁ ἐπίσκοπος) John placed the crown on his head. Justin took the lance and shield, and reappeared in the *kathisma*.

All cried: "Justin August, thou conquerest (σὺ νικᾷς)!" The text of the address (τὸ λιβελλάριον) to be given by the new emperor to the assembly was read by the *magisters a libellis* (παρὰ λιβελλησίων), officers whose original duty was to present petitions to the emperor and to register them, and through whom, as in this case, the emperor announced his manifesto to the people, because neither the *quaestor sacri palatii* nor the *Magister* Celer who should have performed this act could be found. Celer was suddenly afflicted by trouble with his feet and could not come. In his proclamation Justin promised a donation of five nomismata (gold coin) and one pound of silver to each shield (κατασκουτάριν), that is, to each soldier.

Justin's address ran as follows: "Imperator (αὐτοκράτωρ) Caesar Justin, Victorious, ever Augustus [saith]: Having received the imperial power through the will of Almighty God and your unanimous choice, we invoke celestial providence." All cried: "Abundance to the world! Reign as thou hast lived! Abundance to the government! Celestial Lord, save the earthly one! Justin August, thou conquerest! Long live the new Constantine! We are slaves of the emperor!" Imperator, Caesar Augustus [saith]: "May God, through His grace, enable us to achieve everything that is beneficial to you and to the state (τῷ δημοσίῳ)!" All cried: "Son of God, have pity on him! Thou hast elected him! Have pity on him! Justin August, thou conquerest." Imperator Caesar Augustus [saith]: "Our concern is to provide you, by divine grace, with every kind of prosperity, and to conserve all of you with all benevolence, affection, and in a state of full tranquillity." All cried: "Worthy of the Empire! Worthy of the Trinity! Worthy of the City! Long may thou live, Imperator! We demand honest (ἀγνοὺς) magistrates for the world." The emperor: "Because of the celebration of our happy enthronement I will grant every one of you (ὑμῖν καταχάσμα) five nomismata and a pound of silver." All cried: "May God protect a Christian emperor! Such are the unanimous vows of the world!" The emperor: "God be with you!" Here Peter the Patrician's text on Justin's election and coronation ends with the following words: "The rest of the ceremony was performed according to the ceremony of [the coronation] of Anastasius of blessed memory." [51]

[51] *Constanti Porphyrogeniti De cerimoniis aulae byzantinae*, I, 93; CSHB, pp. 426–430. The edition of the *Ceremonies* and its French translation by Albert Vogt has not yet been carried out to this particular section of the text. In his letter of April 22, 519, to the Pope Hormisdas, the patriarch recalls that he

The official description of Anastasius' election and coronation has survived in the same compilation *De Cerimoniis* and also belongs to Peter the Patrician. There, after his final words, "God be with you!" Anastasius, and accordingly later Justin, proceeded to St. Sophia (εἰς τὴν ἐκκλησίαν) where, before entering the church itself through the narthex, he took off his crown in the mutatorium, a special room where the emperors changed their garments; so the emperor entered the church without his crown to show his veneration for the temple. Then the grand chamberlain (*Praepositus sacri cubiculi*) took the crown and gave it to Justin, who placed it on the altar of St. Sophia. After offering gifts to the church, the emperor went again into the mutatorium, put on the crown, and then returned to the palace. There he dismissed the assembly, keeping some high officials to eat with him in the palace. This last act concluded the election and elevation of the new emperor.[52]

---

placed the crown on the head of Justin. *Collectio Avellana*, p. 612, 18–19 (no. 161): quoniam talem verticem meis manibus tali corona decoravit. For the name of the Magister Peter as the author of a series of records included in the compilation *De cerimoniis* see I, 84 and 85 (p. 386, 388). On the supposed Latin original of Peter's records see D. T. Beliaev, *Byzantina*, II (St. Petersburg, 1892), 4, n. 1 (in Russian), *Zapiski* of the Russian Archaeological Society, new series, VI, 1–2. On the special meaning of οἱ στρατιῶται in the sixth century see Bury, *op. cit.*, II, 76; regular Roman soldiers, distinguished from the other sections of the army. On mouse-colored garments see N. P. Kondakov, *Sketches and Notes on the History of Mediaeval Art and Culture* (Prague, 1929), p. 300 (in Russian). Those garments were of a gray shade on violet tissue, or ash-colored, and were worn in case of mourning or sometimes for general wear as well. See also Reiskius, *Commentarii ad Const. Porph. De cerim.* II, 446. D. 6. In addition to the ash-colored garments, Reiske mentions *vestes* embroidered with mice which were called μυωτοὶ χιτῶνες. The latter have no connection with our case. In the same note Reiske by an oversight remarks: Parimodo habebant talpas, genus murium, intextas; vid Du Cange, v. *Talpa*. But under the word *talpa* Ducange deals with *machina ad suffodiendos muros*. Apparently Reiske took *muros* for *mures*. On στρατηλάτης — magister militum see R. Grosse, *Römische Militärgeschichte*, p. 183. On the later significance of the title στρατηλάτης see Σ. Π. Κυριακίδης, Βυζαντιναὶ Μελέται, II–V (Thessalonica, 1939), 291–295. On the location of the Ivory Gate the best information in D. Beliaev, *Byzantina*, I 49–50, n. 1 (in Russian), *Zapiski*, V, 1–2. Cf. Bury, *op. cit.*, II, 17. On μανιάκιον — the chain, see A. Vogt, *Constantin VII Porphyrogénète, Le Livre des Cérémonies: Commentaire*, I (Paris, 1935), 114. Bury, I, p. 315. On campiductores (campidoctores) Bury, I, 315, n. 2. Grosse, *op. cit.*, pp. 126–127 (Nachfolger des alten centurio).

[52] The concluding part of Anastasius' election and coronation which interests us is in *De cerimoniis*, I, 92 (p. 425). On the *Mutatorium* (Mitatorium, and some other spellings) see Beliaev, *Byzantina*, II, 128–132; see also *Index*, p. 274, s. v. St.

The date of Justin's election and proclamation is exactly recorded as July the ninth, eleventh indiction, which means the year 518; the date has also sometimes been given, especially by Greek chroniclers from Syria, according to the local Antiochene era, which gives the ninth of the month of Panemos, corresponding to July, and the year 566. On the basis of this example and some others for which the Antiochene era was used, it has been established that the era of Antioch was counted from 49 B.C. The first day of the era was originally calculated as October 1, but in the fifth century it was changed to September 1.[53]

To the contemporaries of Justin his elevation to the imperial throne was absolutely unexpected, according to Evagrius, "beyond any ex-

Sophia. Vogt, *Commentaire*, I, 61. A concise description of Justin's election, on the basis of the record of Peter the Patrician, is to be found in G. Manojlović, "Le peuple de Constantinople," *Byzantion*, XI (1936), 691–692 (transl. into French by H. Grégoire; originally this very important study was published in Croatian in the Review of Zagreb, *Nastavni Vjestnik* [1904], part XII, pp. 1–91); Kulakovsky, *History of Byzantium*, II, 3–4 (in Russian); A. E. R. Boak, "Imperial Coronation Ceremonies of the Fifth and Sixth Centuries," *Harvard Studies in Classical Philology*, XXX (1919), 39–40; Bury, *op. cit.*, II, 16–18; O. Treitinger, *Die oströmische Kaiser und Reichsidee nach ihrer Gestaltung im höfischen Zeremoniell* (Jena, 1938), pp. 11–12. In his study "Byzantine Imperial Coronations," F. E. Brightman fails to enlarge on Justin's election: *Journal of Theological Studies*, II (1901), 359–392. He remarks only: "Leo I and Justin I assume rest both together after the elevation, under cover of a testudo formed by the soldiers with their shields" (p. 376). For his study Brightman uses the accounts of the elevation of Anastasius and Leo II. Cf. A. Diakonov, "The Byzantine Demes and Factions in the Fifth–Seventh Centuries," *Vizantisky Sbornik*, ed. by Levchenko (Moscow-Leningrad, 1945), p. 218 (in Russian).

[53] Malalas, XVII (*CSHB*, p. 410). The era of Antioch was used by Evagrius, IV, 1; ed. Bidez and Parmentier, p. 153. *Chron. Pasch.*, *CSHB*, p. 611. Malalas and the *Easter Chronicle* in addition say that Justin was elevated during the consulship of Magnus. Niceph. Callistus, *Hist. Eccles.*, XVII, 1, abridges Evagrius (Migne, *PG*, CXLVII, col. 220). It is interesting that the Slavonic version of Malalas gives much more than the printed Greek text, adding: during the consulship of Magnus, in the month of Panemos (Janem), July the ninth, the eleventh indiction, 669 years after the foundation of the Syrian Antioch. *Chronicle of John Malalas*, books VIII–XVIII, transl. by M. Spinka, p. 120. The printed Greek text fails to mention the era of Antioch. V. Istrin, "Chronicle of John Malalas in a Slavonic Version," *Sbornik Otdeleniya Russkago Yazyka i Slovesnosti*, XCI, 2, 17. Theophanes (p. 164) gives the wrong month for the death of Anastasius, April the ninth. On the Antiochene era see Glanville Downey, "The Calendar Reform at Antioch in the Fifth Century," *Byzantion*, XV (1940–1941), 39–48. E. Honigmann, "The Calendar Change at Antioch and the Earthquake of 458 A. D.," *ibidem*, XVII (1944–1945), 336–339.

pectation." Among the kinsmen of the late Anastasius, there were many distinguished men who by their wealth and influence would have been entitled to obtain the highest power. But, as Procopius says, they were forced aside. Anastasius never intended to designate Justin, his *comes excubitorum*, as his successor; nor did his relatives take Justin into account. Apparently everything was decided by a stroke of fortune. Justin's low social origin was not exceptional in the history of Byzantium, however, but rather something he shared with a number of emperors, as we have noted above. Napoleon stated that every soldier had a marshal's baton in his knapsack. We may paraphrase this statement to read that every man in the Byzantine Empire had an imperial scepter in his hands,[54] and illustrate it by Justin's elevation.

The text of Peter the Patrician is extremely important because among other things it clearly indicates the four fundamental bases of the unwritten constitution of the Byzantine Empire: the Senate, the army, the demes, and the Church. All these vital elements in the life of the empire took part in the election and inauguration of Justin. The upper classes, the Senate, and the high officials of senatorial rank in general (ἡ σύγκλητος, οἱ συγκλητικοί, οἱ ἄρχοντες) and the Patriarch (ὁ ἀρχιεπίσκοπος, ἐπίσκοπος) assembled in the palace, in the Great Hall, the Triclinos of the Nineteen Akkubita. The army, represented by the troops stationed in Constantinople, and the people of the capital, the demes (ὁ δῆμος, οἱ δημῶται) met in the Hippodrome. The personal imperial guards, the candidates and scholarians, and the palace guards, the excubitors, apparently fulfilled their duty of guarding the palace so well that in spite of the confusion the precincts of the palace were not assailed or molested by the populace. The guards took part in the discussions, and when the scholarians put forward their own candidate and broke into the palace to crown him, a violent conflict arose between scholarians and excubitors, who refused to accept this nominee.

It is very important to point out that the Senate and the high officials, including the Patriarch, finally agreed upon Justin and were backed by the army and the people, represented by the demes (οἱ δημόται). In

---

[54] Evagrius, IV, 1 (p. 153): πάσης ὑπέρτερον ἐλπίδος. Nic. Call., XVII, 1, col. 220: παρ' ἐλπίδα πᾶσαν. Procopius, BP I, 11: ἀπεληλαμένων αὐτῆς (βασιλείας) τῶν Ἀναστασίου ξυγγενῶν ἀπάντων, καίπερ πολλῶν τε καὶ λίαν ἐπιφανῶν ὄντων.

other words, the new dynasty was established by the nobility, and this fact is to be remembered when one deals with the epoch of Justin I and Justinian. That Justin's candidature was supported by the army and the people is not surprising; his obscure origin as a peasant or shepherd appealed to the masses. But that the Senate, high officials, and the Patriarch should agree upon him is rather unexpected. Of course, the religious sympathies of the Count of the Excubitors in favor of the Council of Chalcedon were well known, and this may have served as an essential motive to elect Justin as a counterpoise to his monophysite predecessor, Anastasius. Before his ordination the patriarch John II, who took part in the election of Justin, had condemned the Council of Chalcedon. But he was not an irreconcilable monophysite, and he was called "desirous of adopting a deceitful middle course" by the ardent monophysite patriarch of Antioch, Severus.[55] We know that under Justin I, whose chief aim in his religious policy was reunion with Rome, John supported the new trend.

One of the most active elements in the election of Justin was the people, represented by the demes. In the record of Peter the Patrician they are named *demos* (ὁ δῆμος), *demotai* (οἱ δημόται) and the Blues and the Greens (οἱ Βένετοι and οἱ Πράσινοι). The four circus parties were named after their colors, Blues, Greens, Reds, and Whites. But beyond racing in the Hippodrome, only two parties, the Blues and the Greens, played a fundamental part in the political, social, and religious life of the empire. The account of Justin's election once more shows that the Hippodrome was more than a race course. It was "the only place for a free expression of public opinion, which was at times compelling for the government" (Uspensky), "a substitute for the vanished comitia, the last asylum of the liberties of the Populus Romanus" (Baynes).[56] As we know now, the term *demos* (ὁ δῆμος) meant not only the people in general, and not only in a narrower sense a deme or faction of the Hippodrome, but also the city militia, an armed and well organized urban military body which was used when necessary for the defense of the city or for the execution of public works. The *demotai* (δημόται)

[55] *The Sixth Book of the Selected Letters of Severus*, transl. by E. W. Brooks, II (London, 1904), 361.
[56] T. Uspensky, *History of the Byzantine Empire*, I, 2, 506. N. H. Baynes, *The Byzantine Empire* (New York, London, 1926), p. 31.

were the permanent urban militia. The penetrating study of Manojlović whose results I am ready to accept, together with some other scholars, leads us to the following conclusions: the factions of the Blues and the Greens represented two different social classes of the population of Constantinople: the Blues, the upper wealthy classes, and the Greens, the lower poor classes. Very often their class antagonism led to violent clashes and revolutionary tumults. But sometimes, as in the case of Justin's election, the two factions put aside social contradictions and came to a common agreement. We must also take into consideration the result of a new treatment of this problem by the late Russian professor A. P. Diakonov, who convincingly proved that the terms *deme* (ὁ δῆμος) and *faction* (τὸ μέρος; sometimes ἡ μοῖρα) are not identical, as had before been believed; but that factions are divided into demes, or demes are united into factions.

Returning to Justin's election, one very important detail may be pointed out. After the election, the *demos* did not confine itself to laudatory acclamations only, but it clearly expressed its demand for better administration. It cried: "We demand honest magistrates for the world," indirectly but clearly criticizing the abuses of the previous regime. This detail, in addition to many others, shows once again the political importance of the *demos*.

In religious affiliations, the Blues were mostly orthodox and were sometimes called Chalcedonians; the Greens were mostly monophysites.[57]

---

[57] E. Manojlović, "Carigradski narod ("demos") od god. 400–800. po. Is. (s osobitim obzirom na njegove vojne sile elemente njegove i njegova ustavna prava u ovoj periodi)," *Nastavni Vjestnik* XII (1904); *Casopis za srednje škole*, XII (Zagreb, 1904), 323–332 (in Serbo-Croatian). Translated into French by H. Grégoire under the title "Le peuple de Constantinople," *Byzantion*, XI, 644–655. This is chapter V. The whole study in the original Serbo-Croatian, *Nastavni Vjestnik*, XII (1904), 155–185, 323–347, 485–496, 624–647. In French, *Byzantion*, XI, 617–716. Some scholars have not accepted Manojlović's thesis. In 1921 E. Stein wrote that his thesis as to the social class contrasts of the factions was entirely without reliable foundation. But, as Stein says himself, owing to his want of knowledge of Serbo-Croatian, he became acquainted with the content of Manojlović's study through the kindness of one of his colleagues, Franz Kidrić. E. Stein, "Bericht über die Literatur des Übergangs vom Altertum zum Mittelalter (V. und VI. Jahrhundert) aus den Jahren 1894–1913," *Jahresbericht über die Fortschritte der klassischen Altertumswissenschaft*, CLXXXIV, 86 (1921), 38–39. Apparently later Stein became inclined to change

A very interesting question is the role of the patriarch who crowned Justin. It has often been asserted that in performing the ceremony of imperial coronation the patriarch was acting not as the representative of the church but as the representative of the state. The emperors seemed unwilling to receive the diadem from the hands of a subject, who in the eyes of other officials might gain too much importance by conferring the symbol of sovereignty on the emperor. If the emperor received the diadem from one of his laic subjects, he himself might feel an encroachment on the omnipotence of his imperial power. To assign the duty of coronation to the patriarch seemed successfully to solve this delicate problem, at least in the fifth century. But although this theory has been brought forward and supported by many eminent historians, it has not been universally accepted.[58]

Before Patriarch John II who crowned Justin, Patriarch Anatolius

---

his opinion. See E. Stein, "Justinian, Johannes der Kappadozier und das Ende des Konsulats," *Byz. Zeitsch.*, XXX (1929–1930), 378. In 1937 in his critical note on Grégoire's translation, F. Dölger said that Manojlović in a clear and convincing manner had shown the importance of the Blues as a party of the upper classes, and of the Greens as a party of the lower and middle classes. *Byz. Zeitsch.*, XXXVII (1937), 542. In 1940, without mentioning F. Dölger's note, G. Ostrogorsky dismissed Manojlović's thesis, saying it rested upon weak grounds. G. Ostrogorsky, *Geschichte des byzantinischen Staates* (München, 1940), p. 41, n. 1; also p. 51, n. 2. In my opinion, Manojlović's proofs for assigning these two factions to two different social groups are quite convincing and very stimulating for a further study of class interests and class interrelations in the Byzantine Empire. See the excellent study in Russian by A. P. Diakonov, "The Byzantine Demes and Factions from the Fifth to the Seventh Centuries," *Vizantisky Sbornik*, pp. 144–227. Diakonov not only accepts Manojlović's point of view (p. 145) but goes farther and deeper into the study of the complicated problem of the demes and factions in Byzantium.

[58] The patriarch as the representative of the State: W. Sickel, "Das byzantinische Krönungsrecht bis zum 10. Jahrhundert," *Byz. Zeitsch.*, VII (1898), p. 519. J. B. Bury, *The Constitution of the Later Roman Empire* (Cambridge, 1910), pp. 10–11; reprinted in *Selected Essays of J. B. Bury*, ed. by H. Temperley (Cambridge, 1930), p. 105. *Idem, History of the Later Roman Empire*, I, p. 11. Against this point of view, P. Charanis, "The Imperial Crown Modiolus and its Constitutional Significance," *Byzantion*, XII (1937), p. 193; *Idem*, "The Crown Modiolus Once More," *ib.*, XIII (1938), p. 381. Cf. O. Treitinger, *Die oströmische Kaiser-und Reichsidee*, pp. 27–28; 36. *Idem, Von oströmischen Staats-und Reichsgedanken, Leipziger Vierteljahrsschrift für Südosteuropa*, IV, 1–2 (1940), p. 12. Cf. Bury, *A History of the Eastern Roman Empire* (London, 1912), p. 39: the coronation of the Patriarch may be said to have definitely introduced the new constitutional principle that the profession of Christianity was a necessary qualification for holding the Imperial office.

(449–458) had performed the ceremony of coronation of Emperor Leo I, in 457, and he had perhaps taken some part in the coronation of Marcian in 450. This new patriarchal function was not secular in its character. The secular element was represented by the Senate, high officials, the army, and the *demos*. In the eyes of the masses, the choice of a new emperor must be sanctified from heaven, by God, and the new emperor as a Christian emperor must live in accordance with the church. The participation of the patriarch Euphemius in the coronation of Anastasius I in 491 is extremely important. He refused to participate in the coronation unless definite assurance was given to him by the new emperor to maintain the faith inviolate and "introduce no innovations into the holy Church of God" (Evagr., III, 32). The emperors themselves shared this conception. The newly elected emperor Marcian wrote in 450 to Pope Leo I (440–461): "We have reached the greatest Imperial power through the providence of God and the choice of the most excellent Senate and the whole army."

During Justin's coronation, as we have seen above, the emperor announced that he had received the imperial power through the will of Almighty God. The assembly cried that the Son of God had chosen Justin. In his letter to Pope Hormisdas (August 1, 518) Justin announced: "We have been elected to the empire first by the favor of the indivisible Trinity, then by the choice of the highest ministers of the sacred palace and of the most venerable senate, and by the election of the most powerful army." In another letter to the same Pope (September 7, 518) Justin wrote that the government of the empire was entrusted "to his piety" from heaven. In September 518 Justinian, the future emperor, also wrote to Pope Hormisdas that "our lord, the unconquerable Imperator . . . has gotten the highest insignia by celestial power." In 520 Justinian *Illustris* wrote to Pope Hormisdas that "by the favor of our Lord Jesus Christ, in the world reigns one who founds his empire on the basis of sacred religion. . . . Your most clement son Imperator has obtained the scepter *aeternitatis beneficio*." The same idea was expressed in his Code by Justinian after he became emperor: "Since the Roman Empire has been conferred upon us through the favor of the Almighty." So Patriarch John, placing the diadem on the head of Justin, was acting not as representative of the state but of the church, and it was in precisely this way that the participation of the patriarch was accepted and interpreted by Justin and Justinian.[59]

Not all Greek sources dealing with Justin's election mention all four elements which were concerned; but none omit the army and the *demos*. The Latin tradition reports that Justin was elected by the Senate only.

As we have mentioned above, Justin promised the troops at the inauguration of his reign a donation of five nomismata and one pound of silver for each soldier; this was exactly the same amount which the elected emperors Leo I in 457, the infant Leo II in 474, and Anastasius I in 491 had promised to their troops.[60]

[59] Valentinian's and Marcian's *Letter* to Pope Leo I in Migne, *PL*, LIV, col. 900 (ep. LXXIII): Εἰς τοῦτο τὸ μέγιστον βασίλειον ἤλθομεν Θεοῦ προνοίᾳ καὶ ἐπιλογῇ τῆς ὑπερφυοῦς συγκλήτου, καὶ παντὸς τοῦ στρατοῦ; in Latin (col. 899): Dei providentia et electione senatus excelentissimi cunctaeque militiae. Justin's and Justinian's letters to Pope Hormisdas: Aug. 1, 518: declaramus, quod primum quidem inseparabilis trinitatis favore, deinde amplissimorum procerum sacri nostri palatii et sanctissimi senatus nec non electione fortissimi exercitus ad imperium nos licet . . . electos fuisse et firmatos. Mansi, *Conc. Coll.* VIII, col. 434 B; *Coll. Avellana*, ep. 141 (p. 586). Sept. 7, 518: proque nobis et re publica, cuius gubernatio nostrae pietati caelitus credita est. Mansi, VIII, 435 C; *Coll. Avell.*, ep. 143 (pp. 587–588). September, 518, Justinian to Hormisdas: Dominus etenim noster invictissimus imperator . . . mox ut adeptus est caelesti judicio infulas principales. Mansi, VIII, 438 C; *Coll. Avell.*, ep. 147, (pp. 592–593). Justinian Illustris to Hormisdas, in 520: Domino nostro Iesu Christo favente regnat in saeculo, qui sacra religione suum fundat imperium . . . filius etenim vester amplissimus imperator aeternitatis beneficio sceptra sortitus. Mansi, VIII, 503 D; *Coll. Avell.*, ep. 196 (p. 655). *Cod. Just.*, I, 29, 5: Imperator Justinianus Zetae . . . magistro militum per Armeniam et Pontum Polemoniacum et gentes: cum propitia divinitate Romanum nobis sit delatum imperium (ed. P. Krueger, p. 82). In English by S. P. Scott, XII, 139. See W. Ensslin, "Das Gottesgnadentum des autokratischen Kaisertums der frühbyzantinischen Zeit," *Studi bizantini e neoellenici*, V (Rome, 1939), 160 (Atti del V Congresso Internazionale di Studi Bizantini, I).

[60] Evagr., IV, 2: ὁ δῆμος and the excubitors. Malalas, 410, 3–5: "στρατὸς ἐξκουβιτόρων ἅμα δήμῳ." Zon., XIV, 5, 3: "παρὰ τῶν στρατιωτῶν καὶ τοῦ δήμου" (*CSHB*, III, p. 145). *Marcellini comitis Chronicon, s. a.* 519: "Iustinus a senatu electus imperator continuo ordinatus est." *Chr. Minora*, II, p. 101. *Iordanis De summa temporum vel origine actibusque gentis Romanorum*, ed. Mommsen, p. 47 (360). *MGH, AA*, V, 1 (1882): ex comite scubitorum a senatu imperator electus. Modern historians generally omit to mention the participation of the patriarch. For example, C. Lécrivain, *Le Sénat romain depuis Dioclétien à Rome et à Constantinople* (Paris, 1888), p. 222: the Senate with the factions and the militaries of the Palace. S. Runciman, *Byzantine Civilization*, p. 71: the demes with the army. Diehl-Marçais, *Le monde oriental*, p. 47: the Senate backed by the army and the people. K. Amantos, Ἱστορία τοῦ Βυζαντινοῦ Κράτους, I, 176: the

As we have noted above, on the basis of the official record of Peter the Patrician, Justin's elevation to the throne took place by mere chance, "beyond any expectation," as Evagrius says. We know from Greek and Syriac sources that Amantius, the high chamberlain (*praepositus sacri cubiculi*), could not as a eunuch, according to Evagrius, claim the throne for himself, but attempted to secure it for his *comes domesticorum* Theocritus, otherwise unknown. For this purpose Amantius gave money to Justin, who we know was *comes excubitorum*, to bribe the troops in favor of Theocritus. According to the story Justin distributed the money among the demes, or among the excubitors, or among both in order that they might support the candidature of Theocritus. But in spite of the money in their hands, they failed to do so and elected Justin himself.

This story is reported from so many sources that it is hard to believe it a mere fiction; something similar must have taken place. Amantius' intrigue in favor of his *comes domesticorum* Theocritus is perfectly probable; and it is quite possible that he gave Justin money which Justin distributed among his excubitors. The money they received from Justin may have led the excubitors to begin to think of him as a potential candidate for the throne, ignoring its real source. But the events which led to Justin's election passed too rapidly, practically within one day (July 9), to allow enough time for an elaborate plan, for "a subtle and dishonorable intrigue," as Runciman says, unless it had been thoroughly worked out and elaborated before Anastasius' death, which seems unlikely. Bury may go too far in his conjecture that "the data seem to point to the conclusion that the whole *mise en scène* was elaborately planned by Justin and his friends;" and Justin himself, in my opinion, may have been quite sincere when in his letter to Pope Hormisdas announcing his elevation (August 1, 518) he wrote that he had been elected against his will.[61] At the moment of Anas-

---

Senate and the army. On the donation see Bury, *op. cit.*, I, 316; II, 17. E. Stein, *Geschichte des spätrömischen Reiches*, I, 89, n. 3. Evidently the donation of five nomismata and one pound of silver was the usual amount at a coronation. See Const. Porph. *De Cerim.* I, 94 (p. 432): Κατὰ τὸ ἔθος (the coronation of Leo II).

[61] Malalas, XVII, 410–411. *Chronicle* of John Malalas, transl. by M. Spinka, p. 120. Evagr., IV, 2. *Chr. Pasch.*, 611–612. Theoph., 165. Zach. of Mityl., VIII, 1; Hamilton-Brooks, pp. 189–190; Ahrens-Krüger, p. 140. John of Nikiu, transl. R. H. Charles, chapter XC, 3 (p. 133). John of Nikiu gives an incorrect account

tasius' death no one could foresee that Justin would be elected emperor. The story of Amantius' machinations during Justin's election receives confirmation from the plot which was discovered and nipped in the bud by Justin after his accession, which we shall discuss below.

One detail more may be pointed out in connection with Justin's elevation. Celer, the master of offices who controlled the bodyguards of the imperial person, the candidates, and other scholarians, and who had taken an active part at the beginning of the discussion about the new emperor, suddenly disappeared and could not be found when Justin's elevation became an accomplished fact. In other words, when the excubitors, the opponents of his scholarians, had won the argument, Celer advanced as an excuse for his absence some trouble with his feet. But it is more probable that this was a sort of diplomatic illness, a reluctance or even fear to face his triumphant antagonists.

JUSTIN'S ILLITERACY

One of the deeply rooted legends about Justin has been that he was illiterate and could neither read nor write. The basic evidence for this is the very well known passage in Procopius' *Secret History*, which runs as follows: "Justin . . . had never learned to tell one letter from another, and was, as the familiar phrase has it, 'without the alphabet,' a thing which had never happened before among the Romans. It was the custom for an emperor to sign his edicts with his own hand; but he was unable either to make decrees himself or to understand what was being done." That they might have evidence of the emperor's own hand, the Quaestor Proclus invented the following device. "Taking a small strip of specially prepared wood, they cut into it a sort of pattern of the four letters which mean in the Latin tongue

---

without mention of Theocritus; Amantius gave money to secure his own elevation. Marcellinus calls Theocritus *Amantii satelles* (*s. a.* 519; 2. *Chr. Min.*, II, 101). See Bury's speculations on this story, II, 17–18. E. Stein calls Theocritus Amantius' nephew and *comes domesticorum*. E. Stein, "Justinus," *PW*, X, col. 1315. S. Runciman, *Byz. Civilization*, p. 35. Diehl-Marçais, *Le monde oriental*, p. 47. Justin's letter to Pope Hormisdas, Mansi, VIII, col. 434; *Coll. Avell.*, ep. 141, p. 586: nos licet nolentes ac recusantes electos fuisse. Pančenko regards the palace revolution as a fitting explanation of Justin's elevation, for all sources connect it with the intrigues of Amantius, *praepositus sacri cubiculi*. Pančenko, "On Procopius' *Secret History*," *Viz. Vrem.*, III, 98 (in Russian).

'I have read' (*legi*), and dipping the pen into ink of the color which emperors are wont to use in writing, they would put it into the hand of this emperor. And placing on the document the strip of wood which I have mentioned and grasping the emperor's hand, they moved it and the pen along the pattern of the four letters, causing it to follow all the winding lines cut in the wood, and then went their way, carrying that kind of writing of the emperor." Among other sources, John Malalas and John of Nikiu call Justin illiterate. John Lydus writes that Justin was a good easy quiet man who had no knowledge whatever except of military matters. Michael the Syrian characterizes him as a simple man, uneducated in the Scriptures. Abu-l-Pharagius (Bar Hebraeus) calls Justin rude or ignorant, and old and simple. But Cedrenus, on the contrary, calls him "an old much-experienced man."

Everyone knows Procopius' prejudiced attitude towards Justin and Justinian in his *Secret History*, and that any information coming from this source must be taken with many reservations. No doubt Justin had little formal education; but it is incredible that a man like Justin who had passed through a very long military career in Constantinople, who had been entrusted with several responsible military missions under Anastasius, and who stood at the head of the palace guards, was illiterate. The legend of his illiteracy is due on the one hand to the malicious insinuation of Procopius and on the other to an historical fact. A mechanical device for signing documents is no invention of Procopius. This device actually existed; it reproduced the ornamented *legi* and signature of the emperor, a signature written with so many flourishes that it would have been impossible for one who was not specially trained to satisfy the requirements of the imperial chancellery in making it. We are perfectly familiar with hieroglyphic imperial signatures from many Byzantine manuscripts. And even in our own day the bishops of the Greek Orthodox Church supply us with excellent specimens of signatures preserving the traditions of Byzantine times, signatures so elaborately executed that it is beyond our imagination to conceive how they can be performed by a human hand.

An identical story has been told of the Ostrogothic king Theodoric, a contemporary of Anastasius and Justin, who was sent as a youth to Constantinople as a hostage. Although he received his education there and became imbued with sincere admiration for Greek and Roman civilization, the story says he was illiterate, and like Justin used a mechanical device for signing documents, pierced with the four letters *legi* so that he could sign by drawing a pen through the holes. As the Anonymus Valesianus says, Theodoric's memory was so poor that "in ten years of his reign he was in no wise able to learn the four letters for signing his decree." The only difference in the stories is that Theodoric used a gold stencil plate (*laminam auream*) and Justin a wooden one. Both stories, of course, are equally incredible, but the tradition, like many other unreliable traditions, has more lives than a cat, and even in our own day serious historians often assert that Justin was illiterate.[62]

[62] Procopius, *S. H. VI*, 11–16 (Dewing, pp. 70–73). Suidas, *Lexicon, s. v.* Ἰουστῖνος and ἀμάθητος (from *Hist. Arc.*); ed. I. Bekker (Berlin, 1854), pp. 74 and 535; ed. A. Adler, I (Leipzig, 1928), 131; II (1931), 646. Malalas, p. 410 (ἀγράμματος); this detail is missing in the Slavonic version of Malalas (Spinka, p. 120). John of Nikiu, XC, 2; transl. by R. Charles, p. 133 (unlettered). John Lydus *De magistratibus*, III, 51; ed. Wuensch, p. 140: ἀπράγμων καὶ μηδὲν ἁπλῶς παρὰ τὴν τῶν ὅπλων πεῖραν ἐπιστάμενος. Michel le Syrien, ed. Chabot, XI, 12; II, 169. Armenian version transl. by Langlois, p. 175: Justin had no education whatever and was devoid of intelligence. Abulpharagii *Chronicon Syriacum* II, 80 (rudis). Gregory Abu-l-Faraj, *The Chronography*, ed. W. Budge, p. 73: old and simple. But cf. Cedr., I, 636: πρεσβύτης καὶ πολύπειρος. An interpretation of the mechanical device: H. Gelzer, "Sechs Urkunden des Georgsklosters Zografu," *Byz. Zeitsch.*, XII (1903), 500. Against Justin's illiteracy, E. Stein, in *PW*, X, col. 1328; also in *Byzantion*, VIII (1933), 314. The Russian church historian V. Bolotov long ago called this story an anecdote. V. Bolotov, *Lectures in the History of the Ancient Church*, I (St. Petersburg, 1907), 41 (posthumous edition). Some doubt on Justin's illiteracy: Uspensky, *History of the Byzantine Empire*, I, 2, 410. Bury, *op. cit.*, II, 19. But many recent historians flatly call Justin illiterate; for example, Kulakovsky, *History of Byzantium*, II, 2 (in Russian). Runciman, *Byz. Civil.*, p. 35. W. Wroth, *Catalogue of the Imperial Byz. Coins in the British Museum*, I (1908), XIV. H. Goodacre, *A Handbook of the Coinage of the Byzantine Empire*, II (London, 1931), 63 (wholly illiterate). Holmes, *op. cit.*, I, 303. W. Gundlach, *Quaestiones Procopianae* (Hanau, 1861), p. 14: "Licet verum sit, Justinum nescivisse litteras." Pančenko, "On Procopius' *Secret History*," *Viz. Vrem.*, III, 99–101 (in Russian). W. Wigram, *The Separation of the Mono-physites*, p. 85. A. Bailly, *Byzance*, p. 65. J. Calmette, *Le monde féodal*, p. 62. N. Iorga, *Histoire de la vie byzantine*, I, 36; 134, n. 2; 232. E. Kornemann, *Römische Geschichte*, II, 497. Amantos, Ἱστορία τοῦ Βυζαντινοῦ Κράτους I, 178. C. Gerard, *Les Bulgares de la Volga et les Slaves du Danube*, p. 26. M. Levchenko, *History of Byzantium*, p. 53 (in Russian). G. Ostrogorsky, *Geschichte des byzantinischen Staates*, p. 42. Recently F. Dvornik wrote: "an unlettered man, if we may credit Malalas and Procopius" — "The Circus Parties in Byzantium," *Byzantina Metabyzantina*, I, 1 (New York, 1946), 127. Most recently, L. Bréhier calls Justin "fils de ses oeuvres et peu lettré." *Vie et mort de Byzance*, p. 21. On

Although without much general education, Justin by nature possessed military talents which he displayed during his career under Anastasius and which, as we have pointed out above, are indicated in the sources.[63] Another merit is to be assigned Justin: he gave an excellent education to his nephew, the future Emperor Justinian. The latter, by his interest in various branches of knowledge and by his intelligence, assiduity, and perseverance, considerably facilitated his uncle's task, and in many respects deserves the credit for his own vast intellectual development. Justinian of course was already thirty-six years of age when Justin began to reign, and his training had started before that time, during the reign of Anastasius, a number of years before his uncle became emperor.

JUSTIN'S AGE AND APPEARANCE

When Justin became emperor, he was not a young man; he was about sixty-six or sixty-eight years of age. In the *Secret History*, Procopius characterizes Justin at the moment of his inauguration, as "an old man on the edge of the grave." [64]

Many sources supply us with a description of Justin's personal appearance. They describe him as handsome, old but of fine presence, of average height, slim, well built, with broad shoulders and chest, a well formed nose, a healthy ruddy complexion, and curly gray hair.

A medallion representation of Justin I possibly exists on one of the

---

Theodoric's illiteracy *Anonymus Valesianus*, 79; ed. Mommsen. *Chr. Minora*, I, 326; ed. R. Cessi (Città di Castello, 1913), p. 19 (new ed. of Muratori, *Rer. Italic. Script.*, XXIV, part IV).

[63] On Justin's military skill, in addition to John Lydus (III, 51) mentioned above (n. 62), Malalas, p. 410: ἐν πολέμοις κοπωθείς. Theoph., p. 165: ἐν πολέμοις εὐδοκιμῶν, From him Cedr., I, 636–637: ἐν τοῖς πολέμοις μεγάλως εὐδοκιμῶν. John of Ephesus, F. Nau, "Analyse de la seconde partie de l'Histoire Ecclésiastique de Jean d'Asie, patriarche jacobite de Constantinople," *Revue de l'Orient Chrétien*, II, 467: he was a brave warrior.

[64] On Justin's age, see above, note on Justin's birth date (p. 63, n. 43). Mal., 424 (in 527 he had lived 75 years). *Chr. Pasch.*, 617 (in 527 he had lived 77 years). Proc., *Anecdota* VI, 11: τυμβογέρων μὲν γεγονὼς ἤδη (ed. Dewing, p. 70). See Suidas, *Lexicon*, s. v. τυμβογέρων with reference to Procopius (Arc. 6). For better understanding of the word τυμβογέρων, Suidas gives the Greek words ὁ πέμπελος (a rather obscure epithet applied to an aged person) and ἐσχατόγηρως (in extreme old age). See Bury, *op. cit.*, II, 18: about sixty-six. Stein, *Iustinus*, col. 1314: about sixty-eight.

two extremities of the horizontal bar of a silver cross preserved in the Treasury of St. Peter's at Rome (the other extremity perhaps presents Justin's wife, Euphemia). The cross bears the following inscription: "ligno quo Christus humanum subdidid hostem dat Romae Justinus opem et socia decorem." From the style of the cap of the empress, the German scholar Delbrück has inferred that Justin I and Euphemia (not Justin II and his wife Sophia) are represented. Apparently Bury is inclined to share Delbrück's opinion; but most scholars either continue to identify the medallions as those of Justin II and Sophia, or hesitate to come to any definite conclusion.

Under Justinian, statues of Justin and seven of his relatives, some of marble, some of bronze, were erected in the portico of the Chalce, the entrance to the Imperial Palace. We have no description of these statues. A statue of Justin, which may have represented the emperor genuflecting in adoration (in *proskynesis*), was destroyed during an earthquake in the ninth century.

The figure of Justin alone, and jointly with Justinian after the latter's elevation as Augustus, has been preserved on gold, silver, and bronze coins bearing Justin's name; but it is not easy to identify the real features of the emperor or to compare them with the description of his appearance in literary sources; our difficulty is the greater since the gold coins of Justin I, for example, are rudely worked. But we can say with certainty that Justin is represented on coins beardless and in imperial garb, wearing diadem, cuirass, and paludamentum. On the coins of the joint rule, which are now rare, both Justin and Justinian are represented beardless, nimbated, and draped in long robes, seated facing each other, hands clasped on their breasts. Of course there are some variations.[65]

[65] On Justin's appearance: Malalas, 410. J. A. Cramer, *Anecdota Graeca e codd. manuscriptis Bibliothecae Parisiensis*, II, 318. Πάτρια Κωνσταντινουπόλεως II, 28: Λεπτοειδής — slim. *Scriptores originum constantinopolitanarum*, ed. T. Preger, II, 165, 14-15. Cedr., I, 636. Zach. of Mityl., VIII, 1; Hamilton-Brooks, p. 189; Ahrens-Krüger, p. 140. Michel le Syrien, ed. Chabot, II, 169. *Chronicon Anonymum ad annum Christi 1234 pertinens*, transl. by Chabot, p. 150: "senex visu pulcher." From Greek sources the Russian Annals mention that Ustiyan was of average stature. *The Lvov Chronicle*, PSRL, XX, 32. See J. Ebersolt, *Les arts somptuaires de Byzance* (Paris, 1923), p. 132 (by oversight, referring to Cedr., I, 642, Ebersolt ascribes to Justin I the details Cedrenus gives of Justinian. The reference should be Cedr. I, 636. See the opening lines of this note). On Justin's

FROM SWINEHERD TO EMPEROR

JUSTIN'S SURNAMES

Since in the history of the Byzantine Empire there were two Justins, the sources distinguish Justin I from Justin II by applying to the former various epithets, such as "the Great" in the sense of the Older,

---

medallion on the Vatican cross see R. Delbrück, *Portraits byzantinischer Kaiserinnen, Mitteilungen des K. Deutschen Archaeologischen Instituts,* Römische Abteilung, XXVIII (1913), 340. Bury, *op. cit.,* II, 19, n. 4. With the majority of scholars, Diehl refers the medallion to Justin II. Charles Diehl, *Manuel d'art byzantin,* 2nd ed., I (Paris, 1925), 310; the picture of the cross on p. 309, fig. 155. O. M. Dalton, *Byzantine Art and Archaeology* (Oxford, 1911), p. 548 (bibliography given), fig. 336 337. *Idem, East Christian Art* (Oxford, 1925), p. 220; 331; beautiful plate of the cross, LXI, between pp. 332 and 333. The cross itself is kept in the Volto Santo and is not shown. A. Grabar refers the medallion to Justin I or to Justin II. A. Grabar, *L'empereur dans l'art byzantin* (Paris, 1936), p. 16, n. 3. On the statues of Justin and his relatives Πάτρια Κωνσταντινουπόλεως, II, 28, ed. Preger, p. 165, 14–15. On the statue of Justin destroyed by the earthquake see *Nicetae Paphlagonis Vita S. Ignatii Constantinopolitani Archiepiscopi,* Migne, *PG,* CV, col. 520: τότε δὴ καὶ ἡ στήλη Ἰουστίνου ἐκ τῶν γονάτων κοπεῖσα κατερράγη (in Latin: "Iustini quoque statua a genibus convulsa concidit"). Grabar, who used this information from Du Cange (*Constantinopolis Christiana,* 1729, p. 117) states positively that in one of the public buildings of Constantinople Justin was represented kneeling. Grabar, *op. cit.,* p. 100 and n. 1. Evidently Grabar is quoting here the Venetian edition of Du Cange's *Const. Christ.,* p. 117. In the original Parisian edition of 1680 the quoted passage is to be found on pp. 148–149: "statua geniculata Iustini." But following Du Cange (*ibidem*) Grabar erroneously ascribes another kneeling statue to Justin (p. 100, n. 1; 101, n. 3; 153; 174). This statue represents Justinian II during the second period of his tyrannical reign. Grabar quotes: Codinus, *Topogr. Cpl.* p. 38: γονυκλινὲς (ἀνδροείκελον ἄγαλμα) Ἰουστίνου τοῦ τυράννου. Here the name Justin is evidently an error for Justinian; the term ὁ τύραννος could not be applied to Justin. See G. Codinus, *De Signis Constantinopolitanis, CSHB* p. 39, 7: ἄγαλμα γονυκλινὲς Ἰουστινιανοῦ τοῦ τυράννου. See *Meursii et Lambecii Notae,* ibidem, p. 239: pro Ἰουστίνου τοῦ τυράννου scribendum est Ἰουστινιανοῦ τοῦ τυράννου id est I. Rhinotmeti. G. Codinus, Παραστάσεις σύντομοι, ed. Bekker (*CSHB*), p. 166 = ed. Th. Preger, I, 40 (37): ἀνδρείκελον ἄγαλμα ὑπάρχον χρυσέμβαφον . . . τὸ γονυκλινὲς Ἰουστινιανοῦ ἐστι κατὰ τὸ δεύτερον αὐτοῦ τὴν Κωνσταντινούπολιν τυραννήσαντος. This, of course, refers to Justinian II. On Justin's coins see W. Wroth, *Catalogue of the Imperial Byzantine Coins in the British Museum,* I, p. XIV; 11–24; excellent plates II, III, IV. E. Stein (*PW,* col. 1328) points out that among these coins that on plate II, no. 12, seems to have preserved the best expression of Justin's face. Stein is right; this bust of Justin in profile represents a very good and distinctive picture of Justin. His well-formed nose, which as we have indicated above, is mentioned in the sources, is particularly noteworthy on this coin. See J. Sabatier, *Description générale des monnaies byzantines,* I (Leipzig, 1930 [a reprint from the original Parisian edition of 1862]), 159–170. H. Goodacre, *A Handbook of the Coinage of the Byzantine Empire,* part II, "Anastasius to Michael VI," pp. 63–67. J. Tolstoy, *Byzantine Coins,* III (St. Petersburg, 1913), 228–263 (text in Russian).

or the "Old Man," or, as is done in present usage, "the First." [66]
Justin II is called Justin the Younger (ὁ μικρός).

PREDICTIONS OF JUSTIN'S ELEVATION

As often happens in cases like that of the unexpected elevation of
Justin, after-the-fact stories were fabricated of predictions, sometimes
supernatural, of the event. Byzantine literature is full of stories of
miraculous omens which prognosticated to the elect Justin's rise to
imperial power. Among these, one motif was very popular — that of
prophetic dreams. I have already related one such story, told by
Procopius, according to which during the reign of Anastasius Justin
and Justinian were accused of high treason, sentenced to death, and
saved by the interference of a supernatural power which manifested
itself in a dream to Anastasius and persuaded him to spare their lives.
Another tradition affirms that the martyrs Sergius and Bacchus, who
had suffered death in the reign of Maximianus in the fourth century,
appeared in a dream to Anastasius and commanded him to spare the
culprits. For this reason the saints Sergius and Bacchus were highly
venerated in the native country of Justin and Justinian, and the latter
erected in their honor a magnificent temple in Constantinople.

There is another legend also connected with a dream. Anastasius,
wishing to know his successor, prayed God to give him a revelation.
One night in a dream he saw a man who said to him: "He who will be
announced first tomorrow morning in your bedchamber, he will receive thine empire after thee." It was Justin, at that time Count of the
excubitors, who was first announced the next morning to Anastasius
by the chamberlain (*praepositus cubiculi*). "And when Anastasius
learned this, he began to express his gratitude to God, who deigned
to reveal his successor to him." [67]

---

[66] Theoph., p. 165, 4: ὁ μέγας; *Anastasii Chronographia Tripertita*, ed. de Boor,
p. 130: "magno imperatori." Const. Porphyr., *De cerimoniis*, p. 642, 19: Ἰουστινιανοῦ
τοῦ μεγάλου. This, however, refers to Justin, not Justinian. See Reiske, *Commentarii
ad Cerimonias*, p. 760. Evagrius, 151: τῆς Ἰουστίνου τοῦ γέροντος βασιλείας. John
of Ephesus, Nau, *Revue de l'Orient Chrétien*, II (1897), 467: Justinian (= Justin)
l'Ancien. In another place Evagrius (p. 148) calls Justin the First: Περὶ τῆς
Ἰουστίνου τοῦ πρώτου βασιλείας. Πάτρια Κωνσταντινουπόλεως, ed Preger, II, 28:
Ἰουστῖνος ὁ πρῶτος (p. 165). Leontius Byzantinus, *De sectis*, actio V, Migne, *PG*,
LXXXVI, 1, col. 1229 C: γίνεται βασιλεὺς Ἰουστῖνος ὁ πρῶτος.
[67] Procopius, *S. H.* VI, 5–9. On SS. Sergius and Bacchus see Du Cange,

FROM SWINEHERD TO EMPEROR

Marinus the Painter, Justin's Biographer

Apparently the amazing career of Justin, who rose from plow and herd to the imperial power, greatly impressed his contemporaries. Some extremely interesting information has been preserved in one source only, a Syriac version based on a lost Greek original. This is the *Chronicle* of Pseudo-Zachariah of Mitylene (VIII, 1). The story runs as follows: A certain Marinus of Apamea, a wise man who was chartulary (*chartularius*), depicted in a public building (δημόσιον) a set of pictures in which he portrayed the career of Justin from his youth upwards — how he came from the fort of Bederiana in Illyricum to Constantinople, how he entered into Constantinople, and how he advanced step by step until he became emperor. When Marinus was challenged by Justin for depicting the early pictures so realistically and felt himself in danger, he, trusting in his astuteness, readily rendered an answer, saying: "I have represented these things in pictures for the consideration of the observant and for the understanding of the discerning, in order that magnates and rich men and men of high family may not trust in their power and their riches and the greatness of their noble family, but in God, who raises the poor man out of the mire, and places him as chief over the people, and ruler in the kingdom of men, which He will give to whom He will, and over which He will set the lowest among men; He who chooses men of low birth in the world, men that are rejected, and those who are nothing in order to bring to naught those who are something." Marinus' reasoning was accepted as valid, and he was released from danger.

This Marinus of Apamea, a *chartularius*, is to be identified with the

---

Constantinopolis Christiana (Paris, 1680), lib. IV, LXXXVIII (pp. 135–136). N. Kondakov, *Byzantine Churches and Monuments of Constantinople*, in *Works (Trudy) of the Sixth Archaeological Congress in Odessa* (in 1884), III (Odessa, 1887), 133–134 (in Russian). A. van Millingen, *Byzantine Churches in Constantinople: Their History and Architecture* (London, 1912), pp. 63–64. Archbishop Sergius, *The Complete Liturgical Calendar (Menologion) of the Orient*, II, 2, 417 (in Russian). On the second dream of Anastasius, *Anonymus Valesianus*, 74–76; ed. Mommsen, *Chronica Minora*, I (1892), 324, 326; ed. Cessi, p. 18. See Holmes, *op. cit.*, p. 305, note. See M. A. Andreeva, "The Political and Social Element in Byzantino-Slavonic Mantic Books," *Byzantinoslavica*, II, 2 (Prague, 1930), 404–405 (in Russian).

Marinus of Apamea, also a *chartularius*, who was, according to the same Syriac source (VII, 9), the friend and confidant of Anastasius, and his counsellor as well, a vigilant and clever man, well versed in business, wise and learned, true in the faith. "When he was walking in the street or sitting anywhere, he would tell his secretaries to commit to writing in concise form whatever thought he had. And at night also, he had a pen-and-ink stand (καλαμάριον) hanging by his bedside, and a lamp burning by his pillow, so that he could write down his thoughts on a roll; and in the daytime he would tell them to the king, and advise him as to how he should act." Such was the man who portrayed in pictures the amazing career of Justin, and probably supplied them with some biographical notes. A *chartularius* was an archivist, keeper of the state or court archives. Marinus' pictures of the earlier stages of Justin's career may have been drawn in one of the archives and discovered there by Justin after his accession.

The question might be raised why Justin took so much exception to Marinus' pictures that the latter fell into disgrace. We may conjecture that Marinus, a friend and confidant of the late Emperor Anastasius, may not have been altogether discreet in portraying Justin's early career, and may have depicted his past with more realism than Justin, in his fresh imperial attire, chose to remember. Like many self-made men, the emperor might have preferred to forget or to ignore certain details of his early life. We do not know what happened to the pictures; probably they were destroyed.

I am rather doubtful about identifying this painter with another Marinus, the Praetorian Prefect of the East probably in 519, who was also the trusted counsellor of Anastasius and as a *scriniarius*, that is, a clerk who kept the tax accounts, was famous for his extortions, although both were from Syria: the painter from the city of Apamea, the prefect from Syria without specification of any particular city.[68]

---

[68] Zach. of Mityl. VII, 9; VIII, 1; Hamilton-Brooks, pp. 177–178; 189; Ahrens-Krüger, pp. 129; 140. In connection with this text cf. Psalms 113, 7. 1 Corinth. 1, 28. I do not know why Hamilton and Brooks call the building in which Marinus' pictures were exhibited the public baths; the Syriac text reproduces the Greek word δημόσιον. J. P. N. Land, *Anecdota Syriaca*, III (Leyden, 1870), 233, 1. 5. The public baths would hardly be an appropriate place for exhibiting

FROM SWINEHERD TO EMPEROR

Euphemia, Justin's Wife

The little we know about the earlier life of Justin's wife, Euphemia, has been told above. After becoming empress, because of her humble background and lack of education and probably also because of her practical mind, she kept aloof from the political life of the empire and was wise enough not to take advantage of her high position. Most of her attention and zeal was concentrated on works of Christian piety and religious devotion. In his letter of April 22, 519, to Pope Hormisdas, the Patriarch of Constantinople, John II, after praising the accomplishment of the religious union between Constantinople and Rome, prays God for "the most clement and most Christian sovereign Justin and his most pious spouse, our daughter, Eufimia."

The most important act in Euphemia's life as empress was her stubborn opposition to the marriage of Justin's nephew Justinian to his mistress Theodora. Neither argument nor entreaty could overcome Euphemia's obstinacy. As Procopius says: "As long as the empress was still living, Justinian was quite unable to make Theodora his wedded wife. For in this point alone the empress went against him, though opposing him in no other matter." It was not till after Euphemia's death that Theodora became the wife of Justinian. The year of Euphemia's death is not known. But undoubtedly she died before April 1, 527, when Justin, old and ill, coöpted Justinian as his colleague, and the latter became the new Augustus. As a matter of course, Theodora was crowned Augusta.

During her lifetime Euphemia built in Constantinople in the region of Olybrius a nunnery and church of St. Euphemia, where she was buried. In this church on an elevation stood a small gilt statue of Euphemia. We have already mentioned that some scholars are inclined

---

such a set of pictures. The public baths has been accepted by W. G. Holmes, *The Age of Justinian and Theodora*, 1st ed., I, 304, n. 1. Ahrens and Krüger give a more plausible translation, *Regierungsgebäude* (p. 140). Marinus of Apamea in Zach. of Mityl. *loc. cit.* The other Marinus the Syrian: Malalas, 407, 10: εἰς τὰ Μαρίνου τοῦ Σύρου; in the Slavonic version of Malalas by V. Istrin, p. 17; M. Spinka, *op. cit.*, p. 118. Lydus, *De magistratibus*, III, 36: Μαρίνου . . . ὃς καὶ αὐτὸς εἰς τῶν τῆς Συρίας σκρινιαρίων ἐτύγχανε (ed. Wuensch., p. 124, 17–19). On the painter Marinus, E. Stein, *PW*, X, col. 1329. Kulakovsky writes that Justin's past was described in detail and seemingly supplied with illustrations by the *chorty-*

to identify Euphemia in a medallion on one of the extremities of the horizontal bar of a silver cross preserved in the Vatican; but most scholars think that the miniature represents Sophia, wife of Justin II.

Unless I am mistaken, no coins bear the figure of Euphemia. Sabatier believed he had found the representation of Euphemia on the reverse of a small bronze coin of her husband. But according to Wroth, this is in the highest degree doubtful, and the coin may be a badly preserved example of a piece with Tyche of Antioch on its reverse.[69]

JUSTIN AND JUSTINIAN

Justin's nephew, Peter Sabbatius, known by his adoptive name of Justinianus, without doubt played a very important part behind the throne during the reign of his uncle from the very beginning. Justin had other nephews and seems to have taken care of their fortunes. They were liberally educated and played parts of varying distinction

---

larius Marinus. Kulakovsky, *History of Byzantium*, II, 1, n. 1 (in Russian). In their English translation of Pseudo-Zacharias, Hamilton and Brooks give for Bederiana a distorted name Mauriana; correct form Bederiana in Ahrens-Krüger.

[69] On Euphemia see a brief and not very complete article by Benjamin in *PW*, VI, col. 1167. The letter of the Patriarch John to Hormisdas in Mansi, VIII, 457; Migne, *PL*, LXIII, 450; Coll. Avell., no. 161 (p. 613). See V. Grumel, *Les regestes des actes du patriarcat de Constantinople*, I, Socii Assumptionistae Chalcedonenses, no. 213 (Kadiköy-Istanbul, 1932), p. 86. Procopius, *H. A.* IX, 47 (Dewing, pp. 116–117). In the spurious life by Theophilus (*Vita Theophili*) it was Justinian's mother Biglenitza (Vigilantia) who opposed his marriage to Theodora; and in spite of her opposition Justinian married Theodora by Justin's order. J. Bryce, "The Life of Justinian by Theophilus," *The English Historical Review*, II, 662. A. Vasiliev, "The Problem of Justinian's Slavonic Origin," *Viz. Vrem.*, I, 477 (in Russian). On the time of Euphemia's death, Bury, II, 29, n. 3 (he says it is unknown); Benjamin: he says it was before April 527. Holmes, *op. cit.*, I, 347: in 524. I do not know his reason for this date. On the nunnery of St. Euphemia and Euphemia's burial place see Πάτρια, III, p. 183; ed. Preger, p. 273. Codinus, *De signis*, ed. Bekker (*CSHB*), p. 33. Suidas, s. v. Εὐφημία; ed. Bekker, p. 449; ed. Adler, I, 2, p. 478. *Anonymi Antiquitates Constantinopolitanae in Banduri, Imperium Orientale*, I (Paris, 1711), reprinted in Migne, *PG*, CXXII, col. 1285. *Breves enarrationes chronographicae*, ed. A. Banduri, *Imp. Orient*, I, reprinted in Migne, *PG*, CLVII, col. 676. Euphemia's statue: Πάτρια, II, 26; ed. Preger, II, 164. Suidas, s. v. Εὐφημία. Codinus, p. 33. Migne, *PG*, CLVII, col. 676. On the Vatican cross see above. Euphemia's coin: J. Sabatier, *Description générale des monnaies byzantines*, I, 167. W. Wroth, *Catalogue of the Imperial Byzantine Coins in the British Museum*, I, p. XIV, n. 4. On the church of St. Euphemia ἐν τοῖς 'Ολυβρίου see R. Janin, "Les églises Sainte-Euphémie à Constantinople," *Échos d'Orient*, XXXV (1932), 276–279.

and importance on the political scene. But Justinian far outstripped them all. We do not know exactly when Justinian was invited to the capital by his uncle. He was about thirty-six years of age when Justin ascended the throne, and at that time was already among the *candidati*, took part in the elevation of his uncle, and was even asked by the excubitors to accept the diadem, an offer which he wisely declined. It was evidently during the reign of Anastasius, when Justin himself had already reached a high military position, distinguished himself in several military campaigns, and possessed great influence, that he invited his nephew to the capital when the latter had reached a suitable age, perhaps about twenty-five. Justin became his guardian. He set two goals for his nephew's future destinies: to give him an excellent and extensive education, and then to prepare him for military service. He worked in fruitful soil. The intellectual talents of Justinian were far above the average; particularly, he was deeply interested in theological questions and studied dogmatic problems independently and systematically so that he had all the confidence of a professional theologian, a fact which inspired Bury's striking remark that a theologian on the throne is a public danger (II, 27). In addition he was undoubtedly much interested in Roman law, as he showed later by his monumental work in this field.

Probably on the completion of his studies Justinian was drafted into the ranks of the *candidati* or personal bodyguards of the emperor. Meanwhile Justin legally adopted Sabbatius, who on this occasion assumed the derivative name of Justinian. The exact date of the adoption is not recorded. During his uncle's reign, Justinian held several important offices. Immediately after Justin's election he was appointed Count of the domestics (*comes domesticorum*), commander of a special body of imperial guards, the *domestici*, who as a rule were stationed at the imperial court but might be sent elsewhere for special purposes. At the very beginning of the year 519 Pope Hormisdas addressed a letter to Justinian as *domesticorum comes*. Then he was created master of soldiers *in praesenti* (*magister militum praesentalium*) or, as it is phrased on his consular diptychs, *magister equitum et peditum praesentalium*, and was invested with the rank of patrician. In 521 he held the consulship, which Marcellinus calls most famous (*famosissimum hunc consulatum*); he entertained the populace with magnificent spectacles, spending 288,000 solidi in gold money and exhibiting twenty lions and thirty leopards in the arena in addition to other wild animals; and he gave to the charioteers many mail-clad horses, "wearing ornaments for the forehead and breast" (*faleratosque*). As Justinian's influence and authority became more powerful, Justin was not without some jealousy and apprehension. This feeling must have considerably increased when the Senate and other high officials, in view of the advanced age of the emperor, petitioned him that the younger man should be formally recognized as his colleague. Justin, as Zonaras reports, grasped his robe and answered, "Be on your guard against any young man having the right to wear this garment," and thus rejected the petition. But the Senate did not abandon their efforts. They passed an order to elevate Justinian to the rank of *nobilissimus* and begged Justin to ratify it. The emperor yielded, and under the pressure of the senate and against Justin's own will, Justin's nephew was elevated to the rank of *nobilissimus*. This distinction must have been bestowed upon Justinian before the year 525, in which he received the highest title, Caesar. In this year, upon the supplication of the senators and once more against his will, Justin made Justinian Caesar.[70] Such was the spectacular career of Justinian during his uncle's reign.

---

[70] *Comes domesticorum*: Mansi, VIII, 447 (ep. XXXVII): "Ad Iustinianum Domesticorum comitem" (the end of January or beginning of February, 519). In *Coll. Avell.* ep. 154 (p. 601), the title of *Domesticorum comes* is omitted. Some historians identify Justinian's title *Com. Dom.* with *Comes Excubitorum*. See Holmes, I, 304, n. 4: Justinian also took over his uncle's post of Count of Excubitors. Holmes refers to the letter of Hormisdas just mentioned. *Magister militum*: Mansi, VIII, 497; *Coll. Avell.*, ep. 230 (p. 696): "filii quoque vestri magistri militum Vitalianus ac Iustinianus." Constantine Porphyrogenitus calls Justinian during his uncle's reign μονοστράτηγος τῶν Ῥωμαϊκῶν ταγμάτων, *i.e.* magister militum. *De thematibus*, p. 34. *Victoris Tonnennensis Chronica, s. a.* 520: "Iustinianus nepos Justini Augusti ex candidato magister militum ordinarius constituitur" (ed. Mommsen, *Chr. Min.*, II, p. 196).

Patrician: Vict. Tonn. *s. a.* 523, 3: "Iustiniani patricii" (*Chr. Min.*, II, p. 197).

Consulship: Marcellinus, *s. a.* 521 (*Chr. Min.*, II, 101–102). Justinian's consular diptychs have been discussed above. Cyril of Scythopolis, a writer of the sixth century, mentions Justinian's three titles together: ἀδελφιδὸν ὄντα ἑαυτοῦ πατρίκιον τυγχάνοντα, καὶ ὕπατον καὶ στρατηγόν. Saint Sabas, *Vita Sabae*, J. B. Cotelier, *Ecclesiae graecae monumenta*, III (Paris, 1686), 337; ed. I. Pomialovsky, with the Slavonic version, 386 and 388; Slav. version, 387 and 389; ed. E. Schwartz,

In reality Justinian's powerful influence started from the year 518 when Justin ascended the throne. The fact of this influence may be attested not only by the data of the *Secret History* but by the evidence of Procopius' other works, *The Wars*, and *On the Buildings*.[71] Of Procopius' statement in the *Secret History*, Pančenko remarks: "The difference was that before 527 Justinian was tyrant, and after this year he covered his violences with the rank of autocrat." [72]

Meanwhile the old emperor, who in 527 was seventy-seven was taken seriously ill. His illness was due to the recrudescence of an old arrow wound in the foot which he had received in one of his previous campaigns. Feeling death approaching, Justin yielded to the solicitations of the Senate to coöpt his nephew as his colleague. The brief contemporary official description of the elevation of Justinian has been preserved in Constantine Porphyrogenitus' compilation *De cerimoniis* and was written by the same Magister Peter who described the elevation of Justin. The ceremony took place on April 4, Easter Day, 527, in one of the great halls of the palace, the so-called great Triklinos. Justin commanded the master of offices, Tatianus, to call

---

Kyrillos von Skythopolis, p. 170. On the petition of the senators to make Justinian Augustus, Zon., XIV, 5, 35 (*CSHB* III, 150).

Nobilissimus: Zon., *ibidem*. Marcellinus, *s. a.* 527: "Iustinus imperator Iustinianum . . . jamdudum a se Nobilissimum designatum." The adverb *jamdudum*, meaning *long before*, shows that Justinian was elevated to the rank of *nobilissimus* several years before 527; in any case before 525, when Justinian became Caesar, a title superior to that of *nobilissimus*.

Caesar: Vict. Tonn. *s. a.* 525: "Post consulatum II Justini et Apionis (they were consuls in 524) Justinus Augustus Iustinianum nepotem suum ad senatorum supplicationem invitus Caesarem facit" (*Chr. Min.*, II, 197). Const. Porphyr., *De thematibus*, p. 34: Ἰουστινιανὸς . . . καῖσαρ ὤν. I do not clearly understand why Bury dismisses the important information of Victor Tonnennensis concerning Justinian's elevation to the rank of Caesar with the blunt statement "But his authority is inferior." Also, overlooking the record of Constantine Porphyrogenitus, Bury says: "We may wonder why Justinian did not receive the higher title of Caesar" (II, 21 and n. 6). Some Syriac sources identify Justin's elevation to the rank of Caesar with his official proclamation as Augustus. Michel le Syrien, II, 189; ed. Langlois, p. 187. *Abulpharagii sive Bar-Hebraei Chronicon Syriacum*, II, 81. *Idem*, *The Chronography*, ed. Budge, p. 73.

[71] This point of view has been particularly emphasized by Pančenko, "On Procopius' *Secret History*," *Viz. Vrem.*, II, 52–53: III (1896), 103 (in Russian).

[72] Pančenko, *op. cit.*, III, 103. Procopius, *Anecdota* IX, 51: τυραννῶν τε αὐτίκα ἐπεβάτευε τῆς τοῦ αὐτοκράτορος τιμῆς προσχήματι συμπεπλασμένῳ τῆς πράξεως ἐπικαλύπτων βίαιον (ed. Dewing, VI, 118).

the Senate, other high officials, the imperial guards (scholarians), and representatives of the army to the Delphax, one of the halls in the building of the Consistorium. The patriarch Epiphanius was present, and, as we may conclude from Magister Peter's contemporary evidence, it was the patriarch who in the absence of the sick emperor placed the diadem on the head of the new Augustus. The ceremony was performed according to the usual procedure, except that it was in the Delphax and not as was usual in the Hippodrome. Thus occurred the formal elevation of Justinian to the throne with the rank of Augustus.[73] At the same time his wife Theodora was as a matter of course crowned Augusta.

JUSTIN AND THEODORA

It would be out of place to discuss at length in this book the early life of Theodora, one of the most famous women in history. Her amazing career has been many times described, discussed, and esti-

[73] For Justin's age, I am inclined to accept the statement of *Chr. Pasch.*, 617, i.e. seventy-seven, because as early as 518 Procopius calls him τυμβογέρων, "with one foot in the grave." As I have noted above, Malalas (424) says that he died at the age of seventy-five. On Justin's illness: Malalas, 424. Zonaras, XIV, 5, 38 (*CSHB* III, 150). John of Nikiu, XC, 47: Justin had a wound in his head; transl. Charles, p. 138. Justinian's proclamation is merely mentioned by Malalas, 422; Slavonic version in Istrin, p. 17; in Spinka, p. 132. Evagr., IV, 9; ed. Bidez-Parmentier, p. 159. *Chr. Pasch.*, 616. Theoph., 173, 15. John of Ephesus, Nau, p. 474. John of Nikiu, XC, 48; Charles, p. 138. Agapius of Menbidj, ed. Vasiliev, *Patr. Orient.*, VIII, 426 (166). Michel le Syrien, II, 189. *Gregorii Abulpharagii Historia Dynastiarum*, ed. E. Pocockius, 149 (94); ed. Salhani, p. 148.

Dating: The contemporary Magister Peter gives April 4, Easter Day, 527. But another contemporary, Procopius, in his *Historia Arcana*, positively states that Justinian took over the Roman Empire three days before the feast of Easter, at a time when it is not permitted either to greet any of one's friends or to say "Peace be unto you" (*S.H.* IX, 53; Dewing, pp. 119–121). I think it improbable that such a ceremony should have been performed during the Passion week, and Procopius' statement is probably to be explained as one of the many examples of his bias against Justinian and Theodora. Our sources give various dates: Easter Day, April 4 (Theoph., 173, 15; Mal. 424, 19–20); April 1 (Evagr., IV, 9; p. 159); April 14 (Cedr. I, 64). Cedrenus erroneously calls April 14 Easter Day. John of Ephesus (Nau, 474) ascribes Justinian's elevation to the year 531. Stein (col. 1326) accepts the date of April 1.

From Magister Peter's description one gets the impression that the emperor was too ill to attend the ceremony so that Justinian was crowned by the patriarch. Some sources report that Justin himself placed the diadem on the head of Justinian. We must, however, give preference to the evidence of the contemporary Peter.

mated from various points of view by historians, biographers, and men of letters in general from Procopius down to writers of our own day.

Procopius' well known description of Theodora's turbulent youthful years marked by voluptuousness and wantonness, as an actress and prostitute of the lowest class has a basis in reality in spite of its high coloring. Theodora was an actress and prostitute at a time when the two terms were almost synonymous. We have no reason whatever to disregard the record of her contemporary, John of Ephesus, who bluntly says that she "came from the brothel" (πορνεῖον). There are no grounds for believing with Bury (II, 28, n. 5) that "those words are certainly an interpolation, for it is incredible that they were written by John, who was a devoted admirer of the Empress." We must not forget that the conception of prostitute in the sixth century was entirely different from that of our own day.

The best authority on John of Ephesus, a Russian scholar, A. Diakonov, remarks that John's high esteem for Theodora is not shaken by his knowledge of her past; "with quiet boldness he calls her one from the brothel." I should like to give Diakonov's account of the subject here, which if I am not mistaken has never been reproduced in any other language than the original Russian. Diakonov writes: "Following Chabot, Diehl is skeptical as to the authenticity of the quoted phrase; but for this [skepticism], it seems, the grounds are not sufficient. Le gros mot sounded rather differently to John from the way it sounds to us. The Greek word πορνεῖον (house of ill-fame) occurs only once in the Syriac text of John; but by analogy with the Greek word πόρνη (a prostitute), which occurs twice with John, the word πορνεῖον admits of a broader interpretation. In the fifty-second story of the *Lives of the Eastern Saints*, the expression 'the garb of a courtesan' (in the Syriac text of John the Greek words σχῆμα πόρνης are used) is applied to a strolling actress (ἡ μιμάς) who had no wish *prostituere in publico*, and called herself the wife of an actor. In the fifty-fifth story of the *Lives of the Saints*, Susina (Sosiana) gives John her precious garments for church use; and in addition she says, "If I spare these [garments], how do I know if courtesans (πόρναι) will wear them?" She was not referring to residents of a house of ill-fame (πορνεῖον).

97

In any case the stage on which Theodora performed was undoubtedly for John a πορνεῖον; and here Diakonov quotes a text from John's *Ecclesiastical History*, where the Hippodrome is named "the church of Satan." By saying that Theodora was ἐκ τοῦ πορνείου John did not intend to emphasize her immorality, as Procopius does, but simply stated a well known fact. It is not necessary to consider this text the mistake of a copyist or an interpolation. From Diakonov's discussion one may conclude that John of Ephesus had no idea of saying that Theodora was from a real brothel; but like any actress of the lower class she undoubtedly did prostitute herself and had many lovers. Even in his highly colored description of Theodora's early life, however, Procopius does not mention that she came from a house of ill fame. It is not to be forgotten that the church paid a great deal of attention to this social evil, and gladly received into its bosom the repentant and converted prostitute. We may cite here a well known passage from John Chrysostom: "In this way the very harlot became more honorable than virgins, when seized by this fire" (namely, by the fire of faith and repentance).

Justinian met Theodora for the first time during his uncle's reign, about 522, in Constantinople. After her wandering existence in the Near East, she had returned to the capital to lead a quiet and retired life, renting a humble tenement, staying at home, and spinning. We do not know how Justinian met her. He fell madly in love with her and she became his mistress. He persuaded his uncle to raise her to the high rank of patrician, and he formed the desire to marry her. Apparently Justin had no objection to his nephew's choice. But an impediment arose from the stubborn opposition of Justin's wife, the Empress Euphemia, who, as Procopius says, "in this point alone went against him, though opposing him in no other matter" (*Anecdota* IX, 47). When the empress died in 523 or 524, there was no further obstacle, and Justinian and Theodora were married. When on April 4, 527, Easter Day, Justin formally raised Justinian to the throne with the rank of Augustus, Theodora automatically became Augusta. When Justin died on August 1, 527, Justinian became the sole emperor and Theodora the basilissa or empress, with an authority almost superior to that of her husband. She brought to the throne her boundless ambition, her greed for wealth, her sympathy with the monophysites, with whom she had become acquainted during her wanderings in the Near East, especially in Egypt, and her own practical mind. All these qualities fully revealed themselves during the rule she, along with Justinian, exerted over the empire. After her marriage to Justinian, Theodora broke entirely with her turbulent and equivocal past and became a faithful wife; Voltaire's caustic remark that Justinian, like his famous general Belisarius, was a silly cuckold, has no historical basis whatever.[74]

[74] Procopius, *Anecdota* IX. John of Ephesus, *Lives of the Eastern Saints*, Syriac text edited and translated by E. W. Brooks, *Patrologia Orientalis*, XVII, 189. In Latin by W. J. van Douwen and J. P. N. Land, p. 68. Diehl is hesitant about accepting the record of John of Ephesus. Diehl, *Justinien et la civilization byzantine au VIe siècle*, pp. 42–43; especially note 2 on p. 42, with Chabot's suggestion. Holmes (I, 345, n. 2) remarks that this sentence in John of Ephesus "has probably been introduced by a copyist, but of what date I cannot surmise." On the incredibility of the sentence, Bury, II, 28, n. 5. Cf. A. Diakonov, *John of Ephesus and his Historical-Ecclesiastical Works*, pp. 63–64, especially n. 109 (in Russian). The best west European authority on John of Ephesus, the English orientalist, E. W. Brooks, says: All studies on John of Ephesus have now been thrown into the shade by the great work of A. Diakonov (*Patr. Orient.*, XVII [1923], III). *Idem, Johannis Ephesini Historiae Ecclesiasticae* 3rd part (Louvain, 1936), p. IV: "Discussio critica admirabilis vitae et operum Johannis." I shall list the references to the more recent edition of the *Lives of the Eastern Saints*, which came out after the publication of Diakonov's work, *Patr. Or.*, XVII (1923), 189 (see the beginning of this note); XIX (1925), 514 (168); 541 (195); cf. story XXI, *ibidem*, XVII (1923), 285: "perhaps it (my wealth) will become the property of men who are prodigal and vicious and of fornicators, and they will squander it in evil fashion." On the Hippodrome as "the Church of Satan" see John of Ephesus, *Ecclesiastical History*, V, 17; transl. by R. Payne Smith (Oxford, 1860), pp. 226–227 (in this translation, chapter V, 17 is included in the third chapter, III, 34); in Latin by Brooks (Louvain, 1936), pp. 202–203: "ecclesia Satanae." Referring to this passage Diakonov (p. 64, n. 109) by an oversight gives IV, 17 for V, 17. In Constantinople one of the streets leading to the theater was called, Πόρναι, i.e. harlots. See *Justiniani Novella* CV, *De consulibus*, a. 537 (536), ed. R. Schoell-G. Kroll, p. 502 (CV, 1): (the consul) καὶ πέμπτην γε ποιήσει πρόοδον τὴν ἐπὶ τὸ θέατρον ἄγουσαν, ἣν δὴ πόρνας καλοῦσιν. Zachariae von Lingenthal (Leipzig, 1881), I, 468 (Nov. LXXXI, a. 537). *Joannis Chrysostomi In Matthaeum Homilia* VI, 5: οὕτω ἡ πόρνη παρθένων ἐγένετο σεμνοτέρα, τούτῳ κατασχεθεῖσα τῷ πυρί. Migne, *PG*, LVII, 69. On the opposition of the Empress Euphemia, Procopius, *Anecdota* IX, 47 (Dewing, 116–117). The exact year of Euphemia's death is unknown. See Alemannus, *Notae in Historiam Arcanam*, CSHB p. 385. Bury, II, 29, n. 3. In his various works on Justinian and Theodora, Diehl gives the year 523 (*Justinien et la civil. byzantine*, p. 39; *Figures byzantines* (Paris, 1909), I, 59; *Theodora*, p. 52). Holmes (I, 347) gives 524. The legendary *Vita Theophili* (see above) reflects another and probably later tradition, according to which Justinian married the beautiful girl Bosidara (this is the Slavonic equivalent of the Greek name of

Procopius in his *Secret History* (IX, 51) says, "Since it was impossible for a man who had attained to senatorial rank to contract marriage with a courtesan, a thing forbidden from the beginning by the most ancient laws, Justinian compelled the emperor to amend the laws by a new law, and from then on he lived with Theodora as his married wife, and he thereby opened the way to betrothal with courtesans for all other men." This passage has been connected with a decree which has sometimes been attributed to the time of Justinian, but which was in reality published during Justin's reign and is now tentatively referred to the years 520–523. This law "On Marriage" (*De nuptiis*) addressed by Justin to the praetorian prefect Demosthenes (A.D. 520–524) will be discussed in detail below. In *On the Wars* Procopius wrote that Theodora's "nature always led her to assist unfortunate women."

According to Procopius, Justinian before marrying Theodora had managed to have her advanced to the rank of patrician, and Procopius has been confirmed by John of Ephesus, who narrates that "the good God directed the virtuous Stephen to Theodora . . . who was at that time a patrician, but eventually became queen also with King Jus-

---

Theodora) by Justin's order, although Justinian's mother Biglenizza (Vigilantia) opposed the marriage, not on account of Theodora's lack of chastity, but because of her too great cleverness and pride. J. Bryce, "Life of Justinian by Theophilus," *The English Historical Review*, II, 662; also in *Archivio della R. Società Romana di Storia Patria*, X 142–145. In Russian, A. Vasiliev, *Viz. Vrem.*, I, 477. Some sources show a curious confusion in regard to Theodora. Theophanes (I, p. 170, l. 29) calls Theodora the wife of Justin. This is probably a defect in the text; such a blunder on the part of Theophanes seems almost impossible. Alemannus noted the error and tried to restore the real text. Alemannus, *Notae in Hist. Arcanam*, CSHB p. 385. Following Theophanes, Cedrenus (I, 639) regards Theodora as Justin's second wife, whom he married after the death of Euphemia. A Syriac chronicle states that after Anastasius, reigned Justinian (as Justin is called in Syriac sources) husband of the pious Theodora, and a little later, after Justinian, Justinian reigned forty years. *Chronicon Miscellaneum ad annum Domini 724 pertinens*, ed. E. W. Brooks, transl. I.-B. Chabot, *CSCO*, Scriptores Syri, 3rd series, vol. IV, *Chronica Minora* (Paris, 1903), 108. See H. F. Clinton, *Fasti Romani*, II (Oxford, 1850), 141–142. Holmes (I, 342, n. 2) quotes *pour rire* a very amusing bit of information which he found in a German work, which I have seen, *Trachten des christlichen Mittelalters* by Hefner-Altneck. The text runs as follows: "Theodora was the daughter of Acacius, Patriarch of Constantinople, and was trained by her mother for the theater, in which she distinguished herself by her art as a pantomimist." (I [Frankfurt am Main, 1879], 124). On Justinian and Belisarius, Voltaire, *Lettre à M. Marmontel*, no. 7082. *Oeuvres complètes*, XLV (Paris, 1881); *Correspondence*, XIII, 441.

tinian." If this is true, even before her marriage Theodora had already ceased to be an actress and bore the high rank of patrician; in this case no special law would be necessary for the purpose of making her marriage possible.[75]

[75] Procopius, *Anecdota* IX, 51 (Dewing, pp. 118–119). The decree *De nuptiis* in *Cod. Just.*, V, 4, 23. The dates of the praetorian prefecture of Demosthenes in Bury, I, 445. On the general trend of Justinian's legislation in favor of women see B. Pančenko, "On Procopius' *Secret History*," *Viz. Vrem.*, III, 105 (in Russian). Procopius, *Bellum Gothicum*, III, 31, 14: ἡ δὲ βασιλὶς ἐπεφύκει γὰρ ἀεὶ δυστυχούσαις γυναιξὶ προσχωρεῖν (ed. Haury, II, 432; Dewing, IV, 418–419). Bury gives an inexact reference to this passage: III, 32 for III, 31 (II, 32, n. 3).

CHAPTER THREE

Justin's Domestic Rule

THE LIQUIDATION OF AMANTIUS' PLOT

At the moment of his elevation the position of Justin was precarious and complicated. A mere chance had raised him to the throne. The late Emperor Anastasius had three nephews, none of whom had been seriously regarded as potential successor to their uncle. But the high chamberlain, the eunuch Amantius, who had attempted to secure the imperial throne for his domestic Theocritus and, as we have pointed out, had for this purpose given money to Justin, at that time Count of the excubitors, to bribe the troops, apparently was unwilling to abandon his plan. Energetic and speedy action by the new government was urgently needed, and action more decisive than was to be expected from an old man like Justin inexperienced in politics. Fortunately his nephew Justinian was young, talented, and highly educated, and even before Justin's elevation Justinian was evidently well prepared to meet emergencies.[1] His influence among the leading elements of the state had already been highly regarded under Anastasius, so highly that, as we have seen, he was even offered the imperial rank, which for the time being he wisely declined. His predominant power behind the throne dated, one may say, from the first day of his uncle's rule. In all three of his works, different as they are from each other, Procopius clearly develops this idea. In his great *History in Eight Books*, which in spite of its slightly laudatory tone in numerous instances tells the plain truth, Procopius writes that even before coming to the throne Justinian administered the government according to his pleasure, for his uncle Justin was very old and not much experienced in matters of state. In another work, *On The Buildings*, a continuous panegyric of Justinian, Procopius relates that Justinian administered the government

[1] I am unable to agree with W. G. Holmes when he writes: "Owing to the suddenness of their elevation both princes were ignorant of the routine of government." Holmes, *The Age of Justinian and Theodora*, I, 304.

on his own authority during his uncle's reign. Finally, in the vicious libel upon Justinian and Theodora, *Anecdota* or *The Secret History*, Procopius says that Justinian, who was still young, used to administer the entire government; another passage of the same work, describing the amazing prodigality with which Justinian handed over huge donations to the leaders of the Huns, remarks: "it was said that he had done this even during the period of Justin's reign." In the same work Procopius mentions a dancing girl, Macedonia, who wrote letters to Justinian while he was still administering the empire for Justin.[2] On the basis of the *Secret History* Bury rightly observes that Procopius treats the reign of Justin as virtually part of that of Justinian (II, 21, n. 4).

Immediately after Justin's elevation the High Chamberlain, the eunuch Amantius, hastily organized a consipracy against him. Evidently supported by his followers, among whom John Malalas mentions Marinus, the trusted counselor of the late Anastasius, he entered St. Sophia for a public denunciation of the new government. But the conspirators met a hostile demonstration on the part of the assembly and, according to John Malalas, "were cried down" (κατεκράγησαν). The plot was quickly nipped in the bud, and the participants were severely punished. Amantius, his protégé Theocritus, and Andreas Lausiacus (ὁ Λαυσιακός) were executed. A particularly severe and humiliating punishment was inflicted upon Theocritus, as the potential claimant to the throne; he was beaten to death in prison by enormous stones, and his body was thrown into the sea. The other two were beheaded. According to a legendary tradition, Amantius in the time of Anastasius had had a dream, a sort of premonition of his destiny; he saw himself seized, thrown down, and devoured by a great pig, which of course symbolized the future emperor Justin, who according to one tradition had been a swineherd in his native country in his youth. Two other conspirators, Misael (Μησαήλ, Mishael, Misahel) and Ardabur, were exiled north to Sardica (Serdica; now Sofia, in Bulgaria).

Strangely enough, Marinus, the devoted counselor of the late

<hr />

[2] Proocpius, *De bello Vandalico* I, 9, 5; Haury, I, 351–352; Dewing, II, 85. *De aedificiis* I, 3, 3; Dewing, VII, 38–39. *Anecdota* VI, 19; XI, 5; XII, 29; Dewing, VI, 75; 131; 155. See also *Joannis Lydi De magistratibus*, II, 28; ed. Wuensch, p. 83.

Anastasius, whose name is also mentioned among the conspirators, not only escaped any punishment but even held high office under Justin as Praetorian Prefect of the East in 519; and later, in Edict XIII of Justinian the Great, which is now dated August 554, Marinus (Μαριανός) is referred to as one who under Anastasius of blessed memory was at the head of the administration, one "of glorious memory." We know also that one of the exiles, Misael (Mishael), after many years of exile, was not only allowed to return to Constantinople but was even restored to his official position; he was appointed chamberlain, and later retired from the world and became a deacon in the church. The Syrian monophysite historian, John of Ephesus, gives an interesting character sketch of Misael. A Christian, merciful, ascetic, and perfect in all spiritual things, he underwent exile for the sake of the truth of the right faith, for he might not communicate with the synod of Chalcedon; he spent many years in exile, was at last invited to come back, was restored to his place, and finally retired, having lived many years devoted to religious practice and works of charity.[3] That the

[3] On Amantius, Theocritus, and Andreas see John Malalas, pp. 410–411; *Hermes*, VI, 375; *Excerpta historica jussu Imp. Constantini Porphyrogeniti confecta*, III, *Excerpta de insidiis*, ed. C. de Boor (Berlin, 1905), p. 170. Slavonic version, Istrin, 17; Spinka, 120. Evagrius, IV, 2 (Bidez-Parmentier, p. 154). *Chr. Pasch.*, 611–612. Theoph. 165. Cedr. I, 637–638. Zonaras, XIV, 5, 4 (*CSHB* III, 145). Nic. Call., XVII, 1 (Migne, CXLVII, col. 220). Com. Marcell., *s. a.* 519, 2 (*Chr. Minora*, II, 101). *Iordanis De summa temporum*, *MGH*, *AA*, V, 1, 47. Vict. Tonnen. *Chronica*, *s. a.* 519 (*Chr. Minora*, II, 196). Malalas and *Chr. Pasch.* call Andreas ὁ Λαυσιακός. His surname may have been derived from the palace of Lausus in Constantinople. See Πάτρια τῆς Κωνσταντινουπόλεως, II, 36 (27). Preger, *Scr. originum Constantinopolitanarum*, II, 170. Amantius' dream is mentioned in *Chr. Pasch.*, 610–611, and in Zonaras, *loc. cit.* John of Nikiu calls all the conspirators eunuchs. He writes: "When Justin became emperor he put to death all the eunuchs, however guiltless they were, because they had not approved of his elevation to the throne; for he thought they would plot evil against him." *The Chronicle of John, Bishop of Nikiu*, XC, 4; transl. R. H. Charles, p. 133. Mention of Amantius and Theocritus is also to be found in a Russian source. *The Russian Chronograph of the version of the year* 1512, ch. 136, in *Complete Collection of the Russian Annals*, XXII, part I, 292. Also J. A. Cramer, *Anecdota graeca parisiensia*, II, 518. On the exile of Misael (Μησαήλ) and Ardaburius ('Αρδαβούριος) Malalas, *Hermes*, VI, 375; ed. de Boor, p. 170. The name of Serdica, the place where they were exiled, is recorded in Comes Marcellinus and Iordanes (*loc. cit.*). On Marinus as a participator in the plot, Malalas, *Hermes*, VI, 375; de Boor, p. 170 (Μαρῖνος ἰλλούστριος). Cf. a corrupt passage in *Joannis Lydi De magistratibus*, III, 51: 'Ιουστίνου δὲ τὴν βασιλείαν παραλαβόντος . . . Μαρῖνος μὲν, καὶ ὅσοι 'Αναστασίου τῆς αὐξήσεως ⟨ἔτυχον, ἀπηλλάτοντο⟩; ed. Wuensch, p. 140; see also III, 36 (Wuensch, p. 124). Marinus as praetorian prefect under Justin in 519 in

Chalcedonian emperor Justinian should recall such an open monophysite as Misael, may help us, in connection with other testimony, to take a new approach to the general religious policy of this emperor.

There is no doubt that the prompt liquidation of the plot against the new emperor was due to the energy of his nephew Justinian. Since religious matters were indissolubly associated with political affairs, in some sources there are indications that the persons involved in the conspiracy also resented Justin's new religious policy, which aimed at the recognition of the Council of Chalcedon and the restoration of friendly relations with the Pope. *Comes* Marcellinus describes Amantius, Andreas, Misael (Misahel) and Ardabur not only as traitors but also as Manichaeans, because at that time the supporters of the Council of Chalcedon often mockingly called Manichaeans all those who tried to reconcile the Chalcedonian doctrine with other religious tenets, as well as those who were suspected of sympathy with the doctrine of Nestorius. Of course a religious protest was included in Amantius' plot, but it was not the leading feature of the movement.

Procopius' presentation is one-sided and incomplete when he writes that Justinian "slew Amantius, director of the palace eunuchs, together with certain others for no cause whatever, charging the man with nothing except that he had spoken some hasty word against John, the

---

Cod. Just. II, 7, 25; V, 27, 7: "Imp. Justinus A. Marino pp" (ed. P. Krueger, p. 101; 217). Justinian's Edict XIII "De urbe Alexandrinorum et Aegyptiacis provinciis," cap. XV (XIII, 15): ἐπὶ τῶν χρόνων 'Αναστασίου τοῦ τῆς εὐσεβοῦς λήξεως, ἡνίκα Μαριανὸς ὁ τῆς ἐνδόξου (μνήμης) ἐπ' αὐτῷ τὰ πράγματα ἔπραττε. *Novellae, Corporis CLXVIII Novellarum appendices, I, Iustiniani XIII edicta quae vocantur*, ed. R. Schoell et G. Kroll, pp. 787–788. Zachariae von Lingenthal, I, no. XCVI, 545. Schoell and Kroll think that this edict was issued between September 538 and August 539 (p. 795, note). Zachariae von Lingenthal, in his edition of the *Edict*, attributed it to the year 538 (p. 529). But later in 1891 in his new edition of this edict he changed his mind and stated that the year 553–554 was the correct one. *De diocesi aegyptiaca lex ab Imp. Iustiniano anno 554 lata* (Leipzig, 1891) preface, p. 5ff. The majority of scholars reject his conclusion. But Gertrude Malz writes that the additional evidence furnished by the papyri of Dioscorus of Aphrodito confirms Zachariae von Lingenthal's final dating of the edict, and its date is August, 554 A. D. Gertrude Malz, "The Date of Justinian's Edict XIII," *Byzantion*, XVI, 1 (Boston, 1944), 135–141. On Misael (Mishael), John of Ephesus, *Lives of the Eastern Saints*, story 57; in Latin by Douwen and Land, pp. 179–180; in English by E. W. Brooks, *Patrologia Orientalis*, XIX 200–201 (546–547). Severus addressed many letters to Misael as chamberlain and later as deacon. See index in *The Sixth Book of the Select Letters of Severus*, transl. by E. W. Brooks, II, 2, 470.

Archbishop (that is, patriarch) of the city." The same point of view
has been taken by Syriac sources. A Syriac chronicle of the sixth
century, the so-called *Chronicle* of Zachariach of Mitylene, relates
that Amantius tried to prevent Justin's new religious attitude. "The
signature of the three patriarchs and the principal bishop of your
dominion, who anathematized the Synod (of Chalcedon) is not yet
dry. . . . And because he (Amantius) spoke with freedom, he was
immediately put to death, and so were Theocritus his domestic and
Andrew the chamberlain." The Syriac writer of the seventh century,
Jacob (James) of Edessa, writes: "Amantius praepositus, Theocritus,
and Andreas cubicularius, who stood against proclaiming the Council
of Chalcedon, were killed." The Syriac historian of the twelfth century, Michael the Syrian, probably referring to Jacob of Edessa, relates: "Then Amantius praepositus, Theocritus, and Andreas cubicularius revealed themselves courageous in piety. These three real
martyrs shone in their orthodoxy and were crowned by the sword,
because they would not consent to proclaim the impious synod." A
very little known anonymous Arabian historian who compiled his
work in the eleventh century briefly mentions that Justin "massacred
Amantius, defender of Severus." In these Syriac and Arabian sources
Amantius and his followers are represented as monophysite martyrs.[4]

It is very possible that in connection with the liquidation of the
conspiracy the property of a certain senator, Patricius, was confiscated,
and that he himself was sent into exile at the beginning of the year 519.
This fact is recorded in a report of the Roman bishops Germanus and
Iohannes to Pope Hormisdas from the city of Scampae (now Elbasan
in Albania) written at the end of February or at the beginning of
March, 519. They reported that they had this information from the
imperial messengers, Leontius and *comes* Stephanus, who had been
sent by Justin to meet the papal envoys; in their report the bishops

[4] *Comes Marcell., s. a.* 519 (*Chronica Minora*, II, 101). Proc., *Anecdota* VI, 26
(Dewing, VI, 76). Zach. of Mitylene, VIII, 1; Hamilton-Brooks, p. 190; Ahrens-
Krüger, pp. 140–141. The latter translation differs from that of Hamilton-Brooks.
The same story in the *Chronicon ad annum Domini 846 pertinens*, E. W. Brooks,
p. 169, *CSCO*, Scriptores syri, *Chronica minora. Chronicon Iacobi Edesseni* transl.
by E. W. Brooks, p. 239, *CSCO, ibidem. Michel le Syrien*, Chabot, IX, 12; 16
(II, 170; 180). *Histoire nestorienne, Chronique de Seert*, transl. Addai Scher,
Patrologia Orientalis, VII, 139 (47).

wrote that they could not say the real cause of Patricius' disgrace, "because it is not easy to learn the truth about such matters."

We have pointed out above that during the troubled hours of the election of the new emperor, there was a moment when the excubitors proclaimd John, a tribune and a friend of Justin; but his candidature was violently opposed by the Blues. Although John was thus a possible rival, Justin, perhaps moved by their former friendship, did not execute him but instead merely obliged him to take orders; in 520 he was ordained Bishop of Heraclea in Thrace.[5]

All these measures putting an end to political opposition to the new government were taken immediately upon or very shortly after Justin's elevation. He was proclaimed emperor on July 9, 518. According to Procopius, Amantius and his close followers were executed when Justin had not yet been ten days in power (*Anecdota* VI, 26), that is, in July, 518. In connection with Procopius' dating, I wish to refer to the fact that on July 16, 518, the crowd in St. Sophia during their turbulent altercation with the patriarch and the other clergy, of which I shall speak later, cried to the patriarch: "Eject the new Tzumas. The new Tzumas is Amantius. Eject the braggart from the palace."[6] In other words, on July 16, 518, either Amantius was still alive or the crowd thought that he was. Combining this record with Procopius' statement that Amantius and his followers were executed when Justin had not yet been ten days in power, we may conclude

[5] *Collectio Avellana*, ed. O. Günther (Vienna, 1895), no. 213, p. 672: "qui nobis nuntiaverunt Patricium senatorem proscriptum et in exilio missum; pro qua tamen causa, nisi quo modo ad nos pervenerit, nom possumus dicere, quia non est de talibus rebus facile deliberare. Exemplum suggestionis Germani et Johannis episcoporum Felicis et Dioscori diaconorum et Blandi presbyteri." CSEL, vol. XXXV. In a note to p. 671, other editions of this letter are indicated. The letter was written at the end of February or the beginning of March (p. 671, note). Cf. a brief letter of Pope Hormisdas, written in January 519 to *Celer et Patricius a pari* (*ib.*, no. 152, pp. 600–601). On the meaning of *a pari* see p. 926 (Index). On John Bishop of Thracian Heraclea, Const. Porphyr., *De cerimoniis*, I, 93: ἀναγορεύουσιν βασιλέα Ἰωάννην τινὰ τριβοῦνον, οἰκειούμενον τῷ τῆς θείας λήξεως Ἰουστίνῳ, ὃς μετὰ ταῦτα ἐπίσκοπος Ἡρακλείας ἐγένετο (CSHB I, p. 427). *Victoris Tonnennensis Chronica*, s. a. 520: "Johannes, qui ante Iustinum ad imperium erat electus, Heracliae Thraciae episcopus ordinatur" (*Chr. Minora*, ed. Mommsen, II, 196. MGH, AA, vol. XI).

[6] Mansi, *Conciliorum Collectio* VIII, 1063–1064. The eunuch Chrysaphius Τζουμᾶς, the all-powerful favorite under Theodosius II (408–450), was executed by his successor Marcian. See below.

that the execution took place between July 16 and 18 (the ninth day from Justin's proclamation as emperor). The new government, guided by the energetic Justinian, thus managed to seize control of the political situation so promptly that at the end of 518 it had no political danger to fear. The measures taken against the most influential members of the church who opposed the new orientation of the government in its religious policy will be discussed below.[7]

THE RECALL OF EXILES AND ASSASSINATION OF VITALIAN

At the same time, the new government directed by Justinian took measures to recall those who had been unjustly exiled by Anastasius. Our sources have preserved the names of some eminent exiles. The patrician Appion (Apion), and Diogenianus and Philoxenus, both of senatorial rank, returned to the capital and were reinstated in their official functions, and later promoted. Appion was made praetorian prefect of the East, a post he held perhaps in 518–519, when he was succeeded by the above-mentioned Marinus. Severus dedicated one of his treatises to Appion and Paul, who "were very renowned patricians." Diogenianus became master of soldiers in the East, and Flavius Theodorus Philoxenus, together with Probus Junior, was honored with the consulship in the West in 525. Several bishops whom Anastasius had deposed and exiled were brought back by Justin: from Syria Prima, John of Paltos; from Syria Secunda, Severianus of Arethusa and Eusebius of Larissa.[8]

But the most important personage who was allowed to return was Vitalian, the influential leader who had nearly overthrown Anastasius. Posing as an ardent champion of orthodoxy and an energetic opponent of the monophysite policy of Anastasius, Vitalian had held the post of Count (*comes*) of the Federates in the Balkans, and had the support of the population of Illyricum, the Danubian regions, Scythia

---

[7] Procopius, *Anecdota* VI, 26 (Dewing, VI, 76). *Comes* Marcellinus and Victor Tonnennensis tell the story of the liquidation of the plot under the year 519. On the tumult of July 16, 518, see Mansi, *Conciliorum Collectio*, VIII, 1063–1064. At the Synod of Tyre, September 16, 518, the crowd shouted: "The rebel against the Trias, Amantius, is dead!" Mansi, VIII, 1089–1090. See H. F. Clinton, *Fasti Romani*, I, 736 (under the years 518 and 519).

[8] See Devreesse, *Le patriarcat d'Antioche* (Paris, 1945), pp. 170; 182; 183.

(now Dobrudja) and lower Moesia, where the orthodox element pre-
dominated. But his orthodox championship was only the outward pretext for the revolt. His real object was to dethrone Anastasius and become emperor himself. He had twice revolted, and there was a
moment when with his army and fleet he occupied the suburbs of the
capital and was making sallies against the Golden Gate itself. Anastasius
opened negotiations with Vitalian, and gave him promises of a change
in his religious policy, which he had no intention of fulfilling. Finally
Vitalian was routed and fled with the remnants of his troops. Vitalian's
defeat was regarded by the monophysites as a glorious event, and the
head of the monophysite movement, the Bishop of Antioch, Severus,
wrote a special hymn in commemoration of the brilliant victory of
the imperial troops, "On Vitalian the Tyrant, and on the Victory of
the Christ-loving Anastasius the King." At the moment of Justin's
elevation, Vitalian, in spite of his defeat, was still at large and, as W. G.
Holmes writes, "apparently, if not in reality, master of the forces in
Thrace and in Illyria" (I, 306).

Justin's government decided to apply to Vitalian its policy of re-
calling those who had been exiled under Anastasius. But it is clear that
Vitalian's case could not be compared with that of the other exiles
whose names have been indicated above. Vitalian was not merely a
supporter of Justin and Justinian's new religious policy in favor of
the restoration of the decrees of the Council of Chalcedon and the
resumption of relations with the papacy; he was a potential political
rival of considerable magnitude, whose name was popular among the
masses in the Balkans and even in Constantinople. One cannot help
surmising that the invitation to return to the capital may have covered
the secret hope on the part of Justin, and particularly Justinian, that
it would be much easier, in case of necessity, to dispose of him near at
hand. Evagrius (IV, 3) plainly says that Justin — in other words,
Justinian — when he invited Vitalian to Constantinople, feared his
power, his experience in military matters, his fame, and his aspiration
to imperial power. And Justin — behind him, Justinian, — very well
knew that he would be able to match Vitalian in strength and influence "in no other way so well as by pretending to be his friend."
Vitalian understood the situation well and was on the alert.

When the invitation to come to Constantinople reached him, Vitalian clearly remembered the ambiguous policy of the late emperor, who had failed to keep his promises. He accepted the proposal on condition that an assurance of good faith on the part of the emperor and Justinian should first be given with solemn religious formalities. The meeting took place at Chalcedon, in the Church of St. Euphemia so beautifully described by Evagrius (II, 3), where in 451, sixty-seven years before, the great Council of Chalcedon had been held. There Justin, Justinian, and Vitalian swore oaths to one another, partook of the holy sacraments, and then entered Constantinople. Safety was pledged to Vitalian. He was immediately created master of soldiers *in praesenti*, and in 520, with his colleague Rusticus in the West, he was consul for the year. This reconciliation had a very important political significance: it pacified the Balkan Peninsula, where Vitalian, as we have noted above, was very popular. In religious policy Vitalian was a strict Chalcedonian and a sworn enemy of all dissident denominations, particularly of monophysitism. It was said that he demanded that Justin cut out Severus' tongue for the offensive language the patriarch had directed against him in writings and homilies. We have already mentioned Severus' hymn "On Vitalian the Tyrant." This abuse was now a thing of the past. In the correspondence dating from the years 519 and 520 which has been preserved in the *Collectio Avellana*, Vitalian is called *magnificus vir*, and his name is connected with the name of Justinian: *Vitalianus, Pompeius et Justinianus*, or *Vitalianus ac Justinianus*. In one of his letters to Pope Hormisdas Justinian calls Vitalian "our most glorious brother" (*frater noster gloriosissimus Vitalianus*).

But two such strong personalities as Justinian and Vitalian could not get along well together. At that time Vitalian was much more experienced politically than Justinian; and his ascendancy and popularity grew so rapidly that there was danger that his presence might overshadow and even nullify the authority of the aged Justin and of Justinian. As consul in 520, Vitalian officially opened the games in the Hippodrome. And then suddenly, according to the Escurial manuscript of John Malalas — we do not know the real cause — during the evening races riotous demonstrations of the Blues and the Greens burst out and spread over the city with some loss of life. Peace was restored; the factions came to a friendly understanding and returned to the Hippodrome to attend the tenth race, presided over by the prefect of the city, Theodorus; and after the performance both factions in a merry-making mood (παίζοντες) left the theater to assemble again in the Hippodrome next morning. The factions asked the emperor to attend the games and began to shout demands for their favorite dancers: the Greens demanded Caramallus (Καράμαλλον), the Blues a certain Porphyrius from Alexandria, the Reds and the Whites their favorites, who in Malalas' text are called τοὺς πρώτους. The emperor satisfed all demands, and the factions, wearing mantles (μετὰ παλλίων) of their particular colors, joyfully paraded in the Hippodrome and in the city. In their excitement, apparently, they seized some bystanders (τινας τῶν παρακενότων?) and threw them into the sea. And then, without any apparent connection with his preceding text, Malalas makes this statement: "Vitalian, consul and magister militum, was slain in the palace, and Celerianus, his secretary (κελλάριος; probably should be καγκελλάριος) as well."

The names of the dancer and mime Caramallus, whom the Greens demanded, and Porphyrius, the favorite of the Blues, are known from other sources. In one of his *Letters* (the ascription, however, is doubtful) Aristaenetus, a writer of the fifth or sixth century, mentions the famous dancer Caramallus. In this letter an imaginary personage, Seusippus, praises the talent of a certain girl, Panarete (Παναρέτη), also imaginary, who could exactly imitate in her dancing "the most famous Caramallus." The Latin poet of the fifth century, Apollinaris Sidonius, also mentions the famous mime Caramallus. This presents some chronological difficulties. The time of the writer Aristaenetus, who mentions the name of the famous dancer Caramallus, has not been definitely fixed. Supposedly he lived either at the end of the fifth century or in the sixth century. If the Caramallus mentioned by Apollinaris Sidonius is identical with the famous dancer Caramallus in Aristaenetus' letter, Aristaenetus must have lived in the middle of the fifth century, because Apollinaris Sidonius died about 479; but, according to W. B. Anderson, a somewhat later date seems probable. The riot under Justin with which we are dealing occurred in 520. It is hard to believe that there were two Caramalli, one a dancer and the other a mime. At any rate, the record of the Escurial version of Malalas is strong evidence that the famous dancer Caramallus was still alive and performing in 520.

Porphyrius, the favorite of the Blues, was the famous charioteer who during a long life won so many victories in racing that in one epigram he is praised as follows: "Cytherea was in love with Anchises and Selene with Endymion, and it seems that Victory is in love with Porphyrius." His bronze statue was erected when he was young "with the first down on his cheeks," according to another epigram. The marble base of this monument, once in the Hippodrome, has survived; for many years the base was to be found in the atrium of St. Irene, and it is now preserved in the Museum of Antiquities in Istanbul (Constantinople). On each of the four sides of the monument Porphyrius is represented either in his chariot or on foot, in his driving costume with palm and wreath. On each side are laudatory Greek inscriptions in his honor. On the basis of the style of the reliefs and of the character of the letters of the inscriptions, the scholars who have studied the monument have come to the rather tentative conclusion that the approximate date of the monument is A. D. 490–510, or the end of the fifth century. Without doubt the Porphyrius claimed by the Blues in 520 is the Porphyrius of this monument. We have pointed out above that the Blues called Porphyrius' town Alexandria. One of the inscriptions on the base of the statue and an epigram confirm the identification by calling him a Libyan (Λίβυς), that is, an African. Surprisingly, the evidence of the Escurial version of Malalas has not been utilized by the numerous scholars who have studied Porphyrius' monument, but it should be taken into consideration.[9]

Let us return to Vitalian's murder. According to the Oxford manuscript of Malalas (412), he was slain after "his first *mappa*," the napkin which the consul held in his right hand and threw down as the signal for the commencement of the games or races in the circus. We have seen that a riot burst out; then both factions came to a friendly under-

---

[9] Even A. M. Woodward and A. J. B. Wace have overlooked this record. "The Monument of Porphyrius," in W. S. George, *The Church of Saint Eirene at Constantinople* (Oxford, 1912), p. 84.

standing and in a state of exuberant joy and exaltation paraded around the city. This exalted mood of the factions may well have been inspired by the popularity of the new consul who had made his first public appearance. The dangerous height of the popular enthusiasm in his favor no doubt alarmed Justin and Justinian and made them hastily decide to do away with a political rival of such caliber. As they were leaving the baths, Vitalian and his two lieutenants, Celer (Celerianus) and Paul were invited by the emperor to a banquet. All plans had been made for Vitalian's assassination, and men were posted ready to stab him. As they entered one of the banqueting rooms of the Great Palace, which was called Delphax (Δέλφαξ), Vitalian and his two lieutenants, Celer and Paul, his notary and his domestic, were set upon and slain.

Two contemporary sources, Greek and Latin, Procopius and Victor Tonnennensis, supported by a later Greek historian, Zonaras, make Justinian responsible for Vitalian's murder. A Syrian monophysite chronicler from his own particular point of view concludes his story of Vitalian's violent death with the remark: "God requited him for the evil which he had done in the days of Anastasius and the violation of his oaths." A Greek chronicler of the ninth century, Theophanes, says that Vitalian was killed by the Byzantines to avenge those who had perished through his insurrection under Anastasius. This attributes the crime to the people of Constantinople rather than to Justin and Justinian, and is evidently a later report circulated to cover Justinian's guilt. The conclusion that Justinian premeditated and participated in Vitalian's murder is inescapable. The old Justin only followed his nephew's directions. After the imposing figure of Vitalian had been eliminated, Justinian had no other competitors or rivals, and became the all-powerful ruler, entirely overshadowing Justin. Vitalian was murdered in the seventh month of his consulship, in July, 520. After his death Justinian was appointed master of soldiers *in praesenti*, the office which had been granted Vitalian on his arrival in Constantinople.[10]

[10] Diakonov has recently given another interpretation of the riot of 520. After remarking that Malalas' account is rather puzzling, he writes: "Probably the *demotai* of the faction of the Blues who supported Vitalian, in spite of their leaders (including Justinian), joined the Greens and abandoned Vitalian, and this enabled Justinian to do away with Vitalian, his potential rival." A. Diakonov,

The nephews of the late Anastasius, Probus, Pompeius, and Hypatius, were loyal to Justin during his life. The influential and incorruptible minister Proclus the Quaestor, whom, according to Procopius, it was impossible to bribe, and who therefore, as Bury writes, had the reputation of an Aristides, was singlemindedly devoted to his work for the benefit of the empire, and possessed no desire for political power. Justinian knew this and did not regard him as dangerous.[11]

"The Byzantine Demes and Factions in the Fifth to the Seventh Centuries," *Vizantisky Sbornik*, p. 207, n. 1 (in Russian).

[11] On the recall of exiles see Malalas, 411; no names in the Slavic version (Istrin, 17; Spinka, 121). *Chr. Pasch.*, 612. Theoph. 166. Cedr. I, 638. Zon, XIV, 12 (*CSHB* III, 146). On Severus' treatise addressed to Appion see Zacharias the Scholastic, *The Life of Severus*, in French by F. Nau, *Opuscules Maronites, Revue de l'Orient Chrétien*, V (1900), 92; and by M.-A. Kugener, *Patrologia Orientalis*, II (1907), 105. See also *The Sixth Book of the Select Letters of Severus*, transl. by E. W. Brooks, I, VII. The most recent descriptions of Vitalian's rebellion under Anastasius in Bury, I, 447–452; P. Charanis, *Church and State in the Later Roman Empire. The Religious Policy of Anastasius the First* (Madison, Wisconsin, 1939), pp. 51–56; 63–65. Severus' Hymn "On Vitalian the Tyrant," transl. by E. W. Brooks, *The Hymns of Severus and others in the Syriac version of Paul of Edessa as revised by James of Edessa, Patrologia Orientalis*, VII, 710 (298). Description of the church of St. Euphemia at Chalcedon in Evagrius, II, 3 (ed. Bidez-Parmentier, pp. 39–40); from him in Nic. Callistus, XV, 3 (Migne, CXLVII, 16–17). On the demand to cut out Severus' tongue see Evagrius, IV, 4 (p. 155). *The Syriac Chronicle known as that of Zachariah of Mitylene*, VIII, 2; in English by Hamilton and Brooks, p. 191; in German by Ahrens and Krüger, p. 142). John of Nikiu, XC, 8; Charles, p. 133. For Vitalian's name in the correspondence see *Collectio Avellana*, ed. O. Günther, nos. 167 (p. 619), 217 (pp. 678, 679), 230 (p. 696). Justinian's letter to Hormisdas, in Mansi, VIII, 483. The best information on the riot in 520 in the Escurial version of Malalas, *Hermes*, VI (1872), 375; *Excerpta historica jussu Imp. Constantini Porphyrogeniti confecta*, III, *Excerpta de insidiis*, ed. C. de Boor pp. 170–171. See G. Manojlović, "Carigradski narod" *Nastavni Vjestnik*, XII, 342 (in Serbo-Croatian); in French by H. Grégoire, *Byzantion*, XI, p. 667. Caramallus' name: *Aristaeneti Epistolae*, Liber I, 26: μιμουμένη τὸν Καράμαλλον τὸν πάνυ ἁπάντων ἔχεις τὴν μίμησιν ἀκριβῆ. R. Hercher, *Epistolographi Graeci* (Paris, 1873), p. 155. *Gai Sollii Apollinaris Sidonii Epistulae et Carmina*, ed. Chr. Lvetjohann, Carmen XXIII, Ad Consentium, vv. 268–272:

> coramte Caramallus aut Phabaton
> clausis faucibus et loquente gestu
> nutu, crure, genu, manu, rotatu
> toto in schemate vel semel latebit. . .

MGH, AA, VIII (1887), 256. In the *Index personarum* (p. 422) we read: "Caramallus. Pantomimus aetatis incertae." An English translation of this poem in *Sidonius, Poems and Letters*, with an English translation, introduction and notes by W. B. Anderson, I (Cambridge, Mass. — London, 1936), 300 (text); 301 (trans-

JUSTIN'S DOMESTIC RULE

JUSTIN AND THE FACTIONS

As we have pointed out above, the new family on the Byzantine throne represented by Justin was vigorously supported at the moment of his election by the nobility who came to an accord with the other elements involved in this unexpected elevation. At first sight we might

lation). On Aristaenetus' time see *Pauly-Wissowa*, II, 851–852: "at the end of the fifth century" (article by W. Schmid). W. Christ, *Geschichte der griechischen Litteratur*, W. Schmid and O. Stählin, II, 2 (München, 1924), 1048–1049 dates him in the fifth century. F. A. Wright, *A History of Later Greek Literature* (New York, 1932), p. 403: about 560. On the charioteer Porphyrius, see G. Kaibel, *Epigrammata graeca ex lapidibus conlecta* (Berlin, 1878), p. 388, no. 9351 "Porphyrius Calliopas natione Afer celeberrimus quinti sextique saeculi apud utramque factionem auriga." Mordtmann, *Das Denkmal des Porphyrius* (Hierzu Tafel XVI), *Mittheilungen des Deutschen Archäologischen Instituts* V (Athens, 1880), pp. 295–308; Πορφύριος Λίβυς οὗτος . . . (p. 299). The monument belongs to the period just before the accession to the throne of Anastasius; at the most, to the beginning of his rule (pp. 302–303). J. Ebersolt, "A propos du relief de Porphyrios," *Revue archéologique*, II (1911), 76–85. The monument is the work of the end of the fifth century (p. 76). See also J. Ebersolt, "Céramique et statuette de Constantinople," *Byzantion*, VI (1931), 559–563. Dumont erroneously called this monument "a curious specimen of Byzantine sculpture in the epoch of Justin II." A. Dumont, "Le Musée Saint-Irène à Constantinople," *Revue archéologique*, XVIII (1868), 255. On the epigrams to Porphyrius, see *The Greek Anthology With An English Translation* by W. R. Paton, V (New York, London, 1918), book XV, Miscellanea of the Anthologia Palatina, and book XVI, Epigrams of the Planudean Anthology not in the Palatine Manuscript, nos. 44 (pp. 150–151), 46 (pp. 150–153), 47 (pp. 152–153) and 27 epigrams of the Planudean Anthology, nos. 335–362 (pp. 361–375). A. Vasiliev, *The Monument of Porphyrius in the Hippodrome at Constantinople*, Dumbarton Oaks Papers, no. 4 (Cambridge, Massachusetts, 1948). In calling Delphax a banqueting room of the Great Palace, I follow D. Beliaev, *Byzantina*, I 118, note; 120 (in Russian). Cf. J. Ebersolt, *Le Grand Palais de Constantinople et le Livre des Cérémonies* (Paris, 1910), pp. 66–67; he disagrees with Beliaev and Paspatis. On Justin and Justinian's participation in Vitalian's murder, Procopius, *Anecdota* VI, 28 (Dewing, VI, 76). Victor Tonnennensis, *s. a.* 523: "Iustiniani patricii factione dicitur interfectus fuisse" (*Chronica Minora*, II, 197). Victor errs in his chronology by three years. Zonaras, XIV, 5, 15 (CSHB III, p. 147). *The Syriac Chronicle of Zachariah of Mitylene*, VIII, 2 (Hamilton-Brooks, 192; Ahrens-Krüger, p. 142). The monophysite John of Nikiu, after saying that Justin gave orders for the execution of Vitalian, adds: "God punished him speedily, even as Severus had prophesied regarding him that he should die a violent death" (XC, 12; Charles, p. 133). Another version in Theophanes, 166. Nic. Call., XVII, 1 (Migne, CXLVII(221). Holmes (I, 307) believes in Justin and Justinian's participation. Kulakovsky is also inclined to accept Justinian's participation. *History of Byzantium*, II, 12 (in Russian). I do not know why Kulakovsky gives the exact date for Vitalian's murder, the 17th of January. Bury (II, 21) writes: "For this crime, rightly or wrongly, Justinian was also held responsible." In 1939, Bailly says flatly that Vitalian was assassinated through Justinian's order. "It was one of those necessi-

think the dynasty of such humble origin as that of Justin should have been despised or hated as an upstart house by the Byzantine aristocracy. Two reasons may be adduced for the support Justin received from the nobility. On the one hand, they may have hoped and wished to play an important role in the new government under an inexperienced man, a role which had been denied them under the preceding regime of Anastasius. On the other hand, most of the nobility were adherents of the Chalcedonian doctrine and knew Justin's devotion to it.

One fact is absolutely clear: with Justin's elevation orthodoxy, in the form of the Chalcedonian decrees, prevailed, and with that came the triumph of the faction of the Blues. This shows once more that the Blues were not only the representatives of one of the powerful parties in the Hippodrome, not only the advocates of a certain religious trend, but also the representatives of a certain social group, that of the upper classes and of the Byzantine high bureaucracy. Considering what they had done for the promotion and elevation of a poor and uneducated peasant from a backward province, the Blues came to the conclusion that the most essential influence in the new government would be theirs, and that it would be their right to interfere arbitrarily anywhere they wished in the empire in any internal affairs which seemed to infringe upon their own interests. A contemporary source, John Malalas, writes that in the second year of Justin's reign in 519, the party of the Blues caused disorders in all the cities of the empire, particularly, however, in Antioch in Syria; they stoned, attacked and killed private citizens and assaulted city officials, even in the capital itself. I have already described a riot in Constantinople, when Vitalian as consul in 520 opened the games in the Hippodrome. I have tried to interpret this riot when both conflicting factions, the Blues and the

---

ties which are sometimes binding on the aspirants and sovereigns in virtue of the public interest." A. Bailly, Byzance, p. 68. On Justinian's increasing power after Vitalian's murder, see B. Pančenko, "On the Secret History of Procopius," Viz. Vrem., III, 103 (in Russian). On the sources for Vitalian's murder see a note by G. Krüger, in Die sogenannte Kirchengeschichte des Zacharias Rhetor, in German by Ahrens and Krüger, p. 354. On Proclus the Quaestor see Procopius, Bell. Pers. I, 11; Anecdota, VI, 13. Lydus, De magistratibus, III, 20: "Πρόκλος ὁ δικαιότατος" (ed. Wuensch, p. 108, 24–25). Cod. Just., XII, 19, 13: Imp. Iustinus A. Proculo quaestori sacri palatii (ed. Krüger, p. 460). See Bury, II, 23.

Greens, came to an agreement and in a state of exuberant joy and exaltation paraded around the city, on the basis of the popularity of the new consul and the popular enthusiasm in his favor. The manifestation of this enthusiasm alarmed Justin and Justinian, who hastily decided to do away with their political rival, and in July, 520, assassinated Vitalian. The leading part in these riots belonged to the Blues. According to the not very reliable record of John of Nikiu, Justinian himself was involved in these violent acts, "helping the Blue Faction to commit murder and pillage" (XC, 16).

Apparently the government failed for several years to take any decisive measure to put an end to the violence of the Blues. Finally in 523 Justin appointed as prefect of the city a certain Theodotus, who had formerly been the *comes orientis*, and whose nickname was "pumpkin" (κολοκύνθιος). He was to punish all who were guilty of crime. Justin made him swear that he would show no partiality. In his new function Theodotus punished many guilty persons and succeeded in putting down excesses. One episode is particularly noteworthy. Theodotus arrested among other guilty persons a certain Theodosius Ztikkas, an extremely wealthy man bearing the very high rank of *illustris* who so ardently served the interests of the Blues that Theodotus, on his own authority without bringing his decision to Justin's knowledge, put him to death. This was too much impartiality. Justin was infuriated. He immediately dismissed Theodotus from his office and exiled him to the east; fearing further punishment Theodotus escaped to Jerusalem and ended his life in seclusion. According to the unreliable record of John of Nikiu, Theodotus, as one of the ardent sympathizers of the Blues, wished to execute even Justinian himself. Theodotus was replaced in his position as prefect of the city by Theodorus, surnamed τηγανιστής (literally, frier, broiler). In 523 the troubles caused by the Blues came to an end.[12]

[12] Malalas, 416–417. Slavonic version: Istrin, p. 19; in English, Spinka, pp. 123–124. Theoph., 766, Cedr., I, 638. In these Greek texts the usage of the verb δημοκρατέω in the sense *turbas factionum agere*, to make factional troubles, and of the noun δημοκρατία in the meaning *turbae factionum*, factional troubles, is worthy of notice. Malalas: (Theodotus) κατεδυνάστευσε τῆς δημοκρατίας τῶν Βυζαντίνων . . . ἡσύχασεν ἡ δημοκρατία τοῦ Βενέτου μέρους τοῦ ποιεῖν ταραχάς. Theophanes: τῷ δ'αὐτῷ ἔτει ἐδημοκράτησε τὸ Βένετον μέρος. Cedrenus: ἐδημοκράτει τὸ Βένετον μέρος. His original source is Malalas. On Theodotus' nickname and the

The suppression of the riots and violence of the faction of the Blues, although it was Justin's party and supported his government, was not exceptional. The emperors in general considered it necessary to suppress excesses and acts of violence of any faction, no matter what their sympathies, if these acts were causing serious disturbances; the emperors, to use the language of the epoch (see the preceding note), "suppressed democracy" (κατεδυνάστευσε τῆς δημοκρατίας). In other words, they put an end to factional troubles which interrupted the normal course of life. Justin's predecessor, Anastasius, had in the same manner pitilessly suppressed "the democracy" of his own faction of the Greens, who confident in the imperial favor had allowed themselves to much liberty. In 527 Justinian sent orders to all cities to punish severely all those who were provoking disorders or committing murders, "regardless of whatever faction to which they might belong." [13]

The decisive step undertaken by Justin in 523 was the turning point in the attitude of Justin and Justinian towards the faction of the Blues, in other words towards the upper classes who had supported Justin in his elevation. Apparently the victory of the government over the

---

way he was saved by the quaestor Proclus, see Procopius, *Anecdota*, IX, 37–42; ed. Haury, III, 1, pp. 62–63; Dewing, pp. 114–116. John of Nikiu, XC, 16–19; ed. Charles, pp. 134–135. He gives information on Justinian's personal participation in the factional troubles. Com. Marcellinus, a. 523: Plerique lapidatorum, percussorum urbisque depopulatorum sua ob scelera deprehensi ferro, igni suspendioque expensi sunt, gratum bonis civibus spectaculum exhibentes (ed. Mommsen, p. 102). On the episode of Ztikkas see G. Manojlović, "Carigradski narod," *Nastavni Vjestnik*, XII, pp. 326–327 (in Serbo-Croat); in French by H. Grégoire, *Byzantion*, XI, pp. 648–649. See also G. Bratianu, *Études byzantines d'histoire économique et sociale* (Paris, 1938), p. 101. E. Stein, "Justinus," *PW*, X, col. 1319. A. Diakonov, "The Byzantine Demes and Factions in the Fifth to the Seventh Centuries," in *Vizantisky Sbornik* (1945), p. 177 and n. 12, with an incorrect reference to the book of Bratianu cited above (pp. 90–91 for 100–101). M. V. Levchenko, "The Venetoi and Prasinoi in Byzantium in the Fifth–Seventh Centuries," *Vizantisky Vremennik*, I, XXVI, (Moscow, 1947), 164–183 (on the basis of Diakonov's study). Both in Russian.

[13] Malalas, p. 422: ἐν ἑκάστῃ δὲ πόλει κατέπεμψε θείας σάκρας, ὥστε τιμωρηθῆναι τοὺς ἀταξίας ἢ φόνους ποιοῦντας, ὁποίου δ'ἂν ὑπάρχωσι μέρους, ὥστε μὴ τολμᾶν τινα τοῦ λοιποῦ τὴν οιανδήποτε ἀταξίαν ποιῆσαι. See Diakonov, *op. cit.*, pp. 177–178 (in Russian). See also F. Dvornik, "The Circus Parties in Byzantium, Their Evolution and Their Suppression," *Byzantina Metabyzantina*, I, 1, p. 127: (Justin) had the good sense to stop their persecution (i.e. by the Blues) of the Greens and to curb their violence.

turbulent Blues was decisive because Procopius several times points out that after their disorderly activities had been crushed, the Blues became "the most discreet men in the world"; and he also says that Justinian *previously* was an enthusiastic supporter of the Blues.[14] This clash with the Blues under Justin was the beginning of the considerable change in the relations between the government and the upper classes which resulted later, after Justin's death, in the energetic struggle of Justinian with the large landowners.

Because of the excesses of the Blues all over the empire and especially at Antioch in Syria whose population was always very turbulent and unruly, Justin, at the end of 520 or in 521, commanded that the Olympian games, a very popular and ancient festival in the city, should no longer be held. Various causes for this measure have been adduced. It has been said that this festival, going back to ancient times, illustrated a survival of pagan superstition. A Christian writer of the fifth century, Basil of Seleucia in Isauria, called it "a demonic festival wantonly insulting the cross." It has also been said, as we shall explain below, that the government felt the need to economize and save unnecessary expenses. Neither of these, I believe, is the true cause. The Olympian games in Antioch were suppressed, in my opinion, because the government was determined to put an end to the excesses of the factions. Following the same policy, the government prohibited other spectacles in the eastern regions of the empire and sent into exile from the east all the dancers who appeared at them. As in religious matters, concessions were also made in this respect to Alexandria in Egypt so that the dancers and other entertainers continued to perform there. The Alexandrian spectacles remained undisturbed by imperial decrees and continued to amuse and divert the population of the Egyptian capital, whose tranquillity and satisfaction were essentially important for the tranquillity and prosperity of the empire as a whole.[15]

[14] Procopius, *Anecdota*, VII, 3: (οἱ Βένετοι) προϊόντος ἤδη τοῦ δεινοῦ σωφρονέστατοι ἔδοξαν εἶναι ἀνθρώπων ἁπάντων. The same adjective σωφρονέστατοι Procopius uses in two other places in *Anecdota*, IX, 43 and X, 19. See also *Anecdota*, VII, 1: ἡ (μοῖρα Βενέτων) οἱ καὶ τὸ πρότερον κατεσπουδασμένη ἐτύγχανε.

[15] Malalas, 417. Istrin, 19; Spinka, 124. He gives the exact date of the last Olympian games at Antioch: the fourteenth indiction = Sept. 1, 520–August 31, 521. See Φ. Κουκουλές, "'Αγῶνες, ἀγωνίσματα καὶ ἀγωνιστικὰ παιγνία κατὰ τοὺς βυζαντινοὺς χρόνους," 'Επετηρὶς τῆς 'Εταιρείας Βυζαντινῶν Σπουδῶν, XIII (1937),

In Justin's period the brilliant charioteer Porphyrius Calliopas from Alexandria, who had become famous in his youth under Anastasius, resumed his successful driving in spite of his sixty years and was again enthusiastically acclaimed by the spectators. In addition to thirty-two epigrams praising Porphyrius' exploits under Anastasius, six epigrams composed by Leontius Scholasticus deal with his activities under Justin, and two epigrams by a certain Thomas were written soon after Porphyrius' death, which probably occurred at the end of the reign of Justin or at the beginning of that of Justinian. Porphyrius resumed his career under Justin as charioteer with the dominant faction of the Blues. But his fame was so overwhelming that even "the rival faction (the Greens) in admiration of his glory applauded him loudly." "He alone gained an unwonted mark of honor, a bronze statue in the grounds of each faction." One epigram compares him with Alexander the Great. Referring to Justin's period, epigram 360 proclaims: "Thy old age has surpassed thy youth in victories, and thou didst ever overcome all, Calliopas. Therefore do the Emperor (i.e. Justin) and the free faction (i.e. the Blues) again raise this honor for thee, a monument of thy skill and valor." [16] The original bronze statue representing Porphyrius which had been erected under Anastasius has not come down to us; but the rectangular base of white marble which originally

---

p. 71. Cottas gives the year 520. V. Cottas, *Le théatre à Byzance* (Paris, 1931), p. 6. *Basilii Seleuciensis oratio* XXVII, Εἰς τὰ ᾿Ολύμπια: τί γὰρ ἕτερόν ἐστιν ἀγὼν ᾿Ολυμπιακὸς ἢ δαίμονος ἑορτὴ τὸν σταυρὸν καθυβρίζουσα. Migne, *PG*, LXXXV, col. 309. On the economic reason see G. Downey, Ephraemius, Patriarch of Antioch, *Church History*, VII (1938), p. 365 (he ascribes the suppression of the games to the year 520). Downey refers in his judgment to Procopius, *Anecdota*, XXVI, 6–9, where Procopius says (XXVI, 6) that Justinian took "all the revenues which the inhabitants of all the cities had been raising locally for their own civic needs and for their public spectacles, transferred and dared to mingle them with the national income" (Dewing, VI, 303). Among recent writers A. Schenk also refers the suppression of the Olympic games at Antioch to the year 520. Alexander Schenk, Graf von Stauffenberg, *Die römische Kaisergeschichte bei Malalas, Griechischer Text der Bücher IX–XII und Untersuchungen* (Stuttgart, 1931), p. 438. E. Bouchier ascribes the end of the games to the year 522. *A Short History of Antioch* (Oxford, 1921), p. 181. See Charles Diehl, "L'Egypte chrétienne et byzantine," in Gabriel Hanotaux, *Histoire de la nation égyptienne*, III (Paris, 1933), p. 483.

[16] *The Greek Anthology*, book XVI: Epigrams of the Planudean Anthology not in the Palatine Manuscript, Nos. 338; 351; 345; 360 (῎Αναξ καὶ δῆμος ἐλεύθερος), ed. with an English translation by W. R. Paton, V, 362–363; 368–369; 366–367; 374–375.

supported the statue has been preserved in Istanbul.[17] Porphyrius' exploits probably ended in 523 under Justin, when the emperor carried out his punitive measures against the Blues.

JUSTIN'S COLLABORATORS AND COUNSELORS

Since Justin himself possessed no special education or training as a statesman, he needed reliable collaborators and counselors. During his whole reign Justin of course was under the predominant influence of his nephew Justinian, who was already very powerful behind the throne, and whose strong will and already well formulated plans for the future guided the policy of his elderly uncle.

At the very beginning of Justin's reign the most powerful figure was Vitalian, who was brought back from exile by the edict of the new emperor granting pardon to those who had been sent into exile by Anastasius. Vitalian, a strict Chalcedonian, extremely popular among the masses, whose personality overshadowed the personality of Justinian, held towards dissidents a stern and rigid policy without any flexibility or possibility of conciliation. His irreconcilable attitude was not in complete harmony with Justin and Justinian's policy, whose relative moderation may be noticed in their correspondence with the Pope and in some acts. If we add to this the unavoidable political rivalry between the two strong men, Vitalian and Justinian, we are not surprised that Vitalian soon disappeared from the historical stage. As described above, he was assassinated in July 520, and his dominant and rather ominous influence was short lived.

We have some information on several other counselors and collaborators of Justin in various aspects of the administrative machinery, and some of these did not always perfectly discharge their duties and responsibilities.

Next to Justinian the most influential minister was Proclus the Quaestor *sacri palatii*. A man of independent judgment, perfect honesty, and courage, just and incorruptible, with the reputation of

[17] See A. M. Woodward and A. J. B. Wace, *The Monument of Porphyrius*, in W. S. George, *The Church of Saint Eirene at Constantinople*, pp. 79–84. A. Vasiliev, *The Monument of Porphyrius in the Hippodrome at Constantinople*. See above, in the section *Recall and Assassination of Vitalian* (more sources and literature).

Aristides, Proclus according to John Lydus was an adornment to the empire by his good qualities.[18] We shall discuss at some length how as a lawyer he represented to Justin and Justinian the danger of granting the request of Kawad that Justin adopt his son Chosroes, and how he induced them to refuse the Persian demand. Procopius calls him, as counselor to Justin, a just man and manifestly incorruptible, one who attended to all matters with independent judgment.[19]

Justin's undated decree on the reorganization of some offices (*scrinia*) is addressed to Proculus (Proclus) *quaestor sacri palatii*. Another decree addressed jointly by Justin and Justinian to Tatianus, *magister officiorum*, refers to Proclus as *magnificae memoriae*. The names of Justin and Justinian used together mean that the decree was issued between April and the first of August 527, when Justin died, and the words *magnificae memoriae* mean that at that time (in 527) Proclus was dead.[20]

Another very important official of Justin's time was Euphraemius (Ephraim) from Amida in Mesopotamia.[21] The monophysite chronicler Pseudo-Zacharias of Mitylene, in spite of Euphraemius' strict orthodoxy, writes that in the authority which he exercised in various countries he was a man just in his deeds, not greedy after bribes, able and successful.[22] During Justin's reign Euphraemius had a very suc-

---

[18] *Joannis Lydi De magistratibus*, III, 20: Πρόκλος ὁ δικαιότατος Τριβωνιανός τε ὁ πολυμαθέστατος . . . οἱ δὲ ἄμφω κυαίστορες γενόμενοι τὴν πολιτείαν ἐκόσμησαν (*CSHB* pp. 214–215; ed. Wuensch, pp. 108–109). See Bury, II, p. 23.

[19] Proc., *B. P.* I, 11, 11: ἀνὴρ δίκαιός τε καὶ χρημάτων διαφανῶς ἀδωρότατος. *Anecdota*, VI, 13: αὐτὸς δὴ αὐτονόμῳ γνώμῃ ἅπαντα ἔπρασσεν (Haury, III, 1, 40; Dewing, VI, 72–73).

[20] *Cod. Just.*, XII, 19, 13; ed. Krueger, p. 460 (undated); XII, 19, 15, 2: "idem magnificae memoriae Proculus ad nos retulit"; ed. Krueger, p. 461 (a. 527). Since our Proculus was dead in 527, the Proculus who according to Procopius held the office of quaestor under Justinian was another man. Procop., *Anecdota*, IX, 41 (Haury, III, 1, 63; Dewing, VI, 114–117). See E. Stein, "Justinus," *PW*, X, 1317.

[21] The best information in G. Downey, "Ephraemius, Patriarch of Antioch," *Church History*, VII, pp. 364–370. Jülicher, *Pauly-Wissowa*, VI, col. 17. See also C. Karalevskij, article in French "Antioche," in Baudrillard, *Dictionnaire d'histoire et de géographie ecclésiastiques*, III, col. 577. Patriarch Photius, in his *Bibliotheca* (228–229) calls Euphraemius a Syrian (Σύρας) and deals at length with his theological writings. I. Bekker, *Photii Bibliotheca*, I, pp. 245–266; Migne, *PG*, CIII, coll. 957–1024. R. Duval erroneously calls Euphraemius "Ephrem le Mede," i.e. the Mede, for "Ephrem d'Amid", R. Duval, *Histoire politique, religieuse et littéraire d'Edesse jusqu'à la première croisade* (Paris, 1892), p. 199.

[22] Zachariah of Mitylene, VIII, 4; transl. by F. Hamilton and E. Brooks, p. 205; K. Ahrens and G. Krüger, pp. 156–157. Cf. this characteristic with that of

cessful career. Justin appointed him prefect of Constantinople; and "by great efforts and severity he put an end to civil war among the citizens, made feuds to cease, and established peace." [23] A dated inscription shows that at one time he was *comes sacrarum largitionum*, that is head of the central treasury of the empire dealing especially with taxes; afterwards he became *comes orientis* late in 522 or early in 523, and still held this office in November 524, when according to the dated inscription found in Seleucia Pieria, in Northern Syria, he built three bridges there.[24] As Count of the East Euphraemius was the civil administrator of Palestine and Syria, with his headquarters at Antioch, one of the most turbulent cities of the East. Euphraemius had a very hard task to perform. The discontent of the unruly population of Antioch at the recent suppression (520 A. D.) of the local Olympic game, a great fire at Antioch which broke out in October 525 and devastated a considerable part of the city, and ultimately a catastrophic earthquake, which visited the city in May, 525 and almost completely destroyed it — Euphraemius seems to have met effectively and energetically all these troubles and disasters.[25] In the disaster of 526 the Patriarch of Antioch, Euphrasius, perished, and the civil administrator, the *comes orientis*, Euphraemius, was chosen in 526 or 527 to be his successor. Such a case was not exceptional, and the sixth century saw the appointment to high ecclesiastical offices of several laymen chosen from the upper ranks of the army and the civil service.[26] Malalas says that Euphraemius had to accept the election; the local clergy canonically ordained him, and his choice was approved

---

Proclus which I have adduced above. See also Michel le Syrien, IX, 16: Euphraemius passed for a sage and eloquent man; Chabot, II, p. 181.

[23] *The Chronicle of John, bishop of Nikiu*, transl. Charles, XC, 23 (p. 135). See also Malalas, pp. 416–417.

[24] V. Chapot, "Inscription de la Séleucie, de l'année 524," *Antiquités de la Syrie du Nord, Bulletin de correspondance hellénique*, XXVI (1902), pp. 166–167. H. Seyrig, "Antiquités Syriennes, 30. Inscriptions, 7. L'inscription d'Éphrem," *Syria*, XX (1939), pp. 309–312. See Downey, "Euphraemius," *Church History*, VII (1938), p. 364 and n. 2. See Theophanes, p. 173: κόμης ἀνατολῆς. Cedr., I, p. 642. Also Photius, *Bibliotheca*, 228 and 229. Migne, *PG*, CIII, pp. 957–1024. See also G. Downey, *A Study of the Comites Orientis and the Consulares Syriae* (Princeton, 1939), pp. 14–15. R. Devreesse, *Le patriarcat d'Antioche*, p. 168.

[25] See Downey, *op. cit.*, pp. 364–365.

[26] See examples in J. Maspero, *Histoire des patriarches d'Alexandrie* (Paris, 1923), pp. 256–257.

by Justin and Justinian.[27] To his new ecclesiastical office Euphraemius brought his usual energy as a state functionary. His patriarchate lasted from 526 to 545 so that his activities in his new functions belong to the time of Justinian. As a convinced Chalcedonian, he persecuted monophysites and as a consequence has been severely judged by monophysite writers. Downey calls him a "warrior bishop"; Bury says that he acted as a grand inquisitor.[28] His adversaries called him *quaestionarius fidelium*,[29] that is the torturer, executioner of the faithful.

Among other eminent personages whom Justin returned from exile was a man of senatorial rank (συγκλητικός), Theodorus Philoxenus Sotericus, who had a brilliant career under the new emperor. He was appointed to occupy an important military post in Thrace, *magister militum per Thraciam*; then, perhaps in 520, he was elevated to the post of *comes domesticorum*, and in 525 was nominated consul, *consul ordinarius*.[30] For his official career we have valuable monumental evidence; four consular ivory diptychs of Philoxenus; the most important among them is preserved in the Bibliothèque Nationale of Paris (from the church Saint-Corneille at Compiègne). The diptych represents the consul twice in the upper medallions, beardless, curled hair falling on his forehead, dressed in the toga, holding in his left hand a scepter and in his raised right hand the *mappa circensis*, the napkin thrown down as the signal for the commencement of the games. E. Weigand wrote of this picture: "His portrait shows us a man with fatigued face, pendant cheeks, sensual mouth, in short a grand seigneur au déclin de son age." [31] In the lower medallions there are two figures of a woman, presented only above the waist, holding in both hands a small standard with a crown of laurel at the top. So far, this woman has not been satisfactorily explained. The inscriptions on this diptych are in both Latin and Greek. In the two intermediate medallions the names and titles of the consul are engraved in Latin capital letters. On

[27] Malalas, pp. 423–424. The Slavonic version of Malalas omits this record.
[28] Downey, *op. cit.*, p. 364. Bury, II, p. 377. J. Lebon, "Ephrem d'Amid patriarche d'Antioche, 526–544," *Mélanges d'histoire offerts à Charles Moeller* (Louvain-Paris, 1914), pp. 197–214.
[29] Seyrig, *Syria*, XX, p. 310.
[30] Malalas, p. 411. *Chr. Pasch.*, p. 612. See E. Stein, *PW*, 1316: as *comes domesticorum* he may have succeeded Justinian in 520.
[31] See P. Waltz, "Mélétê," *Byzantion*, XIII (1938), p. 189, n. 1.

Consular Diptych of Philoxenus. Ivory.
Probably Constantinople. A.D. 525.

the right leaf we read: "Fl(avius) Theodorus Filoxenus Sotericus Filoxenus vir illustr(is)"; on the left: "Com(es) Domest(icorum) ex Magistro M(ilitum) per Thracia(m) et Consul Ordinar(ius)." In the field of the panel a Greek inscription of four lines is engraved, also in capital letters. On the right leaf: ΤΟΥΤΙ ΤΟ ΔΩΡΟΝ ΤΗ ϹΟΦΗ ΓΕΡΟΥϹΙΑ; on the left leaf: ΥΠΑΤΟϹ ΥΠΑΡΧΩΝ ΠΡΟϹΦΕΡΩ ΦΙΛΟΞΕΝΟϹ. The other three diptychs of Philoxenus fail to give any more information.[32]

The opinion has been sometimes expressed that Philoxenus in addition to the offices indicated in the diptych also three times held that of Prefect of the City of Constantinople. This opinion is based on two Christian epigrams which mention under Justin a consul Theodorus who was three times Prefect of the City and who erected a chapel and set up statues to Justin and Justinian.[33] It is natural to identify the consul Theodorus of the epigrams with the consul of 525 Theodorus Philoxenus, supposing that his office as of the Prefect of the City

[32] The diptychs of Philoxenus have many times been reproduced and described. The most recent publication is by R. Delbrück, *Die Consulardiptychen und verwandte Denkmäler*, pp. 144–148 (Nos. 29–31). Three diptychs: two from Paris and one from Milan (Trivulzio collection). Delbrück regards the fourth diptych of Liverpool as a forgery, a copy of the diptych of Trivulzio Collection, no. 30 (p. 278). Excellent plates of Nos. 29–31 in Delbrück's album of plates, 29–31. Delbrück wrote (p. 146, n. 2) that the diptych of the Trivulzio Collection was inaccessible (unzugänglich). It is now to be found in the Dumbarton Oaks Research Library and Collection, Washington, D.C. See *Handbook of the Collection* (Georgetown, Washington, D.C., 1946), p. 77 (No. 155); reproduction, p. 83. See also E. Molinier, *Histoire générale des arts appliqués à l'industrie du Ve à la fin du XVIIIe siècle*, I: Ivoires (Paris, 1896), pp. 29–32 (Nos. 29–32). L. von Sybel, *Christliche Antike. Einführung in die altchristliche Kunst*, II (Marburg, 1909), p. 234. See also W. Meyer, "Zwei antike Elfenbeintafeln der K. Staats-Bibliothek in München," *"Abh. der philos.-philolog. Classe der Bayerischen Ak. der Wiss.,* XV, 1, pp. 59–60 (Nos. 26–28). H. Graeven, *Entstellte Consulardiptychen. Mittheilungen des K. Deutschen Archaeol. Instituts. Römische Abtheilung*, VII (Rome, 1892), pp. 206–209. Meyer and Graeven mention only three diptychs of Philoxenus. Cabrol-Leclercq, *Dictionnaire d'archéologie chrétienne et de liturgie*, IV, 1 (1920), pp. 1124–1125. Excellent plate of the first diptych which we have just described is to be found also in C. Diehl, *Justinien et la civilisation byzantine au VIe siècle*, p. 456. In regard to the figure of the woman Delbrück affirms that she cannot be a living person and sets forth two hypotheses: 1) she may be a personification of Constantinople; 2) she may be a personification of the Gerusia (pp. 145–146). Molinier (p. 29) suggests tentatively that she may be the wife of the consul.

[33] *The Greek Anthology*, transl. Paton, I, pp. 40–43 (Nos. 97–98). See P. Waltz, "Mélété," *Byzantion*, XIII, pp. 189–190.

was omitted in the diptych. But in my opinion H. Grégoire is right in rejecting this identification and referring the data of the epigrams to another Theodorus, surnamed Teganistes, who during Justin's reign was Prefect of the City and *consul honorarius*.[34]

In 521 the office of *praefectus praetorio* was held by Demosthenes, whose activities were severely criticized by his contemporaries. He had formerly occupied the post of Prefect of Constantinople. Three decrees exist issued by Justin which are addressed to Demosthenes as Praefectus Praetorio, including the famous decree *De nuptiis*. The time of Demosthenes' prefecture may be approximately put in the years 520–524.[35]

In the last years of Justin's reign, 524–527, the Praetorian Prefect Archelaus is often mentioned. Several decrees were addressed to him in the name of Justin, and one, with great probability, may be attributed to the joint rule of Justin and Justinian.[36] Six edicts issued by Archelaus were indicated by Borghesi (392–393). Later on, under

---

[34] Malalas, 416: προήχθη ἔπαρχος πόλεως Θεόδωρος ὁ ἀπὸ ὑπάτων, ὁ ἐπίκλην τηγανιστής. See H. Grégoire, "Notules épigraphiques," *Byzantion*, XIII (1938), p. 176 and n. 1. Idem, "L'ἔπαρχος Ῥώμης. A propos d'un poids-étalon byzantin," *Bulletin de correspondance hellénique*, XXXI (1907), p. 325. Based on Alemannus' commentary on Procopius' *Historia Arcana* (Procopius, CSHB, III, p. 448) Borghesi erroneously calls this Theodorus Praetorian Prefect in 524. See E. Cuq, in his edition of Borghesi's monograph *Praefecti Praetorio*. B. Borghesi, *Oeuvres complètes de Bartolomeo Borghesi*, X (Paris, 1897), 390–391. I may add that John of Nikiu also mentions the Prefect of the City Theodore, who was appointed by Justin. *The Chronicle of John, Bishop of Nikiu*, XC, 23; Charles, p. 135.
[35] Criticism of Demosthenes' activities in J. Lydus, *De magistratibus*, III, 42 (CSHB, p. 236; Wuensch, p. 131). Procop., *Anecdota*, XII, 5 (ed. Haury, III, 1, p. 78; Dewing, VI, pp. 144–145). Prefect of the City, in *Novella* 166: Φλάβιος Θεόδωρος Πέτρος Δεμοσθένης, ὁ μεγαλοπρεπέστατος ἔπαρχος τῶν ἱερῶν πραιτωρίων καὶ ἀπὸ ἐπάρχων τῆς βασιλίδος πόλεως (ed. R. Schoell, p. 753). Cod. Just., V, 4, 23: *De nuptiis* (no date; a. 520–523); VI, 22, 8 (a. 521, *Justiniano et Valerio conss.*); VII, 62, 34 (no date; a. 520–524); ed. P. Krueger, pp. 196–197; 252–253; 323. In his commentary on Procopius' *Anecdota* Alemannus says that Demosthenes was Praetorian Prefect for the first time under Justin in 521, and later for the second time under Justinian. In *Hist. Arcanam Notae Alemanni*, CSHB, p. 410; 448. See Borghesi, *op. cit.*, pp. 389–390. Bury, I, p. 445: A.D. 520–524.
[36] See Cod. Just., II, 7, 27 (8), a. 524; V, 3, 19 (a. 527?); VI, 23, 23 (a. 524; cf. I, 3, 30 (41), where a fragment of this decree is found; VII, 39, 7 (a. 525). Charles Diehl, "Rescrit des empereurs Justin et Justinien en date du ler juin 527," *Bulletin de correspondance hellénique*, XVII (1893), 508–509. In this inscription, which is from Asia Minor, neither the names of the emperors nor the name of the Praetorian Prefect to whom the decree was addressed have been preserved; but it is dated *Mavortio viro clarissimo consule*, who was *consul solus*

Justinian, Archelaus as a general under the command of Belisarius took part in the Vandal expedition; and Procopius, telling the story, noted that Archelaus, a man of patrician standing, had already been pretorian prefect both in Byzantium and in Illyricum.[37] From this survey we may see that Archelaus was a very prominent high official both in the civil administration as Praetorian Prefect and in the military administration as general.

Among other exiles whom Justin returned to Constantinople was the patrician and kinsman of the empress, Diogenianus, one of the generals who had put down the Isaurian revolt under Anastasius. On his return Diogenianus was appointed *magister militum per orientem*. We have no information about his activities in this new position.[38]

To the same class of returned exiles belonged Apion. He belonged to the wealthy Egyptian Apion family, on which we have our first clear evidence in 497, and whose first head is already known as a large landowner. This family was to play some part in the sphere of imperial politics for three generations. Most of the political career of the Apion who is connected with Justin's time belongs to the reign of Anastasius, when Apion clearly manifested his high qualities.[39] He served as quartermaster general of the Persian expedition in 503. Procopius gives this picture:

As manager of the finances of the army Apion, an Aegyptian, was sent, a man of eminence among the patricians and extremely energetic; and the emperor in a written statement declared him partner in the

---

in 527. On this basis Diehl has restored the opening lines of the decree as follows: "Impp. Justinus et Justinianus AA Archelao pr. pr." See Borghesi, *op. cit.*, p. 392, n. 6 (E. Cuq). On Diehl's restoration see E. Stein, "Justinus," *PW*, X, 1315. E. Kornemann, *Doppelprinzipat und Reichsteilung im Imperium Romanum* (Leipzig-Berlin, 1930), p. 159, n. 1 (this chapter compiled by G. Ostrogorsky). In his commentary on Procopius' *Historia Arcana* Alemannus places Archelaus as Pretorian Prefect in 524 (Justinus Aug. II and Opilio conss.). Alemannus, *CSHB* p. 448. See also Borghesi, p. 391 (incorrect reference to Alemannus: p. 488 for p. 448.).

[37] Procop., *B. Vand.*, I, 11, 17 (ed. Haury, I, p. 363; Dewing, II, pp. 106–107): τῆς αὐλῆς ἔπαρχος ἔν τε Βυζαντίῳ καὶ Ἰλλυριοῖς γεγονώς.

[38] Malalas, p. 393; 411. *Chr. Pasch.*, 612. Theoph., 166. See Bury, I, p. 433, n. 2.

[39] See E. R. Hardy, *The Large Estates of Byzantine Egypt* (New York, 1931), pp. 25–28. See the very detailed note on the members of the Apion family, filled with interrogation marks, giving the first list of the members of the family, in *The Oxyrhynchus Papyri*, ed. by B. Grenfell, A. Hunt, and H. Bell, XVI (London, 1924), pp. 4–6 (note 24 to Pap. 1829).

royal power, in order that he might have authority to administer the finances as he wished.[40]

The failure of the expedition ended his career for a time. John Lydus writes that Anastasius grew angry with Apion, an excellent man, who was taking part in public affairs at the time when Kawades was infuriated. Apion was dismissed, taken to Nicaea, and there by force ordained presbyter.[41] In 518, soon after Justin's accession, Apion among many others was recalled by the new emperor to Constantinople, and became Praetorian Prefect, a position practically equivalent to that of prime minister. He held it on December 1, 518, because a decree of Justin of this date is addressed to Apion Praetorian Prefect.[42]

As we know, from the religious point of view the new government meant a change from monophysitism to orthodoxy. Apion is an interesting though not very rare example of a change of religious doctrine. Apion's son described his father's "conversion" some years later in a speech to a group of monophysite bishops: "You yourselves know that my father Appius [sic] of glorious memory, himself a native of the province of Egypt and a follower of your sect and of that of the Alexandrians [the bishops addressed were Syrians] hesitated to communicate with the holy great church established in this city [Constantinople], but the most pious and faithful emperors persuaded him, by this argument, that the most reverend bishops, who had met at Chalcedon, had handed down to us no other creed or other faith than that which had been confirmed at Nicaea, at Constantinople, and at Ephesus, — they also had established the faith and condemned Nestorius and Eutyches, who had been introducing new heresies; persuaded by this argument he communicated with the Holy Church."[43]

---

[40] Proc., *B. P.* I, 8, 5; Dewing, I, pp. 62–63.

[41] John Lydus, *De magistratibus*, III, 17: κινηθέντος κατὰ 'Απίωνος, ἀνδρὸς ἐξοχωτάτου καὶ κοινωνήσαντος αὐτῷ τῆς βασιλείας. *CSHB*, pp. 210–211; Wuensch, p. 104. Theoph., p. 166: 'Απίωνα τὸν πατρίκιον, ὃν ἐν Νικαίᾳ πρεσβύτερον βίᾳ ἐχειροτόνησεν. *Anastasii Chronogr. Tripertita*, p. 130.

[42] Malalas, 411. *Chr. Pasch.*, 612. Theoph., 166, 2–5. *Anast. Chr. trip.*, 130. *Cod. Just.*, VII, 63, 3; ed. Krüger, p. 325. See Hardy, *op. cit.*, pp. 26–27. See B. Borghesi, "Les préfets du prétoire," *Oeuvres complètes de Bartolomeo Borghesi*, X, 387–388.

[43] Letter of Innocent, Bishop of Maronia, in Mansi, VIII (Florence, 1762), col. 818. I have used Hardy's translation (p. 27). Innocent himself heard this

At the end of 518, when he reached the dignity of prefect, Apion was probably already quite old. He may have been dead by November 9 of the following year (519) when Marinus held the office of Praetorian Prefect.

Marinus the Syrian also came to Justin from Anastasius, under whom he had done brilliantly and whose most trusted adviser he had been. He had begun his career as *scriniarius* (σκρινιάριος), a financial clerk under the Count of the East, then attained the post of head of the tax department of the Praetorian Prefect, and ultimately was elevated to the Praetorian Prefecture itself.[44] His reputation as an official connected with taxes and finances in general, however, was not immaculate; his greediness for money and extortions was well known.[45] He also had a very bad influence upon the emperor himself. Anastasius, who entrusted all the finances to Marinus, became very unpopular with the masses on account of Marinus' abuses and greediness.[46] Marinus' injustice, arbitrariness, and excessive haughtiness were sharply criticized by Saint Sabas, who under Anastasius visited Constantinople, met the emperor, and in his presence had a conflict with Marinus, whom he called "a most unjust man." [47]

Pseudo-Zacharias is probably depicting this same Marinus when he refers to Marinus of Apamea (in Syria). He says that in Anastasius' days Marinus was a vigilant and clever man, well versed in business, wise and learned, who was moreover true in his faith, the friend and confidant of Anastasius, a chartularius and his counselor. The chronicler adds, as I have noted above, that at night Marinus had a pen-and-ink stand (καλαμάριον) hanging by his bedside, and a lamp burning

---

speech at the conference of 533. On this conference see J. Maspero, *Histoire des patriarches d'Alexandrie*, p. 99, n. 3. Hardy, p. 29.

[44] John Lydus, *De magistratibus*, III, 36: ὑπὸ τῷ 'Αναστασίῳ εἶτα καὶ Μαρίνου τὴν ὅλην ἀναζωσαμένου τῶν πραγμάτων διοίκησιν; also III, 49–51 (*CSHB* 229; 242–244; ed. Wuensch, 124; 139–140). See E. Stein, "Justinus," *PW*, X, 1316. Bury, I, 443, and especially 470. A few words in B. Borghesi, *op. cit.*, X, pp. 388–389.

[45] J. Lydus, *De mag.*, III, 49: πονηρὸς ὡς ἐπιεικὴς τούς φόρους . . . καὶ γίνεται μὲν πολύχρυσος, εἴπερ τις ἄλλος, ὁ βασιλεὺς (Anastasius) καὶ μετ' αὐτὸν ὁ Μαρῖνος καὶ ὅσοι Μαρινιῶντες ἁπλῶς (*CSHB* 242; Wuensch, 138; see also III, 46 (*CSHB*, 239; Wuensch, p. 135).

[46] Lydus, III, 45–46, *CSHB*, 238–240; Wuensch, 134–136.

[47] *The Life of Saint Sabas*, ed. Cotelier, III, pp. 304–305; Schwartz, pp. 146–147: Μαρῖνός τις ἀδικώτατος.

by his pillow, so that he could write down his thoughts on a roll; and in the daytime he would tell them to the emperor, and advise him as to how he should act.[48] Marinus' portrait as given by Pseudo-Zacharias entirely coincides with other information which asserts that he was Anastasius' counselor and confidant; and Marinus' office of chartularius may be compared with that of scriniarius in other sources. Pseudo-Zacharias' remark that he was true to his faith indicates that he was a monophysite and was true to monophysitism.

A defective passage of John Lydus (III, 51) seems to indicate that Marinus' influence came to its end with Justin's accession. But on the other hand we know that in November and December 519 he was again Praetorian Prefect, because two decrees were issued in 519 by Justin addressed to Marinus Praetorian Prefect.[49] One may suppose that he experienced a "conversion" similar to Apion's to have been allowed to hold such a high position under the Chalcedonian emperor. Marinus as Praetorian Prefect must have succeeded Apion, who probably died in 518 or 519.

In later times Marinus' activities were highly appreciated by Justinian, who in one of his edicts remembers "the times of Anastasius of blessed memory, when Marianus (i.e. Marinus) of glorious memory was at the head of the administration." [50]

---

[48] Zachariah of Mitylene, VII, 9; Hamilton-Brooks, pp. 177–178; Ahrens-Krüger, p. 129. According to the same chronicle, this same Marinus of Apamea, as we have reported above, represented the career of Justin from his youth on. Cf. above.

[49] Cod. Just., II, 7, 25 (6); V, 27, 7; ed. P. Krueger, p. 101 and 217: Imp. Justinus A. Marino pp. See J. Maspero, Histoire des patriarches d'Alexandrie, p. 67: In the first days (of Justin) Marinus and his Syrians must have abandoned their posts.

[50] Justiniani Edict XIII, 15: ἐπὶ τῶν χρόνων 'Αναστασίου τοῦ τῆς εὐσεβοῦς λήξεως, ἡνίκα Μαριανὸς ὁ τῆς ἐνδόξου (μνήμης) ἐπ' αὐτῷ τὰ πράγματα ἔπραττα. Corpus Juris civilis, III, Novellae, ed. R. Schoell and G. Kroll, p. 788; ed. Zachariae von Lingenthal, no. XCVI, 15, I, p. 545. The date of the edict, as we have noted above, has been accepted as between Sept. 538 and August 539 (Schoell-Kroll, p. 795, note). In 1891 Zachariae von Lingenthal concluded that the year 553–554 was the correct date of the edict (De diocesi aegyptiaca lex ab Imp. Justiniano anno 554 lata), praefatio, p. 5ff. His conclusion has been rejected by the majority of scholars. But Gertrude Malz now believes that the additional evidence furnished by the papyri of Dioscorus of Aphrodito confirms Zach. v. Lingenthal's final dating of the edict as August 534 A.D. G. Malz, "The Date of Justinian's Edict XIII," Byzantion, XVI, 1, 135; 140. See E. Stein, "Justinus," PW, X, col. 1316. Bury, I, p. 470.

Magnus, the consul in 518, the year in which Anastasius died and Justin ascended the throne, strictly speaking does not belong to Justin's reign. He was one of the younger relatives of Anastasius. Four diptychs mention his name, one original, two Carolingian copies, and the fourth apparently modern. One Carolingian copy gives Magnus' full name: "H (*sic*) (= Flavius) Anastasius Paul(us) Prob(us) Moschian(us) Prob'us Magnus." We have no further information about him.[51]

[51] See R. Delbrück, *Die Consulardiptychen und verwandte Denkmäler*, pp. 134–141 (nos. 22–25), plates 22–25, 3. Lieferung (1927). Other works have been listed in connection with Philoxenus' diptychs. See also J. Strzygowski, *Die Tyche von Konstantinopel, Analecta Graeciensia* (Graz, 1893), p. 148: "The Tyche appears with a staff (mit dem Stabe) on the consular diptychs of Clementinus (513), Magnus (518), and Orestes (530)."

CHAPTER FOUR

The Religious Policy of Justin

The accession of Justin to the throne meant a new era in the religious history of the empire. The two preceding emperors, Zeno and Anastasius, had been monophysitically inclined. In 482, when Zeno issued his *Henoticon*, which by means of compromise aimed at reconciling dissenting parties in the church, relations were broken between Constantinople and Rome. This was in reality the first breach between the Eastern and Western churches. In 518 the policy of strict orthodoxy established at the Council of Chalcedon started. This was the signal for an orthodox reaction all over the empire. The decrees of the Council of Chalcedon, which in 451 completed the alienation of Constantinople and Rome from the Orient, came into effect again in 518. It was impossible for such a policy to be carried out smoothly without opposition.

Monophysitism, which had been protected and supported during the two preceding reigns, was the most stubborn and energetic opponent of Justin's policy. Egypt was the real center of monophysitism and Alexandria the bulwark of opposition. The bishops or patriarchs of Alexandria possessed enormous power and influence. Taking advantage of the great distance which separated Egypt from the imperial capital, they felt themselves independent. One writer calls them the uncrowned kings of Roman Egypt; sometimes they were given the title of Pope or even "the blessed Pope." The twenty years after the Council of Ephesus (431–451) were the period of the supremacy of Alexandria in the east. But in 451, when the Council of Chalcedon worked out and passed its decisions, the whole structure of Alexandrian supremacy, according to N. Baynes, fell like a house of cards. The Council condemned monophysitism, and in addition, by giving the Patriarch of Constantinople the rank next below that of the Pope of Rome, it "insulted" the See of Alexandria, which by this act was reduced to third place. After 451, therefore, monophysitism became for the population of Egypt not only a national creed but also a sign and symbol of their political alienation and separation from the Roman Empire. They even had a separate language predominant in the country, the Coptic tongue. By the year 518 Egypt was already almost ripe for political separation under favorable circumstances. Justin's new government, in opening a new religious policy, faced a very complicated problem in managing Egypt. And, as we shall see later, the government understood the situation and treated Egypt in a different way from that accorded other regions of the empire. Monophysitism was less strongly represented in Syria than in Egypt. But this province also gave much trouble to Justin's government, and the head of the monophysite movement at the time, Severus, was Patriarch of Antioch. It should not be forgotten that Armenia also was faithful to monophysitism.

Justin's religious policy met much less difficulty in dealing with Nestorianism. In spite of the official condemnation of Nestorianism by the Third Ecumenical Council at Ephesus in 431, there still remained numerous followers of this teaching in Syria and Mesopotamia. But when the main center of Nestorianism, the famous school of Edessa, was destroyed in 489 during the reign of Zeno and the teachers and students were driven out of the city, they emigrated to Persia and under the protection of the King of Persia founded a new school at Nisibis. After this blow Nestorianism as a dangerous and disturbing element within the empire disappeared and is almost entirely ignored by the church historians, despite the fact that, as F. W. Buckler writes, its missionary activities extended to the uttermost parts of the world. So Justin in his aggressive religious policy had no organized opposition to encounter on the part of the few Nestorians who still remained in the territory of the empire.

When one reviews today all the heated disputes and irreconcilable controversies of the fifth and sixth centuries, which struggled in vain to reach unity on the insoluble problem of the union of the two natures in Jesus Christ, divine and human, and finally almost brought the empire to the brink of political and economic disaster, one cannot help citing at random various comments on those doctrines to be read in writings of our own day. One modern scholar considers the monophysite doctrine of incarnation, especially as scientifically presented by Severus, exactly the same as the christology of Cyril, the Patriarch of Alexandria, a contemporary of the Third Ecumenical Council, the sworn enemy of Nestorius and defender of the true orthodox faith. As to Nestorius himself, one scholar maintains that he was not a Nestorian at all but perfectly orthodox. Another scholar asks: "Was his doctrine really in harmony with that of the Council of Chalcedon? Was this heretic a rudely maltreated exponent of orthodoxy?" And a third writer testifies that Nestorius "has provided a name for a heresy which he did not originate, possibly did not even hold, and for a church which he did not found." If modern historians with the advantage of historical perspective find it difficult to resolve the ideological confusion of the time, we can not wonder that contemporaries found it impossible.

But not only the East occupied the attention of the new government. In the West in Italy, Justin's strictly Chalcedonian policy faced another religious problem in the person of the powerful and highly educated Ostrogothic king Theodoric who was an Arian. The existence in Italy of the Arian Ostrogothic kingdom amid the local orthodox population close to the papal residence in Old Rome created another very delicate and complicated situation.

The slowly dying paganism was not dangerous, although in a few outlying places the population still indulged in heathen practices. It is not to be forgotten that the famous philosophic school in Athens, "the most notorious home of uncompromising Hellenists" (Bury, II, 369), although in a state of decay, still existed during Justin's reign. But a real persecution of the remnants of paganism started only after Justin's death under Justinian, who in 529 closed the Athenian school.

This was the general situation in the empire in religious matters at the time of Justin's accession to the throne.[1] But before starting to

[1] On the development and fall of the Alexandrian supremacy see a very interesting article by N. H. Baynes, "Alexandria and Constantinople: A Study in Ecclesiastical Diplomacy," *The Journal of Egyptian Archaeology*, XII (1926), 145–156; esp. 155. On the extension of Nestorianism, F. W. Buckler, "Regnum et Ecclesia," *Church History*, III (1934), 38. On the monophysitism of Severus and Cyril of Alexandria, J. Lebon, *Le monophysisme sévérien* (Louvain, 1909), p. XXI.

deal with the new religious policy which began in 518 I wish to make my stand perfectly clear. I shall very often use for convenience such terms as "Justin's government," "Justin's new religious policy," and so on. By these I do not mean at all to imply that the real inspirer and leading spirit of the new period was Justin himself. Of course he was a convinced Chalcedonian. But he was too old and had too limited an education to be able to carry out a definite policy. The policy of his period, in this particular section of our study the religious policy, was organized, worked out, and put in practice by other men: till 520 by Vitalian and Justinian, who as we know had an excellent theological education, and after Vitalian's assassination in 520 by Justinian himself. I entirely agree with the opinion that "from the accession of Justin in 518 to the death of Justinian nearly fifty years later, the ecclesiastical policy of the empire was Justinian's own." [2]

It is not irrelevant to note that in spite of Justin's drastically new religious policy, the Patriarch of Constantinople, John II, who had been patriarch under the late emperor Anastasius apparently without offering opposition to his monophysite sympathies, was not deposed and continued to act under the new regime. John became patriarch on April 17, 518, less than three months before Anastasius' death (on the night of July 8–9, 518). Just after his elevation to the patriarchal rank the crowd, rebellious and seditious, shouted demands to him to anathematize Severus.[3] This amounted to a warning that very shortly after he would be compelled to anathematize the head of the mono-physite movement. Evidently before Anastasius' death John had no time to make clear his religious policy. In any case John as Patriarch of Constantinople after 518 was also an entirely acceptable person to the Pope, who wrote him very cordial letters. The monophysites themselves were suspicious of the firmness of John's monophysite convictions, and in reference to his nomination to the highest post in the Byzantine church under Anastasius, the famous head of the mono-

---

On Nestorius: J. Bethune-Baker, *Nestorius and His Teaching* (London, 1908), p. 198. F. Loofs, *Nestorius and His Place in the History of Christian Doctrine* (Cambridge, 1914), p. 26. Aubrey R. Vine, *The Nestorian Churches* (London, 1937), p. 21.
[2] Rev. W. A. Wigram, *The Separation of the Monophysites*, p. 106.
[3] Theoph., p. 164.

physite movement at the time, Severus of Antioch, wrote: "As to the man who has just been instituted and holds the prelacy of the royal city, we have learned that he is John . . . who is thought to be inclined to the right opinions, and holds out some pleasing hopes to the orthodox [i.e. monophysites], but is more desirous of adopting a deceitful middle course." A little farther on in the same letter, however, Severus says of an assembly of clergy convoked by the new patriarch on New Sunday, April 22, 518: "However on New Sunday an assembly of orthodox [i.e. monophysites] was purposely collected so that those who were gathered by the gleaning process by the heretics [i.e. orthodox] did not dare even to appear, but only to slink away and hide, and they were in great fear, and by flight gained freedom from all harm." [4] Whatever John's real views may have been, no question arose under the new government of deposing him and finding a successor. Apparently John was emboldened immediately after Anastasius' death to reveal his genuine religious sympathies, took an active part in the ceremony of Justin's elevation, and even placed the crown on his head. The text of John's synodical letter written before July 20, 518 is lost. But from the first passage in the letter of Severus given above, one may infer that the document was not compiled in strong Chalcedonian form.[5]

With these introductory remarks, let us now turn to the presentation and interpretation of the new religious trend which started in 518.

The Meeting in St. Sophia on July 15

The first reaction of Constantinople and the Near East, especially of Syria and Palestine, to Justin's new religious policy may be completely traced from detailed, almost stenographic records by unknown contemporary authors, probably eyewitnesses. When we read these records, we can almost see the disorderly crowd which thronged the great Church of St. Sophia, and hear the reverberation of their incoherent shouts and exclamations, sometimes rising even to open insult of the patriarch, showing total disregard of his presence or of

---

[4] *The Sixth Book of the Select Letters of Severus*, transl. E. W. Brooks, II, 360–361: 362.
[5] See Grumel, *Les regestes*, I, 84 (no. 207).

the mention of the names of the emperor and empress. A noted Russian church historian, V. Bolotov, remarks that these records show what the church was for Christians in the sixth century and adds that "the conception of church decorum (at that time) was entirely different from that which exists in our own day." [6] This series of extremely interesting documents on the subject is reproduced among the Acts of the Constantinopolitan Synod of 536 A. D., which was summoned under Justinian by Patriarch Menas, anathematized the patriarch Anthimus, Severus, and some others, and condemned their writings.[7]

Of course the first reaction to the new policy is obvious among the people of Constantinople, the organ most sensitively reflecting all important events and essential changes in the life of the empire. Two stormy days, July 15 and July 16, 518, the crowd spent in St. Sophia in their turbulent altercation with the patriarch and other clerics.[8] We are fortunate in having a complete record of these days. Although the text contains many repetitions, it so vividly brings to the modern reader the excited mood of the crowd, who after many years of restraint and suppression were taking advantage of free expression of their Chalcedonian sympathies, that I should like to give here an almost complete reproduction of these extremely interesting and vigorously written documents. On Sunday, July 15, 518, that is, six days after Justin's elevation, a religious service was held as usual in St. Sophia. When the Patriarch John with his clergy made his solemn entrance from the altar and was near his pulpit (ἄμβωνα), the congregation began to cry:

"Long live the patriarch! Long live the emperor! Long live the

[6] V. Bolotov, "Lectures in the History of the Ancient Church, III, A History of the Church in the Period of the Ecumenical Councils," *Christianskoe Chtenie* (June, 1915), Addenda, p. 360 (in Russian). I quote the Addenda. There is a separate edition of Bolotov's *Lectures* in four volumes.

[7] Documents in Mansi, VIII, coll. 1037–1136. By an oversight, L. Bréhier states that these documents were reproduced in the Acts of the Fifth Ecumenical Council. *Histoire de l'église*, ed. A. Fliche and V. Martin, IV, 426, n. 2.

[8] A contemporary description of the proceedings of the meeting of July 15 in Mansi, VIII, coll. 1057–1062; of July 16, VIII, coll. 1061–1066. See V. Bolotov, *op. cit.*, pp. 360–361. S. Salaville, "La fête du concile de Nicée et les fêtes de conciles dans le rit byzantin," *Echos d'Orient*, XXIV (1925), 455–458. Salaville writes that it seems very probable that the oldest among all the commemorations of the councils in the Byzantine liturgical texts is that of the Council of Chalcedon (p. 455). Cf. M. Jugie, *Le schisme byzantin* (Paris, 1941), p. 8.

Augusta! Long live the patriarch! Why do we remain without communion? Why haven't we taken communion for so many years? We want to have communion from your hands. Oh, mount the pulpit! Oh, comfort your people! For many years we have wanted to take communion. You are orthodox; of whom are you afraid, [you who are] worthy of the Trinity? Long live the emperor! Long live the Augusta! Throw out Severus the Manichaean! Whoever does not say this is a Manichaean himself. The bones of the Manichaeans must be exhumed! Now proclaim the holy synod [i.e. the Council of Chalcedon]! Long live the emperor! Long live the patriarch, worthy of the Trinity! The Holy Mary is the Mother of God [θεοτόκος] — [you who are] worthy of the (patriarchal) throne — the Holy Mary is the Mother of God. The Holy Synod proclaimed it. Whoever does not say this is a Manichaean himself. The faith of the Trinity prevails; the faith of the orthodox prevails. Now proclaim the Holy Synod! The orthodox (emperor) reigns. Of whom are you afraid? The faith of the emperor prevails; the faith of the Augusta prevails.

"Long live the new Constantine, long live the new Helen, long live the patriarch, worthy of the Trinity. Justin Augustus, you are triumphant! Long live the new Constantine! Either leave or proclaim [the Synod]! Long live the emperor! Justin Augustus, you are triumphant! Now proclaim the Synod of Chalcedon! Justin reigns, of whom are you afraid? Throw out Severus the Manichaean. Now proclaim the Synod of Chalcedon! Whoever does not anathematize Severus is a Manichaean himself. Anathema to Severus the Manichaean! Whoever does not say this is a Manichaean himself. Throw out Severus, throw out the new Judas. Throw out the traitor to the Trinity! Now proclaim the Holy Synod! Oh, I testify: either proclaim [it] or get out. Oh, Christian brethren, the faith is one soul; it is impossible to cast doubt upon it. Justin Augustus, you are triumphant! If you love the faith, anathematize Severus. Oh, I testify! I sweep you out (σύρω σε)! I lock the door! He who does not say this is a Manichaean himself. . . . The Holy Mary is the Mother of God, the Synod said so!"

To these turbulent, daring, and even presumptuous exclamations the patriarch answered: "Be patient, brethren; first we shall worship at the holy altar and after that I will give you your answer."

As he approached the altar, the crowd continued to shout: "Long live the emperor! Long live the Augusta! Oh, I testify: you shall not leave unless you anathematize Severus. Say openly: anathema to Severus! Oh, shut him out (ἀπόκλεισον)! I testify! Long live the emperor!"

Then the patriarch ascended the pulpit and addressed the congregation as follows: "You know my labors, beloved ones, which I endured when presbyter; and I have been and am devoted to the orthodox faith (τῆς ὀρθοδοξίας) till death. Therefore there is no need of confusion or tumult, because no damage whatever has been done to the true faith. No one dares anathematize the Holy Synod. We acknowledge all the holy synods which have confirmed the sacred symbol of the three hundred and eighteen Holy Fathers who assembled at Nicaea as orthodox, and particularly the three holy synods, those of Constantinople, Ephesus, and the great Synod of Chalcedon. Those three synods have unanimously confirmed the symbol of the three hundred and eighteen Holy Fathers in which we are baptized."

In spite of the patriarch's address, the crowd remained in the church for very many hours, uttering the same exclamations: "You can not come down (from the pulpit) unless you anathematize. Long live the patriarch, worthy of the Trinity! Long live the emperor, long live the Augusta! Now announce the celebration of the Synod of Chalcedon! I shall not go away unless you announce it; we shall stay here until late in the day. Announce the celebration for tomorrow; announce the commemoration of the Fathers for tomorrow. . . . If you announce it today, it will be held tomorrow. We shall not go away unless you announce it. Tomorrow proclaim those who anathematized Nestorius and Eutyches! Unless I get an answer, I shall stay here till late."

Thereupon the Patriarch said: "Since you have demanded a religious service (σύναξιν) to be held in commemoration of the Holy Fathers of Chalcedon, you should know that we will do it at the wish of our most pious and Christ-loving Emperor."

In spite of the mention of the necessity of imperial authorization, the crowd continued to cry: "By the Holy Gospels, I will not go away! Proclaim the service in commemoration of the Fathers now; hold the service in commemoration of the Fathers tomorrow; hold the service in commemoration of the Chalcedonian Fathers tomorrow!"

Then through the deacon Samuel the service was announced thus: "We notify your love (ἀγάπη) that tomorrow we shall celebrate the memory of our Holy Fathers and Bishops who assembled in the metropolis of Chalcedon, and who along with the Holy Fathers who had assembled in Constantinople and Ephesus confirmed the symbol of the three hundred and eighteen Holy Fathers who had assembled at Nicaea. We shall assemble here."

Even after the announcement of the ceremony, the people continued to stay and cry again and again: "Severus is to be anathematized now; the traitor to the Trinity is to be anathematized now; the adversary of the Fathers is to be anathematized now! He who anathematized the Synod of Chalcedon is himself to be anathematized now. I shall not go away unless I get an answer now. I protest: you are orthodox, anathematize (him) now. Either anathematize (him) or I shall have nothing to do with you (ἢ οὐδὲν παρ'ἐμέ; aut nihil ad me attinet)."

Under the pressure of the excited congregation the patriarch and the bishops who were present in the church consulted, and finally reached a decision. Our document gives here the list of bishops present: Theophilus of Heraclea, Theodotus (in the Latin text Theodorus) of Gangra, Hypatius of Claudiopolis, John of Bosporus, Pythagoras of Sinope, Isaac of Pentapolis in Greece, John of Semneon (Σεμνέων; in Latin Commocorum) in the region of Pamphylia, Amantius of Nicopolis, Ammonius of Abydus, Plato of Cratianai (τῆς Κρατιανῶν, Cratianus), Eustathius of Philadelphia, Pelagius of Azanitai (τῆς Ἀζανιτῶν, Azanitanus), and some others. The decision follows: "It is clear to all that Severus, who has separated himself from this Holy Church, has submitted himself to condemnation. Therefore we, following the divine canons and the Holy Fathers, regard him as alien, and on the basis of the divine canons anathematize him as one who has been condemned on account of his blasphemy." Apparently it was only after this solemn announcement, practically forced from the clergy by the uncontrollable congregation, that the crowd quitted the church. Thus ended the first meeting of the Patriarch John with the people of Constantinople, a meeting which took place on Sunday, July 15, 518 A. D.

THE MEETING IN ST. SOPHIA ON JULY 16

Next day, on Monday, July 16, 518,[9] according to the announcement of the Patriarch on the previous day, the commemoration of the Holy Fathers was performed. When after the service the Patriarch approached the pulpit ($\check{\alpha}\mu\beta\omega\nu$os), the whole congregation burst forth in a shout: "Long live the patriarch, long live the emperor, long live the Augusta, long live the new Constantine, long live the new Helen! Restore the relics of Macedonius to the church! Justin Augustus, you are triumphant! Euphemia Augusta, you are triumphant! Return to the church those who are in exile on account of the faith. The bones of the Nestorians must be exhumed; the bones of the Eutychians must be exhumed!

"Who Nestorius is, I do not know; anathema to him from the Trinity. Who Nestorius is, I do not know; anathema to him along with Eutyches. Throw out all the Manichaeans. Justin Augustus, you are triumphant! Throw out Severus the Judas; throw all Manichaeans out of the church; throw out the two Stephens! Now bring the relics of Macedonius! We pray the emperor unanimously that the name of Macedonius be now restored. Throw out the new Tzumas ($\tau\zeta o\nu\mu\hat{\alpha}\nu$)![10] The new Tzumas is Amantius. Throw the braggart ($\tau\grave{o}\nu$ $\lambda\hat{\eta}\rho o\nu$, *nugatorem*) out of the palace! Restore Euphemius and Macedonius to the church. Send the decrees of the Council to Rome at once![11]

"Long live the patriarch! Long live the new John! Justin Augustus, worthy of the Trinity, you are triumphant! Long live the Augusta!

[9] A contemporary description of the proceedings of the meeting of July 16, 518, in Mansi, VIII, 1061–1066. There is some deterioration in the text, but the meaning is quite clear: $\tau\hat{\eta}$ $\kappa\upsilon\rho\acute{\iota}\alpha$ $\tau\hat{\eta}$ $\dot{\epsilon}\xi\hat{\eta}s$ $\mathring{\eta}\tau\iota s$ $\dot{\epsilon}\sigma\tau\grave{\iota}\nu$ $\dot{\epsilon}\xi\kappa\alpha\iota\delta\epsilon\kappa\acute{\alpha}\tau\eta$ $\tauο\hat{\upsilon}$ $\iotaο\upsilon\lambda\acute{\iota}ο\upsilon$ $\mu\eta\nu\grave{o}s$, $\mathring{\eta}\mu\acute{\epsilon}\rho\alpha$ $\delta\epsilon\upsilon\tau\acute{\epsilon}\rho\alpha$; in Latin: sequenti dominica quae est XVI, mensis Julii, indictione undecima. Mansi, VIII, 1061–1062. See Salaville, *op. cit.*, *Echos d'Orient*, XXIV, pp. 458–461.

[10] This, as we have noted above, is the eunuch Chrysaphius T$\zeta ο\upsilon\mu\hat{\alpha}s$, the all-powerful favorite under Theodosius II (408–450), who was executed by his successor, Marcian. Theoph., p. 100 (T$\zeta ο\upsilon\mu\hat{\alpha}s$). Malalas, p. 363; 368 (Z$\tauο\mu\mu\hat{\alpha}s$, Z$\tauο\upsilon\mu\mu\hat{\alpha}s$). Slavonic version by M. Spinka, *Chronicle of John Malalas*, Books VIII–XVIII, pp. 84; 88 (Chumlva, Chumva).

[11] $\tau\grave{\alpha}$ $\sigma\upsilon\nuο\delta\iota\kappa\grave{\alpha}$ $\epsilon\iota s$ $'P\acute{\omega}\mu\eta\nu$ $\check{\alpha}\rho\tau\iota$ $\dot{\alpha}\pi\acute{\epsilon}\lambda\theta\omega\sigma\iota$; in Latin: *Synodica Romana modo valeant.*

Restore the relics of Macedonius to the church! If you do this, you will always be victorious. The names of Euphemius and Macedonius should now be restored for perfect celebration in the church. Throw out the false witnesses against Macedonius. Inscribe the four synods in the diptychs; inscribe Leo the Bishop of Rome in the diptychs! The Holy Mary is the Mother of God; the Synod said so. Bring the diptychs to the pulpit! He who does not say this is a Manichaean himself. Justin Augustus, you are triumphant! You have no master above you (κουράτωρα οὐκ ἔχεις).[12] Now bring the diptychs. Justin reigns, bring the diptychs now! Long live the orthodox emperor; long live the new Helen! Now we have the [orthodox] emperor (τὸν δεσπότην); bring the diptychs now. Now we have the Augusta; bring the diptychs now. The canons have not thrown them out. Oh, settle this, settle it, settle it!"

Then the patriarch addressed the congregation. "Yesterday we sufficiently satisfied your love; and now, clearly feeling your zeal, we have hastened and will haste to do that which pleases God and fully satisfies you. I think that by your own experiences in various times and various circumstances, your love has recognized that nothing would be removed by us from the true faith. Therefore by the grace of our Lord and Saviour Jesus Christ, we have endeavored that the foundation of the faith established by the tradition of the Holy Fathers should remain unbroken (ἀρραγῆ), hoping through Him to unite the dissident churches and keep firmly (ἐνθέσμως) everywhere the rules of the divine canons. It is not allowed, indeed, that the faithful remove anything or indulge in idle talking and subtle discussion; but we must hold to the holy symbol, in which we were all baptized, which the Synod of Nicaea acting through the Holy Spirit declared, which the assembly of the Holy Fathers in Constantinople ratified, which the Holy Synod in Ephesus confirmed, and which the great Holy Synod at Chalcedon equally sealed. And no one will be able in any way to violate it in order to deprive the heterodox of any pretext (for change). So keeping this faith unchangeable — have no doubt about this — and rejecting any idle talking, innovations (καινοτομία;

---

[12] Salaville translates these words "Puisque vous êtes les maîtres" (p. 459). The meaning is, "You can do it," or "You are free to do so."

vocum novitas), or subtleties (subtle discourse, λεπτολογία), let us unanimously glorify the holy and consubstantial Trinity, which shall guard in peace the life of our most pious and Christ-loving emperor and (the lives of) all of us. Glory to the Father, the Son, and the Holy Ghost, now and for evermore, to all eternity. Amen."

Even after this address, the crowd still continued to cry out: "If anyone goes out, — I protest — I shall close the door. Orthodox brethren, one soul; brethren in faith, one soul! Justin Augustus, you are triumphant! He who does not say this is a Manichaean. Holy, holy, holy! The Trinity has triumphed! From now on do not fear Amantius the Manichaean. Justin reigns! Why are you afraid of Amantius? He who loves the Synod is held in high esteem. Long live the emperor, long live the Augusta, long live the patriarch! The faith of the orthodox prevails!"

When the crowd continued to shout, a new appeal was made to them: "You well know that we have by all means (διὰ πάντων) tried to satisfy you and not to offend you. But since it is necessary that everything should be done canonically and in good order, allow us to congregate the bishops beloved of God in order that everything may proceed according to the divine canons and through the order of our most pious emperor. And we shall report to His Serenity all your exclamations (ἐκβοήσεις)."

But the crowd locked the doors and continued to shout. Then the Patriarch took the diptychs and ordered that there should be inscribed in them the four holy synods held at Nicaea, at Constantinople under the Patriarch Nectarius, at Ephesus on the expulsion of Nestorius, and at Chalcedon on the expulsion of Eutyches and the same impious Nestorius, as well as the names of the late archbishops of the imperial city, Euphemius and Macedonius, and also the name of the Archbishop of Rome, Leo.

Then the whole congregation aloud as if from one mouth exclaimed: "Blessed be the Lord God of Israel; for He hath visited and redeemed His people (Luke I, 68)." While both factions sang this chant (ἀντιφωνούντων ἑκατέρων τῶν μερῶν, καὶ ψαλλόντων τὴν ψαλμῳδίαν ταύτην) the choir made their appearance and began to recite the Trisagion. Hearing this, the whole crowd became quiet and listened. Then the liturgy was

143

celebrated; and after the reading of the Holy Gospels, when the doors had been closed and the Holy Symbol of the Creed (τὸ μάθημα) had been read as usual, at the time for reading the diptychs the whole congregation in perfect silence gathered close to the altar and listened. And as soon as the names of the four holy synods and of the archbishops of blessed memory, Euphemius, Macedonius, and Leo, had been read, all exclaimed aloud: "Glory to Thee, oh Lord!" And after this, the divine liturgy was celebrated in perfect order.

The result of the two tumultuous meetings of July 15 and 16 was, then, full concession on the part of the patriarch and the clergy to the demands of the excited and unruly people of Constantinople. But this concession, however important and gratifying to the people it may have been, was merely provisional. The final word was to be left to the synod, and the Patriarch John determined to summon a synod in Constantinople, which convened on July 20. The members of this synod had to discuss not only the report of the meetings in St. Sophia, July 15 and 16, but also the memorandum of the monks of the Constantinopolitan monasteries, which was presented to the synod.

The meeting of July 16 was further memorable because it was here that there was instituted the first solemn commemoration of the Council of Chalcedon, as well as that of the Councils of Nicaea, of Constantinople, and of Ephesus.[13] The two remarkable contemporary reports of the meetings of July 15 and 16 certainly possess a high degree of general interest. In addition, I wish to repeat a few detailed points I have already made. The name of Amantius, leader of the plot against Justin, is three times mentioned in the description of the proceedings of July 16. In other words, as I have noted above, this document shows that on July 16, 518, Amantius was still alive or was at least thought to be so by the people. It is not surprising that among the exclamations of the crowd Justinian's name is missing. In the few days which had elapsed since Justin's elevation on July 9, Justinian had not had the opportunity to manifest himself as a leading figure, and his name was as yet almost unknown to the population of the capital at large.

[13] Salaville, op. cit., pp. 460–461; also p. 468.

144

THE RELIGIOUS POLICY OF JUSTIN

MEMORANDUM OF THE CONSTANTINOPOLITAN MONKS

We come now to a discussion of the memorandum of the Constantino-politan monks, of which I have just spoken above. This memorandum (Λιβέλλος, libellus) [14] which was presented to the synod, was addressed to the fathers and bishops Theophilus, Basiliscus, Anastasius, Marcianus, Theodotus, Hypatius, Theodorus, John, Pythagoras, and to the whole Holy (εὐαγής) Synod which is held in the imperial city, by Alexander, Constantine, Diogenes, Evethius, Antonius, Acacius, John, Domnus, Leontius, Julianus, Alexander, Jacob, Christinus, John, Basiliscus, Babylas, Hypatius, Marcus, and other presbyters and archimandrites of the holy monasteries situated in the Christ-loving imperial city as well as by the whole monastic order.

The memorandum pays due honor to the religious zeal of His Sanctity the Patriarch and "our victorious Emperors" (sic) as well as to the decisions which were formulated on July 15 and 16. The monks then remark that it would be necessary and useful to consider also the monastic point of view, which concurs with these decisions. They are in full agreement with the idea of restoring in the diptychs the names of the Patriarchs Euphemius and Macedonius, and Pope Leo, as well as the names of the Four Ecumenical Councils; they de-mand excommunication of the impious Severus; they require that the bishops, clergymen, archimandrites, monks, and laymen who had been expelled for their religious doctrine should be recalled by the most holy Archbishop and Ecumenical Patriarch John and by our most pious and victorious Emperors, and be returned to their former order and position. At the end of the memorandum, "not to enlarge too much on our own supplications," they approve the shouts and acclamations of "the Christ-loving people" which were heard in the great church of St. Sophia, and the addresses of the Patriarch John, which have been confirmed by "our victorious Emperor." The memorandum was signed by fifty-six representatives of the Byzantine monastic order: fifty-four presbyters and archimandrites (πρεσβύτερος καὶ ἀρχιμανδρίτης), one deacon and archimandrite of the monastery of the Akoimetoi (Evethius), and one presbyter of the Holiest Great Church (St.

[14] Mansi, VIII, 1049–1056.

145

Sophia) and abbot ($\dot{\eta}\gamma\epsilon\mu\dot{\omega}\nu$, prior) of the Church of St. Eusebius (Joannes-John).

The memorandum twice mentions the emperor in the plural ($\beta\alpha\sigma\iota\lambda\epsilon\hat{\iota}s$, *imperatores*) and once in the singular ($\beta\alpha\sigma\iota\lambda\dot{\epsilon}\omega s$, *imperatoris*). If the plural "emperors" is not a misprint, it may be explained as signifying that the empire henceforth was to be ruled by the "pious emperors," that is, by the Chalcedonians.

A very important addition to the title of the patriarch seems to have been definitely established in Justin's reign. In this memorandum the Constantinopolitan Bishop John is called Ecumenical Patriarch. If I am not mistaken, the title of the Patriarch of Constantinople as Ecumenical first occurs officially in our documents in 518. This title, which seemed to be very derogatory to the prestige of the Bishop of Rome, is used in 518 without any ostentation, almost as a matter of course, so that we may suppose that it had been used before this date and was not new. The formal title of the Patriarch of Constantinople on this date was "The most holy, godly, and wise (John), Lord Archbishop of Constantinople, which is New Rome, and Ecumenical Patriarch." [15]

THE SYNOD OF CONSTANTINOPLE

The Synod, consisting of forty-three or forty-four bishops who were present in Constantinople and in the neighborhood, was held in the capital on July 20, 518 ($\dot{\eta}$ $\sigma\acute{v}\nu\omega\delta\omega s$ $\dot{\epsilon}\nu\delta\eta\mu\omega\hat{v}\sigma\alpha$).[16] The patriarch him-

[15] See H. Gelzer, "Der Streit über den Titel des ökumenischen Patriarchen," *Jahrbücher für protestantische Theologie*, XIII (1887), 568–569; 572. Idem, "Das Verhältnis von Staat und Kirche in Byzanz," *Historische Zeitschrift*, LXXXVI (1901), 207–208. A. Fortescue, "John the Faster," *The Catholic Encyclopedia*, VIII (New York, 1910), 493–495. Rev. W. A. Wigram, *The Separation of the Monophysites*, p. 93, n.t. On the papal title as "ecumenical patriarch" see C. Hefele, *Conciliengeschichte*, 2nd ed., II (Freiburg im Breisgau, 1875), 544–545; Hefele-Leclercq, II, 2 (Paris, 1908), 834–835. M. Jugie, *Le schisme byzantin*, pp. 22–24. See V. Laurent, "Le titre de patriarche oecumenique et la signature patriarcale," *Revue des études byzantines*, VI, 1 (1948), 26: the title of Ecumenical Patriarch had been added timidly (*timidement*) in the fifth century, and definitely at the outset of the sixth.

[16] Mansi, VIII, 1041–1050. The date, coll. 1043–1044. I have not seen the new edition of the documents on this synod published by E. Schwartz, *Acta conciliorum oecumenicorum*, vol. III (Berlin-Leipzig, 1940). The anonymous Arab chronicle of the eleventh century, the so-called Chronicle of Seert, mentions this synod and writes that it consisted of 143 bishops, who assembled to anathematize

self was not present, and the decrees of the synod were sent to him for consideration and confirmation. The synod was presided over by Theophilus, Bishop of the European Heraclea, whose signature stood at the head of the list of the members of the synod in their letter to the patriarch. The business of the synod was to consider the demands of the people which had been brought forward on the stormy days of July 15 and 16, and the memorandum or petition of the monks of the monasteries of Constantinople, which has been discussed above, in order to confirm them canonically. The synod found the petitions of the people and of the monks right and reasonable, and without much discussion or dispute decreed that they should be communicated by the patriarch to the emperor, the empress, and "their most glorious and great Senate." According to the demands which were included in the petitions, the synod divided its decisions into five items, as follows:

1. That the names of the patriarchs who had died in exile, Euphemius and Macedonius, should be restored into the list ($\tau\hat{\omega}$ $\kappa\alpha\tau\alpha\lambda\acute{o}\gamma\omega$) of the bishops of Constantinople, and into the diptychs, and that everything which had been done against them should be annulled.

2. That all those who had been condemned and banished on account of their adherence to Euphemius and Macedonius should be returned and restored to their appropriate positions.

3. That the Synods of Nicaea, Constantinople, Ephesus, and Chalcedon should be inscribed in the diptychs.

4. That the name of Pope Leo should also be put in the diptychs with the same honor as that of St. Cyril, "the Christ-loving shepherd of Alexandria," whom the Synod of Chalcedon considered orthodox, and whose name had already been inscribed in the diptychs.

5. Finally, that in accordance with the demand of the monks and the people, deposition and anathema should be pronounced against Severus of Antioch, who had repeatedly reviled the Synod of Chalcedon.

This fifth section is lengthy, and for this particular provision the synod used a new and additional document: a special letter of com-

---

Severus, his adherents, and all those who professed one nature in Christ. *Histoire nestorienne. Chronique de Seert*, ed. Addai Scher, *Patrologia Orientalis*, VII, 139 (47).

plaint from the clergy and monks of Antioch, addressed to the Patriarch John and the synod. The letter rejoices that the empire is ruled by "the pious and Christ-loving emperors" (*sic*) and presents a long list of various accusations against Severus, who intruding as "a wolf instead of a shepherd," killed many monks and "with Judaic hands ('Ιουδαϊκαῖς χερσί) carried out this massacre." Specifically he is accused of embezzlement, because he misappropriated church property; among other things, he had taken the gold and silver doves in the form of the Holy Ghost from the altar under the pretext that the Holy Ghost should not be presented in the form of a dove. This document was signed by twenty-six representatives of the church of Antioch.[17]

Copies of the synodal decrees were sent by the Patriarch John to other bishops of distinction, requesting their concurrence and acceptance. The copies were accompanied by his personal letters. Two such letters have survived: one addressed to the Archbishop (Patriarch) John of Jerusalem, and to all the metropolitans who were at that time congregated there; the other, to the Bishop Epiphanius of Tyre.

In his brief letter to Patriarch John of Jerusalem, Patriarch John of Constantinople states that "the Christ-loving population of the capital in their exclamations were inspired from heaven," and their demands had his sanction. He notified the Patriarch of Jerusalem of the decrees of the Synod of Constantinople supported by "the whole monastic order." [18] In this letter we may note that the turbulent behavior of the crowd in St. Sophia on the stormy days of July 15 and 16 is presented as divinely inspired.

THE SYNOD OF JERUSALEM

In response to the letter of the Patriarch of Constantinople, John, the Patriarch of Jerusalem, summoned the Synod of Jerusalem which was held on the sixth of August, 518. The decrees of the Synod, signed by thirty-three bishops, are known from the report (ἀντίγραφον, rescriptum) of John of Jerusalem to John of Constantinople, which is

---

[17] Mansi, VIII, 1037–1042. See Devreesse, *Le patriarcat d'Antioche*, p. 71.
[18] Mansi, VIII, 1065–1068: θεία τις οὐρανόθεν γέγονε κίνησις τοῦ φιλοχρίστου λαοῦ τῆς βασιλίδος ταύτης πόλεως. See V. Grumel, *Les regestes*, I, 84 (no. 208).

in complete accordance with the decrees of the Synod of Constantinople, July 20. The report, which is full of biblical references, recognizes the Four Ecumenical Councils, and the Letter of Pope Leo, and condemns heretics, especially Severus, "a disgust of desolation and a shameless monster." The renowned Palestinian hermit of the period, Sabas, attended the synod and represented a very large number of monks and laymen who had come to Jerusalem on this occasion.[19]

After the synod, the Patriarch of Jerusalem charged Sabas and some other monks to go to Caesarea and Scythopolis to announce the imperial decree and those of the Synods of Constantinople and Jerusalem regarding the entry of the Four Ecumenical Councils in the diptychs. At Caesarea they were met by the bishop of the city, John the Khuzibites (Khozibites). After carrying out their commission there, they went to Scythopolis, where the whole population came to meet them, headed by the metropolitan Theodosius. Chanting psalms they proceeded to the old Church of St. Thomas, where a solemn service was celebrated, the imperial decree announced, and the Four Synods put in the diptychs.[20]

THE SYNOD OF TYRE

As we have noted above, the Patriarch of Constantinople sent the decrees of the Constantinopolitan Synod with a personal letter to

[19] Mansi, VIII, 1057–1074. On Severus: τὸ γὰρ βδέλυγμα τῆς ἐρημώσεως, τὸ τέρας τὸ ἀνερυθρίαστον (col. 1070). The date of the synod (August 6) is indicated in the *Life of St. Sabas*: καὶ ἑορτῆς γενομένης, τῇ ἕκτῃ τοῦ Αὐγούστου μηνός. Cotelier, *Ecclesiae Graecae monumenta*, III (Paris, 1686), 326; ed. I. Pomyalovsky (St. Petersburg, 1890), p. 356 and 358 (Slavonic version, p. 357 and 359); E. Schwartz, *Kyrillos von Skythopolis* (Leipzig, 1939), p. 162. See also Mansi, VIII, p. 578. The Arab *Chronicle of Seert* mentions the Synod of Jerusalem, of thirty bishops, who excommunicated Severus. *Patr. Or.*, VII (1911), 139 (47).

[20] *The Life of St. Sabas*, Cotelier, III, 326–327; Pomialovsky, pp. 358–361; Schwartz, pp. 162–163; also p. 387. On St. John the Khozibites, who is commemorated by the Greek Orthodox Church on October 3, see Archbishop Sergius, *The Complete Menologium of the Orient*, II, 1, 411–412 (in Russian). See also M. Abel, "Mélanges, VII, Beisan," *Revue biblique*, new series, IX (1912), 418–419. Abel erroneously calls the Metropolitan of Scythopolis Theodorus (for Theodosius). Abel's text has been literally reproduced by Alan Rowe, *The Topography and History of Beth-Shan* (Philadelphia, 1930), p. 51. A miraculous story of the cure by John Khuzibites performed on the eye of the wife of a nobleman of Palestinian Caesarea, Arkesilaos, is told by Evagrius, IV, 7; ed. Bidez and Parmentier, pp. 157–158. From Evagrius, Nicephorus Callistus Xanthopulus, XVII, 4; Migne, *PG*, CXLVII, pp. 228–229.

Epiphanius, Bishop of Tyre. In his letter he notified Epiphanius of the decrees in order that Epiphanius after reading them might be "of the same opinion and of the same mind (σύμψηφος καὶ ὁμόψυχος)" and "if some enemies are found around him he should get rid of them" (κἂν ὀψέποτε τῶν κυκλωσάντων σε ἐχθρῶν λυτρωθείης).[21]

In response to the patriarchal letter, Epiphanius summoned a synod at Tyre September 16, 518.[22] Two documents referring to this synod have survived: 1) the synodal letter of Epiphanius of Tyre and of the bishops under him to the Synod of Constantinople, which was addressed to "the most Christ-loving and holiest brethren and fellow ministers, Theophilus, Basiliscus, Marcianus, and to the entire Holy Synod"; and 2) a document appended to it which contains a detailed account of the proceedings which took place in the principal church of Tyre, at the opening of the synod, an account which strikingly reminds us of the anonymous description of the stormy days of July 15 and 16 in St. Sofia in Constantinople. I shall reproduce the proceedings below in a somewhat condensed form.

The long synodal letter of Bishop Epiphanius of Tyre to the Synod of Constantinople [23] was addressed, as we have seen above, first to Theophilus, Bishop of Heraclea, because Patriarch John was not present at the synod which was presided over by Theophilus. The letter presents a long list of canonical transgressions and various other crimes of Severus, not only in Antioch but also in other cities, including Tyre. At the end of the letter Epiphanius writes of the joy of the orthodox population of Tyre which manifested itself in the principal church of the city after the decrees of the Constantinopolitan Synod had been announced. In addition, the people of Tyre expressed their special demand to receive back into their city the bodies of their "Holy Fathers" Euphemius and Macedonius, to have their names inscribed in the diptychs, to receive the body of the late Patriarch of Antioch, Flavianus, and to have his name restored in the list of other "Holy

---

[21] Mansi, VIII, 1067–1068. See Grumel, *Les regestes*, p. 84 (No. 209).

[22] Mansi, VIII, 1081–1092. See C. Hefele, *Conciliengeschichte*, 2nd ed., II (Freiburg im Breisgau, 1875), p. 695; Hefele-Leclercq, II, 2 (Paris, 1908), 1048–1049. The Arab *Chronicle of Seert* mentions the Synod of Tyre, of forty bishops, who excommunicated Severus. *Patr. Or.*, VII, p. 139 (47).

[23] Mansi, VIII, 1073–1082.

Fathers." The letter expresses the hope that "the pious and serene emperor" will grant their demands" for the glory of the Undefiled and Consubstantial Trinity." This synodal letter was subscribed by five bishops only; but the list is not complete, as is shown by the words "and others" (καὶ οἱ λοιποί, *et reliqui*) at the close.

The document appended to this synodal letter, which we have already mentioned above, is a very vivid presentation of what took place in the principal church of Tyre September 16, 518, after the reading of the letters which had come from Constantinople, and before the opening of the Tyrian Synod. Here is the account.[24] On September 16, the twelfth indiction, that is, 518, in the ancient church of Tyre a solemn service was held. After the reading of the Gospels, the deacon of the church, Sergius, read three letters: those of Patriarch John of Constantinople, of Bishop Theophilus of Heraclea, and of the members of the Synod of Constantinople, which were addressed to Bishop Epiphanius of Tyre. After this the same deacon Sergius read the decree of the Constantinopolitan Synod, which anathematized Severus. Immediately the congregation burst out in exclamations:

"Long live Augustus, Augusta, the Senate, the Eparchs (Prefects), the *comes* John, the patriarch Epiphanius! Do what the synod has done! Long live the orthodox John (of Constantinople)! This empire forever! The faith of Augustus prevails. This empire is from God! Long live the new Constantine, long live the orthodox father! He who does not say this is not faithful. One God, one faith, for the peace of the churches, for the peace of the orthodox. Long live Patriarch John! What the synod has done, do you likewise. The faith of Augustus prevails. This empire forever! Long live the patrician Vitalian; long live the orthodox Vitalian! Long live the orthodox Epiphanius! Anathematize, like the Fathers; anathematize, like the synod; anathematize Severus and Mandrites; anathematize Severus and Joannes!"[25]

---

[24] Mansi, VIII, 1081–1092. In the text the year is indicated according to Tyrian reckoning: 643 (Mansi, 1083–1084).

[25] Mandrites. On the basis of these two exclamations, I identify *Mandrites* in the first with *Joannes* in the second. Mandrites — μανδρίτης is a surname meaning "belonging to a mandra — μάνδρα," *i.e.* to a monastery, or monk: in other words, John the Monk. Several monophysites with the name of John appear in the correspondence of Severus. Since a little further on in our document the crowd shouts, "Why is Mandrites' workshop open?", I may quote here Severus' letter

When Epiphanius mounted the pulpit (ἄμβωνι), the congregation exclaimed: "God has welcomed you (καλῶς ὁ Θεὸς ἤνεγκέ σε; *Bene Deus tulit te*)! One God, one faith! One God who has done this! Bring back the bishops; bring back the orthodox (ἄνω βάλε τοὺς ἐπισκόπους; ἄνω βάλε τοὺς ὀρθοδόξους)!"

And when Bishop John of Ptolemais, Bishop Theodorus of Porphyreon (Πορφυρεῶνος) [26] and Bishop Helias of Rachlenai ('Ραχληνῶν, Rachlenus) [27] had mounted the pulpit (ἄμβωνι), the congregation exclaimed again: "Long live patriarch Epiphanius! As the saints have borne witness, you have borne witness and triumphed! He (our Lord) alone died for the faith; He alone endured labors (ἀπέλαβε καμάτους; *labores assumpsit*). You have borne witness and triumphed! He alone has triumphed (ἐνίκησεν; *vicit*) through the faith! You have borne witness and your faith has triumphed! The Trisagion has rejected them (ἔβαλεν αὐτούς; *emisit ipsos*)! The Mother of God has rejected them! The Mother of God rejected Severus, who had put asunder the churches. The mystery [of the Eucharist] expelled them. One whom they had stoned expelled them. Throw them out of the city! There is no city for schismatics. Throw out the Egyptians (Αἰγυπτίους)! [28]

"Now we have the orthodox emperor! May this empire live forever! Destroy the cavern of robbers, destroy the cavern of schismatics; burn them. Drive out all deceivers! Drive out Romaicus ('Ρωμαϊκόν; *Romanum*); [29] bring back those whom you have pitied. Drive out

---

to Victor, bishop of Philadelphia, in which he mentions "the devout John . . . who has lapsed into love of money and the vileness of filthy lucre." *The Sixth Book of the Select Letters of Severus*, E. W. Brooks, II, pp. 378–379; also I, p. 102.

[26] Porphyreon, a bishopric which formerly was thought to be located between Sidon and Beirut (Berytus), and recently has been identified with Haifa, the port of Jerusalem. E. Honigmann, "L'évêché phénicien de Porphyreon (Haifa)," *Annuaire de l'Institut de philologie et d'histoire orientales et slaves*, VII (New York, 1944), 381–394. Honigmann mentions Theodorus of Porphyreon (p. 386).

[27] Rachle, a bishopric in Phoenicia Prima, under the jurisdiction of the Archbishop of Tyre. See, for instance, E. Honigmann, "Studien zur Notitia Antiochena," *Byz. Zeitsch.*, XXV (1925), 73: "ὁ 'Ράχλης." R. Dussaud, *Topographie historique de la Syrie antique et médiévale* (Paris, 1927), p. 394. Devreesse, *Le patriarcat d'Antioche*, p. 200.

[28] Egyptians, i.e. monophysites.

[29] Romaicus, Romanus. Perhaps Romanus, mentioned by Zach. of Mitylene, IX, 13; Hamilton-Brooks, p. 244; Ahrens-Krüger, p. 188; also p. 370. Romanus was

Synthecarius (συνθηκάριον; Synthecarium or Sinaicarium)[30] and the Manichaean! Romaicus (ὁ Ῥωμαϊκός) is a deceiver! Drive out Romaicus; drive out the Manichaean! Purify the churches! Anathema to Severus, to those who agree with him, and to Mandrites! Anathema to Severus, Eutyches, Nestorius, and Mandrites! Why is Mandrites' workshop (ἐργαστήριον; officina) open? Anathematize, like the Patriarch of Rome, Helias of Botrys (Βοτρυηνόν),[31] anathematize the baker (ἀρτοκόπον; pistorem).[32] Send a bishop there in his stead. Expel the heretic bishops!

"Justin reigns: there is nothing to fear; He is orthodox. Long live Augustus; may his empire be forever! He is the new Constantine; there is nothing to fear. Long live the new Helen! Long live the patrician Vitalian; long live the stratelates Vitalian! Long live the prefect (ἐπάρχων), long live the magister, long live all the Senate, long live the curator (κουράτωρ) Hlias,[33] long live the archbishop Epiphanius! Victory to Augustus! Depose the Botryenos (Helias of Botrys) as a Manichaean! The city does not want Egyptian wood-merchants (ξυλεμπόρους)![34] Expel the Acephaloi ('Ακεφάλους)! If they prevail, we shall die![35] Put the patriarch Flavianus into the diptychs!

---

a follower of Julian of Halicarnassus and his doctrine, which was known as aphthartodocetism, and therefore was an odious figure to both the Chalcedonians and Severus, who in his letters mentioned "the hateful opinions of Romanus," and spoke of "the mad dogs who have followed the witless Romanus and the stony Julian." *The Sixth Book of the Select Letters of Severus*, E. W. Brooks, II, p. 288; 356. Cf. Hefele's note that the Ῥωμαϊκός mentioned here is not the Pope of Rome. *Conciliengeschichte*, 2d ed., II, p. 691, n. 6; Hefele-Leclercq, II, 2, 1049, n. 4.

[30] Synthecarius, συνθηκάριος, Sinaicarius. On the margin of the Acta are the words "locus suspectus."

[31] Botryenus. Βότρυς — Botrys, a city in Phoenicia Prima. Malalas, 485. Theoph., 227. See R. Devreesse, *Le patriarcat d'Antioche*, p. 198. He says that Helias of Botrys is known only by the maledictions which were bestowed upon him at the Synod of Constantinople (*sic*) in 518.

[32] Baker — ἀρτοκόπος — pistor?

[33] Curator — κουράτωρ Hlias. Probably he was the *curator civitatis*, whose business was to superintend the finances of the municipality. Bury, I, 60.

[34] These "Egyptian (*i.e.* monophysite) wood-merchants" may perhaps be connected with the above mentioned "Mandrites' workshop" and with "the devout John . . . who had lapsed into love of money," whom Severus mentions in his letters. In other words, the Tyrians resented the monophysite John Mandrites, who was making money by his wood trade. See note above.

[35] *Acephali, Akephaloi*, 'Ακέφαλοι, the extreme monophysites, who refused to recognize the Alexandrian patriarchs who accepted the Henoticon.

The Trinity has triumphed. Accept the Mother of God! The emperor commanded what the synod had said; the emperor ordered as did the entire synod. Accept the Mother of God! Ascend and purify the holy house! He who does not say this is not faithful! Let us go to the church of the Mother of God (εἰς τὴν θεοτόκον ἄγωμεν; *ducimus*). Announce [it] and we shall go.

"Long live Augustus! One God, one faith! Send the relics (λείψανον) of Flavianus; we shall bring them to the church of the Holy Mary. Ho, they have closed the interior of the church (δεύτερον ἔφραξαν τὰ ἔσω) again; give us the cross (σταυρίον; *cruciferum*)! they have stoned the cross and closed the interior [of the church]. In what city do such things occur? There is one faith; there is no confusion. The Trinity has triumphed and there is no confusion. The Trinity has triumphed and the Acephalus withdrawn. Justin has triumphed! Let us go to the church of the Mother of God (ἄγωμεν εἰς τὴν θεοτόκον). Justin triumphs! Let us go; let us enter. Justin triumphs! Let us now go inside. Justin triumphs; announce the synod. Justin triumphs, proclaim (*praedica*) this day. Long live the patriarch John, the patriarch Epiphanius, the Augusta, the Augusta Euphemia. The stronghold is firm (καστέλλιον ἐγγύετο; *castellum factum est*); accept the Mother of God! The church is firm (συναγωγὴ ἐγγύετο; *conventus factus est*), accept the Mother of God!

"Let us go; let us enter and there anathematize. Let us go; let us enter. The Acephalus [Severus] has gone. Let us go, let us enter, the Acephalus has been deposed. Give command, and we will go carrying the cross. The Augustus triumphs! Whom are you waiting for? Are you orthodox? Let us pray there (λιτανείαν κἀκεῖ); let us enter. Justin triumphs, let us go inside. I assure you, they have left nothing inside (οὐδὲν ἀφῆκαν ἔσω). *Ille modiarii* (?) took the valuables (τὰ κειμήλια ἔλαβεν ὁ τοῦ μοδιαρίου; *cimelia accepit ille modiarii*).[36] Proclaim a celebration (σύναξιν)! Victory to the Augustus! Peace (ἀργίαν) to the city, peace to the orthodox faith! Ascend [the pulpit]; purify the building.

---

[36] I do not understand this phrase. It is evidently a reference to Severus, who, as we have seen above, took from the altar several valuable pieces, including the gold and silver dove which was the emblem of the Holy Ghost. In his Greek dictionary Sophocles, referring to our text, writes with an interrogation point, μοδιάριος — maker of modii?

The Acephalus has no place here; the Manichaean has no place here. Long live the archbishop Epiphanius!"

Then the archbishop proclaimed: "I beg your love to tolerate forbearingly (ἀνεξικάκως) and to allow me and the Christ-loving bishops to excommunicate the Acephalus. Here, in the church of the holy Mother of God and Immaculate Mary, and in all churches and in all cities and in the entire world he is excommunicated forever." And the crowd cried again: "Peace to our lord."

Thereupon Epiphanius proceeded: "The right, undefiled, and true faith, which the ancient eyewitnesses and writers have transmitted to us (ὑπηρέται γενόμενοι τοῦ λόγου; ministri sermonis), which the holy apostles have taught us, and, through them, the Holy Fathers of the Councils of Nicaea, Constantinople, Ephesus, and Chalcedon, and other orthodox fathers — such a pure faith we have always preached in the churches, and we preach it to you now, oh beloved ones. And we excommunicate all heretics and their adherents, especially Arius, Eunomius, Macedonius, the enemy of the Holy Spirit (πνευματομάχον), Ebion, Photeinus, Marcellus, Theodotus, Artemas, Paul of Samosata, Nestorius, the man-worshipper (ἀνθρωπολάτρην), the impious Valentinus, Scythianus, Manes, Marcion, Bardesanes, Apollinaris, Eutyches, with all other heretics. And along with all these, we excommunicate the impious Severus the Acephalus, schismatic and hostile to the Holy Catholic and Apostolic Church, and his impious doctrine; he had excommunicated our holy orthodox fathers, and made schism and troubles for the orthodox churches, that is for the entire world." Here the crowd interrupted the archbishop, crying: "One God who has done this; one God; one faith. Excommunicate Mandrites!" And Epiphanius, yielding to the crowd, proclaimed: "We equally excommunicate Joannes (John) Mandrites, the schismatic and God-denying, who took his impious doctrine from Severus. So let the abovementioned Severus the Acephalus be excommunicated and John Mandrites and their impious doctrine with their followers. Anathema (ἀνάθεμα καὶ κατάθεμα) in the name of the Father, the Son, and the Holy Ghost, in heaven and on earth, in this time and in time to come, amen!"

The crowd cried: "Amen, amen, amen! Long live the archbishop

Epiphanius! Long live the Count (*comes*) John. Excommunicate all heretics. Peace to the Mother of God (μίαν ἀργίαν τῇ θεοτόκῳ; *unum otium Dei genitrici*). The Trinity has triumphed. Announce the service (σύναξιν). The cross has triumphed. Return the bishops translated against the canons (ἄνω βάλε τὸν πριγκιπίας [τοὺς πρίνκιπας]; ἄνω βάλε τοὺς μεταβάτας; *sursum mitte principes. Sursum mitte* μεταβάτας). He who does not say this is not faithful. This hour pleases the Fathers, God, and the Augustus. Enter and open [the church] of the Mother of God (τὴν θεοτόκον; *aperi Dei genitricem*); enter and open [the church] which you have received (παρέλαβες). The Jews (Ἰουδαῖοι) rejoice; open the church of the Mother of God. The Jews rejoice because the inside [of the church] is closed (ἠσφάλισται τὰ ἔσω; *quoniam clausa sunt quae intus*). Enter (εἴσβα). Sanctify (the church) which they have defiled (ἣν ἐκοίνωσαν; *sanctifica quam communicaverunt*).[37] There is no Anastasius; the orthodox Justin reigns. There is no Manichaean; the orthodox Justin reigns, the new Constantine; he is no Manichaean, like Anastasius. Long live Patriarch John, long live the orthodox Epiphanius. Excommunicate Mandrites' cousin (ἀνεψιόν; *nepotem*). Excommunicate those who are against you. Peace (ἀργίαν, *otium*) to the city. Open [the church] which they plundered. One God, one faith! The rebel against the Trinity, Amantius, is dead. Put on new clothes [that is, adorn the altar] which they stripped off (ἔνδυσον ἣν ἐγύμνωσαν). Perform the lamplight service (λυχνικόν), announce the congregation. Oh, Holy Trinity, give him health. Long live all orthodox. Excommunicate Helias of Botrys. Long live Patriarch Epiphanius! Long live the Augustus and the Augusta Euphemia. Victory to the emperor, the expeller of the Acephalus, the expeller of heretics."

Then Bishop John of Ptolemais addressed the congregation, saying: "We excommunicate all those whom our archbishop and metropolitan excommunicated, and all heresies as well, particularly Severus the Acephalus and Manichaean, an impious man and an enemy to God, and John Mandrites, an impious man and an enemy to God; we

---

[37] An error occurs in the Latin translation: ἐκοίνωσαν does not mean *communicaverunt* but defiled. Evidently the translators confused the verb κοινόω with κοινωνέω.

turn away from communion with them, and proclaim them hostile to and enemies of the name of Christians. Let them be excommunicated in the name of the Father, the Son, and the Holy Ghost, in heaven and on earth, in this time and in the time to come. Amen."

After him, Bishop Theodorus of Porphyreon and Bishop Helias of Rachlenai ('Ραχληνῶν) made the same proclamation. And the crowd exclaimed: "One God Christ reigns. Long live the bishops; long live the orthodox! 'Blessed be the Lord God, for He hath visited and redeemed His people'" (Luke, I, 68).

Since the crowd remained waiting for the announcement of a religious service in the Church of the Virgin Mary, Archbishop Epiphanius said: "Since now it is late, and since it is time to celebrate the divine liturgy by which we worship God for the profit of our souls, and since there will be many things to be read, it is enough to say that next Sunday in the same Church of the Virgin Mary, we shall read the rest and excommunicate again the Acephalus and all his followers." And after this, the archdeacon Zacharias announced: "We notify your love that next Sunday in the Church of the Holy Mary at Yampsyphis [ἐν Ἰαμψύφοις] [38] we shall celebrate a religious service to the glory of our Lord Christ, the holy Virgin Mary, the safety, victory, and long life of our Christ-loving emperor Justin, the most pious empress Euphemia, and the high officials (τῶν μειζόνων ἐξουσιῶν), the most holy archbishop John of the imperial city, and the holy Synod which is held there. On the morning of the same Sunday, we shall meet here, in order to come with psalm-singing, candles, and incense to that church and celebrate the liturgy. Let us meet all of us, men and women!" After the deacon's announcement, the archbishop himself made the same announcement. Then the crowd exclaimed: "Expel the ephorus (ἔφορον); expel all schismatics. Anathema to schismatics, anathema to those who accept one of them. No one shall accept any clerical schismatic. No one shall accept those who fight against the cross." Then the Archbishop Epiphanius to close the meeting said: "On Saturday evening in the Church of the Holy Mary we shall celebrate a lamp-

---

[38] Ἰάμψυφα or Ἰάμψυφοι is probably a certain quarter at Tyre. I have as yet found no information about it.

light service (λυχνικόν)." [39] And when the crowd had quieted, the meeting came to an end.

This vivid contemporary report of the stormy meeting of September 16, 518, in the chief church of Tyre, compiled by an unknown writer, is interesting in several respects. The many exclamations in honor of Justin, Empress Euphemia, and Patriarch John of Constantinople are not surprising; such exclamations always occur on similar occasions. But some of them are rather unusual. The crowd four times shouted the name of the patrician *stratelates* orthodox Vitalian, who was evidently very popular in Palestine; and while the name of Vitalian with his new titles was uttered four times, the name of Justinian, as was the case also at the turbulent meetings of July 15 and 16 in Constantinople, was not uttered at all. Evidently in the popular imagination at the outset of Justin's reign the name of Vitalian, especially because of the orthodox sympathies which he had revealed under Anastasius, quite overshadowed the name of Justinian. The report also gives a very interesting chronological detail: the crowd cried that Amantius was dead. In other words, on September 16, 518, the inhabitants of Tyre knew that Amantius had already been executed. The report gives the name of the local Count (*comes*) John. The archbishop Epiphanius of Tyre is several times called the patriarch. We learn that the local Tyrian cleric John Mandrites, one of Severus' adherents, who was involved in trade operations, was excommunicated. Severus himself is often called Severus the Acephalus or simply the Acephalus.

Also from the text we learn that the solemn religious service of September 16, 518, continuously interrupted by tumultuous scenes of popular exclamations and demands, took place in the ancient church of Tyre. The same source reveals that another church, that of the Mother of God, had been closed, evidently by monophysites, and robbed of its valuables. The crowd several times urged the bishop and the clergy to go and open the church, and finally the bishop announced that the following Saturday and Sunday a lamplight service and the liturgy would be celebrated there.

---

[39] In the Greek ritual, λυχνικόν is the introductory part of vespers, which begins when all the candles and lamps have been lit.

THE SYNOD IN SYRIA SECUNDA

Along with the Synods of Jerusalem and Tyre, a similar synod was held by the Bishop of Syria Secunda under the presidency of the "humblest" bishop of this region, Cyrus of Mariamne (Μαριάμνη). In their synodal letter [40] to the "Archbishop and Ecumenical Patriarch," John of Constantinople, the bishops express their joy that now "the most pious and orthodox emperor" is reigning, who will pay heed to their letter and "liberate the holy churches of God from injury which corrupts the soul; so that the pure grain will remain uncorrupted in his pious empire after the darnel has been weeded out." Declaring their unconditional adherence to the decree of the Synod of Constantinople, they stated that they had excommunicated and deposed not only Severus of Antioch but also his associate the impious bishop Peter of Apamea who "against any ecclesiastical sanction had snatched (ὑφαρπάσαντα) the episcopate of Apamea." Listing the many crimes of Peter, they requested from the Patriarch of Constantinople and his synod confirmation of their sentence and submission of the matter to the emperor. The letter was subscribed by the president of the synod, Bishop Cyrus of Mariamne, and by Zoilus of Recphane (Raphanensis), Severianus of Arethusa, Cosmas of Epiphania, Eusebius of Larissa. This list of course is not complete, as is shown by the words at the close "and others" (καὶ οἱ λοιποί).

The accusations against Peter of Apamea and the enumeration of his crimes and transgressions which are found in the synodal letter were based on many documents. A very large dossier contains testimonies and opinions of a vast number of clericals and monks of Syria Secunda, compiled during the administration of the "most magnificent prefect of the province" (ἐπὶ τοῦ μεγαλοπρεπεστάτου τῆς ἐπαρχίας ἄρχοντος). These documents appended to the synodal letter draw a very vivid picture of general resentment among the clerics against the hated Peter of Apamea; the testimonies are sealed by numerous signatures.[41] There are two special documents: the address of the clergy of the metropolitan Church of God of Apamea to the most holy fathers and bishops

---

[40] Mansi, VIII, 1093–1098.
[41] Mansi, VIII, 1097–1136.

of the province of Syria Secunda (VIII, 1097–1120), and the Libellus of the monks of Apamea to their bishops concerning Peter's crimes (VIII, 1129–1136).

Some signatories in addition add their vows for the "long life" of the emperor. Flavius Joannes Palladius Eutychianus, *comes et praeses*, who also testified against Peter, wished "long life" also to the *magister militum* Vitalian, who is worthy of the emperor (*dignus imperatore*; ἄξιος Βιταλιανὸς τοῦ βασιλέως).[42] These vows once more indicate that at this time the figure of Vitalian completely overshadowed that of the emperor's nephew Justinian.

There is no doubt that about the same time in many other cities of the Byzantine Empire similar synods took place for the rejection of the monophysitic heresy and its adherents. Emperor Justin, after confirming the decrees of the Synod of Constantinople, expressly demanded this rejection.[43]

JUSTIN AND POPE HORMISDAS IN 518

The restoration of the decrees of the Synod of Chalcedon which became the center of the policy of Justin's government inevitably raised the question of reëstablishing normal relations with the Pope. Justin's contemporary in Rome was Hormisdas (514–523). His church relations with the monophysitically inclined Anastasius, Justin's predecessor, had been frequent and tense; and they had ended with the emperor's blunt letter of July 11, 517, in which he wrote: "From henceforth we shall suppress in silence our requests, thinking it absurd to show the courtesy of prayers to those who, with arrogance in their mouth, refuse even to be entreated. We can endure insults and contempt, but we cannot permit ourselves to be commanded." [44] After this letter there was no further correspondence between Hormisdas and the old emperor, who died a year later on the night of July 8, 518.

---

[42] Mansi, VIII, 1119–1120.

[43] Hefele, *Conciliengeschichte*, II, 692 (§ 233). Hefele-Leclercq, II, 2, 1049–1050. English translation by W. Clark, IV, 120.

[44] *Coll. Avellana*, no. 138 (p. 565): "injuriari enim et adnullari sustinere possumus, juberi non possumus." On the *Collectio Avellana* see the following note. See E. Caspar, *Geschichte des Papsttums von den Anfängen bis zur Höhe der Weltherrschaft*, II (Tübingen, 1933), 147–148. P. Charanis, *Church and State in the Later Roman Empire: The Religious Policy of Anastasius the First*, p. 76.

The new orientation in Constantinople was exceedingly welcome in Rome, and the Pope impatiently waited for official confirmation of such a momentous change.

In the eyes of a monophysite Syrian historian of the sixth century, John of Ephesus, the new Constantinopolitan orientation appeared thus: "After the decease of the believing King Anastasius who is among the saints, when Justin was set over the kingdom, he made a beginning of divisions and contentions in the church of God by introducing the impious Synod of Chalcedon; and from that time forward by order of the same schismatic king everyone who did not assent to the reception and introduction of the Synod lived under persecution and expulsion." [45] According to another monophysite writer, Michael the Syrian, at the very outset of Justin's reign a comet appeared, which filled everyone with fear; and in the superstitious medieval imagination of the masses of the Near East, this heavenly body portended apostasy, destruction, and the ruin of the church, all of which disasters would shortly occur.[46]

THE CHALCEDONIAN REACTION UNDER JUSTIN AND THE PAPACY

In Justin's religious policy his most cherished aim was to resume normal relations with Rome as soon as possible.[47] As early as the first

[45] W. J. van Douwen and J. P. N. Land, *Joannis episcopi Ephesi Syri Monophysitae Commentarii de beatis orientalibus,* Verhandelingen der Koninklijke Akademie van Wetenschappen, Afdeeling Letterkunde, XVIII (Amsterdam, 1889), 67. John of Ephesus, *Lives of the Eastern Saints,* E. W. Brooks, I, *Patrologia Orientalis,* XVII, 187.

[46] *Michel le Syrien,* IX, 12; transl. by Chabot, II, p. 170.

[47] Our best source on relations between Constantinople and Rome is the copious correspondence between these two cities. A valuable mine of information is found in the so-called *Collectio Avellana,* which contains a rich selection from papal records, but which unfortunately breaks off in the year 521 so that it fails to give any letters from Pope Hormisdas for the last two years of his pontificate (he died on August 6, 523). In the *Collectio Avellana* the letters are not presented in chronological order. *Epistulae imperatorum pontificum aliorum Avellana quae dicitur Collectio,* ed. Otto Günther, I–II (Vienna, 1895–1898), CSEL, vol. XXXV. Altogther 244 letters and other documents, beginning with the year 367, are included. The name *Avellana* has no justification for existence today; it was given to the collection in the eighteenth century by the two learned brothers Ballerini, because the collection had once been in possession of the monastery S. Crucis in Fonte Avellana in Umbria (Italy). The collection now should be called "The Collection of the Vatican manuscript 3787." But for

of August, three weeks after his elevation and ten days after the Synod of Constantinople which was held on July 20, 518, Justin sent his first message to Pope Hormisdas through one of his high officials (*vir spectabilis*), Alexander. In the letter he informed the Pope of his election. He wrote as follows: "We declare by this sacred letter to your Sanctity that first of all with the benevolent help of the indivisible Trinity, as well as through the election of the highest officials of our sacred palace, the most venerable Senate, and the most powerful army, we have been elected and confirmed against our will and in spite of our protest. Therefore we beg that by your saintly prayers you may supplicate the divine power that the beginnings of our rule be strengthened." [48] In this letter three elements which raised Justin to the throne are plainly indicated: the palace officers, the Senate, and the army. The people (ὁ δῆμος) are not mentioned.

Five weeks later on September 7 three letters to Pope Hormisdas were drawn up in Constantinople: one from the Patriarch John, the second from the emperor himself, and the third from his nephew Justinian. Gratus, *sacri consistorii comes*, was commissioned to deliver these messages to the Pope. We do not know exactly when he left Constantinople on his mission; but we do know that the letters reached Rome on December 20 of the same year, 518; in other words, three

---

convenience scholars continue to use the old name. O. Günther, *Avellana-Studien, Sitzungsber. der philos.-hist. Classe der Ak. der Wiss. zu Wien*, CXXXIV (1896), 1. Another collection: A. Thiel, *Epistolae romanorum pontificum genuinae et quae ad eos scriptae sunt*, I, A. S. Hilario usque ad S. Hormisdam, ann. 461–523 (Brunsbergae, 1868). This volume contains 150 letters and some additions going up to the year 521. But Thiel's text must always be verified by Günther's edition. See Duchesne, *L'église au sixième siècle*, p. 48, n. 1. These documents have also been published in older collections: Mansi, Migne, Baronius. For information the following are very useful: P. Jaffe-G. Wattenbach, *Regesta pontificum roman-orum*, I (Leipzig, 1885), 104–110. V. Grumel, *Les regestes des actes du patriarcat de Constantinople*, I, 83–89. O. Günther, "Beiträge zur Chronologie der Briefe des Papstes Hormisda," *Sitzungsberichte der philosophisch-historischen Classe der Akademie des Wissenschaften zu Wien*, CXXVI, XI (1891), pp. 50. The correspondence of Pope Hormisdas from 514 to 521, which is of the greatest value as a source for our study, has survived only in the *Collectio Avellana*, with the exception of a very few pieces. The best presentation of the material which the *Collectio Avellana* contains on the opening years, 518–521, of Justin's reign is found in Erich Caspar's work *Geschichte des Papsttums*, II, 149–181.

[48] *Coll. Avell.*, no. 141 (p. 586). Thiel, no. 41 (pp. 830–831), Mansi, VIII, 434. Baronius, *s.a.* 518, 67.

and a half months passed before they were delivered to the Pope. In
his message (*relatio*) the Patriarch John, saluting the Pope as his
dearest brother in Christ, professed his own faith according to the
acts of the four Ecumenical Councils and expressed the hope that the
true faith would be established for ever by their joint efforts. Then
he added that the name of the former Pope Leo and that of Hormisdas
himself would be inserted and commemorated in the diptychs. He
ended by asking the Pope to send to Constantinople as legates men
"peaceable and worthy of the Apostolic See, in order that in this part
too our God Christ, who through you has preserved this peace to the
world, may be glorified." [49]

In his letter Justin speaks of the Patriarch John and other bishops
who assembled in Constantinople to establish the union of the churches
on the basis of the true and orthodox faith, and begs Hormisdas to
support their effort and pray for them and the empire whose rule has
been entrusted to him from heaven. Then Justin asks the Pope to send
legates to Constantinople, and very highly recommends to his attention Gratus, who would deliver the letters in Rome.[50]

The letter of Justin's nephew, Justinian, of the same date is much
more interesting than the letters of the patriarch and the emperor. The
general tone of his letter is much more definite and decisive than theirs,
and shows once more that although for the time being he was behind
the throne, he was still the leading figure from the very beginning of
his uncle's reign. He says: "As soon as our lord the invincible emperor,
who has always most ardently held to the orthodox faith, had by the
will of God received the princely fillet (*infulas principales*), he announced at once to the bishops that the peace of the church must be
restored, and this has already in a great degree been accomplished."
In dealing with the name of the Patriarch Acacius they must have the
papal consent. Therefore "our most serene emperor" had sent in
charge of the imperial letter Gratus, "a sublime man" and Justinian's
closest friend (*unanimum mihi amicum*). Justinian asks the Pope to

[49] *Coll. Avell.*, no. 146 (pp. 591–592). Thiel, no. 43 (pp. 832–833). Mansi, VIII,
436–437. PL, LXIII, 429. Baron., 518, 72. See Grumel, *Les regestes*, no. 210 (pp.
84–85).
[50] *Coll. Avell.*, no. 143 (pp. 587–588). Thiel, no. 42 (p. 831). Mansi, VIII, 435.
PL, LXIII, 428. Baron., 518, 71.

come to Constantinople for final settlement of the union (*ad reliqua concordiae componenda*). Then he proceeds: "We expect your advent without delay; but if some obstacle — which should not be — may detain (*retinuerit*) your coming, then in the meantime do not delay to send suitable plenipotentiaries (*sacerdotes idoneos*), because all the people of our country converted to the union will not endure delay. Therefore do hasten, *domine sanctissime.*"

Justinian's letter differs considerably from the letters of the patriarch and the emperor. While the two latter ask the Pope only to send legates, Justinian rather categorically asks him to come personally without delay, as if anticipating his future autocratic policy towards Pope Vigilius, who later was summoned to Constantinople by the emperor and forced to remain there for more than seven years. The letter closes with a very interesting remark that the same *vir sublimis* Gratus has also been commanded to visit "the most invincible king." These words clearly indicate that Gratus was commissioned before reaching Rome to call on the powerful Ostrogothic king Theodoric, who is not named in Justinian's letter, but who without doubt is referred to by the words "the most invincible king"; corroboration of this is furnished in an earlier document, 516 A. D., addressed by the Senate of Rome to Emperor Anastasius, in which the name of Theodoric is given in the following terms: "Our lord the most invincible king Theodoric your son." I shall return to this passage a little later.[51]

Pope Hormisdas, most probably in October, 518, answered Justin's short letter of August 1 announcing his election. The Pope expresses the congratulations of the Catholic Church and the hope that religious peace will be reestablished "in the parts of the Orient." Referring to Justin's words that he was elected against his will, the Pope thinks

[51] *Coll. Avell.*, no. 147 (pp. 592–593). Thiel, no. 44 (pp. 833–834). Mansi, VIII, 438. Baron., 518, 74–75. Excerpts from this letter in Caspar, *Geschichte des Papsttums*, II, 150. See O. Günther, "Beiträge zur Chronologie der Briefe des Papstes Hormisda," *Sitzungsberichte der philosophisch-historischen Classe der Ak. der Wiss. zu Wien*, CXXVI (1892), Abh. XI, 19, n. 1. On Theodoric, *Coll. Avell.*, p. 593: "propter causam saepius memoratam ad invictissimum regem religionis quoque negotium filio vestro viro sublimi Grato est injunctum favente domino nostro Iesu Christo." Cf. no. 114 (p. 508): "maxime cum ad hoc et animus domini nostri invictissimi regis Theoderici filii vestri . . ."; also no. 199 (p. 658): "quem ad praecelsum regem Theodoricum super negotiis quibusdam transmisimus." This is Justin's letter to Pope Hormisdas, August 31, 520.

that Justin was elected by heaven (*coelesti judicio*), according to the Apostle: "There is no power but of God; the powers that be are ordained of God" (Romans XIII, 1). "Let those disappear who oppose the peace of the church; let those grow calm (*quiescant*) who, in the shape of shepherds, try to scatter the flock of Christ! This correction (*correctio*) strengthens the power of your empire; because, where God is worshipped rightly, opposition will take no effect." At the close of his message Hormisdas says that he sends this letter of congratulation (*gratulationis paginam*) through the *vir spectabilis* Alexander, who brought Justin's letter to Rome, and hopes to go into details concerning the reunion of the churches through the *vir spectabilis* Gratus.[52]

I am inclined to attribute this letter with most probability to October, 518 on the following grounds. This *gratulationis pagina* of the Pope is his answer to Justin's letter of August 1. Three other letters to the Pope, those of the Patriarch John, Justin, and his nephew Justinian, which are dated September 7 and were commissioned for delivery to Gratus, reached Rome on December 20; as we have noted above, it took three and a half months for them to reach the Pope, too long a time even for the crude transportation facilities of the sixth century. Since the Pope in his letter to Justin mentions not only the name of Alexander, who delivered to him Justin's notification of his elevation, but also that of Gratus, who delivered the letters on December 20, most scholars have believed that Hormisdas wrote this letter after December 20. But such procrastination on the part of the Pope in answering Justin's letter would be unexpected and hard to explain. Justin's announcement was welcome news to the Pope, who certainly would have wished to open negotiations as soon as possible for the reunion of the churches. Now, since we know that on his way to

---

[52] *Coll. Avell.*, no. 142 (pp. 586–587). Thiel, no. 45, p. 834 (*a. 518 c. fin. vel initio a. 519*). Mansi, VIII, 434. P.L., LXIII, 427. Baron., 518, 68–69. See Jaffe-Wattenbach, *Regesta*, I, 104 (801). Apparently referring to this papal letter, Bolotov writes: "Rome wanted no union; it wanted victory and domination; it wanted to play the part of the protector of orthodoxy and executioner of heretics. To the declarations of the embassy Rome replied that measures on its side would be taken for the restoration of the union." Bolotov, "Lectures," III, *Christianskoe Chtenie* (June, 1915), p. 361 (in Russian).

Rome Gratus paid a visit to Theodoric at Ravenna, where he apparently was detained for some time, the problem is solved. Hormisdas may easily have heard of Gratus' arrival at Ravenna and his sojourn there at the court of the Ostrogothic king before he came to Rome. In other words, the Pope's answer to Justin's first letter of August 1 was sent from Rome not after December 20 but before, most probably in the middle of October, when Gratus was still at Ravenna.[53]

THE QUESTION OF THE COUNCIL OF ROME IN 518

In connection with Gratus' arrival at Rome when he brought three letters to the Pope received on December 20, 518, there is a rather vague indication that Hormisdas held a synod in Rome to take counsel on the subject of the reunion with Constantinople. In Mansi's *Collection of the Councils* we read: "The Roman Council concerning expunging from the diptychs the names of the Constantinopolitan Bishops Acacius, Euphemius, and Macedonius is celebrated in Rome under Hormisdas in the year 518." Then the text runs as follows: "After receiving the letters of Patriarch John of Constantinople, Justin, and Justinian, the Pope for a little while (*paulisper*) detained Gratus in Rome; then he convoked an assembly (*conventum*) of bishops, who after diligent examination of the question came to the conclusion that it would be possible to receive the Oriental Church to the communion of the Apostolic See, if the schismatic Acacius should be condemned, and his name eliminated from the diptychs, and then, if the names of Euphemius and Macedonius, who were defiled by the same stroke of schism, should also be eliminated and expunged from the diptychs. After that a pontifical legation was designated which should carry into effect the decree of the synod. Then the papal embassy left for Constantinople" (Mansi, VIII, 579–580).

In his *Ecclesiastical Annals* Cardinal Baronius gives the same account with some additions. He says that the Pope retained Gratus till the following year, when he sent legates to Constantinople. Then Baronius reports that for more successful and more documented discussions at

---

[53] See a very convincing discussion in Günther, *Beiträge*, pp. 16–18. *Coll. Avell.*, no. 142 (p. 586): "mense Octobri vel Novembri." After December 20 supported by Baron., 518, 69. Thiel, 45, p. 834. Jaffe-Wattenbach, I, 104 (801).

the Council, the letters of the former Popes Simplicius, Felix, Gelasius, and Symmachus, which had dealt with the same subject, were brought from the church archives; and on the basis of this material the final decree was made at the Council of 518 (Baron. 518, 82–83).

But since Baronius does not mention the source of his information and since in the rather numerous letters of Hormisdas for this period there is no reference to any council, many scholars are inclined to believe that no council was held in Rome in 518, that neither in Constantinople nor in Rome was the question raised of any council, and that the Pope, happy to see the matter settled more simply, was entirely satisfied if his formula or *libellus* was merely signed by both sides. The text of this formula or *libellus* had already been prepared during the negotiations with Constantinople under Justin's predecessor, Anastasius.[54]

In my opinion, after Pope Hormisdas received Gratus, he must without doubt have consulted some prelates on the subject. The consultation, however, was not an official council, but merely a sort of assembly of the representatives of the Roman Church presided over by the Pope. Baronius and Mansi did not invent their information. An assembly was held with most probability at the end of December of 518 or at the beginning of January 519. It was not, however, a formal council.

The legates to Constantinople carried with them the papal formula or *libellus* which the Patriarch of Constantinople and all the bishops of the empire were to sign as a condition of reunion with Rome. The most essential part of this document runs as follows: "The first condition of salvation is to keep the rule of the true faith and not to deviate in anything from the constitutions of the Fathers. As the sentence of our Lord Jesus Christ cannot be passed in silence who says, 'Thou art Peter, and upon this rock I will found My church' (Matthew XVI, 18), these words are effectively proved by reality, because it is in the Apostolic See that the catholic religion has always been preserved without blemish (*extra maculam*). Unwilling in any way to be sepa-

[54] See Hefele, *op. cit.*, II, 694; Hefele-Leclercq, II, 2, 1051; English, IV, 121. Duchesne, *L'église au sixième siècle*, pp. 49–50. Fliche-Martin, *Histoire de l'église*, IV, 423, n. 5. The papal formula in *Coll. Avell.*, no. 116b (pp. 520–521): March 18, 517. See Günther, *Beiträge*, p. 4, n. 2.

rated from this hope and this faith, and following the constitutions of the Fathers, we anathematize all heresies (Nestorius, Eutyches, Dioscorus of Alexandria, Aelurus, Acacius). On the other hand we accept and approve all the epistles of the blessed Pope Leo on the Christian religon, following in everything, as we have said above, the Apostolic See and proclaiming all its constitutions. And I hope to be admitted in communion with the Apostolic See, in which is found the entire, true, and perfect stability of the Christian religion, promising not to recite henceforward in the sacred mysteries the names of those who have been separated from the communion of the Catholic Church, i.e. who disagree with the Apostolic See. If I try, in some way, to deviate from my profession, I declare by my (this) sentence (*sententia*) myself to agree with those whom I have condemned. I have signed with my own hand this my profession and sent it to thee, to Hormisdas, the holy and venerable Pope of the city of Rome." [55]

THE PAPAL EMBASSY TO CONSTANTINOPLE IN 519

As we know, in their letters to the Pope Patriarch John and Justin asked him to send legates to Constantinople, and Justinian urged him to come personally, and only if this was impossible, to send legates. Hormisdas did not go himself, but decided to send a delegation with definite instructions concerning reunion. The imperial messenger Gratus had left Rome for Constantinople some time before the papal delegation, and reached the capital before it, so that the opinion sometimes advanced that Gratus and the legates traveled east together is to be absolutely discarded.[56] Owing to the great power and influence

---

[55] This *libellus* is to be found among other documents in the Letter of Pope Hormisdas to all the bishops of Spain: *Dilectissimis fratribus universis episcopis per Hispaniam constitutis Hormisda*. In this letter the Pope explains to the Spanish bishops what they should do if someone of the Oriental clerics asked to be admitted into their communion. See the text of the *libellus* in Mansi, VIII, 467; Migne, *PL*, LXIII, 459–460; *Coll. Avellana*, No. 116b (pp. 520–522). A portion of the *libellus* in a French translation is reproduced by M. Jugie, *Le Schisme byzantin*, pp. 73–74. In Russian, the *libellus* is reproduced by V. Bolotov, "Lectures," III, *Christianskoe Chtenie* (June, 1915), pp. 362–363. One Greek writer remarked, "The demands of Rome were hard and excessively unjust." Ἰωάννης Εὐστράτιος, Σευῆρος ὁ Μονοφυσίτης, πατριάρχης Ἀντιοχείας (Leipzig, 1894), p. 56.

[56] The best account on this question in Günther, *Beiträge*, pp. 18–24. See also Caspar, *Geschichte des Papsttums*, II, 150–151. *Coll. Avell.*, no. 159 (p. 607):

of Theodoric in Italy the Pope sent these legates to the Byzantine court with his knowledge and on his advice.

Gratus left Rome at the beginning of January, 519, carrying two letters from Hormisdas: one to Justin and one to the Patriarch John. In his letter to the emperor, the Pope urges him to be firm in his initial task of obtaining religious peace, refers to the memorandum which he was sending at the same time in his letter to the patriarch, explaining what they should do, and at the end mentions the name of the messenger Gratus.[57] In his letter to the patriarch, the Pope expresses general satisfaction at his letter, calls his attention to Patriarch Acacius whose memory should be condemned, and then writes: "We expect from your love, with the help of the all-powerful God, better acts." Then he notifies the patriarch that a special memorandum has been appended to the letter, and asks him to sign it and send it back to Rome. At the end, he warmly compliments the imperial messenger Gratus.[58]

It is strange that Gratus was not entrusted with a letter from Hormisdas to Justinian in answer to the one of September 7. There is no reason to surmise that the Pope might have been a little offended by Justinian's demand that he come personally to Constantinople, however, a demand rather blunt from the point of view of papal etiquette. The papal letters to Justinian which have survived show no such feeling. Probably the answer was sent but has not survived or

---

"Redditis mihi litteris vestrae sanctitatis, in Christo frater carissime, per Gratum clarissimum comitem et nunc per Germanum et Johannem reverentissimos episcopos . . ." From this text it is clear that Gratus and the legates did not go to Constantinople together. The *Liber Pontificalis* erroneously relates that the papal legates entered Constantinople *una cum Grato*. Duchesne, I, 270; ed. T. Mommsen, *Gestorum pontificum romanorum*, I, 129 and 259 (Epitome Feliciana) in *MGH; The Book of the Popes (Liber Pontificalis)*, transl. by L. R. Loomis, I (New York, 1916), 128. Cf. Duchesne, *L'église au sixième siècle*, p. 49: the legates went with Gratus.

[57] *Coll. Avell.*, no. 144 (pp. 588–589). Thiel, 46, 835–836. Mansi, VIII, 435–436. Bar., 518, 77–78. Jaffe-Wattenbach, *Regesta*, I, 104 (no. 802).

[58] *Coll. Avell.*, nol. 145 (pp. 589–591). Thiel, 47, 836–837. Mansi, VIII, 437. Bar., 518, 79–81. Jaffe-Wattenbach, I, 104 (no. 803). Among other things, Hormisdas writes: "de caritate siquidem tua meliora dei omnipotentis expectamus auxilio" (*Coll. Avell.*, p. 590, line 11–12). On the attitude of Pope Hormisdas towards Patriarch Acacius, see W. Haacke, "Die Glaubensformel des Papstes Hormisdas im Acacianischen Schisma," *Analecta Gregoriana*, XX (Rome, 1939), 22–26.

for the time being has not been discovered. In any case, the letters of Hormisdas which we do have to Justinian contain no mention of Justinian's demand for the Pope's personal visit to Constantinople. The letters carried by Gratus make no mention of the forthcoming papal embassy; hence we may conclude that at the moment of Gratus' departure from Rome, at the beginning of January, 519, the question of the embassy had not yet been definitely decided. As has been noted above, Theodoric had to be consulted on the matter and his authorization secured.

Soon after Gratus' departure, all formalities were settled and the members of the embassy were designated. They were as follows: two bishops, Germanus of Capua and John (See unknown), the priest Blandus, the deacon Felix, and a notary Peter. But the most important figure in the group was the deacon Dioscorus, a Greek from Alexandria, who of course was master of the Greek language, was very familiar with Byzantine life and customs, and had already distinguished himself as an ingenious diplomat. He enjoyed Hormisdas' absolute confidence, and had already proved his talents of eloquence and persuasion as a diplomat at the Roman court in 506. Dioscorus was attached to the embassy as interpreter, skillful negotiator, and subtle observer.[59]

The embassy left Rome in all probability in the middle or at the end of January, 519. They carried eight letters and a secret instruction (*indiculus*) as to their line of conduct; among the letters was one to be delivered on their way to the capital to the Praetorian Prefect of Illyricum who resided at Thessalonica. The rest of the papal letters were to be brought to Constantinople.[60] I shall give in a very concise form their contents.

In his lengthy and rather verbose letter to Justin, Hormisdas, using the text of the Epistle of St. Paul to the Philippians (4, 18), says: "The odor of your sweet smell has reached us," and then proceeds to de-

---

[59] *Lib. Pont.*, Duchesne, 270; Mommsen, 128 and 259; Loomis, 127. See Caspar, *op. cit.*, II, 151 and n. 4. Duchesne, *L'église au sixième siècle*, p. 49. On Dioscorus' earlier activities, Caspar, p. 116; Loomis, p. 118, n. 1.

[60] See Günther, *Beiträge*, p. 21. Caspar, II, 151 (seven letters). *Coll. Avell.*, no. 153 (p. 601): "Hormisda praefecto praetorio Thessalonicensi et ceteris illustribus a pari." Mansi, VIII, 448.

velop the usual subjects of the Council of Chalcedon and the *constituta* of Pope Leo. He condemns Acacius, and after a complimentary mention of Gratus announces the sending of his embassy; he gives the names of his official legates, omitting Dioscorus, who as we know was attached to the embassy as interpreter.

In a brief and commonplace letter to Justinian, the Pope mentions only one name to be condemned, that of Acacius, and concludes with the announcement of his legation. To the Patriarch John he writes: "You know by which way you must come to the communion (*consortium*) with the blessed Apostle Peter." After stereotyped references to the Synod of Chalcedon and the dogma of the Blessed Leo, he insists on the necessity of the condemnation of Acacius and his followers, and asks: "If you praise everything with us, why do you not condemn everything with us? Then you will love with us what we venerate, if along with us you will abhor what we detest." At the end the Pope lists the names of his legates, including Dioscorus. In his letter to the Empress Euphemia, the Pope says: "Since the sacred resolution (*sanctum propositum*) of your husband is known, we confidently (*fiducialiter*) send this letter to your Clemency (*clementia*) in order that through you (*per vos*) your husband's piety may be more stimulated to make peace in the church."

The papal letters to the Constantinopolitan Archdeacon Theodosius, to Celer, who as we know had taken part in Justin's elevation, to Patricius, and to two Byzantine ladies, Anastasia and Palmatia, contain requests for help in the matter of reunion and announce the sending of the legates.[61]

The special instruction (*indiculus*) on how to behave when they

---

[61] The letter to Justin: *Coll. Avell.*, no. 149 (pp. 594–598). Thiel, 50, 840–843. Mansi, VIII, 442–444. Baron., 519, 9–13. The letter to Justinian: *Coll. Avell.*, no. 148 (pp. 593–594). Thiel, 48, 837. Mansi, VIII, 440–441. See also *Coll. Avell.*, no. 154 (pp. 601–602): the same notification; an answer to Justinian's lost letter. The letter to the Patriarch: *Coll. Avell.*, no. 150 (598–599). Thiel, 52, 845. Mansi, VIII, 445–446. Baron., 519, 18–20. See also *Coll. Avell.*, no. 151 (p. 600): on the same subject; an answer to John's lost letter (after September 7). Grumel, *Les regestes*, I, 85 (no. 211). The letter to the empress: *Coll. Avell.*, no. 156 (pp. 603–604). Thiel, 51, p. 844. Mansi, VIII, 444–445. Baron., 519, 15. The letters to Theodosius, Celer, Patricius, Anastasia, Palmatia: *Coll. Avell.*, nos. 155, 152, 157 (pp. 602–603, 600–601, 604–605). Thiel, 53, 54, 56, pp. 846, 847, 848. Mansi, VIII, 447–449. Baron., 519, 23, 28, 32. Anastasia, of course, is not Theodora's sister.

reached the territory of the empire advised the legates that if on their way to the capital they met bishops who were ready to subscribe the instruction, they should accept them and give them the holy communion; if some bishops did not want to accept the instruction, they should nevertheless be treated mildly (*sub sacerdotali affectione*); but the legates were not allowed to eat together with them or take victuals from them, except that in case of need they might accept means of transportation or hospitality lest these bishops think themselves disdainfully despised. At their arrival in Constantinople, they should take up their abode in the building assigned by the emperor, and before they saw him receive no one but those sent by him or those known to belong to the Roman church.[62] Then they should present their letters of salutation to the emperor and express all their joy on what he is doing for the benefit of reunion. If the emperor suggests that they see the Bishop of Constantinople, they should answer that in this respect they have exact directions; so that if the bishop is ready to follow them, they will meet him with pleasure; but if he fails to follow the exhortation of the Apostolic See, there is no reason to meet him, because they have not come for disputes or discussions. If the emperor wishes to become acquainted with their instruction, they should show it to him. And if the emperor agrees to excommunicate Acacius but says that his successors who sent into exile several bishops for their defense of the Synod of Chalcedon should be mentioned in the diptychs, the legates should explain that they are not authorized to change anything in the instruction, which condemns Acacius' successors as well as himself. If they are unable to make the emperor change his mind, they may come to a compromise: Acacius must be excommunicated according to the instruction, but the names of his successors may be passed over in silence and simply erased from the diptychs. If the bishop of Constantinople agrees to this formula, he may be admitted to the reunion with Rome.

The instruction (*libellus*) must be announced in the presence of the people (*praesente populo*); if this cannot be done, at least in a consistory (*in secretario*) in the presence of clerics and archimandrites.

---

[62] *Indiculus quem acceperunt legati nostri qui supra. Coll. Avell.*, no. 158 (pp. 605–607). Thiel, 49, 838–840. Mansi, VIII, 441–442. Baron., 519, 3–7.

After this the legates should ask the emperor to notify the Bishop of Constantinople to proclaim his own confession in full accord with the *libellus* in order to be accepted into the union of the Apostolic See. Other bishops should do the same thing. If the emperor meets some difficulties in this respect, the Bishop of Constantinople should notify his parochial and other metropolitans what he himself has done. The legates by any means whatever should exact from him that all, even those who live in far off regions, should be informed about this fact.

We see from the instruction that the legates were subject to some restrictions as to their behavior in Constantinople; but on their way thither they were authorized to admit to the reunion and Holy Communion those who were ready to accept the papal formula.

In all probability, the legates left Italy at Brundisium, crossed the straits, landed at Aulona (Valona), a port on the western coast of the Balkan Peninsula, in the Byzantine province of New Epirus (*Epirus Nova*), and started their journey east along the great Via Egnatia which through Thessalonica led to Constantinople. The route of the legation and the duration of the journey are well known from the letters sent by the legates to the Pope from various places on their way east. In the papal interests, their journey through the Balkan Peninsula, at the beginning at least, was very successful. In Aulona the bishop of the city welcomed the legates and was ready to accept the papal *libellus*. But it was at Scampae (*Scampina civitas*, now Elbasan, in Albania) that the legates had a real triumph. The bishop of the city, Troius, came out to meet them accompanied by his clergy and people. He wrote his confession in accord with the papal instruction, which was read by the papal notary Peter, a member of the embassy, in the presence of the clergy and the nobility of the city. A solemn service was celebrated in the Church (*basilica*) of St. Peter. The legates were overwhelmed with joy. They wrote: "It is difficult to see in any other people such devotion, such praises to God, such tears, such joy. Almost the whole population welcomed us, men and women with candles, soldiers (*milites*) with crosses. Masses were celebrated. No name obnoxious to religion was recited. The papal bishop Germanus celebrated mass; and they promised to recite no names but those which the Apostolic See has accepted."

173

In addition, in the same city of Scampae the imperial messengers, the count (*comes*) Stephanus, a relative of Vitalian, and Leontius met the legates. The messengers had been ordered by the emperor to go as far as Italy to meet the papal envoys, and they did not know that the latter had already reached the territory of the empire; the meeting at Scampae was by mere chance. As has already been noted, the messengers brought news from Constantinople; they reported that the property of a certain senator Patricius had been confiscated, and that he himself had been exiled. The legates write that they cannot tell the real cause of Patricius' disgrace, "because it is not easy to learn the truth about such matters." It is quite probable that this disgraced senator Patricius was the same man to whom the Pope had addressed a letter (see above). The legates were also told that some officers (*apocrisiarii*) of the church of Thessalonica had been arrested because certain letters had been found in their possession. A man named Filuminus, the *magistrianus* Demetrius, and some other persons, whose names the legates did not know, had also been arrested. I am inclined to believe that these punitive measures were taken in connection with the liquidation of the plot at the very beginning of Justin's reign, which has been described above.

From Scampai the legates went to Lignidus (Lychnidus, now Ochrida) and they were cordially welcomed there also. In their letter to the Pope sent from this city on March 7, 519 (*die Nonarum martiarum*) the legates say that the Bishop of Lignidus, Theodoritus, subscribed the *libellus*, which was then read in one of the churches of the city, so that "everything has been done according to the papal constitution." They close with an expression of their hope that after such successful beginnings God may help the Pope to reach the final "correction of the churches" (*in correctione ecclesiarum*).[63]

At their arrival in Thessalonica the legates delivered to the Praetorian

[63] On the route of the legates before they reached Thessalonica, *Coll. Avell.*, nos. 213–215 (pp. 671–674). Thiel, 59–60, 849–852. Mansi, VIII, 449–450. Baron., 519, 34–38. See Günther, *Beiträge*, p. 22 and n. 1. Caspar, *op. cit.*, II, 152. P. Leporsky, *History of the Exarchate of Thessalonica down to its Annexation to the Constantinopolitan Patriarchate* (St. Petersburg, 1901), pp. 165–166 (in Russian). Bolotov writes that the "ceremonial" train of the papal embassy "savored of terrible Pharisaism." Bolotov, "Lectures," III, *Christianskoe Chtenie* (June, 1915), p. 362 (in Russian).

Prefect of Illyricum, whose residence was there, the brief papal message which we have mentioned above. The Pope, addressing the Prefect as *"vestra amplitudo"* and *"vestra celsitudo,"* asks him to support the papal task and assures him that through his support he will "acquire the fruit of great glory" (*fructum tantae laudis acquirere*). The message was addressed to the Praetorian Prefect of Thessalonica and other *illustres*. The legates were lodged at Thessalonica at the home of Joannes (John), a convinced Catholic and defender of the Council of Chalcedon. The local bishop Dorotheus, however, disappointed the legates. After many disputes on the subject, finally convinced outwardly at least, he declared himself ready to subscribe to the *libellus;* but since the other bishops of his diocese were not present, he proposed to postpone the decisive step until after the Holy Week and Easter (*post dies sanctos*), when a congregation of local bishops would be convoked; and then the bishops also would subscribe to the *libellus*. The future decided otherwise. A few months later Dorotheus appeared openly against the *libellus*, and serious troubles broke out in the city. We shall discuss this deplorable incident later.[64]

From Thessalonica the legates proceeded to Constantinople. On Palm Sunday, March 24, 519, they were quite close to the imperial city. They reached it on Monday of Holy Week, March 25. The capital welcomed the legates with great pomp, reverence, and enthusiasm. At the tenth milestone from the city, the so-called Round Castle (*Castello Rotundo*), the legates were met by Vitalian, Pompeius, nephew of the late Anastasius, and Justinian, as well as by many other illustrious persons. In procession with lighted candles, surrounded by a jubilant crowd, they entered the capital. On Tuesday, March 26, the legates were received by the emperor himself, in the presence of the senate and four bishops whom the Patriarch John had sent in his own name. The legates delivered the papal message to Justin, who received it "with great reverence" (*cum grandi reverentia*). He suggested that the legates meet the patriarch and settle the matter with him peaceably (*pacifico ordine*). But the legates said: "Why should we go to the

---

[64] The letter to the Praetorian Prefect of Thessalonica: *Coll. Avell.*, no. 153 (p. 601). Thiel, 55, 847. Mansi, VIII, 443. Baron., 519, 30. On the arrival of the legates in Thessalonica, *Coll. Avell.*, no. 167 (p. 618). Thiel, 65, p. 858. Mansi, VIII, 454. Baron., 519, 42–43.

bishop for discussion? Our most blessed lord Pope Hormisdas, who has sent us, has ordered us not to dispute (*certare*). But we have in our hands the *libellus*, which all bishops willing to have reconciliation with the Apostolic See have drawn up. If Your Piety orders, it may be read." After the document had been read, the legates immediately added: "Let the four bishops who are here present as representatives of the Constantinopolitan bishop, say if this which is read in the *libellus* is contrary to the true faith." The bishops answered that everything was true. Then the legates said: "Oh Lord Emperor, the bishops have relieved us from great labor and given you a good opportunity to say the truth." And the emperor said to the bishops present, "If this is true, why do you not do so?" Several senators also said: "We are laics. You say that it is true. Do it, and we will follow you."

Another day passed, however, before the patriarch came to a decision. According to the *Liber pontificalis*, he and the clergy of Constantinople "shut themselves up in the great church which is called Santa Sophia and held a council" to discuss the situation. At the beginning the patriarch was unwilling to yield and sent word to the emperor, saying: "Unless the reason be expounded to us why Acacius, the bishop of our city, was condemned, we make no agreement with the Apostolic See." A council was held in the presence of Justin, all the nobility, and the legates. We know that the *libellus* did not allow the legates to enter into any disputation on the subject, but a very ingenious method of solving this difficulty was found. The legates chose the deacon Dioscorus from among themselves to expound the reason, because he was not an official member of the papal delegation but merely attached to it as interpreter and negotiator. By selecting him to speak the legates themselves did not transgress their instructions. And Dioscorus set forth to the emperor and the council the guilt of Acacius so clearly that they all, including Justin, exclaimed together, saying: "Damnation to Acacius here and in eternity."

Such was Justin's will. In vain John attempted to write a special letter to explain his attitude. He was allowed to write only a brief preamble adjoined to the *libellus*, and by this act only was allowed to preserve the fiction of his coming to an independent decision. According to the detailed report of the deacon Dioscorus, this triumph of the papal policy was reached only "after much struggle" (*post multa certamina*). At last on Maundy Thursday in Holy Week, March 28, at the imperial palace in the presence of Justin, the Senate, and the clergy, the Patriarch John signed the libellus. The names of the Patriarch Acacius and his four heretical successors as well as the names of the Emperors Zeno and Anastasius were expunged from the diptychs. In the official reports to the Pope from the members of the embassy on this significant event, Justinian and Vitalian are not mentioned; but without doubt both men were present among the other high officials of the court. The document of the reunion was compiled in Greek and Latin, and a copy in two languages was sent to Rome. According to the *Liber pontificalis*, the original document was kept in the archives of the church.[65] Bolotov makes the comment that the union signed on March 28 was "a disgusting (*omerzitelnaya*) ceremony" (III, 363).

Easter Sunday, March 31, 519, and the holidays of the Easter Week passed in an atmosphere of religious elation and mutual satisfaction that finally the reunion between the two Romes had been achieved. From the far West, the Bishop of Vienna on the Rhone, Avitus, sent the Patriarch of Constantinople his congratulations on the restoration of

---

[65] On the reception of the legates and on the reunion, *Coll. Avell.*, no. 223 (pp. 683–684); no. 167 (pp. 619–621). Both letters of April 22, 519. *Liber Pontificalis*, ed. Duchesne, I, 270; ed. Mommsen, pp. 128–129 and 259–260; transl., by Loomis, pp. 128–129. The author of the *Lib. Pont.* erroneously says that the Emperor Justin himself was among those who met the legates and escorted them to the city. Another blunder of the *Lib. Pont.* has been indicated above; the messenger Gratus in reality came to Constantinople not with the legates but some time earlier. The *Lib. Pont.* relates that the legates were escorted into the city from the so-called Round Castle. This was a fort, Κυκλόβιον, Cyclobion, Στρογγύλον Καστέλλιον, *Castrum Rotundum*, which derived its name from its circular form (Procopius, *De aedificiis*, IV, 8, 4). It was located at or close to the Hebdomon (now Makri-Keui), on the shore of the Sea of Marmora, and stood some two and a half miles from the Golden Gate; it was a link in the chain of coast fortifications defending the approach to the city. A. van Millingen, *Byzantine Constantinople* (London, 1899), pp. 326–327. Millingen erroneously says that the legates were met at the Golden Gate (p. 67). See also D. Beliaev, *Byzantina*, III (St. Petersburg, 1907), 78–86 (in Russian). See Caspar, *op. cit.*, II, 155–157. In his report to the Pope the deacon Dioscorus writes that the patriarch and the clergy discussed the situation not in St. Sophia but in the palace: *in palatio* (*Coll. Avell.*, p. 620). The union was signed on Maundy Thursday — "*hoc est cena domini*" (*Coll. Avell.*, no. 223, p. 683, 28). Only the Latin text of the union has survived. Grumel, *Les regestes*, I, 85 (no. 212). On the archives of the church, *Lib. Pont.*, Duchesne, p. 270; Mommsen, p. 130 and 260; Loomis, p. 129.

peace with the Roman bishop as a symbol of what the two Apostolic Princes should grant to the world. "Who among those who may be called catholics," Avitus proceeds, "would not rejoice at the peace between such great churches (*tantarum et talium ecclesiarum*), at which the world looks as at a double star (*pro gemino sidere*) fixed in the heaven like a sign of faith (*religionis signum*)." [66]

I shall cite some passages from the report of the deacon Dioscorus to Hormisdas which was sent to Rome on April 22, 519 through the subdeacon Pullio. Pointing out again that the satisfactory result was reached "after much struggle" (*post multa certamina*), Dioscorus writes that it would be beyond his capacity to describe the joy over the union, how God was glorified, what praises were made to the Apostle Peter and the Pope. "Nothing occurred according to the wishes of our enemies: no sedition, no bloodshed, no tumult, which our enemies had foretold to terrify us. The Constantinopolitan clerics, themselves admiring and showing their gratitude to God, say that they never have seen so many people partake of Holy Communion." [67] The other members of the papal legation write of the same event to the Pope: "Peace has been returned, through your prayers, to Christian minds; one soul of the entire church, one joy: the sole enemy of the human race is mourning, struck by the force of your prayer (*vestrae precis expugnatione collisus*)" [68]

The Pope realized well the very important part Dioscorus had played in the matter of the reunion and wished to reward him for his service; in his letters to Dioscorus himself and to Justin the Pope expressed his desire that Dioscorus be appointed Patriarch of Alexandria, in other words of his native city, where at the time the See was vacant. It would be very appropriate to have at the head of the church there a Chalcedonian such as Dioscorus, and not a monophysite, as had formerly been the case. But negotiations dragged on and came to nothing.[69]

About a month had passed before the Pope was officially informed

[66] Avitus, *Alcimi Ecdicii Aviti Viennensis episcopi opera quae supersunt*, ed. R. Peiper (Berlin, 1883), ep. IX (7), p. 43. *MGH, AA*, VI.
[67] *Coll. Avell.*, no. 167 (pp. 620–621). See Caspar, II, 156.
[68] *Ibidem*, no. 223 (p. 684).
[69] Hormisdas' two letters to Dioscorus, *ib.*, no. 173 (pp. 629–630); no. 175 (pp. 631–632). See J. Maspero, *Histoire des patriarches d'Alexandrie*, p. 74.

of the reunion. The copious mail on the subject is dated April 22, 519. It contained the general report of all the members of the legation, the private report of the deacon Dioscorus, the letters of Emperor Justin, his nephew Justinian, Patriarch John, Pompeius, nephew of the late Emperor Anastasius, and finally two Byzantine ladies, Anastasia and Juliana Anicia. I have already given some extracts from the two letters written by the members of the legation. Justin announces that the *libellus* was signed without any discord by Patriarch John, "the most blessed bishop of our new Rome," and his clergy; he says that the Sees of Rome and Constantinople are now "illuminated by the flashing gleam of the truth"; he mentions again that those who are hesitant about accepting the union must be "corrected" (*aliorum correctis*). Then he says that all the regions of the empire are to be advised to imitate the example of "the imperial city," and that by reëstablishment of religious peace he will be able "to conciliate his subjects." [70]

In a very brief letter the Count Justinian (*Justinianus comes*) after a few words on religious peace begs the Pope to pray "for our holiest Augustus, the patron of the whole faith (*totius fidei fautore*), for his empire, and for ourselves as well." Justinian fails to mention the patriarch. [71]

Patriarch John addresses his letter "To my lord the most holy and God-loving brother and cominister Hormisdas (*Domino meo per omnia sancto et Deo amabili fratri et comministro Hormisdae*)." His letter is both interesting and important as a document for proving once more the reality of the caesaro-papistic idea in the Byzantine Empire, where the emperor was the head of the church. The patriarch, almost entirely ignoring the papal role in the reëstablishment of the church union, attributes everything to the emperor. After quoting Psalms 106, 2: "Who can utter the mighty acts of the Lord? Who can shew forth all his praise?" the patriarch proceeds: "The Lord has raised such a pious prince to the Roman state, whom long ago the Catholic Church needed and the whole human race wanted to see. Through the Lord's grace from heaven, compassion has been poured

---

[70] *Coll. Avell.*, no. 160 (pp. 610–611). Thiel, 66, 861–862. Mansi, VIII, 456–457. Baron., 519, 58–59.
[71] *Coll. Avell.*, no. 162 (p. 614). Thiel, 68, 864. Mansi, VIII, 458. Baron., 519, 65.

in abundance upon his head, and at the time of his elevation, all in a loud voice glorified God, the master of everything, while the crown decorated such a head from my hands." [72] Then the patriarch points out three achievements of Justin during the first year of his rule: "First, he has manifestly displayed a brilliant victory in his struggle (*primam suorum certaminum palmam*) against the defeated enemy; [73] the second merit of his virtue: he has most wisely prepared the union of the holiest churches; the third blessing of his reign: he has joined what had been spread abroad, and has most wisely taken care of the peace of the world. . . . What had been divided, has been united; what had been dispersed, has been collected. As it behooves us to say and as once I wrote: clearly perceiving that both churches of the older and new Rome are one, and rightly designating that the See of both churches is one, I, in full soundness of my mind (*cum judicii integritate*) acknowledge the indivisible union and harmonious consolidation (*consonam confirmationem*) of both of us. Therefore I pray God that through the prayers of the Holy Apostles and those of your Sanctity, the church may remain forever indivisible, and that the most clement and most Christian prince Justin, and his most pious wife, our daughter, Euphemia may be granted to us in peace for many years." The patriarch closes his letter with warm compliments to the members of the papal legation. [74]

From these three very important letters one may clearly see that if the Pope by means of the reunion hoped to obtain a preponderant influence in the religious, and to a certain extent in the political, affairs of the empire, he missed his aim. The central figure of the religious and political life remained the emperor, who had no idea whatever of surrendering any of his prerogatives based on "the unwritten constitution" of the Byzantine Empire.

The rest of the letters are of little significance. Pompeius, nephew of the late Anastasius, devotes the greater part of his brief letter to

[72] As was noted above, it was John who placed the crown upon the head of Justin.

[73] Here the patriarch has in view the suppression of the plot just after Justin's elevation. See above.

[74] *Coll. Avell.*, no. 161 (pp. 612–613). Thiel, 67, 862–864. Mansi, VIII, 457–458. Bar., 519, 60–62. Grumel, *Les regestes*, I, 86 (no. 213).

extolling the emperor and begging the Pope to pray for him. The Byzantine ladies Juliana Anicia and Anastasia who were honored with papal letters, pay much more attention to the Pope and his influence in the reunion; in her brief note Juliana fails to mention the emperor at all, while Anastasia writes of "pontifical intercession" (*de pontificali intercessione*) and begs the Pope to pray for the safety and prosperity of "our lord Augustus." [75] All the letters, dated April 22, 519, were carried to Rome by the subdeacon Pullio, and reached the Pope on June 19.

We know that the legates had sent letters to the Pope from various places on their way to Constantinople. But he had not received them. At the end of April, 519, Hormisdas had still heard nothing from his legates, and had become worried at this unexpected silence and rather impatient. Three papal letters exist on this subject: one of April 25 and two of April 29. It may be interesting to note that these three letters were written after the mail of April 22 had already left Constantinople for Rome. In the first the Pope writes: "We wish to hear from you; we wish that you may in more detail notify us of everything that has been done; by which persons and in which places you were well received as we believe, or where and in what celebration you spent the day of the Resurrection of our Lord, and what you have then achieved." In his first letter of April 29, the Pope plainly expresses his worry: "Our mind (*animus noster*) is full of anxiety because of daily expectation; particularly since you had been sent to such a great prince, you should have quickly informed us. And we thought that your letters could have reached us before Ascension Day (May 10)." This letter and some others, both to the emperor (*principi*) and to certain individuals, were sent by the hands of the *ecclesiae Romanae defensor*, Paulinus. Another letter also dated April 29 and sent at the same time, not through a messenger connected with the curia but by a trader, Stephen (*Stephanum negotiatorem*), deals with the same concern on the part of the Pope which "makes him take advantage of any opportunity of writing to the legates." Evidently on April 29 the worried and impatient Pope tried to make use of two

[75] *Coll. Avell.*, nos. 163–165. Thiel, 69–71, 864–866. Mansi, VIII, 458–459. Baron., 519, 66, 68–69.

methods of communication with the Orient: one, the usual papal channels; the other, a trader, who was probably going to Constantinople on a business trip. Perhaps the second might be the more successful. Paulinus, however, had a fast trip and was already back in Rome by July 9, 519.[76] This delay in delivering the mail sent to Rome by the legates from various places on their way to Constantinople may perhaps be ascribed to appropriate preventive measures of the Byzantine government. They may have wished not to forward the correspondence in order to prevent any influence on the course of the coming official negotiations in the capital.

Without question Pope Hormisdas rejoiced deeply on receiving all the letters notifying him of the reunion of the churches. He answered them meticulously. From his letters, especially those to the most important personages involved, we realize at once that he regarded the fact of the reunion which had taken place in Constantinople as a beginning for further activities in the same spirit; he was particularly interested in the potential incorporation into the reunion of Antioch and Alexandria. In his congratulatory letter to the members of his legation, he not only writes of the Alexandrian and Antiochene Churches, but also urges the legates with the help of Christ, of the most clement emperor, and of his wife the most pious Augusta, to act in such a way that all churches, no matter in what part of the world they are located, may be recalled to communion with the Apostolic See.

In his lengthy complimentary letter to the emperor, the Pope with several Biblical references says: "Certain of divine support, most excellent emperor, you will fight and subdue to the yoke of your empire the necks (*colla*) of the most ferocious peoples; but no victory can be more remarkable than that when you overthrow the enemy of the human race . . . this victory (*palma*) encompasses the entire human race . . . and what is dearest to divine piety is that those who are a little before were acting harshly (*grassabantur*) at the command of the devil, now are overcome without bloodshed for their own salva-

---

[76] Three papal letters: *Coll. Avell.*, nos. 219–221 (pp. 680–682). Thiel, 72–74, 866–868. Mansi, VIII, 460–461. Bar., 519, 70–71. Jaffe-Wattenbach, *Regesta*, I, 105 (nos. 815, 816, 818; see also no. 817). Günther, *Beiträge*, p. 29 and n. 2. Caspar, *op. cit.*, II, 152–153.

tion." Hormisdas' phrase "overcome without bloodshed" reminds us of the similar wording in Dioscorus' report, which has been recorded above. At the close of his letter, the Pope says that "correction (*correctio*) of the Alexandrian, Antiochene, and other churches is in no way to be neglected." In his letter to the patriarch, the Pope develops the theme that subjects may not be allowed to think otherwise from their chiefs (*praepositos*) who have come to an agreement on the subject; and he expresses the hope that with such a patriarch as John the union with the Apostolic See will be firm and lasting (*mansuram*). At the end of the letter, together with his wish that the emperor with the aid of God may "destroy (*compresserit*) the poison of the old serpent," the Pope, as in his other letters, shows his concern for the Antiochene and Alexandrian Churches. The other papal letters in the same mail, to Justinian Illustris, to the two Byzantine ladies Juliana Anicia and Anastasia, to Pompeius, to an unknown high official, and to Gratus, the former messenger to the Pope from the emperor, are brief, of general character, and without particular interest. In the letter to Gratus the Pope says that he is saddened because of Gratus' long silence.[77]

After the union had been reëstablished, the legates remained in Constantinople until about July 10, 520, that is, a year and three and a half months. Their task after March 28, 519, was to observe how the union was applied to the various regions of the empire, which from the religious or dogmatical point of view were far from presenting a homogeneous whole. This prolonged sojourn of the legates in Constantinople, accordingly, did not pass entirely in the calm atmosphere of an achieved success, but was marked at times by troubles which threatened to undermine the foundations of the religious peace. Moreover, the legates realized more and more clearly that in spite of the assurances given by the Byzantine government of its wish to live in

---

[77] Letter to the legation: *Coll. Avell.*, no. 170 (p. 627). Thiel, 87, pp. 884–885. Mansi, VIII, 468. Bar., 519, 77 (text itself not reproduced). Letter to the emperor: *Coll. Avell.*, no. 168 (pp. 622–624). Thiel, 79, 877–879. Mansi, VIII, 462. Bar., 519, 73–77. Letter to the patriarch: *Coll. Avell.*, no. 169 (pp. 624–627). Thiel, 80, 879–881. Mansi, VIII, 463. Other letters: *Coll. Avell.*, nos. 174, 176, 177, 178, 179, 180. Thiel, 882, 881, 882, 884, 883 (81–86). Mansi, VIII, 465, 463, 457, 466. Baron., 519, 77 (a mere mention).

peace and harmony with the Apostolic See, Emperor Justin, supported and guided by his nephew Justinian, was an autocrat who was in no wise willing to give up any of his prerogatives either in favor of the Pope or in favor of the patriarch. Therefore, it is not surprising that messages from the legates to the Pope were not consistently encouraging or triumphant, but often full of anxiety, disquiet, and uncertainty about the future.

In several places discontent manifested itself on account of the general imperial order that not only the names of the Patriarch Acacius and his successors be erased from the diptychs but also the names of all those prelates who had remained in communion with Acacius, in other words all prelates after the year 484, when Zeno's *Henoticon* was issued. Troubles broke out at Ephesus. Although in his report the deacon Dioscorus calls this incident "not a very serious trouble" (*modicum scandalum*), at the same time he points out that the Synod of Chalcedon was defied and insulted there (*contempta est et injuriata*). The Bishop of Ephesus, Theosebius, was summoned to Constantinople to accept the Synod of Chalcedon. He asked for a delay of three days, prostrated himself before an altar and prayed; on the third day he was found dead.[78] In his letter to the Pope of January 19, 520, Justin stated that various Oriental provinces (*ex diversis Eois provinciis*) had sent to the emperor their own interpretation of the problem of the Trinity, and declared that they would firmly hold to it. The deacon Dioscorus had become acquainted with the Oriental interpretation and found that it was not entirely correct.[79] Patriarch John wrote a letter to the Pope on the same subject, also dated January 19, 520, referring to the Oriental provinces (*ex Orientalium partium regionibus*) which had presented supplications saying what they wanted. The Patriarch

[78] On general discontent: *Coll. Avell.*, no. 216 (p. 675). Thiel, 868–871 (75). Mansi, VIII, 479–480. Baron., 519, 78. On the Bishop Theosebius: Michel le Syrien, ed. Chabot, IX, 13–14 and 30 (II, 172, 250–251). A. Diakonov, *John of Ephesus*, p. 79 (in Russian): Theosebius probably died soon after the year 518. H. G. Kleyn, *Bijdrage tot de Kerkgeschiedenis van het Oosten geburende de zesde eeuw, Feestbundel aan Prof. M. J. de Goeje* (Leiden, 1891), p. 67. K. Ahrens and G. Krüger erroneously ascribe the episode of Theosebius to the Synod of Constantinople in 536. *Zacharias Rhetor*, p. 361 (note to p. 158, 13).

[79] *Coll. Avell.*, no. 181 (636–637). Thiel, 108, 908–909. Mansi, VIII, 487–488. Baronius, 520, 3.

would examine the matter more thoroughly and then inform the Pope in more detail.[80] Some days later, indeed, at the end of January, 520, through Paulinus, *vir honestus defensor*, the patriarch notified the Pope that some difficulties had arisen. And evidently these difficulties were of more than a minor character, because the patriarch suggested mild and proper treatment, "as it is becoming those who have been chosen to pasture the flocks of God." Paulinus was to inform the Pope of all details.[81]

A very disconcerting occurrence broke out at Thessalonica. As we have mentioned above, when the legates were passing through on their way to Constantinople, the bishop of the city, Dorotheus, proposed to postpone the signing of the *libellus* until a congregation of local bishops could be convoked. Trusting in his promise and according to the previous agreement, the legates sent to Thessalonica one of their colleagues, Bishop John, accompanied by his brother, the presbyter Epiphanius. An officer (*comes scholae*) Licinius, whom Justin had sent to Thessalonica previously on another matter, was there to meet them. But Dorotheus had after all resolved against signing the *libellus*. He stirred up the local population by spreading the rumor that the time of religious persecution was drawing near. Two days before the arrival of Bishop John from the capital, Dorotheus baptized over two thousand people who streamed to the city in fear; baskets were filled (*canistra plena*) with sacramental wafers for distribution among the multitude. Accordingly the messengers from Constantinople found Thessalonica in a state of extreme excitement. Dorotheus sent to them his confidential agent, the presbyter Aristides, accompanied by two bishops, to say that some points in the *libellus* needed emendations. The messengers refused to make any changes. Next day an infuriated crowd burst into the building where they were staying, killed their host John, a true Catholic and defender of the Synod of Chalcedon, two servants of Bishop John, and badly wounded the Bishop himself,

---

[80] *Coll. Avell.*, no. 183 (638–639). Thiel, ep. 136, pp. 958–959 (a. 520 *post* 9 Sept.). Mansi, VIII, 514. See Günther, *Beiträge*, p. 41. Grumel, *Les regestes*, I, 87 (no. 215).

[81] *Coll. Avell.*, no. 184 (640–641). Thiel, 147, 985–986 (a. 521 *m. Jul.*). Mansi, VIII, 514–515. See Grumel, *Les regestes*, I, 87 (no. 216). Bolotov, "Lectures," III, *Christianskoe Chtenie* (June, 1915), pp. 363–364.

who would certainly have perished, had not the local police (*manus publica*) saved him. The matter was reported to the emperor, who promised to examine it and punish the culprits. The legates announced to him that "the blessed Pope can in no wise receive Dorotheus among bishops and in communion with the Apostolic See." [82]

The disastrous news of the Thessalonican incident reached the Pope, who on October 13, 519, wrote to the legates in Constantinople on the subject. In his letter he mentions with deep sorrow the attempt on Bishop John and the violent death of John, his host. Regarding the presbyter Aristides as the chief instigator of sedition, he asks the legates to do their best in order to make the emperor send Dorotheus to Rome for the purpose of "receiving dogmatic instruction from the Apostolic See" (*ab apostolica percipiat sede doctrinam*). If he is ready to join the Catholic Church, the latter is ready to instruct well those who ask for, and to return those who have gone away from, the right path of the faith. At the same time the Pope also wants to have Aristides in Rome in order to make him feel "the medicine of Catholic wisdom" (*catholicae scientiae cupimus sentire medicinam*). This papal message, if we take into consideration the gravity of the offense inflicted in Thessalonica upon the papal authority, is striking in the mildness of its tone.

Another letter from the Pope to the legates, dated December 3, 519, is very interesting in which he urges them to exert their influence once more on the emperor on the subject of the trouble in Thessalonica. Evidently he had had no satisfaction from his first letter; therefore he writes with considerable more severity. He mentions again his deep sorrow at the violent death of the host John, "murdered, according to your report, through the insanity of the heretic Dorotheus, who afterwards, by the emperor's order, was summoned to Constantinople," and declares that their duty is to insist with "our most clement emperor" that Dorotheus should not return to Thessalonica, but should be deprived of his episcopal rank — "he never was a good bishop" —

---

[82] On the trouble at Thessalonica: *Coll. Avell.*, no. 186 (pp. 642–644); no. 225 (pp. 688–690). Letters of October, 519. Thiel, 901–903 (102); 898–900 (100). Mansi, VIII, 489–490. Baronius, 519, 137–139; 128–132. See Caspar, II, 165. P. Leporsky, *History of the Exarchate of Thessalonica*, pp. 166–170. V. Bolotov, "Lectures," III, 364–366. Both in Russian.

dismissed from the city, and then sent to Rome for suitable prosecution (*sub prosecutione congrua*). "You must also pay special attention to the point that Aristides, the instigator and accomplice of the whole evil, should on no account by any surreptitious means be ordained in his stead. For it is no use to change the man if his odious vileness continues to exist (*si ejus deformis nequitia perseveret*). But you must choose a man whom, in your opinion, the entire congregation of the Catholics may welcome." But the Pope was about to meet a new and very great disappointment. In answering his letters, the legates on January 19, 520, informed him that Dorotheus of Thessalonica had been removed to Heraclea where he was to stay until the end of his case. They had urged the emperor to send Dorotheus and Aristides to Rome "for perceiving the doctrine of Catholic purity." But the emperor answered that there was no reason to send them to Rome where "without debates with the accusers, they might more easily justify themselves." Then the legates proceed: "But suddenly, while this was going on, Dorotheus, as far as we have learned, was permitted to leave Heraclea, where he was detained: why and for what reason or on what condition and at whose pressure, we do not know."

This was not all. Evidently Dorotheus not only managed to justify himself, but succeeded in being reinstated as Bishop of Thessalonica, and his confidential agent the presbyter Aristides, whom the Pope considers the chief instigator of all the trouble, returned with him there. After Dorotheus' death, Aristides became his successor. In the Greek *Life* of St. David of Thessalonica (died between 527 and 535) both prelates, Dorotheus and Aristides, are called "the holiest archbishops." In August 520 the reinstated Dorotheus went so far as to write a letter himself to Hormisdas in which he presented the affair of Thessalonica from his own point of view; he claimed that he had saved the life of the Bishop John, "who had been sent by your venerable crown," at the risk of his own life, and closed the letter with the assurance to the Pope that he was in complete harmony with the Catholic Church. The Pope answered Dorotheus' letter on October 29, 520, by a rather cold and brief message in which he mentioned the cruelties of the Thessalonica incident and only at the close of his note did he express the hope that Dorotheus would finally come to a reconciliation with the true faith.[83]

Hormisdas suffered another setback in his intercession on behalf of three bishops, Elias of Caesarea, Thomas, and Nicostratus, who, according to papal information, were almost the first to join the reunion with Rome but nevertheless had not been restored to their former positions before their deposition. Five papal letters on the subject have survived, dated September 2, 519, which were sent to Constantinople through an official, Eulogius. In his letter to Justin, the Pope calls attention not only to the high moral qualities of the deposed bishops, but also to the points that by this action the constitutions of the venerable canons have been despised and that the humiliation (*abjectio*) of the bishops has done considerable injury to the Apostolic See. In a letter to the Empress Euphemia (Eufimia) the Pope asks her to join him in his attempt to intercede on behalf of his "venerable brethren and cobishops (*coepiscopos*)" with the emperor. On the same subject he writes to Justinian *illustris* and his nephew Germanus *illustrissimus*. Finally in a letter to Thomas and Nicostratus themselves the Pope notifies them of the sending of the four preceding letters. Receiving no response to his letters of September 2, Hormisdas three months later (December 3) wrote to his legates in Constantinople and separately to Dioscorus urging them to take up the case more energetically. In December of the same year (519) the Pope asked Bishop John of Constantinople and the deacon Dioscorus to exert great efficiency without delay in order that "it may not be thought that we have been

---

[83] Two papal letters referring to the trouble in Thessalonica: *Coll. Avell.*, nos. 226 and 227 (pp. 690–692). Thiel, 97 (892–894); 102 (901–903). Mansi, VIII, 474; 477. Baron., 519, 125–127; 134. Letter of the legates, Jan. 19, 520: *Coll. Avell.*, no. 185 (pp. 641–642). Thiel, 110, 910–911. Mansi, VIII, 488–489. Bar., 519, 141–142. Hormisdas' letter of Oct. 29, 520: *Coll. Avell.*, no. 209 (pp. 668–669). Thiel, 134, 956–957. Mansi, VIII, 508. Bar., 520, 63. The letter of Dorotheus, *Coll. Avell.*, no. 208 (pp. 667–668). Thiel, 128, 940–941. Mansi, VIII, 507–508. Baron., 520, 61–62. A very fine presentation of the Thessalonica affair in Caspar, *Geschichte des Papsttums*, II, 164–169. V. Rose, *Leben des heiligen David von Thessalonike griechish nach der einzigen bis her aufgefundenen Handschrift herausgegeben von V. Rose* (Berlin, 1887), pp. IV–V; 7; 9. O. Tafrali, *Thessalonique des origines au XIVe siècle* (Paris, 1919), pp. 265–267. P. Leporsky, *History of the Exarchate of Thessalonica*, pp. 166–172 (in Russian), is a very fine presentation. A. Vasiliev, "Life of David of Thessalonica," *Traditio*, IV (New York, 1946), 134. Bolotov, "Lectures," III, 364–366 (in Russian).

still more despised" (*contempti*). At the same time he notifies Thomas and Nicostratus of the letter he has just sent and suggests that they meet Dioscorus and talk with him in order that he may be better informed of their case.

At last, on June 7, 520, Justin informed Hormisdas of his decision. The Bishop Elias could not be reinstated, because his successor, the present Bishop of Caesarea, was extremely popular, not only with the local population, but more generally; "almost the entire Orient, without doubt, venerated him." It would be unjust and even dangerous to remove him. Therefore Elias must live in quiet; and after his popular successor's death he could be reinstated according to "the most sacred rules" (*regularum*), and with the consent of the Roman See, of this "most flourishing city" (Constantinople), and of other churches concerned. The case of "the most religious bishops" Thomas and Nicostratus was to be postponed till a final settlement was reached on the question of the union.

Of course this answer of Justin was not satisfactory to the Pope, who felt that he had failed in his intercession. Hormisdas' letter of March 26, 521, to the new Patriarch of Constantinople, Epiphanius, John's successor, reverts to the same case and asks the patriarch to admit the three bishops to communion with the Byzantine Church. If we compare this letter with Hormisdas' previous messages in which he spoke of the violation of ecclesiastical canons and the humiliation of the Apostolic See, we realize that in this case at least he definitely yielded ground. Caspar aptly remarks: "A very modest demand after the original fanfare as to the violation of canons and insult to the Apostolic See" (II, 167).[84] We have noted above that the Pope also

---

[84] Hormisdas' five letters of Sept. 2, 519: *Coll. Avell.*, nos. 202 (p. 661); 203 (p. 662); 207 (666–667); 221 (669–670; 210 (669). Thiel, 889; 890; 891; 892; 888. Mansi, VIII, 471; 472; 473; 474. Baron., 519, 134 (a mere mention). Caspar (II, 164) erroneously calls Germanus Justinian's brother (for nephew). Hormisdas' letters of Dec. 3, 519 to the legates and to Dioscorus: *Coll. Avell.*, nos. 227 (692–693) and 175 (631–632). Cf. no. 173 (629–630) which seems to be a draft of no. 175. Günther, *Beiträge*, p. 32. Caspar, II, 167, n. 4. Thiel, 903 and 905. Mansi, VIII, 477; 469. Hormisdas' letters to the Patriarch John and to the Bishops Thomas and Nicostratus, *Coll. Avell.*, nos. 171 (627–628); 172 (628–629). Thiel, 106–107, 907; 908. Mansi, VIII, 470; 471. Justin's letter of June 7, 520: *Coll. Avell.*, no. 193 (pp. 650–651). Thiel, 114, 914–916 (see his note 1). Hormisdas' letter of March 26, 521, to Epiphanius: *Coll. Avell.*, no. 204 (p. 663). Thiel, 144, 982–983. Mansi, VIII,

had no success in recommending to Justin the deacon Dioscorus as candidate for the vacant See of Alexandria, Dioscorus' native city.

THE SCYTHIAN MONKS

The legates faced another and much more serious danger which might have undermined the very foundations of reunion. This was the case of the Scythian monks and their Theopaschite doctrine.[85] This doctrine goes back to the second half of the fifth century, when the doctrinal decrees of the Council of Chalcedon (451 A. D.) raised violent theological discord in the Near East, which was ardently devoted to monophysitism. Timothy Aelurus, an energetic monophysite, was set up as a rival patriarch in Alexandria; another monophysite, Peter the Fuller, was raised to the patriarchal throne of Antioch. In 482 the Emperor Zeno issued his famous Act of Union, or the *Henoticon* (ἐνωτικόν). Its inspirer and author was the Patriarch of Constantinople, Acacius, whose cherished idea was to find some way of reconciling dissenting parties and putting an end to religious discord. The *Henoticon*, therefore, was an attempt at compromise, which failed to satisfy either the orthodox or the monophysites. The Pope of Rome not only protested against this document but even excommunicated and anathematized Acacius, who in his turn ceased to mention the Pope in his prayers. This was in reality the first breach between the Eastern and Western churches. This was the period of the Acacian schism, which ended with Justin's accession to the throne.

The case of the Scythian monks is another attempt to reconcile the dissenting parties. At the beginning of the year 519 a group of Scythian monks appeared in Constantinople. They were from the province of Scythia Minor, on the Lower Danube (now Dobrudja) and came to Constantinople to settle their local conflict with their Bishop of Tomi, Paternus. They were led by John Maxentius, a very skillful disputant

---

501. Bar., 520, 65–66. See Günther, *Beiträge*, p. 41 and 50 (after March 26). Jaffe-Wattenbach, *Regesta*, I, 108 (no. 854): under Oct. 29, 520. Caspar, II, 180 and n. 5.

[85] See a very comprehensive and accurate article by G. Krüger, "Theopaschiten," in A. Hauck, *Realencyklopädie für protestantische Theologie und Kirche*, XIX (1907), 658–662. A rather superficial chapter by G. Glaizolle, *Un empereur théologien Justinien. Son rôle dans les controverses, sa doctrine christologique* (Lyon, 1905), pp. 20–36.

and writer. Another member of their group was Leontius, a relative of Vitalian, who at that period was the most powerful figure at court; as a result the monks had very effective support there and were treated accordingly.[86] But they came to Constantinople not only for the settlement of their christological conflict with their bishop. They also brought their formula of conciliation for the dissenting parties, which is known as the Theopaschite doctrine. The thesis was that "one of the Holy Trinity suffered in the flesh" (*unum ex trinitate passum esse carne*; ἕνα τῆς Τριάδος πεπονθέναι σαρκί). They hoped that this formula would satisfy both the strict orthodox devoted to the Synod of Chalcedon, and the monophysites. But this formula meant that there must be some changes or modifications in the decrees of the Synod of Chalcedon, which was absolutely inadmissable from the viewpoint of the Pope and his legates. Therefore it is not surprising that the latter were unfavorably impressed. In addition, the formula was denounced as heretical by the powerful monastic organization in the capital, the Akoimetoi (Acoemeti) that is, the Sleepless, whose monasteries enjoyed enormous influence.

Disappointed at their failure in Constantinople, the monks in the summer of 519 went to Rome to submit their views to the Pope. The members of the papal legation and the deacon Dioscorus in his personal letter reported their own impressions to the Pope. The letters are dated June 29, 519. In the joint letter the legates relate how at the order of the emperor and the master of the soldiers, Vitalian, several discussions were organized in order to reconcile the monks with their bishop Paternus. Against their will, the legates were involved in discussions, which was contrary to the *libellus*. Discussions led to nothing; and finally the emperor himself "conciliated" (*reduxit ad gratiam*) Paternus

---

[86] Since Vitalian, the chief upholder of the Scythian monks, was himself a native of Lower Moesia, a semibarbarian, probably a Goth or even perhaps a Hun, whom *Comes* Marcellinus (*s.a.* 514) calls a Scyth, some scholars are inclined to consider the Scythian monks Goths. The French historian, J. Zeiller, writes that they might have been Goths, or there might have been some Goths among them, from the Cimmerian Bosporus (from the Tauric Peninsula). *Les origines chrétiennes dans les provinces danubiennes de l'Empire Romain*, p. 383 and n. 9. The German scholar E. Schwartz plainly calls Scythia the Gothic province (die Gotenprovinz) and the leader of the monks John Maxentius "the Gothic monk." *Die sogenannten Gegenanathematismen des Nestorius, Sitzungsber. der Bayer. Ak. der Wissensch., philosoph.-philologische und historische Klasse* (1922), I, 9.

and Vitalian, who evidently had previously upheld the monks' accusations against the bishop. But the monks "preferred to flee from the city rather than to come to an agreement." They went to Italy carrying several of their theses, among them "unum de trinitate crucifixum," hoping that "your Beatitude may confirm them, and that the church has had enough suffering during sixty years on account of Eutyches." The monks "have insinuated themselves (*subripuerunt*) into the favor of Vitalian, and put all sorts of obstacles in our way." At the close of the letter, the legates warn the Pope to be very cautious, "because the Catholic Constantinopolitan Church is struck with horror at all of this."

In his individual report on the same subject to the Pope, the deacon Dioscorus is more decisive and frank in his statements. He writes: "The old lurker (*insidiator*, the devil) has excited the monks of Scythia, who are related to the master of soldiers Vitalian (*de domo . . . Vitaliani*); they are adversaries of the prayers of all Christians, and their lack of calm (*inquietudo*) has generated considerable delay to the union of the churches and particularly to the ordination (of a new bishop) to the Church of Antioch. Those monks, among whom is also Leontius, who claims to be a relative of the master of the soldiers (Vitalian) are speeding to Rome in the hope that certain theses of theirs will be confirmed by your Beatitude. . . Their teaching has never been introduced by the Fathers in the Synods, because doubtless it could in no wise be in harmony with the Catholic faith." [87]

In a letter to the Pope also dated June 29, 519 Justinian as well gives a very unfavorable account of the monks, who had evidently left the capital for Rome shortly before. "We know," Justinian writes, "that certain monks by name, who care more for discord than for love and the peace of God, wishing to make troubles, started from here on their journey (*iter arripuisse*). Aware of their malice by this letter, your Beatitude should receive them as they deserve, and drive them far away from you . . . after striking them with worthy correction (*ipsos digna correctione perculsos*)." Justinian gives the names of four

---

[87] Letters of the legates and Dioscorus: *Coll. Avell.*, nos. 217 (677–679); 216 (675–676). Thiel, 871–873; 868–871. Mansi, VIII, 480–482; 479–480. Baron., 519, 85; 78.

monks who went to Rome: Achilles, Johannes, Leontius, and Mauritius. The Pope must have delayed his answer, as he received another letter from Justinian dated at the beginning of July of the same year 519, which put him in a very delicate position. Within a few days Justinian fundamentally changed his attitude towards the doctrine of the Scythian monks. The change may be explained by the influence of Vitalian, who supported the Scythian movement and who in most probability urged Justinian to support it too. After some vacillation, Justinian concluded that the formula of the Scythian monks might really be the panacea which could reconcile the dissenting parties and finally grant his empire a durable and steadfast peace. It is important to note that even after Vitalian's assassination, Justinian continued to favor the Scythian doctrine.

In a letter to the Pope written at the beginning of July 519, Justinian says plainly of his previous letter: "Both our brother the most glorious Vitalian and we have written to your Beatitude through the defender of your church Paulinus." Obviously something unexpected and important had happened that made Justinian write another letter and send it by a special carrier, the brother of one Proemptor, whom he expected to travel to Rome very fast and arrive before Paulinus with Justinian's and Vitalian's letters. The messenger was to tell the Pope all the details. In this new brief letter, Justinian says: "Therefore we beg, if it is possible, to give us a speediest answer, and after giving satisfaction to the pious (*religiosis*) monks Johannes and Leontius, to send them back to us. If this question has not been solved by your prayers and diligence, we are afraid that the peace of the holy churches may not be established. Treat the matter diligently and send to us a most definite (*firmissimum*) answer through the above-mentioned pious monks; and if it is possible before our (special) messenger (*legatus*) (Paulinus) comes to your Beatitude. The whole matter (*intentio*) depends entirely on this." [88]

Meanwhile the Scythian monks were not idle in Rome. During almost fourteen months of their sojourn there, they showed intense activity and spread a good deal of propaganda for their formula among

[88] Justinian's letters to the Pope: *Coll. Avell.*, nos. 187 (644–645); 191 (648–649). Thiel, 78; 89; 875; 885. Baron., 519, 96–97.

the population in general, and even in the Roman Senate. They met there their compatriot, a Scythian monk Dionysius Exiguus, whose name is always linked with the origin of our Christian Era, and who translated for the Scythian comers the epistle of Cyril of Alexandria against Nestorius. They even entered into relations with the African bishops in Sardinia, whom the Vandal king Thrasamund (Trasamund) had banished from Africa into this island, and whom the Scythian monks consulted on account of their deep theological insight and great fame.[89]

Apparently Hormisdas was annoyed by their presence. On September 2, 519, he writes to Justinian that he would be glad to send them back to Constantinople; but they refused to leave, fearing some ambush on their way home which might threaten their lives. Therefore the Pope, unwilling to go so far as to expel them by force, decided to retain them till the return of his legates from Constantinople, in order to examine their case more thoroughly.[90] In his letter the Pope fails to make clear his own stand on their doctrine. This vagueness irritated Justinian, who in his letter of October 15, 519, to the Pope presses for an exhaustive answer on the doctrine *carne crucifixus unus de trinitate*, that is, the doctrine of the Scythian monks, because it was for this very purpose that they had come "to your See." He asks the Pope to order the monks to return, and adds that they have nothing to be afraid of.[91]

Meanwhile the Pope evidently changed his mind and was inclined to remit the case to the Patriarch of Constantinople, as we learn from the letter of October 15, 519, from the deacon Dioscorus to the Pope. In this letter Dioscorus again has nothing good to say of the monks or their leader Maxentius. He writes: "if somebody asks Maxentius, who asserts that he is an abbot in some congregation, among what monks he lived, or in what monastery, or under which abbot he

---

[89] By an error, Bréhier names Sicily for Sardinia. Fliche-Martin, *Histoire de l'église*, IV, 430.

[90] *Coll. Avell.*, no. 190 (647–648); cf. no. 189 (646–647) which is almost identical. The latter is probably a draft for no. 190 and was never dispatched. See Günther, *Beiträge*, p. 29, n. 1. Thiel, 90–91; pp. 886, 887. Mansi, VIII, 485. Baron., 519, 117–118.

[91] *Coll. Avell.*, no. 188 (645–646). Thiel, 99, 897.

became monk, he cannot say. The same darkness is about Achilles." In the same letter Dioscorus tells the story of the "so-called" deacon Victor, whom the monks accused of heresy. According to Dioscorus, the master of soldiers Vitalian and the patriarch, without informing the legates (*sine nobis*), summoned Victor and conversed with him. "What they decided among them, we do not know. Later Victor did not come to see us, nor has his cause been told to us." [92] This episode clearly shows that the legates were ignored in all decisions about the Scythian monks.

Meanwhile the Scythian monks in Rome became very anxious to return to Constantinople, probably after learning that their way east would be safe. From the papal letter of December 3, 519, to the legates we see that the monks did not want to wait for the arrival in Rome of the legates; they even tried to leave Rome secretly and the Pope was compelled to take them into custody.[93] We have Hormisdas' letter of August 13, 520, to the African bishop Possessor in reply to Possessor's letter of unknown date to the Pope, received in Rome on July 18. Possessor's letter does not refer directly to the case of the Scythian monks, and they are not mentioned by name. But he writes in a most elaborate style about religious difficulties in Constantinople. "I presume that your Beatitude knows well from how many ambushes (*insidiae*) the Church in the Constantinopolitan city suffers, and how as in the case of an old illness, its wound bleeds again." [94]

This letter is of interest because it mentions the master of soldiers, Vitalian, and Justinian. In other words, when the letter was written, Vitalian was still alive or Possessor thought that he was. But, as I have noted above, the exact date of the letter is unknown; it was probably written at the outset of July. In his reply (August 13, 520) Hormisdas lets loose his indignation at the Scythian monks and speaks of them with reproach and irritation in no uncertain terms. Apparently the monks had already left Italy but had not yet arrived in

[92] *Coll. Avell.*, no. 224 (685–687). Thiel, 98, 894–896. Mansi, VIII, 485–487. Bar., 519, 122–123. On the deacon Victor see also no. 189 (647). See note above. See also Caspar, II, 164, and n. 4.

[93] *Coll. Avell.*, no. 227 (693, 6). Thiel, 103, 903–904. Mansi, VIII, 477. Baron., 519, 134.

[94] *Coll. Avell.*, no. 230 (695–696). Thiel, 115, 916–917. Mansi, VIII, 497. Baron., 520, 12–14. See E. Schwartz, *Konzilstudien* (Strassburg, 1914), p. 52.

Constantinople. They are monks, he says, "only in name, not in fact; in profession only, not in deed; they are scatterers of poison under the pretence of religion." They only "love strife and the obstinacy of pertinacious pride." The Pope writes about them as he does lest, if they should return to Constantinople, they might deceive those who did not know how they had conducted themselves in Rome.[95] He does not, however, commit himself to any definite opinion about their doctrine.

This letter indicates not only that the Scythian monks had not yet reached Constantinople, but that they had already left Rome, not of their own occord. According to a statement given by their leader John Maxentius, they were violently expelled from Rome by the papal officials (defensores) at the order of the Pope.[96] Of course Hormisdas' severe letter to Bishop Possessor was not overlooked by John Maxentius. He wrote a reply in which in his turn he attacks the Pope. First of all, he refuses to believe that the letter could have been written by Hormisdas; whether it was or not, its author was a "heretic and enemy of the Catholic truth." [97] After this, we hear nothing more of Maxentius and the Scythian monks until after the death of Hormisdas. Since Hormisdas' letter to Possessor is dated August 13, 520, the Scythian monks must have been expelled from Rome before this date, that is, at the beginning of the month. There is no record of their return to Constantinople. But without doubt they did return, for it must have been from them that Maxentius got the detailed information of their unhappy experiences in Rome which he reveals in his reply to the papal letter.[98]

[95] *Coll. Avell.*, no. 231 (696–700). Thiel, 124, 926–931. Mansi, VIII, 498. Baron., 520, 16–21. Caspar, II, 178.

[96] "Joannis Maxentii Ad epistolam Hormisdae Responsio: Romanus episcopus . . . postquam comperit reverti Dioscorum, volens ei praestare hoc beneficium, ne in publico ab eisdem monachis argueretur haereticus, missis defensoribus cum ingenti violentia eos ab urbe Roma subito exire compulit." Migne, *PG*, LXXXVI, 1, col. 104. E. Schwartz, *Acta Conciliorum Oecumenicorum*, vol. IV, 2 (1914), p. 54 (36). Caspar, II, 177–178.

[97] *Joannis Maxentii Responsio*: "Nunc certe auctorem hujus Epistolae haereticum esse, quisque ille est, et inimicum catholicae veritatis." *PG*, LXXXVI, 1, col. 96. E. Schwartz, *op. cit.*, IV, 2, 48 (9). Caspar, II, 179.

[98] See F. Loofs, *Leontius von Byzanz und die gleichnamigen Schriftsteller der griechischen Kirche* (Leipzig, 1887), p. 259. A very fine article on Maxentius in *A Dictionary of Christian Biography*, III (1882), 865–868.

It seems possible that Justinian later made Maxentius bishop of his home province of Scythia Minor. In 523 A. D., or a little earlier, Justinian issued an edict which explicitly asserted that one of the Trinity suffered in the flesh; this edict formally approved Maxentius' orthodoxy.[99] Harnack says: "Thus as matters stood, the formula, 'one of the Holy Trinity suffered in the flesh,' was a *henotikon*." [100]

THE DEATH OF THE PATRIARCH JOHN II
AND THE DEPARTURE OF THE PAPAL EMBASSY IN 520

During the sojourn of the legates in Constantinople Patriarch John II the Cappadocian died in February, 520, according to Hergenröther "renowned in holiness" (*im Rufe der Heiligkeit*). In the ninth century Patriarch Photius in his *Bibliotheca* calls him "an abode of virtue" (ἀνὴρ ἀρετῆς οἰκητήριον). His name was included in the Greek Orthodox Menologion. The Bishop of Vienna in the West, Avitus, addressed him as "the Constantinopolitan Pope" (*papa Constantinopolitanus*). The new patriarch, Epiphanius, a presbyter and former syncellus, was ordained on February 25, 520, occupied the patriarchal throne during the whole reign of Justin, and died on June 5, 535.[101]

The legates had no exact information on the personality of the new patriarch because they were not consulted in the appointment. Shortly after Epiphanius' ordination, the deacon Dioscorus notified the Pope

[99] See Loofs, *op. cit.*, p. 260. Bury, *History of the Later Roman Empire*, II, 376. E. Schwartz, *Die sogenannten Gegenanathematismen des Nestorius*, 9. W. C. Bark, "John Maxentius and the Collectio Palatina," *The Harvard Theological Review*, XXXVI (1943), 94; cf. p. 104. J. Lebon, *Le monophysisme sévérien*, p. 70. P. W. Rugamer, *Leontius von Byzanz* (Würzburg, 1894), pp. 54–56. V. Ermoni, *De Leontio Byzantino et de ejus doctrina christologica* (Paris, 1895), p. 8.

[100] A. Harnack, *Lehrbuch der Dogmengeschichte*, 4th ed., II (Tübingen, 1909), 416; *History of Dogma*, transl. from the third German ed. by E. B. Speirs and James Millar, IV (London, 1898), 242. See also Caspar, II, 179. Bolotov, "Lectures," III, *Christianskoe Chtenie* (June, July, and August, 1915), pp. 366–373 (in Russian).

[101] Hergenröther, *Photius*, I (Regensburg, 1867), 150. *Photii Bibliotheca*, cod. 231 (from Σωφρονίου Ἱεροσολύμων συνοδικὴ Ἐπιστολή); I. Bekker, p. 287; Migne, *PG*, CIII, col. 1089. Archb. Sergius, *The Complete Liturgical Calendar (Menologion) of the Orient*, II, 1, 258. According to Archb. Sergius, the Patriarch John died on February 21. *Aviti Viennensis episcopi opera quae supersunt*, ed. R. Peiper, p. 43, ep. IX (7): "Avitus episcopus papae Constantinopolitano." The date of Epiphanius' ordination in Theophanes, p. 166.

of the event. After speaking in high terms of the late patriarch, who "among the catholics and participators (communicatores) of the Apostolic See has departed from this life to the next," Dioscorus says that the new patriarch seems to be making a good beginning; "he speaks sensibly and promises not only not to destroy (*dissipare*) peace and unity but even to increase them (*magis augere*)." Dioscorus cannily qualifies his praise: "This is what he promises; however, we do not know what he will be able to carry out in practice." [102]

The new patriarch was in no hurry to notify the Pope of his election. Not until July 9, 520, that is four and a half months after his election, did he write a letter which with some other mail was conveyed to Rome by the legates, who had by that time left Constantinople. Epiphanius says that the new high rank of Bishop of Constantinople was conferred upon him by decision and election of "the most Christian and most just Emperor Justin and the most pious Empress . . . and with consent of the clergy, monks, and the most faithful people. . . . Being nurtured from early youth (*ex teneris unguibus*) in the Holy Catholic Church," he assures the Pope that he accepts the Four Ecumenical Synods and the letters of Pope Leo, and consents to have erased from the diptychs all the names which the Pope had demanded should be erased. He does not give the specific names. At the close he repeats that he has no intention "to rend asunder (*dilacerari*) the Holy Church of God." Epiphanius' letter reached the Pope on September 17, 520.[103]

Some time after September 17 (the exact date is unknown) Hormisdas answered Epiphanius' letter. He was apparently offended by Epiphanius' delay in writing, and his message is brief and rather cold. Epiphanius had kept him in suspense too long in announcing the

[102] *Coll. Avell.*, no. 222 (682–683). Thiel, 111, 911–912. Baron., 520. 7. This letter was probably written at the beginning of March, and received in Rome on April 7. See Günther, *Beiträge*, p. 37. Caspar, *Geschichte des Papsttum*, II, 168, n. 2. The letter itself reads: "has si quidem litteras quartum post ordinationem ejus diem reperta occasione transmisimus" (*Coll. Avell.*, p. 682). On this account Thiel (p. 911) ascribes the letter to February 29.

[103] *Coll. Avell.*, no. 195 (652–654). Thiel, 121, 923–925. Mansi, VIII, 502–503. Bar. 520, 30–34. See Günther, *Beiträge*, pp. 38–39: there was no earlier letter from Epiphanius. Caspar, II, 168 and n. 4. Grumel, *Les regestes*, I, 88 (no. 217).

beginning of his episcopate, and the Pope was astonished that the old custom had been neglected.[104] His congratulations on this special occasion, therefore, are formal and fail to conceal his dissatisfaction.

In the same bundle of letters which contained Epiphanius' letter of July 9, 520, were five other letters to the Pope, those of Justin, Empress Euphemia, Justinian, Celer *illustris*, and a Byzantine lady Juliana. The name of the other Byzantine lady Anastasia, who as we know had formerly corresponded with the Pope, is missing in this list. It may be that she died in the interval, or that her letter has not come down to us. Justin warmly compliments the activities of the legates in Constantinople, and agrees with the Pope on the names of the bishops to be removed from the diptychs. Some other bishops, he says, are so much beloved by the population of their cities that they will need to receive milder and more cautious treatment. Justin notifies the Pope that he is planning to send to Rome before long a special envoy for more detailed discussion on this matter.[105]

A much more interesting letter is that of Justinian *illustris*.[106] Of the reunion he frankly says: "Since the enemy of the human race often tries to hamper the prosperous course (of events), a part of the Orientals can be compelled, neither by exile nor by sword or fire, to condemn the names of the bishops who died after Acacius; this difficulty involves delay for general agreement." It would be better, he thinks, to drop (*sopita*) the question of the names of the other bishops, "in order that you may release from blood(shed) the people whom our Lord has entrusted (to us) to rule, and that you may conciliate the people not by persecutions and bloodshed but by priestly patience, in order that, willing to win souls, we may not lose both bodies and souls of many. . . . That doctor is justly praised who hastens (*deproperat*) to heal old sicknesses in such a way that new wounds may not appear from them." This letter shows that in July, 520, Justinian had already attained great power. A statement like "the

[104] *Coll. Avell.*, no. 205 (664). Thiel, 113, 913–914. Mansi, VIII, 500–501. Bar., 520, 9. Jaffe-Wattenbach, *Regesta*, I, 107 (no. 851): "post September 17."
[105] *Coll. Avell.*, no. 192 (649–650). Thiel, 116, 918–919. Mansi, VIII, 494. Excerpt in Baron., 528, 28.
[106] *Coll. Avell.*, no. 196 (655–656). Thiel, 120, 920–922. Mansi, VIII, 503–504. Baron., 520, 35–38.

people which our Lord has entrusted (to us) to rule," without mention of Justin, shows that he felt secure in his own achievement. Moreover, his suggestions and advice to the Pope are amazingly daring and altogether without precedent in the diplomatic correspondence of the time. They are a clear foreshadowing of the future Emperor Justinian and his attitude towards the Apostolic See. This letter is even more striking than that of September 7, 518, in which he urged Hormisdas to come to Constantinople. The letters of Celer *illustris*, the Empress Euphemia, and Juliana Anicia are of little significance. Juliana calls the adversaries of union "mad dogs." [107]

The legates left Constantinople about July 10, 520. In the same month Vitalian was assassinated. Some scholars, for instance Duchesne, wonder whether his assassination was carried out a few days before or after the departure of the legates.[108] In my opinion, there is no doubt that Vitalian was murdered after the legates had quitted the capital. In the correspondence which has come down to us and which extends to the very day of their departure, there is no mention or even any hint of this momentous fact. Justinian himself, in spite of his authoritative and impetuous character, might well have preferred to postpone the perpetration of the act until after the legates had left. As we know, Vitalian was always referred to by the legates and the Pope in a manner appropriate to his high position.

CORRESPONDENCE BETWEEN CONSTANTINOPLE AND ROME AND THE DEATH OF POPE HORMISDAS IN 523

I shall discuss later the situation in the eastern provinces of the empire during the first years of Justin's reign. We shall see then how stubbornly and sometimes fanatically the East reacted to the new religious orientation of Justin's government. I wish to show here how Oriental difficulties were reflected in the formal correspondence between Constantinople and Rome after the legates had left the capital.

Justin's letter to the Pope of September 9, 520, shows how con-

---

[107] *Coll. Avell.*, nos. 194 (652); 197 (657); 198 (657–658). Thiel, 117–119, 919–920. Mansi, VIII, 495–496.

[108] Duchesne, *L'église au sixième siècle*, p. 63.

cerned the emperor was about removing certain names from the diptychs. We read: "Some cities and churches both Pontic and Asian and particularly Oriental, whose clerics and people have been tested (*pertemptati*) by threats and persuasions, have been however in no way prevailed upon to annul and remove the names of the priests (*antistitum*) whose views are in high esteem among them. They consider life harder than death, if they condemn the dead on whose lives those who are alive pride themselves. Thus, what can we do to such pertinacity, which fails to obey orders and despises tortures (*tormenta*) to such an extent that they think it would be great and joyous for them to abandon their bodies rather than their religious opinions? It seems to us, indeed, it is necessary to act more mildly and more gently. . . . Willing to avoid blood and tortures (*suppliciorum*) we have accepted the *libellus*." Some concessions would be desirable and useful, especially as to removing from the diptychs those names which were particularly venerated among the population of the eastern regions. Justin quotes one of Hormisdas' predecessors, Anastasius II (496–498), who openly and plainly declared that it would be enough for reconciliation if only the name of Acacius should not be mentioned.[109]

From this letter we see that Justin had a mind of his own and did not want to be a mere tool in the papal hands, as he has sometimes been represented by historians.[110] To this letter was appended a petition (*deprecatio et supplicatio*) to Justin from the clerics, the abbots of Jerusalem, Antioch, and Syria Secunda, as well as the *possessores* of the province of Syria. This petition contained the profession of faith of these regions, which in many details agreed with the formula of the Scythian monks.[111] Justinian enlarged on the same subject in his letter to the Pope, also dated September 9, 520. He also refers to the statement of the late Popes Anastasius and Leo the Great, and to that of

[109] *Coll. Avell.*, no. 232 (701–703): "verum nonnullae fuerunt urbes et ecclesiae tam Ponticae quam Asianae ac praecipue Orientales, quarum clerici vel populi omnibus pertemptati minis atque persuasionibus tamen nequaquam flexi sunt . . . nam neque sanguinis et suppliciorum cupidi, quod dictu etiam grave est, libellum suscepimus." Thiel, 129, 941–944. Baron., 520, 54–57. See Caspar, II, 172–173.

[110] See for instance A. Bailly, *Byzance*, pp. 67–68: "The docile Justin worked on this with the vigor of a soldier."

[111] *Coll. Avell.*, no. 232 a (703–707). Thiel, 944–947. See Caspar, II, 173.

the Emperor Leo I, and urges Hormisdas to follow them in their milder policy towards the dissenting regions.[112]

Also on September 9, 520, is dated the letter of the patriarch Epiphanius, who strongly emphasizes the decisive part which the emperor and his "most faithful wife flourishing in all good" have taken in achieving the union. Like Justin, Epiphanius points out the stubborn resistance of Pontus, the province of Asia, and particularly of the Orient (*tam Ponti quam Asiae provinciae et maxime Orientis*), and suggests milder management. Epiphanius twice expresses in passing the idea of the equality of the two patriarchates, Constantinople and Rome. Along with this letter, Epiphanius sent to the Pope several presents: a golden chalice adorned with gems, a golden paten, another chalice, this one of silver, and two veils of pure silk (*vela holoserica duo*).[113]

The members of the synod convoked in Constantinople for the ordination of Epiphanius also sent the Pope their report. They express the hope that peace will be restored between the churchs both of the Older and of the New Rome (*tam senioris quam novellae Romae*), praise the new patriarch, and point out the part taken by the emperor, the empress, and "the most glorious senators" (*gloriosissimorum . . . procerum*). They also express the hope that the union may be restored by mild measures. As Caspar remarks, the Pope was allowed to inter-

---

[112] *Coll. Avell.*, no. 235 (715–716). Thiel, 132, 954–955.

[113] *Coll. Avell.*, no. 233 (707–710). Thiel, 130, 947–950. Mansi, VIII, 500–506. Baron., 520, 46–51. Grumel, *Les regestes*, I, 88 (no. 218). The *Liber Pontificalis* indicates many presents, saying that they were offered by Justin to the Pope in order that he should pray for the emperor (ed. Duchesne, pp. 270–271; 274, n. 24; 275–276; ed. Mommsen, pp. 130–131; a curtailed list in Loomis, *Book of the Popes*, p. 131). One of the presents was *gabata helectrina, pens. lib. II*, a suspended lamp for the church, which weighed two pounds. Most scholars translate the adjective *helectrina* as "of enamel," and state that the art of enameling already existed in Byzantium in the sixth century. See J. Labarte, *Histoire des arts industriels au moyen âge et à l'époque de la renaissance*, III (Paris, 1865), 512; 514. E. Garnier, *Histoire de la verrerie et de l'émaillerie* (Tours, 1886), p. 376. J. Ebersolt, *Les arts somptuaires de Byzance*, p. 26. But N. Kondakov is inclined to see here not enamel but an alloy of gold and silver, which was called *electron* even in antiquity. *History and Monuments of Byzantine Enamel* (St. Petersburg, 1892), p. 19. (I am using the Russian edition of this work). In his *Glossarium mediae et infimae latinitatis*, Du Cange writes: "gabatae in hoc loco lances seu disci in Ecclesiis, a laquearibus pendentes, cereis vel lampadibus instructi." But *gabata* may mean also a *plate, platter*.

vene on behalf of the general tranquillity of the orthodox churches only if he was in agreement with "his brother and cominister, our lord and patriarch." The report was signed by twenty bishops, most of them from Asia Minor. Three of them were metropolitans. Among the signatures is that of the bishop Paternus, of provincia Scythia, who has been mentioned above in connection with the Scythian monks.[114]

But the Pope was silent concerning suggestions as to the milder treatment of the Oriental recalcitrants. Shortly after September 9 Justinian sent another brief letter to the Pope which revealed his impatience. He wrote: "Recently we sent most reverend priests to Rome, that they might come to full agreement as to the points about which some doubt existed. But we do not know what difficulties have arisen to prevent the settlement of things which seem to be very simple." [115]

Only on March 25 or 26, 521, did the Pope answer the letters of September 9, 520, although they had reached Rome on November 30. The Byzantine government must have found the papal reply unsatisfactory, for it was vague and evasive as to the suggestions from Constantinople, and virtually unyielding as to the Pope's religious position. In his lengthy letter to Justin, which was virtually the answer to the petition of Jerusalem, Antioch, and Syria, although the document itself was not mentioned, the Pope expounded the orthodox dogma of the Trinity, indirectly declined the formula of the Scythian monks, and once more proclaimed the decrees of the Ecumenical Synods (*synodica constituta*) and the dogmas of Pope Leo as the only weapon against all heresies.[116]

In his still lengthier answer to Patriarch Epiphanius, also of March 25 or 26, which has come down to us in the *Collectio Avellana* in both Latin and Greek, the Pope holds to his usual standpoint that "our faith and integrity must be preserved immaculate of any contagion . . . We shall free ourselves of the error of Severus, his participants, or

[114] *Coll. Avell.*, no. 234 (710–715). Thiel, 131, 950–954. Mansi, VIII, 500–506. Baron., 520, 42–45. Grumel, *Les regestes*, I, 88–89 (no. 218). Caspar, II, 174.
[115] *Coll. Avell.*, no. 243 (743). Thiel, 135, 957. Mansi, VIII, 517–518. Baron., 521, 3. See Caspar, II, 174.
[116] *Coll. Avell.*, no. 236 (716–722). Thiel, 137, 959–965. Mansi, VIII, 520. Baron., 521, 16–24. Jaffe-Wattenbach, *Regesta*, I, 108 (857). See Caspar, II, 177.

any one of such a sort (*aut similium*), and we will not bear the loss of those who can be cured." The Pope takes his stand against the suggestions of the clergy and monks of Jerusalem in their petition. "Either the constitutions of the Holy Fathers are complete (*perfecta*) as they are, they need no addition, or they are thoroughly effective (*bene valida*), then they are not to be altered." On the formula of the Scythian monks, who "as if willing to add a fourth person to the Trinity" suggest some changes, the Pope quotes the First Epistle of Paul to the Corinthians (I, 11, 16): "If any man seem to be contentious, we have no such custom, neither the churches of God"; and then he proceeds: "To sum up, it is not appropriate to doubt about the points concerning the faith which have been several times defined, and almost superfluous is a plea to improve that which has been arranged; I have often touched upon this subject (in writing) to our son the most clement emperor." [117]

Hormisdas' second letter to Justin, also dated March 25 or 26, is one of the most interesting pieces in the *Collectio Avellana*. It clearly reveals that the unyielding attitude of the Pope was absolutely incompatible with the new and more flexible religious policy of Justin's government which manifested itself in the letters from Constantinople. The letter is long and rather verbose. The most characteristic points follow: "It is a comfort to me," the Pope writes, "that the world exults with me in your benefactions, and the hitherto lacerated members of the church rejoice at being restored to its structure. You have returned faith to the peoples and persecuted error. The arrogance of the enemies of the church of God has abated, and the humbleness of the faithful has been exalted. A great thing has fallen to your lot, oh emperor! . . . The peace which Jesus Christ gave His disciples, the world has found through you. There is no doubt that the heavenly angels congratulate you. . . . You are the destroyer of schism and arrogance, and the restorer of the old cult. . . . By sending your pious letters you have awakened me, who after so many continuous troubles was almost discouraged to the point of despair, to new tranquillity.

[117] *Coll. Avell.*, no. 237 (722–733). Thiel, 141, 970–979. Mansi, 1029–1036 (Latin and Greek). Jaffe-Wattenbach, *Regesta*, I, 108 (no. 861): April 26. See Caspar, II, 177.

. . . I pray that you may not fail in so good a work, and that you may not keep your hands which you lift to God from finishing the work begun." Eulogies so boundlessly flattering do not often occur even in documents of this sort, but they occupy a full half of this particular letter.

The Pope then expounds his theory concerning the relationship between the ruler and his subjects. He asks: "Is it unjust that those who are not stimulated by the example of a religious emperor should be subdued to his power? . . . May it be more just if the emperor should follow the will of his subjects against (his own) salvation (*contra salutem*) than if the subjects of the emperor should obey his power for the sake of their own salvation (*pro sua salute*)? . . . At the beginning leniency may have been suitable; but unfortunately, as it is known, in later times, errors have augmented. . . . Then, oh most clement emperor, do not compel me either to desert that which for long has been well agreed upon or to change it. For the following saying incessantly sounds (*immurmurat*) in my ears: "no man having put his hand to the plow and looking back is fit for the kingdom of God" (St. Luke, IX, 62).

At the close of his letter the Pope declares that the allegations presented by the imperial ambassadors, the bishop John, the presbyter Heraclianus, and the deacon Constantine, have persuaded him to transmit to the patriarch Epiphanius the cases of the innocent and ignorant who have been deprived of communion, in order that the latter may admit them to the Holy Communion, provided the papal *libellus* be preserved.[118]

Hormisdas' brief letter to Epiphanius, also on March 26, 521, is a commonplace note in which he compliments the patriarch and the Byzantine ambassadors, "the brother and cobishop" John, the presbyter Heraclianus, and Constantine, and acknowledges, in his own handwriting, receipt of the presents for the *basilica beati Petri* which Epiphanius had listed in his letter to Hormisdas of September 9, 520 (see above).[119] Of the same commonplace complimentary character is

[118] *Coll. Avell.*, no. 238 (734–738). Thiel, 140, 967–970. Mansi, VIII, 518. Baron., 521, 7–14. Jaffe-Wattenbach, I, 108 (no. 860): April 26. See Caspar, II, 179–180.
[119] *Coll. Avell.*, no. 239 (738–739). Thiel, 138, 965. Mansi, VIII, 513. A discrepancy between these two letters is that Epiphanius wrote he had sent the Pope a

Hormisdas' answer, March 26, 521, to the letter of the Constantinopolitan synod on Epiphanius' ordination.[120]

In their letters of May 1, 521, Justin and Epiphanius notified the Pope that Bishop Paul of Antioch, who had been appointed to this important city at the instance of the papal legates, had resigned. The prelate had incurred the displeasure of the Antiochese clergy and community, and "being overwhelmed (*victus*) by the testimony of his bad conscience and in addition in fear lest in case of examination his affair might have graver consequences, he had presented his resignation." The resignation was accepted because "it is and will be dear to Justin that the bishop should always be beloved by the community" which he has been chosen to guide.[121] To Paul of Antioch we shall return later; but we must note here that his resignation was a blow to the prestige of the papal legates, who, as we have mentioned above, were to some extent responsible for his appointment.

With these two letters of May 1, 521, closes the valuable collection of Hormisdas' correspondence which the unknown compiler of the *Collectio Avellana* has drawn from the papal registers. No letters for the last two years of Hormisdas' pontificate have survived.

Hormisdas died and was buried in the basilica of Saint Peter August 6, 523. His son Silverius, who himself became Pope in 536 (536–537), wrote his epitaph, consisting of twelve lines, of which five to ten are historically interesting. They are as follows:

You have healed the body of the fatherland lacerated by schism
By restoring the torn members to their appropriate places.
Greece, vanquished by pious power, has yielded to you
Rejoicing that she has recovered the lost faith.
Africa, which was in captivity for many years, is joyful
To have won again her bishops through your prayers.[122]

---

golden paten, and the Pope acknowledges the receipt of a silver one. Jaffe-Wattenbach, I, 108 (858).

[120] *Coll. Avell.*, no. 240 (739–740). Thiel, 139, 966. Mansi, VIII, 512. Jaffe-Wattenbach, I, 108 (no. 859).

[121] *Coll. Avell.*, nos. 241–242 (740–742). Thiel, 145–146, 983–984. Mansi, VIII, 524. Baron., 521, 37–38. Grumel, *Les regestes*, I, 89 (no. 219). See Duchesne, *L'église au sixième siècle*, pp. 66–67. Caspar, II, 181 and note 3.

[122] This epitaph was recognized by G. B. de Rossi among the poems of Alcuin. *Poetae latini aevi Carolini*, ed. E. Dümmler, I (Berlin, 1881), 114. Here the

The epitaph ascribes to Hormisdas the credit not only of healing schism at home and in Greece, that is, in the Byzantine Empire, but also of restoring the Catholic Church in the Vandal Kingdom in Africa, where after the death of the pro-Arian King Trasamund on May 23, 523, orthodoxy was restored. This news might have reached Rome still in the lifetime of Hormisdas, who as we know died at the beginning of August of that year. But it is always possible that the passage on Africa is to be ascribed to the exaggeration of a panegyrical epitaph. The sentence "Greece vanquished by pious power has yielded to you" reminds us of the famous passage of Horace in his letter to Augustus: "Captive Greece took captive her fierce conqueror" (*Graecia capta ferum victorem cepit.* Epist. II, 1, 156).

Now that we are familiar with the contents of the *Collectio Avellana*, from the correspondence between Rome and Constantinople during the years 518 to 521, we can see how the tone of the papal letters gradually changed from a rather authoritative beginning to milder and much more moderate claims, and how strong and unyielding, under the cover of diplomatic courtesy and finesse, on many essential points were the letters of Justin and even more of Justinian. The idea that the union of 519 was a triumph for the Roman See has been deeply rooted with several scholars. We read of "an unheard of triumph of unarmed Rome over the Byzantine Empire and the patriarch of Constantinople." [123] Another scholar writes: "On March 31, 519, the Patriarch of Constantinople John signed the formula of Hormisdas, the dogmatic submission to Rome. In comparison with this solemn act, it did not matter if in a letter John tried to save the co-ordination of the churches of the Old and New Rome, which had been established at Chalcedon." [124]

But not all writers emphasize the triumph of the Apostolic See. Long ago Cardinal Hergenröther, after giving a concise but very

---

epitaph was reproduced without the mention of any name, either of Hormisdas or of Silverius. See also Duchesne, *Liber Pontificalis*, I, 274, n. 25. On Hormisdas' death and burial, *Liber Pontificalis*, Duchesne, 274; Mommsen, 131–132 and 261; in English, Loomis, I, 131.

[123] K. Müller, *Kirchengeschichte* (Tübingen, 1905), p. 273; sec. ed. I (Tübingen, 1929), 754. See Caspar, II, 182.

[124] Hans von Schubert, *Geschichte der christlichen Kirche im Frühmittelalter* (Tübingen, 1921), p. 56. See Caspar, II, 182.

accurate presentation of the material which is contained in the correspondence for the years 518–521, made no mention of papal triumph; he only wrote that the emperor and the patriarch remained in friendly correspondence with Hormisdas, and the agreement concluded bore good fruit.[125] Caspar is also moderate: If you examine thoroughly the Western-Eastern correspondence after the conclusion of peace, he says, you will sense from it not only "a testimony of a cordial and profuse exchange of good feeling between Byzantium and Rome, such as for a long time had not occurred," as Pfeilschifter notes,[126] "but also as the dominating note, the diplomatic wrestle (Ringen) which marked the relations between Rome and the eastern state church." [127] Harnack wrote: "It was not intended that Rome should triumph in the East, but that the emperor of the East should once more become the Lord of Rome." [128] An American writer, M. Hasset, correctly says that "to regard the outcome merely as a triumph of an ambitious Papacy over the civil power, as is frequently done, is wholly to mistake the character of the issue between Eastern and Western Christendom at the beginning of the sixth century." But Hasset is wrong in estimating the result of the union of 519 as follows: "Briefly stated, it was the right of the Church to freedom of action in its own sphere, a right ignored and set aside in a more flagrant manner by Zeno, Basiliscus and Anastasius than even by any of their predecessors." Of course Justin's restoration of the Chalcedonian Creed did not mean that the Byzantine Church obtained the right to free action in its own sphere. The author of this rather popular study has entirely overlooked the influence and power of the emperor.[129]

In our own day M. Jugie returns to the idea of the triumph of the Apostolic See. After reproducing the most important part of the papal *libellus*, he writes: "It was difficult to affirm more clearly and more peremptorily the sovereign authority of the Pope both in the

---

[125] Hergenröther, *Photius*, I, p. 152.

[126] See G. Pfeilschifter, *Der Ostgotenkönig Theoderich der Grosse und die katholische kirche* (Münster i. W., 1896), p. 153.

[127] Caspar, II, 182.

[128] Adolf Harnack, *Lehrbuch der Dogmengeschichte*, 4th ed., II, 414–415; Eng. transl. by E. B. Speirs and James Millar, IV (London, 1898), 241.

[129] M. Hasset, "Church and State, VII, The Monophysite Controversy," *The American Catholic Quarterly Review*, XXXVI (Philadelphia, 1911), 609.

doctrinal matter and in the disciplinary matter. If there was, here and there, some resistance, it was not at all on the substance itself of the formula, but on the secondary question of certain names to be erased from the diptychs, for instance, those of the patriarchs Euphemius and Macedonius II. The events which followed down to the Controversy of the Three Chapters only consecrated the triumph of the Roman supremacy (la primauté) in the Orient." [130]

Russian, that is Orthodox, Byzantinists do not concern themselves particularly with the union as a triumph for one or the other side. They tell the story of the union, emphasizing the severe persecutions in the East of those who did not consent to accept the decrees of Chalcedon. Kulakovsky alone mentions that the Pope firmly defended his demands and yielded no point in spite of all exhortations and prayers; and then he writes: "Persecutions of those who failed to accept the Synod of Chalcedon began through all the east." According to Uspensky, "Justin settled this long dispute; but the price of his agreement with the Pope was horrible sacrifices upon the altar of church unity. About fifty Syrian monophysite bishops were deposed and sent into confinement, and the churches of Syria suffered terrific losses." A historian of our own time in Russia, Levchenko, writes that the reëstablishment of church unity with Rome could not have been brought about without a decisive rupture with the monophysites. [131]

Let us turn to the Russian church historians whose works deal especially with the history of the Byzantine Church. I shall give here three names: A. Lebedev, F. Ternovsky, and the very noted scholar V. Bolotov.

Professor A. Lebedev ends the first part of his *History of the Oecumenical Councils* with the following statement: "The Chalcedonian Council paralyzed once and for all the ambition of the popes towards the East. The church established a barrier against which the traps of the Roman pontiffs split." At the beginning of the second volume of

---

[130] M. Jugie, *Le schisme byzantin*, p. 74. W. Haacke states that "the Papacy triumphed over the whole front" (Das Papsttum siegte auf der ganzen Linie!). *Analecta Gregoriana*, xx (1939), 90.

[131] J. Kulakovsky, *History of Byzantium*, II, 12. Uspensky, *History of the Byzantine Empire*, I, 411. M. Levchenko, *History of Byzantium*, p. 54. All in Russian.

the same work, Lebedev remarks that the activities of Emperors Zeno and Anastasius served to spread monophysitism more widely in the East, and then immediately passes to the Fifth Ecumenical Council held under Justinian in 553 without referring to the new religious policy of Justin or even mentioning his name.[132]

In a rather old but still valuable book, *The Greco-Eastern Church in the Period of the Oecumenical Councils*, Professor F. A. Ternovsky of Kiev writes of the union of 519 as follows: "The relations of Justin to the Roman Pope are worth noting. Perhaps the vast plans for the unification of the whole Roman empire under one scepter which manifested themselves in the later activity of Justinian, directed his uncle in his attempts at a rapprochement of Byzantium with Rome; however this may have been, Justin took much trouble to put an end to the thirty-four-year church separation between the Pope and the Constantinopolitan patriarch, and immediately after his accession to the throne he was in active correspondence with Pope Hormisdas on this subject. His efforts were crowned with success. The legates came to Constantinople, and there on March 28, 519, the union of the churches was solemnly proclaimed; the Pope inscribed in the diptychs the patriarch Acacius, under whom the break between the churches had begun,[133] and the Constantinopolitan patriarch inscribed the Roman popes." [134] There is no word in Ternovsky's text as to the triumph of one or the other side. We are given the impression of compromise.

Bolotov, on the contrary, acknowledges the triumph of the Pope in the union. "The Patriarch bowed his head and with it also the head of the whole Constantinopolitan church under the power of the

---

[132] A. Lebedev, *Collection of the Church-Historical Works*, III and IV, *History of the Oecumenical Councils*, part I: *The Oecumenical Councils of the Fourth and Fifth Centuries*, 2nd ed. (Sergiev Posad, 1896), 284; part II: *The Oecumenical Councils of the Sixth, Seventh, and Eighth Centuries*, 2nd ed. (Moscow, 1897), 9–10.

[133] Ternovsky makes a grave blunder here: as we know, the name of Acacius was expunged from the diptychs.

[134] F. A. Ternovsky, *The Greco-Eastern Church in the Period of the Oecumenical Councils*, in the *Accounts* (*Izvestiya*) of the University of Kiev, XX (September, 1880), Addenda, chapter VIII, p. 263. There is a separate edition of the work. Ternovsky accepts the data of the legendary *Vita Iustiniani*, which we have discussed above, and Justin's illiteracy as well (pp. 261–262).

Roman Pope. . . . The legates solemnly entered the Cathedral of Saint Sophia, and they themselves on the altar expunged the names of the dead patriarchs. The Bishop of Constantinople, John, was cruelly forced (*primoochili*) to give his signature to the union with Rome. But this triumph was only temporary; and when more propitious times came, the names erased were restored in the diptychs, and the patriarchs Euphemius and Macedonius were proclaimed saints." [135]

The text of Hormisdas' *libellus*, which in its most essential part I have reproduced above, and which was signed by Patriarch John and many oriental bishops, at first sight appears a great triumph for the Apostolic See. The Byzantine Church, the emperor himself, his nephew Justinian and other high authorities of the empire acknowledged that the Catholic religion has always been preserved without blemish in the Apostolic See, in which the entire, true, and perfect stability of the Christian religion is found. The Byzantine Church like a strayed lamb seems to return to the fold which it has temporarily forsaken. But the strong and vivid desire of Rome was not only to restore normal relations with the Byzantine Church on the basis of the uniformity of religion and dogma but also to establish the superiority of the Old Rome over the New Rome in rank and priority in time as the church founded by the Apostle Peter. The ambitions of the Apostolic See went far beyond the matters of pure religion; they aimed at spreading the papal influence in the internal life of the Oriental empire in general, upon its politics and upon other sides of the complicated governing machinery. Theoretically, Maundy Thursday in Holy Week, March 28, 519, when in the imperial palace in the presence of Justin and Justinian, the Senate, the clergy, and other dignitaries, Patriarch John signed the *libellus* — theoretically this day was a triumph for the Apostolic See under Pope Hormisdas.

But in reality this was not the case. Actual events shortly revealed the reverse of the medal. Neither the Byzantine Church nor the imperial power were able to overcome the stubborn, fanatical resistance of the monophysite elements in the eastern regions of the empire; the severe measure of implacable persecution came to nothing. We see clearly in the correspondence between Rome and Constantinople, how

[135] V. Bolotov, "Lectures," III, *Christianskoe Chtenie* (June, 1915), 362–363.

Justin, Justinian, and the patriarch gradually became persuaded of the uselessness of this policy and began to suggest to the Pope a milder and more flexible line of conduct towards the opponents of the Chalcedonian Council. In other words, Byzantium was unable to keep the pledge to which it had committed itself by signing the *libellus*. Though the Byzantine Church and government did not deviate from their Chalcedonian tenets, they gradually extricated themselves from the papal pressure and finally regained a free hand in their own methods of managing religious life and religious difficulties within the empire. The Pope understood the situation but could not alter it. His discontent and irritation, as we have noted above, are clearly shown in his letters to Constantinople.

The reunion with Rome in 519 failed to deprive the Byzantine Empire of its independence in religious matters. There is no sufficient ground for speaking of the eventual triumph of the Apostolic See. It was a triumph of the moment, that is of the day of the signing of the *libellus*: a day which gave a great if temporary satisfaction to the Pope. But no matter what consequences resulted from the reunion of the two churches, the fact itself was of momentous significance both for the empire and for the papacy.

POPE JOHN I IN CONSTANTINOPLE, 526

Hormisdas' successor was John I (August 13, 523–May 18, 526). The *Liber pontificalis*, the semi-official source on papal biographies, is very meager concerning the brief pontificate of this Pope; besides the detailed description of his voyage to Constantinople, which is very essential for our study, the *Liber* gives only a few words on his building activities in Rome.[136]

[136] Duchesne in his edition of *Liber Pontificalis* I, is certain that the *Life* of Pope John I was compiled by a contemporary writer who lived in the sixth century. In his more recent edition, Mommsen, following the old opinion of Waitz, attributes the original text of the earlier part of the *Liber* to the later date (the seventh century). See Mommsen's lengthy *Prolegomena* to his edition. *Gestorum pontificum romanorum*, I, *Libri Pontificalis pars prior*, VII–CXXXIX (*MGH*). In English, a clear presentation of this question in L. R. Loomis, *The Book of the Popes (Liber Pontificalis)* pp. IX–XXII. Loomis' English translation is based upon the text edited by Mommsen. Mommsen's thesis has not been generally accepted. See for example R. Cessi, *La Vita di Papa Giovanni I nel*

The Pope undertook his voyage to the Byzantine court at the instance of the powerful Ostrogothic king, Theodoric, who, an Arian himself, strongly wished to establish relations with Justin, who had opened a new religious policy in defense of the Chalcedonian Creed and had within the territory of his empire a considerable number of Arian subjects. The position of Theodoric, an Arian ruler in an Arian Germanic kingdom, among an orthodox indigenous population, was rather complicated. The religious trend of similar Germanic kingdoms in the west and south inspired in him a feeling of apprehension and anxiety. In the far distant northwestern corner of Europe, the Franks under Clovis in 496 became orthodox Roman Catholics. In 516 the new king of the Burgundians, Sigismund, Theodoric's son-in-law, was converted to Catholicism by Avitus, Bishop of Vienna. In the Arian Vandal state of Africa, when the new king Hilderic came to the throne in 523, persecution of the Catholics ceased, and under his mild rule the peace of the church throughout the Vandalic dominions at length became assured; in fact, after Justin's death, he was received as the guest and friend of Justinian. Finally in 518 the Chalcedonian creed triumphed in Constantinople. Theodoric was surrounded by anti-Arian countries.

When persecution of anti-Chalcedonians broke out in Byzantium, the Arians as well as other dissidents suffered. In addition to the pure religious causes, some economic reasons may also have been involved in the persecution, for the dissidents apparently possessed too much wealth. In Procopius, at least, we come across the following passage: "the shrines of these heretics, as they are called, and particularly those who practised the Arian belief, contained wealth unheard of." [137] When the severe measures adopted against the Arians in the Eastern empire were reported in Italy, Theodoric determined to come forward as the protector of his fellow heretics, and send a special embassy to

---

"Liber Pontificalis" e nell' *Anonimo Valesiano, Archivio Muratoriano*, 19–20 (Bologna, 1917), pp. 463–488. Cessi supports Duchesne's point of view. In *Appendice* (p. 488) Cessi gives the text of the *Vita Johannis* in its potential original form. I am inclined to accept Duchesne's conclusions.

[137] Procopius, *Anecdota* XI, 16: τούτων δὲ τὰ ἱερὰ τῶν αἱρετικῶν καλουμένων, καὶ διαφερόντως οἷσπερ ἡ τοῦ Ἀρείου ἤσκητο δόξα, πλοῦτόν τινα εἶχεν ἀκοῆς κρείττω (ed. and transl. by Dewing, p. 134–135).

Constantinople. He chose very carefully the members of the mission, and the choice shows that he attached exceptional importance to it. At the head of the embassy stood the Pope himself, who was summoned by Theodoric to Ravenna to receive detailed instructions.

A contemporary source, an anonymous Chronicle of Ravenna, which has unexpectedly just here incorporated another source hostile to Theodoric, reproduces a very interesting conversation between the king and the Pope, which in spite of the evident prejudice of the author may reflect historical reality. The king said: "Go to Constantinople, to the Emperor Justin, and among other things tell him to bring back (to Arianism) those who have accepted the Catholic faith." The Pope answered: "Oh king! What thou doest, do quickly (John, 13, 27). Here I stand before you: I do not promise you to do this, nor shall I tell this to him (the emperor). But as far as other things are concerned which you charge me to obtain from him, with the aid of God I shall be able (to do)."

Caspar conjectures that on John's refusal to transmit his demand to Justin, Theodoric may have charged some other members of the embassy with it (II, 186), but this seems to me rather improbable. Another commission of Theodoric to his embassy was that they should ask Justin to restore to their former cult the Arian churches converted into Catholic ones. Theodoric ordered ships to be made ready for the embassy, which, beside the Pope, consisted of both clerics and laymen: the bishops Ecclesius of Ravenna, Eusebius of Fano (Fanestrus), Sabinus of Canosa (Sabinus Campanus) and two others; then the Roman senators, Theodorus, Importunus, Agapitus, and another Agapitus.[138] At the moment of departure, the Pope, according to the *Liber Pontificalis*, was in a bad state of health (*egrotus infirmitate*).

The route of the embassy was different from that taken by the previous papal embassy sent by Pope Hormisdas. The latter as we

---

[138] *Liber Pontificalis*, ed. Duchesne, p. 275; ed. Mommsen, pp. 133–135; 260–261; in English, Loomis, pp. 132–133. On the identification of Sabinus of Canosa with Sabinus Campanus see Caspar, II, 185, n. 2. Anonymus Valesianus, ed. Mommsen, *Chronica Minora*, I, 328; ed. Cessi, p. 20 (*Raccolta degli storici italiani* by Muratori, new edition, XXIV, part IV, 1913). The statement of *Liber Pont.* that before sending the embassy Theodoric was so angered that he threatened to put all Italy to the sword, is exaggerated.

know landed at Aulora (Valona) and went east along the Via Egnatia. Pope John's embassy landed at Corinth, in Greece, a detail which has survived in one of the *Dialogues* of Pope Gregory the Great (590–604). This *Dialogue* contains a very amusing legendary episode, the story of a sort of miracle which supposedly occurred at Corinth on the Pope's arrival. When "the holiest man John, the pontiff of this Roman Church, on his way to the Emperor Justin Senior, had arrived in Corinth," he needed a horse for his journey. One of the local nobles offered him one, a horse which on account of its tameness his wife habitually rode. The Pope mounted the horse and rode it to a point where he could get a fresh mount to continue his journey; from there he sent the horse back to Corinth. But when the wife of the nobleman tried to ride it again, she could not, because the horse by neighing, blowing, and shaking its body, apparently wished to say that after carrying the patriarch it could not endure to carry a woman; so finally the man sent the horse back to the patriarch to be at his permanent disposal.[139] I have quoted this amusing anecdote of a later time because it is the only text which gives a hint of Pope John's itinerary. It throws light on traveling conditions, too, by indicating that even such a high personage as the Pope in spite of his bad health was forced to ride on horseback.

The embassy reached Constantinople early in the spring, 526, since on Easter Sunday, which in this year fell on April 19, the Pope had already arrived.[140] Without doubt this was an event of great magni-

---

[139] Pope Gregory, *Gregorii Papae I Dialogi*, liber III, cap. II, Migne, *PL*, LXXVII, coll. 221–224 (in Greek and Latin).

[140] There has been much discrepancy concerning the chronology of the embassy. I follow here the conclusions of Duchesne, which have also been accepted by Caspar (II, 766). See Duchesne, *Lib. Pont.*, I, 277, n. 8; *L'église au sixième siècle*, p. 74, n. 2. It seems to me that the report of *primicerius* Bonifatius to Pope John on his consultation with Dionysius Exiguus concerning the date of Easter in 526 clearly shows that the Pope was still in Rome at the end of 525 or at the beginning of 526. Bruno Krusch, "Die Einführung des griechischen Paschalritus im Abendlande," *Neues Archiv der Gesellschaft für ältere deutsche Geschichtskunde*, IV (1884), 108–109. Cf. Pfeilschifter, *Der Ostgotenkönig Theoderich der Grosse und die katholische Kirche*, p. 167; 169: The Pope left Ravenna for Constantinople between September 1 and the end of November 525 and returned to Ravenna in May, 526, where he passed away on May 18 of the same year. J. Sundwall, *Abhandlungen zur Geschichte des ausgehenden Römertums* (Helsingfors, 1919), pp. 256–257 (he follows Pfeilschifter). Comes Marcellinus attributes

tude for the Eastern Empire; it was the first time the Pope had ever come to Constantinople.[141] This was the opening of the Byzantine-dominated period of the papacy, which ended with the last Greek upon the papal throne, Zacharias (741–752).[142]

The embassy was received in the capital with an exceptionally brilliant welcome. According to the *Liber Pontificalis*, the whole city with candles and crosses came to meet them at the twelfth or fifteenth milestone, probably near the same Round Castle where the previous embassy of Pope Hormisdas had been met. This time the emperor himself met the Pope and bowed himself to the ground before the vicar of St. Peter (*humiliavit se pronus et adoravit*) as if he were the Apostle himself. Justinian is not mentioned in our source; but without doubt he was among those who met the Pope. Through the Golden Gate the procession entered the city; and here, according to a later legend, in the presence of all a miracle was performed: by putting his hand upon the eyes of a blind man who appealed to him, the Pope restored his sight.[143] Every sort of honor and favor was showered upon the Pope: he was seated on a throne higher than that of the patriarch; he celebrated the Easter service in Latin in St. Sophia on Easter Sunday, April 19, 526; and finally, Justin, though long since duly crowned by the patriarch, caused the Pope to crown him again.[144]

the arrival of the embassy to the year 525 (ed. Mommsen, *Chronica Minora*, II, 102). Bury accepts this year: "The Pope set forth some time between the beginning of September and the end of November A. D. 525" (II, 156–157 and n. 1, p. 157). Some confusion in Jaffe-Wattenbach, *Regesta*, p. 110. See also W. Ensslin, *Theoderich der Grosse* (München, 1947), pp. 322–323: the Pope began his journey to Constantinople early in the spring, 526. This is inexact.

[141] Comes Marcellinus, a. 525: "solus dumtaxat Romanorum sibimet decessorum urbe digressus Constantinopolim venit" (ed. Mommsen, p. 102). The record of the *Liber Pontificalis* that "the ancients among the Greeks bore witness, saying that in the time of Constantine Greece had been accounted worthy to receive the blessed Silvester, Bishop of the Apostolic See," has no historical ground whatever. Duchesne, p. 275; ed. Mommsen, p. 134; Loomis, p. 133.

[142] See G. Schnürer, "Die erste päpstliche Kaiserkrönung," *Festschrift Felix Porsch zum siebzigsten Geburtstag dargebracht von der Görres-Gesellschaft* (Paderborn, 1923), p. 211.

[143] *Gregorii Papae I Dialogi*, lib. III, cap. II (*PL*, LXXVII, col. 224): ἐν Κωνσταν-τινουπόλει, εἰς τὴν πύλην τὴν καλουμένην χρυσίαν, ἐλθόντος αὐτοῦ. It is only in this legend that we have any mention of the Golden Gate, through which the Pope entered the city.

[144] Comes Marcellinus, a. 525: "plana voce romanis precibus"; ed. Mommsen, p. 102. Theoph., p. 169. *Anastasii Chronographia Tripertita*, p. 132. Niceph. Call.,

During his very short sojourn in Constantinople, the Pope manifested great activity. He had time enough to communicate with many bishops from various regions of the empire, most of whom were apparently orthodox or inclined to accept the Chalcedonian decrees. Egypt, however, was beyond his influence and out of his reach; he had no communication with Patriarch Timothy IV of Alexandria.[145] Egypt remained firmly faithful to monophysitism, and its patriarch apparently made no attempt to meet the Pope.[146]

The papal visit was to some extent successful. We can discard the

---

XVII, 9 (Migne, *PG*, CXLVII, col. 241). The information that the Pope crowned Justin is mentioned only in *Lib. Pont.*: "de cujus manibus cum gloria coronatus est Iustinus Augustus" (ed. Duchesne, p. 275; ed. Mommsen, p. 135; 261; Loomis, p. 134). I do not clearly understand the doubt cast by Iorga: "je crois qu'il faut rattacher 'romanis' à 'precibus.'" N. Iorga, *Histoire de la vie byzantine*, I, 235, n. 2.

[145] Theoph.; Anastasius; Nic. Call., *loc. cit.*

[146] In connection with the papal visit to Constantinople we may mention a Greek document which is regarded as a forgery fabricated during the seventh century and attributed to an imaginary Bishop of Tyre, Dorotheus. In this piece, which contains a number of brief notes on the prophets, Apostles, disciples of Jesus Christ, and so on, we come across the story of a dispute concerning precedence which arose between Pope John and the patriarch of Constantinople. During the Pope's sojourn in the capital the patriarch asked him to officiate jointly with him on Christmas Day. Pseudo Dorotheus, Bishop of Tyre, Σύγγραμμα ἐκκλησιαστικὸν περὶ τῶν ο' μαθητῶν τοῦ Κυρίου, *Selecta ad illustrationem Chronici Paschalis*, in *Chronicon Paschale*, CSHB II, 136. Lequien, *Oriens Christianus*, I (Paris, 1740), coll. 203–205. *Prophetarum vita fabulosa, indices apostolorum discipulorumque Domini Dorotheo, Epiphanio, Hippolyto aliisque vindicata*, ed. Theodorus Schermann (Leipzig, 1907), pp. 151–152. Also in Migne, *PG*, XCII, 1059–1076. This forged document reflects an actual fact, a dispute between the two patriarchs of Old and New Rome as to precedence, which is confirmed by Theophanes and his followers (see preceding note). This text gives Christmas Day as the date of the religious service performed by these two prelates, while *Comes* Marcellinus gives the Day of Resurrection, Easter Day. Combining these two sources, some historians believed that the Pope spent in Constantinople a much longer time than is now admitted; that is, that he attended the services on both December 25 (Christmas Day) and Easter Day (March 30 in 525 or April 19 in 526). See for instance Bury, (II, 157): "He celebrated Christmas and Easter in St. Sophia . . . and remained there at least five months." More recently, C. Amantos, Ἱστορία τοῦ βυζαντινοῦ κράτους, I, 179. But the forged document ascribed to Dorotheus of Tyre probably errs in giving Christmas for Easter. Duchesne positively states that this document is a forgery of the seventh century. *L'église au VIe siècle*, p. 76, n. 3. See also Caspar, II, 748. This forgery is sometimes invoked to prove the chronological priority of the See of Constantinople over the See of Rome, as having been established by the Apostle Andrew, the first disciple whom Jesus Christ sent on a mission. See S. Vailhé, "Origines de l'église de Constantinople," *Echos d'Orient*, X (1907), esp. 289–293. Jugie, *Le schisme byzantin*, p. 22.

exaggerated statement in the *Liber Pontificalis* that Pope John and the ambassadors obtained everything they asked from Justin, but we may be positive, on the basis of Anonymus Valesianus, that Justin promised to do everything, with one exception: he refused to bring back to Arianism those who had accepted the Chalcedonian Council.[147] From this record we may conclude that Justin restored to the Arian cult most of the churches — possibly not all — which had been confiscated and converted to the orthodox creed. The rare distinctions granted the Pope, such as his precedence over the patriarch in the Easter service, and the great honor of crowning the emperor, manifest high veneration and great diplomatic courtesy towards such a distinguished guest; but though they were highly flattering to papal ambition they had no real political significance whatever. The emperor had no need of any new confirmation of his coronation, which had been duly performed by Epiphanius' predecessor, Patriarch John II, in 518. But it is not improbable that Justin himself was pleased to be crowned once more, this time by the Bishop of Rome, who represented the western part of the Roman Empire, which had been separated from Constantinople for many years by religious dissent. At any rate the crowning of Justin by the Pope is an historical fact, and not a "clumsy fabrication" (*eine plumpe Erdichtung*), as J. Langen once wrote.[148]

The Pope received from Justin several gifts for the adornment of various Roman churches: the basilica of the Holy Apostles Peter and Paul, the Church of the Holy Mary, and the Church of St. Laurentius. Here is the list: a golden paten adorned with gems, weight twenty pounds; a golden chalice also adorned with gems, weight five pounds;

---

[147] *Liber Pontificalis*: "Johannes venerabilis et senatores cum gloria, dum omnia obtinuissent a Iustino Augusto" (ed. Duchesne, p. 276; Mommsen, p. 136; Loomis, p. 136). Anonymus Valesianus, 29 (90): "cui (to the Pope) data legatione, omnia repromisit facturum praeter reconciliatos, qui se fidei catholicae dederunt, Arrianis restitui nullatenus posse" (ed. Mommsen, *Chr. Min.*, I, 328; Cessi, p. 20).

[148] See G. Pfeilschifter, *Der Ostgotenkönig Theoderich der Grosse und die katholische Kirche* pp. 194–195. Pfeilschifter quotes Langen's book, *Geschichte der römischen Kirche*, (Bonn, 1881–1893), p. 300, n. 3. Caspar, II, 189. See also an old book by R. Baxmann, *Politik der Päpste von Gregor I. bis auf Gregor VII*, I (Elberfeld, 1868), 29: "the Pope came to Constantinople in 525; the ceremony was not an imperial coronation, but as was usual in Germany in later times a means of embellishing a banquet." G. Schnürer, "Die erste päpstliche Kaiserkrönung," *Festschrift Felix Porsch*, p. 216: he says it was a pure religious ceremony.

five silver cups; and fifteen pallia interwoven with gold (*pallea auro texta*).[149]

A permanent trace of the result of the Pope's visit to Constantinople appears in the legislation of Justin. We possess the edict against heretics, Manichaeans and Samaritans, issued by Justin and Justinian in 527. The edict is extremely severe towards all heretics and religious dissidents, but it contains one exception, that in favor of the Goths, who were permitted to serve as usual among the *foederati*.[150]

The embassy returned home by Via Egnatia, because we read in the *Liber Pontificalis* that one of its members, the patrician Agapitus, died in Thessalonica.[151] The other members, traveling rapidly, reached Ravenna safely, probably at the beginning of May. Theodoric, apparently dissatisfied with the results of the mission, particularly with Justin's refusal to restore to their old faith those Arians who had been converted to orthodoxy, received the Pope and his companions very sternly and detained them at his court for further investigation. The Pope, who, as we have noted above, had been in poor health from the time of the departure of the mission from Italy, died shortly after their arrival at Ravenna, May 18, 526, without seeing Rome again. His body was taken to Rome and interred in St. Peter's. His epitaph of eight lines contains no allusion to his mission to Constantinople but calls him "a victim of Christ" (victima Christi).[152] The usual story that on his return to Ravenna the Pope was thrown into prison and died there a few days later, is now, in my opinion, to be discarded. Theodoric kept the Pope not in confinement but only under rigorous surveillance. But very probably the stern reception which he met at Ravenna may have accelerated his death.[153] It is clear that Theodoric

---

[149] *Liber Pontificalis*, ed. Duchesne, p. 276; Mommsen, 137; 262. Loomis omits the list (p. 138).

[150] *Cod. Iust.* I, 5, 12, 17. We shall speak later of this important edict in the section dealing with religious persecution under Justin.

[151] *Lib. Pont.*, ed. Duchesne, p. 276; Mommsen, 135: "et Agapitum patricium defuncto Thessalonica"; in Epitome Feliciana: "defuncto in Grecias" (Mommsen, p. 262). Loomis, p. 136: "was dead in Greece."

[152] Epitaph in Duchesne, *Lib. Pont.*, I, 278, n. 15. See Loomis, *op. cit.*, p. 138, n. 2.

[153] *Lib. Pont.*: "rex Theodoricus hereticus cum grande dolo et odio suscepit eos, id est, papam Iohannem et senatores, quos etiam gladio voluit interficere; sed metuens indignationem Iustini Augusti, quos tamen in custodia omnes adflictos

had the success of the mission very much at heart. The stay in Constantinople was markedly short, which is perhaps to be explained by the efforts of the ambassadors to return to Ravenna to report as soon as possible. Theodoric was impatient to learn the results of the mission and would not have tolerated a long sojourn in the East.

Curiously enough, at the end of the sixteenth century a French historian and politician, Jacques-Auguste de Thou (1533-1617), whose name is connected with the registration of the Edict of Nantes, 1598, which secured partial freedom of religion to the Protestants, in his book *Continuation of the History of his Time*, told the story of the embassy of Pope John to Constantinople to represent the Pope as the defender of Arianism. Thou says that Justin decided to abolish the "Arian pest" (*Arianorum luem*) which at that time raged vigorously (*vigebat*) in the eastern regions, and that Theodoric, himself "polluted

---

cremavit (tortured), itaque ut beatissimus Iohannes episcopus primae sedis papa in custodia adflictus deficiens moreretur. Qui tamen defunctus est Ravennae in custodia XV kal. Iun. martyr" (Duchesne, p. 276; Mommsen, pp. 136-137; 262; on pp. 136-137 is another version with a few insignificant variants; Loomis, p. 137: "he confined them in prison." Anonymous Valesianus, 31 (93): "revertens Johannes papa a Iustino: quem Theodericus cum dolo suscepit et in offensa sua eum esse jubet: qui post paucos dies defunctus est" (ed. Mommsen, *Chr. Min.*, I, 328; Cessi, p. 20). The words *custodia* and *offensa* do not necessarily mean "prison." See Cessi, *Studi critici preliminari*, p. CLIX (in his edition of Anonymus Valesianus). Bury, II, 157, n. 4; although in the text of his book Bury writes that the Pope and his companions were thrown into prison (p. 157). In 1925 Duchesne wrote that the entire mission was thrown into prison, *L'église au sixième siècle*, p. 77. As early as the end of the sixth century, a later tradition not without legendary element states that Pope John was imprisoned and even killed by Theodoric. *Sancti Gregorii Dialogi*, lib. IV, cap. 30: "(Theodoricus) Joannem papám affligendo in custodia occidit"; in Greek, εἰς φυλακὴν ἐφόνευσε (Migne, *PL*, LXXVII, 369-370). Gregory of Tours, *Gregorii episcopi Turonensis Liber in Gloriam Martyrum*, 39: "Theodericus posuit in carcerem . . . positus in carcerem . . . obiitque in carcere," *Scriptores Rerum Merovingarum*, I, 513 (*MGH*). See Caspar, II, 189-191. Caspar gives some other examples of later legendary tradition. Recently the Italian scholars, G. Romano and A. Solmi, wrote that the Pope died in prison: *Le dominazioni barbariche in Italia* (Milan, 1940), p. 217. See also an older monograph by M. Rosi, "L'ambasceria di Papa Giovanni I a Costantinopoli, secondo alcuni principali scrittori," *Archivio della R. Società Romana di Storia Patria*, XXI (Rome, 1898), 567: "the Pope died in prison." Diehl-Marçais, *Le Monde Oriental de 395 à 1081*, p. 50: "emprisonné au retour de sa mission." L. Bréhier, *Vie et mort de Byzance*, p. 22: "jeta le pape dans une prison où il mourut." W. Ensslin, *Theoderich der Grosse* (München, 1947), 324: the Pope was not imprisoned. The same opinion in O. Bertolini, *Roma di fronte a Bizanzio e di Longobardi* (Bologna, 1941), 92.

by this pest," sent an embassy headed by Pope John demanding that his legates in his own name should insist with Justin upon the return of the Arian churches to the Arians, allowing them to live in peace; otherwise Theodoric would slaughter by the sword the whole population of Italy. With many tears they obtained from Justin the satisfaction of Theodoric's demands so that the Arians were granted their rights. And here Thou gives his sources: Book XV of *Miscella Historia* of Paul of Aquileia and Cedrenus.[154] The aim of the French historian was to show the extent of the tolerance of the Pope himself in that he went to Constantinople to plead with the emperor for the security of the heretical doctrine of Arianism. It is worth our notice that Thou chose the fact of Pope John's mission as an example of admirable tolerance, and as a support for the promulgation of the Edict of Nantes in France. Voltaire wrote of Thou's story: "The striking image of a Pope going himself from Rome to Constantinople to speak in behalf of heretics produced such a powerful impression on public opinion that the Edict of Nantes passed unanimously and was afterwards registered in all the parliaments of the kingdom." [155]

RELIGIOUS PERSECUTION UNDER JUSTIN

Religious persecution under Justin, which was inspired by the strong pro-Chalcedonian policy of the new emperor, his nephew Justinian, and the powerful Vitalian, and which was supported and stimulated by the suggestions of Pope Hormisdas that measures of "correction" be applied to the recalcitrant opponents of the new movement, passed through three stages.

The first stage was apparently characterized by violent measures taken by the government in the Near East. At this time, as often happens in history, those who carried out the orders on the spot were

---

[154] Jacques-Auguste de Thou, *Continuation of the History of His Time, Illustris viri Iac. Augusti Thuani regii in Sanctiore Consistorio Consiliarii, et in suprema Regni curia praesidis Historiarum sui temporis continuatio*, vol. III (Frankfort, 1621), lib. CXXII, p. 876 (under the year 1599). Paul of Aquileia is Paulus Diaconus. See *Scriptores rerum langobardicarum et italicarum* (Hannover, 1878), p. 410 (*Gesta episcoporum neapolitanorum*, part I).

[155] Voltaire, *Histoire du parlement de Paris*, chap. XL, *Oeuvres complètes de Voltaire*, nouvelle édition, XV (Paris, 1878), 572.

much more severe, cruel, and unyielding than those who had framed the policy intended or wished them to be. Although for this period we depend almost entirely on monophysite information, which obviously cannot be objective and often exaggerates, — even making allowances for this bias, we must admit that generally speaking it reflects the harsh reality fairly well. Many unnecessary and deplorable excesses were reported during the opening stage of, in the words of John of Ephesus, the "violent storm of persecution."

The second stage has not been emphasized in monophysite tradition, but is indicated several times in the correspondence between Constantinople and Rome, in which as we have noted above, Justin, Justinian, and Patriarch John notified the Pope that on the basis of their experience they believed a milder management of the religious difficulties in the Near East would be desirable. The cause of this change, in the opinion of the leading men of Constantinople, is clearly explained in the letters: the stubborn resistance of the clergy, monks, and masses of the population to the aggressive policy of the central government. The authorities on the one hand apparently felt respect and admiration for the vast self-sacrifice and boundless devotion of the Near East to the cause of their religion; on the other, they feared that if the stubborn and rigid persecution continued, the Near East might be politically and economically lost to the empire. It may be plausibly surmised that the change in the ideology of the government depended to some extent on Vitalian's disappearance from the scene when he was assassinated in 520; before then, on his return from exile to the capital, he had been the most ardent adherent of the Chalcedonian Creed and the most powerful personage in the empire, just as in his previous career under Anastasius. In addition, it is not to be forgotten that the stronghold of monophysitism, Egypt, remained absolutely untouched by persecution, and many persecuted clerics, monks, nuns, and even laymen took refuge there.

Since, on the basis of the sources which have come down to us, it is almost impossible to draw a distinct line between these two periods, almost all historians have emphasized only the picture of continuous religious persecution under Justin and marked a change only with Justinian's accession to the throne. This is historically wrong, for

Justinian was only continuing and developing the religious policy of the later years of his uncle's reign which he had himself considerably affected. The correspondence which has survived permits us to fix the precise date of the change. The first suggestions to the Pope concerning milder treatment of religious difficulties in the Near East are found in the letters of July and September, 520. Vitalian, the most ardent supporter of energetic measures against the monophysites, was assassinated in July, 520. The activities of the Scythian monks, whose doctrine as we know also had for a time considerable influence on Justinian's ideas, belong to the years 519 and 520. These dates obviously show that with Vitalian's violent death in July, 520, the chief obstacle to opening a new policy in the East disappeared. During the first two years of Justin's reign, 518–520, the government had come to realize the uselessness and even the political danger of an irreconcilable and aggressive policy against the East, and determined to apply new methods, those of mildness, persuasion, and a degree of tolerance.

The third and last stage in the religious policy of Justin's period, however, belonging to the last years of his reign, marked a return on the part of the two Augusti, Justin and Justinian, to the policy of coercion and persecution and culminated in 527 in the issue of the famous edict against heretics.

Since our abundant monophysite evidence has naturally not stressed the milder period, historians dealing with the religious policy of Justin have often confined themselves to a general statement that his reign represents merely a continuous and rigorous persecution, which abated somewhat in severity only with the accession of Justinian. A monophysite historian of the twelfth century, Michael the Syrian, wrote: "At the end of six and a half years the fury subsided, because the emperor had changed." [156] Gibbon said that "Justin trod the narrow path of inflexible and intolerable orthodoxy." According to Bury, "the persecution continued throughout the reign of Justin. But Justinian determined to essay a different policy." Maspero writes: "This was a general rout of the monophysite clergy, which began in the autumn of 518 and extended during the whole reign of Justin;" in another

[156] Michael the Syrian, IX, 15; Chabot, II, 177.

place he remarks: "The Orientals do not use against Justinian such words of hatred as they address to Justin I." [157]

We may now, however, adduce some examples of Justin's relative tolerance, for sometimes in his religious ideology he seems to have differed clearly from the Pope in the direction of moderation. In several cases he left prominent monophysites unharmed. Not only did he refrain from deposing the Patriarch of Alexandria, Timothy, but he even employed him for various purposes. Egypt of course was economically extremely important, the richest granary of Constantinople and a large source of state revenues, so that the central government needed to be very cautious in carrying out its new religious policy there. This shows once more that the new religious policy was directed not by fanatical impulses only, but also by other motives of an economic, financial, and political character. As we shall see below, Jacob (James) of Sarug, appointed bishop though a monophysite, in his letter to Paul, Bishop of Edessa, chose words of highest praise for Justin. Soterichus was allowed to retain the See of Caesarea of Cappadocia, contrary to the Pope's wish. There are also other examples of Justin's tolerance.[158]

I admit that these examples are not striking enough to solve the question, and some scholars are not convinced of the new trend towards mildness in Justin's policy. For instance, Lebon asserts that the proofs alleged by Guidi fail to convince him: Paul of Edessa was brought back to his See because he was converted to the Synod of Constantinople; moreover when Jacob of Sarug was ordained Bishop of Batnan in 519 the imperial order to enforce the synod had not yet reached the Orient.[159] But Lebon failed to take into consideration the correspondence between Constantinople and Rome, which in my opinion is strong evidence for the theory that Justin showed some tolerance.

[157] Gibbon, ch. XL; ed. Bury, IV, 208. Bury, II, 373. Jean Maspero, *Histoire des patriarches d'Alexandrie*, p. 71; 109. Also J. Lebon, *Le monophysisme sévérien*, p. 73.

[158] These examples are cited in I. Guidi, *La lettera di Simeone Vescovo di Bêth-Aršâm sopri i martiri omeriti*, in *Atti della R. Academia dei Lincei. Memorie della classe di scienze morali, storiche e filologiche*, VII, 474. From Guidi, H. G. Kleyn, *Het Leven van Johannes van Tella door Elias*, p. 24, note.

[159] J. Lebon, *Le monophysisme sévérien*, p. 69, n. 4.

An additional proof of Justin's attempt to follow a lenient policy towards the heretics is the first lines of the edict on heretics, which was issued in 527 shortly before Justin's death. We read in its preamble: "Therefore we have permitted the heretics to assemble and have their own denomination, that they feeling shame because of our patience may voluntarily become sound of mind and turn to the better. But unbearable recklessness has laid hold of them." [160] Unfortunately the very beginning of this law, in which the emperor indicated his reasons for granting concessions, is lost. But that it contained these reasons is clear from the word "therefore" (διὰ τοῦτο; *ideo*) which occurs in the text given above.

From this preamble we may not only draw the conclusion that an attempt at religious leniency was made, but also that it failed. This is the explanation of the fact that this law was issued so late, in the last months of Justin's rule, and its extreme severity. It was the infliction of punishment for the stubborn resistance of heretics and various religious dissidents. It was a manifestation of the imperial anger inspired by ruined hopes. And without doubt this law once more reflects the influence of the impetuous and energetic coemperor Justinian, who, now about forty-five years of age, was destined very shortly to ascend the throne to replace the old and ill Justin.

Justin had ascended the throne with the strong determination to reëstablish the decrees of the Council of Chalcedon all over the empire. In his letters to Constantinople Pope Hormisdas, as we know, suggested several times that religious dissidents should be "corrected"; and by "correction" the Pope meant that if persuasion failed coercion should be applied. A dark period of persecution opened in the Near East, in Asia Minor, and particularly in Syria and Palestine. Egypt only was spared and remained a refuge to the persecuted monophysites. Deposition and exile, very often accompanied by severe punitive measures, were ordinary proceedings. Not only the clergy, recalcitrant bishops, monks, clerics in general, but also laymen, men, women,

---

[160] Τοὺς αἱρετικοὺς ἡμεῖς μὲν διὰ τοῦτο καὶ συνιέναι καὶ προσηγορίαν ἔχειν ἰδίαν συνηχωρήσαμεν, ἵνα τὴν καρτερίαν ἡμῶν αἰσχυνθέντες σωφρονήσωσιν ἑκόντες καὶ πρὸς τὰ καλλίω μεταβάλωσιν. Τοὺς δὲ εἰσῆλθέ τις οὐκ ἀνεκτὴ τόλμα. *Cod.* I, 5, 12, preamble; ed. Krueger, p. 53.

and even children, sank beneath the wave of persecution. In addition to many deposed and exiled bishops whose names have not survived, there is a list of about fifty-four bishops who were deprived of their sees and sent into exile. Most of them belonged to the territory of the patriarchate of Antioch, but three were from Cappadocia and several from the provinces of Asia and Caria. The list of the bishops from the patriarchate of Antioch clearly shows how successful had been the work of Severus, who occupied the patriarchal throne six years only (512–518). Here is the list: Cilicia Secunda: Ethericus of Anazarbe, Julius of Aegae, John of Mopsuestia, Paul of Epiphania, John of Irenopolis, Paul of Alexandretta. Syria Prima: Constantine of Laodicea, Antony of Alep, Nonnus of Seleucia, Isidore of Chalcis. Syria Secunda: Peter of Apamea.[161] Phoenicia Secunda: Thomas of Damascus, Alexander of Abila, Thomas of Iabroud, John of Palmyra, John, Bishop of the Arab monks of Hawarin (Evaria). Euphratesia: Philoxenus of Hierapolis, Sergius of Kyrros (Κύρρος), Thomas of Germanicia, Eustathius of Perre (Πέρρη). Osrhoene: Paul of Edessa, John of Harran, Thomas of Himeria,[162] John of Tella, Peter of Resaina, Nonnus of Circesium, Paul of Callinicus, Marion of Sura. Mesopotamia: Maras of Amida, Thomas of Dara, Akhron of Arsomosata.[163]

From the point of view of the Chalcedonians, the most odious figure and formidable adversary was Severus, Patriarch of Antioch (512–

[161] Devreesse calls him "one of the leaders (coryphei) of Severian monophysitism." Le patriarcat d'Antioche, p. 180.

[162] Himeria's location is unknown. Devreesse, op. cit., p. 298.

[163] Mich. le Syr., IX, 13 (Chabot, II, 170–173). He reproduces the data of John of Asia (of Ephesus). See also a list of the banished bishops in the Chronicle of Pseudo-Dionysius of Tell Mahre (a. 809–889). H. G. Kleyn, Bijdrage tot de Kerkgeschiedenis van het Oosten geburende de zesde eeuw, Feestbundel aan Prof. M. J. de Goeje, pp. 65–67. M. l'abbé Nau, "L'histoire ecclésiastique de Jean d'Asie," Revue de l'Orient Chrétien, II (1897), 467–468 (a list in Syriac). Gregorii Barhebraei Chronicon Ecclesiasticum, ed. J. B. Abbeloos et T. J. Lamy, I, 196 (55 bishops). The Arab historian and geographer of the tenth century, Masudi, laconically says: "The sixteenth (Christian emperor) is Justin who reigned nine years; he persecuted the Jacobites by death and exile." Kitâb at-Tanbîh, Bibliotheca geographorum arabicorum, ed. de Goeje, VIII (Leiden, 1894), 152. Maçoudi, Le livre de l'avertissement et de la revision, transl. into French by Carra de Vaux (Paris, 1896), p. 209. The list of the exiled bishops is also reproduced in R. Devreesse, Le patriarcat d'Antioche, p. 72, note; individual names are given in several places.

518), the real leader and inspirer of the monophysite resistance, "the rock of Christ, and guardian of the pure faith" (Zach. IX, 24). As we have noted above, his name was shouted many times by the turbulent crowd during the stormy days of July 15 and 16 in Constantinople and at the Synod of Tyre, September 16, 518. It was rumored that under pressure from Vitalian Justin had ordered Severus' tongue to be cut out. It is a fact according to Evagrius (IV, 4), that Justin commanded one of his officials, Irenaeus, to arrest Severus. But in September, 518 Severus received a warning from some friends and succeeded in quitting Antioch secretly by night; at Seleucia Pieria, which was the port of Antioch, he boarded a ship and then reached Alexandria in safety, where he was warmly welcomed by the monophysite patriarch of the city, Timothy IV.[164] One of the biographers of Severus and his contemporary, John, abbot of the monastery of Bar-Aphtonia, himself a monophysite, wrote "After the shepherd had been banished, his flock was handed over to the wolves. False shepherds have replaced the true ones. They neither have spared the flock (cf. Acts 20, 29) nor fortified the sick, nor bound up the wounded, nor recovered those who were driven away (cf. Ezekiel 34, 4); but they made fall into heresy those who were sound in faith (cf. Titus II, 2)." In a hymn on Severus supposedly written by an Alexandrian poet, he is called "the sage Severus, a great pillar of the church and a true teacher of the entire universe." [165]

It is not surprising that Justin and his government should single out as their main object of attack such a personage as Severus. Even stripped of all the exaggerated enthusiasm of the monophysite writers, he still remains a great man, an honest defender of his religious doctrine, and an amazingly prolific writer. It was unfortunate for Justin

---

[164] Liberatus Deacon, *Liberati Diaconi Breviarium*, XIX. Migne, *PL*, LXVIII, col. 1033. Evagr., IV, 4; ed. Bidez-Parmentier, pp. 154–155. *Nic. Call. Eccles. Historia*, XVII, 2; Migne, *PG*, CXLVII, coll. 221–224. See a very useful list of excerpts on Severus from Greek, Latin, and Arab sources by M.-A. Kugener in *Patr. Orient.*, II (1907), 336–400 (252–316). See also a discussion of Severus' flight and its chronology in Jean Maspero, *Histoire des patriarches d'Alexandrie*, pp. 70–71, n. 3.

[165] "Vie de Sévère par Jean supérieur du monastère de Beith-Aphtonia," par M.-A. Kugener, *Patr. Or.*, II (1907),248 (164). F. Nau, "Opuscules Maronites," *Revue de l'Orient Chrétien*, V (1900), 298. Severus, "Une hymne sur Sévère qui a été composée, dit-on, par un poète d'Alexandrie, *Patr. Or.*, II, 330 (246).

and his new religious orientation that energetic and talented theologians who could effectively defend the Chalcedonian Creed were entirely lacking. Not only were there none to equal Severus, but there were not even any to approach him in talent or energy.

There were several prominent figures among the banished bishops in addition to Severus. One was Julian of Halicarnassus, a friend of Severus, who fled at the same time with him to Egypt and later engaged in passionate polemics with Severus concerning his doctrine of the indestructibility of the body of Christ from the moment at which it was assumed by the Logos (the so-called aphthartodocetism).[166] Some bishops who signed the anti-Julian manifesto were banished by Justin and later returned by Justinian; for instance, John of Constantine (Tella), Peter of Resaina (Theodosiopolis), and Thomas of Dara.[167]

The most prominent monophysite leader after Severus was Philoxenus-Xenaias (in Syriac Aksenaya), Bishop of Hierapolis-Mabbug (Mabbôgh, Menbidj) in eastern Syria, who in the Greek Orthodox tradition is named "the slave of Satan." He was first banished to Philippopolis in Thrace, whence he wrote two letters, the most important of his dogmatic works, which show that the sufferings and privations of his exile had no power to change the opinions for which he had been fighting ever since he left Edessa, where he had studied over half a century before. Probably on account of his dogmatic writings, he was taken from Philippopolis to a place even farther distant from the capital, Gangra in Paphlagonia, where he died, probably in 523. According to Pseudo-Zacharias, at Gangra he was imprisoned over the kitchen of the local inn (ξενοδοχεῖον) and suffered greatly from the smoke, as he himself states in his epistle; in fact it eventually brought about his death.[168] Philoxenus-Xenaia, who before

---

[166] Zach. Mityl. IX, 9–13; Hamilton-Brooks, pp. 232–244; Ahrens-Krüger, 177–188 (epistles between Severus and Julian). Michel le Syrien, IX, 13; Chabot, II, 172. *History of the Patriarchs of the Coptic Church of Alexandria*, ed. and transl. by B. Evetts, *Patr. Or.*, I (1907), 454 (190): "Julian did not cease to send his writings into the country to lead men astray and draw them to himself." *Liberati Diaconi Breviarium*, Migne, PL, LXVIII, 1033–1034. Theoph., p. 165: τὸν περὶ φθαρτοῦ καὶ ἀφθάρτου λόγον κινήσαντες.

[167] Devreesse, *op. cit.*, pp. 297; 299; 302.

[168] Zach. of Mityl., VIII, 5; Hamilton-Brooks, p. 207; 211; Ahrens-Krüger, pp.

his ordination as bishop had lived a considerable time in the monasteries of Amida in the far off province of Mesopotamia, had a powerful influence with the local monks. As a Syrian chronicler says, he "urged the believing and zealous monks of the East" and was in correspondence with them. When under Justin persecution broke out in the East and finally reached the remote confines of Mesopotamia, Philoxenus' religious agitation bore fruit, and the monks of the monasteries of Amida and the Eastern monks in general became the most stubborn and most fanatical adversaries of the new policy. It is not to be forgotten that the true leaders of the religious life were not the bishops but the monks, who had enormous influence with the uneducated masses of the population, men, women, and children, stimulated their religious ardor, and formed out of them a solid and compact whole which at times the government found very difficult to manage. Considering the strength of Philoxenus' influence and his organizing ability, we are not surprised that Justin applied very severe measures to him. Greek tradition also mentions among exiled bishops Peter of Apamea.[168]

It is interesting to note that apparently Justin's persecution did not at once embrace all the Near East, particularly such distant provinces as Mesopotamis, with cities like Amida, Tella, Sarug. There may have been the practical problem that it took more time to reach them than to reach Syria and Palestine, which were nearer; or the government might have hesitated for some time before undertaking the more difficult task of striking the regions which were most deeply affected

---

158-159. Mich. le Syr., IX, 13; II, 171. *Chronique de Seert, Patr. Or.*, VII, 139 (47): "Philoxenus was suffocated at Philippopolis." *Gregorii Barhebraei Chronicon Ecclesiasticum*, I, 198. Theoph., p. 134: ὁ δοῦλος τοῦ Σατανᾶ; also p. 165: μανιχαιόφρονα ὄντα. Cedr., I, 637. *Anastasii Chronographia Tripertita*, p. 116: "servus Satanae." Nic. Call., XVI, 27 (Migne, *PG*, CXLVII, 169-172). See Assemani, *Bibliotheca Orientalis*, II (Rome, 1721), 10-46. A. A. Vaschalde, *Three Letters of Philoxenus, Bishop of Mabbôgh* (Rome, 1902), pp. 1-23. J. Lebon, *Le monophysisme sévérien*, p. 68. A. Baumstark, *Geschichte der syrischen Literatur*, pp. 141-144. E. Tisserant, *Philoxène de Mabboug, Dictionnaire de théologie catholique*, XII, 2 (Paris, 1935), 1509-1532. Excellent article.

[169] On Philoxenus, Zach. of Mityl., VII, 10. Hamilton-Brooks, p. 179; Ahrens-Krüger, p. 130. On Philoxenus' influence with the masses see some very instructive pages in A. Diakonov, *John of Ephesus*, p. 23 ff. (in Russian). On Peter of Apamea, Theoph., p. 165. Cedr. I, 637.

by monophysitism and where the population was excessively fanatical. I shall give here some examples. The monophysite bishop Nonnus (in Syriac, Nuna) was banished by Justin from Seleucia Pieria, near Antioch. He went to distant Amida, his native city, and there after the death of Bishop Thomas occupied the episcopal see for three months, at the end of which he died; after his death three local bishops ordained as bishop of the city another monophysite, Mara (Moro). Both were ordained at Amida without the knowledge of the patriarch. Only later, two years after the persecution had started (at the end of 520, or at the outset of 521) was Mara banished to Petra, and then from Petra to Alexandria. His place at Antioch was assumed by Abraham Bar-Khaili, who was a sworn enemy of monophysitism and had been ordained at Antioch.[170]

In *Lives of the Eastern Saints*, in a passage which deals with Mara, Bishop of Amida, and his three companions, John of Ephesus tells a very interesting story which probably has some foundation in fact. Mara from the place of his exile, Petra, sent his deacon Stephen to Constantinople "in the hope that he might perhaps by the intercession of anyone whom God might put in his way" be able to obtain permission to leave Petra for another more hospitable place. In the capital "the good God" directed Stephen to Theodora, the wife of Justinian who was at that time master of the soldiers ($\sigma\tau\rho\alpha\tau\eta\lambda\acute{\alpha}\tau\eta\varsigma$). Theodora asked her husband to present the case to the emperor. Her intercession was successful, and "an order went out to them to come to Alexandria," where "the blessed men were quietly settled." [171] In this story Mara's move from Petra to Alexandria is represented as due to special favor on the part of the emperor, while other sources merely state that he was banished from Petra to Alexandria. In my opinion, John of Ephesus' story is the more plausible explanation, since the government

---

[170] Zach. of Mit., VIII, 5; Hamilton-Brooks, pp. 208–209; Ahrens-Krüger, pp. 158–159. Mich. le Syr., IX, 13. Chabot, II, 173–174. Assemani, *Bibl. Or.*, II, 48–51. Diakonov, John of Ephesus, pp. 24–25 (in Russian). Chabot, *Littérature syriaque* (Paris, 1934), p. 71: "Mara was banished by Justin in 519." Devreesse, *op. cit.*, p. 301.

[171] John of Ephesus, *Lives of the Eastern Saints*, ch. XIII; in Latin by van Douwen and Land, pp. 67–68; in English by E. W. Brooks, *Patr. Or.*, XVII (1923), 187–190. In this story occurs the famous statement that Theodora came from the brothel.

had no power to "banish" him to Alexandria, which was at that time a haven for refugees, and not under Justin's control.

In the regions near Amida, two monophysites, John of Tella (John Bar Cursus) and Jacob (James) of Sarug, received their episcopal sees after the beginning of the persecution but "before it crossed the Euphrates." John of Tella, who according to Michael the Syrian was so abstemious that he "did not eat as much bread as a child," was banished, probably in 519. His life was written by John of Ephesus, and if we discount some miraculous and edifying passages, we can rely on it for some historical data. "When the severe persecution originated by the partisans of the schismatic synod of Chalcedon was wafted like smoke everywhere, and blinded everyone whose spiritual eyesight was not founded upon a sound basis, and concealed the light of their truth," John was driven from his see with all the other bishops, and "they endured the severe labors and grievous hardships of banishment, and wanderings in every place." One of the questions which worried the exiled "believing bishops" was that of ordination ($\chi\epsilon\iota\rho o$-$\tau o\nu\iota\alpha\varsigma$). Candidates could be ordained only in three places, at Marde, where John of Tella stayed, probably till about 527, in Persia, and at Alexandria. And it is interesting to note that candidates for ordination came from Armenia, Arzanene, Cappadocia, and the seacoasts, which usually means the province of Phoenicia Maritima. John outlived the period of Justin's reign, and finally suffered martyrdom in 538.[172] Ac-

---

[172] On John of Tella see his *Life*, by John of Ephesus. Latin translation by W. J. van Douwen and J. P. N. Land, *Joannis episcopi Ephesi Commentarii de beatis orientalibus* (Amsterdam, 1889), cap. XXIV, pp. 108–113. In Syriac and English by E. W. Brooks, *Lives of the Eastern Saints*, Patr. Or., XVIII, 513–526 (312–324); see also *Patr. Or.*, XVII (1923), p. 228. Another *Life* of John of Tella by Elias, one of his companions, is published with a Dutch translation by H. G. Kleyn, *Het Leven van Johannes van Tella door Elias*, pp. XIX–LXXXVIII (translation); 1–83 (Syriac text). In Latin by E. W. Brooks, *Vita Johannis Episcopi Tellae auctore Elia*, transl. E. W. B., CSCO, *Scriptores syri*, 3rd series, vol. XXV, *Vitae virorum apud Monophysitas celeberrimorum* (Paris, 1907), pp. 21–60. Michel le Syrien, IX, 14; Chabot, II, 173. See Assemani, *Bibliotheca Orientalis*, II, 53. Kleyn, *op. cit.*, p. VII. Both say that John was banished in 519. Brooks, *Patr. Or.*, XVIII, 514 (312): probably in 521. Chabot, *Littérature syriaque*, p. 70: in 521. On Tella-de-Mauzelat-Constantina see Honigmann, *Die Ostgrenze*, p. 4; 22; 24. The name of this city Constantina derives from the name of the Emperor Constantius, who in the fourth century fortified the place. E. Stein erroneously calls this city Tela d'manzalat. *Studien zur Geschichte des byzantinischen Reiches*, p. 69 and others (see index).

cording to Chabot, Jacob of Sarug was ordained Bishop of Batnan in 519 and died in 521.[173]

These few examples indicate that even in the first years of Justin's reign the government was not absolutely ruthless towards the monophysites. The policy, if sometimes severe, was not reckless. The first and most severe period of persecution lasted from 518 to 520, when Vitalian was assassinated.

We have little information on the followers of Nestorius who were condemned at the Council of Ephesus, 431. They were also subject to persecution; but they were far less numerous than the monophysites, and most of them at that time lived beyond the confines of the empire, in Persia, out of reach of Constantinople.[174]

An interesting episode occurred at Cyrrhus connected with one of the most conspicuous theologians of the fifth century, Theodoret, Bishop of Cyrrhus, in the province of Euphratensis, who died in 457 or 458. His memory was still very vivid in Justin's period and he had warm admirers, especially at Cyrrhus. Under Justin two clerics of Cyrrhus, the presbyter and defensor Andronicus and the deacon George, took Theodoret's image, put it upon a chariot, and, singing psalms, organized a procession. Up to very recently the episcopal chair of Cyrrhus had been vacant, but Sergius had been appointed to fill it shortly before. Sharing the sympathies of his new flock, he ordained a special celebration in honor of his renowned predecessor. This episode was reported to Justin, who in his edict in the name of the then *magister militum Orientis*, Hypatius, August 7, 520, ordered him to investigate the matter. In the official document referring to the case Theodoret is characterized as one "who is everywhere accused of the error of faith" (*qui undique inculpatur propter fidei errorem*).

---

[173] On Jacob of Sarug, Michel le Syrien, IX, 15; Chabot, II, pp. 175–176. See Diakonov, *John of Ephesus*, p. 25 (in Russian). Lebon, *Le monophysisme sévérien*, pp. 68–69. Chabot, *Littérature syriaque*, pp. 62–63. Baumstark, *Geschichte der syrischen Literatur*, pp. 148–158 (detailed information on Jacob's literary work). E. Tisserant, "Jacques de Saroug," *Dictionnaire de théologie catholique*, VIII, 1, 300–305. A very fine article.

[174] It is worth noting that later Russian sources which took over information from Greek evidence incorporate a mention of severe persecution of Nestorians opened by Justin. *The Russian Chronograph of 1512*, PSRL, XXII, 1, 292. *The Chronograph of Western-Russian Version*, PSRL, XXII, 2, 108.

After investigation Sergius was ejected from his chair, although he later attended the colloquium of 531 (533) in Constantinople.[175]

The new religious trend also affected the army. In the second year of Justin's reign, in 519 or 520, an edict was issued in virtue of which soldiers must adhere to the Chalcedonian Creed; otherwise they would be deprived of their rations and other privileges connected with military service. The majority of the soldiers accordingly complied with the imperial demand.[176] And we shall see later that in several cases the military force aided the civil authorities to drive the monks out of their monasteries and take coercive measures against the recalcitrant populace. Our sources make no mention of any revolts in the army on account of the new religious policy.

An interesting episode took place at Edessa in November 519. At that time the bishop of this city was a monophysite, Paul. By order of the government a certain Patricius came to Edessa to offer Paul an alternative: either to subscribe to the Chalcedonian Creed or to be dismissed from his episcopate. The bishop refused to subscribe and took refuge in a baptistery. Patricius, following the emperor's edict and fearful of being accused of excessive mildness, ordered Paul to be dragged out of the baptistery and deported to Seleucia. When Justin heard of the sacrilege with which the carrying out of his order had been attended, he changed his mind and returned Paul to his see, hoping that he would finally accept the synod. Forty-four days later Paul returned to Edessa and remained there as bishop, although he did not accept the synod, till the end of July, 522. Only then did Justin, recognizing his tenacity, send him into exile, to Euchaïta in Pontus. Three months after he had left Edessa, his successor, the monophysite Asclepius, came into the city (October 23, 522).[177]

[175] This episode is told in the *Acts of the Fifth Ecumenical Council*, which also mentions Justin's dated edict to Hypatius. See Mansi, IX, 348–350; 364–365. See N. Glubokovsky, *The Blessed Theodoret, Bishop of Cyrrhus*, I (Moscow, 1890), 312–313. G. V. Florovsky, *The Byzantine Fathers of the Fifth-Eighth Centuries* (Paris, 1933), p. 81. Both in Russian. See R. Devreesse, *Le patriarcat d'Antioche*, p. 285.

[176] On this edict see below, p. 242.

[177] *Chronicle of Edessa*, LXXXVIII; Hallier, pp. 126–127; Guidi, p. 9; in English, Cowper, p. 37 (LXXXIX). *Chronicon Anonymum ad A. D. 819*, transl. I.-B. Chabot, CSCO, Scriptores syri, 3rd series, vol. XIV, 5. Cf. Michel le Syrien, IX, 13–14; II, 172; 174; 176. *Chronique de Michel le Grand*, by Langlois, pp. 176–178

On Paul's return to Edessa at Justin's order we have a very interesting letter by Jacob (James) of Sarug, a monophysite, to Paul himself, which confirms this story as told in the *Chronicle of Edessa.* Jacob of Sarug highly praises Justin's attitude towards the unjust treatment of Paul. "The faithful emperor, indeed, and worthy of victory, hearing that which had been done against you, was moved and hastened to return you to your see; he covered your enemies with shame and confusion, and clearly said to everyone that he in no way approved those who, by their violence, had outraged baptism (perhaps the baptistery?) and persecuted your religion. The whole country is now in joy on account of this event, and the little herd is delighted that the shepherd has been brought back to his flock. All assemblies pray with all their hearts for the faithful emperor and for your Holiness. . . . This pure belief agrees with that of the blessed Constantine and the faithful Abgar. Now all the Eastern churches are joyous and thank God for having given us a faithful and powerful emperor, able to confess his faith. It was the meed of the Bishop of Edessa to make shine the faith of our emperor and to prove that it was in harmony with the faith of the disciples of the cross. Indeed, if the emperor failed to believe that the Crucified One was God, how could he wear the cross on the top of his crown? If it were simply the cross of a man, as those pretend who wish to deceive the emperor and outrage God, the emperor would never have wished to wear the cross of a man on the top of his crown. It was proper that the belief of the emperor should shine like the sun all over the world through the Bishop of Edessa, for Edessa is the first bride of Christ, and it must always be the first in virtue." This letter was one of the last written by Jacob of Sarug. He was an old man at the time, and he died a few months later, probably in 521. Jacob wrote another letter, probably about 520, addressed to the Himyarite Christians in South Arabia, in which he made the following striking statement: "We Romans, who live quietly under Christian kings, praise your most glorious life." [178]

(a passage from John of Asia, i.e., John of Ephesus). See R. Duval, *Histoire politique, religieuse et littéraire d'Edesse jusqu'à la première croisade*, p. 198.

[178] M. l'abbé Martin, "Lettres de Jacques de Saroug aux moines du Couvent de Mar Bassus, et à Paul d'Edesse," *Zeitschrift der Deutschen Morgenländischen Gesellschaft*, XXX (1876), 274 (Syriac text and French translation); see also

I have given these two quotations because they are very little known among Byzantine scholars, because they are additional evidence for some degree of tolerance in Justin's religious policy, and because it is amazing to hear from a monophysite writer such high praise given to the emperor who in most monophysite writings, as we know, is very harshly judged. The idea was advanced in the eighteenth century by Assemani that Jacob himself might have been orthodox; but it has not been accepted, and Jacob of Sarug, whom in their admiration the Syrians call "the flute of the Holy Ghost and the harp of the Orthodox Church," has generally been recognized to have been a monophysite. But most recently, Paul Peeters has come to a very plausible conclusion, that Jacob was orthodox.[179]

I shall give an account of how persecutions under Justin have been presented by monophysite writers, especially by two sources of the sixth century, the *Syriac Chronicle* known as that of Zachariah of Mitylene, which was completed in 569, and, even more important, John of Ephesus, who died probably in 585.[180]

The most hateful figure in monophysite tradition was Patriarch Paul of Antioch, surnamed the Jew (519–521), Severus' successor, a former innkeeper in the quarter of Eubulus, in Constantinople (ὁ ξενοδόχος τῶν Εὐβούλου, Theoph., 165. Mal., 411). According to John Malalas, he ordered that the names of the six hundred and thirty bishops of the Council of Chalcedon be included in the diptychs in

---

p. 219. On Jacob of Sarug see above, p. 231–232. R. Schröter, "Trostschreiben Jacob's von Sarug an die himyaritischen Christen," *Zeitschrift der Deutschen Morgenländischen Gesellschaft*, XXXI, 388.

[179] Paul Peeters, "Jacques de Saroug appartient-il à la secte monophysite?" *Analecta Ballandina*, LXVI (1948), 134–198; especially pp. 194–198.

[180] The second part of the *Ecclesiastical History of John of Ephesus* which contains the time of Justin, and which has not yet been published and translated in its entirety, I use here in a Latin translation of some of its fragments by van Douwen and Land (Amsterdam, 1889). The analysis of the second part of the *History of John of Ephesus* has been made by M. l'abbé Nau, "Analyse de la seconde partie inédite de l'Histoire Ecclésiastique de Jean d'Asie," *Revue de l'Orient chrétien*, II, 455–493. Diakonov disagrees with some of the results of Nau's study: *John of Ephesus*, p. 3 (in Russian). By misprint Diakonov (p. 165) gives in the text of his book the probable year of the death of John of Ephesus as 595 or 596; see his own correction on p. 404 (585–586). Many details of the life of the monks and anchorites in Justin's time in the eastern regions can be found in various *Lives of the Eastern Saints* also compiled by John of Ephesus.

every city.[181] He opened severe persecution all over the territory of his patriarchate in the districts of Antioch, Apamea, Mabbug, in all Arabia and Palestine, in all southern and northern cities, as well as among the anchorites living in the desert down to the Persian border. The whole Orient suffered persecution. Men were killed, tortured, banished, expelled from their homes, pursued from place to place, deprived of property and food. Not only clerics and monks suffered but also laymen, men, women, and even children. Those who one day were dwelling in one place, were driven out from there the next day and sometimes even the same evening; they roamed without direction and could not find a place to pass the night. Wandering in fields and mountains like wild beasts, they bore the rigors of rain, snow, and cold. Monks were expelled from cloisters; stylites were compelled to descend from their columns. And here John of Ephesus inserts: "The emperor seeing that on account of Paul's violence men were withdrawing from the church, and realizing that some other crimes had been perpetrated by him, removed him from Antioch. Soon after Paul the Jew died." This information from a monophysite writer, which is confirmed by the data of the correspondence between Rome and Constantinople, is very valuable again in showing us that in religious policy Justin and his advisers were not mere fanatics, but were inclined to moderation.[182]

John of Ephesus vividly describes what happened at Edessa, when Paul's successor Asclepius, appointed by Patriarch Paul the Jew, took possession. The Monastery of Edessa refused to carry out the order of Paul the Jew to accept the Chalcedonian Synod and the *Tome of*

[181] Malalas, 411. Istrin, *Chronicle of John Malalas*, XCI, 17–18. *Chronicle of John Malalas*, Books VIII–XVIII, transl. M. Spinka, p. 121.

[182] Fragments of John of Ephesus by Douwen and Lánd, pp. 217–218. Zach. of Mit., VIII, 1: "Paul the Jew was driven out, because he celebrated the memory of Nestorius." Hamilton-Brooks, p. 190; Ahrens-Krüger, p. 141. Michel le Syr., II, 173–174. John of Nikiu, XC, 9–10; transl. by R. H. Charles, pp. 133–134; Zotenberg, p. 502. *Notices et extraits*, XXIV. See *Coll. Avell.*, no. 241 (pp. 740–741). Justin to Hormisdas (May 1, 521): "sacerdotio praeditus Antiochenae civitatis ita versatus esse dicitur in multis causis quae religionis alienae sunt episcopis . . . (Paulus) territus recusatorios libellos obtulit . . . quoniam cordi nobis et est et fuit, ut semper civitatum antistites in amore sint omnium communiquorum regendas accepisse creduntur animas." Also *Coll. Avell.*, no. 242 (pp. 741–742). Epiphanius to Hormisdas. On the same subject, Evagrius, IV, 4: παῦλος μὲν οὖν ἐθελούσιος ἀναχωρήσας (Bidez-Parmentier, p. 155).

Leo, and to take Holy Communion with Asclepius. The inhabitants of Edessa and Amida joined the monks. The new Bishop of Edessa, Asclepius, "the most wicked man" (*vir scelestissimus*) applied for help to the military power. The *praefectus militiae* Pharesmanes, in spite of the fact that it was midwinter, at Christmas time, commanded the monks to quit their monastery. The monks, among whom there were many sick and old, protested, saying that even barbarians would not have done such a thing. Then Pharesmanes took pity on them and ordered Asclepius to supply them with beasts of burden and camels. The whole population of the city, young and old, men, women and children, ran together to see their departure and ask for their blessing. Courageously bearing their cross, they left their abode. The brotherhoods of several other monasteries joined them in their exodus. Proceeding east from Edessa they reached the city of Tella de Mauzelat (now Viranshekhr), whose population met them with incense and torches. Finally they arrived in a monastery called En-Hailaph, south of Marde (Mardin, Μάρδης) where they stayed for nearly six years. At this time Justinian had assumed the throne, and Theodora permitted them to return to their own monastery at Edessa.[183]

Asclepius did not remain long at Edessa. In the winter of 524–525, during a disastrous inundation of the river of Daisan, the people of Edessa drove him out and he took refuge with Patriarch Euphrasius at Antioch. There, according to Michael the Syrian (II, 180), Euphrasius

---

[183] Fragmenta, pp. 219–220. Zach. of Mit., VIII, 4: "Asclepius was a Nestorian; but he was just in his deeds, and showed kindness to the tillers of the soil, and was gentle towards them, and was not greedy after bribes. In his body he was chaste, and in outward matters he did much good to his church, and paid its debts. But he was active and violent against the believers; and many were banished by him and outraged with every kind of torture, or died under the hard treatment inflicted on them at the hands of Liberarius [Liberius], a Goth, a cruel governor, who was called 'the bull-eater.'" Hamilton-Brooks, pp. 203–204; Ahrens-Krüger, pp. 153–154. We have seen in our text that the name of Liberarius (Liberius) is given here for that of Pharesmanes in John of Ephesus. See note in Ahrens–Krüger, p. 356 to p. 154, 2. The *Chronicle of Edessa* merely mentions the fact of the banishment of the monks by Asclepius under December 24, 522. L. Hallier, *Untersuchungen über die Edessenische Chronik mit dem syrischen Texte und einer Uebersetzung*, LXXXIX (XC), 128; *Chronicle of Edessa* transl. by I. Guidi (Paris, 1903), p. 9. CSCO, Scriptores syri, *Chronica Minora*, I. In English: *The Chronicle of Edessa*, by B. H. H(arris) C(owper). *The Chronicle of Sacred Literature and Biblical Record*, V, 37, § 90. Michel le Syrien, II, IX, 13; Chabot, II, pp. 176–177.

made Asclepius mount the ambo (pulpit) with him and said to the congregation: "Come to see a new Noah, who also escaped the deluge, as if in the Ark." Seventy days later on June 27, 525 Asclepius died and was buried at Antioch. But on September 4 of the same year his body was brought back to Edessa and deposited in the church of Mar Barlaha, close to the tomb of Mar Nonnos.[184]

When he heard of Asclepius' death, the former Bishop of Edessa, Paul, wrote a supplication to the Patrician Justinian, and sent his profession of faith (*libellus*) to Patriarch Euphrasius, which declared his adherence to the Chalcedonian Creed. And the "glorious and God-loving" Justinian reëstablished him in the see of Edessa. He returned to Edessa and died there on October 30, 526. His successor Andreas arrived at Edessa on February 7, 527.[185]

John of Ephesus describes another episode similar to the expulsion of the monks from Amida and its vicinity. The Amida community at that time "was composed of a combination of the convents great and small round the city and those inside it, and those of its territory"; this community contained not less than a thousand men. Since they "entered valiantly and heroically and courageously into the struggle against the defenders of the corrupt synod of Chalcedon," they were driven out of their convents in 521. Roaming "from place to place and from region to region," they arrived "at the great and famous convent" of the blessed Mama, in the village of Hazin (Hzyn) in the region of Tishpa (Tyšf), probably not far from Edessa, in the northern part of Osrhoene near the Euphrates. At that time the archimandrite of the convent was Sergius. There they remained five years (521–526). After five years of all sorts of spiritual labors, they determined to take up their abode in the neighborhood of Amida, though as John of Ephesus remarks "by reason of the persecution it was only by necessity (ἀνάγκη) that they could appear in the same province." Then they

---

[184] *Chronicle of Edessa*, XCI (XCII); Hallier, p. 130; Guidi, pp. 9–10; in English, Cowper, p. 37 (§ 92). Zach. of Mit., VIII, 4; Hamilton-Brooks, p. 204 (the river Scirtus); Ahrens–Krüger, p. 154 (the river Daisân). Michel le Syr., IX, 16; II, 180–181; 182–183. See Duval, *Histoire d'Edesse*, p. 198.
[185] *Chronicle of Edessa*, XCII (XCIII)–XCIV (XCV); Hallier, pp. 130–131; Guidi, p. 10; in English, Cowper, p. 38 (§ 93–95). Cf. Mich. le Syr., IX, 15; II, 176. As usual in the Syriac texts Justin is called Justinian. See Duval, *op. cit.*, p. 199. Devreesse, *Le pontificat d'Antioche*, p. 292.

left the convent of St. Mama and settled in the district east of Amida, in a monastery called the monastery of the Poplars, on the border of the territory of Amida, in the district opposite the hot spring (in Syriac, Hamimtha) of Abarne (now Chermük, Čermük). Since the monastery was too small for so many monks, they "were compelled all the summertime to set up tents for themselves outside on the mountains and under the wild trees surrounding the convent, and erect huts in extended and varied lines for themselves to dwell in"; at the same time they built great houses for winter habitation. They stayed in this place four years and a half. At the beginning of the reign of Justinian in 530, they were allowed to return to their own monasteries of Amida, which they found "destroyed, demolished, and knocked to pieces." In all, after they had been driven out of the Amida monasteries, the monks spent nine years and a half in exile.[186]

On the basis of the migrations of the persecuted monks, the so-called *Chronicle* of Zacharias of Mitylene draws an idyllic picture of religious life at that time in the Syrian deserts. We read: "And so the desert was at peace, and was abundantly supplied with a population of believers who lived in it, and fresh ones who were every day added to them and aided in swelling the numbers of their brethren, some from a desire to visit their brethren out of Christian love, and others again because they were being driven from country to country by the bishops in the cities. And there grew up, as it were, a commonwealth (πολιτεία) of illustrious and believing priests, and a tranquil brotherhood with them; and they were united in love and abounded in mutual affection; and they were beloved and acceptable in the sight of everyone." [187]

According to John of Ephesus, the successors of Paul the Jew as Patriarch of Antioch, Euphrasius of Jerusalem (521–526) and Ephraim

---

[186] John of Ephesus, *Lives of the Eastern Saints* ch. XXXV; van Douwen and Land, pp. 130–135; Brooks, *Patr. Or.*, XVIII, 607 (405)–623 (421). On the location of Hazin in Tishpa, see Douwen-Land, p. 77, n. 2. Diakonov, *John of Ephesus*, p. 27 (in Russian). On the location of Abarne, Diakonov, *op. cit.*, p. 28; E. Honigmann, *Die Ostgrenze des byzantinischen Reiches* (Bruxelles, 1935), p. 35; 139, n. 6. The Archimandrite Sergius is mentioned in *Lives*, ch. 58; van Douwen-Land, p. 187; Brooks, *Patr. Or.*, XIX, 221 (567). General presentation of this episode in Diakonov, *op. cit.*, pp. 27–28. See also Brook's Introduction, in *Patr. Or.*, XVII (1923), IV.

[187] Zach. of Mitylene, VIII, 5; Hamilton-Brooks, p. 211; Ahrens-Krüger, pp. 159–160.

of Amida (526–545), were most cruel persecutors of all those who refused to accept the Chalcedonian Creed (frag. 218). But the previous reputation of Euphrasius himself was not immaculate: he had removed from the diptychs the Synod of Chalcedon and the name of Pope Hormisdas, and only later, seized by fear of Justin and his new policy, had he proclaimed the four synods.[188] This record, which has been preserved by the Byzantine Chronicler, once more shows that Justin's religious policy was not stubbornly fanatical. Proof of this is that he maintained in such a responsible post as that of Patriarch of Antioch, with a vast territory under its jurisdiction, a man who had struck out of the diptychs the Chalcedonian Synod and the name of Pope Hormisdas, who was at that time still alive (he died in 523). As often happens with proselytes, however, after his conversion Euphrasius became more zealous than the original believers, and was a very severe persecutor of monophysites. The Egyptian chronicler of the seventh century, John of Nikiu, who of course as a monophysite himself shows marked bias, relates: "This man hated the Christians attached to the teaching of Severus. And many of the orthodox were put to death. He stirred up civil war throughout all the Roman Empire, and there was much shedding of blood. In the city of Antioch there were great tumults during five years; and no one could speak owing to fear of the emperor." [189] Euphrasius met a shocking and spectacular end: during the earthquake of 526, which struck Antioch severely, "he fell into a cauldron blazing with aromatic wax, and perished." [190]

His successor, Ephraim of Amida, who in his previous brilliant

---

[188] Theoph., p. 167. *Anastasii Chronographia Tripertita*, p. 131. As Devreesse writes: "Euphrasius was of a rather unsteady orthodoxy" ("d'une orthodoxie un peu chancelante"). *Le Patriarcat d'Antioche*, p. 118.

[189] *The Chronicle of John, Bishop of Nikiu*, XC, 14–15; 32; transl. Charles, p. 134; in French, by M. H. Zotenberg, p. 503.

[190] Zach. of Mit., VIII, 1, 4, 6; Hamilton-Brooks, p. 190; 205; 212–213; Ahrens-Krüger, p. 141; 155; 161. John of Ephesus in Nau, "Analyse," *Revue de l'Orient Chrétien*, II, 473: "in a cauldron of tar." *Chronicon anonymum, ad ann. p. Chr. 846 pertinens*, transl. by Chabot, p. 169: "in ardenti lebete cerati unguentarii." CSCO, Scriptores syri. *Chronica Minora. Nicephori Chronographia Compendiaria*: Εὐφράσιος, ὁ ἐν τῇ πτώσει τῆς πόλεως χωσθείς. CSHB, p. 784. John of Nikiu, XC, 14; Zotenberg, p. 505; Charles, p. 136. *Mal.*, p. 423: ἐν τῇ θεομηνίᾳ πυρίκαυστος ἐγένετο. Cedr., I, 640–641. Nic. Call., XVII, 3; PG, CXLVII, 224. Michel le Syrien, IX, 16; Chabot, II, 181. See Ahrens-Krüger, *Einleitung*, p. XXXIX. Diakonov, John of Ephesus, p. 240: a cauldron of slaked lime (in Russian).

career had reached the high dignity of *comes Orientis*, occupied the
See of Antioch for about nineteen years (526–544 or 545–546), which
is an exceptionally long time in the turbulent history of the patriarchate
of Antioch. According to John of Ephesus, "by persecution he thoroughly disturbed all the Orient, and the Church of God, and all Syria."
The Byzantine chronicler Theophanes relates that "Ephraim of Amida,
who was at that time *comes Orientis*, was ordained and revealed divine
zeal against the renegades." [191] Ephraim was also a polemist and writer.
The greater part of his patriarchate, of course, belongs to the time of
Justinian. He was canonized, and his name is included under June 8 in
the Greek Orthodox calendar.[192]

THE EDICT ON HERETICS, 527

Let us resume once more the general course of the religious policy
of Justin and Justinian. On the basis of the data which we have discussed above, the general picture of Justin's religious policy presents
itself thus: Justin ascended the throne with the firm decision to enforce the Chalcedonian Creed and restore normal relations with the
Pope. His policy falls into three periods. The first period, extending
from 518 to 520, was marked by extreme severity and harsh persecution. During this period, the powerful Vitalian, an ardent Chalcedonian,
was the leading spirit of the persecution. After his assassination in 520,
Justin, supported and guided by Justinian, entered a new path, a
certain degree of mildness and tolerance, as is decisively proved by the

---

[191] *Fragmenta*, p. 221. Theoph., 173: Ἐφραίμιος ὁ Ἀμιδηνός, κόμης ἀνατολῆς ὢν
ἐν τῷ χρόνῳ ἐκείνῳ, ἐχειροτονήθη ἀντ' αὐτοῦ (i.e. Euphrasius), ὅστις ζῆλον θεῖον κατὰ
τῶν ἀποσχιστῶν ἐνεδείξατο. Mal., p. 424. Evagr., IV, 6; Bidez-Parmentier, p. 156.
Nic. Call., XVII, 3; PG, CXLVII, 224. Zach. of Mityl., VIII, 4: "comes Orientis";
Hamilton-Brooks, p. 205; Ahrens-Krüger, p. 155. John of Nikiu, XC, 32; Charles,
p. 136; Zotenberg, p. 505. Mich. le Syr., IX, 19; Chabot, II, p. 181. F. Nau, Ahrens-
Krüger, Diakonov; see the preceding note. For chronology see H. F. Clinton,
Fasti Romani, I, 747: As Ephraimius was appointed after Justinian's elevation, his
appointment is brought to April 527, eleven months after the death of his prede-
cessor, and his eighteen years are completed in 545. See the special study by J.
Lebon, "Ephrem d'Amid patriarche d'Antioche 526-544," *Mélanges d'histoire
offerts à Charles Moeller* (Louvain-Paris, 1914), pp. 197-214. Photius devotes to
Ephraim two lengthy articles in his *Bibliotheca*, codd. 228 and 229. Migne. *PG*,
CIII, 957-1024. R. Devreesse, *Le patriarcat d'Antioche*, p. 118: 527-545.
[192] Sergius, *The Complete Liturgical Calendar* II, 1, 173; II, 2, 214 (in Russian).

correspondence between Constantinople and Rome, and by the preamble of the edict of 527 against heretics. This new policy, however,
failed because it met with a stubborn and often fanatical resistence on
the part of heretics and other religious dissidents, and another change
resulted. Realizing the failure of compromise and leniency, Justin and
Justinian, the two Augusti, in 527 decided to return to the policy of
coercion and persecution, the result of which was the edict of 527
against heretics. Undoubtedly the leading part in this decision and in
the writing of the edict itself belongs to Justinian.

Justin's new religious policy had repercussions in his legislation.
An extremely important edict was issued at the very beginning of
Justin's rule, in 519 or 520, before Vitalian's assassination in July 520;
it is permissible to surmise that Vitalian's powerful influence as a
strict and fanatical defender of the Chalcedonian doctrine is reflected
in this edict. The new law prescribed that all soldiers should adhere
to the Synod of Chalcedon; otherwise they would be deprived of
their rations and other privileges due to military service. The majority
of soldiers followed the imperial order and declared themselves in favor
of the Chalcedonian doctrine. This information is given us from the
monophysite Syriac sources: from the *Chronicle* of Jacob (James) of
Edessa, who died at the very beginning of the eighth century, and from
Michel the Syrian, who gives some supplementary details from the
second part of the *History of John of Ephesus*.[193]

That such an edict was published by Justin we have clear evidence
in the edict issued jointly by Justin and Justinian Augusti in 527, after
the first of April of that year, when Justinian was proclaimed augustus
and co-emperor. The edict of 527 (whose opening lines are missing)
deals with heretics and promises severe punishments to those who by
their unbearable recklessness disregard the laws and contrary to the
forbidding imperial ordinances intrude into the army.[194]

[193] *Chronicon Iacobi Edesseni* (under the second year of Justin's reign), transl.
Brooks, *CSCO*, Scriptores syri, 3rd series, vol. IV, *Chronica minora*, p. 240: "Exiit
(ab imperatore de) militibus mandatum ut omnes (synodo) Chalcedonis con-
sentirent; et revera consenserunt." On Jacob of Edessa and his *Chronicle* see A.
Baumstark, *Geschichte der syrischen Literatur*, pp. 248–256; on his *Chronicle*,
p. 254. He died in 708 (or 704). Michel le Syrien, IX, 16; Chabot, II, 180.

[194] *Cod. Just.* I, 5, 12, 1: τοὺς δὲ εἰσῆλθέ τις οὐκ ἀνεκτὴ τόλμα, καὶ τῆς τῶν νόμων
ἀμελήσαντας παραγγελίας στρατείας, ὧν οὐκ ἐᾷ μετεῖναι τοῖς τοιούτοις αὐτὰ τὰ τῶν

I am now able to state that the edict itself has been preserved, but has without any grounds erroneously been inserted among the edicts issued by Justinian (I, 4, 20). This is an undated and, strictly speaking, anonymous document, because the title Αὐτοκράτωρ ᾿Ιουστινιανὸς A. is printed in brackets, showing that it is tentative. I shall give the text of the edict, so far as I understand it, in English: "Nobody can be enrolled into the army unless three witnesses on the Holy Gospels testify that he is an orthodox Christian; the transaction is to take place in the presence of the commander under whom he is to serve; and a fee of two nomismata is to be paid for this (transaction). But if this (edict) is violated, the commander shall pay fifty pounds of gold, his staff twenty, and the person enrolled ten; he shall be dismissed, and the false witnesses shall undergo corporal punishment. And penalties are to be paid to the imperial treasury at the peril of the *comes*.[195]

Without doubt this is the edict issued by Justin in 519–520 which has been recorded in the Syriac monophysite evidence and is referred to in the law of 527. The very stern tone of the edict would indicate almost with certainty that it was issued before Vitalian's assassination in July 520, after which time the government somewhat mollified its severity.[196]

Of course this law did not apply to all the armed forces of the empire; it was restricted to the regular Roman soldiers, who in the sixth century were distinguished as *stratiotai* from the other sections of the army, the *limitanei*, the *foederati*, the allies (σύμμαχοι). These terms in the sixth century were applied to the bands of barbarians, such as Goths, Huns, Heruls, Gepids, Slavs (Sclavenes and Antae) who supplied the empire with armed forces, usually under the command

---

βασιλικῶν συμβόλων δηλοῖ γράμματα παρενέβαλον αὐτούς; also I, 5, 12, 6: οὔτε πολιτικὴν οὔτε στρατιωτικὴν οὔτε εἰς τάξιν τελεῖν οὐδεμίαν (ed. P. Krüger, p. 53).

[195] Cod. I, 4, 20; ed. Krueger, p. 41: Οὐδεὶς στρατεύεται, εἰ μὴ ἐν ὑπομνήμασι μαρτυρηθῇ ἐπὶ τριῶν ἐπὶ τῶν ἁγίων εὐαγγελίων Χριστανὸς ὀρθόδοξος, συνισταμένης τῆς πράξεως παρὰ τῷ ἄρχοντι, ἔνθα μέλλει στρατεύεσθαι, δύο νομισμάτων ὑπὲρ αὐτῆς διδομένων. εἰ δὲ τοῦτο παραμεληθῇ, δίδωσιν ὁ ἄρχων πεντήκοντα λίτρας καὶ ἡ τάξις αὐτοῦ κ' καὶ ὁ στρατευσάμενος ι' καὶ ἐκβάλλεται καὶ οἱ ψευδομαρτυρήσαντες σωματικῶς τιμωροῦνται καὶ αἱ ποιναὶ τοῖς πριβάτοις εἰσάγονται κινδύνῳ τοῦ κόμητος. The κόμης of the edict is κόμης τῶν πριβάτων, or, in Latin, *comes rerum privatarum.*

[196] Those who mention this edict attribute it to the epoch of Justinian. See, for example, Hamilcar S. Alivisatos, *Die kirchliche Gesetzgebung des Kaisers Justinian I* (Berlin, 1913), p. 32.

of their native chiefs.[197] These sections of the army were not affected by Justin's law, which applied only to the regular Roman soldiers.

Apparently the regular army accepted this drastic measure quietly, in full obedience, as military units are accustomed to accept the orders of their highest commanding officer, the emperor. We do not know what effect if any this law had on the discipline and fighting qualities of the Byzantine troops.

Now let us turn to another document, which represents the final step in the nine years of Justin's religious policy. Although his central purpose never changed, there was considerable vacillation as to the methods by which that purpose might best be attained. Throughout the period, of course, the policy, although proclaimed by Justin, was inspired by Justinian.

For a clear understanding of the religious policy of the period, the edict on heretics (I, 5, 12) is of the utmost importance. It is incorporated in the section of the *Code* "on Heretics, Manichaeans, and Samaritans" (*De haereticis et Manichaeis et Samaritis*), and has been preserved in the Greek and Latin languages. The beginning of the edict is lost. But the names of Justin and Justinian Augusti, who issued it, can be restored with full certainty from Justinian's later edict (I, 5, 18, 4) dealing with heretics, in which he refers to "the law made by us and our father of blessed memory." [198] Thus the edict was issued during the joint rule of Justin and Justinian, in 527, between April 4 and August 1.

The general tenor of the edict is very severe. "From those who are not orthodox in their worship of God, earthly goods should also be withheld." [199] At the beginning of his own reign, Justinian proclaimed that heretics should be "deprived of all earthly advantages, so that

---

[197] On the *stratiotai* and the auxiliary barbarian troops in the sixth century, see for instance Albert Müller, "Das Heer Justinians (nach Procop und Agathias)," *Philologus*, LXXI (1912), 101–102; 111–114.

[198] In his *Novel* CIX (ed. Schoell, p. 517) of 541, "De privilegiis dotis haereticis mulieribus non praestandis," Justinian evidently refers to the same edict but attributes it to Justin alone: Ἰουστῖνος ὁ τῆς θείας λήξεως ἡμῶν πατήρ. . . . In English by Scott, XVII, 27. Justinian's edict on heretics (I, 5, 12) has been incorporated in the *Basilics*, I, 1, 30; ed. C. Heimbach, I (Leipzig, 1833), 21–23; ed. Ἰωάννου Δ. Ζέπου, I (Athens, 1896), 19. Justinian was Justin's adopted son.

[199] I, 15, 12, 5: τοῖς μὴ τὸν θεὸν ὀρθῶς προσκυνοῦσι καὶ τὰ τῶν ἀνθρωπίνων ἀγαθῶν ἐπέχεται (Krueger, p. 53).

they might languish in misery." [200] A long list of restrictions and penalties for heretics is enumerated in the edict. They were excluded from all offices of dignity in the state, as well as from any magistracy or military post except those of the least important military offices of *curtalini* (κοορταλίνων; this is the Latin word *cohortalini* or *cohortales*); as we read in the edict, heretics who held this office would have no promotion, and would be unable to harm orthodox Christians.[201] Among the magistracies from which they were excluded are specifically mentioned those of public advocate (ἔκδικος; *defensor*) and "father of the city" (πόλεως πατήρ; *pater civitatis*), the *praefectus urbi* (ὁ ἔπαρχος τῆς πόλεως), "lest they (the heretics) might be constituted as judges of Christians and particularly of the most God-loving bishops" (I, 5, 12, 7). Heretics were debarred from practising the liberal professions of law and teaching (12, 8) "for fear of their imparting to others their own fatal errors" (I, 5, 18, 4). All these rules were to be strictly observed not only in "this glorious city," Constantinople, but also in all the provinces and all over the empire (12, 10). If some heretics have managed to circumvent the law and obtain a forbidden office, they should not only be deprived of it but also fined thirty pounds of gold; and those officials who were aware of their religious errors and notwithstanding let them hold office should be fined eight pounds of gold (12, 13–14). The duty of "the *comes* of the most sacred treasury" (ὁ μεγαλοπρεπέστατος κόμης τοῦ ἱερωτάτου ταμείου) was to collect the fines and enter them into the treasury of the *res privata* (τοῖς θείοις εἰσοίσει πριβάτοις) (12, 16).

In cases where the parents held differing religious views, or the children of pagan parents were inclined to be Christians or were Christians, every effort should be made to help and support the Christian side (12, 18–19). Restrictions were also established as to dowry and donations before marriage (12, 20). The last paragraph of

[200] I, 11, 1: παντὸς ἀφαιρεθέντες πράγματος ἐν ἐνδείᾳ καταλειφθήσονται (Krueger, p. 64). I use here Holmes' translation (II, 693); his reference *Cod.* I, 11, 10 is incorrect.
[201] See *cohortales, cohortalini, curtalini*, in Du Cange, *Glossarium mediae et infimae latinitatis*. See also Lydus, *De magistratibus*, III, 3; ed. Wuensch, p. 90. Also Bury, I, 31, n. 5: "cohortalini is sometimes applied to members of the officium, to those of the least important offices."

the law (21) lists those in charge of observing the strict enforcement of it; they are all the officials whom it concerns in "this greatest city" and the provincial governors, as well as "the most blessed archbishop and patriarch of this greatest city and the holiest bishops of other cities who occupy the patriarchal and metropolitan sees or the smaller ones." All these authorities should watch that the law be firmly kept, and inform the emperor if still more severe measures should be taken against violators. The law presents strong evidence of the disabilities imposed on heretics, whose religious status had been investigated and proved not only by the civil authorities but also by the clergy.

If we consider the definition of a heretic in terms of this law, the answer is very simple: a heretic was anyone who was not an orthodox churchman,[202] that is, a Chalcedonian. The following categories of heretics and religious dissidents are listed specifically in this law: Manichaeans, Samaritans, Jews, and Hellenes, that is, pagans.

The Manichaeans were always regarded as the worst enemies of humanity and the laws applied to them were exceedingly severe. Even before Justin's time, in the year 487 or 510, a law had proclaimed that the followers of the pernicious error of Manichaeanism had no right to exist in any region of the empire, and that wherever they were found they should be condemned to death (I, 5, 11). Justin's law begins its list of heretics with "the execrable Manichaeans" (12, 2) and "those who resemble them" (τοὺς τούτοις παραπλησίους), who should not even be named nor appear anywhere nor defile that which they have touched"; they should be expelled, "so that their very name might perish among the people"; they should be subject to the severest punishment wherever found (12, 3). It was a crime to possess Manichaean books and not to hand them over to a public official to be burnt. According to the *Liber Pontificalis*, during Justin's reign Manichaean books were burnt in front of the Constantinian basilica, probably in front of St. Sophia.[203]

[202] I, 5, 12, 4: αἱρετικὸν γὰρ πάντα καλοῦμεν, ὅστις μὴ τῆς καθολικῆς ἐκκλησίας καὶ τῆς ὀρθοδόξου καὶ ἁγίας ἡμῶν ὑπάρχει πιστεως. See a similar definition of heretic in one of the earlier rescripts of Justinian, I, 5, 18, 4.

[203] *Cod. Just.* I, 5, 16, 3: κἀκεῖνο δὲ θεσπίζομεν, εἴ τις ἔχων βιβλία τῇ πανταχόθεν ἀσεβεῖ τῶν Μανιχαίων πλάνῃ προσήκοντα μὴ ταῦτα δῆλα ποιήσειεν, ἐφ᾽ ᾧ καταφλεχθῆναι καὶ παντελῶς ἐξ ἀνθρώπων ἀφανῆ γενέσθαι, ἢ καὶ καθ᾽ οἱανοῦν πρόφασιν εὑρεθείη

The Samaritans, who were very numerous in Palestine, and the Jews were religious dissidents and therefore subject to the same disabilities as heretics. According to Justin's law, the government decided not only to renew and make more effective the laws already existing concerning them but also to issue more laws "through which greater security, order, and consideration of the adherents of our holy faith might be assured" (12, 4). Pagan as well as Jews and Samaritans (12, 4) are included as heretics in general. "Hellenic impiety" was subject to the same penalties.

The edict of 527, which is extremely severe towards all heretics and religious dissidents, contains one apparent exception in favor of the Goths. The relevant item (12, 17) reads as follows: "Taking, however, into consideration that we had often enrolled the Goths in the *devo-tissimi* (καθωσιωμένοις) *foederati*" and that their behavior has been corect, "we have decided to relieve them somewhat of the severity (of the edict), and permit them to be among the foederati and enjoy their honors insofar as we please." [204]

It has been pointed out many times that this particular item granted a special favor to the Goths residing on the territory of the empire; and this favor has been regarded as the result of the visit to Constantinople of the Pope, sent by the Ostrogothic king Theodoric, an Arian himself, on behalf of his coreligionists. But the Goths are mentioned and praised as Federates, who in the fifth and sixth centuries were drawn indifferently from foreign peoples, not from the Goths alone, were commanded by Roman officers, and formed a distinct section of the military establishment. And as such, as we have noted above, they

---

παρ᾽ αὐτῷ τὰ τοιαῦτα βιβλία, ὁμοίως καὶ αὐτὸν ποινὴν ὑποστῆναι τὴν προσήκουσαν (ed. Krueger, p. 56). *Liber Pontificalis*, ed. Duchesne, I, 270–271: "Hic (Justinus) invenit Manicheos, quos etiam discussit cum examinatione plagarum, exilio deportavit; quorum codices ante fores basilicae Constantinianae incendio concremavit." Later Russian sources of the sixteenth century, which took information from Greek sources, also mention that "the pious and wise old man Justin, burning with the zeal of pious faith" opened a severe persecution on Manichaeans. *The Russian Chronograph of 1512*, PSRL, XXII, 1, 292 (ch. 136); *The Chronograph of Western-Russian Version*, PSRL, XXII, 2, 108.

[204] *Cod. Just.* I, 5, 12, 17: συγχωρῆσαί τι τῆς ἀκριβείας αὐτοῖς (Γότθοις) συνείδομεν καὶ γινομένων ἀνέχεσθαι φοιδεράτων καὶ τιμωμένων, ὃν ἂν ἡμῖν παρασταίη τρόπον. In Latin: "de severitate nonnihil eis remittere decrevimus et foederatos eos fieri honoribusque decorari permittimus, quem admodum nobis visum fuerit."

were affected neither by the above-mentioned law of 519–520 nor by this law of 527. Some compliment to Theodoric may be seen, however, in the fact that the law singles out the Goths by name, while no other of the various nationalities are specified.[205]

We notice that the term monophysite or Nestorian is not used in Justin's law. Even in the item which deals with the Goths, too, the term of Arian is not employed. In the first decade of Justinian's rule these heretics were not yet pronounced against by name. Monophysites were called either Eutychians or Acephali (Akephaloi or "Headless"). In this respect Justinian's *Novella* issued in 541 is interesting. In it the emperor mentions those "who follow the Jewish madness of Nestorius, as well as Eutychians and Acephali, who suffer the heresy of Dioscorus and Severus." [206] In this novel Justinian still does not use the name Nestorian or monophysite. But the title of one of the works of Leontius of Byzantium who died in 543 is "Three addresses against Nestorians and Eutychians." [207]

It is noteworthy that the sect of the Montanists in Phrygia, which under Justin and particularly under Justinian was subject to very severe treatment, is not mentioned in Justin's law. They were the greatest fanatics of all, who, according to Procopius, shut themselves up in their sanctuaries and then set fire to them so that all perished together.[208]

---

[205] Cf. E. Caspar, *Geschichte des Papsttums*, II, 184, n. 3.

[206] *Nov.* CIX, preface; ed. Schoell, p. 517.

[207] Leontius of Byzantium, Λεοντίου Μοναχοῦ λόγοι Γ΄ κατὰ Νεστοριανῶν καὶ Εὐτυχανιστῶν, Migne, *PG*, LXXXI, 1, 1267 foll.

[208] Proc. *Anecdota* XI, 23; Dewing, VI, 136. The Montanists were so severely persecuted that some scholars thought it hardly likely that Montanism survived the persecution of Justinian. See W. Smith and H. Wace, *A Dictionary of Christian Biography*, III (London, 1882), 945. This opinion, however, is not correct, for their name occurs in later texts. A very well known passage referring to the period of Leo III (717–741) is given by Theophanes, *s. a.* 6214 (p. 401, ed. de Boor). He reproduces the same story of their burning themselves alive that Procopius tells. *Anastasii Chronographia Tripertita*, ed. de Boor, p. 260. From Theophanes, Cedranus, I, 793. The identity of these two passages in Procopius and Theophanes is so striking that Baronius (*Ann. Eccles.*, *s. a.* 722, n. 1) was inclined to think that Theophanes had by mistake misdated the occurrence. But most historians have accepted Theophanes' statement as an independent story of an event which took place under Leo III. See for example J. B. Bury, *A History of the Later Roman Empire*, II, 431. E. J. Martin, *A History of the Iconoclastic Controversy* (London, 1930), p. 26. In addition to Theophanes, see *Ecloga legum*,

Very interesting information is supplied by the Roman deacon Rusticus, a contemporary, the nephew of Pope Vigilius with whom he came to Constantinople under Justinian. He attacked the compromising policy of Justinian and his uncle. Rusticus relates that under Justin about 2500 bishops (sacerdotes) had in writing declared their recognition of the Council of Chalcedon.[209] According to Hefele, at that time the church numbered more than six thousand bishops.[210] Although this figure is tentative, it may be surmised that under Justin less than half the bishops in the empire officially recognized the Council of Chalcedon.

Rusticus' record is important as reflecting the Roman or papal reaction to Justin's religious policy, and once more confirms our thesis of its temporary mildness and moderation. Rusticus — in other words, the papal court — was dissatisfied with the concessions of Justin and Justinian, and their reluctance to carry out Pope Hormidas' suggestions that they "correct" the heretics. Our figures are not accurate enough to allow us to conclude with certainty that less than half the bishops in the empire accepted the Chalcedonian Creed. We may, however, be sure that not all bishops did. This state of affairs was obviously not satisfactory to Rome.

At the moment of the death of Justin, on August 1, 527, the sees of only three oriental patriarchates were occupied by Chalcedonians:

XVII, 52: Οἱ μανιχαῖοι καὶ οἱ μοντανοὶ ξίφει τιμωρείσθωσαν. *Jus Graeco-Romanum*, ed. J. Zepi and P. Zepi, II (Athens, 1931), 61. *Vita Nicephori Constantinopolitani Archiepiscopi*, βάλλει δὲ καὶ τὴν τῶν Φρυγίων τερατώδη ἐρεσχελίαν. Migne. PG, C. col. 69; ed. de Boor (Leipzig, 1880), pp. 158–159. In the Justinian Code there are several enactments referring to the Montanists, from Justinian's period. I, 5, 18, 3; 19, 4 (529); 20, 3 (530); 21, 1–2 (531).

[209] Rusticus, S. Rom. Ecclesiae Diaconus, *Contra Acephalos Disputatio*: "Licet sufficeret tibi unica auctoritas synodi universalis, quae numero superat universas, quae toties cunctarum ecclesiarum consona sententia confirmata est, tam per encyclicas epistolas regnante Leone, quam per libellos sacerdotum forsan duorum millium et quingentorum, imperante Justino post schisma Petri Alexandrini et Acacii Constantinopolitani." Migne, PL, LXVII, 1251–1252. Mansi, VIII, 578–579. *Baronii Ann. Eccl.*, s. a. 518, no. 37. See Hefele, *op. cit.*, II, 692 (§ 233); Hefele-Leclercq, II, 2, 1050; Eng. transl. by Clark, IV, 120. Duchesne, *L'église au sixième siècle*, p. 192. Caspar, *Geschichte des Papsttum*, II, 256–257; 271; 278; 281. *Histoire de l'église*, Fliche and Martin, IV, 465–466. Article "Rusticus" by Stech, in PW, 2nd series, I (1920), 1243 (no. 20).

[210] Hefele, *op. cit.*, II, 692, note; Hefele-Leclercq, 1050, n. 2; Eng. transl., IV, 120, n. 1.

these men were Epiphanius of Constantinople, Ephraim of Antioch, and Peter of Jerusalem. During the whole period of Justin the Alexandrian See was occupied by a monophysite patriarch, Timothy IV, who after Justin's death continued to hold his high office for several years under Justinian (518–536 or 517–535).

JUSTIN'S RELIGIOUS POLICY OUTSIDE THE EMPIRE

In 1888 a French historian, A. Gasquet, wrote: "Missionary activity — this was the new element which gives to the Byzantine policy its distinctive character. The priest, the monk, precede, in the barbarian countries, the diplomat and the soldier. By the route which the first will open, the second will not take long to penetrate." [211] Justin's religious interests were not confined to the limits of his own empire. He was supporting, protecting, and spreading Christianity outside the empire.

An historian of the sixth century whose text has survived in Syriac tells a very interesting story of Justin's period, which in spite of its legendary and miraculous elements has a real historical foundation. An angel appeared to a man named Kardutsat (which when translated into Greek is Theocletus [Theokletos]),[212] Bishop of the country Arran (the Caucasian Albania), and, as the bishop himself related, said to him: "Take three pious priests and go out into the plain and receive from me a message sent to thee by the Lord of spirits, because I am guardian of the captives who have gone from the land of the Romans to the land of the pagans and have offered up their prayer to God. And he told me what to say to thee." They went, and four others went with them, to the country of the Huns Sabirs who lived north of the Caucasus near the Caspian, where the Roman captives were kept. And when they reached the place, they told these things to the captives and many were baptized; they made also converts among the Huns, and translated books into the Hunnic tongue. At that time, Probus, the nephew of the late emperor Anastasius, who had been sent on a mission to Bosporus in the Crimea by Justin, was in the country of the Huns.

[211] A. Gasquet, *L'empire byzantin et la monarchie franque* (Paris, 1888), p. 75.
[212] Kardutsat from two Armenian words kardal, to shout, to call, and Astwatz, God; hence the Greek name Theokletos (Hamilton-Brooks, p. 329, n. 2).

When he heard from the Huns about these holy men and understood their story also from the captives, he was very eager to see them. He saw them, received a blessing from them, and showed them much honor before the eyes of the pagans. When Justin heard the facts recorded above, he loaded thirty mules from the territories of the neighboring Roman cities and sent them to the captives, and also flour, wine, oil, linen cloths, and other commodities and sacramental vessels.

On Theocletus' departure from the Huns some years later, an Armenian bishop named Maku(?), stirred to emulation by his noble deeds, also went of his own accord to the Hunnic country and some of his priests with him. He built a brick church, set out plants, sowed various kinds of seeds, and baptized many people. When the rulers of these nations saw something new happening, they admired the men and honored them, each one among them inviting them to his own district and his own people, and beseeching them to instruct him.[213]

Ignoring the miraculous and legendary element of this story, and considering the fact that the Armenian bishop Maku (?) went to the Huns in the time of Justinian, we can conclude that the mission of his predecessor Theocletus must have taken place under Justin. Justin's religious interest is proved by the fact that he sent to the Hunnic country various commodities and sacramental vessels for religious services which were to be celebrated in a new Christian community established in this distant region. Other examples also show that Justin's religious interests spread far beyond the confines of his own empire. He supported and protected Christianity against the pressure of the Persian Zoroastrianism in Lazica. Within the empire the champion of the Chalcedonian Creed, outside its official boundaries Justin was the protector of Christianity in general, no matter whether the outlying countries subscribed to his religious dogmas or not. He supported the Emperor of Abyssinia, Elesboas, a monophysite, in his

---

[213] Zach of Mityl., XII, 7; Hamilton-Brooks, pp. 329–331; Ahrens-Krüger, pp. 254–255 (the name of the Armenian bishop is given as Mak). See C. Diehl, *Justinien*, pp. 376–377. On Probus' mission A. Vasiliev, *The Goths in the Crimea* (Cambridge, Massachusetts, 1936), p. 70. For bibliography on the Huns in the sixth century see G. Moravcsik, *Byzantinoturcica*, I, 40–41.

struggle against the Jews in South Arabia.[214] Justin's attitude towards South Arabia and Abyssinia proves once more that in his religious policy outside his empire, as also within it, he was no mere fanatic but took a general view of all considerations, including economic and political ones.

JUSTIN AND MONASTICISM

The *Lives* of several saints who lived in the sixth century tell naive stories of their journeys for the sake of relieving the needs of their eparchies to Constantinople, where they were welcomed by the emperors themselves, who almost always were amazed at their saintly life and experiences and fulfilled all their demands. Saint Sabas came twice from Palestine to Constantinople: on his first visit he saw the Emperor Anastasius and his wife the Empress Ariadne; on his second he was welcomed by Justinian and Theodora. Saint David of Thessalonica was sent by the Thessalonicans to the capital, where he was entertained by Justinian and Theodora. The bishop of the small city Bitilion (τοῦ Βητυλίου) in the south region of Palestine, Theognius, also visited Constantinople twice: in the time of Anastasius and in the time of Justin. The story recorded in the *Life* of Theognius of his meeting with Justin runs as follows: In the reign of the Emperor Justin for the sake of certain needs Theognius again arrived in Constantinople and was praised above all the bishops who at that time were there. It happened that since some senators (τῶν τῆς συγκλήτου) were showing reverence to him, the emperor himself became thoroughly aware of the virtues of the man and fulfilled the request for which he had come to Byzantium; then after bestowing upon him the greatest honors the emperor, along with the whole Senate, respectfully dismissed the sainted man.[215]

There is no doubt that the visits of the hermits to Constantinople

---

[214] Justin's policy in Lazica and South Arabia we shall discuss in detail below, in the chapter on his external policy in general.

[215] Παύλου τοῦ Ἑλλαδικοῦ καὶ Κυρίλλου Σκυθοπολίτου Βίοι τοῦ ὁσίου Θεογνίου ἐπισκόπου Βητυλίου, ed. A. Papadopoulos Kerameus, in the *Palestinsky Sbornik*, XI, 2 (St. Petersburg, 1891) 15–16 (ch. 23); Russian translation, p. 43. *Acta Sancti Theognii episcopi Beteliae Paulo Elusensi et Cyrillo Scythopolitano auctoribus*, ed. J. van den Ghein, *Analecta Bollandiana*, X (1891), 104 (ch. 21); Greek text with a Latin translation.

recorded in hagiographic texts are historical facts. They did go to Constantinople and saw the emperors and empresses there. But without question the stories of their visits are presented embellished and piously adorned in conformity with the style and aims of hagiographic literature. The welcome extended by Justinian to Saint Sabas, for example, exceeds all our expectations.[216] That such meetings of the hermits with the emperors and empresses did take place, however, shows the enormous influence of monasticism in the Oriental Empire in the sixth century, and for the period of Justin the visit of Theognius may serve as one of the striking examples of this influence. In such meetings the emperor and empress cease to represent the highest power in the empire, and become, outwardly at least, humble and faithful worshipers who treat with veneration the ascetics and hermits from distant deserts.

[216] *Vita S. Sabae*, ed. Cotelier, *Ecclesiae graecae monumenta*, III, 341–342; ed. E. Schwartz, *Kyrillos von Skythopolis*, pp. 173–174. This story has been fully taken over by C. Diehl, *Justinien* pp. 524–525. Also W. G. Holmes, *The Age of Justinian and Theodora*, II, 696–697.

CHAPTER FIVE

Justin's External Policy

The external affairs of the period of Justin present great interest and remarkable variety. Their focus was concentrated, as in previous times of the empire, on relations with its permanent foe and rival, Persia. But during the first four years of Justin's rule there were no troubles with the Persian king; difficulties broke out only in the latter period of his reign. Since the West, for example the Ostrogothic Kingdom in Italy and the Vandal Kingdom in North Africa, was quiet during almost the whole reign of Justin, the chief events of the external activities of the empire took place in the north, east, and south. And the territory covered by these activities was enormous: from the Danube in the far north, from the Crimea in the northern region of the Black Sea, from the northern slopes of the Caucasian range, military, diplomatic, religious, and commercial activities embraced Lazica, Iberia, Persia, the Kingdom of the Ghassanids in Syria, and the Kingdom of the Lakhmids in Irak, and went far south down to Abyssinia and Yemen in South Arabia. Armenia at the time was under the double domination of Byzantium and Persia. According to the treaty of 387 A. D. or 384 between Theodosius I and Sapor III, Armenia had been partitioned into two client states, of which the smaller was ruled by a governor dependent on the empire, and the larger a vassal prince of Persia. This arrangement continued during Justin's time.[1] But in Persian Armenia in 428 the last Arsacid King of Armenia, Ardashir, who was a vassal of Persia, was deposed by the Persian monarch, and the country thereafter was ruled by Persian governors (*marzpans*). During Justin's entire reign Asia Minor remained quiet, and it was possible to forget such disturbing events as the rebellion of Illus under Zeno or the Isaurian War under Anastasius.

[1] See Bury, I, 94 (387 A. D. has been generally recognized as the date of the treaty). But see Jean Doise, "Le partage de l'Arménie sous Théodose Ier," *Revue des études anciennes*, XLVII (1945), 274–277 (the year of the treaty as 384).

JUSTIN, LAZICA, AND PERSIA

The Byzantine Empire enjoyed formal peace with Persia till the end of the reign of Justin, when a real war broke out. The previous war with Persia, under Anastasius, had ended in 505 with the conclusion of a peace to last seven years, which was in reality a truce rather than a peace. Since this armistice had not been renewed, under Justin the two powers were legally still in a state of war; and this view was held by the contemporaries of Justinian, Justin's successor, as may be inferred from the statement of John Malalas (XVIII, 478) that the peace of 532 which Justinian made with Persia terminated a war which had lasted for thirty-one years, that is, from the year 502, the year of the beginning of the Persian war under Anastasius.

Justin's contemporary in Persia was Kawad (487–498 and 501–531), whose second reign, after his restoration to the throne in 501, covered the reigns of Anastasius, Justin, and Justinian. Kawad was one of the most interesting figures of his time, a clever and subtle politician who quickly adjusted himself to any surroundings, a brave and able diplomat. At the moment of his death the prestige and power of Iran were very high, and he left behind him a very well trained army to fight his enemies. Diplomatic courtesy and elaborate style are reflected in the sixth century correspondence between the two sovereigns of Byzantium and Persia; and we have no ground whatever for questioning the authenticity of their letters, as they have survived in our sources. Kawad addresses Justinian as follows: "Kawad, the king of kings, the lord of the sun of the east, to Flavius Justinian the Caesar, the lord of the moon of the west." Kawad also had some correspondence with Justin, because in the same letter to Justinian he also mentions: "We have written this to the emperors Anastasius and Justin." In his letter to Kawad concerning the treachery of a Hunnic chief, Justin names himself and Kawad "brothers."[2]

[2] A eulogistic picture of Kawad's talents in N. Pigulevskaya, "The Mazdakite Movement," *Izvestiya* [Accounts] *of the Academy of Sciences of USSR*, I, no. 4 (1944), 174 (in Russian). P. Sykes, A History of Persia, 2nd ed., I (London, 1921), 447. Letters in Malalas, 449: Κωάδης βασιλεὺς βασιλευόντων ἡλίου ἀνατολῆς, Φλαβίῳ Ἰουστινιανῷ Καίσαρι σελήνης δύσεως; also p. 450; 415. See K. Güterbock, *Byzanz und Persien in ihren diplomatisch völkerrechtlichen Beziehungen im Zeitalter Justinians* (Berlin, 1906), p. 6, 7, and n. 1. R. Helm, *Untersuchungen über den*

The peaceful relations between the two empires during most of Justin's reign are to be explained by the internal situation in both countries. After the termination of the war with Anastasius in 505, Kawad was occupied till 513 with the war with the White Huns, which was very successful for him but required strenuous attention. Then Kawad faced the so-called Mazdakite movement, whose founder and organizer, Mazdak, converted thousands to his doctrine which was not only religious in character, but also social, a revolutionary theory and an early form of communism. Since the restoration of Kawad in 501, the Mazdakites had steadily increased in numbers; and finally they engaged in a conspiracy to persuade Kawad to abdicate in favor of his son. The plot was revealed to Kawad, who in 523 summoned the leading Mazdakites to be present at a ceremony where he massacred them. As a dangerous element in Persia, Mazdakism was crushed, and henceforth it existed only as an underground doctrine. Not until he was relieved from the Mazdakite peril, could Kawad have found it possible to form plans against Byzantium.[3]

Justin himself was thoroughly occupied with his new Chalcedonian religious orientation, which created many troubles and ardent altercations of vital significance for the empire far beyond their purely religious aspect. We have also some very interesting information of an economic character: the Persian wars, among many others, cost too much money for the treasury. A large reserve amounting to 320,000 pounds of gold, which by his economical policy and financial

---

auswärtigen diplomatischen Verkehr des römischen Reiches im Zeitalter der Spätantike, Archiv für Urkundenforschung, XII (1932), 385.

[3] On the Mazdakite movement under Kawad, see, among recent publications, Arthur Christensen, "Le règne du roi Kawadh I et le communisme Mazdakite," Historisk-filologiske Meddelelser udgivne af det Kgl. Danske Videnskabernes Selskab, IX, 6 (Copenhagen, 1925), p. 123; 124; 127 (the Mazdakites were destroyed in 528 or at the beginning of 529). N. Pigulevskaya, op. cit., pp. 171–181 (in Russian). See also T. Nöldeke, Geschichte der Perser und Araber zur Zeit der Sasaniden, p. 465 (Mazdakite catastrophe in 528–529). This later dating is based on Malalas. I am inclined to accept the earlier dating given by Theophanes (p. 170), who mentions the event under Justin. See Cedr., I, 639. Zon., XIV, 5, 27; CSHB, III, 148–149. Otherwise I should be unable to explain the active military policy of Kawad during the last years of Justin. Such a policy may be explained only by the fact that he was already relieved from the Mazdakite peril in his own country. G. Rawlinson (The Seventh Great Oriental Monarchy, p. 364) and P. Sykes (A History of Persia, I, 443) accept the year 523.

reforms Anastasius had been able to leave in the treasury at his death, was, according to Procopius (*Hist. Arc.* 19, 7–8), already practically spent before Justinian's accession to the throne. John Lydus, a writer of the sixth century, gloomily remarks: "There was need of money, and nothing which was needed could be done without money." [4]

Only when he was relieved from the Mazdakite peril in his own country was Kawad able to make war against Justin. This war began before Justin's death. This time the war became more complicated than previous conflicts between the two rivals because it was concentrated in the Caucasus and involved the participation of Lazica and Iberia. The episode which finally broke the outward peace in the East took place in Lazica in 522 and brought about serious complications with Persia. [5]

Lazica of the sixth century is not to be confused with Lazistan of later and our own days. Lazica, according to Procopius, was a later name for Colchis of the classic writers, and was situated on the eastern shores of the Black Sea, roughly speaking between the rivers Phasis (now Rion, Rioni) in the north and Chorokh (Chorokhi) in the south, extending eastward down to the border of Iberia. Lazica was rather an unproductive country. As Procopius says, "neither corn nor wine nor any other good thing is produced there. . . Salt is produced no-

---

[4] John Lydus, *De magistratibus populi romani libri tres*, ed. R. Wuensch (Leipzig, 1903), III, 51 (p. 140); 52 53 (pp. 140–142, a brief sketch of the Byzantino-Persian wars from the third century); 54 (p. 143): ἔδει δὲ χρημάτων, καὶ οὐδὲν ἦν ἄνευ αὐτῶν πραχθῆναι τῶν δεόντων.

[5] Even today the old collection by I. G. Stritter is still very useful for our Greek sources on Lazica, Iberia and other adjoining regions. *Memoriae populorum, olim ad Danubium, Pontum Euxinum, Paludem Maeotidem, Caucasum, Mare Caspium, et inde magis ad septemtriones incolentium, e Scriptoribus Historiae Byzantinae erutae et digestae a Ioanne Gotthilf Stritters*, IV (St. Petersburg, 1779). The collection reproduces Greek sources in a Latin translation with very substantial notes (on Lazica, pp. 21–170). The events in Laxica and Iberia during Justin's reign are well presented in old books; for example, Lebeau, *Histoire du Bas-Empire*, ed. M. de Saint-Martin, VIII, 25–44. F. Dubois de Montpéreux, *Voyage autour du Caucase*, II (Paris, 1839), 80–83. M. Brosset, *Additions et éclaircissements à l'histoire de la Géorgie depuis l'antiquité jusqu'en 1469 de J.-C.* (St. Petersburg, 1851), Addition IV: Sur le royaume de Lazique, pp. 81–107. In more recent works, I. Kulakovsky, *History of Byzantium*, II, 23–25 (in Russian). Kulakovsky erroneously identifies Tzath of Lazica with Gurgenes of Iberia. A few words in Bury, II, 80. No mention in W. E. D. Allen, *A History of the Georgian People* (London, 1932), p. 70.

where in Lazica, nor indeed does grain grow there nor the vine nor any other good thing." Only "by furnishing skins, hides and slaves did the Lazi secure the supplies which they needed. . . Lazica is everywhere difficult to traverse both to the right and to the left of the river Phasis. For there are on both sides of the river exceedingly high and jagged mountains, and as a result the passes are narrow and very long." But Lazica was "a bulwark against the barbarians dwelling in the Caucasus," and the Persians knew very well its importance in this respect; therefore they were anxious to possess that region in order to check the Huns, "who lived next to Lazica." The Lazi had erected some forts.[6] On the basis of his very problematic figures of the extent of the Byzantine Empire and the various regions adjoining it, E. Foord wrote that in the fifth and sixth centuries Lazica comprised a territory of 15,000 square miles.[7]

In the sixth century, also according to Procopius, the Lazi were friendly to the Romans as well as to other Caucasian peoples who dwelt north of Phasis like the Abasgians (Abasgi, Abkhaz) and Alans, "who are Christians and friends of the Romans from of old." Thus the conditions along the eastern shore of the Black Sea seemed to be very favorable for the penetration and extension of Byzantine influence.

The kings of Lazica, however, stood in a peculiar relation to the empire. They were vassals of the empire, but they did not have to meet heavy obligations towards their suzerain. They did not pay the Romans any tribute nor, to use Procopius' wording, did they obey "their commands in any respect"; they did not join the Roman armies in their military expeditions. After the death of the Lazic king, however, the Roman emperor sent the emblems of the royal office to him who was about to succeed to the throne. From this statement of Procopius we should not conclude that the emperor chose the new king. The successor was elected by the Lazi themselves, and by sending

---

[6] Procopius, *B. P.* I, 12, 15 (Dewing, 98–99); II, 18, 27; 15, 5; 29, 24–25; 28, 22 (Dewing, 522–523; 386–387; 534–535; 520–521). See Bury, II, 100.
[7] E. Foord, *The Byzantine Empire — The Rearguard of European Civilization* (London, 1911), p. 417. Foord's figures have been reproduced by André M. Andreades, "περὶ τοῦ πληθυσμοῦ καὶ τοῦ πλούτου τῆς Κωνσταντινουπόλεως κατὰ τοὺς μέσους χρόνους," *Oeuvres*, I (Athens, 1938), 417–418. Originally this study was published in Ἐπετηρὶς τοῦ φιλολογικοῦ συλλόγου Παρνασσοῦ (1917).

the appropriate emblems to the new king the emperor only confirmed the fact of election, by a sort of investiture. Bury, then, is hardly correct in saying that the Lazi "committed the choice of their kings to the wisdom of the Roman Emperor" (II, 100).

But it was extremely important for the empire to be on a friendly footing with the Lazic kingdom, which was, as we have mentioned above, an essential barrier against the trans-Caucasian invaders, especially against the Huns. And the Lazic king, according to Procopius, "together with his subjects, guarded strictly the boundaries of the land in order that hostile Huns might not proceed from the Caucasian mountains, which adjoin their territory, through Lazica and invade the land of the Romans." It is worth noting that the Lazi defended the mountain passes without receiving money or troops from the Romans. This security in the north, then, cost the empire nothing for a while. But of course all such security depended on the relations between the empire and Persia.[8] The Persian king also realized very well the importance for his own empire either of living in peace with Lazica or even of possessing it for the same purpose of protecting his own land against invasion and plunder at the hands of the Huns beyond Lazica. Procopius strikingly says that the Persian king thought of Lazica in no other light than that of a bulwark ($\epsilon\pi\iota\tau\epsilon\iota\chi\iota\sigma\mu\alpha$) against the barbarians dwelling in the Caucasus.[9]

During the reign of Justin's predecessor, Anastasius, and during the first years of the rule of Justin himself, the Persian king Kawad had great influence in Lazica. In the time of Anastasius a certain Damnazes (Zamnaxes) had been chosen from among the Lazi and crowned by the Persian king, who intended to introduce into Lazica the rites of the Zoroastrian religion. Damnazes' son and heir Tzath, during his father's life, is characterized in our sources as Kawad's friend.[10] But

---

[8] Procopius, *B. P.* II, XV, 2–4; Dewing, I, 384–387.

[9] Procpius, *B. P.* II, XXVIII, 22; Dewing, I, 520–521. See above.

[10] Malalas, pp. 412–413 (Δαμνάξης; Ζτάθιος); 427 (Ζτάθιος). Slavonic version, Istrin, pp. 18–19; 25; in English by M. Spinka, p. 122; 134 (Chaphios). *Chr. Pasch.*, p. 613 (Τζάθιος ὁ υἱὸς Ζαμνάξου). Theoph., de Boor, p. 168 (Τζάθιος). *Anastasii Hist. Tripertita*, p. 131 (Zathus). Codd. give Τζάθον. Zonaras, XIV, 5, 24; *CSHB*, III, 148 (Τζάθος). Cedrenus, I, 638 (Τζάθος). John of Nikiu, XC, 40; transl. by Charles, p. 137 (Tzathius). The name of Tzath's father, Damnazes (Zamnaxes), is given only by Malalas and the *Chronicon Paschale* (*Easter Chronicle*).

apparently the Persian domination in Lazica was too heavy a burden for Tzath to bear.

In 522,[11] immediately after his father's death, instead of going to the Persian court to be inaugurated and crowned by the king there, Tzath, fearing lest Kawad might force him to accept the Zoroastrian religion, took refuge with Justin. He fled to Constantinople and asked the emperor to have him proclaimed King of the Lazi and baptized. According to John of Nikiu, he said to Justin: "We wish thee to make us Christians like thyself, and we shall then be subjects of the Roman empire." Justin received Tzath cordially. Tzath was baptized and married a Roman lady, Valeriana, daughter of Nomos, a patrician and curopalates, one of the highest dignitaries in the empire in the fifth and sixth centuries.[12] Finally Justin crowned Tzath and gave him elaborate royal robes, which our sources describe at some length. He wore a royal diadem of the Roman fashion and a white mantle all of

---

The best established form for the son's name is Τζάθος — Tzathus. Surprisingly enough, Procopius fails to tell the story of Tzath. According to A. Gugushvili, Damnazi (sic) was the second king of Lazica, a contemporary of Kawad, King of Persia (488–496; 499–531) and the Roman Emperor Anastasius (491–518). A. Gugushvili, "The Chronological-Genealogical Table of the Kings of Georgia," *Georgica: A Journal of Georgian and Caucasian Studies*, I, 2–3 (London, October, 1936), 152. In note 2, the author refers to S. Gorgadze, *An Ancient History of Georgia* (Tiflis, 1920), p. 94. I am not acquainted with this book, which was published, as far as I know, in Georgian. To this reference Gugushvili adds: "The writer, however, has found no mention of this king in any of the sources consulted by him." In this case, where did he find the name itself? An old Greek book calls Tzath a son of Zamnaxes, the king of Trebizond. Μεταξοπούλου Ἡ θεία καὶ ἱερὰ ἀκολουθία τῶν ὁσίων καὶ θεοφόρων Πατέρων ἡμῶν Βαρνάβα καὶ Σωφρονίου (Leipzig, 1775), pp. 57–58.

[11] Exact date in *Chr. Pasch.*, 613: the 15th indiction, consulship of Symmachus and Boethius, i.e. the year 522. H. F. Clinton, *Fasti Romani*, I, 740.

[12] Malalas, 412–413 (the name of the patrician, Νόμος). Slav. version: Istrin, 18–19; Spinka, 122 (patrician Iotion). *Chr. Pasch.*, 613 (the name of the patrician, Ὄνινος). Theoph., 168. Briefly in *Anastasii Chronographia Tripertita*, 131; Cedr., I, 638; Zonaras, XIV, 5, 24 (*CSHB* III, 148). John of Nikiu, XC, 37–38; R. Charles, p. 137 (he calls the patrician Ionios). Gugushvili lists Tzathos-Dsat'e I as the third king of Lazica. "Kings of Georgia," *Georgica*, I, 2–3 (Oct. 1936), 153. He ascribes his reign to the year 520 and gives an absolutely unnecessary note which says, "According to Gorgadze Dsat'e was the son of Damnazi." This record is given by our sources, Malalas and Chr. Pasch. Nomos or Oninos as curopalates, see J. B. Bury, *The Imperial Administrative System in the Ninth Century*, p. 33 (16).

silk, which had not a purple fringe but a royal golden fringe, with the figure of Justin embroidered on the front; he also wore a white tunic, the paragaudion (παραγαύδιον) with royal golden embroideries also including a picture of the emperor. His boots adorned with pearls according to the Persian fashion he had brought from his own country, as well as a belt, also adorned with pearls. In addition to these particular presents, which especially in their use of the emperor's picture sufficiently indicated his dependent position, he and this wife Valeriana received from Justin many other gifts.[13] Lazica then must be regarded during the reign of Justin I as a vassal state, and its King Tzath I as a client prince of the Byzantine Empire. That Tzath wore the picture of Justin embroidered on his royal robes reminds the Rumanian scholar Iorga of the Rumanian princes who in the nineteenth century wore the picture of the Sultan Mahmud.[14]

One episode in the history of the relations between Justin and Tzath is open to question: this is Tzath's baptism. The question has been raised as to why Tzath felt it necessary to be baptized. The Lazi were not a pagan people. Christianity appeared there in the fourth century and became firmly established in the fifth. In that century the King of Lazica Gubaz I (Γαβάζης), contemporary of the Emperor Leo I (457–474) was zealously devoted to Christianity. When he came to Constantinople, he was taken by the emperor to visit the famous stylite Daniel who lived on a pillar close to Constantinople for thirty-three years; Gubaz was immensely impressed by this sight and on his return to his own country spread the praises of the saint, as the author of the *Life* of Daniel learned from the Caucasian envoys who later came to the capital.

At the beginning of the sixth century and perhaps even as early as the fifth, the Lazi had a monastery in the desert of Jerusalem, which

---

[13] Malalas, 413. Slavonic version: Istrin, 18–19; Spinka, 122 (χλαμύς, mantle, in Slavonic *ukril*). *Chr. Pasch.*, 613–614. Theoph., 168–169. John of Nikiu, XC, 38, p. 137, mentions only "a robe of honor." Agathias, III, 15 (*CSHB*, p. 172) describes the similar royal robes granted by Justinian to the Lazic king Tzath II, about 555. See Bury II, 119. See A. Grabar, *L'empereur dans l'art byzantin*, p. 6 and n. 2.

[14] N. Iorga, *Histoire de la vie byzantine*, I, 133. See R. Helm, *Untersuchungen über den auswärtigen diplomatischen Verkehr des römischen Reiches im Zeitalter der Spätantike, Archiv für Urkundenforschung*, XII, 391; 393.

was later restored by Justinian.[15] Therefore Tzath must have been a Christian; it was not necessary for him to be baptized into that faith. But he may have feared that Kawad might put pressure on him to introduce Zoroastrianism into his own country, and wished to confirm once more his own adherence to the Christian faith by a solemn ceremony of his baptism, or rebaptism, to be performed by the emperor himself. In my opinion, it would be unjustifiable to reject flatly a fact which has been testified to by our best sources. The religious ceremony of Tzath's baptism performed by Justin is an historical fact. The ceremony was important for Tzath by way of insurance against Kawad's aggressive religious policy. Our only other alternative would be that we have here the case of a pagan prince ruling over a people predominantly Christian, among whom some continued faithful to paganism.[16]

Justin's interference in the domestic affairs of Lazica was unjustified from the point of view of the Persian king, for Lazica had been dependent on Persia from old times. Kawad was irritated, and the friendly relations established between Byzantium and Persia by the treaty of

[15] On Gubaz see N. H. Baynes, "The *Vita S. Danielis* Stylite," *The English Historical Review*, XL (1925), 397–398. See the text in H. Delehaye, *Les Saints Stylites* (Bruxelles-Paris, 1923), p. 49. On the monastery of the Lazi, Procopius, *De aedificiis* V, 8, 7: τὸ τῶν Λαζῶν (μοναστήριον) ἐν τῇ ἐρήμῳ Ἱεροσολύμων (Dewing-Downey, VII, 358–359). See N. Marr, "The Conversion of the Armenians, Iberians, Abkhaz, and Alans by Saint Gregory," (An Arabian Version), *Zapiski* of the Oriental Section of the Russian Archaeological Society, XVI (1904–1905), 165, n. 4 (in Russian).

[16] More than a hundred years ago, F. Dubois de Montpéreux wrote on this point: Tzathius wished to remain faithful to Christianity, which his subjects professed. *Voyage autour du Caucase*, II, 81. Kekelidze, "Historico-Hagiographic Fragments," *Khristiansky Vostok*, II (1913), 190 (in Russian). Güterbock states that Tzath's pretended baptism is very doubtful. K. Güterbock, *Byzanz und Persien in ihren diplomatisch-völkerrechtlichen Beziehungen im Zeitalter Justinians*, p. 52, n. 2. Dvornik is not quite correct in saying that the Lazi were converted under Justin. F. Dvornik, *Les Slaves, Byzance et Rome au IXe siècle* (Paris, 1926), p. 65. Bury positively states that Tzath was baptized a Christian and crowned by Justin (II, 80, n. 2). Tzath's story is told in the most recent textbook for Georgian high schools in the Caucasus. N. Berdzenishvili, I. Djavakhishvili, S. Djanashia, *History of Gruzia*, I (Tbilisi, 1946), 116–117 (in Russian). According to this book, Tzath was a pagan. The emperor invited him to Constantinople and consented to grant him the crown of the Lazic kings if he would accept Christianity. As we have pointed out, however, the population of Lazika had been familiar with Christianity for a long time. *Gruzia* is the Russian name for Georgia.

505 A. D. were greatly disturbed. Although in 505 no formal peace had been made but only a truce for seven years, which apparently had not been renewed at the end of that period, nonetheless the two empires exchanged no hostilities for seventeen years until 522, the date of Tzath's baptism. In this year it was thought that war would break out. But evidently neither Justin nor Kawad wanted an immediate rupture. Before taking a decisive step, Kawad explained the cause of his dissatisfaction to Justin in a letter which his special envoy brought to Constantinople. We can be sure of the very interesting fact that a correspondence existed between the two most powerful rulers of that time, although the text of their letters as it has been preserved in our evidence is hardly to be regarded as an original text.

Justin's answer to Kawad is especially noteworthy in its distortion of historical realities. Kawad's letter to Justin reads as follows: "In spite of friendship and peace which has been established between us, thou actest as an enemy. Lo! thou hast inaugurated my own subject as king of the Lazi, who was not under the Roman dominion but had been from time immemorial (ἐξ αἰῶνος) under the power of the Persians." Justin also despatched his answer to Kawad by a special envoy. Unwilling to complicate the tense relations with Persia, he avoided discussion of the very delicate question of the political influence of either empire in Lazica and merely explained Tzath's baptism. "We have annexed no one of the subjects of thy empire nor urged him to come. But a man named Ztathios came to us, to our empire, humbly begging us to set him free from the pagan religion (τοῦ Ἑλληνικοῦ δόγματος), impure sacrifices and diabolical errors, and to make him Christian worthy of the grace (δυνάμεως) of the Eternal God and Maker of all things. How could I prevent one who desired from entering better conditions and from knowing the true God? And after he became a Christian and worthy to receive the holy mysteries, we sent him back to his own country." From this time on, according to our sources, there was enmity between Romans and Persians.[17] Justin's answer, of

---

[17] The text of the letters in Malalas, 414; *Chr. Pasch.*, 614–615; Theoph., 169; *Anastasii Chronographia Tripertita*, 131–132; Cedr., I, 638–639. John of Nikiu, XC, 39–41; Charles, pp. 137–138. The text of the letters is also reproduced in the Slavonic version of Malalas. Istrin, pp. 18–19; Spinka, p. 123. On the authenticity of the letters see Güterbock, *Byzanz und Persien* p. 7.

course, strongly indicates that Tzath was a pagan before his baptism, and therefore may be taken as support for the second theory advanced above on this problem.

Both empires looked for allies in case of the impending war and, curiously enough, both opened negotiations with the Huns who at that time occupied a large territory of presentday southern Russia. For both empires amity with the Huns was very essential, especially because the possessions of both empires in the north bordered upon the Caucasian mountains, and through the Caucasian passes the Huns could be dangerous to the vital interests of both empires in Iberia and Lazica.

Both Kawad and Justin entered into negotiations with the ruler (king) of the Huns Zilgibi (Zilgbis, Zilgbi, and some other variants). Kawad was the first to do so and had opened negotiations in which he was apparently successful, for Zilgibi pledged himself to take the field against Justin with an army of twenty thousand men. But Justin in his turn opened negotiations with Zilgibi, who accepted from him rich gifts and gave his promise on oath to help him in his struggle with Persia. When Justin became aware of the Hunnic king's perfidy, he endeavored to turn it to his own advantage. He sent a friendly letter to Kawad in which he disclosed Zilgibi's duplicity and perjury, informing the Persian king that Zilgibi had taken money from him in order to betray the Persians in favor of the Romans. "As brothers we should be on friendly terms and not be duped by those dogs" ($\mu\grave{\eta}$ $\dot{\upsilon}\pi\grave{o}$ $\tau\hat{\omega}\nu$ $\kappa\upsilon\nu\hat{\omega}\nu$ $\tauο\acute{\upsilon}\tau\omega\nu$ $\pi\alpha\acute{\iota}\zeta\epsilon\sigma\theta\alpha\iota$. Malalas, 415). Justin's message has been preserved at length in the Chronicle of John of Nikiu, where we read: "Behold, it is fitting that we should be brothers in friendship, and not be mocked by our enemies. And behold, we wish to inform thee that Zilgibi the Hun has received large sums from us with a view to helping us in the time of war, and behold now he has gone to thee with treacherous intent, and in the time of war he will come to our side and slay the Persians. And now, as thou sayest, let there be no enmity between us, but peace." On receiving this information the enraged Kawad summoned Zilgibi to his court and inquired whether he had really accepted money from Justin to fight against the Persians; and when the Hun acknowledged this, Kawad killed him and most of the twenty thousand Huns who were with him and who were taken unawares. Only a few escaped to their own country. Justin's friendly gesture greatly pleased Kawad, and through his special envoy Labroinus (Broinus) he informed Justin that he was ready to open negotiations for peace. Of this affair, John of Nikiu piously remarks: "But the Christians had the help of God, who always wars against their enemies." The Hunnic episode took place in 522.[18]

Kawad was so impressed with the openness and friendliness Justin had shown in this affair that somewhat surprisingly he asked Justin to adopt one of his sons, Chosroes. The idea itself was not absolutely new; relations of this sort between the two empires can be found in older times. It is known that the Emperor Arcadius, who died in 408, left a testament in which he recommended his young son and successor Theodosius to the protection of the Persian king, Yezdegerd I, fearing that the courtiers might deprive Theodosius of the throne; and Yezdegerd accepted the charge and during all his reign remained faithful to his commitment. Many scholars deny the authenticity of the story; but since similar instances are to be found during other periods of history, there seems to be no good reason for rejecting it.

Kawad's plan belongs to the same category. The story is related at length by the contemporary writer Procopius. If some details are not entirely exact, the fact itself seems firmly established and not to be rejected as a fabrication. The plan was conceived in 522, and was inspired by the friendliness of feeling that Justin's informing Kawad of the duplicity of the Hunnic king germinated in him.

Kawad was at this time especially anxious about the succession. He had four sons, Kaoses, Zames, Phthasuarsas, and Chosroes. Kaoses as the eldest was according to the Persian law successor to the throne.

[18] Malalas, 414–415 (Ζιλγιβί); the Slavonic version omits this episode. *Chr. Pasch.*, 615–616 (Ζιλγβί; Βροῖνου); this chronicle gives the date (p. 613). Theoph., 167 (Ζιλγβί). Theophanes erroneously tells the Hunnic episode as preceding Tzath's story, ascribing it to the year 521. *Anastasii Chronographia Tripertita*, 131 (Zelicbes). Some other variants of this name are indicated on p. 611 (Theoph., de Boor, II). Zonaras, XIV, 5, 18–22; *CSHB*, III, 147–148 (as in Theophanes, this episode precedes the story of Tzath). Cedrenus omits the Hunnic episode but writes that in the third year of his reign Justin made peace with Kawad (I, 638). John of Nikiu, XC, 42–46; Charles, p. 138. On the name of this Hunnic ruler see G. Moravcsik, *Byzantinoturcica*, II, *Sprachreste der Türkvölker in den byzantinischen Quellen* (Budapest, 1943), p. 121.

But this choice did not please Kawad, although, as Procopius says, "the father's judgment did violence to the law of nature and of custom as well." The second son Zames had lost one of his eyes, and therefore was ineligible by law as an invalid. Kawad's affections were fixed on his fourth son, Chosroes. Seeing, however, that the Persians felt extravagant admiration for the military talent of Zames, he feared lest they should rise against Chosroes. He therefore proposed to Justin that he should adopt Chosroes and aid him against his country-men, if his right of succession should be disputed; for only in this way, according to Procopius, "could he preserve stability in the govern-ment." Accordingly, his special envoys were sent to Justin in Con-stantinople, carrying the letter whose text has been preserved in Procopius and reads as follows: "Unjust indeed has been the treatment which we have received at the hands of the Romans, as even you yourself know, but I have seen fit to abandon entirely all the charges against you, being assured of this, that the most truly victorious of all men would be those who with justice on their side are still willingly overcome and vanquished by their friends. However, I ask of you a certain favor in return for this, which would bind together in kinship and in the good-will which would naturally spring from this relation not only ourselves but also all our subjects, and which would be calculated to bring us to a fulness of the blessing of peace. My pro-posal is this, that you should make my son Chosroes, who will be my successor to the throne, your adopted son."

When this message was brought to the emperor, Justin and Justinian at first were overjoyed and attracted by the proposal; they were quite ready to perform the act and set down the adoption in writing. But the influence of the quaestor Proclus, "a just man and one whom it was impossible to bribe," induced them to refuse. As a lawyer, in a long speech reproduced by Procopius, he represented the request as dangerous and insidious. "Nothing else is before our con-sideration at the present time than the question how we may hand over the Roman Empire to the Persians on a seemly pretext. For they make no concealment nor do they employ any blinds, but explicitly ac-knowledging their purpose they claim without more ado to rob us of our empire. . . And yet both of you ought to repel this attempt of the barbarians with all your power; thou, O Emperor, in order that thou mayst not be the last emperor of the Romans. . . . This embassy openly and straight from the very first words means to make this Chosroes, whoever he is, the adopted heir of the Roman Empire." Proclus' energetic warning was very clear: the adopted son might assert a claim to the father's inheritance; the Persian king might claim the Roman Empire.

In the meantime Kawad sent another letter to Justin, asking him to send men of repute in order to establish peace with him, and to indicate by letter the manner in which it would be his desire to accomplish the adoption of his son. This letter increased suspicion still more. It was decided to send the noblest men for this purpose, who must answer plainly to Kawad, when he enquired in what manner the adoption of Choroes should be accomplished, that it must be of the sort befitting a barbarian, and this meaning was that the barbarians adopt sons, not by a document, but by arms and armor (οὐ γράμμασιν οἱ βάρβαροι τοὺς παῖδας ἐσποιοῦνται, ἀλλ᾽ ὅπλων σκευῇ). The Persian envoys who had brought Kawad's letter were instructed to inform him that the noblest of the Romans would follow them not long afterwards, and that they would arrange in the best possible way a settlement regarding the peace and the adoption of Chosroes. Justin also answered Kawad by letter to the same effect.

Accordingly there were sent from the Romans the following men: the patrician Hypathius, nephew of the late Emperor Anastasius, who also held the office of General of the East; Rufinus, the son of Silvanus, a man of note among the patricians and known personally to Kawad; and an old man of exceptional ability as a warrior, Pharesmanes, a native of Colchis (Lazica). From the Persians came a very high official, Seoses, and Mebodes, who held the office of magister. All these men came together at a certain spot on the boundary line between the land of the Romans and the land of the Persians. Chosroes himself came to the Tigris River, which is distant from the city of Nisibis about two days' journey, in order that when the details of the peace should be definitely arranged, he might betake himself to Byzantium.

In the meantime the negotiations dragged on. The question of Lazica arose. Seoses claimed Lazica had been subject to the Persians from of old and that the Romans had taken it from them by violence and held it on no just grounds. When the Romans heard this, they were indignant to think that even Lazica should be disputed by the Persians. And when they in turn stated that the adoption of Chosroes must take place as is proper for a barbarian, this seemed to the Persians unbearable. The two parties therefore departed homeward with nothing accomplished, and Chosroes returned to his father. Thus the negotiations led to no result; and Kawad deeply resented the refusal of the request to adopt his son. After his return home, Seoses was accused by Mebodes of exceeding his power in discussing the question of Lazica and therefore frustrating the peace, and he was executed.[19]

It is not quite clear what Procopius meant in this story by the *adoptio per arma*, the manner in which the barbarians adopted their sons. It may be surmised that the ceremony of adoption was carried out by the giving of costly and elaborate armor. The one who received the arms therefore became an arm-companion of, and entered into a certain family relationship with the giver; but this was not the formal act of real adoption and would not involve rights of inheritance. If Justin had accepted Kawad's proposal and adopted Chosroes by this process, Chosroes would not have become his legal son with all rights resulting from legal adoption. Nonetheless, complications might of course have arisen between the two empires had an adequate occasion presented itself.[20]

[19] Detailed story in Procopius, *B. P.* I, 11; Dewing, I, 83–95. I have made free use of Dewing's excellent English version. Constantinus Porphyrogenitus, *Excerpta de legationibus*, ed. de Boor, I (Berlin, 1903), p. 91. Theoph., 167–168 (concise presentation). In his *Chronographia Tripertita* Anastasius omits the story. The Patriarch Photius tells it in his *Bibliotheca*, 63; ed. I. Bekker, 23; Migne, *PG*, CIII, 125. Zonaras, XIV, 5, 22–23; *CSHB*, III, 148 (a few words only). Kawad's third son Phthasuarsas is mentioned by Theophanes only, a little later (p. 170). Zachariah of Mitylene, VIII, 5; Brooks-Hamilton, p. 206; Ahrens-Krüger, pp. 157–158. This story has been reported in almost all general histories of the Byzantine Empire or in the histories of Persia. For Persia, see G. Rawlinson, *The Seventh Great Oriental Monarchy*, pp. 363–364. Sir Percy Sykes, *A History of Persia*, 2nd ed., I, 444. Nöldeke erroneously states that Kawad asked the Emperor Anastasius to adopt Chosroes. T. Nöldeke, *Geschichte der Perser und Araber zur Zeit der Sasaniden*, p. 76, note to p. 74. A. Christensen, *L'Iran sous les Sassanides* (Copenhague, 1936), p. 350.

[20] See K. Güterbock, *Byzanz und Persien*, pp. 29–30. R. Helm, *Untersuchungen über den auswärtigen diplomatischen Verkehr des römischen Reiches im Zeitalter des Spätantike, Archiv für Urkundenforschung*, XII, 432.

JUSTIN, IBERIA (GEORGIA, GRUZIYA), AND PERSIA

This setback resulted in Kawad's renewed decision to take possession of Lazica. But for the time being he was forced to change his policy towards Lazica because of new complications with another Caucasian country, Iberia. If these countries were extremely important to Persia, they were also vitally essential to Byzantium. Thus from 524, the last years of the reign of Justin, the full strength of the two contending empires was concentrated in the Caucasus, in Lazica and Iberia.

. Procopius draws a very interesting picture of the Persian position in the sixth century. To have secure possession of Lazica would be advantageous to the Persians in many ways. In the first place, they would also be permanently secure of Iberia also, for the Iberians would have no one to help them if they should revolt. And it was evident that the Iberians would be most thoroughly dissatisfied and that they would attempt a revolution shortly if they could only seize upon some favorable opportunity. Furthermore, the Persian Empire would be forever free from plunder by the Huns who lived beyond Lazica, and the Persian king would be able to send them against the Roman domains more easily and readily, whenever he should so desire. For the Persian king considered Lazica merely as a bulwark against the barbarians dwelling in the Caucasus. And then Procopius reveals one of the most ambitious plans and hopes of the Persian king. After the subjugation of Lazica, the Persians might with no trouble overrun both by land and by sea the countries along the Euxine Sea and thus win over the Cappadocians, Galatians, and Bithynians who adjoined them, and capture Byzantium (Βυζαντίους) herself by a sudden un-opposed assault.[21] Thus the final aim of the Persian kings was to conquer the Byzantine Empire by capturing Constantinople, with Lazica as a starting point. If we envisage the Lazo-Ibero-Persian con-flicts of the sixth century from this point of view, they cease to be mere local incidents and take their place in the history of the disastrous series of wars between two world powers whose ultimate destinies sometimes hung in the balance.

Apparently after Kawad determined to make war on Iberia, he

[21] Procopius, B. P. II, 28, 18–23; Dewing, I, 518–521.

looked about for a pretext for invasion. He issued a command to the
Iberians to adopt the rites of his own religion, and, in particular, under
no circumstances to bury their dead in the earth but to throw them all
to the birds and dogs. The Iberian nation was Christian and, as Procopius states, they guarded the rites of this faith more closely than any
other men known. Gurgenes, the Iberian king, turned to Justin for
protection; and the emperor gave him pledges of support against
Kawad's aggressive policy. As the first step in helping Gurgenes,
Justin sent Probus, nephew of the late Emperor Anastasius, with a
great sum of money to the city of Bosporus in the Crimea, which at
that time was subject to the Huns, in order to bribe an army of Huns
and send them as allies to the Iberians. But Probus, though, as we
have noted above, reached the Hunnic country north of the Caucasus,
was ultimately unsuccessful in his mission and departed without
accomplishing anything, since the Huns, torn by internal strife, were
not in a condition to respond to the emperor's request.[22]

At the same time Justin was able to raise some Hunnic troops which
he sent under the command of Peter as general to Lazica to fight "with
all their strength for Gurgenes." Meanwhile Kawad sent a powerful
army against Iberia under the command of a Persian general, Boes.
Since the help from the Romans was insufficient, and Gurgenes was
too weak to withstand the Persian attack with his own forces, he fled
to Lazica, taking with him his wife, his children, of whom Peranius
was the oldest, his brothers, and all the Iberian nobility as well. When
they reached the boundaries of Lazica, they remained there and took
advantage of the roughness of the country to make a stand against
the enemy. At that time there were two fortresses of the Lazi almost
on the very boundary of Iberia, Skanda or Skende (now Skanda) and
Sarapanis or Sarapa (now Shorapan), situated in an extremely rugged
and mountainous country and extraordinarily difficult of access. Before the time of Justinian the Lazi had great difficulty in garrisoning
them, for no food at all grew there, and supplies had to be brought
in on the shoulders of porters. It was probably in one of these

---

[22] On Probus' mission to Bosporus see A. Vasiliev, *The Goths in the Crimea*,
p. 70. R. Helm, *Untersuchungen über den auswärtigen diplomatischen Verkehr
des römischen Reiches im Zeitalter der Spätantike, Archiv für Urkundenforschung*, XII (1932), 433: about 527–528.

fortresses that Gurgenes and his numerous suite tried for a while to take their stand. But ultimately they were forced to yield before the numerical superiority of the Persians and they proceeded to Constantinople. At the same time the Byzantine commander in Lazica, Peter, was also summoned by Justin to the capital. Iberia was occupied by the Persians and lost its independence. As Procopius states, "the Persians from that time on did not permit the Iberians to set up a king over themselves" (*B. P.* II, 28, 20). A few years later, during the reign of Justinian, the Iberians tried to put on the throne a new king by the name of Jamanarsé (Ζαμαναρζός), who in his turn went to Byzantium and received assurance of friendship from Justinian.[23] But none of these attempts on the part of the Iberians led to any result, and the Persian king stubbornly denied them the right to enthrone their own king.

Justin's influence thus suffered a considerable blow in the Caucasian regions, in Lazica and Iberia. Therefore he determined to strike Kawad in his own territory, in Persarmenia and Mesopotamia. In 526, at the very end of Justin's reign, he opened hostilities on Persia. The Roman troops under the command of Sittas and Belisarius, made an inroad into Persarmenia. Both commanders at that time were young, "wearing their first beards," as Procopius says (I, 12, 21), and occupying the rather modest position of bodyguard (δορυφόρω) to Justin's nephew, the general Justinian. At the beginning their campaign seemed successful; they plundered a large tract of the country and withdrew with a great multitude of Armenian captives. But when Sittas and Belisarius made a second inroad into Persarmenia, two Persian generals, Narses and Aratius, unexpectedly confronted them with a considerable force, engaged them in battle, and gained the advantage. Such was the not very promising result of this expedition. As we can judge from our source, this was not a campaign undertaken on a large scale, but merely a raid. It is to be noted that the name of Belisarius, the future national hero of the epoch of Justinian, occurs for the first time in connection

---

[23] Theoph., p. 216 (under the eighth year of Justinian's rule). Malalas, p. 429: τῶν δὲ Ἰβήρων Σαμαναζός. Spinka, p. 137 (Zamala). Allen writes that Jamanarsé's flight to Byzantium occurred in 527. W. Allen, *A History of the Georgian People*, p. 377. Gugushvili, "The Chronological-Genealogical Table of the Kings of Georgia," *Georgica*, I, 2–3 (1936), 148.

with these military operations. This is his first appearance upon the historical scene.

Simultaneously another Roman army under the command of a certain Libelarius (Λιβελάριος) of Thrace invaded Mesopotamia near the city of Nisibis. But here something strange happened: Libelarius' army retired abruptly in flight, although no one came out against them. Because of this Justin reduced Libelarius from his office and appointed Belisarius commander of the troops in the very important frontier city and fortress of Dara, which had been built by the late Emperor Anastasius. Belisarius, going to the place of his new destination, received as his adviser (ξύμβουλος) or secretary, Procopius, the renowned historian of the epoch of Justinian, to whom we are indebted for most of our information on Justin's policy towards Iberia and Persia.

The Mesopotamian campaign occurred in 527, the last year of Justin's rule, so that the continuation and conclusion of the so-called First Persian War (527–532) took place under Justinian. The final treaty of 532 is known as "the Endless Peace." Among other clauses of the treaty it is to be noted here that the Iberian refugees at Constantinople might, as they chose, either remain there or return to their own country. Many returned, but many also, mistrusting the Persians, remained in Byzantium (*B. P.* I, 22, 16). King Gurgenes, his family and suite preferred to remain in Constantinople and never returned to their own country. Their final destiny in exile is unknown, with the exception of Gurgenes' oldest son Peranius. He entered the Roman service and died many years after of injuries received from falling from his horse while he was out hunting (*B. P.* II, 28, 1).[24]

[24] For Justin's relations with Persia we are almost entirely dependent on Procopius. *B. P.* I, 12; Dewing, I, 94–101. Constantinus Porphyrogenitus, *Excerpta de legationibus*, ed. de Boor, I, 90–91. On the fortresses Scanda and Sarapanis, Proc., *B. G.* IV, 13, 15–16; Dewing, V, 186–187. Brosset, *Additions et éclaircissements à l'histoire de la Géorgie* (St. Petersburg, 1851), pp. 103–104. On Gurgenes' son, Peranius, *B. P.* II, 28, 1; Dewing, I, 514–515. On the adoption, in addition to Procopius, see Zach. of Mityl., VIII, 5: "the old man Farzman, and Asthebid" (Hamilton-Brooks, p. 206; Ahrens-Krüger, pp. 157–158). Asthebid is the title of the Persian commander-in-chief Spahpat ('Ασπεβέδης); see Hamilton-Brooks, p. 206, n. 5; Zach. IX, 4; p. 225 and n. 7. The Arab Christian historian of the tenth century, Agapius (Mahbûb), probably refers to the inroad into Persarmenia when writing: "In the seventh year of his [Justin's] reign, the Greeks and the

It is very possible that to this Persian campaign refers a Greek inscription discovered by R. P. Mouterde in 1927 at Ghour, on the direct road from Emesa (Homs) to Apamea in Syria. The inscription was found on a lintel which belonged to "an encampment (μητᾶτον) of the saints Longinus, Theodore, and George," destined for troops passing by. If the date of the inscription, 524–525, is correct, the building, Mouterde assumes, may have served as a resting place under the patronage of these three military saints for soldiers brought there to fight the Persians and occupy the line of the river Orontes.[25]

After the conquest of Iberia, the new Persian frontier reached in the north the Caucasian mountain passes, through which the northern barbarians, especially the Huns, penetrated into the territory of Iberia and Lazica; accordingly these passes or "the gates facing the land of the Huns" (Zach. of Mityl., VIII, 5) had to be very watchfully guarded by the troops settled in Iberia. So long as the Romans were overlords of Iberia, they had guarded these danger points. But now that they had abandoned Iberia to Persian influence, they were no longer responsible for the defense of the passes and were no longer in a position to keep garrisons there. But apparently Kawad was inclined to believe that they should still help him to guard the passes, if not by a military force at least by donating a certain amount of money. He demanded from Justin the considerable sum of 550 centenaria (κεντηνάρια, talents) of gold, which the Persians had been

---

Persians engaged in a battle on the banks of the Euphrates; and many Greeks drowned"; ed. A. Vasiliev, p. 425 (165). Also *Gregorii Abulpharagii Historia Dynastiarum*, ed. E. Pocockio, p. 149 (93); ed. Salhani, p. 147. In this text Chaboras, on which Nisibis lay, would be a better reading than the Euphrates, which flows with it. In the fifteenth century, in his famous *Encomium* of Trebizond, Bessarion of Nicaea mentions the Persian invasion of Iberia under Kawad and gives the name of Gurgenes. Bessarion of Nicaea, Βησσαρίωνος Ἐγκώμιον εἰς Τραπεζοῦντα νῦν τὸ πρῶτον ἐκδιδόμενον ὑπὸ Σπυρ. Π. Λάμπρου, Νέος Ἑλληνομνήμων, XIII (1916), 178; separate edition (Athens, 1916), p. 36. Bessarion's source is Procopius; see Lampros, *op. cit.*, p. 59. Kulakovsky erroneously states that Gurgenes is to be identified with Tzath. *History of Byzantium*, II, 23 (in Russian). Clinton correctly places the expedition to Persarmenia in the year 526. *Fasti Romani*, I, 746.

[25] See R. P. Mouterde, *Rapport du R. P. Mouterde à l'Académie des Inscriptions sur la mission épigraphique en Haute-Syrie*, Syria, IX (1928), 167. As we have seen, the Persian War started in 526. The date of the inscription is not absolutely certain. See also R. Devreesse, *Le patriarcat d'Antioche*, p. 205.

accustomed to give for the rations of the troops who guarded the gates against the Huns. Justin refused to pay it, and his refusal was another cause of trouble between Byzantium and Persia.[26]

JUSTIN AND THE ARABS: THE LAKHMIDS AND THE GHASSANIDS

The Persian king had another way to make Byzantium feel his dissatisfaction and wrath. In the sixth century the Lakhmid kingdom was under his suzerainty in Irak with its capital at Hira (al-Hira; in Syriac, Herta) about three Arab miles south of the future city of Kufa. The Lakhmids were Arabs, of Yemen origin. Christianity in the form of Nestorianism was widespread among the population. During the reign of Justin lived the most illustrious ruler in the Lakhmid annals, al-Mundhir III (in Greek sources Ἀλαμούνδαρος) whose long rule (ca. 505–554) covered the periods of the reigns of Anastasius, Justin, and Justinian. He himself was apparently not a Christian. The Lakhmids were very well known by their continuous war with another Arab dynasty in Syria, the Ghassanids, also of southern origin, who were monophysite Christians and were under the suzerainty of the Byzantine emperors; their ruler, probably in the sixth century, was honored with the title of phylarchus (φύλαρχος). The Ghassanids had no fixed residence, and their frontiers had to depend on the Persians and their vassals the Lakhmids. Their history is one of the most obscure portions of Arab history. Both dynasties, the Lakhmids and the Ghassanids, were obedient tools in the hands of the two competing monarchs of Byzantium and Persia when they opened hostilities on each other.

But they did not neglect their own interests. In the Syrian desert, south of the city of Palmyra, lay a country which according to Procopius (B. P. II, 1) was called Strata (Στράτα). In the sixth century this

---

[26] See Zach. of Mityl., VIII, 5: demands for the payment of the tribute of 500 lbs. weight of gold which was paid to him by the king of the Romans. Hamilton-Brooks, p. 206; Ahrens-Krüger, pp. 157–158. Michel le Syrien, IX, 16; Chabot, II, 178: "5 mille 5 cents κεντηνάρια d'or." Michel le Grand, *Chronique* by Langlois, p. 179: "5500 quintaux d'or pour les remettre au général chargé de la garde de la porte de l'Albanie." Gregory Abû'l Faraj, commonly known as Bar Hebraeus, *The Chronography*, transl. Budge, I, 73 (550 kantinare talents of gold). *Abulpharagii Gregorii sive Bar-Hebraei Chronicon Syriacum*, Bruns and Kirsch, II, 81 (550 quintalia auri).

country was claimed by "both tribes of Saracens," that is, by both Lakhmids and Ghassanids, who tried to turn the Roman-Persian wars to their advantage by getting possession of Strata, which, although a burned-up country, exceedingly dry and producing not a single tree nor any of the useful growth of cornlands, had been from of old used as a pasturage for a few flocks of sheep. It is interesting to point out that when a conflict arose between the two tribes under Justinian, the Ghassanid ruler of the time, Arethas, Procopius writes, maintained that the place belonged to the Romans, supporting his assertion by the name Strata which had long been applied to it by all and which signifies in the Latin tongue "a paved road." [27] But his rival sheik, al-Mundhir, son of Sakkike, who was, according to Procopius, "by no means inclined to quarrel concerning the name," contented himself with the more practical argument that for years back the shepherds had paid him tribute. Justinian entrusted the settlement of the dispute to two arbitrators.[28]

The Byzantine emperors, Justin among them, took measures against the assaults of the Saracens by building forts on the eastern border. The place which drew the attention of the emperors as a convenient site to protect the frontier was the desert of Thannuris (Θαννούριος), east of the river Habur (Aborras) on the edge of the border. The fortification, which was already listed in the *Notitia dignitatum* (Thannuri), had evidently been built by Justin's predecessor Anasta-

[27] Proc., *B. P.* II, 1, 6–7; Dewing, I, 260–263. The Strata of Procopius has been now identified with the Strata Diocletiana indicated by some milestones; this was the Roman road from Damascus to the Euphrates by way of Palmyra. See P. René Mouterde, "La Strata Diocletiana et ses bornes militaires," *Mélanges de l'Université Saint-Joseph Beyrouth* (Liban), XV (1930–1931), 222. Alois Musil, *Palmyrena* (New York, 1928), pp. 247–248 (American Geographical Society. Oriental Explorations and Studies, no. 4). Also Bury, *History of the Later Roman Empire*, II, 92. R. Dussaud, *Topographie historique de la Syrie antique et médiévale*, p. 255 and n. 4.

[28] Proc., *B. P.* II, 1, 8–9; Dewing, I, 262–263. See also Proc., I, 17, 1: Ἀλαμούνδαρος ὁ Σακκίκης (Dewing, I, 144). Theoph., p. 178: ὁ Ζεκικῆς. *Anastasii Chronographia Tripertita*, p. 134: "Alamundarus Zecices." The name of al-Mundhir's mother is an Arabic proper name Šaqîqa; the mother of one of the earlier kings of Hira also bore this name. See T. Nöldeke, *Geschichte der Perser und Araber*, p. 79; 169–170, n. 4. Cf. Saint Arethas, *Martyrium Sancti Arethae et sociorum in civitate Negrana, Acta Sanctorum, Octobris*, X (Bruxelles, 1861), p. 742, § 25: Ἀλαμούνδαρον τὸν λεγόμενον Σακίκαν. The commentator (p. 688, § 88) noted that Sjakika was the name of the first wife of Amundari I.

sius, but probably destroyed soon after by the Saracens. According to a contemporary source (Zach. of Mityl., IX, 2), Justin learned that Thannuris was a convenient place where a city could be built as a place of refuge in the desert and a military force could be stationed in order to protect the Byzantine Arabs against the marauding bands of Saracens, that is, the Persian Arabs. Accordingly, Thomas the silentiary, a native of Aphphadana (evidently Ἀπάδνας), was sent to build, or it is probably better to say to rebuild, such a city. But he had made but inconsiderable progress when his unfinished work was destroyed by the Saracens and Kadisenes (Καδισηνοί in Proc., B. P. I, 14, 38–39) from two nearby points, Singara and Thebetha.

Justin's successor, Justinian, set to work again; and among many other places, Procopius tells us, he built and fortified on the eastern border two Thannourios, one large and one small, which the emperor made, like many other places, "truly formidable and altogether unapproachable for their assailants" (De aed. II, 6, 13–14). The name of Thannuris still survives in the modern Tell Tenenir (Tell Tuneinir).[29] Pilgrims who in the sixth century visited the Holy Land testify that south of Palestine in the north of Arabia, cities, monasteries, and isolated hermits were assailed by Saracens, so that pilgrims had to make their way under the protection of the military forces of the empire.[30]

After Justin had refused to pay money for keeping garrisons at

[29] Zach. of Mityl., IX, 2: "Concerning the battle which was fought in the desert of Thannuris"; Hamilton-Brooks, pp. 222–223; Ahrens-Krüger, p. 165. Proc. B. P. I, 14, 38–39 (Καδισηνοί); De aed. II, 6, 13–14 (Θαννούριος); II, 4, 20 (Ἀπάδνας). Thannuris under Anastasius in Michel le Syrien, IX, ch. XI; Chabot, II, 167. See Pigulevskaya, Syriac Sources for the History of the Peoples of USSR, pp. 161–162 (in Russian). E. Honigmann, Die Ostgrenze des byzantinischen Reiches, p. 10; 15 and n. 2; 17. See Honigmann's map: "Mesopotamia et Armenia Quarta, ann. 600." R. Dussaud, Topographie historique, pp. 488–489 (Touneinir).

[30] See Sanctae Silviae Peregrinatio, ed. P. Geyer (Vienna, 1898), p. 47: "sic tamen per heremum, ut cata mansiones monasteria sint cum militibus et praepositis, qui nos deducebant semper de castro ad castrum," CSEL, vol. XXXIX. I attribute this pilgrimage to the sixth century. Antonini Placentini Itinerarium (circa a. 570), ed. P. Geyer, p. 185: (in the countries between Sina, Abila (Aila) and Clysma, is) "custodia monasteriorum et heremitarum propter insidias Saracenorum, ante quorum timorem non exagitantur Saraceni. Nam exeuntes de ipsa civitate a foris illi serant et claves tollent secum. Et illi qui sunt ab intus similiter faciunt propter insidias Saracenorum, quia non habent, ubi exeant foris, praeter caclum et harenam," CSEL, XXXIX.

the Caspian gates to protect Iberia, now in Persian hands, from Hunnic raids, and after the Roman troops had made inroads into Persarmenia and Mesopotamia, Kawad determined to devastate the Roman border provinces by sending his Lakhmid vassals under command of al-Mundhir. Some Greek sources contemptuously call this man "a little king of the Saracens," but his contemporary Procopius highly praises his talents; Alamoundaros, he says, holding the position of king, ruled alone over all the Saracens in Persia, and was able to make his inroads with the whole army wherever he wished in the Roman domain, and no commander of the Roman troops was strong enough to array himself against him.[31] In 523 al Mundhir made two evidently very devastating inroads into Byzantine territory. In the first he thoroughly pillaged the frontier region along the two tributaries of the Euphrates, al-Balikh which the Greeks knew as the Bilecha, and Khabur ('Αβόρρας).[32] Then, after the Roman inroads into Persarmenia and Mesopotamia, Kawad ordered al-Mundhir to make another expedition which was very devastating indeed. Al-Mundhir invaded the region of Emesa and Apamea and in his drive pillaged the district of Antioch in Syria. He carried off many captives. Our sources relate the revolting fact that in one day in honor of an old Arabian goddess, al-Uzza (the Arabian Aphrodite-Venus) he sacrificed four hundred nuns made captive among the congregation in the Church of the Apostle Thomas at Emesa.[33]

[31] *Martyrium Sancti Arethae et sociorum in civitate Negrana, Acta Sanctorum,* Octobris, X, 742, § 25: τὸν βασιλίσκον πάντων τῶν ὑπὸ Πέρσας Σαρακηνῶν. Theoph., p. 178: ὁ βασιλίσκος τῶν Σαρακηνῶν, *Anastasii Chronographia Tripertita,* p. 134: "regulus Saracenorum." Cf. Procopius, B. P. I, 17, 45–46; Dewing, I, 158–159.

[32] On Balikh see G. Le Strange, *The Lands of the Eastern Caliphate* (Cambridge, 1905), pp. 102–103. E. Honigmann, *Die Ostgrenze des byzantinischen Reiches,* p. 13, n. 7 (Balih). On Khabur, or Greater Khabur, see Le Strange, p. 87; 95–97. This river is not to be confused with the other Khabur, or the Little Khabur, which flower into the Tigris.

[33] Zach. of Mityl., VIII, 5; Hamilton-Brooks, pp. 206–207; Ahrens-Krüger, pp. 157–158. Michel le Syrien, IX, ch. XVI; Chabot, II, 178–179. Armenian version by Langlois, p. 179 (the goddess is called Couzia). *Gregorii Abulpharagii sive Bar Hebraei Chronicon Syriacum,* Bruns and Kirsch, II, 81. Gregory Abu'l Faraj commonly known as Bar Hebraeus, *The Chronography,* Budge, p. 73. The Syrian chronicler of the seventh century, Jacob (James) of Edessa, notes that "Persians and Arabs reached the regions of Antioch and Apamea." *Chronicon Iacobi Edesseni,* transl. E. W. Brooks, CSCO, Scriptores syri, 3rd series, vol. IV, *Chronica minora,* 240. On al-Uzza, an old Arabian goddess, who was especially

Among other captives, al-Mundhir took two Roman generals, Timostratus and John. Timostratus was a very prominent figure in Byzantino-Persian relations; he had taken part in the war with Persia during the reign of Justin's predecessor Anastasius and was for a time the Duke of Callinicum (Καλλίνικον) on the Euphrates, the Roman market for Persian merchandise. It is not easy to identify exactly the second captured general, John, son of Lucas, as Procopius calls him (*B. P.* I, 17, 44). He may have been John, Duke of Mesopotamia, who participated in the second Persian war during the reign of Justinian (540–545).

Justin decided to negotiate peace with al-Mundhir, and at the very end of 523 sent an embassy to Hira, his capital.[34] Abram (Abraham,

worshipped outside Arabia proper by the Lakhmids of Hira, see *Encyclopaedia of Islam*, IV, 1069–1070 (by Fr. Buhl); also G. Rothstein, *Die Dynastie der Lahmiden in al-Hîra* (Berlin, 1899), p. 140. T. Nöldeke, *Die Ghassanischen Fürsten aus dem Hause Gafna's, Abhandlungen der Akademie der Wissenschaften zu Berlin*, 1887, II, 18. See Proc., *B. P.* II, 28, 13 (τῇ 'Αφροδίτῃ); Dewing, I, 518. In the Latin translation of Abulpharagins (II, 81) we read: "Mondarus, rex Arabum, depopulatus est omnem Dalmatiam," i.e. Beliham et Haburam. I believe that in the distorted form of Dalmatia we should recognize the name Dabanas mentioned in the *Notitia dignitatum*, XXXV, 6, 18, which according to Honigmann is presumably located in Osrhoene. *Die Ostgrenze*, p. 13, n. 7. Chronological confusion in Rothstein, *op. cit.*, p. 81. This invasion of Mundhir III undoubtedly belongs to the period of Justin and not to that of Justinian. See Devreesse, *Le patriarcat d'Antioche*, p. 259; Cyril of Scythopolis has preserved the memory of this bloody incursion of al-Mundhir. Devreesse confounds Amida with Emesa and refers to the *Vita* of John Hesychastes, p. 211, ed. Schwartz. If I am not mistaken, however, the *Vita* speaks of the Saracen invasion and capture of Amida which took place under Anastasius in 502–503. E. Schwartz, *Kyrillos von Skythopolis*, p. 211.

[34] Our best authentic source on this embassy is the Syriac letter of Simeon, Bishop of Beth-Arsham, one of the members of the embassy, on the Homerite martyrs. The authenticity of the letter has often been questioned; but its chronological and topographical data and the names of various persons who took part in the negotiations are so exact that its main genuineness is beyond doubt. Of course in the text which has survived there are some inventions, for instance, the fabricated lengthy texts of the letters included in this document; but the fact itself that letters were sent and received remains firmly established. The abridged Syriac text of the letter with a Latin translation was published by J. S. Assemani in his *Bibliotheca Orientalis*, I (Rome, 1719), 364–386. The much more complete text with an Italian translation and commentary was published by I. Guidi, *La lettera di Simeono vescovo di Bêth-Arsâm sopra i martiri omeriti, Atti della R. Acēademia dei Lincei*, CCLXXVIII, 3rd series, *Memorie della classe di scienze morali storiche e filologiche*, VII (Rome, 1881), 471–515. Assemani took the text of the letter from John of Ephesus. The text is also to be found in the so-called

'Aβράμης), the son of Euphrasius and the father of the historian Nonnosus, who later under Justinian was employed on similar diplomatic missions, headed it. Several sources call Abram a presbyter, which may imply that towards the end of his life he took holy orders. It is possible that as envoy to the Arabian ruler he could speak Arabic.[35] On his mission to Hira, Abram was accompanied by Sergius (or George), Bishop of al-Resafa (Bejt-Resâfa) who later probably became the author of the Syriac version of a report on the martyrs of Nagran (Nadjran) in south Arabia.[36]

Chronicle of Zachariah of Mitylene, VIII, 3; Brooks-Hamilton, pp. 192–203; Ahrens-Krüger, pp. 142–153. See also Michel le Syrien, IX, 18; Chabot, II, 184. Michel le Grand, *Chronique*, pp. 185–186 (the name of the king is given as Mentour). J. Halevy came out decidedly against the authenticity of the letter. "Examen critique des sources relatives à la persecution des chrétiens de Nedjran par le roi juif des Himyarites," *Revue des études juives*, XVIII, 16–42; 161–178. According to Halevy, the letter attributed to Simeon of Beth-Arsham is a fanciful story (un roman fantaisiste) written at the end of Justinian's reign in order to extend to the Jews the persecutions which had already been ordered by the court of Byzantium against the monophysites (p. 178; also pp. 41–42). Halevy's skeptical attitude has not been accepted. In Arabic: Agapius (Mahboub) de Menbidj, Kitab al-'Unvan, *Histoire universelle*, ed. with a French translation by A. Vasiliev, *Patrologia Orientalis*, VIII, 425 (165). *Gregorii Abulpharagii Historia Dynastiarum*, ed. Pocockio, p. 149 (text); 93 (transl.); Arabic text only by Salhani, p. 148. *Histoire nestorienne*, *Chronique de Seert*, ed. with a French translation by Addai Scher, *Patrologia Orientalis*, VII, 142–145 (50–53). In Greek: Nonnosus, *Excerpta* preserved in *Photii Bibliotheca*, Cod. III: *Nonnosi Historia legationum*, Migne, *PG*, CIII, col. 44; *CSHB*, pp. 478–479; C. Müller, *FHG*, IV, 179; L. Dindorf, *Historici graeci minores*, I (Leipzig, 1870), 473 (contemporary but unfortunately a very meagre fragment). Proc., *B. P.*, I, 17, 44 (a few words on one result of the negotiations). *Martyrium Sancti Arethae et sociorum in civitate Negrana*, Acta Sanctorum, Octobris, X, 742 (§ 25); 743 (§ 27) (substantial report). I have placed the embassy to Hira at the very end of 523, because according to the letter of Simeon, the embassy had already left Hira on the twentieth of January, 524, to meet al-Mundhir ten days later at Ramlah. Guidi, p. 480. Zach. of Mityl., VIII, 3; Hamilton-Brooks, p. 192; Ahrens-Krüger, p. 142. On Hira see also Franz Altheim, *Die Krise der alten Welt im 3. Jahrhundert n. zw. und ihre Ursachen*, I. *Die ausserrömische Welt* (Berlin-Dahlen, 1943), 138–139.

[35] Bury, *op. cit.*, II, 326, n. 2. In the same note Bury also conjectures that Abram was of the Saracen race. I do not see any reason for such a conjecture.

[36] Nonnosus: ὁ πατὴρ Νοννόσου ('Αβράμης δ'ἦν αὐτῷ ὄνομα) πρὸς 'Αλαμούνδαρον φύλαρχον Σαρακηνῶν ἐπρεσβεύσατο. Guidi, *Le lettera*, p. 480: "Abram, priest, the son of Euphrasius"; pp. 486–487: "Abram, priest, the son of Euphrasius along with the venerable and holy bishop of Resafa, Sergius (or George)." On Sergius as the potential author of the Syriac report on the martyrs of Nagran see Guidi, p. 499; also A. Musil, *Palmyrena* (New York, 1928), p. 267 (American Geographical Society, Oriental Explorations and Studies, no. 4). Musil is quite positive in his assertion. *Martyrium Arethae*, p. 742 (§ 25): 'Αβράμιον τὸν εὐλα-

The embassy arrived in Hira in January, 524, but did not find al-Mundhir there, who was at that time in one of his encampments in the Syrian desert. Accordingly, on the twentieth of January Justin's envoys left Hira. They traveled a ten-day journey through the desert towards the southeast, and on the thirtieth came upon al-Mundhir in his camp, over against the hills called "the hills of sand," in the Saracen language "Ramlah."

Their reception was not very promising. When the envoys were entering the encampment, some pagan Arabs met them with insults, saying: "What can you do? for behold! your Christ has been expelled by the Romans and by the Persians and by the Himyarites (Homerites)." And Simeon of Beth-Arsham himself in his letter remarks, "And when we were insulted by the Saracens it distressed us." [37]

At Ramlah there was present a very large and manifold gathering. The Persian king sent representatives of various Christian doctrines who dwelt in his empire, mostly Nestorians. *Martyrium Arethae* gives their names: the priest (presbyter) and apocrisiarius, that is, ambassador, Simeon, for the orthodox Christians in Persia; the subdeacon John (Ioannes) Mandinos; the *comes* Angaios ('Αγγαῖος), son of Set (Σήτ), who was a Christian and ethnarch (governor) of the whole region of Ramlah. Silas (Σίλας), bishop of the Nestorians in Persia, arrived with a large suite wishing "to strike upon and defend their own doctrine against the Roman and Persian Orthodox" and in this way "to be agreeable to the pagans and Jews." [38] Along with

βέστατον καὶ θεοφιλέστατον πρεσβύτερον. Duchesne has conjectured that Sergius was the author of the *Martyrium Arethae*. Duchesne, *Eglises separées*, p. 325. Bury, *op. cit.*, II, 324, n. 1. In transliteration the name of the place where the massacre was carried out has various forms: Nagran, Nadjran, Nejran. For the sake of uniformity I use the form Nagran throughout.

[37] Simeon's letter, Assemani, *Bibl. Or.*, I, 365. Guidi, p. 481. Zach. of Mityl., VIII, 3; Hamilton-Brooks, p. 193; Ahrens-Krüger, p. 143. Mich. le Syr., IX, 18; II, 184–185. On the location of Ramlah (Ramle) see Alois Musil, *Northern Neğd, A Topographical Itinerary* (New York, 1928), p. 71 and note 30.

[38] Zach. of Mityl., VIII, 3; Hamilton-Brooks, pp. 192–193; Ahrens-Krüger, p. 142. *Martyrium Arethae*, p. 472 (§ 25). Simeon-Guidi, pp. 480–481. The dating of January is supplied by Zachariah and Simeon. Lebeau says that the embassy went to Hira at the outset of February, 524. Lebeau, *Histoire du Bas-Empire*, ed. Saint-Martin, VIII, 58. Correct date in G. Rothstein, *Die Dynastie der Lahmiden in al-Hira*, p. 80. R. Helm, *Untersuchungen . . . Archiv für Urkundenforschung*, XII, 432. Devreesse, *Le patriarcat d'Antioche*, p. 255. Le P. Henri

Abram, Simeon, Bishop of Beth-Arsham, the future author of the famous letter addressed to Simeon Abbot of Gabula, arrived at Ramlah from Hira. Abram and Simeon belonged to two opposing denominations: as Justin's chief envoy Abram was a Chalcedonian or a diophysite, and Simeon a monophysite, famous for his propaganda for monophisitism in Sassanian Persia.[39]

The commission with which Justin charged Abram was complex. First of all, his objective was to make peace with al-Mundhir, put an end to disastrous devastations of the frontier region of Syria by a treaty of amity, and obtain the release of two Byzantine generals, Timostratus and John, who, as we know, had been captured by al-Mundhir in 523. In the last respect Abram's mission was entirely successful, and the two generals were released.[40]

Another objective of Abram's mission was to establish peaceful relations with al-Mundhir on behalf of the Christians who dwelt in his territory; in other words, Justin was making an attempt here to interfere with the religious matters of a foreign country.[41] If we consider more closely the general situation in al-Mundhir's kingdom, we shall see that the problem entrusted to Abram was very complicated and delicate.

Justin's new strictly orthodox or Chalcedonian policy had resulted

---

Charles, *Le christianisme des Arabes nomades sur le limes et dans le désert syro-mésopotamien aux alentours de l'hégire* (Paris, 1936), p. 59.

[38] Assemani's attempt to prove that Simeon was orthodox, i.e. Chalcedonian, has not been accepted. Assemani, *Bibl. Or.*, I, 342-343. See Bury, II, 324: "Simeon Beth Arsham, the head of the Monophysites of the Persian empire . . . having come on the part of the Emperor Justin." Baumstark, *Geschichte der syrischen Literatur*, p. 145.

[40] Peace negotiations in Zach. of Mityl., VIII, 3. *Martyrium Arethae*, p. 742 (§ 25). Agapius of Menbidj, p. 425 (165). Michel le Syrien, IX, 18; Chabot, II, 184. Michel le Grand, Arm. version, pp. 185-186. The names of two generals in Nonnosus; Proc., *B. P.* I, 17, 44. With certainty, in Zach. of Mityl., IX, 1-2, we can say that Timostratus should be substituted for Timus as master of the soldiers. Hamilton-Brooks, pp. 222-223; Ahrens-Krüger, p. 168: "Timostratos." The Russian translation of the excerpts from the *Chronicle* of Zachariah by Miss Pigulevskaya gives Timostratus without mention of the form Timus. N. Pigulevskaya, *Syrian Sources on the History of the Peoples of USSR*, pp. 160-161. See R. Helm, *Untersuchungen* . . . , *Archiv für Urkundenforschung*, XII, 395, n. 4. Devreesse, *op. cit.*, pp. 258-259.

[41] *Martyrium Arethae*, p. 742 (§ 25): προτρέψαι αὐτὸν σπονδὰς εἰρηνικὰς ποιῆσαι πρὸς τοὺς ὄντας ὑπὸ τὴν αὐτοῦ ἐξουσίαν χριστιανούς.

in the persecution of other denominations, especially monophysites. Many monophysites escaped persecution by fleeing into Persia, and special orders were given by Justin to the border authorities to keep their eyes open for fugitives. Some escaped to Hira. The local bishop Silas (Sila) whom, as we have noted above, the *Martyrium Arethae* designated as the Nestorian bishop in Persia, was informed of the arrival of monophysite fugitives from Byzantium. Silas found them and told them to choose one of three things: to profess the doctrine of the Christians who dwelt in the Persian Empire, that is, Nestorianism; to accept public discussion on their faith; or to be exiled. Supported by a certain "heretic" monophysite, al-Hadjdjadj, son of Qaïs, of Hira, who was one of al-Mundhir's courtiers, they rejected his proposition. Therefore al-Mundhir commanded the refugees to leave his country. Some of them fled; some remained hidden; and some proceeded south into Arabia, where they established themselves in Nagran. Soon after the bishop Silas, who as we know took an active part in religious matters in Persia, died. The expulsion of the monophysites from al-Mundhir's kingdom must have been a great source of satisfaction to Justin's ambassador Abram and to Justin himself.[42]

A very interesting episode with an important result occurred during the conference at Ramlah. A Himyarite leader in south Arabia, Dhu-Nuwas (Novas) of the Jewish faith, "this second Pharaoh," as the *Martyrium of Arethae* calls him, dispatched an envoy to al-Mundhir bearing a lengthy letter in which he described how he had massacred all the Christians in his land and urged the Saracen emir to do likewise. This letter was read in the presence of all the members of the meeting. The Christians were horrified by the news; the pagans and Hebrews were cheered. Simeon of Beth-Arsham immediately transmitted the news to Simeon, Abbot of Gabula, by his famous letter asking him to arrange that "the faithful," i.e. the monophysites,

---

[42] It would be difficult to accept the information of the late Nestorian *Chonicle of Seert* that the expulsion of monophysites by al-Mundhir was carried out under special pressure from Justin. The measure was desirable to both al-Mundhir and Justin. Justin probably entrusted Abram with this delicate diplomatic mission. *Histoire nestorienne; Chronique de Seert*, Addai Scher, *Patr. Or.* VII, 142–145 (50–53). The chronicler says that Silas passed away in the thirty-fourth year of the reign of Kawad, in 522–523. But we know that he was still alive in 524.

of Antioch, Tarsus of Cilicia, Caesarea of Cappadocia, Edessa, and other cities of "the faithful" should be informed of what had happened in the Himyarite land.[43]

In general from the point of view of Justin's interests, the conference of Ramlah may be considered successful in spite of its unpromising beginning. Justin's envoys succeeded in concluding peace with al-Mundhir and releasing the two generals. They were very much pleased with the expulsion of monophysite refugees from the kingdom of al-Mundhir. They had, however, to bring to Justin the terrible news of the massacre of the Christians in the far-off south Arabian land of the Himyarites.[44]

JUSTIN, ABYSSINIA, AND SOUTH ARABIA

As we know, the beginning of Justin's reign was marked by a new orientation of religious policy. The first task of the new government was to restore the intercourse of the church with the papal throne. From the point of view of the emperor and the Pope, this new orientation should not only have created unity within the empire but also embraced the whole world. In 519 the Patriarch of Constantinople wrote that Justin had very wisely provided for the peace of the world; and in the same year Pope Hormisdas exhorted his envoys in Constantinople to exert their influence and persuasion upon "the most clement emperor and the most pious Augusta his consort that they might restore to the communion with the Apostolic See all the churches in whatever part of the world they may be located." It was no matter that Justin was orthodox, adhering to the Chalcedonian doctrine, and his contemporary, King Elesboas of Abyssinia, was monophysite. The common cause of Christianity and common political interests united them and made them allies and friends. At that time

---

[43] Guidi, p. 493. *Martyrium Arethae*, p. 742 (§ 25). Zach. of Mityl., VIII, 3; Hamilton-Brooks, pp. 193–202; Ahrens-Krüger, 143–153 (a very long letter). See Michel le Syrien, IX, 18; Chabot, II, 185–189. Armenian version by Langlois, pp. 186–187. Axel Moberg, *The Book of the Himyarites*, p. CII (XXV).

[44] *Martyrium Arethae*, p. 743 (§ 27): Τότε οἱ δοῦλοι τοῦ Θεοῦ, ποιήσαντες εἰρηνικὰς συνθήκας πρὸς 'Αλαμούνδαρον, ὑπέστρεψαν, καὶ τὴν δύναμιν τῶν γραφέντων ὑπὸ τοῦ 'Ομηρίτου ἀνήγαγον καὶ τὰ κινηθέντα εἰς τὰς ἀκοὰς τοῦ δούλου τοῦ Θεοῦ 'Ιουστίνου, βασιλέως 'Ρωμαίων.

the Byzantine Emperor was regarded as the protector of Christians everywhere.[45]

In the sixth century Byzantium considered Abyssinia a vassal state, and an historian of the fifth century, Theodoret of Cyrus, named it among the peoples who "gladly accepted the Roman power," the Ethiopians, a number of the tribes of Ismaël (Arabs), the Lazi, Sanni, Abasgians (Abkhaz), and other barbarians.[46]

Relations between Byzantium under Justin I and Ethiopia were carried on through Egypt, particularly through the Patriarch of Alexandria. As we know, monophysite Egypt was not disturbed by the orthodox policy of Justin. When after the death of the monophysite patriarch Dioscorus II in 518 (or possibly 517), perhaps still during the reign of Anastasius, the monophysite Timothy III (IV) was appointed, his patriarchate lasted from 517 to 535; in other words, Justin did not remove him from his position. It may be added that immediately after Dioscorus' death Pope Hormisdas recommended to Justin that he appoint as Patriarch of Alexandria the Alexandrian deacon Dioscorus who took part in the papal embassy to Constantinople, a Chalcedonian. But in spite of the papal suggestion, Egypt received another convinced monophysite in the person of Timothy, and this "heretical patriarch occupied the throne without opposition during

[45] *Exemplum Relationis Johannis Episcopi Constantinopolitani* a. 519 die 22 Apr.: (Justin) pacem mundi sapientissime procuravit," *Coll. Avell.*, no. 161 (p. 612). Thiel, *Epistolae romanorum pontificum*, no. 67 (p. 863). Mansi, VIII, 457–458. Baronius, a. 519, 60–62. Hormisdas' letter, a. 519, July 9: "hortamur, ut clementissimo principi et piissimae Augustae conjugi ejus officiis imminere competentibus debeatis et agere auxiliante Christo nostro, ut . . . omnes ecclesiae, quae in qualibet mundi parte sunt positae, ad communionem sedis apostolicae revocentur," *Coll. Avell.*, no. 170 (p. 627). Thiel, no. 87 (p. 884). Mansi, VIII, col. 468. See A. Vasiliev, "Justin I (518–527) and Abyssinia," *Byz. Zeitsch.*, XXXIII (1933), 73. P. K. Hitti, *History of the Arabs* (London, 1937), p. 62. C. Amantos, Ἰστορία τοῦ Βυζαντινοῦ Κράτους, I, 179 (reference to my study cited above).

[46] Theodoret of Cyrus, *Theodoreti Episcopi Cyrensis Graecarum affectionum curatio*, Migne, *PG*, LXXXIII, col. 1037 (Sermo IX: De legibus): ὅσοι τὴν Ῥωμαίων ἀσπάζονται δεσποτείαν. In his fundamental Russian work on Theodoret of Cyrus, N. Glubokovsky gives a detailed discussion on this work. N. Glubokovsky, *The Blessed Theodoret, Bishop of Cyrus*, II, 202–242. He fails, however, to mention our passage; but on p. 215 he remarks: "There are quite a few records to be found in his work which for the time being have not been studied in detail"; and in note 129 on this page among other examples he gives our reference: *Sermo IX*, 1037.

the whole reign of Justin." There is some information that after Dioscorus' death Justin appointed as Patriarch of Alexandria an orthodox, Asterius; but since this information is vague and rather confusing, it has not been accepted as authentic.[47]

Direct relations between Egypt and and Ethiopia by land were not very easy in the sixth century. From the reign of Diocletian, Upper Egypt had been exposed to the incursions of two African peoples, the Blemyes, who lived above the First Cataract and who were immediate neighbors of Egypt, and the Nobadae (Nubians), whose territory was south of the Blemyes and who were immediate neighbors of Ethiopia. About 450, after Nestorius had been banished to Oasis in Upper Egypt, he was for some time prisoner among the Blemyes. Justin's predecessor Anastasius wrote to Kawad that the wars which he had to carry on with many barbarians, among them the Blemyes, were not trifling.[48] Almost with certainty we may attribute to the fifth century fragments of a heroic poem on a war with the Blemyes, preserved on a papyrus and edited under the title of Blemyomachia, which mentions "the dense phalanges of the Blemyes." On the basis of our evidence, and particularly on that of the papyri, a French scholar, P. Jouguet, says that we may construct

[47] On the patriarchs Timothy and Asterius and their part in the relations between Ethiopia and Byzantium see J.-B. Coulbeaux, *Histoire politique et religieuse d'Abyssinie, depuis les temps les plus reculés jusqu'à l'avènement de Ménélick* II, I (Paris, n. d.), 178–179 (the preface is dated 1928). Coulbeaux apparently believes in the existence of Asterius and thinks that the name of Timothy has been substituted for that of Asterius in later times by a monophysite monk "to do honor by this step to a patriarch of his own sect." Villard regards the text of Timothy's letter to Elesboas as "certainly fictitious." U. M. de Villard, *Storia della Nubia Cristiana* (Rome, 1938), p. 58 (*Orientalia Christiana Analecta*, 118). By an oversight Villard names Justinian for Justin. See also a long note on Timothy and Asterius in Assemani, *Bibl. Or.*, I, pp. 382–383. Bury thinks that Justin's letter to Elesboas is without doubt an invention (II, 324, n. 2). See J. Maspero, *Histoire des patriarches d'Alexandrie*, pp. 74–75; cf. p. 344 and n. 2. L. Bréhier, *Histoire de l'eglise* IV, 432 and n. 3. The name of Asterius is mentioned neither in Le Quien, *Oriens Christianus*, II (Paris, 1740), 428–430, nor in the list of the Alexandrian Patriarchs compiled by Sergius, *The Complete Menologion of the East*, II, 2, 685. Le Quien says that Symeon Metaphrastes invented (finxisse) Asterius.

[48] *The Chronicle of Joshua the Stylite*, with a translation into English and notes by W. Wright (Cambridge, 1882), ch. XX (pp. 13–14). A Russian translation of the chronicle by N. Pigulevskaya, *Mesopotamia on the Threshold of the Fifth and Sixth Centuries*, p. 135.

a Blemyan dossier for the period from the third century down to the reign of Justinian and call this period that of the Blemyan "terror." [49]

Probably during the reign of Justin the Blemyes again troubled Upper Egypt. Papyrologic evidence relates that about 522 the authorities of the city of Omboi in Upper Egypt addressed a petition to the Duke of the Thebaid, Flavius Marianus, to protect them against a certain Kollouthos, evidently a pagan, who had aroused the Blemyes against their city which had been plundered by the barbarians. In another petition to the Duke of the Thebaid the inhabitants of the city of Antaiopolis complain of exactions of a certain *strategos* Florentius who apparently called in the Blemyes to plunder their city.[50]

The vanity and boasts of the petty potentates of the Blemyes and Nobadae (Nubians) were amazing. One of them, Silko, in the time of Justinian set up an inscription composed in Greek in which he calls himself the "kinglet" (βασιλίσκος) of the Nobadae (Nubians) and all the Ethiopians who jointly with the Blemyes had fought the Romans and to whom God had granted victory in capturing their cities. In this inscription we read the following lines, which, as Bury says (II, 330), might be appropriate in the mouth of Attila or of Tamerlane:

[49] *Blemyomachiae fragmenta*, ed. A. Ludwich, I, 191, l. 17: καὶ γὰρ δὴ Βλεμύων πυκιναὶ κλονέοντο φάλαγγες. *Eudociae Augustae, Procli Lycii, Claudiani carminum graecorum reliquiae; Accedunt Blemyomachiae fragmenta*, ed. Arthurus Ludwich (Leipzig, 1897), p. 191. The editor himself is inclined to deny the historical foundation of the poem, thinking that the hostilities described are imaginary and contain no more "historical color" than the epic *Dionysiaca*, "Adventures of Dionysus," written by the poet of the first half of the fifth century, Nonnus. But on the other hand, at the end of his introduction to Blemyomachia, Ludwich admits that particularly in their wars against the Romans the Blemyes obtained great glory as warriors (p. 189). P. Jouguet, *L'histoire politique et la papyrologie*. W. Otto und L. Wenger, *Papyri und Altertumswissenschaft* (München, 1934), p. 87. A very good survey of the Blemyan danger from Diocletian to the seventh century in U. Wilcken, *Grundzüge und Chrestomathie der Papyruskunde*, I (Leipzig-Berlin, 1912), 68–70. On the Blemyans as nomads using dromedaries see F. Altheim, *Die Krise der alten Welt im 3. Jahrhundert n. zw. und ihre Ursachen*, I; *Die ausserrömische Welt*, 161–164.

[50] *Catalogue général des antiquités égyptiennes du Musée du Caire: Papyrus grecs d'époque byzantine*, ed. M. Jean Maspero, I (Cairo, 1911), no. 67004 (pp. 16–18, ll. 7–8: σκανδαλα ποιησαμενος εν τω αυτον τα ιερα τοις βαρβαροις ητι Βλεμυσι διακαινισασθαι ll. 11–12: και επραιτευσαν ημας παντελως και αοικητος τας ημετερας ἐξεπορθησαν οικιας, λεηλατησας τα παντοια ημων πραγματα; no. 67009 (pp. 36–39), ll. 18–19: Βλεμυων βαρβαρων επι των παλαι ημων γονεων παραλαβοντων την ημετεραν πολιν και πορθησαντων δεινως ... The tentative date of the papyri is 522 (?).

"When I became kinglet (βασιλίσκος), I did not however go behind other kings (βασιλέων) but positively I was ahead of them. I am a lion in the lands below, and a goat [bear?] in the lands above . . . As to the sovereigns of other peoples who struggle with me, I do not allow them to rest in the shade unless they submit to me, with no one to bring them water to their home." During Justin's time, the Blemyes and Nobadae were mostly pagans, and they were converted to the monophysite doctrine under Justinian and Theodora.[51]

The danger from the southern neighbors, both Blemyes and Nubians, was so great for the Byzantine frontier in Upper Egypt that even in the sixth century Justin still tolerated the celebration of old pagan rites in the temple of Isis, in the Nile island of Philae which belonged to the empire. According to Procopius, Diocletian decreed that to the Nubians and the Blemyes a fixed sum of gold should be given every year with the stipulation that they should no longer plunder the land of the Romans. And this emperor went so far as to select a certain island in the Nile close to the city of Elephantine and there construct a very strong fortress in which he established certain temples and altars for the Romans and these barbarians in common, and he settled priests of both nations in this fortress, thinking that the friendship between them would be secure by reason of their sharing the things sacred to them. And for this reason he named the place Philae. These sanctuaries in Philae, Procopius writes, were held by these barbarians even up to his time.[52]

---

[51] *Corpus Inscr. Graec.*, ed. A. Bocckh and J. Franz, III, no. 5072 (p. 486); G. Lefebvre, *Recueil des inscriptions grecques chrétiennes d'Egypte*, no. 628 (pp. 118–119): ὅτε ἐγεγονέμην βασιλίσκος, οὐκ ἀπῆλθον ὅλως ὀπίσω τῶν ἄλλων βασιλέων, ἀλλὰ ἀκμὴν ἔμπροσθεν αὐτῶν (ll. 10–12) . . . ἐγὼ γὰρ εἰς κάτω μέρη λέων εἰμὶ καὶ εἰς ἄνω μέρη αἴξ [Lefebvre αρξ] (l. 14) . . . οἱ δεσπόται τῶν ἄλλων ἐθνῶν, οἳ φιλονεικοῦσιν μετ'ἐμοῦ, οὐκ ἀφῶ αὐτοὺς καθεσθῆναι εἰς τὴν σκιὰν, εἰ μὴ ὑποκλίνουσί μοι (υπο ηλιου εξω). καὶ οὐκ ἔπωκαν (ἔδωκαν) νηρὸν ἔσω εἰς τὴν οἰκίαν αὐτῶν (ll. 18–20). Lefebvre's text differs from the old edition of Boeck and Franz in three places: he gives αρξ for αιξ; ει μη υπο ηλιου εσω for εἰ μὴ ὑποκλίνουσί μοι; and ἔδωκαν for ἔπωκαν. A partial translation of the inscription in Bury, *op. cit.*, II, 330. In his translation we read: "I am a lion for the lands below, and a bear for the lands above." Evidently he read ἄρκτος for Lefebvre's text αρξ. See J. Krall, "Beiträge zur Geschichte der Blemyer und Nubier," *Denkschriften der Wiener Ak. der Wiss., philos.-hist. Classe*, XLVI (1900), 6; 10. Lepsius (*Hermes*, X, 1876, 129) has shown that this inscription was set by a Copt.

[52] Proc., *B. P.* I, 19, 31–36; Dewing, I, 186–189.

Under the Christian emperors who followed Diocletian down to the sixth century when Justin began his new religious policy, according to Procopius, the Blemyes and Nubians still continued to reverence Isis and Osiris, and not least of all Priapus (I, 19, 35) in that remote part of the empire. Justin must have tolerated this pagan cult undisturbed. But after his death, Justinian early in his reign sent his general Narses to destroy the sanctuaries. The priests were arrested and their sacred images sent to Constantinople (Proc., I, 19, 36–37). A mediocre Egyptian poet of the sixth century, a Copt by birth, Dioscorus, son of Apollôs, glorifies Justinian's military triumphs thus: "One will no longer see the race of the Blemyes nor that of the Saracens; thine eyes will no longer be afraid of the aspect of murdering robbers; because the divine peace has blossomed everywhere for everyone." [53]

When Justin decided to support the Ethiopian king Elesboas in his expedition to south Arabia, the disquieting border element of the Blemyes and Nubians became exceedingly important. The original plan was to send troops to Ethiopia from Egypt not only by sea but also by land, in other words through the territory of the Blemyes and Nubians. As we shall see below, Justin acted through the agency of the Patriarch of Alexandria, Timothy, who after receiving the imperial instructions sent a letter to Elesboas to inform the latter that it was planned to equip special Blemyan and Nubian troops to take part in the Arabian expedition.[54]

The sixth century is the high point of the medieval history in Ethiopia or Abyssinia. Her relations with the Byzantine Empire allow us to know something about this mysterious country, whose Christianity goes back to the fourth century. After the Arab conquest Abyssinia almost entirely disappears from the historical horizon. Gibbon very strikingly wrote: "Encompassed on all sides by the enemies of their religion, the Ethiopians slept near a thousand years, forgetful of the

[53] J. Maspero, "Un dernier poète grec d'Egypte, Dioscore, fils d'Apollôs," *Revue des études grecques*, XXIV (1911), 430–431.
[54] *Acta martyrii Arethae*, Acta Sanctorum, Octobris, X, p. 743, § 27: ἡμεῖς δὲ διὰ Κόπτου καὶ Βερονίκης τῶν λεγομένων Βλεμμύων καὶ νομάδων πλῆθος στρατευμάτων ἐκπέμψαντες . . . For νομάδων — nomads in the text I read Νοβαδῶν or Νουβαδῶν, i.e. Nobadae, Nubians.

world, by whom they were forgotten. They were awakened by the Portuguese who, turning the southern promontory of Africa, appeared in India and the Red Sea, as if they had descended through the air from a distant planet" (in the sixteenth century).[55] And then the "sheep of Ethiopia" were attacked, in the words of the native anthem, by the "hyenas of the West."[56] In the *Song of Roland* Ethiopia is called "a horrible (cursed) land" (*une tere maldite*); and for Dante (*Inferno*, XXIV, v. 89) Ethiopia was full of serpents.[57] "The Kingdom of the Abyssinians or Ethiopians, who were also known as the Axumites, from the name of their capital city Axum, approached Suakim on the north, stretched westwards to the valley of the Nile, and southwards to the Somali coast. Their port of Adulis was reckoned as a journey of fifteen (or twelve) days from Axum where the king resided" [Bury, II, 322].

Political conditions in the Kingdom of Axum were not very well stabilized in the sixth century: in the north the new state of the Nobades, Nubia, was a very disquieting neighbor;[58] eastwards across the straits the Himyarites of Yemen in south Arabia were also not always peaceful; and some conflicts had already broken out between these two countries before the hostilities of the sixth century. But during periods of peace the commercial relations of the Abyssinians with the Himyarites were close, and the former sought to obtain political control over southwestern Arabia. This was no doubt one of the causes of the conflict between these two countries during the reign of Justin.

Christian missions had for a long time been active in Yemen, and the fact of the existence of Christianity among the Himyarites was well known in the north, in Syria and Mesopotamia. The community of Nagran (Nadjran), even before the massacre of the Christians

[55] Gibbon-Bury, V, 165 (Chapter XLVII).

[56] See C. R. Beazley, *The Dawn of Modern Geography, from the Conversion of the Roman Empire to A. D. 900* (London, 1897), p. 211.

[57] L. Olschki, *Storia letteraria delle scoperte geografiche, Studi e ricerche* (Florence, 1937), p. 202

[58] On Nubia in the sixth century see Ugo Monneret de Villard, *Storia della Nubia Cristiana* (Rome, 1938), pp. 52–58 (*Orientalia Christiana Analecta*, 118). See also a very brief article by I. Guidi, "Bisanzio ed il regno d'Aksum," *Studi Bizantini*, I (Rome, 1925), 137.

there which we shall discuss later, had been the most important Christian center in south Arabia. James of Sarug, who died in 521, wrote a letter about 520 to the Himyarite Christians, comforting them in their faith: "We Romans, who live quietly under Christian kings, praise your most glorious life." [59] But Yemen as a whole is not to be regarded as exclusively Christian. Parallel to Christianity was Judaism, as well as the ancient paganism, which still continued to exist although it probably was steadily losing more and more ground. But in spite of the existence of Judaism and paganism in Yemen in the sixth century, Christianity was well represented there, and H. Grégoire, in my opinion, is right in saying that "in this epoch the sole Christian community, powerful and organized, in the Arabic peninsula, was the Church of the Homerites (Himyarites), the Christian center of Himyar and especially Nagran (Nadjran)." [60]

The Byzantine emperor at that time, especially in Abyssinia, was acting not only as protector of Christians everywhere and not only as a sovereign interested in developing commercial relations with Abyssinia and, through the latter, with south Arabia, but he also showed interest and participation in the war between Abyssinia and the Himyarite Kingdom in Yemen which fell within the network of international politics of that epoch, where Persia, the permanent rival and foe of the Byzantine Empire, played the most essential part. Byzantium hoped through Abyssinia to bring the Arabian tribes under the influence of the empire and use them against Persia.

We know that in the north in Syria and Mesopotamia, the two Arabian dynasties of southern origin, the Ghassanids and Lakhmids, of the same blood as the Yemenites, were fighting on the side of Byzantium and Persia respectively, and both governments were very anxious to extend their political influence over the Arabian peninsula as far

[59] See R. Schröter, "Trostschreiben Jacob's von Sarug an die himjaritischen Christen," *Zeitsch. der Deutschen Morgenländischen Gesellschaft*, XXXI, 360–405; the passage quoted, p. 388.
[60] H. Grégoire, "Mahomet et le Monophysisme," *Mélanges Diehl*, I, 114. Vasiliev, *Justin I and Abyssinia*, pp. 69–70. The article of Ida Peterson Storm, "Early Christianity in Arabia," *The Moslem World*, XXX (1940), 7–13, written at Bahrain on the Persian Gulf, is based on the book by Axel Moberg cited above and has no value. The names of Aryat, Abraha, Masruq or Dzu Nowass are mentioned.

and as soon as possible. Arabia was becoming a flank for military operations, the right flank for Byzantium, the left for Persia. Thus, viewed against the background of the general political situation of the first half of the sixth century, the events in far-off Abyssinia and Yemen lose their local character and are drawn into the lengthy and strenuous struggle between the two empires. Byzantium was alarmed at the prospect of imminent Persian penetration into Arabia and made an attempt to bar it through Abyssinia; and the alarm of Constantinople before the impending Persian peril to south Arabia proved fully justified by subsequent events. In 570–572 Yemen was actually conquered by the Persians.

Justin's contemporary in Abyssinia was the king whose name is transliterated in various ways, according to our sources. His original name in Ethiopic was Ela Atzbeha. Of the Greeks, Cosmas the Indicopleustes gets nearest to it with his Ellatzbaas ('Ελλατζβάας); Procopius has Hellestheaeus ('Ελλησθεαῖος); Malalas, Elesboas ('Ελεσβόας); Nonnosus and Theophanes, Elesbaas ('Ελεσβαᾶς); *Martyrium Arethae*, Elesbas ('Ελεσβάς).[61] For the sake of uniformity I shall use the form Elasboas. In some sources he is called Caleb (Kaleb), a name also given in the Ethiopian translation of the *Acta Arethae*, which belongs to the very oldest form of the tradition.[62]

Elesboas' enemy in Yemen was, we are told in Arab tradition, Dhu-Nuwas, of the Jewish faith, whose name is easily recognizable in the Greek text of the *Martyrium Arethae* in the form Dounaas (Δουναάς).[63] Just as Elesboas has been called in some sources by another name, Kaleb, so likewise Dhu-Nuwas is evidently also known by another

---

[61] *The Christian Topography of Cosmas Indicopleustes*, ed. by E. O. Winstedt, lib. II, p. 72. Procopius, *B. P.* I, 20, 1; Dewing, I, 188–189. Malalas, p. 458, 17. Nonnosus, *CSHB*, p. 479, 10; *FHG*, IV, 179. Theophanes, p. 169, 14. *Martyrium Arethae*, § 1 (pp. 721–722). See Steindorff, "Elesbaas," in *PW*, V (1905), col. 2327. Nöldeke, *Tabari*, p. 188, note. Bury, II, 323, n. 2. Winstedt, *op. cit.*, p. 338.

[62] F. M. E. Pereira, *Historia dos Martyres de Nagram, Versão ethiopica* (Lisbon, 1899), pp. XLI–LVIII (Kaleb, rei de Aksum); pp. 33–76: a Portuguese translation of the *Martyrium Arethae*; pp. 77–122 (an Ethiopic text); see also pp. 191–193 and 195–198 (the Emperor Kaleb; the holy King Kaleb). Axel Moberg, *The Book of the Himyarites*, p. XLII, n. 1; LXXII.

[63] See Nöldeke, *Tabari*, p. 175, note. *Martyrium Arethae*, § 1 (pp. 721–722). Dhu-Nuwas has sometimes been wrongly identified with King Damianus (Δαμιανός) in Theoph., p. 223, 6. See Nöldeke, *ibidem*.

name, Masruk.[64] This is the same Dhu-Nuwas whose letter, as we have mentioned above, was received and read at Ramlah during the conference in the presence of the Byzantine envoys.

I do not intend to give here a detailed account of the Himyaro-Abyssinian war, in which Justin indirectly, and Elesboas of Axum and Dhu-Nuwas of the Himyarites directly, were belligerents. This has been done many times; and its sources, Greek, Syriac, and Arabic, have been thoroughly studied. The traditions of this war in old literature differ considerably according to whether one consults an ecclesiastical or profane work, Muhammedan or Christian. Although the ecclesiastical works in general deal particularly with the persecution of the Christians, the *Martyrium* of S. Arethas in its Greek text is our best source for Justin's interest and indirect participation in the war as well as for the chronology of events.[65] For the time of Justin, Procopius' record of the war is brief and uneventful (*B. P.* I, 20, 1–2), and the contemporary work of Cosmas Indicopleustes, valuable as it is in many other respects, supplies us only with a short note. Other

[64] As long as the name of Masruk appeared only in one of the hymns of John Psalter which has come down to us in a Syriac version of James of Edessa (about 600), one might naturally doubt its authenticity, or simply assume it to be a mistake. But this appearance received confirmation from a note in the *Nestorian History* or the *Chronicle of Seert* (in Arabic) and ultimately from the *Book of the Himyarites* (in Syriac), which I consider authentic. The name Masruk accordingly has been firmly established. Its origin, however, is obscure. John Psalter in James of Edessa, *The Hymns of Severus of Antioch and others in the Syrian version of Paul of Edessa as revised by James of Edessa*, ed. and transl. by E. W. Brooks, *Patr. Or.* VII, 613 (201). *Histoire nestorienne* (*Chronique de Seert*), ed. Addai Scher, *Patr. Or.*, V, 330–331 (218–219). Axel Moberg, *The Book of the Himyarites*, pp. XLI–XLIII. See R. Schröter, *Hymne des Iohannes Psaltes auf die himyaritschen Märtyrer, Zeitsch. der Deutschen Morgenländischen Gesellschaft*, XXXI (1877), 403–405; Masruk's name, p. 403.

[65] In addition to the original Greek text of the *Martyrology* of S. Arethas there exists a fragment of its Latin version of the ninth century (*ASS, Oct.*, X, 761–762), an Ethiopic version published by F. E. Pereira with a Portuguese translation (*Historia dos Martyres de Nagran*, [Lisbon, 1899], 33–76; 77–122 (Ethiopic text)), an abridged Armenian version in the Armenian Synaxarium of Ter Israel published and translated into French by G. Bayan, *Patr. Orient.*, XV, 343 (407)–348 (412). See also a very small portion of the *Martyrium* in Georgian. R. Blake, "Catalogue of the Georgian Manuscripts in the Cambridge University Library," *The Harvard Theological Review*, XXV (1932), 216–219. In old Slavonic, in the *Great Russian Menologion of Macarius: Velikiye Minei Chetii* compiled by the Metropolitan of All Russia, Macarius, October, Days 19–31 (St. Petersburg, 1880), coll. 1839–1863. See also *Bibliotheca Hagiographica Orientalis* (Bruxellis, 1910), pp. 24–26.

historical works, Byzantine and Syriac, are devoid of value for this purpose as independent historical sources. The Muhammedan relation, reporting Justin's interest in the war, fails to give us material of real value, and fills out its narrative with some fantastic details.

The central event which brought on the conflict between Abyssinia and Yemen was the massacre by Dhu-Nuwas in October, 523, of a large number of Christians in the fortified city of Nagran, which was their headquarters in south Arabia. Contrary to his promise to spare all the inhabitants who would capitulate, Dhu-Nuwas, irritated by their refusal to apostatize and accept Judaism, massacred them to the number of over three hundred, among whom the most conspicuous was the emir of the tribe, Harith ibn-Kilab, a name which in Greek texts has been changed to Arethas. Evidently the persecution spread out into other regions of the Himyarites, and our evidence mentions martyrs and the burning of churches in the chief center of south Arabia Zafar (Tafar), in the town of Hadramaut, and in the town of Marib. The massacre of Nagran produced a tremendous shock among the Christians of other countries; fully a thousand years later a Russian source of the sixteenth century, the so-called *Stepennaya Kniga*, tells the story of the treacherous capture of the city of Nagran by "Dunas the Zhidovin" (the Jew) and the massacre of Arethas and his companions, and compares "Dunas" with the impious Tartar Khan Tokhtamysh, who took by cunning "the glorious city of Moscow." [66]

As we know, Justin's ambassador to al-Mundhir on his return to Constantinople reported to the emperor what had happened at Nagran. According to Arabian evidence, the King of Ethiopia was informed by a certain inhabitant of Nagran, Daus Dhu Thalaban by name, who had escaped massacre. He brought to the King of Ethiopia the news of the disaster of his own city, carrying with him as a visible symbol

---

[66] All sources speak in more or less detail of the massacre of Nagran, which is commemorated in the *Menologia* under October 24. The date in the *Martyrium Arethae*, § 20 (p. 737): οἱ ἅγιοι, κλίναντες τοὺς αὐχένας, ἐτελειώθησαν πάντες, ἐν μηνὶ ὑπερβερεταίῳ, ὅς ἐστιν ὀκτώβριος, κδ, ἰνδικτιῶνος δευτέρας. On the martyrs in Hadramaut, Zafar and Marib, see Moberg, *The Book of the Himyarites*, pp. CII–CIII. Stepennaya Kniga, *Complete Collection of Russian Chronicles (PSRL)*, XXI (1908), 399–400. The Stepennaya Kniga is the *Book of Rank of the Genealogy of the Tsars*. See Georg Graf, *Geschichte der christlichen arabischen Literatur*, pp. 22–23.

a half-burnt copy of the Gospel. He begged Elesboas (Kaleb) and the Abyssinian Bishop Eupremius to help his country by making war on Dhu-Nuwas. But Elesboas said to him: "I have many men, but I have no ships. I shall write to the emperor asking him to send me ships that I may transport men." And he wrote a letter, evidently through Timothy, Patriarch of Alexandria, and in addition sent to Justin the half-burnt Gospel. The Nagrarian who was in charge of the mission went to Constantinople, saw Justin, and on behalf of Elesboas asked him for help against Dhu-Nuwas and his troops. The emperor said: "Your land is too far away from ours to reach it with our troops. But I shall write to the King of Abyssinia, because he is of our faith and is nearer to your country than we; he must help and defend you and take vengeance for the wrong done." Justin wrote a letter, and Daus Dhu Thalaban brought it to Elesboas.[67]

At the same time Justin wrote to Timothy, the monophysite patriarch of Alexandria, a letter whose contents have been preserved in the *Martyrium Arethae*. In it he asked the patriarch to write to Elesboas urging him to make war on the King of the Homerites, Dounaan, and "destroy all the violators of law with their king." Following the imperial order, the patriarch convoked in Alexandria in April, 525 a meeting of the representatives of the Egyptian clergy and monks to consider the situation. And then he sent a message to Elesboas urging him to take the field, by sea and by land, against "the abominable and lawless Jew." The patriarch proceeds: "If your Majesty hesitates to do so, God from the heavens will be wroth with you and your kingdom." Then he assures Elesboas that through the Byzantine towns of Koptos on the Nile and Beronice on the Red Sea

---

[67] I have combined here two Arab traditions, one by Hisham ibn Muhammed (ninth century), the other by Ibn Iskhaq (eighth century, which are embodied in the *Chronicle of Tabari*. Tabari, *Annales*, ed. de Goeje, I, 2, 925–927. In German, Nöldeke, *Geschichte der Perser und Araber*, pp. 188–190. Tabari, *Chronique de Tabari traduite sur la version persane d'Abou-'Ali Mohammed Bel'ami par Hermann Zotenberg*, II (Paris, 1869), 181–182. A Syriac source calls the man who brought the news from south Arabia to Elesboas (Kaleb) "the free-born Umayyah." Moberg, *The Book of the Himyarites*, p. CIV (XXXIX–XL). Of the half-burnt Gospel which Elesboas sent to Constantinople, Graf remarks: "But whether the Gospel was written in the Arabian language is not firmly established." G. Graf, *Die christlich-arabische Literatur bis zur fränkischen Zeit* (Freiburg im Breisgau, 1905), p. 2.

they would send troops consisting of Blemyes and Nubians to help in the extermination of the Himyarite king and the destruction of his kingdom.[68] It is not to be forgotten that a road existed across the desert from Coptos to Beronice. The promised Byzantine troops apparently made no appearance in Ethiopia or south Arabia. At any rate, there is no record of such an expedition. But it is certainly true that Justin supplied Elesboas with a considerable number of ships for transportation of Ethiopian troops to south Arabia.[69] Of course these were not warships, but commercial ships which Byzantium had in great numbers for her commercial transactions in the Red Sea and the Indian Ocean. The list of a vast number of such vessels is reported in the *Martyrium of Arethas* from various points: from the city of Aila (now Akaba, Aqabah) in the bay of Akaba, 15 vessels; from Clysma (now Suez), 20; from the island of Yotabe (Iotabe) close to the Sinai peninsula, 7; from Beronice on the Red Sea, 2; from the island of Farsan in the Red Sea, 7; from India, 9. Justin kept his word and, according to Arabian evidence, sent many ships to Elesboas.[70]

[68] *Martyrium Arethae*, § 28 (p. 743): 'Ἐν Ἀλεξανδρείᾳ, ἀπριλλίῳ μηνὶ, ἰνδ. τρίτης, συνάξας Τιμόθεος ὁ ἐπίσκοπος πάντας τοὺς ὀρθοδόξους καὶ πλῆθος τῶν ἐν τῇ Νιτρίᾳ καὶ Σκήτει μοναχῶν; see §§ 27-28 (p. 743). The third indication of April is the month of April, 525. The Armenian Synaxarium of Ter Israel reports that Justin wrote a letter not to Timothy of Alexandria but to John, Patriarch of Jerusalem. Arethas, *Le synaxaire arménien de Ter Israel*, Bayan, *Patr. Or.*, XV, 347 (411). The version of the *Martyrium* by Simeon Metaphrastes says that Justin wrote a letter to the Patriarch of Alexandria, Asterius. Migne, *PG*, CXV, 1280. Asterius is supposed to have been the orthodox patriarch whom Justin appointed to succeed Dioscorus (about 519), whereas Timothy was the monophysite patriarch of Alexandria, but doubts of his existence are probably well founded. On Asterius, see *Dictionnaire d'histoire et de géographie ecclésiastiques*, IV (1930), col. 1163. This article by G. Bardy ends with these words: "It seems well that Asterius should be struck out from history." See doubts about Asterius in Jean Maspero, *Histoire des patriarches d'Alexandrie*, pp. 74-75; also 344 and n. 2. Baronius (*Annales Ecclesiastici ad an.* 521, no. XL) identifies Asterius with the Coptic (monophysite) patriarch Timothy who might have borne the "surname" of Asterius. This, however, seems difficult to believe. On Asterius, also see above, p. 285.

[69] See *Martyrium of Arethae*, § 29, p. 747. Also Cosmas Indicopleustes, II, 72: Ἐλλατζβάας μέλλων ἐξιέναι εἰς πόλεμον πρὸς τοὺς Ὁμηρίτας τοὺς πέρας.

[70] List of vessels in the *Martyrium Arethae*, § 29, p. 747. Tabari, I, 2, 926, 10-11. Nöldeke, p. 188. Tabari-Bel'ami, p. 181. I do not well understand why Bury hesitates to accept the fact of the coming of the Byzantine ships. He says: "Huart (*Hist. des Arabes*, p. 53) suggests that the Ethiopians had no ships and that the Romans must have supplied them with transports for their expeditions to Yemen." Bury, II, 323, n. 1.

The center of assembly for troops and vessels was Gabaza (Γαβαζά), a port in the vicinity of Elesboas' chief city of Adulis. In the winter of 524–525, seventy vessels were ready for transporting troops to Arabia. When the winter season with its stormy weather was over, the expedition started late in the spring of 525, after Pentecost, which in this year was celebrated on May 18.[71] In April of the same year, as we have seen above, the Patriarch of Alexandria sent his message to Elesboas urging him to take the field by sea and by land. A French historian remarks: "From the date of April 525 on, it was a true crusade which was organized in these regions." [72]

In my study I have sought to combine the evidence of our Greek, Arabian, and Syriac sources. I know well that our sources do not literally reproduce the text of the letters of Elesboas and Justin and their speeches. But the sources do state the undeniable fact that such letters referring to the conflict between Ethiopia and South Arabia are not a fiction, as some scholars think, but were actually written and sent. Some discussions and interchange of opinions concerning the situation must have taken place. If we consider this question purely from the Byzantine side we may state positively that Justin was well informed of the Christian persecution in south Arabia; that urged by his religious sympathies with Abyssinia and by political and commercial interests as well, he sent a considerable number of his commercial fleet stationed in the Red Sea and in the Indian Ocean to Elesboas, who himself had not ships enough; that he wrote a letter to the Patriarch of Alexandria, Timothy, through whom Elesboas had originally informed Justin of his difficulties; and that ultimately Justin's land forces took no part in the war. This rapprochement between Justin and Elesboas had its reflection in later times in a rather unexpected way, as we shall see below.

At first sight it may seem strange that Elesboas and Justin got in touch with each other through the mediation of the monophysite Patriarch of Alexandria, Timothy, who would have been acceptable

---

[71] *Mart. Arethae*, § 29 (p. 747): πεποίηκε δὲ καὶ αὐτὸς Ἰνδικὰ πλοῖα ἐν τῇ χειμῶνι τῆς αὐτῆς τρίτης ἰνδ. δέκα, φιλοκαλήσας τὰ ἑβδομήκοντα . . . καὶ μετὰ τὴν ἁγίαν Πεντηκοστὴν εὐτρεπίσας ἅπαντα καὶ μέλλων κινῆσαι . . . The third indiction lasted from September 1, 524, to August 31, 525. Easter in 525 fell on March 30.
[72] Devreesse, *Le patriarcat d'Antioch*, p. 258.

to Elesboas, a monophysite himself, but not to Justin, a convinced Chalcedonian. But this apparent contradiction must be explained, as we have already pointed out above, by the common cause of Christianity and common political interests which united both of them and made them allies and friends.

The two campaigns undertaken by Elesboas ended in the final defeat of Dhu-Nuwas. Elesboas took possession of the Himyarite capital, Tafar (Zafar) and killed Dhu-Nuwas, the last Himyarite monarch, who terminated the period of the independence of Yemen. According to a legendary Arab tradition embodied in Tabari, when Dhu-Nuwas realized what had happened to his kingdom, he turned his horse towards the sea, set spurs to it, plunged into the waves of the ocean, and was never seen again. In his stead a new Himyarite Christian named Esimiphaios was set up as tributary king, and Christianity was reestablished in Yemen. Occupied with the restoration of Christianity and the building of churches in the various cities of Yemen, Elesboas probably remained there about three years, according to the *Life* of Saint Gregentius; he must have returned to his country in 528, after Justin's death.[73]

[73] Procopius, *B. P.* I, 20, 1 ('Εσιμιφαῖος). D. Nielsen sees in the Greek name 'Εσιμιφαῖος the Ethiopic name Shumaipa. D. Nielsen, *Die altarabische Kultur, Handbuch der altarabischen Altertumskunde*, I (Copenhagen, 1927), p. 105: "Die letzten Zeiten des sabäischen Königtums." Malalas (p. 457) gives the name of Anganes ('Αγγάνης), a man of Elesboas' own family. The *Martyrium Arethae* calls the new Christian king in Yemen Abraam ('Αβραάμ), § 38, p. 758. The *Life* of Saint Gregentius, following the *Martyrium*, also calls the new king Abramius ('Αβράμιος). Vasiliev, "The Life of St. Gregentius," *Viz. Vrem.*, XIV, pp. 65–66. Chronology of the expeditions varies with writers. Sometimes the first campaign is dated 523. Hitti, *op. cit.*, p. 62, and some others. I have followed the chronological data of the Greek *Martyrium of Arethas*, combining them with the date of the conference at Ramlah. See above. Legend on Dhu-Nuwas' death in Tabari, de Goeje, I, 2, 927 (19–20)–928. Nöldeke, p. 191. Tabari-Bel'ami, II, 184. Abul-Faradj-al-Isbahani, *Kitab-al-Agani*, XVI (Bulak, 1285–1868), pp. 71–72. A new edition in 21 volumes came out in Cairo, 1905–1906. I use the first edition. On the author, *Encyclopaedia of Islam*, I, 85. C. Brockelmann, *Geschichte der arabischen Literatur*, I, 146. *Idem, Erster Supplementband* (Leiden, 1937), pp. 225–226 (many bibliographical additions). In Brockelmann's new edition, I, 152–153. For the bibliography of this war see A. Vasiliev, "Justin I and Abyssinia," *Byz. Zeitsch.*, XXXIII, 69, n. 2. A. Moberg, *The Book of the Himyarites*; E. A. Wallis Budge, *A History of Ethiopia, Nubia, and Abyssinia*, I, 261–262 (the war in 523). Steindorff and Kampffmeyer, "Elesbaas," *Pauly-Wissowa*, V (1905), 2327–2328. Tkač, "Homeritae," *PW*, VIII (1913), 2182–2188; on the time of Justin, 2186–2187.

It is probable that through the Patriarch of Alexandria a certain Gregentius was sent from Alexandria to be Bishop of Tafar (Safar), the capital of the newly conquered Yemen. Gregentius was a Byzantine monk who had been born far north, in the Balkans, possibly in Dardania (Moesia); in other words, he signified a religious link between South Arabia and Byzantium. The name of Gregentius, as we know, is connected with the code of laws which he supposedly drew up in the name of the Christian king Abram, and which have been preserved. Although their authenticity has sometimes been questioned, Dareste, who published a special study of them, believes there is no real reason to doubt that they were issued and enforced in Yemen after 525.[74]

[74] On St. Gregentius and his *Life* see Vasiliev, "The Life of St. Gregentius," *Viz. Vrem.*, XIV, 23–67 (in Greek and Russian). Bury employed the *Life* in his *History of the Later Empire* (II, 327 and n. 1; 413). The *Life* calls the Patriarch of Alexandria Proterius; this man is never mentioned in any records except in connection with Gregentius. See for example *Propylaeum ad Acta Sanctorum Novembris*, p. 328: Προτερίῳ τῷ πάπᾳ ᾽Αλεξανδρείας. In my opinion the name of Proterius is a deteriorated form of Asterius, whose existence is doubtful. This question has already been discussed. On the Code of Laws of the Himyarites see R. Dareste, "Lois des Homérites. Νόμοι τῶν ᾽Ομεριτῶν," *Nouvelle revue historique de droit français et étranger*, XXIX (1905), 157–170; esp. 158–159. It is not quite clear why Dareste states that the Homerite laws were enforced from the year 522 (p. 159). This date cannot be justified. Bury (II, 413) says that doubts of the authenticity of the laws have been entertained; "but even if they were never issued or enforced, they illustrate the kind of legislation at which the ecclesiastical spirit, unchecked, would have aimed." See a misleading statement in J. T. Bent, *The Sacred City of the Ethiopians*, new ed. (London-New York-Bombay, 1896), p. 178: Bishop Gregentius was sent to regulate the Church in Ethiopia. Confusion in the *Dictionaries of the Saints*. The Right Rev. F. G. Holweck, *A Biographical Dictionary of the Saints*, p. 445: Gregentius, native of Milan; Elesboas overcame Dunaan in 528; Gregentius was sent by Asterius, patriarch of Constantinople, to restore Christianity. Dom Baudot, *Dictionnaire d'hagiographie mis à jour à l'aide des travaux les plus récents* (Paris, 1925), p. 311: Grégence, Bishop of Taphas (for Tafar) in Arabia, was turned out of his see in 520 by the Jew Dunaan who had been made King of Yemen; S. Elesboas reinstated him after overcoming Dunaan; Grégence died on December 19, 552, and left a treatise against the vices. Baudot refers to the old out-of-date publications of Pétin (1853) and R. Ceillier (1865). It is not to be forgotten that the full and very verbose text of the *Life* of St. Gregentius has not been published. The most interesting parts, preserved in a Sinaitic manuscript, have been published with a Russian translation and comment by A. Vasiliev. See the first lines of this note. In his study "Mahomet et le Monophysisme," *Mélanges Charles Diehl*, I, 115, Grégoire, as we have noted

After his victory over Dhu-Nuwas, Elesboas sent two high officials (συγκλητικούς) and two hundred other men to Alexandria, and through the Augustalis of Alexandria, Licinius, informed Justin of the result of his campaign in south Arabia.[75]

The Himyaro-Abyssinian war which resulted in the rapprochement between Justin and Elesboas had an unexpected repercussion in later times. It is extremely interesting that it was not Justinian, one of the greatest emperors of Byzantium, who left his stamp upon later Abyssinian tradition, but Justin I, who appears in the *Kebra Nagast* (*The Glory of the Kings*).[76]

In Abyssinia at the end of the thirteenth century, a new dynasty ascended the throne. This new dynasty proclaimed itself the Solomonian dynasty, tracing its lineage back to the time of Solomon and the Queen of Sheba, and claiming descent from their son Menelik. To justify this claim and to glorify the new dynasty a special book was composed, *Kebra Nagast* (*The Glory of the Kings*), one of the most important works of Ethiopian literature. In all probability, the book was definitely compiled between 1314 and 1322.[77] Even today this compilation is regarded in Abyssinia as one of the foundations of her political might and of her claim to be governed by the oldest dynasty in the world.

This book contains a collection of legends of great interest. In the

above, flatly denies any significance for the *Life* of Gregentius; he calls it "an obvious forgery" ("le faux patent") which is to be "condemned without appeal" ("condamnée sans appel"). But see G. Graf, *Geschichte der christlichen arabischen Literatur*, I, die Uebersetzungen, 22–23; 370 = *Studie testi*, 118.

[75] L. Cantarelli, *La serie dei prefetti di Egitto, III: Dalla morte di Teodosio I° alla conquista araba* (395–642), 5th series, *Atti della R. Accademia dei Lincei*, XIV (1909), 412–413. Cantarelli's dating 520 is inadmissible. See Malalas, p. 434, 6: καὶ ἐμηνύθη τῷ βασιλεῖ Ἰουστινιανῷ πάντα διὰ Λικινίου, αὐγουσταλίου Ἀλεξανδρείας. Malalas erroneously gives the name of Justinian for Justin. See *Codex Justinianeus*, XII, 33, 5 (ed. Krüger, p. 468), s.a. 524, a rescript of Justin to A. Licinio *magistro officiorum*. This *magister officiorum* Licinius is to be identified with Malalas' Licinius *augustalis* of Alexandria, who had in the meantime reached higher rank.

[76] I will follow here my own study, "Justin I and Abyssinia," *Byz. Zeitsch.*, XXXIII, 73–75.

[77] See Conti Rossini, "Aetiopica," *Rivista degli studi orientali*, X, 508. W. Budge calls *Kebra Nagast* an historical romance. E. A. Wallis Budge, *A History of Ethiopia, Nubia, and Abyssinia*, II, 567. I. Guidi thinks that it was compiled in the second half of the thirteenth century. I. Guidi, *Storia della letteratura etiopica*, p. 45.

first place it utilizes for the sake of the dynasty a legend which was long in circulation in southern Arabia and Abyssinia, the legend of Solomon, the Queen of Sheba, their son Menelik, and the Tabernacle which Menelik carried away to Axum. The Ethiopians are an elect people, a new Israel; their kingdom is the highest among all the kingdoms of the world; it is even higher than the Roman Empire, the only state with which the Ethiopian Kingdom may be on an equal footing and with which it divides the earth. The Ethiopian Kingdom is higher, because at its head stands the older line of the Solomonian dynasty. Ethiopia has risen still higher, since Rome has fallen into heresy and Ethiopia has remained orthodox. Rome has lost its spiritual treasures; Ethiopia will keep in safety her own treasures till the completion of the ages.[78] In various parts of the *Kebra Nagast* occur references to the history of Byzantium which are intended to show that the whole world belongs to the Emperor of Rome and to the Emperor of Ethiopia, and that the Ethiopian faith, which is pure and not distorted compared with the heresies of the Byzantine Empire, is superior to all other religions in the world.

I shall give from the *Kebra Nagast* a few important passages referring to the Roman or Byzantine Empire in general and to the reign of Justin I in particular.[79] According to the authors of this book, the document dealing with the division of the world between the Emperor of Rome and the Emperor of Ethiopia was found in the Church of St. Sophia, in Constantinople. The passage runs as follows: "Domitius, the archbishop of Rome (that is, Constantinople), said: I have found in the church of (Saint) Sophia among the books and the royal treasures a manuscript (which stated) that the whole kingdom of

---

[78] See B. Turayev, *From Abyssinian Historical Legends*, essays presented to D. A. Korsakov (*Mélanges Korsakoff*) (Kazan, 1913), p. 307 (in Russian).

[79] There are two complete translations of the *Kebra Nagast*, one in German and one in English. Carl Bezold, *Kebra Nagast: Die Herrlichkeit der Könige, Abhandlungen der philos.-philol. Kl. d. Bayer. Akad. d. Wiss.*, XXIII (München, 1905), I, I–LXII (introduction), 170 and 160 (Ethiopic text and German translation). E. A. Wallis Budge, *The Queen of Sheba and Her Only Son Menyelek*, English translation from Ethiopic MSS. in the British Museum. More literature in Vasiliev, "Justin I and Abyssinia," p. 74, n. 1. See also F. Kampers, *Vom Werdegange der abendländischen Kaysermystik* (Leipzig-Berlin, 1924), p. 126, with reference to Fr. Praetorius, *Fabula de regina Sabaea apud Aethiopes* (Halle, 1870), p. 29.

the world (belonged) to the Emperor of Rome and the emperor of Ethiopia." [80]

After a brief account of the persecution of the Christians by the Jews in Nagran (Nejran) (§ 116; Bezold, pp. 135–136; Budge, p. 225), the *Kebra Nagast* gives the most important passage which refers directly to the reign of Justin I. "And the King of Rome, and the King of Ethiopia, and the Archbishop of Alexandria will inform each other in order to destroy them (the Jews); since the Romans are orthodox. And they were to rise up to fight, to make war upon the enemies of God, the Jews, and to destroy them, the King of Rome to destroy Enya (in Armenia) and the King of Ethiopia to destroy Phinehas (in south Arabia); [81] and they were to lay waste their lands, and to build churches there, and they were to cut to pieces the Jews at the end of this Cycle in twelve cycles of the moon. Then the kingdom of the Jews shall be made an end of and the kingdom of Christ shall be constituted until the advent of the False Messiah (Antichrist). And those two kings, Justinus the king of Rome and Kaleb the king of Ethiopia, shall meet together in Jerusalem. And their Archbishop shall make ready offerings, and they shall make offerings, and shall establish the Faith in love, and they shall give each other gifts and salutations of peace, and they shall divide between them the earth from the half of Jerusalem, even as we have already said at the beginning of this book. And for love's sake they shall have jointly the royal title (of King of Ethiopia). They shall be mingled with David and Solomon their fathers. The one whom in faith they chose by lot to be named from the Kings of Rome is to be called "King of Ethiopia" and the King of Rome likewise is to bear the name of "King of Ethiopia." [82]

This exceptionally interesting passage clearly shows that the epoch and the activities of Justin I left a deep impress upon Abyssinian histori-

---

[80] *Kebra Nagast*, § 19; Bezold, p. 10; Budge, p. 16.
[81] Phinhas, Phinehas, Finhas, or Finehas is a distorted form of Dhu-Nuwas. See F. M. Esteves Pereira, *Historia dos martyres de Nagran* (Lisbon, 1899), p. 38; the name of Finehas is given in *Synaxarium Ethiopicum, ibidem*, p. 175 (Portuguese translation). See also A. Kammerer, *Essai sur l'histoire antique d'Abyssinie* (Paris, 1926), p. 111, n. 1. C. Conti Rossini, *Storia d'Etiopia* (Bergamo, 1928), p. 175. For the time being, I am unable to explain the name Enya.
[82] *Kebra Nagast*, § 117; Bezold, p. 136; Budge, pp. 225–226.

cal tradition. At one of the most important periods in the national history of Ethiopia, when the Solomonian dynasty ascended the throne in the thirteenth century, Abyssinian writers turned to the origin of the political power of their country. They emphatically stated that the political power of Abyssinia originated from the fact of the division of the earth between Justin I and Kaleb, which had occurred at the holiest place of the Christian world, at Jerusalem. But Abyssinia not only possessed a dynasty going back to the remote time of Solomon and a history of political grandeur from the sixth century; she also preserved in her church the purest and most orthodox form of Christianity.

In the sixteenth century in Russia the theory was proclaimed: "Moscow is the third Rome." Moscow began to be regarded as "the new city of Constantine," and the Grand Prince of Moscow became "Tsar of all Orthodoxy." A Russian scholar, Turayev, writes: "Ethiopian scholars came to a similar conclusion two centuries earlier, but their formula was still more ambitious." [83]

JUSTIN AND THE SLAVS

The period of Justin I is a very important epoch in the history of Slavo-Byzantine relations. Especially at the present time this question has had a renaissance of interest in connection with the present Slavophile movement in Soviet Russia, reminiscent of the Slavophile movement in Russia in the middle of the nineteenth century, but which in certain points goes much further. The Slavophiles of Imperial Russia always laid stress upon the extreme importance of Byzantine historical studies for the Slavonic world. One of the deep thinkers of the time, A. S. Khomyakov, wrote: "In our opinion, to speak of the Byzantine Empire with disdain means to disclose one's own ignorance." In 1850 T. N. Granovsky, noted professor of the University of Moscow, pointed out the importance of Byzantine history for Russians, who had taken over from Tsargrad their religious beliefs and the beginnings of their civilization; and he adds a statement, very characteristic of the Slavophile movement, that the Russians

---

[83] B. Turayev, *From Abyssinian Historical Legends*, p. 307 (in Russian).

are bound up with the destiny of the Byzantine Empire by the mere fact that they are Slavs. He concludes: "It is our duty to study the phenomenon to which we are so much indebted." [84] This, of course, was written a century ago.

In 1939 a modern Russian historian, B. Goryanov, made a statement which is clearly similar in spirit to the statements of these historians. "By their clan organization and by the vigor of their barbarism, the Slavs rejuvenated the Empire, prolonged its existence a thousand years, became the intermediary between the world of antiquity and the epoch of the late Medieval Renaissance, and transmitted to Europe the powerful heritage of ancient culture. The Slavs, the ancestors of the great Russian people, have transmitted to our fatherland the high culture of the Byzantine Empire, its literature, religion, and juridical norms. This is the reason why Soviet historical science, the most progressive in the world, must have and shall have among its most important branches the branch of Byzantine studies." [85] He says elsewhere: "That Byzantium could exist ten centuries more after the fall of the Western Roman Empire; that she fulfilled the great historical role of intermediary between the world of antiquity and the epoch of the Reformation, humanism, and the Renaissance — this merit is due not to the abstract idea of the Greek Empire, as the representatives of bourgeois historical science have called it, but to the Slavs, their clan organization (*rodovoy stroy*) and their commune (*obschina*)." [86]

Modern Russian historians have turned their attention to the famous theory of Fallmerayer, who in 1830 declared that not one drop of real Hellenic blood ran in the veins of the modern Greeks. This theory, in spite of its bias and evident exaggeration, was very important in drawing scholarly attention to a most interesting and at the same time very obscure question, that of the part played by the Slavs in Greece

[84] A. Vasiliev, *History of the Byzantine Empire*, I, 43–44; in French, I, 38–39; in Spanish, I, 38.
[85] B. Goryanov, "The Slavs and Byzantium in the Fifth and Sixth Centuries of Our Era," *Historical (Istorichesky) Journal*, no. 10 (October, 1939), p. 111; the whole article, pp. 101–111 (in Russian).
[86] B. Goryanov, "Slavonic Settlements of the Sixth Century and Their Social Organization," *Vestnik (Messenger) of Ancient History*, 1 (6) (1939), 318; the whole article, pp. 308–318 (in Russian). See also *Twenty-Five Years of Historical Studies in USSR* (Moscow-Leningrad, 1942), pp. 232–233 (in Russian).

during the Middle Ages. Surprisingly enough, before 1898, when I published my study on the Slavs in Greece during the Middle Ages, Fallmerayer's theory had been almost entirely overlooked in Russian literature. Today in Soviet Russia, however, much attention is devoted to this theory and to the interpretation of its importance for the history of Slavonic influence in Byzantium.[87] In a very recent publication, we find the following statement: "Only a few German scholars, like Fallmerayer, found the courage to point out the historical role of the Slavs in the formation of the Eastern Roman Empire, which he, following the Byzantine Emperor Constantine Porphyrogenitus, considered "entirely slavonized." [88] As a matter of fact, of course, this statement is inaccurate. The famous passage of Constantine Porphyrogenitus refers to the Peloponnesus only, and not to the whole empire.

I have enlarged on the recent movement in Soviet Russia for two reasons: first, several of the studies noted above are entitled as dealing with the Slavs in the sixth century, in other words, with the period of Justin and Justinian, and therefore legitimately fall within the scope of this study; and secondly I have wished to emphasize this new movement since it is almost unknown outside of Russia. In spite of some exaggerations, the movement seems to me gratifying and promising in the historical life of Russia and likely to lead to further investigation and clarification of Slavo-Byzantine relations and of the essential part which the Slavs played in the internal history of the empire. Vladimir Lamansky, a noted Russian scholar and great authority on Slavonic studies in general, once wrote: "The historical life of the Slavonic race begins only with the end of the fifth and the beginning of the sixth century, and even then only for their considerable minority, for their southern and western branches. . . . For the enormous majority of the Slavonic tribes (Russia, Poland), true history starts with the second half of the ninth century, and even later." [89]

[87] See A. V. Mishulin, "The Ancient Slavs and the Destinies of the Eastern Roman Empire," *Vestnik of Ancient History*, 1 (6) (1939), 294; the whole article, pp. 290–307. Goryanov, "The Slavs and Byzantium in the Fifth and Sixth Centuries," *Istorichesky Journal* (1939), p. 103. Both in Russian.

[88] *Twenty-Five Years of Historical Studies in USSR* (Moscow-Leningrad, 1942), p. 232

[89] V. Lamansky, *On the Historical Study of the Greco-Slavonic World in Europe* (St. Petersburg, 1871), p. 53 (in Russian). He also remarks: "The differ-

There is no doubt that the sixth century is the first stormy period of Slavonic invasions in the Balkan Peninsula with the invaders appearing under their own name of Sclavenes. But this was not their first actual appearance in the peninsula. The name Sclavenes (Σκλαυηνοί) as an ethnographic term for the Slavonic race occurs for the first time in the theological questions and answers which are often attributed to Caesarius of Nazianzus, the younger brother of Gregory the Theologian. It is of minor importance to us whether or not this work really belongs to Caesarius; but it is essential to know that it is a writing of the very end of the fourth century or of the beginning of the fifth, and that it places the Sclavenes in the Danubian region.[90] If at the end of the fourth century the Slavs were already known in the Danubian region, this may imply that they had come to the Balkan Peninsula, the northern part at least, before this time. The old theory of the Russian-Bulgarian scholar M. Drinov is worth remembering, who in 1872 on the basis of geographical and personal names in the peninsula placed the beginnings of Slavonic colonization there in the late second century A. D. Drinov's theory, which has not been generally accepted by many scholars, was accepted by the Bulgarian historian Shishmanov in 1897, and is now strongly seconded by Russian scholars in Soviet Russia.[91] It has been definitely proved that another people

---

ence in their historical ages is one of the most important distinctions between the Romano-Germanic and the Greco-Slavonic worlds." (p. 55).

[90] Caesarius, *Caesarii sapientissimi viri fratris Gregorii Theologi Dialogus II*, interrogatio CX, responsio: οἱ Σκλαυηνοὶ καὶ Φυσωνῖται, οἱ καὶ Δανούβιοι προσαγορευόμενοι. Migne, *PG*, XXXVIII, col. 985. On Caesarius see O. Seeck, *Pauly-Wissowa*, III (1899), 1298–1300. O. Bardenhewer, *Geschichte der altkirchlichen Literatur*, III, 174. See also A. Vasiliev, "The Slavs in Greece," *Viz. Vrem.*, V (1898), 406. Caesarius' passage was unknown to Šafarik when he wrote his *Slavonic Antiquities*. If I am not mistaken, this text was first pointed out by Mullenhoff, "Donau-Dunav-Dunaj," *Archiv für slavische Philologie*, I (1876), 290–298, and again in his great work *Deutsche Altertumskunde*, II (Berlin, 1887), 367. Max Vasmer, *Die Slaven in Griechenland* (Berlin, 1941), p. 12.

[91] M. Drinov, *The Slavic Occupation of the Balkan Peninsula*, p. 135 (in Russian); reprinted in Drinov's *Works*, edited by V. Zlatarsky, I (Sofia, 1909), 139–364. Shishmanov, *Slavonic Settlements in Crete and Other Islands* (Sofia, 1897), p. 18 (pagination of an offprint from the Bulgarian *Pregled*, 1897. In Bulgarian). N. Derjavin, "Slavs and Byzantium in the Sixth Century," *Yazyk i literatura (Language and Literature)*, VI (Leningrad, 1930), p. 29. Cf. A. Mishulin, "The Ancient Slavs and the Destinies of the Eastern Roman Empire," *Vestnik (Messenger) of Ancient History*, I (6), 1939, p. 294: Though not under their

renowned for their warlike qualities, the Antes or Antae, were kin to the Sclavenes. In other words, a greatly enlarged territory for Slavonic activities in general has been opened up.

On the basis of historical, topographical, and linguistic evidence concerning the Balkan Peninsula, we must conclude that Slavonic settlements in the Balkans had begun before the sixth century. The statement attributed to Caesarius of Nazianzus dealing with the Sclavenes in the Danubian region at the end of the fourth century must not be forgotten. But the sixth century Slavonic raids and incursions produced a new development. Generally speaking, they were operated not by the local Slavonic settlers in the peninsula but by new Slavonic emigrants from beyond the Danube, who, along with other barbarians, formed a wave which rushed into the Balkan provinces of the empire. Bury is incorrect in saying that permanent Slavonic settlements on imperial soil did not begin till about twenty years after Justinian's death (II, 298).[92] They had begun long before that time. The predatory Slavonic movements in the peninsula in the sixth century from outside, combined with the Slavonic settlements there dating from older times, formed a powerful Slavonic bloc which was to determine the future history of southeastern Europe.

The Slavonic incursions into the Balkans in the sixth century have a close connection with the fall of the Hunnic Empire. With the death of Attila in 453, his empire, which had no natural cohesion, split into pieces and the numerous and varied tribes which had been incorporated in his empire emerged from it as disorganized and scattered elements. The Antes and Sclavenes were among them. The barbarians who from the end of the fifth century infested the Balkan Peninsula are called in our sources Scythians, Bulgarians, Getae, and Huns. It is natural that our sources, among them the Latin chronicler of the sixth century, Comes Marcellinus, had no exact notion of the race of all

---

own name, the Slavs had been in the Balkan Peninsula long before the sixth century.

[92] In 1930 the Russian scholar Derjavin wrote the same thing: "Of course, a 'solid' settlement of the Slavs in the peninsula towards the end of the sixth century is not to be spoken of." "The Slavs and Byzantium in the Sixth Century," *Yazik i Literatura*, VI, 25. In 1937, F. Lot also asserted that the settlement of the Slavs upon the soil of the empire began after 581. *Les invasions barbares et le peuplement de l'Europe*, I (Paris, 1937), 221.

those invading barbarians; it would be hazardous to try to define exactly whom they meant by these terms. But in my opinion, one statement of a writer of the beginning of the seventh century, Theophylact Simocatta, is to be given special consideration; he identifies the Getae with the Slavs, saying that Getae is the name of the Slavs.[93]

All the barbarian tribes from Attila's fallen empire, the Huns themselves, the Gepids, Rugians, Scirians, and others, rushed into the Roman Empire, devastating, raiding, and seeking military service in its armies. Like all these tribes, the Antes and Sclavenes also devastated, raided, and supplied auxiliaries for the Roman army. But Slavonic incursions of that time into the Balkans from without were much more pregnant with consequences than those of other peoples because the invading Slavs found many settled compatriots in the peninsula who, as we have noted above, had established themselves there a long time before as peaceable colonists. At the beginning of the sixth century, at any rate before the accession of Justin to the throne, bands of Slavs along with other barbarians had infiltrated not only into the provinces of the Balkan Peninsula such as Thrace and Illyricum, but into Greece proper, and in 517 they reached Thermopylae. The capital itself began to feel the impending danger. To increase the security of Constantinople and to protect it from hostile incursions, Justin's predecessor, Emperor Anastasius I, erected in Thrace at a distance of about forty miles west of Constantinople, the so-called "Long Wall," or the Anastasian Wall, which extended from the Sea of Marmora to the Black Sea, "making the city practically an island instead of a peninsula," as one source says.[94] But this wall did not very effectively protect even

[93] Theophylact Simocatta, *Theophylacti Simocattae Historia* III, 4, 7: τὸ δὲ Γετικὸν, ταύτὸν δ'εἰπεῖν, αἱ τῶν Σκλαυηνῶν ἀγέλαι (ed. de Boor, pp. 116–117). Photius mentions this statement in his *Bibliotheca*, cod. LXV. Migne, *PG*, CIII, 148; ed. Bekker, p. 29: Οἱ δὲ Γέται ἤτοι Σκλάβοι τὰ περὶ τὴν Θρᾴκην ἐλυμαίνοντο. See K. Ἄμαντος, Τὰ ἐθνολογικὰ ὀνόματα εἰς τοὺς βυζαντινοὺς συγγραφεῖς, Ἑλληνικά, II (1928), 99. Δ. Ζακυθηνός, Οἱ Σλάβοι ἐν Ἑλλάδι (Athens, 1945), p. 10 and n. 4. G. Moravcsik, *Byzantinoturcica*, II, 105–106.

[94] *Evagrii Historia Ecclesiastica* III, 38; ed. Bidez-Parmentier, p. 136. Contrary to Bury (I, 435, n. 5) who dates the wall in 497, I accept the later date of 507–512. In the nineties of the fifth century there was no pressing necessity for such a wall. See C. Schuchhardt, "Die Anastasius-Mauer bei Constantinopel und die Dobrudscha-Wälle," *Jahrbuch des Deutschen Archäologischen Instituts*, XVI (1901), 107. G. Vernadsky, *Ancient Russia* (New Haven, 1943), p. 162.

the capital, and certainly had no general significance for the peninsula. Most of the peninsula remained entirely defenseless. In addition, terrific earthquakes which struck the peninsula under Anastasius and Justin produced wide havoc and considerably helped the destructive inroads of the barbarians.[95]

In the protection of the central government, the defense of the peninsula was very poorly organized. There were no regular army regiments stationed along the banks of the Danube for protection of the imperial border; the defense of the most essential frontier was entrusted to companies of the *foederati* recruited from various barbarian tribes, men whose compatriots were doing the invading. Bury points out (II, 340) discord which appears to have been incessant between the military and civil officials in Thrace and, as the Thracian provinces constantly suffered from the incursions of the barbarians, want of harmony in the administration was more disastrous there than elsewhere. A striking example of the disorganization of the imperial government in the Balkans was Vitalian's rebellion at the end of the reign of Anastasius; the sources call Vitalian either Scythian, or Goth, or Getian. He might have been a Slav, although his name is not Slavic. Jireček remarks that Vitalian's rebellion is the last great movement on the lower Danube in which the Slavs do not appear.[96]

The most devastating and disastrous barbarian invasion of all, which we have already mentioned above, took place in 517, at the very end of the reign of Anastasius, just before Justin's accession. To indicate more graphically the destructive character of this invasion, the chronicler Comes Marcellinus refers to a passage of Jeremiah. In 517 the Getian raiders — in this case, in most probability, Getian means Slav — devastated Macedonia and Thessaly and reached the old Epirus and Thermopylae. To ransom Roman captives, Anastasius sent to John, Prefect of Illyricum, a large sum of money, which proved to be insufficient. Some prisoners were slain before the walls of captured cities and some were held in captivity.[97] All this makes it clear that

[95] See, for instance, C. Jireček, *Geschichte der Serben*, I, 53–54.
[96] C. Jireček, *Geschichte der Serben*, I, 52.
[97] *Marcellini Comitis Chronicon ad a. 517*: "Duae tunc Macedoniae Thessaliaque vestatae et usque Thermopylas veteremque Epirum Getae equites depraedati sunt." Migne, *PL*, LI, col. 939; Mommsen, *Chronica Minora*, II (1893), 100. See

during the reign of Justin the most dangerous and most vulnerable frontier in the north was the course of the Danube from its mouth up to its confluence with the Sava River and then the territory upwards along the latter. None of this vital frontier was adequately protected.

For a rather long time the point of view prevailed that the Slavs had made their first appearance in the Byzantine Empire during the reign of Justin I. Such was the opinion of the renowned Czech scholar Lubor Niederle, and he was followed by other historians. Jireček wrote that we hear of the invasion of the Slavs across the Danube for the first time under Justin I. In 1914 Uspensky stated that the Southern Slavs have the right to start their national history with the reign of Justin I. In 1938 the Russian historian M. Levchenko said that systematic attacks of the Slavs upon the Balkan Peninsula began under Justin and Justinian.[98]

Conflicts between the Slavs and the Empire during the reign of Justin are mentioned in our evidence. In his *History of the Gothic War*, Procopius comments on the events of the fourth year of Justinian's reign (531): "The Huns and Antae and Sclaveni had already made the crossing (of the Danube) many times and done irreparable harm to the Romans." [99] This passage clearly shows that before the

---

G. Vernadsky, *Ancient Russia*, p. 165: the Getians — definitely Slavs. Jeremiah, 6, 22: "Thus saith Jehovah, Behold, a people cometh from the north country; and a great nation shall be stirred up from the uttermost parts of the earth." C. Jireček calls the invaders of 517 not Getae but Huns. *Geschichte der Serben*, I, 52. Zlatarsky calls them Huns — Kutrigurs. *History of the Bulgarian State in the Middle Ages*, I (Sofiia, 1918), 47 (in Bulgarian). The Kutrigurs were a branch of the Hunnic race near the Maiotis (Maeotis, now the Sea of Azov). On the Kutrigurs see G. Moravcsik, *Byzantinoturcica*, II, 152–153.

[98] Lubor Niederle, *Slovanske Starožitnosti*, II (Prague, 1906), 190–191; 193 (in Czech); in French, *Manuel de l'antiquité slave*, I: *l'Histoire* (Paris, 1923), 61. Among the historians who have followed him see F. Dvornik, *Les Slaves, Byzance et Rome au IXe siècle*, p. 3. M. Spinka, *A History of Christianity in the Balkans* (Chicago, 1933), p. 4. C. Jireček, *Geschichte der Serben*, I, 81. T. Uspensky, *History of the Byzantine Empire*, I, 464–465 (in Russian). M. Levchenko, "Byzantium and the Slavs in the Sixth and Seventh Centuries," *Vestnik (Messenger) of Ancient History*, no. 4 (5) (Leningrad, 1938), p. 37 (in Russian). S. Runciman surprisingly observes that the Slavs made their first excursion across the Danube in 534. S. Runciman, *A History of the First Bulgarian Empire* (London, 1930), p. 22.

[99] Procopius, *B. G.* III, 14, 2 (VII, 14, 2); ed. Haury, II, 354; Dewing, IV, 262–263.

year 531 both Slavonic tribes, Antae and Sclavenes, had already crossed the Danube many times and devastated the peninsula; in other words, these devastating expeditions took place not only in the first four years of Justinian's rule but also earlier, during the reign of Justin. An indirect indication of conflicts between the Slavs and the empire under Justin may also be drawn from another passage in Procopius, where he says that Illyricum and Thrace in their entirety . . . were overrun practically every year by Huns, Sclavenes, and Antae, from the time when Justinian took over the Roman Empire.[100] If we compare this passage of the *Anecdota* with the passage from the *Gothic War*, we may affirm almost with certainty that they refer not only to the period of Justinian but also to the preceding period of Justin.

I shall turn now to one of the stories told by Procopius about Slavo-Byzantine relations under Justinian in order to show that the fact described by Procopius really belongs not to the period of Justinian but to that of Justin. Here follows the story as it is told by Procopius in his book on the *Gothic War* (III, 40, 2–7 = Dewing, VII, 40, 2–7): "The Romans questioned the Sclaveni as to why this army of theirs had crossed the Ister (Danube) and what they had in mind to accomplish. And they stoutly declared that they had come with the intention of capturing by siege both Thessalonica itself and the cities around it. When the emperor heard this, he was greatly agitated and straightway wrote to Germanus, directing him to postpone for the moment his expedition to Italy and defend Thessalonica and other cities and to repel the invasion of the Sclaveni with all his power. But the Sclaveni, upon learning definitely from their captives that Germanus was in Sardica, began to be afraid; for Germanus had a great reputation among these barbarians for the following reason. During the reign of Justinian, the Antae, who dwelt close to the Sclaveni, had crossed the Ister River with a great army and invaded the Roman domain. The emperor had not long before this appointed Germanus Commander (στρατηγός) of all Thrace. He accordingly engaged with the hostile army, defeated them thoroughly in battle, and killed almost all of them; and Germanus, as a result of this achievement, had covered

---

[100] *Anecdota* XVIII, 20; Dewing, VI, 216–217.

himself with great glory in the estimation of all men, and particularly among the barbarians." [101]

This story contains a very interesting episode for our study, that of the defeat of the Sclaveni under Justinian which created such a great reputation for Germanus. All the manuscripts of Procopius give in this place the name of the Emperor Justin, and not that of Justinian. The name of Justinian appeared in this story as a correction of a supposed mistake in the manuscripts, because this story was told by Procopius among the events referring to the time of Justinian. The first to introduce the name of Justinian for that of Justin was the first editor of Procopius' complete works, Maltretus, who lived in the seventeenth century; and his supposed correction was accepted in the later editions of Dindorf, Comparetti, Haury, and of course Dewing, who followed Haury's text. But in all editions there is this reference: Ἰουστινιανός Maltr. Ἰουστῖνος codd.[102] Germanus, then, really gained his brilliant victory over the Slavs who had crossed the Danube during the reign of Justin. From now on, the name of Justin should replace that of Justinian in the text, and the episode must be once and for all eliminated from the activities of Justinian's reign and transferred to its correct place in the period of Justin.[103] We should also modify the following passage in the book by G. Vernadsky: "Justin began his reign by repelling the Slavs, who were pushed north across the Danube and kept quiet during the whole of his reign." [104] We know positively now that during Justin's reign the Slavs were not quiet but

[101] I have used here, with slight changes, Dewing's translation (V, 39).

[102] See ed. Haury, II, 476, l. 17; ed. Dindorf, *CSHB*, II, 450, l. 3, note: Ἰουστινιανός] Ἰουστῖνος. *La Guerra Gotica di Procopio di Cesarea*, ed. D. Comparetti, II (Rome, 1896), 458, l. 14: in the text Ἰουστινιανός; note: Ἰουστῖνος i. codd.

[103] This error in the editions of Procopius has been pointed out several times but without result. See L. Niederle, *Slovanske Starozitnosti*, II, 191 (in Czech); in French, *Manuel de l'antiquité slave*, I, 61. Jireček, *Geschichte der Serben*, I, 81 and n. 2. Without giving any reference A. Shakhmatov says: "In some cases the Antae acted apart from the Slavs; under Justin the Antae by themselves made an incursion into the Roman domain across the Danube." A. Shakhmatov, *The Most Ancient Destinies of the Russian Race* (Petrograd, 1919), p. 7 (in Russian). Bury (II, 298, n. 1) mentions among events under Justinian the victory of Germanus, and adds, "The date is unknown." Vernadsky fails to mention the episode. Diehl only says that the name of Germanus filled the Antes and Slavs with terror. Charles Diehl, *Justinien et la civilisation byzantine au VIe siècle*, p. 101.

[104] Vernadsky, *Ancient Russia*, p. 166.

that they continued their destructive raids, advancing farther and farther southwards to the shores of the Aegean Sea and to the confines of ancient Greece. Under Justin started the powerful and steady process of Slavonic penetration into the Balkans, and it was gradually to determine the later destinies of southeastern Europe.

In spite of the tremendous significance of the Slavonic inroads, so frequent and so devastating, the Slavs under their own name make no appearance in Justinian's official triumphal title where all the nations with whom he had to deal have found their place. The title, which he used in his address to the Constantinopolitan Senate on the occasion of the new edition of his Code in 534, runs as follows: "Christi Imperator Caesar Flavius . . . Iustinianus Alamannicus Gothicus Francicus Germanicus Anticus Alanicus Vandalicus Africanus." There is no surname Slavicus or Sclavenicus here. The Slavs, however, may be traced in the surname Anticus, which may imply that in Justinian's time the Slavs were better and more widely known by their branch of the Antes or Antae than by that of the Sclavenes — Sclaveni.

Justin and Bosporus

The northern border of the empire under Justin was not limited to the course of the Danube and Sava; it extended east, to the northern basin of the Black Sea, and especially to the peninsula of the Crimea, where the situation was rather complicated and was causing the government great anxiety. After the close of the fifth century the Huns occupied the steppe region of the Peninsula; or, as Procopius states of the sixth century, between Bosporus (Panticapaeum) in the east on the Strait itself, and Chersonnesus in the west of the peninsula, "everything is held by barbarians, the Hunnic nations." The city of Bosporus itself became subject to the Huns. There is no ground for speaking, as certain scholars do, of the complete destruction by the Huns of this important center.[105] The Byzantine government, protecting its own

[105] Proc., B. P. I, 12, 7; II, 3, 40; ed. Haury, I, 57; 159–160; Dewing, I, 96–97; 280–281. B. G. IV, 5, 27; Haury, II, 508; Dewing, V, 96–97. I do not know why Mommsen (*Römische Geschichte*, V, 289, n. 2) speaks of the ruin of Panticapaeum during Hunnic attacks. On other holders of this opinion see J. Kulakovsky, "A Christian Catacomb of the Year 491 at Kerch," *Materialy on the Archaeology of Russia*, VI (1891), 24 (in Russian). See also A. Vasiliev, *The Goths in the Crimea*, p. 70.

interests on the far-off borderland of the Tauris as well as those of its vassals and allies, the mountain Goths, could not submit easily to the domination of the Huns in the steppes of the peninsula. These mountain Goths were a remnant of the large Germanic branch which remained in the Crimea after the Hunnic invasion in the south of present-day Russia and was cut off from the main Gothic stock. At the close of the fifth century Dory in the mountains was already the center of so-called Gothia. General danger from the Huns brought together the Byzantine government and the Crimean Goths, who, too weak to defend themselves independently, were forced to seek the protection of the powerful empire and became its vassals and allies.

According to Procopius (*B. P.* I, 12, 8), under Justin I the Bosporites "decided to become subjects of the empire." We do not know the reason for this decision; in all probability they desired to free themselves from Hunnic domination. But under Justin the expectations of the Bosporites were not realized.

We have already related that Justin sent Probus, the nephew of the late Emperor Anastasius, to Bosporus to bribe an army of Huns to help the Iberians, and that his mission was unsuccessful. Justin's policy towards the Huns was not successful either, and it was his successor, Justinian, who took advantage of the Huns' internal strife to capture Bosporus and set to work both to restore the former fortifications in the peninsula and to build new ones.[106]

JUSTIN AND THE HUNS

It is a question of secondary significance which branch of the Hunnic race dominated the Crimean steppes in the sixth century: whether the Onogurs, as Kulakovsky states, or the Kutrigurs, as Gerard and Vernadsky believe.[107] The Huns, who are often mentioned in our

[106] Some historians, in my opinion erroneously, attribute the capture of Bosporus to Justin. See J. Kulakovsky, *The Past of the Tauris,* 2nd ed. (Kiev, 1914), p. 58. *Idem, History of Byzantium,* II, 29–30. F. Dvornik, *Les légendes de Constantin et de Méthode vues de Byzance* (Paris, 1933), p. 152. Chr. Gerard, *Les Bulgares de la Volga et les Slaves du Danube,* p. 26. See Vasiliev, *The Goths,* p. 71, n. 4.

[107] Kulakovsky, *The Past of the Tauris,* p. 58 (in Russian). Gerard, *Les Bulgares de la Volga,* p. 26. Vernadsky, *Ancient Russia,* p. 168. On these Hunnic tribes and their interrelations see J. Moravcsik, "Zur Geschichte der Onoguren,"

sources in the fifth and sixth centuries, did not represent one ethnic unit but included several tribes of Hunnic origin, to which the ancient Bulgarians also belonged. In the sixth century the steppes of present-day South Russia around Maeotis (the Sea of Azov) and to a certain extent the Crimea, were occupied by the Hunnic tribes of Utigurs and Kutrigurs. The tribe of Onogurs, ethnically very close to them, may be considered the ancestors of the Danubian Bulgarians; from the sixties of the fifth century down to the end of the seventh century the Onogurs also were settled in the vicinity of Maeotis in the region of the Kuban River. Their nearest neighbors on the east, in the north Caucasian area between the Euxine and the Caspian Sea, were another people of Hunnic origin, the Sabiri (Sabeiroi, Σάβειροι).

Finally, the great horde of Ephthalites or White Huns, who took Khorasan from the Sassanians and overran Northern India, had established a vast empire over the countries south of the Caspian Sea, and for a short time even reached the banks of the Ganges. In the sixth century Cosmas Indicopleustes wrote that north of India were the White Huns; and another Byzantine chronicler of the sixth century, Theophanes of Byzantium, derived the name of the people of the Ephthalites from the name of their king Ephthalanus (Ἐφθαλάνος). According to Procopius (*B. P.* I, 3, 1–3), "the Ephthalites are a Hunnic people; but they do not mingle with any of the Huns known to us, for they occupy a land neither adjoining, nor even very near to, them . . . they are not nomads like the other Hunnic peoples, but for a long time have been established in a goodly land." [108]

Ungarische Jahrbücher, X (1930), 53–90. *Idem, Byzantinoturcica*, II, 152–153 (Kutrigurs), 189–190 (Onogurs).

[108] The question of ethnic interrelations between various Hunnic tribes is very complicated and has not yet been thoroughly clarified. J. Moravcsik, "Zur Geschichte der Onoguren," *Ungarische Jahrbücher*, X, 53–90; esp. 60–62; 65; 73. A. Cunningham, "Ephthalites or White Huns," *Transactions of the Ninth International Congress of Orientalists*, I (London, 1893), 222; 225; 233. E. Drouin, "Mémoire sur les Huns Ephthalites dans leur rapports avec les rois perses Sassanides," *Le Muséon*, XIV (1895), 74; 83–84; 247. O. G. von Wesendonk, "Kūšān, Chioniten und Hephtaliten," Klio, *Beiträge zur alten Geschichte*, XXVI (1933), 336–346; esp. p. 341; 343; 344 (nationality of the Ephthalites has not been definitely fixed). W. M. McGovern, *The Early Empires of Central Asia: A Study of the Scythians and the Huns and the Part they Played in World History* (Chapel Hill, 1939), p. 404: the origin and exact ethnic affinities of the Ephthalites

The Huns played rather an important role during Justin's reign. Through the Caucasian passes they invaded Iberia and Lazica, and made themselves very acutely felt both by Byzantium and by Persia; on account of this danger both empires were vitally interested in the penetration and firm establishment of their own political influence and even domination in those two countries. On the other hand, when the two empires came to grips with each other, both sought for Hunnic aid, realizing how important Hunnic auxiliary hordes would be in their military operations. In connection with the political combinations of Justin's period, we have already pointed out the treacherous duplicity of the Hunnic ruler Zilgibi (Zilgbis, Zilgbi) and his final fate. The unsuccessful mission of Probus to the city of Bosporus, which was at that time in the possession of the Huns, and to their region north of the Caucasian mountains, has also been told above. Some Huns were included in the Byzantine army as auxiliaries and took part in Byzantine military expeditions; for instance, towards the end of Justin's reign the general Peter was sent to Lazica to fight for the Iberian king Gurgenes against Kawad and his army included some Huns.

In his *Lives* of the Eastern Saints, John of Ephesus several times mentions the hosts of the Huns who, during the period of Anastasius, Justin, and Justinian, devasted the eastern provinces as far as the Euphrates, and disturbed the contemplative life of the hermits. I shall give here a few stories referring to the Huns which are found in John of Ephesus' book. In spite of the fact that this work is to be classed as edifying literature and therefore is not without an element of legend, the passages which I intend to bring forward here are historically significant as indicating the frequency and devastation of the Hunnic incursions in the eastern provinces of the empire. In all probability, the invading Huns were Ephthalites. One story reads: "After

---

are shrouded in mystery. S. P. Tolstov, "Fundamental Questions of the Ancient History of Middle Asia," *Vestnik (Messenger) of Ancient History*, I, 2 (Moscow, 1938), 176–203; esp. 187 (in Russian). Cosmas Indicopleustes, Lib. XI, ed. E. O. Winstedt, p. 324 (449 A): ἀνώτεροι δὲ, τουτέστι, βορειότεροι τῆς Ἰνδικῆς, εἰσὶν λευκοὶ Οὖννοι. *Theophanis Byzantii Fragmenta*, CSHB, p. 447; C. Müller, *FHG*, IV, 270. See G. Moravcsik, *Byzantinoturcica*, II, 118 (Ephthalites, a Hunnic people); 152–153 (Kutrigurs); 189 (Onogurs); 205 (Utigurs); 224–225 (Sabiri).

a space of about twenty years during which the saint stood upon the column, a revelation was shown to him concerning the terrible hosts of barbarians (i.e., Huns), who should come forth to chastise men upon earth . . . And after twenty days the hosts of the Huns came forth, and they covered the land of the East, and none so numerous as they had appeared in the land of the Romans, nor had it even been heard that any Huns except these presumed to cross the Euphrates." Another says: "Again they would often come and cry, 'Flee, flee. Lo! the land is full of Huns.' And Huns appeared to me in various fearful shapes, riding on horses and with swords drawn and flashing . . . Huns cry: 'The cross has protected this man against us!' " In another story we read: "Go and curse these Huns who are coming and making havoc of creation, and let them die." These excerpts probably cover the period from 515 to 531–535, and they leave the impression that at this time in the eastern provinces of the empire as far as the Persian border, destructive Hunnic-Ephthalite incursions were almost continuous.[109]

In addition to the Hunnic tribes in the Crimea and in the southeast, the Byzantine Empire had a dangerous foe in the Huns, the Sabiri (Sabeiroi) who were settled, as we know, north of the Caucasian range, between the Euxine and the Caspian Sea. It was the Sabiri who through the so-called "Caspian Gates" ($\pi\acute{v}\lambda as$ $\tau\grave{a}s$ $\kappa a\sigma\pi\acute{\iota}as$), by which Procopius (B. P. I, 10, 10) meant the Daryal Gorge of today, invaded Iberia and Lazica, forming a disturbing and dangerous element in the north both to Byzantium and to Persia. It was the Sabiri who, three years before Justin's accession to the throne, in 515, made a destructive incursion into the Pontic provinces and devastated Cappadocia. We are not surprised that the guarding of the "Caspian Gates" was the most essential point in political relations between Byzantium, Persia, Lazica, and Iberia. He who guarded the Gates guarded the tranquillity and safety of both empires. The Hunnic ruler Zilgibi, whose treacherous policy has been discussed above, was apparently a Sabirus (Sabeiros).

While the Sabiri were enemies of Byzantium, the Ephthalites or

[109] John of Ephesus, *Lives of the Eastern Saints*, E. W. Brooks, I, *Patr. Or.* XVII, 19–26; 78; 80; 115; 245.

White Huns were sworn enemies of Persia. In 484 (483) the Persian King Perozes (Firuz) was ignominiously defeated and slain by the Ephthalites. Upon his brother and successor Volagases, known to the Byzantines as Balas, the White Hun monarch imposed a tribute, which was apparently paid for two years. Justin's contemporary, Kawad (Kobad), had had better relations with the Ephthalites at the beginning of his reign. In 487 he took refuge with the White Huns after making an abortive attempt to seize the Persian throne. After his deposition in 498 he escaped to the White Huns and was vigorously supported by them in regaining his throne. But in 503–513 he engaged in a war with the Ephthalites which lasted for ten years and in which he was successful. This was already the period of the decline of the Ephthalite Empire, and the White Hun peril which had threatened Iran for so long was in process of disappearing. In the middle of the sixth century the empire of the Ephthalites was overthrown by the Turks, who organized the vast Turkish Empire. It is interesting to point out that Procopius fully understood the particular part which the Ephthalites took in the political life of the sixth century. He wrote: "The Ephthalites have never made any incursion into the Roman territory except in company with the Median (Persian) army" (B. P. I, 3, 4). The invading Huns in the region of the Euphrates mentioned by John of Ephesus in his *Lives* of the Eastern Saints, as we have noted above, were Ephthalites who crossed the Byzantine border from the Persian side.

CHAPTER SIX

Justin and the West

We have described conditions and events in the time of Justin in the north, in the Balkans and the Crimea; in the northeast and in the east, in the Caucasus, in Persia, Syria, and Palestine; in the south, in Egypt; and in the far south, in Ethiopia and south Arabia. Quite a different picture presents itself when we turn to the west, to western Europe, and to the southwest, to Africa. The enormous territory from the estuary of the Rhine in the north to the Pillars of Hercules in the south, Italy with some adjoining regions and Sicily, all other islands in the western Mediterranean, and the littoral of western Africa, belonged to the Germans. On the west and southwest the Byzantine Empire was bordered by a long chain of German kingdoms — the Franks, Burgundians, Visigoths, and Ostrogoths in Europe, and the Vandals in Africa. Of course the Frankish, Burgundian, and Visigothic kingdoms lying west of Italy were far away from Constantinople and, in addition, were separated from the imperial territory by the mighty Ostrogothic kingdom in Italy; they therefore could take no active part in the political life of Byzantium. But the Vandal and Ostrogothic kingdoms, being immediate neighbors of the empire, had vital significance for it. The Ostrogothic kingdom in Italy, whose territory included the city of Rome with the papal residence and the old Roman senate, was of particular interest for the empire, and had to be considered in connection with Justin's new religious policy and with the origin and gradual development of Justinian's political plans for restoring Italy to the empire. It was in the center of the western diplomacy and activities of Justin's government, and this diplomacy from the very first steps was directed by his nephew Justinian.

At the head of the Ostrogothic kingdom stood Theodoric, who after defeating and slaying Odovacar, had become the master of Italy in 493. A very interesting and talented figure, Theodoric had a number of complicated and delicate problems to deal with and decide; and it is not surprising that his personality and activities have been differently estimated, both by his own contemporaries and by later writers down to our own day. Owing to Magnus Aurelius Cassiodorus, who as Quaestor of the Palace conducted the official correspondence of the king and composed the state documents, we have a rich mine of information for the administration and conditions of Ostrogothic Italy.

One of these documents gives the general program of Theodoric's government. The program, which Cassiodorus may have somewhat idealized, strikes us by its vast humanity and breadth of vision. Theodoric proclaims: "Let other kings desire the glory of battles won, of cities and booty taken, of ruins made; our purpose is, God helping us, so to rule that our subjects shall grieve that they did not earlier acquire the blessing of our dominion." [1]

JUSTIN AND THE OSTROGOTHIC KINGDOM

Justin began to rule in 518; the position of Theodoric in Italy and his attitude to the empire had been previously definitely determined in 497 by Justin's predecessor Anastasius.[2] Under this arrangement Italy remained part of the empire, and Theodoric himself was regarded as a viceroy or deputy of the emperor. This particular feature of his position is apparent in the fact that he never used the years of his reign for the purpose of dating official documents, nor did he claim the right of coining money except in subordination to the emperor. Above all, he did not make laws. Ordinances of Theodoric exist, but they are not *leges* in the full sense of the term; they are only *edicta*, which could not originate any new principle or institution.

Another question was the right of naming one of the consuls of the year, which before Odovacar had belonged to the emperor reign-

---

[1] *Cassiodori Variae*, III, 43: "Aliorum forte regum proelia captarum civitatum aut praedas appetunt, aut ruinas; nobis propositum est, Deo juvante, sic vincere, ut subjecti se doleant nostrum dominium tardius acquisisse." In English, Th. Hodgkin, *The Letters of Cassiodorus* being a condensed translation (London, 1886), p. 219.

[2] In the introductory section of this chapter I follow mainly Bury, I, 453–469. Bury himself in some respects depends on Mommsen's study *Ostgotische Studien, Historische Schriften*, III (Berlin, 1910), 362–484 in *Gesämmelte Schriften*, VI, originally printed in 1889–1890, in *Neues Archiv der Gesellschaft für ältere deutsche Geschichtskunde*, XIV–XV.

ing in the West. This right was transferred by Zeno and Anastasius to Odovacar and Theodoric, so that from 498 forward Theodoric nominated one of the consuls. But the stipulation excluded Goths from the consulship. Theodoric could not nominate a Goth; only a Roman could fill the consulship. And before 518 no Goth had been nominated consul. On the same principle, Goths could not belong to the Roman Senate, which under Theodoric continued to meet and perform much the same function which it had performed before his time throughout the fifth century. But though the civil offices were reserved exclusively for Romans, no Roman was liable to military service. As Master of Soldiers (*magister militum*), the office which Zeno had conferred upon him, Theodoric was the commander of the army in his kingdom, and his army was entirely Gothic, both in officers and in soldiers. The old Roman troops and their organization disappeared, and Goths and Romans lived side by side as two distinct and separate peoples. Theodoric made no efforts to bring about fusion.

Like Odovacar, Theodoric adopted the simple title of *rex*, and never styled himself *rex Gothorum* or *rex Romanorum*. Procopius wrote: "He did not claim the right to assume either the garb or the name of emperor of the Romans; but he was called *rex* (ῥήξ) to the end of his life, for thus the barbarians are accustomed to call their leaders." [3] Bury remarks: "To designate the extraconstitutional relation, the word *rex*, which had no place in the constitutional vocabulary of Rome, was appropriate enough. It served the double purpose of his regular relation to his German subjects, and his irregular relation, his quasi-kingship, to the Romans in Italy." [4]

Just as he accepted the duality of legal status among his Italian subjects, Theodoric also accepted a dual religious policy. He had been, before the time of Justin, a consistently tolerant Arian. According to the very well known statement of Cassiodorus, Theodoric's prin-

---

[3] Proc., *B. G.* I, 1, 26; Dewing, vol. III, 10–11 (V, 1, 26); see also II, 14, 38; Dewing, III, 412–413 (VI, 14, 38).

[4] Bury, *op. cit.*, I, p. 458. See Mommsen, *Ostgotische Studien*, pp. 479–480 (539). Cf. A. Gaudenzi, *Sui rapporti tra l'Italia e l'Impero d'Oriente fra gli anni 476 e 554 D. C.* (Bologna, 1888), p. 23: To take the title of *rex* meant that from then on Theodoric intended to rule Italy in his own name, and not to be a subject of the emperor of the Orient any longer. See Mommsen's note on Gaudenzi's book, p. 484 (543–544).

ciple was this: "We cannot impose religion because no one can be compelled to believe against his will" — a maxim which, as Bury says (I, 459) "might well have been pondered on by Roman emperors," and, I may add, by many other rulers. Another very important source for the reign of Theodoric, the Latin chronicle known as Anonymus Valesianus, also reports: "Although he himself was of the Arian sect, he nevertheless made no assault on the catholic religion." [5] Another very important and interesting trait of Theodoric's mind was his sincere recognition of the superiority of Roman culture; his objective was to civilize his own people by submitting them to the influences of Roman civilization (*civilitas*).

But the most fundamental and most vital aim of Theodoric, which he must have kept in abeyance, was his desire not only to secure his unstable position but also to gain his complete independence from the Oriental Empire. For this purpose he undertook some steps to increase his strength and power in the West by establishing matrimonial ties with his German neighbors. Theodoric himself took as his second wife a Frankish princess, Augoflada, sister of Clovis. One of his daughters, Theodegotho, in 494 married Sigismund, who became king of the Burgundians after the death of his father Gundobad. Theodoric married his other daughter, Arevagni, to the Visigothic king, Alaric II. And ultimately, in 500, his own sister, Amalafrida, married Trasamund, king of the Vandals. In addition to these matrimonial ties with the principal Germanic kingdoms, Theodoric's niece, Amalaberga, married Herminafrid, king of the Thuringians; and Theodoric adopted a son of the king of the Heruls.[6] "In that way," Anonymus Valesianus

[5] *Cassiodori Variae*, II, 27: "Religionem imperare non possumus, quia nemo cogitur ut credat invitus." Anonymus Valesianus, 60: "dum ipse quidem Arrianae sectae esset, tamen nihil contra religionem catholicam temptans." According to the recent editor of this *Chronicle*, R. Cessi, this section is highly favorable to Theodoric. R. Cessi, *Studi critici preliminari*, p. CXIX; CLXV sq. *Fragmenta historica ab Henrico et Hadriano Valesio primum edita* (Anonymus Valesianus), *Rerum italicarum scriptores ordinata da L. A. Muratori*, new ed. by G. Carducci and V. Fiorini, vol. XXIV, part IV (1913). See Bury, *op. cit.*, I, 423, n. 1.

[6] The names are indicated in Anonymus Valesianus, ch. 63 and 70. See genealogical tables of the family of Theodoric the Ostrogoth, for instance in Thomas Hodgkin, *Italy and Her Invaders*, 2nd ed., III (Oxford, 1896), p. 320. Bury, *op. cit.*, I, p. XIX. W. Ensslin, *Theoderich der Grosse* (München, 1947), 152. On the adoption of the king of the Heruls, *Cassiod. Variae*, IV, 2: "Et ideo more gentium et conditione virili filium te praesenti munere procreamus."

writes (ch. 70), "he gained peace with all the nations round about."
. . . "Here was a vision of a 'family compact,' binding together all
the kingdoms of the west, from the Scheldt to Mount Atlas, in a great
confederacy, filling all the new barbarian thrones with the sons, the
grandsons, or the nephews of Theodoric, a matrimonial State system
surpassing (may we not say?) anything that Hapsburg or Bourbon
ever succeeded in accomplishing, when they sought to make Venus
instead of Mars build up their empires." [7] At the outset of the sixth
century the Byzantine Empire, facing this family compact in the
West which embraced so enormous a territory, must have realized
that if this agreement were solid and lasting, the empire would be
exposed to serious danger from the West and South, and Italy might
be lost for ever. Therefore it is not at all surprising that relations between Constantinople and Ravenna were never cordial. A spirit of
suspicion and hidden menace was always hovering over both courts.
This was briefly the situation in Italy and in the West in general when
Justin ascended the throne in 518. Some foundation for the possible
complete independence of Theodoric's kingdom had already been
laid. What was to follow depended upon what sort of man Justin was,
and what sort of government would lead the destinies of the empire.

Of tremendous significance for Italy was the religious orientation of
the new emperor: his adherence to the strict Chalcedonian belief and
reunion with the Pope. After many years of uncertainty and vacillation Rome apparently had solid foundations for resuming normal and
friendly relations with Constantinople. In 518 the interests of the
three fundamental elements in the complicated internal life of Italy,
those of the Pope, the Roman Senate, and Theodoric, were identical:
they all wanted to live in peace with Byzantium under the new conditions. The joy of the Pope is both obvious and understandable. The
Roman Senate, living side by side with the Pope and representing
the old Roman aristocracy, had never been inclined to follow the monophysite policy of Justin's predecessors. Theodoric was very anxious
to be on friendly terms with Byzantium from the political point of
view. In this way he hoped to strengthen greatly his own position

[7] Hodgkin, *op. cit.*, III, 321.

and to establish a good peace with the empire, peace which had been threatened more than once under Justin's predecessor, Anastasius. Also, since the question of Theodoric's successor had not been settled, he hoped to get from the new emperor the formal recognition of his son-in-law Eutharic as successor to the lordship of Italy. For these political reasons Theodoric lent a helping hand to the reëstablishment of the reunion of Rome with Constantinople. Relations were very close between Theodoric and Pope Hormisdas. Before sending a special mission to Constantinople for the final settlement of reunion, the Pope called on Theodoric at Ravenna to consult him on the matter, and sent the mission with the king's consent.

But at the same time the new religious policy of Justin must have somewhat concerned Theodoric, who was an Arian. Since the relations of the Pope and the Roman Senate with Justin had been reëstablished on the basis of the Chalcedonian doctrine, it was an extremely vital and still uncertain question what attitude the new government would take to the Arians, who would be dissidents in the empire in general and in Italy in particular. But in this respect, for the time being at least, Theodoric was reassured because the new emperor, especially at the beginning of his reign, had to settle some important internal difficulties and had no intention of creating more troubles elsewhere. On the contrary, in the second year of his reign, in 519, Justin unexpectedly made a friendly gesture towards Theodoric, which he and the Goths highly appreciated: in this year Justin nominated as consul Eutharic, the king's son-in-law. Eutharic was the first Goth to be appointed consul. In a letter to Justin in 526, Athalaric, Eutharic's son, Theodoric's grandson and successor, wrote: "You have adorned my father in Italy with the palm-enwoven robe of the consul." [8] This text expressly records that the nomination was not made by Theodoric, but as a special favor by the emperor. Justin himself in 519 shared the

[8] *Cassiodori Variae*, VIII, 1: "vos genitorem meum in Italia palmatae claritate decorastis." *The Letters of Cassiodorus* . . . by Thomas Hodgkin (London, 1886), p. 347. Some manuscripts and old editions of *Variae* say that this letter was addressed to Justinian. But there can be no doubt that Justin is the right reading. Athalaric's accession took place August 30, 526; the death of Justin, August 1, 527, nearly a year later. Justinian was associated with his uncle in the empire from April 1, 527

consulship with Eutharic. This was the greatest honor which had ever been offered Theodoric and the court of Ravenna, and it might well have afforded Theodoric grounds for regarding Eutharic as his legitimate successor. [9]

When the new Gothic consul visited Rome in order to celebrate the assumption of his consulship, the Senate and the people poured forth to meet him. The games which were organized in the amphitheatre were on a scale of brilliance surpassing anything known before. Rome was particularly surprised and delighted by the magnificent shows of wild beasts procured from Africa, evidently sent by the Vandal king Trasamund and never before seen by the crowd. Even Symmachus the Byzantine, who was present at the time in Rome on a special mission from Justin, confessed his amazement and admiration at the spectacle. When Eutharic's sojourn in Rome came to an end, he returned to Ravenna, where the same shows were exhibited again with even greater magnificence in the presence of his father-in-law. Cassiodorus, who in his *Chronicon* describes these celebrations, chooses the consulship of Eutharic as the concluding point of his literary labor consisting of the history of the world from Adam to the year 519. In conclusion to his *Chronicon* Cassiodorus says that from the beginning of the world down to the consulship of Eutharic there have elapsed 5721 years, thus indicating once more how important in the imagination of the Gothic people was the fact of Eutharic's consulship.[10] It was probably on the occasion of Eutharic's consulship that

[9] See an erroneous presentation of this fact by T. Hodgkin, *Italy and Her Invaders*, III, 297. (Theodoric) conferred upon him (Eutharic) the honor of the consulship. An incorrect translation of Anonymus Valesianus (chapter 80) in Loeb Classical Library: Then Theodoric made Eutharicus consul (p. 559). Eutharic's full name was Eutharic Cilliga. The comma between Eutharic and Cilliga in the text and the English translation of Anonymus Valesianus in the Loeb Classical Library (pp. 560–561) should be deleted.

[10] *Cassiodori Senatoris Chronicon*, Migne, *PL*, LXIX, 1248; ed. Mommsen, *Chronica Minora*, II, 161 (*MGH, AA*, XI). This text is reproduced in Gaudenzi, *Sui rapporti* . . . pp. 63–64. Hodgkin, *Italy and Her Invaders*, III, 297. Anon. Vales., 80: "Ergo Theodoricus, dato consulatu Eutharico, Roma et Ravenna triumphavit." See L. Schmidt, *Geschichte der Wandalen* (Leipzig, 1901), p. 119. F. Gabotto, *Storia della Italia occidentale nel medio evo*, Libro I, 1: Barbari nell' Italia occidentale (Turin, 1911), p. 428. W. Ensslin, *op. cit.*, pp. 309–310. The figure 5721 given by Cassiodorus for the period from the beginning of the world is erroneous. But see H. F. Clinton, *Fasti Romani*, I, p. 737.

Cassiodorus eulogized him in the Senate house in an oration of which a fragment has been preserved.[11] In the West Cassiodorus calls Eutharicus *Dominus noster*; in the *Fasti occidentales*, the name of Eutharic as consul stands before that of Justin.[12] In 519 relations between Theodoric and Sigismund of Burgundy were so strained that Burgundy refused to accept the consulship of Eutharic for use in dating the year.[13]

The year 519 of the consulship of Eutharic was the climax of the political career of Theodoric. The arrival of a special Byzantine ambassador, Symmachus, and the magnificent festivities in Rome and Ravenna seemed definitely to assure the peace between Italy and the Orient and guarantee to the Ostrogothic monarchy a long period of prosperity and security. The reëstablishment of good relations with the Orient was a great success attained by the Gothic king, apparently supported by a group of able and sagacious diplomats.[14] But this promising new period of Theodoric's reign was short-lived. Eutharic, whom Anonymus Valesianus (ch. 80) calls "an excessively rough man (asper) and an enemy to the Catholic faith," died in the course of 522 A. D. Theodoric's cherished idea that he might leave after him a solemnly recognized heir vanished. Eutharic's widow, however, Theodoric's daughter Amalasuntha, had a child, Theodoric's grandson, Athalaric, born in 518, who was destined to become Theodoric's successor.[15]

In 522 Justin made his last friendly and benevolent gesture towards Theodoric: in this year he waived his own nomination of a consul and allowed the Gothic king to name both consuls, Symmachus and Boethius. Whether this act of Justin had any connection with the death of the ex-consul Eutharic, which took place in the same year, we do

---

[11] *Cassiodori Senatoris Orationum reliquiae*, ed. L. Traube (Berlin, 1894), p. 463; 469–470; on the interpretation of the lines in question, p. 463, n. 1 (*MGH, AA*, XII).

[12] See Gaudenzi, *op. cit.*, p. 63. Gabotto, *op. cit.*, p. 428.

[13] *Corpus inscriptionum latinarum*, XII, 1500 (a. 519). See Bury, I, 463. L. Schmidt, *Geschichte der deutschen Stämme bis zum Ausgange der Völkerwanderung* (Berlin, 1907), pp. 395–396.

[14] See G. Romano and R. Solmi, *Le dominazioni barbariche in Italia* (Milan, 1940), p. 195.

[15] Gabotto thinks that Eutharic perhaps died in 521 (p. 435).

not know. We might perhaps consider Justin's rather unexpected concession to Theodoric as his wish to console the latter in the grief which had befallen him. The year 523, in any event, is the turning point in the relations between Ravenna and Constantinople.

We know that from the beginning of Justin's reign, owing to his strictly Chalcedonian policy, a period of religious persecution started in the East. Even if the persecution, as we have tried to emphasize above, was not as severe and ruthless as it has usually been presented by the monophysite evidence, still the persecution did exist and sometimes did extend to cruelty and undesirable excesses. The edict of Justin and Justinian (*Cod.* I, 5, 12) against heretics specifically mentions Manichaeans, pagans ("Ελληνες), Jews, and Samaritans, and, as we have noted above, fails to name Nestorians, monophysites, and Arians, though they were of course regarded as heretics too and were subject to persecution. Some concessions had been granted the Goths. But ultimately these concessions were withdrawn, and Arians also were persecuted in the East.[16] In addition to religious reasons, the enormous wealth of the Arians was possibly a cause of persecution, as we have noted above. Procopius says: "Now the shrines (τὰ ἱερά) of these heretics, as they are called, and particularly those who practised the Arian belief, contained wealth unheard of." [17]

After 523 A. D. the Arians suffered much persecution in the East. Their churches were closed or reconsecrated with Chalcedonian rites; many Arians were compelled to abandon their faith and accept the Chalcedonian dogma. They were excluded from public offices and from service in the army. And to crown all, a political element was involved in the new religious relations between Rome and Constantinople, which had begun in 518–519. Since that time the position of the Papacy had considerably changed. Pope Hormisdas, the first Pope during Justin's reign, was entirely in the confidence of Theodoric; but Hormisdas died in August, 523. His successor, John I, was already associated with those who desired a closer dependency of Italy on the imperial government; the Roman Senate was also inclined

---

[16] Theoph., A. M., 6016; de Boor, p. 169. *Anastasii Chronographia Tripertita*, p. 132.

[17] Proc., *Anecdota*, XI, 16. See above.

to follow this trend. Of course these political aspirations, although for the time being they were kept in secrecy, were directed against Theodoric's power in Italy. Theodoric began to suspect and feel the new danger, whose growth stemmed from Constantinople. Moreover, the all-powerful nephew of the emperor, Justinian, began to realize that the reëstablishment of friendly relations with the Pope might not only have importance for potential religious peace and unity but also might through the support of the Papacy and the Roman Senate lay a foundation for the success of his plan of reconquering Italy to the empire in the future.

During the last years of Justin's reign such a plan had already been definitely formed in the head of Justinian. As I have pointed out above, Theodoric understood this new double danger, religious and political. He feared that the imperial anti-Arian policy which manifested itself in the East might provoke an anti-Arian movement in Italy. These new circumstances deeply affected the character of Theodoric; his famous tolerance and breadth of vision vanished and were replaced by suspicion and mistrust.

I wish to give here a picture of the change of Theodoric's character as it presents itself to a recent Italian historian, G. Romano, although his presentation is not without some romanticism and idealization, as is rather often the case when historians deal with the personality of Theodoric. Romano writes: "In comparison with Theodoric, few men have worked so hard all their lives in order to reach their own ideal. This ideal was for him the kingdom which he had founded, which he had defended, and which he wished to maintain and transmit at all cost to his successors. He had turned to this aim all the strength of his genius, all the dexterity of his political sagacity. He had sought to gain the affections of the Italians, appearing mild and generous to them; he had avowed submission and respect to the emperor; he had interfered as peacemaker in the question of schism, exerting himself for the cessation of any dissention among them and for the reëstablishment of the religious peace. And lo, after thirty years of rule and assiduous and persistent care, a doubt planted itself in his mind that all that he had done had come to nothing, and that the ideal which he had cherished had been but a dream; he saw, or he seemed to see, that the Italians responded to his kindness with ingratitude and treason; that the Italians and the emperor had agreed between them to undermine his throne and tread it under their feet. Since he was too jealous of his own work to permit that others might attempt it, and too much of a barbarian to understand the force of tradition which urged the Italians to cherish a political ideal different from his own, the disillusion which he experienced clouded his mind and made him distrustful and suspicious. The good and loyal king became cruel to those whom he had treated with kindness, and after a glorious reign he allowed himself to indulge in excesses which must cast upon his memory an indelible shadow." [18]

The last three years of Theodoric's rule sullied his fame. In 523–524 took place the famous case of Boethius and Symmachus, who were accused of treason in their communication with the Byzantine court. The whole Roman Senate was involved in the matter, which, on the special order of the King, was taken out of the hands of the Consistory, the usual tribunal for cases of treason. The infuriated Theodoric was determined to teach the Senate a lesson. In 524 Boethius was cruelly put to death, and his father-in-law Symmachus, the head of the Senate, perhaps the only man who remained loyal to Boethius, was arrested, taken to Ravenna, and executed. Bury remarks (II, 155): "It was a foolish act, the precaution of a tyrant." Procopius writes: "This was the first and last act of injustice which he committed toward his subjects, and the cause of it was that he had not made a thorough investigation, as he was accustomed to do, before passing judgment on the two men." [19]

The case of Boethius and Symmachus left the Byzantine government free to act. The Roman Senate, which had already become one of the most important elements in the Byzantine political plans for Italy, was offended and humiliated. At the beginning of 525 the persecution of the Gothic Arians in the Eastern Empire reached its climax; [20] and,

[18] G. Romano and A. Solmi, *Le dominazioni barbariche in Italia*, pp. 212–213.

[19] Proc., *B. G.* I, 1, 39; Dewing, III, 14–15 (V, 1, 39). See an interesting article by William Bark, "Theodoric vs. Boethius: Vindication and Apology," The American Historical Review, XLIX (April, 1944), pp. 410–426.

[20] See J. Sundwall, *Abhandlungen zur Geschichte des ausgehenden Römertums*, p. 169. Ch. Lécrivain, *Le sénat romain depuis Dioclétien à Rome et à Constantinople*, p. 198.

according to Bury (II, 156), severe measures against the Arians had already been adopted and reported in Italy before the autumn of 525 A. D. This was a direct blow at the Gothic kingdom.

Theodoric determined to bring matters to an issue at Constantinople. He selected as his ambassador Pope John, whose mission has already been described in detail. John's objective was to induce Justin to relax his stern policy against Arians and to convey to Justin Theodoric's threat to start persecution of Italian Catholics in reprisal, if he persisted in his anti-Arian activities.

Although the mission was successful in its principal object, John on his return to Ravenna was coldly received by Theodoric and died a few days later (May 18, 526 A. D.).[21] Theodoric's unjustifiable treatment of the Pope is to be explained not so much by religious reasons as by political considerations. Theodoric was very much alarmed at the cordial reception John had received in Constantinople, at his friendly relations with the emperor, and particularly at the fact that he had crowned Justin, a ceremony by which John agreed to recognize publicly and solemnly the Emperor of the Orient as his sovereign and lord.[22]

After a two-month struggle, a new Pope was elected, Felix IV (July 12, 526), and his election was a great source of satisfaction to Theodoric, as we see clearly from the letter of his successor and grandson Athalaric to the Senate of the City of Rome. The opening lines run as follows: "We profess that we hear with great satisfaction that you have responded to the judgment of our glorious lord and grandfather in your election of a Bishop. It was right in sooth to obey the will of a good sovereign, who, handling the matter with wise deliberation, although it had reference to a form of faith alien from his own, thought fit to select such a Pontiff as could rightfully be displeasing to none. You may thus recognize that his one chief desire was that Religion might flourish by good priests being supplied to all the churches." [23]

---

[21] For all details connected with John's mission see above.
[22] G. Pfeilschifter, *Der Ostgotenkönig Theoderich der Grosse und die katholische Kirche*, p. 198. *Idem, Theoderich der Grosse*, p. 94. Romano, *op. cit.*, p. 217.
[23] *Cassiod. Variae*, VIII, 15. English translation by Hodgkin, *The Letters of Cassiodorus*, p. 360.

The month of May, 526, when Pope John returned to Ravenna to die there a few days later, was the time of an open break with Constantinople. Theodoric's own days were numbered; he died on August 30 of the same year. But the last months of his reign were filled with strenuous preparations for war. Theodoric received distressing news from North Africa, from Carthage, where his sister Amalfrida, the widow of the Vandal king Trasamund, was accused of conspiring against the new king Hilderic and thrown into prison to die. All her Gothic followers were killed. Hilderic, himself inclined to Catholicism, leaned more and more towards Constantinople, and the Vandal fleet was strong. Justin and Hilderic became allies in an alliance directed against Theodoric. Theodoric well understood the situation and was especially worried about his lack of an Ostrogothic fleet with which to withstand successfully the mighty strength of the two united fleets. He displayed amazing activity; in a few months he had a fleet of 1000 ships (*dromones*) which were ordered to proceed to Ravenna and assemble there on June 13, 526. For this extraordinary effort there is a great deal of information in Theodoric's letters. In his first letter to the Praetorian Prefect Abundantius he writes: "By divine inspiration we have determined to raise a navy which may both ensure the arrival of cargoes of public corn and may, if need be, combat the ships of an enemy. For that Italy, a country abounding in timber, should not have a navy of her own hath often stricken us with regret. Let your Greatness therefore give directions for the constructions of 1000 ships (*dromones*). Wherever cypresses and pines are found near to the seashore, let them be bought at a suitable price."

In his second letter to Abundantius Theodoric frankly identifies the enemies against whom the fleet is being built. "We praise you for your prompt fulfillment of the orders contained in the previous letter. You have built a fleet almost as quickly as ordinary men would sail one. . . . Now that we have our fleet, there is no reason for the Greek to fasten a quarrel upon us, or for the African to insult us (*non habet quod nobis Graecus imputet aut Afer insultet*). With envy they see that we have now stolen from them the secret of their strength. Let all the fleet be assembled at Ravenna on the next Ides of June." The other three letters, addressed to other persons, but all containing

references to these letters to Abundantius, relate to the same subject —
the formation of the navy, and the meeting of ships and sailors at
Ravenna on the Ides of June.[24] From our sources we learn that in
June, 526, war was on the point of breaking out. But it did not do so
because on August 30 of this year Theodoric died.

Only one source, and that hostile to Theodoric, reports that four
days before his death, on August 25, Theodoric drew up a decree
empowering the Arians to take possession of Catholic churches the
next Sunday; but that he died on the very same day on which he was
rejoicing in his attack on the churches.[25] This statement from the
Anonymus Valesianus, unsupported as it is, has often been accepted.
But historians of our time positively reject the story. Pfeilschifter calls
it a legend; Bury and Romano consider it entirely incredible.[26] Even
if we take into consideration the general extremely tense atmosphere
of the year 526, when it was possible that war between Byzantium and
Ravenna might break out at any moment, a decision such as this by
the king almost on the eve of his death, a decision which would have
thrown Italy into one of the most ominous convulsions in her internal
history, would have been contradictory to all his policy. This contradiction becomes particularly striking when we read of the settlement

---

[24] Cassiod. *Variae*, V, 16–20. Migne, *PL*, LXIX, 656–660; ed. Mommsen, pp.
152–155. English transl. Hodgkin, pp. 274–277. Hodgkin entirely omits letters
18 and 19. See A. Gaudenzi, *Sui rapporti tra l'Italia e l'Impero d'Oriente*, pp. 73–
74. L. Schmidt, *Geschichte der Wandalen*, pp. 121 123; on the Vandal fleet,
pp. 173–174. F. Martroye, *L'Occident à l'époque byzantine: Goths et Vandales*
(Paris, 1904), p. 214. Gabotto, *Storia della Italia occidentale nel medio evo*,
pp. 460–461. Romano-Solmi, *Le dominazioni barbariche in Italia*, p. 218. W. Ensslin,
Theoderich der Grosse, p. 321; notes, pp. 389–390.

[25] *Anon. Valesianus*, 94–95: "Igitur Symmachus, scolasticus Iudaeus, jubente
non rege sed tyranno, dictavit praecepta die quarta feria, septimo kalend.
Septembr. indictione quarta, Olybrio consule, ut die dominico adveniente Arriani
basilicas catholicas invaderent . . . eodem die, quo se gaudebat ecclesias invadere
simul regnum et animam amisit" (ed. Cessi, pp. 20–21).

[26] G. Pfeilschifter, *Theoderich der Grosse*, p. 95. Bury, *op. cit.*, II, p. 158, n. 1.
Romano, *op. cit.*, p. 217. W. Ensslin, *op. cit.*, p. 327 (malevolent invention). As
late as 1938 we read: (Theodoric) imprisoned the Pope and ordered all Catholic
churches in Italy to be handed over to the Arians. On the very day on which
the latter decree was to be carried out, he died. K. S. Latourette, *A History of
the Expansion of Christianity*, II, *The Thousand Years of Uncertainty* A. D. 500–
A. D. 1000 (New York and London, 1938), p. 25. In 1947 L. Bréhier wrote:
"(Theodoric) prepared an edict of confiscation of the Orthodox churches" (*Vie
et mort de Byzance*, p. 22).

of the fortunes of his kingdom after his death, as it is preserved in the *Gothic History* of Iordanes. Shortly before his death Theodoric presented his grandson Athalaric, a child of ten years, son of Eutharic and his daughter Amalasuntha, to the leaders of the Gothic people and declared that he was their future king; and then, as if it were his last will and testament, he earnestly exhorted the Goths to be loyal to their new sovereign, to love the Senate and people of Rome, and to cultivate always peaceful and friendly relations with the Eastern emperor.[27]

The sources contemporary with Theodoric supply us with a very favorable picture of the deceased king. The Anonymus Valesianus says that he "did nothing wrong" (*nihil enim perperam gessit*), and praises his excellent administration and the economic conditions of his country. "He so won the good will of the neighboring nations that they offered to make treaties with him in the hope that he would be their king. Indeed, merchants flocked to him from the various provinces, for his organization was such that if anyone wished to send consignments of gold or silver in his domain, it was deemed as good as if it were within the walls of a city." [28] This picture is given by a chronicler closely connected with Ravenna. The verdict of the Byzantine writer, Procopius, who was to write the detailed story of the reconquest of Italy by Justinian, is as follows: "(Theodoric) was exceedingly careful to observe justice, he preserved the laws on a sure basis, he protected the land and kept it safe from the barbarians dwelling round about, and attained the highest possible degree of wisdom and manliness. And he himself committed scarcely a single act of injustice against his subjects [29] . . . And although in name Theodoric was a usurper (τύραννος), yet in fact he was as truly an emperor (βασιλεύς) as any who have distinguished themselves in this office from the beginning; and love for him among both Goths and Italians

---

[27] Jordanes, *Iordanis Getica*, LIX, 304: "ac si testamentali voce denuntians, ut regem colerent, senatum populumque Romanum amarent principemque Orientalem placatum semper propitiumque haberent post deum" (ed. Mommsen, p. 136). In the text I have not translated the last two words, post deum, which emphasize even more strongly the high respect to the emperor recommended by Theodoric to his people.

[28] Anon. Vales., 60; 72; ed. Cessi, p. 16; 18.

[29] Cf. Anon. Vales., 60: "nihil enim perperam gessit."

grew to be great, and that too contrary to the ordinary habits of men . . . he left to his subjects a keen sense of bereavement at his loss." [30]

Theodoric ruled thirty-three years (493–526), of which only the eight years fall into the period of Justin. Most of his reign had passed during the rule of Justin's predecessor Anastasius (491–518), when, even if relations between Constantinople and Ravenna were not cordial, there was no political or religious danger to Italy. During this happy period the exceptional traits of Theodoric's striking personality could freely reveal themselves: his religious tolerance, his admiration of Roman civilization, his love of justice, and his profound respect for the Eastern emperor. During this time Theodoric laid the foundations for strengthening his political power, especially, as we have pointed out above, through numerous marriage bonds with other Germanic kingdoms, and he created a vast and outwardly well consolidated Germanic political organization. Anastasius had paid no attention to this important factor in the West, probably failing to realize its potential importance.

During the last eight years of Theodoric's rule (518–526) many changes occurred. In the first half of this period Theodoric was encouraged and reassured by the new government in Constantinople: in 519 Justin nominated as his own colleague in the consulship Theodoric's son-in-law Eutharic, and in 522 Justin allowed Theodoric to nominate both consuls. But new forces in the Eastern empire were actively working which became a real danger to the Ostrogothic kingdom: religious persecutions, particularly of Arians, and the ever growing influence of Justin's nephew Justinian, whose very ambitious political plans concerning Italy began to manifest themselves more and more clearly. The last blow to Theodoric's tranquillity was the military alliance between Justin and the Vandal king Hilderic. The last four years of Theodoric's reign (522–526), accordingly, were filled with danger, fear, nervousness, and suspicion on the part of the king already grown old. Theodoric understood that both his own political security and the security of Arianism for his Italian Goths were at stake. In this hectic period the king, strained and exhausted, lost his temper; and to it belongs the deplorable execution of Boethius and Symmachus.

[30] Proc. B. G., I, 1, 26–31 (Dewing, V, 1, 26–31; III, pp. 10–13).

At this period also he maltreated Pope John on his return from Constantinople. But as I have pointed out above, the story of Theodoric's decree that on an appointed day, August 30, 526, the Arians should take possession of the Catholic churches, is not to be accepted.

A medieval legend of Theodoric's death narrates that a hermit, who resided on the Isle of Lipari, told a friend of Pope Gregory the Great that he had seen the Gothic king, beltless, unshod, with bound hands, thrown into the crater of the Isle of Vulcano because he had killed Pope John and the patrician Symmachus. And the pilgrim Willibald, in 721–727, on his way to Palestine wrote that they sailed to the Isle of Vulcano, which is Theodoric's hell (*Infernus Theodorici*).[31]

At the time of his death Theodoric's dominions comprised an enormous territory. They included Italy and Sicily, the two provinces of Raetia, Noricum, part of Pannonia, and Dalmatia; then farther west, Spain and Narbonensis, which, as we shall see later, were consigned to him. Provence was annexed to Italy from Burgundy. In other words, he had almost reëstablished the ancient empire for his own benefit, with the exception of Africa, Britain, and two-thirds of Gaul.

Theodoric's daughter Amalasuntha held the reins of government as regent during her son Athalaric's minority. Immediately after Athalaric's accession Amalasuntha wrote a letter to Justin which clearly reflects the tenseness of the situation, the menace of war, and her ardent desire to preserve peace at all costs. The letter was written in the name of Athalaric. "I might be justly reprehended, oh most clement lord," we read, "if I sought in a lukewarm manner (*tepide*) after your peace, for which my parents are known to have longed ardently (*ardentius*). The purple rank of our ancestors does not make us so famous, nor does the royal chair (*sella*) elevate us so much, as your all powerful grace renders us renowned. . . Hatred should be buried in the tomb; ire should perish." Then with reference to the fact that Athalaric's father Eutharic had been adopted by Justin, Athalaric proceeds: "For he who was born from your son, is by the

---

[31] *Gregorii Papae Dialogi*, IV, 30 (31): "in hanc vicinam Vulcani ollam jactatus est." Migne, *PL*, LXXVII, 369–370 (in Latin and Greek). *The Travels of Willibaldi*, A. D. 721–727, written from his own recital by a Nun of Heidenheim, in *Early Travels in Palestine*, ed. by Thomas Wright (London, 1848), p. 22.

laws of nature no stranger to you. Therefore I seek for peace not as a stranger (*longinquus*) but as a very close kinsman (*proximus*). . . Let our kingdom be obliged to you with ties of grace." Athalaric concludes his letter with the announcement that he would send to the emperor ambassadors who should make a pact of friendship similar to that which "your renowned predecessors had granted to our lord grandfather of blessed memory." [32]

This letter shows that war was in the air. Such words as "hatred" and "ire" of course reflect the tense atmosphere of the last two years of Theodoric's reign. Peace was badly needed and ardently desired by the regent Amalasuntha. A special mission was to go to Constantinople to smooth out difficulties and make peace. Probably Amalasuntha's efforts succeeded in averting war with the empire, for Iordanes in his *Gothic History* asserts that as long as Athalaricus and his mother were alive, they reigned nearly eight years in peace.[33]

The Italian historian Gaudenzi positively asserts that Justin began war on the Goths.[34] Referring to the letter just dealt with, he says that Justin was not moved by these supplications but started war on the Goths. Gaudenzi himself admits that almost no one of the modern writers speaks of this war, because they all relied upon the statement of Jordanes, which I have just quoted, that Athalaric passed his reign in peace and tranquillity. Gaudenzi states that this is a false assertion, and adds that Cassiodorus, in several places of his *Variae*, clearly indicates the wars which troubled the beginning of Athalaric's reign. Gaudenzi quotes two statements from the *Variae*. The first reference is to Athalaric's letter to Bishop Victorinus, which was probably written in 526 (VIII, 8). In this letter Athalaric asks for the Bishop's

[32] *Cassiodori Variae*, VIII, 1. As I have already pointed out above, some manuscripts refer this letter to Justinian; but it is now generally accepted that Justin is the correct reading. I am also inclined to refer the letter to Justin. Only one detail troubles me a little: the plural "your renowned predecessors (*decessores*)." If the letter is directed to Justin, the singular would seem more natural, because Anastasius was the only contemporary of Theodoric before Justin. Hodgkin's translation of this letter is too abridged; many important phrases are omitted (pp. 347–348).

[33] *Iordanis Getica*, LIX, 305: "quod praeceptum quamdiu Athalaricus rex ejusque mater adviverent, in omnibus custodientes pene per octo annos in pace regnarunt" (ed. Mommsen, p. 136).

[34] Gaudenzi, *Sui rapporti tra l'Italia e l'Impero d'Oriente*, pp. 82–83.

prayers "that the King of Heaven may confirm to us the human (*humana*) kingdom, subdue foreign nations before us, forgive us our sins," and so on. Of course, the words *gentes externas atterat* have a general meaning only and are not intended to refer to actual operations of war.[35] Similarly the meaning is general also in Gaudenzi's second reference, which is to Athalaric's letter to all the inhabitants of Reate and Nursia (*Variae*, VIII, 26), where the King writes: "You are so far moulded by the character of our grandfather that you willingly obey both the laws and the judges . . . Our enemies are being conclusively vanquished by our good customs, for they whom celestial power protects cannot have successful adversaries." [36] These two letters, then, give us no grounds whatever for deducing that Athalaric was at war with Justin. Moreover at the end of the same letter (VIII, 26) we have a statement which Gaudenzi evidently overlooked, and which in my opinion proves definitely that there was no war with Justin. "It is for your advantage that the Romans *are* at peace, who, in filling our treasury, multiply your donatives." [37]

Finally I wish to cite here the following words of Procopius: "After his (Theodoric's) death the kingdom was taken over by Athalaric, the son of Theodoric's daughter; he had reached the age of eight years and was being reared by his mother Amalasuntha; for his father had already departed from among men. And not long afterward Justinian succeeded to the imperial power in Byzantium." [38] Procopius, a contemporary writer particularly interested in Gothic affairs, fails to mention any hostilities between Athalaric and Justin. To sum up, Gaudenzi's opinion must be discarded. For one reason or another, the formidable fleet of one thousand dromones which had been so rapidly built during the last years of Theodoric's reign, did not go into action.

[35] *Cassiod. Variae*, VIII, 8: "Favete nunc orationibus sacris, nostris libenter auspiciis, ut Rex caelestis humana nobis regna confirmet, gentes externas atterat, peccata absolvat." In English by Hodgkin, p. 352.

[36] *Cassiod. Variae*, VIII, 26: "Robustius inimici nostri vincuntur moribus bonis. Quia quos superna protegunt, felices adversarios habere non possunt." Cf. a rather confusing translation by Hodgkin, p. 375.

[37] *Cassiod. Variae*, VIII, 26: "quia vobis proficit quod Romani quieti *sunt*, qui dum aeraria nostra ditant, vestra donativa multiplicant"; ed. Mommsen, p. 257. Hodgkin translates (p. 375): "that the Romans *be* at peace." But the text reads *sunt*, not *sint*.

[38] Proc. *B. G.*, I, 2, 1–2 (Dewing, V, 2, 1–2; III, pp. 14–15).

Theodoric's rather sudden death might have been the cause of this, in conjunction with the fact that Amalasuntha, who took over the government after him, wished to preserve peace with Byzantium at all costs.

THE VANDAL KINGDOM

Among other Germanic kingdoms the Vandal kingdom in Africa had very great importance both for the empire and for the Ostrogothic state of Theodoric. The conquest of the whole Roman province of Africa, the foundation of the Vandal kingdom there, and the occupation of many islands in the Mediterranean are connected with the name of the Vandal king Gaiseric, who died in 477. All the islands between Spain and Italy were conquered by the Vandals. A contemporary source, Victor, Bishop of Vita, lists Sicily, Sardinia, Corsica, Majorca, Minorca, Ebusa (now Ibiza), and "many others" (*et alias multas*).[39] Another contemporary writer, Salvianus, a priest of Massilia (Marseilles) points out the economic importance of Vandal conquests: the Vandals took the fiscal granaries such as Sardinia and Corsica, interrupted maritime communication, "cutting vital veins," and took Africa herself, almost "the soul of the state." [40]

The Vandals did not limit themselves to the occupation of these important islands. Their piratical naval expeditions and depredations extended far east. The most famous raid was in 455 when Gaiseric and his Vandals from North Africa entered Rome and for fourteen

[39] Victor Vitensis, *De persecutione vandalica*, I, 4. Migne, *PL*, LVIII, coll. 186–187; ed. K. Halm, *MGH*, *AA*, III, 1 (1879), 4; *CSEL*, VII (1881), 7, 13. Soon after, Gaiseric ceded Sicily to Odavacar. See L. Schmidt, *Geschichte der Wandalen*, p. 95. F. Martroye, Genséric. *La conquête vandale en Afrique et la destruction de l'Empire d'Occident* (Paris, 1907), p. 162.

[40] Salvianus, *De gubernatione Dei*, VI, 12, 68: "vastatis urbibus mari clausis et eversis Sardinia ac Sicilia, id est fiscalibus horreis, atque abscisis velut vitalibus venis, Africam ipsam, id est quasi animam captivavere reipublicae." Migne, *PL*, LIII, coll. 122; ed. C. Halm, *MGH*, *AA*, I, 1 (Berlin, 1877), p. 78; *CSEL*, VIII (1883), 144. See E. Besta, *La Sardegna Medioevale*, I (Palermo, 1908), pp. 2–3. Besta thinks that the capture of Sardinia took place after 455. A very good bibliography of Salvianus' life and works in O. Bardenhewer, *Gesch. der altkirchlichen Literatur*, IV, pp. 573–579. In 1942 a Russian historian, B. Grekov, used Salvian to show the superiority of the barbarians over the Romans. Salvian concludes: "Long live barbarians! Down with Rome!" B. Grekov, "At the Dawn (Na zare) of the Russian State," *Istorichesky Journal* (1942), no. 7, p. 15. By a misprint Grekov calls Salvian Silvian.

days plundered the city. According to Procopius, the Vandals plundered Illyricum, most of the Peloponnesus and the rest of Greece, and all the islands which lie near. From his exile in far-off Egypt, the famous Nestorius in his autobiography mentions that after Africa and Spain, "the great and glorious islands — I mean Sicily and Rhodes and many other great ones — and Rome itself have been delivered over to spoil unto the barbarian Vandal." [41] And the Bishop of Vita, Victor, concludes: "What Gaiseric has done in Spain, Italy, Dalmatia, Campania, Calabria, Apulia, Sicily, Sardinia, Bruttium (Britiis), Lucania, Epirus, or Greece (Ellade, Hellada), those who have suffered there will better narrate (in telling) their deplorable experiences." [42]

Such a powerful state as the Vandal kingdom, possessing not only a vast territory on the African continent but the most important and richest islands in the western Mediterranean and extending their ravages as far east as Rhodes, must have had very great importance both for the eastern empire and for the Ostrogothic kingdom. Matrimonial ties linked the dynasty of Gaiseric both with the empire and with Theodoric. Gaiseric's son and successor Huneric (477–484) married Eudocia, the elder daughter of the Western emperor Valentinian III, who died in 455; so that Gaiseric's fourth successor Hilderic (523–530), Justin's contemporary, was the grandson of Valentinian. Then about 500 Theodoric's own sister Amalafrida married Trasamund, king of the Vandals (496–523).

The third Vandal king, Huneric's successor, Gunthamund (484–496), looked with suspicion and jealousy on any relations between his African subjects and Constantinople. One episode may be mentioned here which pictures his excessive sensitiveness towards the Byzantine emperor. During his time there lived in Africa the poet Dracontius, a mediocre writer but still the most considerable of the obscure Latin poets between Sidonius and Corippus. He exercised his

[41] Proc. B. V., I, 5, 23; Dewing, III, 5, 23 (II, 52–53). Nestorius, Le livre d'Héraclide de Damas transl. by F. Nau (Paris, 1910), p. 331. Nestorius, The Bazaar of Heracleides, newly translated from the Syriac and edited with an introduction, notes and appendices by G. R. Driver and Leonard Hodgson (Oxford, 1925), p. 379.
[42] Victor Vit., I, 17. Migne, PL, LVIII, 202; MGH, AA, III, 1, p. 13; CSEL, VII, 22–23 (51).

rather facile talent of verse unwisely, to his lasting sorrow. In one of his poems he made the mistake of celebrating the Roman emperor, whom he failed to name but who was undoubtedly Zeno, instead of his own master Gunthamund. For this fault, which was magnified into a political offense, his property was confiscated, and he and his family were thrown into prison. The poem itself has not come down to us; but we learn about it from another poem, "Satisfaction to the King of the Vandals, Guntharius," which Dracontius wrote in his own defense. He wrote: "My fault had been to pass over in silence the modest masters, and to praise an unknown one who was not master." [43] But he received no pardon for his fault. I have enlarged on this rather insignificant episode, because it shows the very delicate balance in the relations between Carthage and Constantinople during Gunthamund's reign (484–496), which coincides with the rule of Zeno (474–491).

Under Gunthamund's successor, Trasamund (496–523), relations between Carthage, Ravenna, and Constantinople were satisfactory. Trasamund asked Theodoric to give him his sister Amalafrida to wife; and Theodoric sent him not only his bride but also a thousand notable Goths to serve as bodyguard, followed by a host of attendants amounting to about five thousand fighting men. As a result of this, Trasamund, according to Procopius, was accounted the strongest and most powerful of all those who had ruled over the Vandals. We have mentioned above that Trasamund sent wild animals to Rome for the celebration of Eutharic's consulship in 519. Procopius also states that Trasamund became as well a very special friend of Emperor Anastasius. In his letter to Pope Hormisdas on November 17, 519, Justin informed the Pope that for regulation of the position of the Catholic clergy in the Vandal Arian kingdom he had sent ambassadors "ad regem magnificum

---

[43] Dracontius, Dracontii Satisfactio ad Guntharium regem Vandalorum dum esset in vinculis, vv. 93–94:
> Culpa mihi fuerat dominos reticere modestos,
> Ignotumque mihi scribere, nec dominum.

See vv. 105–108, where the author regrets his poem and begs with tears for pardon. Migne, *PL*, LX, 912–913; 914; ed. Vollmer, *MGH*, *AA*, XIV (Berlin, 1905), p. 119; 120; ed. Vollmer, *Poetae Latini Minores*, V (Leipzig, 1914), p. 98. On Dracontius see Pauly-Wissowa, V, 2 (1905), 1635–1644. Schanz, *Geschichte der römischen Literatur*, IV, 2, 58–68. Bardenhewer, *op. cit.*, IV, 658–661. F. J. E. Raby, *A History of Christian-Latin Poetry from the Beginnings to the Close of the Middle Ages* (Oxford, 1927), pp. 96–99.

Trasamundum" and was waiting for their return.[44] Trasamund seems to have encouraged literature, and one of the poets of his time, Florentinus, wrote a panegyric in verse on Trasamund and his glorious and flourishing capital at Carthage.[45]

If under the Arian Vandal king Trasamund relations between Carthage and Constantinople were satisfactory, under his successor Hilderic (523–530), grandson of Valentinian III, they became friendly and cordial. We already know that Hilderic accepted Catholicism and leaned more and more towards Constantinople. Correspondingly, of course, his relations with Theodoric grew cooler, especially after he imprisoned Theodoric's sister, Amalafrida, the widow of the late Trasamund. One of the poets of his period wrote a panegyric on Hilderic in which he compares the latter's deeds with the achievements of the emperors Theodosius and Honorius, and concludes that in the person of Hilderic, "all-powerful Vandal king, heir of a double diadem," the great virtue of Valentinian brilliantly reveals itself.[46] We have already pointed out that the friendly relations between Hilderic and Justin ended in a formal alliance against Theodoric.

Summing up relations between Carthage and Constantinople, we have the following picture: If Theodoric regarded Italy as a portion of the empire, Gaiseric and his successors tried to establish a kingdom absolutely independent from Roman influence. The aggressive Vandal Arianism and persecution of the Catholic clergy down to the year 523, when Hilderic came to the throne, were also clear manifestations of

----

[44] Proc. *B. V.*, I, 8, 11–14; Dewing, III, 8, 11–14 (II, 76–77). Justin's letter to Pope Hormisdas, A. Thiel, *Epistolae romanorum pontificum genuinae*, I, ep. 101 (pp. 900–901); *Coll. Avellana*, no. 212 (p. 671). See L. Schmidt, *Geschichte der Vandalen*, p. 119. Trasamund had difficulties with some African nomads who successfully used against him a new sort of "cavalry" composed of dromedaries. "Never before had one overcome a cavalry (*ein Reiterheer*) with dromedaries." Fr. Altheim, *Die Krise der alten Welt*, I, 153–154.

[45] *Anthologia Latina*, ed. F. Bücheler and A. Riese, I (Leipzig, 1894), No. 376: "In laudem regis" (pp. 288–289).

[46] *Anthologia Latina*, I, No. 215 (pp. 182–183). The panegyric begins: "Vandalirice potens, gemini diadematis heres," and ends with the two following lines:

Ampla Valentiniani virtus cognita mundo
Hostibus addictis ostenditur arce nepotis.

Bury (II, 125, n. 6) calls the poet Florentinus. In Bücheler-Riese's edition no name is indicated.

their independent religious policy, which differed markedly from Theodoric's tolerance. To maintain control of all the islands in the Mediterranean, the Vandal kingdom must have possessed a strong navy. Thus up to the year 523 Byzantium had always present a mighty enemy who menaced her from the rear. After 523, however, when King Hilderic entirely reversed his policy, the Vandal kingdom became an ally of Constantinople; and in this new combination the Vandal fleet supplied very essential support to Byzantium, whose navy was not strong. Thus during the last four years of Justin's reign, an allied front was ready for further activities against Theodoric and potentially against his successors. But this alliance was not destined to be long-lived.

The Byzantino-Vandal relations were a severe blow to Theodoric. This particularly becomes clear if we catch a glimpse of the previous relations between these countries. From the time of the foundation of the Vandal kingdom, Arianism was the official religion, intolerant and aggressive in Africa, tolerant and mild in Italy. About 500 Theodoric's sister Amalafrida was sent to Africa to marry Trasamund. Between the two countries were no territorial disputes or misunderstandings; Theodoric had nothing to fear from the south. But in 523 everything changed, when King Hilderic completely reversed his policy in favor of the eastern empire and threw Theodoric's sister Amalafrida, now a widow, into prison, where she died. The Vandal kingdom became Theodoric's enemy. A German historian calls this new trend in the Vandal policy "an incredible suicidal shortsightedness which brought about, in fact, the fall first of the Vandals and then of the Ostrogoths." [47]

The Burgundian Kingdom

Unlike the Ostrogothic or Vandal kingdoms, the Burgundian kingdom had no immediate frontier with the empire: the Ostrogothic kingdom of Theodoric lay between the two countries. This was the so-called second Burgundian kingdom, which had been founded in 443 in Sapaudia (Savoy), south of Lake Geneva, on territory which had been assigned by the Roman government to the Burgundians.

[47] G. Pfeilschifter, *Theoderich der Grosse*, p. 90.

Gradually the Burgundian power extended at the expense of the imperial provinces. Arianism was the creed of the Burgundian rulers until the time of Sigismund (516–523), Theodoric's son-in-law and Justin's contemporary, who was converted to Catholicism. Sigismund's father and predecessor, Gundobad, who died in 516, an Arian, had been on friendly terms with Emperor Anastasius.

During Justin's reign there were no direct connections with the empire. But the characteristic feature of Sigismund's policy was his almost servile attitude towards the empire. This is rather surprising because the natural ally of the Burgundians against their powerful neighbor, the Frankish king, was obviously the Ostrogothic king. But, as Hodgkin writes, "instead of recognizing this fact, Sigismund exhausted the vocabulary of servitude in grovelling self-prostration before the Emperor Anastasius, a sovereign whose power was too remote from the scene of action to be of the slightest service to him, when the time of trial should come." [48] I shall give here some statements from a letter of Avitus, Bishop of Vienna, who converted Sigismund to Catholicism, a letter written in the name of King Sigismund himself and addressed to the Emperor Anastasius. "Although we seem to rule over our own people, we believe that we are nothing else but your warriors . . . our fatherland is your country . . . Your people are my people, but I enjoy more serving you than ruling over this (people)." [49] Theodoric was informed of the letter and was alarmed at the prospect of political intimacy between Burgundy and Constantinople; it is not surprising that, according to another letter of Avitus also addressed to Anastasius, he did not allow Sigismund's messengers to travel through Italy to the East.[50]

---

[48] Hodgkin, *Italy and Her Invaders*, III, p. 368.

[49] Avitus, Viennensis episcopus, *Epistola* LXXXIII (Migne, *PL*, LIX, coll. 285); ed. Peiper, ep. XCIII (83); *MGH*, *AA*, VI, 2, p. 100: "Cumque gentem nostram videamur regere, non aliud nos quam milites vestros credimus ordinari . . . patria nostra vester orbis est. vester quidem est populus meus, sed me plus servire vobis quam illi praeesse delectat." See L. Schmidt, *Geschichte der deutschen Stämme*, p. 395.

[50] Avitus, ep. LXXXIV (*PL*, LIX, 287); ed. Peiper, ep. XCIV (84), p. 101: "Interclusum est ergo atque prohibitum relationibus destinatis iter arreptum." This refers to a letter of Sigismund to the Emperor Anastasius. See L. Schmidt, *op. cit.*, p. 395. R. Helm, *Untersuchungen*, *Archiv für Urkundenforschung*, XII, p. 412.

These two letters of Sigismund expressing his devotion to the eastern empire were addressed to Anastasius. The same friendly relations with the empire and strained relations with Theodoric evidently continued when Justin came to the throne. There is no direct evidence on the subject. We know that the consulship granted in 519 by Justin to Eutharic, son-in-law of Theodoric, was not recognized in Burgundy. In 523 the Franks captured Sigismund and his family and subdued a part of the kingdom, and at the same time Theodoric sent his force on Burgundy and annexed the district between the Isère and the Durance to his realm. But these events and those of the following years, till the death of Justin, have no connection whatever with Constantinople. Nor is there any direct connection with Constantinople in the history of the Visigothic kingdom in Spain and in the south of France, and the powerful Frankish kingdom in the period of Justin, nor in their own conflicts with each other, and the participation of Theodoric in those political combinations and changes in western Europe. The fact may be mentioned here that Justin's predecessor, the monophysite Anastasius, conferred upon the Frankish king Clovis, the ardent champion of Catholic orthodoxy, an honorary consulship.[51]

For regarding the ambitious Byzantine plans directed by Justinian concerning Italy and Africa which were to reveal themselves fully after Justin's death, one fact was of very considerable importance: this is the gradual collapse of Theodoric's matrimonial ties with other Germanic kingdoms, which he had hoped would serve as foundation for his political strength and the future complete independence of his own kingdom from Constantinople.

[51] Gregory of Tours, *Historia Francorum*, II, 38.

CHAPTER SEVEN

Economic Condition of the Empire under Justin

Although the following presentation of the rather deplorable economic conditions of the empire during Justin's reign necessarily cannot be too thorough, I wish to indicate the most essential causes of this situation; and these causes are many and various. Almost continuous barbarian invasions in the north, in the Balkans; Arabo-Persian conflicts on the eastern border, in Syria and Mesopotamia; and many natural disasters, such as earthquakes, fires, floods, which struck practically the whole territory of the empire: these may be regarded as the most important causes of the economic decline of the period. We witness also a considerable decline of trade in the south, in the Red Sea and in the Indian Ocean, which was caused by the growing superiority of the Persian commercial fleet, and to a certain extent by the Himyaro-Ethiopic war in South Arabia, which for a time cut off regular trade relations between the Mediterranean and the southern waters. A great deal of money was needed to restore the destroyed and damaged cities as well as to keep alive their ruined inhabitants. If we add to these facts the expenses of the erection of some new buildings, especially churches, and also of the display of magnificent games, such as those organized for the inauguration of Justinian's consulship in 525, we realize that the fund Anastasius had left in the imperial treasury was not large enough to meet all the demands upon it.

NATURAL DISASTERS

The empire under Justin lived through many internal difficulties and disasters which caused deep repercussions in the economic welfare and financial stability of its vast territory. Justin ruled an empire economically ruined and financially disturbed, and the closing years of his reign saw no trace of economic recuperation or financial readjustment. In addition to continuous barbarian invasions in the north from beyond the Danube into the Balkan Peninsula, invasions which continued under

Justin as they had occurred under his predecessors, and in addition to the danger along the long eastern border from the Sassanids and some hostile Arabian tribes, the nine years of Justin's reign were exceptionally unfortunate in natural disasters. Like a destructive avalanche a series of earthquakes, fires, and floods swept over the whole territory of the empire.

Earthquakes, fires, floods, drought, locusts, and plague are all mentioned and described in our sources. Earthquakes occupy the first place; they occurred in all regions, in the Balkans, in Greece, in Asia Minor, in Syria, and in Constantinople itself. A catastrophic earthquake visited Antioch, in Syria, on May 29, 526. The chronicler John Malalas who lived at Antioch and possibly was an eyewitness of the disaster, has left a detailed account of it.[1]

In the consulship of Olybrius, on May 29, 526, the day of the great feast of the Ascension of our Lord,[2] Antioch, the third city in the eastern Roman Empire, after Constantinople and Alexandria, was swarming with a great multitude of people; there were present not

---

[1] Malalas, 419–421. Slavonic version, Istrin, pp. 20–24, IV; in English, Spinka, pp. 125–131. It is to be noted that many details which are lacking in the Greek text are preserved in the Church Slavonic version. Other sources: Proc., B. P., II, 14, 6–7 (Haury, I, 214; Dewing, I, 382–383). John Lydus, De magistratibus, III, 54 (CSHB, pp. 246–247; Wuensch, p. 143). Evagrius, IV, 5 (Migne, PG, LXXXVI, 2, col. 2709–2712; Bidez-Parmentier, pp. 155–156). Theoph., 172. Anastasii Chron. tripertita, pp. 132–133. George Monachus, ed. de Boor, II, 626 (ed. Muralt, pp. 524–525). John of Nikiu, XC, 26 (Charles, p. 135). Cedr., I, 640–641. Com. Marcell., a. 526 (ed. Mommsen, p. 102). Syriac sources: Pseudo-Zach. of Mityl., VIII, 4 (Hamilton-Brooks, p. 205; Ahrens-Krüger, pp. 156–157). Chronicle of Edessa, XCVII (XCVI); XCIX (XCVII); Hallier, p. 132; 134; Guidi, p. 10; Cowper, p. 38. Iacobi Edesseni Chronicon, trans. E. W. Brooks, p. 240. Chronicon Anonymum ad A. D. 819, transl. Chabot (1937), p. 5. Mich. le Syrien, IX, 16; Chabot, II, 181–182. Armenian version by Langlois, p. 181. Gregorii Barhebraei Chronicon Ecclesiasticum, by Abbeloos and Lamy, I, 200. Chronicon Anonymum ad annum Christi 1234 pertinens, transl. by Chabot, p. 151. Russian sources: The Russian Chronograph: I, The Chronograph of the version 1512; II, The Chronograph of Western-Russian Version, PSRL, XXII, 1, pp. 292–293; XXII, 2, p. 108. The Russian account is based on the Chronicle of Georgius Monachus.

[2] The date of this earthquake is absolutely exact. See some doubts, 525, 526, or 527, in A. Perrey, "Mémoire sur les tremblements de terre ressentis dans la péninsule turco-hellénique et en Syrie," Mémoires couronnés et mémoires des savants étrangers, XXIII (Bruxelles, 1850), p. 9. Misprint: 626 for 526 in C. Karalevskij, "Antioche," Dictionnaire d'histoire et de géographique ecclésiastiques, par Baudrillart, XV–XVI (1922), col. 577.

only the citizens but also many strangers who had come for Ascension Day. The splendor of the city, its good climate, and the beauty of its churches were such that those strangers who had seen them called the city the peaceful harbor of the world and the refuge of the universe. In an atmosphere of wealth, prosperity, and festive feeling, as the bells of the church named Kration began to ring for the holy service, at that moment an earthquake began. To crown the calamity, along with the earthquake a terrible fire broke out. Destruction and desolation were complete. According to John Malalas, not a single dwelling, nor any sort of house, nor a stall of the city remained undestroyed. No holy church, nor monastery, nor any other holy place was left unruined. The Great Church, which had been founded by Constantine the Great, and which had no equal even among the Greeks, remained standing for five days after everything else had fallen. But suddenly even it caught on fire and collapsed to the ground.

The great church of the Archangel Michael which had been erected by Emperor Zeno, and the Church of the Holy Virgin Mary, which had remained undamaged by the earthquake, also caught fire and fell. The Church of the Holy Prophets and that of Saint Zacharias fell to the ground. In several places only shattered walls still stood, threatening death; and many of them fell, killing those living among them and burying in the debris the passers-by. Quakes and fires raged furiously; and those dwellings and churches which had not been destroyed by the earthquake were demolished to their foundations by the fire. According to the testimony of witnesses, the number of those who perished, citizens and strangers, men and women, children and old people, ranged from two hundred and fifty thousand souls to three hundred thousand.[3]

As usual in such catastrophes, many deplorable acts of violence and robbery are noted in our sources. Some of the uninjured citizens seized whatever necessities for the future they could, and carrying them ran away. But they were met by soldiers and strangers who happened to be there; and the latter robbed and despoiled the fugitives. They were likewise robbed by bandits, who killed many of those who refused to

[3] Malalas, 420, 6–7: 250,000. Procopius, II, 14, 6: 300,000. John of Nikiu, XC, 29: 250,000.

surrender their property. Having entered the city, strangers pillaged in the ruins. They found caskets of silver plate, as well as silver and gold coins lying scattered about. They found many women bedecked with much gold, precious stones, and pearls, and robbed them. Among the bandits was a certain Thomas, surnamed of Evreos (the Hebrew?), a *silentiarius* by rank, who along with his slaves committed many robberies. He had escaped the earthquake unscathed, and lived outside the city two or three stadia away, opposite the gates of Saint Julian. There he despoiled those who were trying to run away and took much gold from those who were buried in the ruins. He continued this for four days, gathering much gold, silver, and other property. Then he suddenly collapsed, although apparently a healthy and strong man, and died, not having even had time to count up all he had stolen. At his death all his property was dissipated, stolen, and destroyed, so that nothing was left him but the robe he wore. He was buried in the ruins of the same spot where he died, because the authorities were afraid of violence on the part of the citizens who clamored against him.

The pious John Malalas explains this catastrophe as a manifestation of the wrath of God who sent the disaster as punishment for the sins and transgressions of the Antiochenes. According to John, all bandits and robbers met a miserable death, confessing their sins. In his story Malalas tells many wonders connected with the earthquake and fire which he himself calls marvelous and incredible, which no human tongue can express, and of which only immortal God knows the secret. Naive and tinged with legend as it is, the description of John Malalas of the Antiochene catastrophe is nonetheless invaluable to us; in addition to a vivid and appalling picture of the disaster itself, Malalas supplies us with much priceless data on the topography and temples of Antioch.

The Patriarch of Antioch, Euphrasius, perished during the earthquake and fire. According to Pseudo-Zachariah (VIII, 4), he fell into a boiling cauldron of wax and died;[4] according to the *Chronicle of*

---

[4] See also *Chronicon Anonymum ad A. D. 819*, transl. by Chabot, p. 5: "Cum esset in triclinio, cecidit in cadum picis, qui erat in taberna inferiore, et mortuus est in hoc motu." This *Chronicle* also relates that during the earthquake in Antioch the bishop of Edessa, Asclepius, died.

Edessa (XCIX), Euphrasius was buried under a ruined house where his wailing cry sounded from under the debris the whole day through. The great multitude of unburied corpses which in a state of decomposition infected the air threatened the survivors with the danger of an epidemic.[5]

It was a hard task for the prefect of the Orient to restore the ruined city; he needed enormous amounts of money even to clear away the numberless ruins. The government did its best to restore the city: "with strenuous toil, with large sums of money, and with great energy on the part of the workers the city was rising again as if from darkness (from Erebus), for it was unsafe to leave the capital of Syria thrown to the ground." [6] The patriarch Ephraim, Euprasius' successor, in his turn, restored the destroyed Great Church of Antioch and consecrated it for the second time.[7] Most of these repairs and restorations which Justin started were completed after his death under Justinian. But the horrible earthquake of 526 put an end to Antioch's greatness. The finds of excavators of our own day fully bear out the great extent of the catastrophe.

Apparently before the fire and earthquake which destroyed Antioch in 526 there had been another great fire in the city. The section from the Chapel (τοῦ μαρτυρίου) of Saint Stephen down to the palace of the *comes orientis*, Anatolius Carinus, had been burnt and many people had perished. Fires had also burst out in the neighborhood of the city. Through the intercession of the Patriarch of Antioch, Euphrasius, Justin sent to the burned regions two centenaria of gold.[8]

Simultaneously with the Antioch disaster, severe damage occurred

[5] Malalas, 420, 15–16: ἀπέθνησκον βιαίως, οἱ μὲν σηπόμενοι . . . Mich. le Syr., IX, 16; Chabot, II, 182, 1. See H. Zinsser, *Rats, Lice and History* (Boston, 1935), p. 144.

[6] John Lydus, *De magistratibus*, III, 54: οὐδὲ γὰρ ἦν ἀσφαλὲς τὴν Σύρων πρωτεύουσαν παριδεῖν ἐρριμμένην εἰς ἔδαφος. ὡς δὲ κόπῳ πολλῷ καὶ χρημάτων ἀφθονίᾳ καὶ τεχνῶν συνεργείᾳ ὥσπερ ἐρεβόθεν ἡ πόλις ἀνεφύετο (*CSHB*, p. 247; Wuensch, p. 143).

[7] Zach. of Mityl., X, 5; Hamilton-Brooks, p. 311; Ahrens-Krüger, p. 246. Michel le Syrien, IX, 24; Chabot, p. 207. See R. Devreesse, *Le patriarcat d'Antioche*, p. 109.

[8] Malalas, 417; Istrin, 19–20; Spinka, 124. In the printed Greek text of Malalas, this fire is described before the catastrophe of 526; but the name of the patriarch is given as Ephraim, who was appointed after 526. Therefore I am inclined to accept the name of Euphrasius, who is named in the Slavonic version of Malalas, and who perished, as we know, in 526. It is easy to confuse these two names.

in Seleucia in Syria, Daphne, the suburb of Antioch, and their neighborhood for twenty miles around, evidently caused by the same earthquake.[9]

Justin was deeply impressed by these disasters. He sent for the restoration of the ruined cities a large amount of money, more centenaria of gold, according to the Slavonic version of Malalas, than any other emperor had sent before. As soon as he heard of the calamity, he took off his crown and purple robe, mourning and weeping for a long time. All spectacles were cancelled. On the Pentecost [10] he went to Saint Sophia, walking from the palace to the cathedral without his crown and clad only in a purple robe, and he wept before the nobles and citizens. All the nobles following the emperor were also dressed in mourning robes.

Justin sent Comes Carinus with five centenaria of gold to start the work of restoration. At the same time he sent the patrician Phocas, a rich man, in company with the patrician Asterius, "a wise man," instructing them to save all survivors and to restore quickly all the buildings of the city, public baths, the water system, the bridges across the river. The emperor was particularly interested in Antioch, because for a long time he had enjoyed living in this city, when under Anastasius he took part in the war on the Persians.[11]

During the first years of Justin's reign the Balkan Peninsula was visited by earthquakes several times. Dyrrachium in Epirus, the native city of the late emperor Anastasius, which he had adorned with many beautiful buildings including the hippodrome, was badly damaged. Corinth in Greece suffered the same fate. Pompioupolis in Mysia was so severely shaken that half of it with its residents was actually swallowed in the earth, and the men, from under the earth, implored

---

[9] Malalas, 421. Istrin, pp. 23–24; Spinka, p. 131. John of Ephesus, Nau, *Revue de l'Orient*, II, 473–474. John of Nikiu, XC, 33 (Charles, p. 136). *Iacobi Edesseni Chronicon*, Brooks, p. 240. Mich. le Syrien, IX, 16; Chabot, II, 183.

[10] Malalas, 421: ἁγίας πεντηκοστῆς καταλαβούσης. According to Spinka (p. 131) the Slavonic version records: on Holy Thursday of the Great Week. This is absolutely impossible from the chronological point of view. J. A. Cramer, *Anecdota graeca parisiensia*, II, p. 319.

[11] Malalas, p. 422. Istrin, pp. 20–24; Spinka, pp. 131–132. In my description of the Antioch earthquake I have depended largely on Spinka's English translation of the Slavonic version of Malalas, which, as I have noted above, gives many more details than the printed Greek text.

help. Anazarb in Cilicia, Asia Minor, was also badly damaged. And it is worth pointing out that in all these cases Justin took measures for the care of the population of the ruined cities and for the restoration of their buildings.[12] Constantinople itself was visited by an earthquake also; but evidently the capital escaped severe damage.[13]

In addition to the earthquakes, on April 22, 525 A. D. a disastrous flood struck Edessa. The best and principal contemporary authority on this event is John of Ephesus, who vividly describes the disaster, and whose narrative I follow. Towards the third hour of the night, when a great number of people were asleep, while others were washing themselves in the public bathhouses or taking their meals, the water in the river Daisan (Skirtus) which traverses Edessa became unusually high and entered the city. The wall in the upper part of the river suddenly fell into the water and obstructed its course, so that the deluge of water spread over the city; it filled all the places and houses which were close to the river. In one or two hours the entire city was inundated and the water suddenly entered the public bathhouse by all the doors and suffocated all those who were there; when they opened the doors in order to go out and flee, the water entered through these doors and covered all those who were downstairs; they were suffocated and perished like one man; as to those who were upstairs, when they started to flee in order to descend and escape, the water caught them and they were drowned. Some were asleep and saw nothing, but their houses, which were not well built, were washed away, and they themselves were also drowned. Those only were saved whose houses were built of stone and lime in the lower section of the city, near the river, so

---

[12] Dyrrachium: Malalas, 417, 20; Istrin, 19–20; Spinka, 124. Evagr., IV, 8. Theoph., 168. Cedr., I, 638. Mich. le Syr., IX, 16; II, 183. Corinth: Mal. 418; Istrin, 19–20; Spinka, 124. Theoph., 168. Jacob of Edessa, 240. John of Ephesus, Nau, *R. de l'Orient Chr.*, II, 474. Cedr., I, 638. Mich. le Syr., IX, 16; II, 183. Pompioupolis: Georg. Mon., ed. de Boor, II, 626 (Muralt, 525); Slavonic version, Istrin, I, 411. Cedr., I, 641. Zonaras, XIV, 31 (*CSHB*, III, 149). From Georgius Monachus Russian Annals, XXII, 1, p. 293; XXII, 2, p. 108. Anazarb: Mal., 418; Istrin, 19–20; Spinka, 124. Theoph., 171. John of Ephesus, Nau, p. 474. Cedr., I, 639. Zon., XIV, 31 (*CSHB*, III, 149). Mich. le Syr., II, 183. J. A. Cramer, *Anecdota Paris.*, II, 319.

[13] Georgius Monachus, II, 626 (Muralt, 524). J. A. Cramer, *Anecdota graeca Parisiensia*, II, p. 319. Cedr., I, 640. From Georgius Monachus Russian Annals, XXII, 1, p. 292; XXII, 2, p. 108.

that they withstood the water and failed to collapse. The elevated sections or those which were located on the mountain were also safe. The towers of the wall were overthrown and carried away by the water, which also swept away the dead bodies. The palace was carried away. The churches of Edessa collapsed, among them the cathedral, the so-called "Great Church" or Saint Sophia. This famous church, which had been founded in 313 and enlarged in 327–328, was probably given the name of Saint Sophia about 345–346. It is interesting to note that the name of Saint Sophia as applied to the church of Edessa appeared shortly after the foundation of Saint Sophia in Constantinople.

Not only the city proper, but all the surrounding country was inundated and thoroughly devastated. The river Daisan carried the bodies of men and animals, with all sorts of debris, down to the Euphrates. When the flood had receded, the city and its surroundings were deserted for many days, and some survivors were looking for and burying the corpses "with great sorrow and great suffering." The Slavonic version of Malalas narrates that "other old dwellers who were driven from the city asserted that at other times the city had been inundated by this river in a similar manner, but it had never destroyed all, as now." According to a legend which arose in connection with the disaster, some people who, after the cessation of the flood were building foundations of new dwellings near the river, found a large stone slab on which in carved letters was the following inscription: "The river Skirtus (Scirtus) will play bad tricks upon the citizens." As in cases of other similar disasters, Justin sent much money to Edessa and gave generous help to the survivors. He evidently started the restoration of the ruined city. The wall which was erected by Justin at Edessa is still standing today.[14] He even changed the name of the revived city to Justinopolis. We must realize, however, that the city hardly required help on a large scale because so few survivors remained. According to Procopius, the city lost one third of its population.[15] The real credit for the restoration of Edessa, however, is to be given to Justin's successor, Justinian.

[14] See P. Gindler, *Graf Balduin I von Edessa* (Halle a. S., 1901), p. 36. G. Schlumberger, l'épopée byzantine, III (Paris, 1905), p. 108 and note 1.
[15] The second part of the *History* of John of Ephesus, F. Nau, *Revue de l'Orient Chrétien*, II, pp. 470–473 (Syriac text and French translation). On p. 472

Justinian reconstructed in great splendor the destroyed church of Saint Sophia under the Bishop of Edessa Amidonius. A Syriac hymn (in Syriac *sugitha*) of the sixth century describes the magnificence of the new cathedral, whose architects were probably Asaph and Addai.[16] Later Arab historians and geographers celebrated the magnificent cathedral of Edessa as one of the wonders of the world.[17] We may note that the reconstruction of Saint Sophia in Edessa also coincided with the erection of the new building of Saint Sophia in Constantinople.

In Syria a fire broke out in the temple of Solomon in Heliopolis-Baalbek, in the forest of Lebanon. Lightning struck the temple, reduced its stones to powder, overthrew its pillars, and entirely destroyed the

---

of the French translation, 1, 4, by misprint, is given the wrong year (according to the local era), 846 for 836; in the original Syriac the year is correct. The exact date of the flood in Zach. of Mitylene, VIII, 4; Hamilton-Brooks, p. 204; Ahrens-Krüger, p. 154; note p. 356. Brief mention in the *Chronicle of Edessa*, XC (XCI); Hallier, p. 128; Guidi, p. 9; Cowper, p. 37. *Chronicon a. 846*, Brooks, p. 169. Michel le Syrien, IX, 12 (Chabot, II, 169); IX, 16 (Chabot, II, 179–180; from John of Ephesus). Armenian version by V. Langlois, pp. 176–177; 180. *Chronicon Anonymum ad annum Christi 1234 pertinens*, transl. by Chabot (1937), pp. 150–151. Brief story and legendary tradition in Malalas, 418–419; Slavonic version, Istrin, pp. 19–20; Spinka, pp. 124–125. Procopius, *De aedificiis*, II, 7, 5 (one third of the population perished); Anecdota, XVIII, 38: μύριοι. Evagrius, IV, 8: πλῆθος ἀναρίθμητον ἀπολέσθαι; ed. Bidez-Parmentier, p. 159. Theoph., p. 171 (from Malalas) = Cramer, *Anecd. Paris*, II, 319–320. Cedr., I, 639. Zon. XIV, 5, 29–30; *CSHB*, III, 149. See R. Duval, *Histoire d'Edesse*, p. 148.

[16] Procopius, *De aedificiis*, II, 7, 6: βασιλεὺς δὲ Ἰουστινιανὸς μὴ ὅτι ἀνεσώσατο τῇ πόλει τὰ καθηρημένα εὐθὺς ἄπαντα, ἐν οἷς ἥ τε τῶν Χριστιανῶν ἐκκλημία. Procopius' ἐκκλησία must mean the cathedral, *i.e.*, Saint Sophia. On Saint Sophia of Edessa and on the Syriac hymn, which supplies us with the names of the bishop Amidonius and the two potential architects, see A. Baumstark, "Vorjustinianische kirchliche Bauten in Edessa," *Oriens Christianus*, IV (1904), pp. 164–183; especially pp. 165–166; 170. H. Goussen, "Ueber eine Sugitha auf die Kathedrale von Edessa," *Le Muséon*, XXXVIII (1925), pp. 117–136; a German translation of the 'sugitha' with notes, pp. 120–123; the Syriac text, pp. 118–119. A. Dupont-Sommer, "Une hymne syriaque sur la Cathédrale d'Edesse," *Cahiers archéologiques*, II (Paris, 1947), pp. 29–39; a French translation of the hymn, pp. 30–32. A. Grabar, "Le témoignage d'une hymne syriaque sur l'architecture de la Cathédrale d'Edesse au VIe siècle et sur la symbolique de l'édifice chrétien," *Cahiers archéologiques*, II (Paris, 1947), pp. 41–67; especially pp. 41–43.

[17] See R. Duval, *op. cit.*, pp. 15–16. G. Le Strange, *The Lands of the Eastern Caliphate*, p. 104.

building. In place of the destroyed temple, Justin built the church dedicated to the Holy Virgin, the Theotokos.[18]

Towards the end of Justin's reign in the years 525–526 many damaging natural phenomena are mentioned in our sources in various regions of the empire: there was drought in some places; harvests were small; water was lacking in the wells. The flow of the waters of Shiluho, in the southern quarter of Jerusalem, was stopped for fifteen years. Great swarms of locusts devastated the fields. In some places deep snow and heavy frost destroyed trees and vineyards. A terrible plague broke out and lasted six years. Unfortunately, our sources fail to define the regions affected by these calamities.[19] This list of natural disasters which struck the empire, obviously incomplete as it is, clearly shows us that its many regions suffered great devastation and were economically almost entirely ruined.

TRADE AND COMMERCE

If we leave the consideration of the natural disasters of the period and turn our attention to other aspects of the internal situation of Justin's empire, the general picture is still not very encouraging. Under Justin, as under his predecessors, Zeno and Anastasius I, the western region of the Mediterranean did not belong to the empire. Sardinia, Corsica, and the Balearic Islands were lost to the Vandals soon after 455. Sicily passed somewhat later under the dominion of Gaiseric, who seems also to have occupied without resistance the two Mauretanian provinces in North Africa. Then Odovacar induced Gaiseric, who died in 477, to cede Sicily to him. Italy, with a large territory along the eastern coast of the Adriatic Sea, belonged to the Ostrogothic king, Theodoric. These territorial changes were economically very detrimental to the empire, which lost such immensely rich granaries as Sardinia, Sicily, and North Africa.

The northern region of the empire, the Balkan Peninsula, including

---

[18] Zach. of Mit., VIII, 4; Hamilton-Brooks, p. 204; Ahrens-Krüger, pp. 155–156. Mich. le Syr., IX, 16; Chabot, II, 179. According to the Scripture, Solomon built the temple and stored arms in it. I Kings IX, 19.

[19] Zach. of Mit., VIII, 4; Hamilton-Brooks, p. 204; Ahrens-Krüger, p. 154. Agapius (Mahboub), ed. Vasiliev, p. 425 (165). Mich. le Syr., IX, 16; Chabot, II, 179. *Chronique de Seert*, ed. by Addai Scher, p. 140 (48).

Greece proper, for the greater part was devastated and economically ruined. In addition to the Germanic and Hunnic depredations in the fourth and fifth centuries, the Bulgarians and other northern barbarians, including the Slavs, committed severe devastation in the Balkans beginning with the end of the fifth century. Their depredations were frequent and widespread. We have a very important record which tells us that in 517 at the very end of Anastasius' reign, barbarian riders devastated Macedonia and Thessaly, and reached Thermopylae and "the ancient Epirus." [20] Procopius in his *Anecdota* writes that from the time when Justinian took over the Roman Empire, all Illyricum and Thrace, comprising the whole expanse of country from the Ionian Gulf (the Adriatic Sea) to the outskirts of Byzantium, including Greece and the Thracian Chersonnese, was overrun practically every year by Huns, Sclavenes, and Antae, who wrought frightful havoc among the inhabitants of the region.[21] Procopius states that these particular devastations began at the time when Justinian took over the power; but by the words "when Justinian took over the power" he may well have meant to identify the period starting with Justin's accession in 518. Justinian's influence and power began to be felt from the very beginning of Justin's reign. Procopius knew this and pointed it out several times in his works. He reports that barbarian devastations continued, steadily increasing in ferocity and aggressiveness. Justin thus received the northern provinces of his empire in a state of decline and ruin, and so far as their agricultural produce was concerned, they were a liability rather than an asset to him.

Apparently Thessalonica, the most important point of the empire in the Balkans, was spared during the crucial period of barbarian invasions and earthquakes in the fifth century and at the beginning of the sixth; its mint was operating, although probably not very effectively, for only a few gold coins from it, particularly the golden solidi, are known from Justin's time.[22] The great Via Egnatia, which ran through Thessalonica, was not safe, especially in the section between Thessalonica and

---

[20] *Marcellini Chron.* ad a. 517: "duae tunc Macedoniae Thessaliaque vastatae et usque Thermopylas veteremque Epirum Getae equites depraedati sunt." Mommsen, *Chr. Min.*, II, 100. See above.

[21] Proc., *Anecdota*, XVIII, 20; Dewing, VI, 216–217.

[22] See for example Wroth, I, 17. Tolstoy, *Byzantine Coins*, III, pp. 236–237.

Dyrrhachium, which passed through western Macedonia and Epirus, regions which had been several times devastated by barbarian incursions; and it is not to be forgotten that one of the two western terminals of the road, Dyrrhachium, was badly damaged by an earthquake.

Justin's predecessor, Anastasius, realizing the imminent danger to the capital and its immediate neighborhood, had built a Long Wall, the line of which can still be traced from the Propontis to the Black Sea, at a distance of about forty miles west of Constantinople. For a long time, the Anastasian Wall successfully protected the southeast of the peninsula from barbarian raids; and though its fortifications later on proved not sufficiently strong, the Wall for the period of Justin I considerably increased the security of the capital. In addition to its strategic importance, it was of economic importance also in that it at the same time protected from hostile incursions the suburbs and a considerable tract of the rich and populous country outside the Theodosian Walls.

The undated law of Anastasius I, which probably belongs to the first period of his reign, about 491–505, and which was evidently issued before the erection of the Anastasian Wall, has survived, and it well reflects the deplorable situation in the Balkans. The law deals with the region nearest to the capital, Thrace. "In Thrace taxes are not paid in full; because of barbarian incursions the peasants have decreased in number and have not enough (food) to contribute provisions to the soldiers who are stationed there." [23]

This law of Anastasius pictures well the deplorable situation of Thrace during his own reign; but this picture may with complete certainty be referred to Justin's time too, and the conditions in effect in Thrace existed also in many other regions of the peninsula. The ruined population, and particularly the peasant farmers, who were an overwhelming majority, were leaving their homes and idle uncultivated fields, seeking to save their own lives and to find a better

[23] *Cod. Just.*, X, 27, 2, 10: ἐν Θράκῃ γὰρ, ἐπειδὴ οὐκ εἰς ὁλόκληρον εἰσφέρεται τὰ δημόσια, διὰ τὸ προφάσει τῶν βαρβαρικῶν ἐφόδων ἐλαττωθῆναι τοὺς γεωργοὺς καὶ μὴ ἀρκεῖν τὴν ἐν εἴδεσι συντέλειαν τοῖς κατ' αὐτὴν ἱδρυμένοις στρατιώταις. *Imp Anastasius A. Matroniano pp.* (a. 491–505); ed. P. Krueger, pp. 407–408; on the same pages the Latin text of the law is also published. I do not know why S. P. Scott says in his English translation of the Code that this law (X, 27, 2) is not authentic (XV, 112).

future, and this emigration resulted in a considerable diminution of the imperial revenue. The depopulation of the Balkan provinces, the decline of their agricultural produce, and the diminution of the imperial revenue are the characteristic features of the economic condition of the northern provinces of the empire in the sixth century. A striking example among those who had emigrated from their own homeland to try to better their condition is, of course, the future emperor Justin himself; of poor and obscure family, a peasant or herdsman, like hundreds of other country youths, he quitted his homeland and with two companions set out for Constantinople where he later became emperor.[24]

In the far north, in the northern section of the Euxine, the empire had strategic and economic interests in the lonely Tauric Peninsula (the Crimea), where two cities, Chersonesus (Cherson) and Bosporus, which were particularly famous for preserving Greek civilization for centuries, had also considerable economic importance as the centers for the trade between Constantinople and various barbarian tribes who, one after another, occupied the territory of present-day southern Russia, including the peninsula. In Justin's period the Huns occupied the steppe region of the peninsula, or, as Procopius states, in the sixth century, between Bosporus and Chersonesus, "everything is held by the barbarians, the Hunnic nations." [25] Bosporus also became subject to the Huns. But evidently trade relations were still continued, and, according to Jordanes, the Asiatic merchants brought their merchandise to Chersonesus (Cherson).[26] The Huns themselves were interested in exchanging skins for stuffs and jewels. As usual, one of the most important imports of local produce to the empire was salt fish ($\tau \acute{\alpha} \rho \iota \chi o \varsigma$), a commodity for which the two cities, Bosporus (Panticapaeum) and Cherson, were particularly noted. "Bosporus, rich in salt fish" (ὃ

[24] See above.
[25] Procopii *De bello persico*, I, 12, 7; *De bello gothico*, IV, 5, 27; ed. Haury, I, 57; II, 508; ed. Dewing, I, 96–97; V, 96–97. See A. Vasiliev, *The Goths in the Crimea*, p. 70.
[26] *Iordanis Getica*, V, 37: "Iuxta Chersonem Altziagiri, quo Asiae bona avidus mercator importat . . ." ed. Mommsen, p. 63. *MGH, AA*, V, 1 (1882). In English, by Ch. C. Mierow (Princeton, 1908), p. 11. Altziagiri (several variants) are *gens Scythica*; probably one of the Hunnic tribes, whose name has deteriorated in Jordanes' text. Perhaps Utrigurs?

ταριχόπλεως Βόσπορος) had already been cited by Athenaeus in his Deipnosophistae in the third century A. D.[27]

From the economic standpoint the eastern border of the empire was much more important than the northern. This was a very long line from the southeastern coast of the Black Sea as far south as Arabia. In the northern region of this borderland were Lazica, Armenia, and Iberia or Georgia, and along the whole line the most powerful rival of the empire, Sassanian Persia. In the period of Justin I there was some confusion in trade relations in those regions on account of the strife between Byzantium and Persia for Lazica. At that time Armenia was still organized on the basis of the treaty of 387 or 384 between Theodosius I and Sapor III, King of Persia, which had partitioned her into two vassal or client states, of which the smaller (about one-fifth of the whole) was under a prince dependent on the empire, and the larger, the so-called Persarmenia, under a vassal of Persia. In Persarmenia were two important centers, Artaxata (Artashat) and Dvin (Doubios).[28]

During Justin's period, although Persarmenia was under Persian domination, the trade relations between Dvin and Byzantium were still in operation. Procopius writes: "Now Doublos (Dvin) is a land excellent in every respect, and especially blessed with a healthy climate and abundance of good water; and from Theodosiopolis it is removed a journey of eight days. In that region there are plains suitable for

[27] See Kulakovsky, *The Past of the Tauris*, 2nd ed. (Kiev, 1914), pp. 59–60 (in Russian). Bury, II, 310–314. On the commercial and economic importance of salt fish in those regions since ancient times, see the very old but excellent and very little known study (in French) by M. Koehler, "Τάριχος ou Recherches sur l'histoire et les antiquités des pecheries de la Russie Méridionale," *Mémoires de l'Académie Impériale des Sciences de Saint-Pétersbourg*, 6th series, vol. I (St. Petersburg, 1832), pp. 347–490; especially p. 352; 353; 358. Probably by an oversight Koehler attributes the words ὁ ταριχόπλεως Βόσπορος to Strabo (p. 358). Athenaeus, *Deipnosophistae*, III, 116 b; ed. C. B. Gulick, II (London-New York, 1928), pp. 42–43.

[28] Artaxata-Artashat has usually been located on the site of the present-day settlement Ardashar; but after a recent exploration of the spot, according to Russian archaeologists, the site of Artaxata is to be located south of Ardashar, where the ancient Dvin was found, near the monastery Khor-Virap. S. T. Eremyan, "The trade roads of Transcaucasia in the epoch of the Sassanids, according to the *Tabula Peutingeriana*," *Messenger* (*Vestnik*) *of Ancient History*, I, 6 (Moscow, 1939), p. 83; the whole study, pp. 79–97 (in Russian).

riding, and many very populous villages are situated in very close proximity to one another, and numerous merchants conduct their business in them. For from India and the neighboring regions of Iberia and from practically all the nations of Persia and some of those under Roman sway they bring in merchandise and carry on their dealings with each other there." [29] From Procopius' description we see that in spite of unfavorable political conditions, Dvin in the first half of the sixth century was a commercial center of great importance, where the merchants of various countries, among them those of Byzantium, met each other and transacted business on a large scale.[30] Artaxata, which might have been overshadowed by Dvin to some extent, still continued to play a very important role in the eastern trade. The most important articles of exchange in Artaxata and Dvin were probably Chinese silk and Chinese clothes made of silk.[31]

In Roman Armenia on the Persarmenian frontier there stood during Justin's period the very important town of Theodosiopolis (Erzerum), founded in the first half of the fifth century by Theodosius II. Its speedy growth is to be explained by the fact that it was situated on the main road from Artaxata and Dvin to Asia Minor and to the Black Sea, and was not only an administrative center of the empire but also an important junction for internal and international trade relations. On the southern shore of the Black Sea lay the thriving port of Trebizond, which was linked by a road with Theodosiopolis, and through the latter established commercial connections with Persarmenia and Persia proper.[32]

[29] Proc. *B. P.* II, 25, 1–3; Dewing, I, 478–481. See Eremyan, *op. cit.,* p. 90.
[30] See J. A. Manandyan, *On Trade in the Towns of Armenia in connection with World Trade of Ancient Times* (Erivan, 1930), pp. 87–88 (in Russian). K. Güterbock, *Byzanc und Persien,* p. 78.
[31] *Gregorii Turonensis Historia Francorum,* IV, 40 (39): "Ad Justinum autem (this is Justin II, 565–578; some manuscripts read Justinianum) imperatorem Persae-Armeni cum magno serici intexti pondere venerunt, petentes amicitias ejus, atque narrantes se imperatori Persarum esse infensos." Migne, *PL,* LXXI 302; ed. W. Arndt, p. 174, *MGH,* Scr. rer. Meroving., I (1885). In English, by O. A. Dalton, *The History of the Franks by Gregory of Tours,* II (Oxford, 1927), p. 149. This Perso-Armenian embassy, of course, took place either during Justinian's reign or after his death, in any case after the death of Justin I. But the articles of Chinese silk brought by the ambassadors were not something new, but one of the chief items of the regular trade.
[32] See Manandyan, *On Trade in the Towns of Armenia,* p. 101 (in Russian).

During Justin's reign, on the eastern border of the empire the agreement of 408–409 with Persia was still in force. In this year an imperial edict was issued in which the two governments agreed that the Persian towns of Nisibis and Artaxata and the imperial town of Callinicum on the Euphrates (the future Arab Rakkah) should be the only places at which Persian and Roman traders might bring their wares and transact business. The edict plainly explains the motive of the restriction; the governments feared "lest foreigners might find out secrets, which would be improper." [33]

In choosing Callinicum for trade transactions with Persia, the imperial government considered not only its geographical location on the Euphrates but also its very strong fortifications. At the end of the fourth century, Ammianus Marcellinus wrote that Callinicum was "a strong fortress, and most valuable because of its rich trade." [34] It was always safer to receive foreign traders and deal with them in a fortified place. On the Persian side Nisibis also was strongly fortified. We should remember that Justin's predecessor, Anastasius I, in 507, after the conclusion of the treaty with the Persians which ended his war with Kawad, built to replace a simple village the imposing fortified town of Dara, which he named Anastasiopolis, close to the frontier and a few miles from Nisibis. The protests of the Persian king came to nothing; the new town became "for the empire what Nisibis was for Persia." As a strong military fort Dara was not opened to Persian traders. [35]

Sometimes the foundation of Theodosiopolis has erroneously been ascribed to Theodosius I. See Bury, II, 6, n. 2.

[33] *Cod. Just.*, IV, 63, 4: "Mercatores tam imperio nostro quam Persarum regi subjectos ultra ea loca, in quibus foederis tempore cum memorata natione nobis convenit, nundinas exercere minime oportet, ne alieni regni, quod non convenit, scrutentur arcana. Nullus igitur posthac imperio nostro subjectus ultra Nisibin Callinicum et Artaxata emendi sive vendendi species causa proficisci audeat nec praeter memoratas civitates cum Persa merces existimet commutandas." In English by S. P. Scott, XIII, 126: in order to prevent the secrets of either kingdom from being disclosed (which is improper).

[34] Ammianus Marcellinus, XXIII, 3, 7: "Callinicum munimentum robustum et commercandi optimitate gratissimum."

[35] Our best source on the building of Dara is the Syriac *Chronicle* of the so-called Zachariah of Mitylene, VII, 6; transl. Hamilton and Brooks, pp. 164–167; Ahrens and Krüger, pp. 115–118. See P. Collinet, "Une 'ville neuve' byzantine en 507: La fondation de Dara (Anastasiopolis) en Mésopotamie," *Mélanges*

If we turn south, we find the border line located along Syria, Palestine, and the province of Arabia. Except for Nisibis and Singara, which Jovian in 363 had restored to Persia, and the stronghold of Dara, which had been built by Anastasius, the limes traced by Diocletian remained practically unchanged in the Byzantine period down to the Arab conquest.[36] It is rather surprising that the Byzantine Empire, in spite of its conflict with the powerful empire of Persia and its perpetual struggles in Europe, was able to maintain its eastern frontiers for three hundred years without any serious losses. The most important and prosperous economic center in those regions was of course Antioch-on-the-Orontes, where the main route to the East began. But during Justin's reign the terrible earthquake of May 29, 526 and the resulting destructive fire laid the city in ruins. This disaster was a very severe blow to the wealth and trade activities not only of Antioch in particular but also of Syria in general. Also, as we know, at the very end of Justin's reign war with Persia broke out; the terrific devastations inflicted on Syria by the Persians which are so vividly described by John Lydus may have begun in Justin's lifetime.[37] In addition to the Persians, the Nabatean Arabs also raided the Roman territory with impunity. They were known to the Romans as Saracens or Scenites (people of the tents), and they lived in the great desert east of Syria and Palestine, having no fixed abode, "in a continuous flight" or "always on the move," as Ammianus Marcellinus says.[38] In addition, the Arab tribe of Ghassan and their rulers, the Ghassanids, as dependents of the empire, as well as their bitter foes, the Saracens of Hira, who with their rulers the Lakhmides were under the suzerainty of Persia, by their struggles between themselves and by violating the Byzantine boundary, introduced another element of economic ruin and instability. This practically permanent condition of danger on the

---

Schlumberger, I (Paris, 1924), pp. 55–60. Bury, II, 15. W. Ensslin, "Zur Gründungsgeschichte von Dara-Anastasiopolis," *Byzantinisch-Neugriechische Jahrbücher*, V (1927), pp. 342–347 (on sources). No mention of Collinet's article.

[36] See A. Poidebard, "La trace de Rome dans le désert de Syrie. Le limes de Trajan à la conquête arabe." *Recherches aériennes* (1925–1932). Paris, 1934, p. 25. Some more bibliography in A. Piganiol, *L'empire chrétien* (Paris, 1947), p. 18, n. 120.

[37] John Lydus, *De magistratibus*, III, 54; *CSHB*, p. 247; Wuensch, p. 143.

[38] Amm. Marcell., XIV, 4, 4: "Vita est illis semper in fuga."

eastern frontier in the sixth century adversely affected the economic interests of Justin's whole empire.

But apparently these raids failed to penetrate far into the interior of the country. I shall bring forward one example, that of Gerasa, a city of the Roman province of Arabia, in Transjordan, which was practically untouched. A recent archaeologist writes: "Our best evidence for the nature and brilliance of the new epoch which the late fifth and the early sixth century marks in the life of Gerasa is the series of churches built there at this time. The series begins in 464–465 A.D." One church, that of Procopius, was built in 526, just at the moment when the Persian war broke out. "The mosaics of this church both in number and detail rank among the finest found at Gerasa. An inscription in front of the chancel step recorded that the work was carried out under the supervision of Procopius from the benefactions of Bishop Paul and Saul, a deacon and paramonarius, in the year 526 A.D., but the dedication of the church is not mentioned." [39] The dedication may have been postponed or possibly not been performed at all on account of the Persian danger.

We have much more information on trade relations for the south and southeast. Trade with India, the Persian Gulf, Arabia, and the eastern coast of Africa had been in the hands of Roman merchants under the early Roman Empire, in the flourishing period of direct commercial relations between the empire and the eastern countries, with the center in Alexandria, when Roman merchants sailed through the Red Sea into the Indian Ocean in their own vessels. The first break in direct trade through Alexandria took place in 215, when Emperor Caracalla personally directed a carefully thought-out massacre of its inhabitants. Then the anarchy of the third century which had broken out after the death of Alexander Severus and spread over the entire empire also affected Mediterranean and Egyptian com-

---

[39] C. H. Kraeling, *Gerasa, City of the Decapolis* (New Haven, Connecticut, 1938), pp. 65–66; description of the church of Procopius, pp. 260–262 and 338–340; inscription 304, pp. 478–479. The mosaic from the church of Procopius in front of the chancel enclosure is now in the Gallery of Fine Arts, Yale University. In the Hellenistic period Gerasa, a modest Greek city, was called Antioch on the Chrysorhoas. In the atmosphere of the *Pax Romana* Gerasa developed into one of the most brilliant cities of Transjordan. Real excavations were carried out after the first World War (Kraeling, preface, pp. ix–x).

merce so that the trade between the Mediterranean and the East fell under the control of the Abyssinians, the Himyarites of Yemen, in South Arabia, and particularly the Persians who possessed a strong and well equipped commercial fleet. The Abyssinians and Himyarites were often reluctant to help Byzantium in its commerce for fear that such action might involve them in a quarrel with the powerful Persia. Ancient Rome had ceased to be the main focus of commerce even before the foundation of Constantinople. The drastic reforms of Diocletian and the rise of the new capital caused a partial revival of trade with the East; but this was indirect trade, carried out by the intermediation of the abovementioned peoples. Roman coins found in India, especially those struck under and after Theodosius II, were most probably brought there by intermediaries, not by Roman traders. The same situation continued to exist during Justin's reign: Arabians and Abyssinians held control of the trade. But the real trade monopoly belonged to Persia.

In the sixth century the land route across Arabia from south to north was still in operation. It started in Arabia-Eudaemon (Felix) in the south at Adane (now Aden), a prosperous and wealthy meeting place of Greeks from of old, later called a "Roman mart," then as now the only safe and shoal-free harbor between Suez and India. For a long time the Arabians had been known as excellent and natural merchants, and rather poor warriors. Strabo wrote that "the Arabians are not very good warriors even on land, to say nothing of fighting at sea, instead being hucksters and merchants." [40] The trade along this caravan route was the basis for the well-being of Yemen, because the products of India brought to Arabia-Eudaemon (Aden) and the frankincense from the mountains of Hadramaut and some neighboring regions had no other land route by which to reach the Mediterranean; and this monopoly secured prosperity to the stations along the way. This road went across the desert to the important landing place on the Red Sea, Leuke-Kome (Leuce-Come), from which a good road led to the old trading places, Dedan (el-Ela) and Egra (Hegra, Medain Salih), and

---

[40] Strabo, XVI, 4, 23 (C 780): οὐδὲ γὰρ κατὰ γῆν σφόδρα πο).εμισταί εἰσιν, ἀλλὰ κάπηλοι μᾶλλον οἱ Ἄραβες καὶ ἐμπορικοί, μήτι γε κατὰ θάλατταν. Mommsen has emphasized this passage of Strabo. *Römische Geschichte*, V, 605.

then ran northwest to Aila (Aelana, Aqaba) at the tip of the Aqaba Gulf. It has only very recently been discovered that these two points, the biblical Dedan (el-Ela) and Egra, so far south in the desert from the Roman side, about eight hundred kilometers (five hundred miles) south of Bostra, were occupied by Roman troops, and in the Roman and Byzantine periods became a very well established frontier between Hedjaz and Nabataea. From Aila this caravan road went to Petra and then to Gaza, on the shore of the Mediterranean.[41]

The much more important sea route to the south started from Alexandria in Egypt. We have noted above that Egypt, the most precious granary for the empire, the essential balance for its economic stability, received marked preferential treatment under Justin's government. Although monophysitism all over the empire was persecuted, monophysitism in Egypt, where it was the predominant religious doctrine, remained untouched. Although all sorts of games, spectacles, and amusements were forbidden as disturbing elements in all eastern provinces headed by Antioch and all dancers were banished, no restrictions along this line were placed on "the great Alexandria in Egypt" (Malalas, 417). The wonderful prosperity of Alexandria depended not only on its own natural resources but also on its part in the commerce of the empire with the south. Its exceptional importance in the economic life of the empire in the south may be once more emphasized by the fact that not only the Alexandrian and Egyptian merchants in general took part in this commerce, but also that corporations from outside Egypt, for instance from Palmyra, established themselves there and actively participated in commercial transactions in the region of the Red Sea.[42]

---

[41] See Tkatsch, "Saba," *PW*, 2nd series, I (1920), 1423. On the Roman garrisons at el-Ela and Egra H. Seyrig, "Postes romains sur la route de Médine," *Syria*, XXII (1941), 218–223. Moritz, "Λευκὴ κώμη," *PW*, XII, 2262. D. Nielsen, *Handbuch der altarabischen Altertumskunde*, I. *Die altarabische Kultur*, p. 110. On Egra (el-Heger) and el-Ela in general, see A. Kammerer, *Pétra et la Nabatène* (Paris, 1929), pp. 217–219 and 221–222; cf. also pp. 284–285. Philipp Scherti, "Ela-Akaba. Die Geschichte einer altchristlichen Bischofsstadt," *Orientalia Christiana Periodica*, II (1936), pp. 33–77; esp. p. 50.

[42] On the Palmyrians in Egypt see for instance F. Cumont, *Fouilles de Doura-Europos* (Paris, 1926), p. LI. H. Seyrig, "Inscription relative au commerce maritime de Palmyra," *Mélanges Franz Cumont* (Bruxelles, 1936), p. 400 (*Annuaire de*

The starting points in the Byzantine Empire for the southern trade were Clysma (now in Arabic Qulzum), a quarter of a mile north of modern Suez,[43] and the above-mentioned Aila-Aelana (Akaba) at the tip of the Aelanitic Gulf or the Gulf of Akaba, where, according to Procopius, "the Red Sea comes to an end and becomes a very narrow gulf" (B. P. I, 19, 3). In the period of Justin Clysma was apparently a very important commercial and economic center. According to the description in the account of her pilgrimage to Sinai, probably between 533 and 540, the Abbess Aetheria of South Gaul (Gallia Narbonensis) saw at Clysma (in the text Clesma) many large ships sailing to India and arriving from India; "nowhere else on the Roman soil but there (at Clysma) are ships from India admitted. Therefore this port is famous on account of the merchants coming from India." The central government was represented there at that time by a resident *agens in rebus*, known as a logothete, who by order of the emperor to India every year; he had at his disposal at Clysma his own special ships.[44] Another pilgrim of the sixth century,

---

l'Institut de philologie et d'histoire orientales et slaves, IV, 1936, pp. 397–402). Both these studies indicate some literature on this question.

[43] I think that the correct transliteration of the Greek name Κλύσμα is Clysma. Heyd says that the name of this place should be written Clisma. W. Heyd, *Histoire du commerce du Levant*, I, 10, n. 2. Some writers accept this spelling. Some texts give Clesma. See *Itinera Hierosolymitana*, ed. P. Geyer, index, p. 341. *CSEL*, XXXIX (Vienna, 1898).

[44] "Qui portus mittit ad Indiam vel excipit venientes naves de India; alibi enim nusquam in Romano solo accessum habent naves de India nisi ibi. Naves ibi et multae et ingentes sunt; quare portus famosus est pro advenientibus ibi mercatoribus de India. Nam et ille agens in rebus, quem logotetem appellant, id est, qui singulis annis legatus ad Indiam vadit iussu imperatoris Romani, ibi ergo sedes habet, et naves ipsius ibi stant." This particular text of the account of the Abbess Aetheria has been preserved in *Liber de Locis Sanctis*, which was compiled in the twelfth century (a. 1137) by Peter Diaconus, the librarian at Monte Casino. *Itinera Hierosolymitana*, ed. P. Geyer. *CSEL*, vol. XXXIX, 116. I follow here the dating of Aetheria's account given by K. Meister, "Die Itinerario Aetheriae abbatissae perperam nomini S. Silviae addicto," *Rheinishes Museum für Philologie*. LXIV (1909), 363: the account was compiled between 533 and 540. But his dating has not been accepted by all scholars. Before him, P. Geyer had attributed the text to about 385: "circa annum 385 scriptum esse pro certo haberi potest" (p. XIII). More recently, in 1911, E. Weigand, refuting Meister's dating, returned to Geyer's dating and even tried "with great probability" to fix the year 395 as that of the compilation of the *Peregrinatio Aetheriae*. E. Weigand, "Zur Datierung der Peregrinatio Aetheriae," *Byz. Zeitsch.*, XX (1911), pp. 1–26; especially pp. 25–26. In 1887, our text was reproduced by Mommsen in his study "Ueber einen

the so-called Antoninus of Placentia (circa a. 570), also mentions Clysma, where ships arrive even from India. He adds: "We got there plenty of green nuts which come from India, and which, as men believe, come from paradise." He saw at Clysma "in a basilica over eighteen wooden caskets of the holy father hermits." [45] He also noted that in the city of Abila (Akaba), a ship arrived from India loaded with various kinds of incense.[46]

To control commercial shipping to Clysma and Akaba (Aila), the Byzantine government established a customhouse on one of the small islands in the mouth of the gulf of Akaba, Iotabe, in the eastern inlet formed by the promontory of Sinai; this custom house took care of the ships sailing from the south. Procopius writes that "the island called Iotabe was not less than one thousand stades distant from the city of Aila, and that on this island Hebrews had lived from of old in autonomy" (*B. P.* I, 19, 3–4). The island had been mentioned in Byzantine sources before Justin's time. In 473 under Emperor Leo I an Arab adventurer Amorkesos seized Iotabe, drove out the Greek customhouse officers, amassed a considerable fortune by collecting dues, even sent Peter, Bishop of Iotabe, of the Arabian race, to Con-

---

neu aufgefundenen Reisebericht nach dem gelobten Lande," republished in Th. Mommsen, *Gesammelte Schriften*, VI: *Historische Schriften*, III, 612. Mommsen was inclined to attribute the text to the second half of the fourth century, and believed India referred to India proper. Without going into the details of the discussion, I am ready to accept the later dating, because in the sixth century (not in the fourth) trade relations between Byzantium and India were active. Bury (II, 318, n. 1) is also inclined to accept the later dating. On *Agentes in Rebus*, i.e., on the secret police, see *Cod. Theod.*, VI, 29, 8; ed. Mommsen, pp. 292–293. Edict of Emperors Arcadius and Honorius, May 16–June 1, 395: "nec naves debebunt inlicita concussione vexare nec libellas aut contestationes suscipere aut in carcerem quemquam tradere, sed cursui solum vacare." See *Iacobi Gothofredi Commentarius* to this edict.

[45] "Ibi est et civitas modica, quae appellatur Clisma, ubi etiam et de India naves veniunt . . . Illic accepimus nuces plenas virides, quae de India veniunt, quae de paradiso credunt homines esse. . . Infra civitatem ipsam Clisma intus in basilica vidimus locellos ligneos sanctorum patrum heremitarum ultra decem et octo." *Antonini Placentini Itinerarium. Itinera Hierosolymitana saeculi IIII–VIII*, ed. P. Geyer, pp. 187–188, *CSEL*, XXXIIII.

[46] "In Abila descendit navis de India cum diversis aromatibus." P. Geyer, p. 185. At present, Akaba, the only port of Transjordan, is garrisoned by British troops. There the frontiers of Egypt, Palestine (Israel), and Transjordan adjoin. See very interesting data on modern Akaba in *The Illustrated London News* (1949), March 19 and 26, and April 23.

stantinople to negotiate concerning his uncertain position, and finally was asked by the emperor to come to the capital. There he shared the imperial table and was honored with many distinctions. Finally Leo transferred to him the possession of Iotabe, which the empire regained in 498 under Anastasius I. A customhouse for vessels coming from India was then reëstablished as before.[47]

Under church organization the island of Iotabe belonged to the small patriarchate of Jerusalem which comprised the three Palestinian provinces. The island was included in the province *Palaestina tertia* and was its southernmost point. The four bishops of this province attended the Council of Chalcedon and subscribed its decrees: they were the bishops of Aila, Elousa, Zoora, and Iotape. The signature of the latter reads as follows: "Marcianus the most reverent bishop of Iotape." [48] We do not know how large his flock was in the island, which was, as we shall see a little later, very small, or what the relations were between him and the Hebrew settlement there, which Procopius mentions.[49] During Justin's period Iotabe was a commercial station of considerable importance, and the revenues derived from its customs

[47] *Malchi Philadelphensis Fragmenta*, C. Müller, *FHG*, IV, p. 113 (fr. 1). On the restoration of Iotabe to the empire, Theophanes A. M. 5990; de Boor, p. 141. See Bury, II, 8. R. P. F.-M. Abel, "L'île de Iotabe," *Revue Biblique*, XLVII (1938), 526–527; 534.

[48] Μαρκιανὸς ὁ εὐλαβέστατος ἐπίσκοπος Ἰωτάπης. Mansi, VII, 33; E. Schwartz, *Acta Conciliorum*, II, vol. I, 2, 103. Schwartz gives the erroneous and arbitrary spelling Ἰωτάνης. On this spelling see A. Alt, "Beiträge zur historischen Geographie und Topographie des Negeb," *The Journal of the Palestine Oriental Society*, XVII (Jerusalem, 1937), 230–231; especially, p. 231, n. 2. Abel, *op. cit.*, p. 533, n. 4. Abel supposes that the reading Ἰωτάπης for Ἰωτάβης in the Acts of the Chalcedonian Council may have been influenced by the name of the bishopric of Isauria, Iotape, which also occurs in the lists of the Council (*ib.*). See Devreesse, *Le patriarcat d'Antioche*, p. 148: Only one bishop of Iotape, in Isauria, Ammonius is known, who subscribed the Chalcedonian decree.

[49] The best account on the Bishopric of Iotabe is that by Abel, *op. cit.*, pp. 533–535. There is no ground for questioning, as A. Alt does (*op. cit.*, p. 233), whether or not the Hebrews of Procpius are Samaritans. Procopius clearly distinguishes Hebrews from Samaritans. The settlers of Iotabe were Hebrews. Abel, p. 535. Also E. Stein, *Geschichte des spätrömischen Reiches*, I, p. 529. The third and the last known bishop of Iotabe (after Peter and Marcianus) was Anastasius, whose name was listed in the Acts of the Synod of Jerusalem in 536, which were inserted in the Acts of the Council of Constantinople, of the same year (Abel, p. 534); also Alt, *op. cit.*, p. 231 and n. 3. The Greek text of the Acts gives Iotabe, the Latin translation Iotape.

presented in the disrupted budget of the empire a rather important item.

Iotabe has been definitely identified with the rocky island of Tiran of our own day, fourteen kilometers long and seven to eight wide, and possessing no water. In 1914 M. Bourdon visited the island very briefly and found no trace of any building or pottery. But no methodic exploration of the island was made. As M. Abel writes, if a scientific and thorough exploration of the island of Tiran were authorized by the government of Hedjaz, upon which it depends, it is possible that some archaeological testimony of the past existence of the custom station of Iotabe may come to light.[50]

During Justin's period the empire had in the Red Sea a considerable number of commercial vessels, which are listed, as we have seen above, in the *Life* of Saint Arethas as participants in the Abyssinian war against the Himyarite kingdom. Clysma supplied twenty vessels; Aila fifteen; Iotabe seven; the archipelago of Pharsan in the Red Sea seven; Beronice on the Red Sea two; India nine; [51] sixty ships altogether.

A contemporary of Justin and Justinian was Cosmas Indicopleustes, "sailor to India" or "sailor of the Indian Sea," the author of a remarkable book written in the middle of the sixth century, the *Christian Topography*. It is amazing how little we know about him. In a rather substantial article on Cosmas' work in Photius' *Bibliotheca* (*Cod.* 36), the earliest reference to him, his name is not even given; his work is mentioned and summarized under the very indefinite title "the Book of a Christian" or "the Book of Christians," dedicated to a certain Pamphilus. But Photius gives the very valuable indication that the author "flourished in the days of the Roman Emperor Justinus." [52] The Laurentian MS (at Florence) contains the name of Cosmas. On the basis of our meager data we may conclude that he was a native of Egypt, probably of Alexandria, and in early life a merchant. In that capacity

---

[50] Abel, *op. cit.*, pp. 535–538 (VIII, L'île de Tiran).

[51] *Acta Sanctorum*, Oct., X (Brussels, 1861), p. 747 (§ 29). See Abel, *op. cit.*, pp. 528–529.

[52] ἦν δὲ ταῖς ᾿Ιουστίνου τοῦ τῶν ῾Ρωμαίων βασιλέως ἡμέραις ἐνακμάζων (*Cod.* 36); ed. Bekker, I (1824), 7; Migne, *PG*, CIII, 68–69. Photius' passage has also been reproduced by E. O. Winstedt, *The Christian Topography of Cosmas Indicopleustes*, p. 1, n. 2.

he traveled far and wide, visiting Ceylon, the Persian Gulf, the Sinaitic Peninsula, and Ethiopia. Later in life he settled in Alexandria and probably became a monk. There he composed his book, in the middle of the sixth century.[53] There is no doubt that he was a Nestorian, and Gelzer's statement that he was orthodox must be discarded. An English writer refers to Cosmas as "great Nestorian traveller and monk." [54]

Unfortunately Cosmas' work is neither a treatise on geography, nor a plain account of his travels. His main object is to refute the error of pagan science that the earth is spherical, and to prove that the shape of the world is that of the tabernacle of Moses, "the great cosmographer," which was a miniature model of the universe. For us Cosmas' cosmographic speculations are of much less interest than the data contained in his work on the geography and trade of those countries which he visited or about which he heard. The *Topography* is his only work which has survived. The others are known only by name and by mention he himself makes of them. According to Winstedt, two of them may be passed over without further mention and without regret. But the third, a work on geography addressed to a certain Constantinus, is a real and irreparable loss to students of ancient geography, and indeed to the world in general. "The book is much to be regretted, as Cosmas had travelled over a great part of the ground, and here he was not bound to a theological theory." [55] This book may also have had very interesting data on trade and commerce in various countries.

Cosmas was in Ethiopia, in the city of Adulis, "in the beginning of the reign of the Roman Emperor Justin when the Axumite (Ethiopic) king Ellatzbaas (Elesboas) was preparing to invade the country of the

---

[53] See Windstedt, *op. cit.*, p. 338: *ca.* 550. H. Gelzer, "Kosmas der Indienfahrer," *Jahrbuch für protestantische Theologie*, IX (1883), p. 124, n. 1: Cosmas wrote in 547. Bury, II, 319, and n. 1: about A. D. 545–50; for Books I–V which appeared first, about 544–545. See Milton V. Anastos, "The Alexandrian Origin of the *Christian Topography* of Cosmas Indicopleustes," *Dumbarton Oaks Papers*, no. 3 (Cambridge, Massachusetts, 1946), pp. 75–80. A very good bibliography.

[54] See Gelzer, pp. 131–135. Winstedt, p. 4 and n. 4. The English writer is J. Kennedy, "The Child Krishna, Christianity, and the Gujars," *The Journal of the Royal Asiatic Society* (1907), p. 959.

[55] Winstedt, pp. 4–5. Cosmas' text in the Prologue to his work. Winstedt, pp. 37–38; Migne, *PG*, LXXXVIII, col. 53.

Homerites (Himyarites) lying across the sea." [56] Gelzer wrote that Cosmas was at Adulis in 522; Winstedt says that the passage just quoted makes the date of Cosmas' travels in Abyssinia 525 A. D.[57] Cosmas himself says that he was in Abyssinia *in the beginning* of Justin's reign, when the latter was preparing to start the expedition. In other words, he may have visited Abyssinia in 523 or 524, when, as we know, the preparations for the war were in full swing. Besides Abyssinia, Cosmas sailed for his business transactions in the Roman, Arabian, and Persian Gulfs, i.e. in the Mediterranean, the Red, and Arabian Seas, and the Persian Gulf, and knew a good deal about these regions.[58] "We may regard Cosmas, the Indian navigator, as the forerunner of the Moslem writers, for he fills a gap in the history of the Persian Gulf between the latter and the classical writers." [59] Probably during his voyage to the Persian Gulf he passed by the island of Dioscorides (Socotora, Socotra) in the western region of the Arabian Sea, but he did not stop there.[60] In spite of doubts expressed by some scholars, I believe that Cosmas visited Taprobane — Ceylon and gave us an admirable description of the island, "a true pearl," according to Gelzer, "a revelation" to Abel.[61] Cosmas never landed in India.[62]

The experiences of Cosmas, who lived and transacted trade business under Justin and Justinian, clearly show how far south and east

[56] παρόντι οὖν μοι ἐν τοῖς τόποις ἐκείνοις . . . ἐν τῇ ἀρχῇ τῆς βασιλείας ᾿Ιουστίνου τοῦ ῾Ρωμαίων βασιλέως, ὁ τηνικαῦτα βασιλεὺς τῶν ᾿Αξωμιτῶν ῾Ελλατζβάας μέλλων ἐξιέναι εἰς πόλεμον πρὸς τοὺς ῾Ομηρίτας τοὺς πέραν. Cosmas, II; Migne, *PG*, LXXXVIII, col. 101; Winstedt, p. 72.

[57] Gelzer, p. 116. Winstedt, p. 338; cf. p. 3; circa 525 A. D.

[58] ἐμπορίας γὰρ χάριν ἔπλευσα τοὺς τρεῖς κόλπους, τόν τε κατὰ τὴν ῾Ρωμαίαν, καὶ τὸν ᾿Αράβιον καὶ τὸν Περσικόν, καὶ ἀπὸ τῶν οἰκούντων δὲ ἢ καὶ πλεόντων τοὺς κόλπους ἀκριβῶς μεμαθηκώς. Migne, LXXXVIII, pp. 87-88; Winstedt, p. 62.

[59] Sir Arnold T. Wilson, *The Persian Gulf, An Historical Sketch from the Earliest Times to The Beginning of the Twentieth Century* (Oxford, 1928), p. 51.

[60] On Dioscorides I shall speak below.

[61] Gelzer, *Kosmas der Indienfahrer*, p. 124. Abel, *L'île de Iotabe*, p. 519. The Greeks called Ceylon Taprobane; the inhabitants of Ceylon and India, Selediva, Σιελεδίβα, which has become in Arabic, Serendib. In the Russian versions of Cosmas' work Ceylon is called Sielediva or Provani. The latter is, of course, the abridged form of Taprobane. From the Arabic name Serendib, Horace Walpole coined an English word *serendipity*, the ability to find valuable things unexpectedly; from a fairy tale "The Three Princes of Serendip," the heroes of which were continually finding valuable articles by chance.

[62] See also A. C. Moule, *Christians in China before the Year 1550* (London, 1930), p. 23: Cosmas mentions China, which he calls Τζίνιστα (Tzinista).

Egyptian merchants went at that time, and how active trade relations were in the Red Sea and in the Indian Ocean. Of course competition between Roman and Persian traders was acutely felt. Cosmas himself tells an interesting story about a merchant Sopatros (Σώπατρος), who had died thirty-five years before Cosmas wrote his book in Alexandria, that is at the end of Anastasius' reign, and who had himself told the story to Cosmas. With some other traders Sopatros sailed from Adulis to Ceylon, where he met some Persian merchants who had just arrived from Persia. First, as the custom there was, the chief men of the place and the customhouse officers received them and brought them to the king. At the audience occurred the very well known episode of the proving of the superiority of the Roman Emperor over the Persian King by a comparison of their respective coins. The King of Ceylon was convinced of the superiority of the Roman emperor, and the winner Sopatros was set on an elephant and to the sound of drums paraded in honor through the town.[63]

Since Cosmas states that Sopatros had been dead thirty-five years when he was writing his book (between 545–550), this puts his death about 515. There is no reason for supposing that he took this voyage just before his death; it is more probable that he was relating an old adventure. Consequently Sopatros' voyage should probably be dated considerably earlier, near the beginning of the sixth century.[64] Cosmas mentions another merchant and his friend Menas (Μηνᾶς), who later became a monk at Raithu (now el-Tor) on the Sinai Peninsula, and died shortly before 545–550, when Cosmas was writing his book; consequently he was the contemporary of Justin and Justinian. In about 523–524 Cosmas and Menas were both in Ethiopia, and at the request of the king of Axum, the governor of Adulis, Asbas ('Ασβᾶς), directed them to take copies of the inscription on the chair of Ptolemy. Like a pair of modern archaeological tourists, with note book in hand, they set out to copy the inscription which Cosmas records. He writes: "One

---

[63] Cosmas, XI; *PG*, 448–449; Winstedt, pp. 323–324. In English, J. McCrindle, pp. 368–370.

[64] Winstedt, p. 355. Beazley is wrong in saying: "Possibly Cosmas is inaccurate, or our information misleading. Sopater (Sopatrus) probably travelled *after* Justinian's accession (527)." C. R. Beazley, *The Dawn of Modern Geography*, p. 191, n. 1.

set of the copies we gave the Governor; but we kept also like copies for ourselves which I shall here embody in this work, since their contents contribute to our knowledge of the country, its inhabitants, and the distances of the several places." [65]

The two merchants mentioned by Cosmas, **Sopatros**, who had died before Justin's accession, and Menas, who died under Justinian, provide us with a very valuable indication of the competitive commercial activities in the Red Sea and in the Indian Ocean in the first half of the sixth century. It is by mere chance that Cosmas has preserved for us only two names of merchants. There were doubtless many other traders, Roman, Abyssinian, South Arabian, and Persian, who continuously sailed those distant seas to transact business and compete with each other. Competition was not easy and not in favor of the Roman, Abyssinian, and South Arabian merchants; the Persians traded directly with Ceylon, had a commercial colony there, and possessed, as we have noted above, a better equipped and larger fleet.

During Justin's reign the Himyarite-Ethiopic war in 525–526 must for a time have had a bad effect on trade and commerce in the Red Sea and in the Indian Ocean, carried on by Roman, Abyssinian, and South Arabian merchants. The Persians took advantage of this temporary turmoil in the western waters of the Indian Ocean to develop and increase their own trade activities. The Himyarite-Ethiopic war was important not only from the political view of increasing the political power of the Abyssinian king across the sea, in South Arabia, not only from the religious view of the restoration of Christianity there to replace Judaism, but also from the economic point of view. First, as we have just noted, the war interfered for a time in the regular economic activities in the Red Sea and in the western region of the Indian Ocean, the so-called Arabian Sea, and gave more opportunities to the Persian merchants. Then under the pressure of the restoration of Christianity in South Arabia, many Jews probably emigrated north, reinforced their colonies in Hedjaz and spread along the shores of the Elanic Gulf (Gulf of Akaba). Later, in the first half

---

[65] Cosmas, II; *PG*, 101–104; Winstedt, 72–73. McCrindle, p. 56 (he calls the governor Abbas for Asbas). See also Winstedt, p. 14. The Adulis inscription was published in *Corpus Inscriptionum Graecarum*, III, no. 5127 (pp. 508–514); G. Dittenberger, *Orientis Graeci Inscriptiones Selectae*, I (1903–1905), no. 54.

of the seventh century, Muhammed met them in great numbers in Yathrib (Medina) and in some other places. That economic interests prevailed in Ethiopia and South Arabia at that time is, among other things, shown by the fact that the new king Abramus (Abramius) established by the victorious Elesboas over the Himyarites (Homerites), a Christian and a slave of a Roman citizen, was engaged in the business of shipping in Adulis.[66] A Jewish colony lived from early times on the island of Iotabe. According to Procopius, they "had lived in autonomy, but in the reign of Justinian have become subject to the Romans." Since Iotabe as an important customhouse of the empire played an essential part in its economic policy, the Jews who had long established themselves in the island certainly were occupied with commerce and trade and attained great prosperity. Their economic prosperity probably explains the rather vague statement of Procopius that up to the time of Justinian they were autonomous. They must have purchased their autonomy at a price.[67]

We know from Cosmas that the island of Dioscorides was involved in eastern commerce during Justin's reign. Dioscorides, "the Isle of Frankincense," now Socotra (Socotora, Sokotra), lies in the western region of the Indian Ocean, on the east side of the Gulf of Aden, about one hundred and fifty miles from Cape Guardafui.[68] "In the island called the Island of Dioscorides, which is situated in the Indian Sea, and where the inhabitants speak Greek, having been (originally) colonists (πάροικοι) sent thither by the Ptolemies who succeeded Alexander the Macedonian, there are clergy who receive their ordination in Persia, and are sent on to the island, and there is a multitude of Christians. I sailed along the coast of this island, but did not land upon it. I met, however, with some of its Greek-speaking people who had come over into Ethiopia." [69]

[66] Proc., *B. P.* I, 20, 4: ἐν πόλει Αἰθιόπων Ἀδούλιδι ἐπὶ τῇ κατὰ θάλασσαν ἐργασίᾳ διατριβὴν ἔχοντος. Dewing, I, pp. 190–191.

[67] See Abel, *L'île de Iotabe*, p. 529. Proc., *B. P.* I, 19, 4.

[68] According to McCrindle the name Socotra is Sanscrit, from Dvîpa Sukhâdâra, that is, Island Abode of Bliss. J. W. McCrindle, *The Christian Topography of Cosmas*, p. 119, n. 4. Winstedt, *op. cit.*, p. 345. A very fine and detailed article on "Sokotra" in *Encyclopaedia of Islam*, IV, 476–481 (by J. Tkatsch).

[69] Cosmas, III; *PG*, LXXXVIII, 169; Winstedt, p. 119; transl. by McCrindle, p. 119. See Gelzer, *Kosmas der Indienfahrer*, p. 140. Bury, II, p. 320.

From this text we learn that the inhabitants of Dioscorides in the first half of the sixth century spoke Greek and were Christians of Nestorian doctrine, since their clergy received ordination in Persia, a very well known refuge for the Nestorians persecuted in, and exiled from, the empire. In addition the inhabitants of the island visited Ethiopia, doubtless on commercial business, for they had been known from of old as merchants and traders. The anonymous *Periplus* of the Erythraean Sea, compiled about 60 A. D., which contains a very detailed passage on the island of Dioscorides, among other things remarks that its population consisted "of an intermixture of foreigners — Arabs, Indians, and even Greeks — engaged in commerce." Tkatsch says that Arab merchants are still in our own day as in the days of the *Periplus* busy on Sokotra.[70]

It is interesting to mention that coins with the name of Justin I are the latest Roman coins to be found in India. No coins with names of later emperors, so far as I know, have so far been discovered there.[71] One very important fact must be taken into consideration both for the past and for the period of Justin as well. For the empire trade with the East had always been mainly a trade in imports. "The balance of trade was therefore decidedly against the Empire, and there was a constant drain of gold to the East."[72]

[70] *Periplus Maris Erythraei*, c. 30: εἰσὶ δὲ ἐπίξενοι καὶ ἐπίμικτοι Ἀράβων τε καὶ Ἰνδῶν καὶ ἔτι Ἑλλήνων τῶν πρὸς ἐργασίαν ἐπλεόντων. C. Müller, *Geographi Graeci Minores*, II, p. 281. H. Schoff, *The Periplus of the Erythraean Sea: Travel and Trade in the Indian Ocean by a Merchant of the First Century* (New York-London, 1912), pp. 15–16. Like Cosmas, the author of the *Periplus* was a merchant. Tkatsch, in *Enc. of Islam*, IV, 481. See William Vincent, *The Periplus of the Erythraean Sea*, II (London, 1805), pp. 307–310. E. Sachau, "Zur Ausbreitung des Christentums in Asien," Abh. der *preussischen Akademie der Wissenschaften. Philos.-hist. Klasse* (Berlin, 1919), pp. 69–70. F. Pereira, "La Chrétienté de l'île de Socotora," *Aethiops. Bulletin Ge'ez dirigé par Sylvain Grébaut*, II (Paris, January, 1923), pp. 1–4. A. Kammerer, *La Mer Rouge, l'Abyssinie et l'Arabie depuis l'antiquité*, II (Cairo, 1935), p. 114 (Société Royale de Géographie d'Egypte, vol. XVI). Lequien (*Oriens Christianus*, II, 1257–1258) mentions three names connected with the church of Socotra, which belonged to the ninth, eleventh, and thirteenth centuries.

[71] R. Sewell, "Roman Coins Found in India," *Journal of the R. Asiatic Society*, XXXVI (1904), p. 634. E. Warmington, *The Commerce between the Roman Empire and India* (Cambridge, 1928), p. 140; 282. H. Kortenbeutel, *Der ägyptische Süd — und Osthandel in der Politik der Ptolemäer und römischen Kaiser* (Berlin-Charlottenburg, 1931), p. 78.

[72] Bury, II, 317 and n. 5. A long list of taxable items from the South and East is to be found in *Digesta*, XXXIX, 4, 16, § 7 (for the second and third centuries

Some economic troubles may have occurred in Justin's reign within the Empire. In the *Chronicle* of Comes Marcellinus under the year 524 in the consulship of Justinus Augustus II and Opilio, we find the following laconic note: "In these consulships, the scarcity of oil has brought the people into great need." [73] Generally speaking, olive oil was extensively used in the empire for various purposes. Most important for us is the fact that the government was an important consumer of olive oil for free distribution to the people. The amount available for this purpose became scarce and the price advanced considerably. In order to save the situation, in 370–375 a law was issued which flatly forbade the exportation of olive oil beyond the confines of the empire.[74] The scarcity of olive oil for free distribution became a cause of discontent and disturbances among the people. Shortly before Justin's period, under his predecessor Anastasius, an uprising broke out in Alexandria in Egypt caused by the scarcity of olive oil.[75] Such uprisings throw light on Comes Marcellinus' brief statement that "the scarcity of oil has brought the people into great need." It is clear that under Justin, in various regions of the Empire, the people considered the scarcity of olive oil distributed by the government as a great grievance, and the government may have had some troubles to settle.

EXPENSES

At the moment of Justin's elevation, the empire was financially well established. His predecessor Anastasius, a conscientious ruler who had paid personal attention to the control of the finances until he appointed

---

A. D.); ed. Mommsen and Krueger, p. 651. See Diehl, *Justinien*, pp. 533–545. Abel, *L'île de Iotabe*, p. 519.

[73] "His consulibus, inopia olei magnam penuriam in populum inportavit." Mommsen, *Chronica Minora*, II, p. 102.

[74] *Cod. Just.*, IV, 41, 1: "Ad barbaricum transferendi vini et olei et liquaminis nullam quisquam habeat facultatem ne gustus quidem causa aut usus commerciorum" (ed. Krueger, p. 178). In English by S. P. Scott: "No one shall have authority to transport to the country of the barbarians either wine, oil, or other liquids, either for the purpose of consumption or for commercial purposes" (XIII, 98).

[75] Malalas, p. 401: οἱ δῆμοι Ἀλεξανδρείας τῆς μεγάλης ἐστασίασαν . . . διὰ λεῖψιν ἐλαίου, ἰνδ. θ' (Sept. 1, 515–August 31, 516). According to the Escurial excerpt of Malalas, edited by Mommsen, the uprising broke out on account of the scarcity of bread and oil (διὰ λεῖψιν ἄρτου καὶ ἐλαίου). *Hermes*, VI (1872), 374.

Marinus, one of his chief advisers, as head of a new financial reform, left at his death a large reserve amounting to 320,000 pounds of gold (according to Bury, I, p. 446, about 14,590,000 prewar English pounds or about 70,000,000 prewar dollars). In his *Anecdota*, following his prejudice against Justinian, Procopius calls Anastasius both the most provident and the most prudent of all emperors, and then, idealizing Anastasius' motives, writes that the latter, "fearing, as actually happened, lest his future successor to the throne, finding himself short of funds, might perhaps take to plundering his subjects — he had filled all the treasuries to overflowing (κατακόρως) with gold before he died." Procopius mentions the amount of 320,000 centenaria of gold, and writes that during the nine years of the reign of Justin, "while Justinian was inflicting the evils of confusion and disorder upon the government," all this reserve, large as it was for those days, was squandered.[76] John Lydus also shows high appreciation of the financial economy of Anastasius, praising his willingness to help the needs of the people and his ability to manage the problems of taxes "like the master of a family" (*pater familiae*; δίκην οἰκοδεσπότου),[77] and he defines the reserve accumulated by Anastasius as consisting of "countless myriads of pounds of gold."[78] In one of his earlier edicts Justin himself mentions Anastasius' "thrifty (or economical) subtlety."[79]

Thus Justin as the head of the empire inherited from his predecessor a reserve of 320,000 centenaria of gold, which was evidently spent during the nine years of his reign. But when we consider the events of Justin's reign and the financial obligations and needs of the government, we must conclude that Procopius is biased and not without

[76] Procopius, *Anecdota*, XIX, 4–8; Dewing, 228. See M. Krasheninnikov, "Concerning the Manuscript Tradition of the *Secret History* of Procopius," *Viz. Vrem.*, II (1895), p. 421. B. Pančenko, "On Procopius' *Secret History*," *Viz. Vrem.*, III, p. 103, n. 10. Both in Russian. Curiously enough, Bertha Diener (*Imperial Byzantium*, Boston, 1938) writes: "Manifestly the one and a half milliards of reserve accumulated by Uncle Justin I during an uneventful tenure of the throne could not suffice to finance a truly golden era like Justinian's" (p. 211).

[77] Lydus, III, 45; CSHB, 238; Wuensch, 134.

[78] Lydus, III, 51: ἅπας μὲν ὁ πλοῦτος Ἀναστασίου εἰς ἀπείρους μυριάδας χρυσίου λιτρῶν συναγόμενος. CSHB, p. 244; Wuensch, p. 140. See Pančenko, "On Procopius' *Secret History*," *Viz. Vrem.*, III, p. 462 (in Russian).

[79] *Cod. Just.*, II, 7, 25 (6): "parca posterioris subtilitas principis" (i.e. Anastasii); ed. Krueger, p. 101 (a. 519).

prejudice in accusing Justin and Justinian of prodigality, at least in Justin's period. If they spent money freely for magnificent games and other spectacles, an exorbitant and unjustifiable expenditure, they also spent a great amount of money as we know for other purposes which were unavoidable in governing so vast an empire with such manifold and costly problems. Among other things, very heavy expenditures were required for relief for various natural disasters, which were of course entirely beyond the emperor's control.

In 521 after Vitalian's assassination, Justinian assumed the consulship, an event celebrated by the display of magnificent games whose object was to win the favor of the population, but which cost the government a large amount of money. This was the most brilliant inauguration any Oriental consul had ever had. Comes Marcellinus gives a graphic description of the festivities. Two hundred and eighty-eight thousand solidi were spent for the organization of the games and for distribution among the populace. Justinian exhibited in the amphitheater, besides many other wild animals, twenty lions and thirty panthers. In addition, he presented as gifts to the charioteers numerous horses wearing an ornament for the forehead and breast (faleratos-phaleratos). But evidently the behavior of the spectators during the exhibition was so violent and uncontrollable that the consul refused to permit the running of the last race.[80]

On the other hand, the government of Justin took great care of the cities which had been destroyed or damaged by earthquakes, fires, or floods. He spent many centenaria of gold to start the reconstruction of Antioch and its vicinity, Edessa, Dyrrachium, Corinth, Pompioupolis (in Mysia), Anazarb (in Cilicia), and probably other places affected by natural disasters; the people of the ruined places also received effective aid.[81] John Lydus states plainly that Justin used much care and pains and spent a great deal of money for the restoration of Antioch.[82]

Justin's period is marked by his building activities, which likewise

[80] Com. Marcell., a. 521: "una dumtaxat ultimaque mappa insanienti populo denegata" (ed. Mommsen, pp. 101–102).

[81] On the sources see above, in the description of the disasters themselves.

[82] Lydus, III, 54: ὡς δὲ κόπῳ πολλῷ καὶ χρημάτων ἀφθονίᾳ καὶ τεχνῶν συνεργείᾳ ὥσπερ ἐρεβόθεν ἡ πόλις ἀνεφύετο (CSHB, 247, 6–8; Wuensch, 143, 16–18).

were a serious expense. He thoroughly restored and beautifully adorned the famous Church of the Holy Virgin at Blachernae, which had been founded in the fifth century by Pulcheria, the wife of the Emperor Marcian, shortly before her death.[83] Procopius, who doubtless saw it many times, thus describes it: "This church is a most holy and very stately church, of unusual length, and yet of a breadth well proportioned to its length, both its upper and its lower parts being supported by nothing but sections of Parian stone which stand there to serve as columns. . . Anyone upon entering this church would marvel particularly at the greatness of the mass which is held in place without instability, and at the magnificence which is free from bad taste (τοῦ ἀπειροκάλου ἐλεύθερον)." [84] It was a "lovely temple shining with beauty," as we read in an epigram of *Anthologia Palatina* entitled "In the apses of Blachernae." [85] One may be sure that this thorough restoration and beautiful adornment of one of the most famous churches in Constantinople must have cost Justin's government a very considerable amount of money.

Also, during Justin's life, Justinian in his capacity as *comes domesticorum* erected the Church of Saints Peter and Paul, near the Palace of Hormisdas, which was his own residence while Crown Prince; after his accession to the throne, the church was by his orders improved and annexed to the Great Palace. No church of that dedication had previously existed in Byzantium. Thus the Church of Peter and Paul was the basilica connected first with the Palace of Hormisdas and after 527 annexed to the Great Palace.[86] Another contemporary source

---

[83] This tradition has been preserved by a contemporary source, Theodorus Lector, *Eccl. Hist.*, II, 37 (Migne, *PG*, LXXXVI, 1, col. 168). Procopius says that the building was erected by Justin and Justinian (*De aedif.*, I, 3, 3; Dewing-Downey, 38–39). The same information in *Epigrammatum Anthologia Palatina*, ed. F. Dübner, I (Paris, 1871), no. 3, p. 1 (in a note Dübner indicates that the church was built by Pulcheria.) *The Greek Anthology*, with an English translation by W. R. Paton, I, no. 3, p. 2. See Oberhummer, "Blachernai," *Pauly-Wissowa*, III (1899), coll. 554–556. J. Ebersolt, *Sanctuaires de Byzance* (Paris, 1921), p. 44 and note. J. Papodopoulos, *Les palais et les églises des Blachernes* (Thessalonica, 1928), p. 107: The Great Church of Blachernae was built under Justin I, by the care of Justinian.

[84] *De aedif.* I, 3, 3–5; Dewing-Downey, pp. 38–41.

[85] *Anth. Palatina*, ed. Dübner, no. 3, p. 1; Paton, I, no. 3, p. 2: Ὁ πρὶν Ἰουστῖνος περικαλλέα δείματο νηὸν τοῦτον Μητρὶ Θεοῦ, κάλλει λαμπόμενον . . .

[86] Procop., *De aedificiis* I, 4, 1: Dewing-Downey, 42–45.

gives us information on the erection of this church, a letter sent on June 29, 519, to Pope Hormisdas from the papal legates at Constantinople. It begins thus: "Your son, the magnificent Justinian, acting as becomes his faith, has erected a basilica of the Holy Apostles, in which he wishes the relics of the martyr Saint Laurentius to be placed. . ." Justinian himself in a letter of the same date also begs for the chains which bound the Apostles and the gridiron upon which the blessed martyr Laurentius was burnt to death in order to glorify the new basilica. The Pope readily granted the request in the same year.[87] The date of this letter, June 29, 519, is the day of the commemoration of Saints Peter and Paul by the Greek Orthodox Church. It was probably later under Justinian when Pope Vigilius was in Constantinople that the custom arose of placing the Churches of Saints Peter and Paul and Saints Sergius and Bacchus at the service of the Latin clergy in Constantinople, especially when a representative of the Pope or the Pope himself should visit the city.[88] The erection of the basilica of Saints Peter and Paul as a result of the new religious orientation of Justin and Justinian's policy also must have required great expenditure. The foundations of the Church of Saints Sergius and Bacchus, known now as Kutchuk Aya Sofia (Little Saint Sofia), were laid in 527, the year of Justinian's accession, and its erection must have been completed before 536. I mention this church here, although it does not belong to the period of Justin, because some scholars erroneously attribute its construction to his time.[89] With his wife, Empress Euphemia, Justin did build in Constantinople the women's nunnery known as that of the Augusta, where she was buried.[90]

[87] *Collectio Avellana*, no. 218 (pp. 679–680). Thiel, *Epistolae romanorum pontificum genuinae*, epp. 77–78 (pp. 873–874; 877). *Baronii Ann. Eccles.*, a. 519. See A. van Millingen, *Byzantine Churches in Constantinople*, p. 64, note. J. Ebersolt-A. Thiers, *Les églises de Constantinople* (Paris, 1913), pp. 22–24; 253.

[88] Van Millingen, *op. cit.*, p. 67.

[89] See for instance Arch. Sergius, *The Complete Menologion of the Orient*, II, 2, p. 242 (in Russian).

[90] Πάτρια, III, 183. *Scriptores originum constantinopolitanarum*, ed. Preger, p. 273. In his article on Justin, Suidas apparently attributes the erection of the famous Golden Hall (Chrysotriclinos) in the Great Palace to Justin I. But this hall was in reality built by Justin II. *Suidae Lexicon*, ed. Ada Adler, I, 2, 646; ed.

The building activities of Justin were not limited to the capital. They extended to the provinces, where, as we know, he repaired and restored many buildings damaged or ruined by natural disasters. It is very probable that during Justin's reign, most probably in 522–523, the town walls of Bethshan-Scythopolis, the native city of Cyril of Scythopolis in Palestina Secunda, were repaired with a grant "provided by imperial liberality." Two Greek inscriptions which were discovered in the excavation of Tell el-Hosn, in 1921–1923, refer to this fact. The first reads: "With a grant made by Imperial liberality at the instance of Flavius Arsenius, the most glorious (ἐνδοξοτάτου), the entire construction of the wall was repaired in the time of Flavius Anastasius in his ninth year (?) as governor (ἄρχοντος), the third indiction, the year. . . ." The second inscription runs as follows: "With a grant . . . the entire construction of the wall was repaired in the time of Fl. Leo, the most magnificent governor (τοῦ μεγαλοπρεπεστάτοῦ ἄρχοντος), the first (or fourth) indiction." These two inscriptions supply us with the names of the two high local officials of that time, Flavius Arsenius, who supposedly was the dux or military governor of both Palestina Prima and Secunda, and Flavius Anastasius, who is termed archon, the designation of the incumbent of the civil governorship of a province, Palestina Secunda in the present context, and is equivalent to the *praeses* and *consularis* of the contemporary Latin sources. The latest writer on these inscriptions (J. Starr) remarks: "If the identification be correct, the most likely date would be 522–523 A. D." [91]

In addition to these two inscriptions, the excavations directed in 1931 by G. M. FitzGerald discovered at Beisân (Bethshan)-Scythopolis a Greek inscription which records the foundation of a monastery. "The monastery of the abbot and treasurer (ἀποκρισιαρίου) Justin was

---

I. Bekker (Berlin, 1854), p. 535. Generally speaking, Suidas in his article confuses the two Justins.

[91] The first inscription was published by J. Germer-Durand, "Inscription byzantine de Scythopolis," *Echos d'Orient*, XIV (1911), pp. 207–208. The revised reading of the inscription in G. M. FitzGerald, *Beth-Shan Excavations 1921–1923: The Arab and Byzantine Levels*, III (Philadelphia, 1931), p. 47. The second inscription in FitzGerald, *op. cit.*, p. 46, plate XVIII, 2. Both inscriptions have been republished and interpreted by Joshua Starr, "The Byzantine Inscriptions of Bethshan-Scythopolis," *American Journal of Philology*, LVIII, 1 (1937), pp. 83–84. I agree with Starr's opinion.

founded in the 15th indiction in the year 858 on the twenty . . . of the month of Panemos, and in the same year, in the month of September, the first indiction, it was inaugurated. The offering of Nysius the scholasticus. O Lord, help Nysius." From this inscription we learn that the so-called Pompeian era was employed in the sixth century at Scythopolis; and the double dating of the inscription enables us to determine the era for Scythopolis as beginning in 64 B. C.[92] Hence our inscription belongs to the year 522 A. D. In other words, during Justin's reign at Scythopolis, the capital of Palestina Secunda, a certain scholasticus Nysius contributed money for the construction of a monastery whose abbot and treasurer was a certain Justin.

Unfortunately, for the time being we have very few inscriptions which may be attributed to Justin's period. Most of them were discovered in Syria, and they deal with the erection of some church buildings, which were built or repaired not at the emperor's expense, but probably by private organizations or indiivdual citizens. In Göl-Djibrin in the district of Antioch, a church was built in 521.[93] At Kafr Arouq in the same district "under the lord of the universe ($\tau\hat{\omega}\nu$ οἰκουμένων) Fl. Justin Augustus" a refuge (προσφύγιον) was dedicated to Saints Eia (?), Andreas, and Dometius, in 521–522.[94] At Kafr Antin in the same district a certain Damianus erected a building in 523. In the same place on the lintel *in situ* of a building called by the natives id-dukkân, "the shop," was found a Syriac inscription with the names of Mar Damianos and his son Mar Kosmas.[95] At Sudjin in Chalcidica in

---

[92] The inscription was published by L. H. Vincent, "L'ère de Scythopolis d'après une inscription nouvelle," *Revue biblique*, XLII (1933), 555–561; chronological calculations, pp. 560–561. The inscription was republished by J. Starr, *op. cit.*, pp. 85–86. See also G. M. FitzGerald, *A Sixth Century Monastery at Beth-Shan*, University of Pennsylvania, vol. IV, 12 (no. 20); appendix, p. 19; plate XXII.

[93] L. Jalabert and R. Mouterde, *Inscriptions grecques et latines de la Syrie*, II (Paris, 1939), no. 355 (pp. 206–207). See R. Devreesse, *Le patriarcat d'Antioche*, p. 174 and n. 5.

[94] Jalabert-Mouterde, no. 589 (pp. 321–323). Saint Dometius was highly venerated in Syria. He is several times mentioned by H. Delehaye, *Les origines du culte des martyrs*, (Bruxelles, 1933), pp. 192, 206, 213, 241. Devreesse, p. 174 and n. 10. On Kafr (Kefer) Arouq, R. Dussaud, *Topographie historique de la Syrie antique et médiévale*, pp. 238–239.

[95] *Idem*, no. 392 (pp. 223–224). Devreesse, p. 174 and note 8. On the Syriac inscription and discussion on the names of Damianos and Kosmas see Enno

Syria Prima in 527–528 was built the martyrion of Saint Sergius.[96] At Harake (Herakeh) in Syria Secunda was found the lintel of a structure, perhaps a monastery, with a dated inscription, August 524.[97] At Kafr Nabo in Syria Prima was discovered a dated chapel, 525 A. D. [98] Also at Kafr Nabo (Nabū) was discovered a chapel with a lintel *in situ* of 525–526.[99] At il-Burdj in Syria Secunda a large lintel *in situ* was found over the entrance to a tower with an inscription stating it had been built by a centurion (ἑκατοντάρχης) in July, 526 A. D.; the inscription mentions the archangel Michael and the holy Longinus.[100] At Falûl in Syria Secunda a chapel (εὐκτήριον) of the Archangels was discovered built by the most glorious (λαμπρότατος) Diogenes. In the year 838, ind. 5, i.e. in 526–527.[101]

I have given these casual inscriptions from Syria here, because they have never before been collected for Justin's period. They are too few and fragmentary and their origin from one province only is too restricted to give them great importance for the general picture. But they may show to a certain extent that during the monophysite persecution under Justin and in spite of the Persian danger, new churches, new oratories, and new buildings, patronized of course by saints of Chalcedonian trend, were erected in monophysite Syria as a counterpoise to the monophysite shrines, of which many were closed or converted to the orthodox cult. It would be extremely important for

---

Littmann, discussion in *Publications of Princeton University: Archaeological Expeditions to Syria in 1904–5 and 1909*, Division IV, *Semitic Inscriptions*, Section B: "Syriac Inscriptions" (Leyden, 1934), no. 61 (pp. 52–55).

[96] *Idem*, no. 258 (p. 144). Devreesse, p. 167 and n. 3.

[97] *Publications of Princeton University: Archaeological Expeditions to Syria in 1904–5 and 1909*, Division III, *Greek and Latin Inscriptions*, Section B: "Northern Syria" by W. K. Prentice (Leyden, 1922), no. 1029 (pp. 100–101).

[98] *Ibidem*, Division II, Architecture, Section B: "Northern Syria" by H. C. Butler (Leyden, 1920), no. 85 (p. 295). Devreesse, p. 174 and n. 19.

[99] *Ibidem*, Enno Littmann, "Syriac Inscriptions," no. 52 (pp. 42–46). Devreesse, p. 174 and n. 19.

[100] *Ibidem*, "Northern Syria," by W. K. Prentice, no. 1058 (p. 112). It seems to mean that the two saints mentioned were the patrons of the structure. See Devreesse, p. 185 and n. 7.

[101] *Ibidem*, Div. III, no. 1050 (pp. 108–109). Through some misunderstanding the word εὐκτήριον, oratory, place of prayer, was translated as "Resting place of the Archangels" in the same publication. "Northern Syria," part I by H. C. Butler, p. 98: Falûl, the church as the "Resting place of the Archangels." Devreesse, p. 186 and n. 8.

our knowledge of Justin's time to have more inscriptions to study from various regions of the empire.

One of the usual methods of Byzantine diplomacy was to stir up the neighbors of the empire, one against another, in order to alleviate international relations which sometimes became complicated; for this purpose money was needed. For example, Justin, as we have noted above, sent Probus, the nephew of the late Anastasius, with a large sum of money to Bosporus in the Crimea to induce the Huns to help the Iberians, who were at that time fighting against the Persians and badly needed Roman support. Probus was unsuccessful in his mission; nevertheless, it involved the expenditure of money.[102] Moreover, a considerable sum of money was lost through the dishonesty and abuses of Justin's high officials. Marinus and some other officials of the late Anastasius embezzled and squandered considerable amounts of state money taken from the reserve accumulated by Anastasius.

It is possible that Justin himself felt the financial burden his government had to bear and tried to put into effect measures of economy. I hesitate, however, to explain the suppression of the Olympic festival at Antioch as a measure of government economy. It is rather to be explained by political motives, by the desire of the government to put an end to the turbulent excesses of the factions.[103]

To sum up, if we consider all the circumstances — the restoration of the ruined or damaged cities, war expenses, money paid to neighboring peoples such as the Huns in the Crimea, defalcation on the part of high officials, the extraordinary expenses for Justinian's consulship in 521, and probably other items not mentioned in our evidence — we must conclude that Justin's expenditures were unavoidable, and dismiss the biased and highly colored accusation of senseless prodigality and extravagance Procopius brings against Justinian, who, he says, before he became sole emperor squandered the funds "which would last for a hundred years for any other extremely prodigal emperor." The exhaustion of Anastasius' reserve during the reign of Justin, large

---

[102] Proc., *B. P.* I, 12, 6; ed. Haury, I, 57; Dewing, I, 96. See A. Vasiliev, *The Goths in the Crimea*, p. 70.

[103] On the suppression of the festival as a measure of government economy, see G. Downey, "Ephraemius, Patriarch of Antioch," *Church History*, VII, p. 365.

though the reserve was for the time, is easily explained by the causes I have enumerated. The false assumption originated by Procopius dies hard, however. As late as 1928 a Dutch historian still wrote: "They speak of 320,000 pounds of gold. Justin and Justinian, who, since the nephews of Anastasius were still living, must be regarded more or less as usurpers, had squandered (the reserve) on themselves in feasts and gifts to make themselves popular." [104] Opinions like this are absolutely untenable and must disappear from our historical works.

JUSTIN'S COINAGE

Justin's coinage was issued from the following mints: Constantinople, Thessalonica, Nicomedia, Cyzicus, and Antioch, and consists of the same denominations as in the previous reign. The gold coins of his reign, solidi (*nomismata*) are sometimes, as Wroth states, of rather rude workmanship, and it can be difficult to separate them from the numerous "barbarian" pieces that bear the name and head of Iustinus. Many of the coins bearing his name do not belong to the imperial series but were struck at Vandalic, Ostrogothic, Burgundian, and Italian mints. As is often the case in Byzantine numismatics, the coins of Justin I are common in gold and bronze, but rare in silver. As we know, on April 1, 527, Justinian was created Augustus, and reigned jointly with his uncle till August 1, when Justin died. The coins of the joint rule are now rare, especially the bronze pieces, but the gold coins were probably struck in considerable numbers, as there are two varieties of the solidus, each with its own set of officinae (numerals); the Constantinopolitan mint must have been active during the short period of four months when these solidi were issued. The two emperors are represented seated side by side on the reverse with the legend DN IUSTIN ET IUSTINIAN PP AUG. As I have noted above, the alleged representation of Euphemia, the wife of Justin I, on the reverse of a small bronze coin of her husband, reproduced by Sabatier (I, 167) is in the highest degree doubtful. Wroth suspects the coin to be a badly preserved example of the piece with the Tyche of Antioch on the reverse.[105] Unusual simi-

---

[104] J. Romein, *Byzantium* (Zutphen, 1928), p. 21 (in Dutch).
[105] See W. Wroth, *Catalogue of the Imperial Byzantine Coins in the British Museum*, I, p. XIV and n. 4; pp. 21–22; Justin's coins in gold, silver, and bronze,

larity of the heads, postures, and some other details may be noted on the coins of Anastasius, Justin I, Justinian, Justin II (567–578), Tiberius II (578–582) and Maurice (582–602).[106]

Now it is possible to surmise with great probability that, during Justin's reign, the Byzantine coinage passed through a very essential transformation. It is on the reverse of the solidi of his period that the high-girdled standing female figure of Victory used in the preceding reigns is transformed into the frontal archangel clad in the usual male attire with the tunic and pallium. This new figure of the angel of victory becomes the usual reverse of the coins of his nephew, Justinian. The type retains the old inscription VICTORIA AUG, appropriate for the female victory, as well as the cross and staff held in the right hand (cf. Wroth, op. cit., I, plates I, II, and IV; Tolstoy, op. cit., III, plates 16 and 18). The angel, however, also holds a globe surmounted by a cross. The famous and beautiful ivory in the British Museum which represents an archangel holding a staff in his left hand and a cross-surmounted globe in his right, and standing on the steps of an arched doorway under a panel with the Greek inscription + ΔΕΧΟΥ ΠΑΡΟΝΤΑ | ΚΑΙ ΜΑΘΩΝ ΤΗΝ ΑΙΤΙΑΝ (Receive these gifts (?) and having learnt the cause . . .) should have some connection, according to Professor A. Friend, with the type inaugurated on Justin's coinage. Since the gift of the cross-surmounted globe and staff can most appropriately be made only to an emperor, the panel requires an ivory counterpart representing a standing portrait of an emperor to complete the diptych. The date of the ivories then, because of the iconography of the coin types mentioned above, would most reasonably be placed in the reign of Justin I or in that of his nephew, Justinian; so the imperial portrait depicted on the lost panel could have been either of these two emperors.

---

pp. 11–20; Justin and Justinian, pp. 23–24. Hugh Goodacre, *A Handbook of the Coinage of the Byzantine Empire*, II: Anastasius to Michael VI, pp. 64–67. J. Sabatier, *Description générale des monnaies byzantines*, I, p. 167. F. Dvorschak, "Studien zum byzantinischen Münzwesen," *Numismatische Zeitschrift*, XXIX (1936), p. 75.

[106] See A. Grabar, *L'empereur dans l'art byzantin*, p. 9, n. 2 (similarity on the coins of Anastasius, Justin I, and Justinian). J. Babelon, *Le portrait dans l'antiquité d'après les monnaies* (Paris, 1942), p. 171 (he includes Justin II, Tiberius II, and Maurice).

The fineness of the style would favor the earlier emperor Justin I, as Professor Friend believes.[106a]

I wish to submit here a frankly tentative list of various places where supplies of Byzantine coins with Justin's name have been found.[107]

Africa: In el-Djem (ancient Thysdrus), Tunis, in a burial mound in 1903 were found nineteen coins of Justin alone, and one of Justin jointly with Justinian (Mosser, 29).

Egypt: Alexandria, in 1903, in a burial mound, twelve coins of Justin, three *semissis* and nine *tremissis*; in Saqqara, excavations of 1908–1910 (Monastery of Offa), two coins of Justin and three of Anastasius or Justin I (Mosser, 3 and 77).

Palestine: On February 11, 1928, 125 Byzantine folles (bronze coins) were discovered at Khirbat Dubel on Mount Carmel. They range from Anastasius I to Heraclius (611–612), the majority being those of Justin I and Justinian, from the mint at Constantinople. The hoard therefore was probably abandoned not long after that date, perhaps at the time of the Persian invasion. Some of the coins of Justin I and of Justinian show faint traces of restriking; these are generally thinner and on slightly broader flans. There are 109 coins of Justin I: 94 from the mint of Constantinople, 8 from Antioch, and 7 from Nicomedia. The bust of the emperor is presented with the diadem and in military dress; legend DN IVSTINVS PPAVG. Three coins of Justin jointly with Justinian from the mint of Constantinople, legend DNIVSTINE-IVSTINIAN PP AVG.[108]

Jerash: Transjordania. A concise catalogue of some 1407 coins found at Jerash during the excavations of 1928–1934 contains 32 coins of Justin I: 30 struck in Constantinople, one in Nicomedia, one un certain.[109]

[106a] See H. Peirce, and R. Tyler, *L'art byzantin*, II (Paris, 1934), 75–76 and plate 35a: leaf of ivory: Archangel, 500 (?). The translation of the inscription is taken from O. Dalton, *Catalogue of Early Christian Antiquities and Objects from the Christian East in the British Museum* (London, 1901), pp. 53–54. See below a detailed discussion of the ivory in the British Museum: *Excursus*, pp. 418–426.

[107] My chief source of information is S. M. Mosser, *A Bibliography of Byzantine Coin Hoards* (New York, 1935), *Numismatic Notes and Monographs*, no. 67. Some other publications will be indicated below.

[108] C. L(ambert), "A Hoard of Byzantine Coins," *The Quarterly of the Department of Antiquities in Palestine*, I (Jerusalem, 1932), p. 55; 57–59 (nos. 34–145); 68. Mere mention in Mosser, p. 45.

[109] A. R. Bellinger, *Coins from Jerash*, 1928–1934 (New York, 1938), p. 10;

Syria: In Antioch-on-the-Orontes, during the excavations of 1932 were found 124 coins of the Byzantine period. Among them there are none that are particularly noteworthy. Those of Arcadius, Justin I, and Justinian I are the most numerous.[110]

Cyprus: excavation of 1899, burial 633 A. D.: two golden coins (solidi) of Justin with Justinian (Mosser, 23–24; now at the Metropolitan Museum of Art, New York).

Asia Minor and *Anatolia*: In Alishan, 1930, burial c. 527 A. D. three folles of Justin (Mosser, 3–4; see Wroth, pl. III, 5; pl. IV, 1). In Perganon, Excavations 1904–1908, burial, not a hoard: four coins of Justin (Mosser, 64). Priene, burial: one coin of Justin (Mosser, 70). A hoard of Byzantine coins came into the possession of the Department of Antiquities in Palestine in August 1935. They were reported to have been found at Fandaqūmiya, a village north of Sebastya, by a group of laborers who were digging a well for the Public Works Department. They were found together and form a hoard. 69 folles, ranging in date from the time of Anastasius I to the second year of Heraclius' reign (611–612 A. D.), and showing a variety of five mints. But the great majority belong to the reigns of Justin I, Justinian I, and Justin II. The coins of Justin I struck at Constantinople show all the five officina marks A, B, Γ, Δ, and E, and the coin struck at Cyzicus has the obverse legend in retrograde order. There are 16 coins of Justin I (nos. 5–20). On all those coins appears the bust of Justin I, beardless, wearing the diadem, paludamentum, and cuirass. One coin (no. 21) of Justin with Justinian. Justin's 16 coins are from various mints: 11 in Constantinople, one at Thessalonica, three at Nicomedia, one at Cyzicus. Justin's coin with Justinian is from the mint in Constantinople.[111]

---

description of Justin's coins, .pp. 98–100. Numismatic notes and monographs, no. 81. The same information is given by Bellinger in C. H. Kraeling, *Gerasa, City of the Decapolis*, p. 503.

[110] *Antioch-on-the-Orontes*, I: *The Excavations of 1932*, ed. by G. W. Elderkin (Princeton-London-Oxford, 1934), p. 80 (coins by S. H. Weber).

[111] J. Baramki, "A Hoard of Byzantine Coins," *The Quarterly of the Department of Antiquities in Palestine*, VIII (Jerusalem, 1939), published for the Government of Palestine by Humphrey Milford, Oxford University Press (London), pp. 81–85.

India: One golden coin of Justin I (possibly more) was found at Pudankāvu, Travancore, in 1903; no silver or copper.[112]

Europe: The Balkans: Greece, Corinth excavations, 1896–1929, burial, not a hoard; eight coins of Justin I (Mosser, 21). Olympia, Elis, 1875–1877, burial: four Byzantine hoards found in the course of excavations, each c. 1000. No coins later than Maurice Tiberius (582–602). No specific names are indicated (Mosser, 60); but without doubt among 4000 pieces some of Justin's are to be found.

Bulgaria: In 1911 in Aytoska Banja in a burial, one coin of Justin; in 1914, Hadji Sinanlar, Varna, in a burial, several coins of Justin I; in 1914, Mominbrod, in a burial, 105 bronze coins of Justin I; in 1929, Sofia, in a burial, nine bronze coins of Justin (Mosser, 8; 38; 54–55; 81).

Dalmatia: In the ruins of Narona was found the hoard of a certain woman, Urbice, which contained 65 golden coins from Justin I to Tiberius II. This hoard was evidently hidden in the ground in 582 when the Avars conquered Sirmium and had not been disturbed since. In this hoard were six golden coins of Justin I.[113] In Rumania, in 1856, Klein Schelken, Herrmanstadter Kreis, in a burial, was found one golden coin of Justin I (Mosser, 46).

Italy: In Benevento, in a burial, were found two solidi and two tremissi of Justin I; in Cotrone, in a burial, 103 golden coins from Theodosius II to Justinian; in 1888 in Finero, Domodossola, 4 solidi and 8 tremissi of Anastasius, Justin I, and Justinian; in Padenghe, Desenzano, Brescia, 12 solidi of Leo I, Zeno, Anastasius I, and Justin I; Rome, Lateran Palace: among many golden coins were some of Justin I (Mosser, 10; 23; 33; 63; 73).

France: Alise-Saint-Reine, Cote d'Or: several gold coins of Justin; Chinon: 10 gold coins of Justin; commune of Gourdon, Burgundy: 20 solidi of Justin and 5 tremissi; Viviers, Ardèche: burial, soon after 527 A. D.: 18 golden coins of Justin (Mosser, 3; 18; 36; 96).

Germany. Biesenbrow, Brandenburg, burial: some golden coins of Justin (Mosser, 10).

---

[112] R. Sewell, "Roman Coins found in India," *Journal of the Royal Asiatic Society*, p. 634.

[113] C. Jireček, *Geschichte der Serben*, I, p. 96. Mosser, 57.

Netherlands: Friesland, burial: barbaric imitations of Justin's coins; Velsen, burial: 3 solidi of Justin; Wieuwerd, Friesland, burial, c. 612 A. D.: two tremissi of Justin (Mosser, 34; 95; 98).

Sweden. The Island Gotland. In this island alone were found 111 golden Byzantine coins of the period from 395 to 565; at Etelhem, Gotland, in 1929, 8 golden coins of Justin.[114]

According to the *Report* of coins identified by Professor Katharine M. Edwards from the excavations at old Corinth, 1896–1929, beginning with Anastasius I, there are seven coins from the time of Justin I. But in the excavations at Corinth during the years 1930–1935 there are recorded thirty-eight coins from the time of Justin I and one coin from the time of the joint rule of Justin and Justinian.[115]

It would not be out of place to mention here that the Numismatic Collection of Dumbarton Oaks has four solidi of Justin, and one which is to be classed as a "barbarous imitation"; two semisses, four tremisses; one solidus of Justin's joint reign with Justinian; seven silver pieces; eighteen bronze pieces of Constantinople, five of Antioch, and one of Nicomedia.

[114] *Gotskiy Sbornik* (Leningrad, 1932), p. 42, n. 1 (in Russian). Mosser, p. 32. See also T. J. Arne, "Deux nouvelles découvertes de solidi en Gotland," *Acta Archaeologica*, II (Copenhagen, 1931), 9 (three coins of Justin I).

[115] See John H. Finley, "Corinth in the Middle Ages," *Speculum*, VII, 4 (October, 1932), p. 499. Katharine M. Edwards, "Report on the Coins Found in the Excavations at Corinth during the Years 1930–1035," *Hesperia*, VI, 2 (Athens, 1937), p. 255.

CHAPTER EIGHT

Justin and Legislation

The legislative acts which were issued either under Justin's sole rule or during the short period of the joint rule of Justin and Justinian deserve much more attention than has been paid to them by previous writers. It is quite unjust to dismiss this legislation by a flat statement like E. Stein's that "as lawgiver Justin was not of great importance," and that "his laws deal mainly with juridical matters without historical significance." [1] Not all the laws, of course, are of great importance; but some are significant turning points in the history of various institutions, and traces of their influence may be discovered in the later periods of Byzantine law. I must admit, however, that these laws are difficult to interpret clearly and appreciate properly for those who like myself are not specially trained in Roman and Byzantine jurisprudence. [2]

Most of Justin's legislative acts reflect development of trends in public life and administration which go back to previous times. Only one law — that against heretics — was apparently called forth directly by the new religious policy of Justin, whose main objective, as we know, was to restore in full strength the Chalcedonian credo and normal relations with the Roman See. Most laws, however, represent grades of progress. Even the famous law "On marriage" (De nuptiis) which has almost always been connected with Justinian's eager desire to marry Theodora, was but a further step in the long process of legislation in favor of women.

We have tried above to explain why the only edict against heretics — and a very severe one — which was published during Justin's reign, was issued at the very end of his reign, during his joint rule with Justinian. The late date of the law and its rigidity must be explained by the failure

---

[1] E. Stein, "Justinus," PW, X, 1320: "als Gesetzeber ist Justinus nur wenig hervorgetreten."
[2] In this chapter I am greatly indebted to Professor Clyde Pharr, Vanderbilt University, and to Mrs. Mary Brown Pharr for their help and suggestions.

of a milder and more conciliatory policy towards heretics upon which the government had embarked after Vitalian's assassination in 520. This policy failed, and the law of 527 was the result of this failure, marking the return of the government to a religious policy of force and coercion.

Twenty-eight laws of Justin's reign have survived in the Justinian *Code*. In addition, it has been pointed out that one Greek constitution has been lost either before or after the rescript of August 21, 524 (II, 7, 27 (8); Krueger, pp. 101–102); this lost constitution is indicated in the modern editions of the Code by the three opening words in brackets Ὁ αὐτὸς βασιλεύς (II, 7, 28; Krueger, p. 102). Apparently it is Justin's constitution *De advocatis praefecti praetorio Orientis* which is mentioned in Justinian's rescript, in Latin, to the Praetorian Prefect John (Iohannes) issued about 531–534.[3] There is also the edict issued in 519–520, in which all soldiers are directed to adhere to the decrees of the Council of Chalcedon. This edict recorded in the Syriac evidence has been preserved, as I have tried to prove above, in the Justinian *Code*, among the edicts issued by Justinian (I, 4, 20). Finally there is a bilingual rescript of Justin and Justinian of June 1, 527, which has been preserved in an inscription. This rescript is addressed to the Praetorian Prefect Archelaus, whose name is often mentioned in the Code.[4] Most of the laws are written in Latin; but several are compiled in both languages, Latin and Greek.

Sixteen of Justin's laws, out of the total of twenty-eight, are exactly dated: thirteen by the names of the consuls, and three by the joint rule of Justin and Justinian (April 4–August 1, 527); six have been tentatively attributed to the year 527, though this attribution can not be considered absolutely certain; and six laws bear the name of Justin only and therefore can be assigned to no fixed year.

The magistrates to whom the laws are addressed are as follows: *Praetorian Prefects*; Apion, 518; Marinus, 519; Demosthenes, 527, also in two undated rescripts and in a tentatively dated rescript of 527;

[3] *Code* II, 7, 29 (9); Krueger, p. 102: "De constitutione divinae recordationis Iustini patris nostri super togatis amplissimae tuae sedis prolata." This lost constitution is also mentioned in *Basilica*, VIII, 1, 35; ed. Heimbach, I (Leipzig, 1833), 353; ed. Zepos, I (Athens, 1896), 385 (an interpretation is added to the constitution).
[4] Diehl, "Rescrit des empereurs Justin et Justinien en date du 1er juin 527," *Bulletin de correspondance hellénique*, XVII, pp. 501–520.

Archaelaus, 524, 525, in a tentative rescript of 527, and in the rescript of 527 in Ch. Diehl's inscription. *Magistri officiorum*: Tatianus, 520, 527, and in an undated rescript; Lucinius, 524. *Praefecti urbi*: Theodorus, 524, 526; Theodotus, undated.[5] *Quaestor sacri palatii*: Proculus, undated.

Two years of Justin's reign may be singled out for the number of the laws issued therein: the year 524, when five rescripts were issued, and even more the year 527, when five exactly dated rescripts and six tentatively attributed to this year were published. Even if some of the latter laws do not belong to this year, the last year of Justin's reign, specifically the period from April 4 to August 1, when Justin and Justinian were jointly ruling the empire, was the most fruitful in the number of laws published.

No doubt Justinian was deeply interested in legislation even before he was coöpted as Justin's colleague and became Augustus, when his interest in legal work became more intense. There is probably no doubt that at that time Justinian had already conceived the idea of compiling a new code and was meditating upon the measures which he later took, after Justin's death; it is quite possible that Justinian had already fixed his eyes on the men he planned to use as instruments, such as Tribonian and his two learned coadjutors, Theophilus, professor at Constantinople, and Dorotheus, professor at Berytus. Otherwise it would be hardly possible to understand how Justinian could have set to work so promptly after his accession. Evidently the general plan of his colossal work had already been conceived before Justin's death. It is possible that this interest of Justinian in legislative work explains the fact that the largest number of Justin's laws fall within the short time of his joint rule with Justinian. Even before Justinian's accession, we can discern some foreshadowings of his great legislative work.

Most of Justin's laws which have been preserved in the *Code* — twelve out of twenty-eight — deal with the practice of the law courts and specifically with the appeal courts and the procedure of appeal, as well as with advocates (advocati, συνήγοροι) who along with notaries (*tabularii*) were public officers under the president of the court

---

[5] There is some confusion as to these two names, Theodorus and Theodotus. See Krueger, p. 101, n. 7; 170, n. 5 (*Cod.* IV, 30, 13).

($\pi\rho o\kappa a\theta\eta\mu\epsilon\nu os$) and whose business was to plead in court on behalf of the parties concerned. These laws introduce some changes in the general administration of the courts as to staff and remuneration; they lay stress upon speedy and unbiased trial; and they supply us with information about witnesses and their duties. One among these twelve rescripts which was addressed to the Praetorian Prefect Demosthenes, a. 520–524 (VII, 62, 34) announces that the cases which were to be submitted for final decision to the emperor (*consultationes*) should be considered and settled by a special board, instituted on such occasions by a special imperial decree (*per sacram pragmaticam nostri numinis jussionem*); the board should consist of the *quaestor sacri palatii* and *duo magnifici viri vel patricii vel consulares vel praefectorii*; decision of the board should be final, and no appeal against it admitted. Some of these laws have been incorporated in the *Basilica*. A detailed investigation of these twelve laws and an evaluation of them must be made in connection with the general question of the development of the civil Romano-Byzantine Law and the history of the law courts, which I am not equipped to do.[6] In addition, Justinian's law addressed to the Praetorian Prefect Iohannes and attributed to the years 531–534, mentions "the constitution of Justin of blessed memory, father of ours," concerning legal advisers or attorneys in Johannes' Prefecture.[7]

Decree on Marriage and Illegitimate Children

Although almost half of Justin's decrees concern the practice of the law courts and appeals, the most significant laws of his period are two: "On Marriage" (*De nuptiis*) and "On Heretics." The latter law has already been discussed in detail above. The decree "On Marriage," an undated, unusually lengthy and detailed piece of juridical literature, is

---

[6] Here are the twelve laws under review: 1) VII, 63, 3; Krueger, 325, Dec. 1, 518. 2) VII, 63, 4; Kr. 325, May 28, 520. 3) II, 7, 25 (6); Kr. 101, Dec. 1, 529. 4) II, 7, 26 (7); Kr. 101, Febr. 13, 524. 5) II, 7, 27 (8); Kr. 101–102, Aug. 21, 524. 6) II, 7, 28; Kr. 102. Only these three words have been restored: Ὁ αὐτὸς βασιλεύς. 7) I, 15, 2; Kr. 68–69, a. 527. 8) VII, 62, 34; Kr. 323, a. 520–524. 9) III, 1, 12; Kr. 120, a. 527? 10) IV, 20, 16; Kr. 159, a. 527?; in the *Basilica*, XXI, 1, 40; Heimbach, II, 411; Zepos, II (Athens, 1898), 1832–1833. 11) VII, 62, 35; Kr. 323–324. 12) VII, 62, 36; Kr. 324, a. 527? in the *Basilica*, IX, 1, 126; Heimbach, I, 440; Zepos, I, 460.

[7] *Cod. Just.* II, 7, 29 (9): "De constitutione divinae recordationis Iustini patris nostri super togatis amplissimae tuae sedis prolata" (ed. Krueger, p. 102).

addressed to the Praetorian Prefect Demosthenes; and since his first prefecture is attributed to the years 520–524, the law itself must be ascribed to the same period.[8]

The law consists of a preamble and eight paragraphs. In the preamble after mentioning that it is a peculiar duty of imperial benevolence not only to consider the convenience of subjects but also to improve it (*eis mederi*), the law turns to its main subject, i.e. the women "who through the weakness of their sex" (*imbecillitate sexus*) have fallen into unworthy living. The chief aim of the law is to help them abandon their immoral customs and return them to an honest life. "If we fail to act in this manner in reference to the subjects of our empire, we should seem to be unworthy of pardon." The first paragraph of the new law opens with an interesting contrast between manumitted slaves (*servos libertate donatos*), who after manumission become full citizens and live "as if they were free-born" (*quasi . . . ingenui nati essent*), and women who after being actresses (*quae scaenicis quidem sese ludis immiscuerunt*) and then wishing to abjure their errors and "escape a dishonest profession" have no hope of resuming normal life "as if they had not been in error." In accordance with "the present most merciful law," women who have relinquished their evil and dishonest condition and are anxious "to embrace a more virtuous and more honest life" are permitted to contract legal marriage. And all the men, no matter of what rank, who marry them shall have no apprehension whatever that their marriage may be considered invalid on account of the past of their wives. The latter shall be regarded as free women who "shall have no difference whatever from those who had never erred in a similar way" (*neque differentiam aliquam eas habere cum his, quae nihil simile*

---

[8] *Cod. Just.* V, 4, 23; ed. Krueger, pp. 196–197. One of the manuscripts calls the author of this decree Justinian, not Justin (see ed. Krueger, p. 196, n. 18); but this is incorrect, because in a later decree of Justinian's period, there is a reference to the decree *De nuptiis* which had been issued by the late Justin. *Cod. Just.* V, 4, 29, 8: οὔτε ἐκ τῆς ᾿Ιουστίνου τοῦ τῆς θείας λήξεως διατάξεως (Krueger, p. 198). Procopius also testifies that Justinian compelled Justin to amend the ancient law forbidding a man of senatorial rank to marry a courtesan. Proc., *Anecdota*, IX, 50–51 (Dewing, pp. 118–119). The full text of Justin's decree *De nuptiis* has also been reproduced by Alemannus in his *Notae in Historiam Arcanam*. Procopius, *CSHB*, III, 387–389. An English translation of this law in *The Civil Law*, by S. P. Scott, XIII, pp. 150–153.

peccaverunt), provided, however, that the marriage can be proved by dotal contracts reduced to writing.

The children by these marriages shall be legitimate children to their father, with all hereditary rights (par. 2). The same hereditary rights (par. 3) shall be granted those women who after the publication of this rescript have changed their way of living but have not yet contracted marriage (*ad matrimonium venire distulerint*). Paragraph 4 runs as follows: "But it is our will that those women also shall be of similar status to the women who obtain such benefit from the emperor, who even though they have not supplicated the Most Serene Emperor, have nevertheless obtained some high rank by voluntary grant (from the emperor) before their marriage. As a consequence of this high rank, every other blot (*stigma*) also must be completely abolished through which such women are prohibited from being legally married to certain men." In par. 6 we find a further step for the improvement of the status of women in the empire. If a daughter born to a mother actress, who till her death practiced in her profession, petitions after the latter's death for "Imperial clemency" and obtains it, she shall be freed from "maternal wrong doing" and be allowed to marry; and she also can without fear of previous laws contract matrimony with those who were formerly forbidden to marry the daughter of an actress. Par. 7, dealing with a more general case, repeals what in former laws had been somewhat obscurely (*licet obscurius*) constituted, that matrimony contracted between persons of unequal rank shall not be valid unless dotal instruments referring to it (*dotalia instrumenta*) were executed; now such matrimony shall be absolutely valid without any distinction of persons, provided the women are free and free-born, and that no suspicion of any nefarious or incestuous union arises; "for we under all circumstances annul nefarious and incestuous unions as well as those which were especially forbidden by the provision of former laws, with the exception, however, of the union which we have permitted by the present law, that is to say that by the right of lawful matrimony." The law closes (par. 8) with the statement that matrimonial unions which have been contracted according to this decree from the beginning of Justin's reign (*ab initio nostri imperii*) shall be lawful so that the father of the children who were born, or are to be born, to his wife shall have them as real and legitimate successors, entitled to succeed to their father's estate without a will as well as under one (*tam ab intestato quam ex testamento*), and the wife, as well as any children hereafter born to her, shall also be considered legitimate.

As I have noted above, Procopius refers to this law when in his *Anecdota* he speaks of Justinian's marriage with Theodora. "Since it was impossible for a man who had attained to senatorial rank to contract marriage with a courtesan, a thing forbidden from the beginning by the most ancient laws, Justinian compelled the Emperor (i.e. Justin) to amend the laws by a new law, and from then on he lived with Theodora as his married wife, and he thereby opened the way to betrothal with courtesans for all other men." [9] Procopius' interpretation of this law, especially in the *Anecdota*, would give us the impression that the only reason for the promulgation of the new law was Justinian's eager desire to marry Theodora. But as we know such a law was merely one step in the process of the emancipation of women, which goes back to the fourth and fifth centuries and was in accordance with Christian sentiment. Also, as I have emphasized above, Theodora, who had been raised to the high rank of patrician, according to the terms of par. 4 of the law "On Marriage" [10] did not need any modification of the existing legislation which forbade marriage with actresses and prostitutes. But even if Justinian officially needed no special decree for his marriage, the decree would explain and justify to the people in general a case which was in complete accord with the general trend of legislation in favor of women. In my opinion, this is the most plausible interpretation of the decree *De nuptiis*, the main objective of which was to combine Justinian's personal interest with the general trend of legislation. [11]

Generally speaking, the legislation of Justin's period paid considerable attention to matrimonial questions, both with reference to the regulation of the position of illegitimate children and with reference to some financial adjustments connected with the conclusion of marriages. Shortly after his accession to the throne, Justin issued in 519 a decree

[9] Proc. *Anecdota*, IX, 51 (Dewing, VI, 118–119). See *In Historiam Arcanam Notae Alemanni*, Procopius, *CSHB*, III, p. 386.

[10] See above.

[11] Ernst Stein says that this law made it possible for Justinian to marry Theodora. *PW*, X, 1320–1321.

addressed to the Praetorian Prefect Marinus, which is inserted in the Justinian *Code* in the section "Concerning natural children and their mothers, and for what reasons they become legitimate." [12] This law was issued as a counterpoise to the short-lived constitution of Justin's predecessor Anastasius, who at the end of his rule in 517 had shown himself favorable to natural children by granting them rights of inheritance from their fathers if legal offspring were lacking and if the father should desire them to inherit. This law deals with "those who having no children by their legitimate wife keep in the latter's stead women who may bear them children." [13] In this case such children shall be entitled to succeed to the paternal estate as his legitimate children would have succeeded.

But two years later in 519 Justin abrogated Anastasius' rule. Acknowledging the validity of all the cases which on the basis of Anastasius' decree had happened from the time of its promulgation down to November, 519, when the new law was issued, Justin announced that henceforward only offspring of legitimate unions should be taken into consideration "as if the above-mentioned Constitution had never been published" and that "no excuse can henceforth be alleged for the unlawful desires of lust," so that every effort shall be exerted to prevent the violation of the new law.[14] This strict law reminds us of the old law of Constantine the Great, who in 326 proclaimed that "no permission shall be granted anyone to have a concubine in his house during marriage." [15] It is worth noting that in the opening lines of Justin's law, which refer to Anastasius' decree, there is the striking discrimination between children born from women who helped childless husbands

---

[12] "De naturalibus liberis et matribus eorum et ex quibus casibus iusti efficiuntur." *Cod. Just.* V, 27, 7; ed. Krueger, p. 217. English translation by S. P. Scott, *The Civil Law*, XIII, p. 218.

[13] "eos, quibus nullis legitimis existentibus liberis in praesenti aliquae mulieres uxoris loco habentur." *Cod. Just.* V, 27, 6; Krueger, p. 217. English translation by Scott, XIII, pp. 217–218.

[14] *Cod. Just.* V, 27, 7; Krueger, p. 217: "ac si praedicta constitutio lata non esset . . . injusta namque libidinum desideria nulla de cetero venia defendet . . ." In English by S. P. Scott, XIII, 202.

[15] *Cod. Just.* V, 26: "Nemini licentia concedatur constante matrimonio concubinam penes se habere" (ed. Krueger, p. 216). Cf. opinions of some ancient jurists on concubines in *Digesta*, XXV, 7 (ed. Mommsen-Krueger, p. 369). Transl. by Scott, XIII, 213.

create a family and therefore children who could be legitimatized, and children born "from nefarious and incestuous union." The latter were barred from all privileges.[16] But this law of the old and rather strict emperor was not in force for long, and nine years later, in 528 at the beginning of his reign, Justinian restored the former claim of natural children to the extent of one half of their father's possessions: [17] later in 539 he supplemented the law by enacting that the father could leave all his possessions to his natural children if he had none who were legitimate.[18]

DECREE ON WEDDING GIFTS

Another law of Justin connected with the institution of marriage deals with a very essential element in the process of contracting marriages, that of wedding gifts, and is included in the Justinian *Code* in the section *De donationibus ante nuptias vel (et) propter nuptias et sponsaliciis* (V, 3, 19; ed. Krueger, p. 194; English transl. by Scott, XIII, 143–144). I shall put aside here the very complicated problem of the origin, sources, gradual development, and real meaning of the *donatio propter nuptias*. This rather obscure question reminds Mitteis of "a calculation with many unknown quantities" and causes him to emphasize "our unprecedented uncertainty in this field," while another authority on Byzantine law, Zachariae von Lingenthal, remarks that even the Justinian Law is not very clear (*etwas unklar*) on the question of *propter nuptias donatio*.[19] Although undated, this law of Justin is usually attributed to the very end of his rule, about 527, and may be explained by the influence of Justinian, whose general objective was to supply the

---

[16] "ita tamen, ut non aliunde progenitis subvenisse credatur quam non ex nefario nec incesto conjugio." See also *Novella* LXXXIX, 15 (ed. Scholl-Kroll, p. 444).

[17] V, 27, 8: "sed etiam ex duplici portione, id est sex unciis, heredes scribere" (Krueger, p. 217). Translation by Scott, XIII, 219.

[18] *Novella* LXXXIX, 12, 3: "testatori licentia sit etiam in duodecim uncias scribere filios naturales heredes" (ed. Schoell-Kroll, p. 441); also LXXXIX, 15 (Schoell-Kroll, p. 444). Transl. by Scott, XVI, 333; 335.

[19] L. Mitteis, *Reichsrecht und Volksrecht in den östlichen Provinzen des römischen Kaiserreichs* (Leipzig, 1891), p. 256; see a long list of various opinions on this question expressed before 1891, on pp. 256–264. K. Zachariae von Lingenthal, *Geschichte des griechisch-römischen Rechts*, 3rd ed. (Berlin, 1892), p. 83. See also a rather confusing article, "Donatio," by R. Leonhard, in *Pauly-Wissowa*, V (1905), 1538–1539.

institution of marriage with more flexibility and more independence on both sides, that of wife and husband alike.

It was the custom that before the final contract was made the bride brought to her future husband a dowry (*dos*; in Greek προίξ, φερνή), and in his turn the bridegroom brought to his fiancée a portion of his possessions as an antenuptial donation of *donatio ante nuptias* (in Greek πρὸ γάμου δωρεά or προγαμιαία δωρεά). In other words the *donatio ante nuptias* was a gift on the part of the future husband, and the *dos* a gift on the part of the future wife. If I am not mistaken, we first come across the exact term *donatio ante nuptias* in a constitution of Theodosius II and Valentinian III of 449 addressed to the Praetorian Prefect Hormisdas. "If a woman in contempt of the law should attempt to repudiate (her husband), she shall lose her dowry and her antenuptial donation; and she shall not be permitted to marry again within five years." [20]

Justin's law (V, 3, 19) allows wives and husbands, if they wish, to increase after marriage the amount of the original dowry or the donation before marriage. We have here an indication that it sometimes happened that the bridegroom brought no donation before marriage at all, and only the wife brought a dowry. But the law proclaims that if the wife nonetheless later wishes to have her dowry increased, the husband at that time likewise may give his first donation to his wife of an amount equal to that by which the dowry is increased. The same law even permits wives and husbands voluntarily to diminish their dowry and donation respectively; but if they have children by a former marriage, no diminution of the dowry and antenuptial donation is to be permitted. This provision, of course, is included to protect the interests of these children.

From this law we see that the *donatio ante nuptias* could be increased or diminished after marriage; therefore the term itself, *donatio ante*

---

[20] *Cod. Just.* V, 17, 8, 4: "nam mulier si contempta lege repudium mittendum esse temptaverit, suam dotem et ante nuptias donationem amittat nec intra quinquennium nubendi habeat denuo potestatem" (ed. Krueger, p. 212). Cf. an earlier constitution of the Emperors Valentinian, Theodosius, and Arcadius, of the end of the fourth century, in the section *De incestis et inutilibus nuptiis* (V, 5, 4): "nihil ex eodem matrimonio, sive ante nuptias donatum sive deinceps quoquo modo datum fuerit." English transl. by Scott, XIII, 204; 156.

nuptias, lost its original meaning and failed to apply to the new modified custom. The term itself had to be changed. We find the full presentation of this change of terminology in the *Institutes* of Justinian, which clearly attribute it to the reign of Justin. This extremely interesting passage of the *Institutes* is as follows: "There is another kind of donation *inter vivos* entirely unknown to the ancient lawyers (*prudentibus*), and subsequently introduced by the more recent emperors. It was termed the *donatio ante nuptias*, and was made under a tacit condition (*tacitam in conditionem*) that it should only take effect when the marriage had followed on it. Hence it was called *ante nuptias*, because it preceded the marriage, and never took place after its celebration. But as it was permitted that *dotes* might be increased even after marriage, the divine Justin, our father,[21] was the first to permit by his constitution that in case the *dos* was increased, the donation *ante nuptias* might be increased also, even during the marriage; but the donation still retained an improper name, and was called *ante nuptias*, while this increase was made to it after marriage. Wishing, therefore, to perfect the law on the subject, and to make names appropriate to things, we have enacted that such donations may not only be increased, but may also be first made during marriage, and that they shall be termed, not *ante nuptias*, but *propter nuptias*, and that they shall be placed on the footing of *dotes*, so far that, as *dotes* may be not only increased but first made during marriage, so those donations which are introduced during marriage (*propter nuptias*) may not only precede marriage, but, even after the tie of marriage has been formed, may be increased or made."[22]

Thus Justin's constitution considerably clarified the terminology of Byzantine jurisprudence: the term *donatio ante nuptias* which was inconsistent with the new modified practice disappeared, and the old term of more general character, *donatio propter nuptias*, donation on account of marriage, was legalized by Justin to replace the now obsolete term, antenuptial donation. The general term now covered both dona-

---

[21] Justin was Justinian's uncle and adoptive father.

[22] *Institutiones*, II, 7, 3; ed. P. Krueger, p. 15. I have used here for this passage the fine English translation by Thomas Collett Sandars, *The Institutes of Justinian*, p. 151. See *Cod. Just.* V, 3, 20 (a. 531–533): "sancimus nomine prius emendato ita rem corrigi et non ante nuptias donationem eam vocari, sed propter nuptias donationem" (Krueger, p. 194). Engl. transl. by Scott, XIII, p. 144.

tions on the part of the husband, *ante* and *post nuptias*. The *donatio propter nuptias* may be identified with the Greek term ἕδνα, which from time immemorial meant the wedding gift presented by the suitor to the bride or her parents. Fresh papyrological material today supplies us with very interesting data on how the constitution of the *donatio propter nuptias* was applied to the ordinary life of the citizens of the empire.[23]

DECREES ON LAST WILLS

Two of Justin's decrees deal with the question of last wills (*testamenta*). The first one, issued in 521 and addressed to the Praetorian Prefect Demosthenes, is inserted in Justinian's *Code* in the section "who can make a will and who cannot" (*qui facere testamentum possunt vel non possunt*); it describes in detail the procedure of making wills by the blind in the presence of seven witnesses and a public notary (*tabularius*); since the latter official is not to be found in all places, he may be replaced by an eighth witness.[24] The second law issued in 524 is inserted in the section of the *Code* "On wills: In what way they should be drawn up" (*De testamentis: Quemadmodum testamenta ordinantur*), and addressed to the Praetorian Prefect Archelaus. This decree enacts that wills which had been executed "in this imperial city" (*in hac regia urbe*, i.e. in Constantinople) should not be opened after the death of the testator unless in the presence of the *magister census*, and that if the amount of property does not exceed the value of a hundred golden coins (*summa centum aureorum pretium non excedit*), no one of the officials who took part in the ceremony of opening the will should

[23] H. Kreller, *Erbrechtliche Untersuchungen auf Grund der graeco-aegyptischen Papyrusurkunden* (Leipzig, 1919), p. 25 and note 5. G. Scherillo, "Studi sulla donazione nuziale," *Rivista di storia del diritto italiano*, II (Rome, 1929), p. 476. R. Taubenschlag, "The Legislation of Justinian in the Light of the Papyri," *Byzantion*, XV (1940–1941), pp. 282–283. This article is based on chapter V of Taubenschlag's study in German, "Geschichte der Rezeption des römischen Privatrechts in Aegypten," *Studi in onore di Pietro Bonfante*, I (Milan, 1930), pp. 335–340; especially pp. 422–423, and note 414. R. Taubenschlag, *The Law of Greco-Roman Egypt in the Light of the Papyri* 332 B. C.–640 A. D. (New York, 1944), pp. 90–91; 96–97. Taking into consideration what we have said, Piganiol's statement that under Constantine (the Great) appears a new matrimonial custom, the *donatio propter nuptias*, must be corrected. A. Piganiol, *L'Empire Chrétien*, p. 407.

[24] *Cod. Just.* VI, 22, 8; ed. Krueger, pp. 252–253. Engl. transl. by Scott, XIII, pp. 326–327.

exact any fee or make any charge for expense for their work; violators of this law should be fined fifty pounds of gold (*poena enim feriendis temeratoribus praesentis sanctionis quinquaginta librarum auri*).[25] In this decree there is no mention of any inheritance tax. The interests of the deceased testator have clearly been taken care of. Only one condition is necessary to make legal the fact of opening a will made in Constantinople, that it should be done in the presence of the magister census. Mentioning the former tax on inheritances, the so-called *vicesima hereditatum*, one of our best authorities on the Byzantine law remarks: "What had formerly been enacted in the interest of the treasury (*aerarium*), now has been enacted in the interest of a testamentary successor."[26]

DECREE ON THE SCHOLARIANS

On April 22, 527, that is, eighteen days after Justinian's coronation as Augustus and Justin's coemperor, was issued a rescript to the Magister Officiorum Tatianus concerning his duties. The law deals with the Scholarians, the imperial mounted guard troops organized by Constantine the Great or by one of his predecessors; they were better equipped and better paid than the ordinary cavalry, and were under the control of the *magister officiorum* (master of offices). Till the middle of the fifth century they were chiefly Germans. At that time the Emperor Leo I (457–474) with the aid of numerous warlike Isaurians residing in the capital, dealt a final blow to Germanic influence at the court of Constantinople. According to Agathias, the decline of the Scholarians started when the Emperor Zeno (474–491), an Isaurian himself, bestowed appointments on his Isaurian relatives of no military experience or valor.[27]

The law of April 22, 527 [28] enacts that in the case of vacancies among

[25] *Cod. Just.* VI, 23, 23; ed. Krueger, p. 255; Engl. transl. by Scott, XIII, 336. A fragment of this decree, where *defensores ecclesiarum* are mentioned, is also reproduced in *Cod. Just.* I, 3, 40 (41); ed. Krueger, p. 25 (in the section *De episcopis et clericis*).

[26] Zachariä von Lingenthal, *Geschichte des griechisch-römischen Rechts*, p. 157. In the Roman administration the *magister census* occupied an important position: among other functions it was he who decided at which rate of taxes each senator should be liable. Bury, *Hist. of the Later Roman Empire*, I, 50, n. 3.

[27] Agathias, *Historiae*, V, 15; CSHB, p. 310.

[28] *Code* I, 31, 5; Krueger, p. 83; Engl. transl. by Scott, XII, 141.

the Scholarians new men should be admitted into their ranks only by a special imperial rescript, not by the order of their immediate chief, the master of offices. "Whoever dares to assume this rank without a sacred rescript shall not only be deprived of it but shall also be subjected to a fine of twenty pounds of gold." And then the law emphasizes the two following points: 1) if a vacancy among the Scholarians occurs, it can be filled only by one whom "our piety through a sacred rescript will designate"; 2) for better information, the master of offices every four months shall present to the Bureau of Registers (*sacro scrinio laterculi*) a report of the condition of the Scholarians.

This law may be explained by the desire of Justin and Justinian to keep stronger control over the Scholarians. As we have said above, in 518 the Scholarians resented Justin's choice and in the heat of altercation, one of them struck the future emperor with his fist and slit his lip. The emperors did not forget such an offense, and in 527 they decided to establish their own personal control over the dangerous element in their own palace guard. Probably owing to this reform, when the new candidates elected by the emperor had filled up the ranks of the Scholarians, the whole character of the imperial guard was changed. Under Justinian the Scholarians ceased to have any military significance and were employed purely for purposes of parade. Bury writes: "Young men who had a little money and desired to lead an idle life in splendid uniform invested it in purchasing a post in the guards, and the high pay was a satisfactory annuity for their capital" (II, 359, note).

OTHER DECREES

Several rescripts deal with administration. One undated rescript is addressed to Proculus, *quaestor sacri palatii* (XII, 19, 23; Krueger, p. 460), whose chief duties under Justin were still as in earlier times to draft the imperial laws and deal with the petitions addressed to the emperor. The change in his functions occurred during Justinian's reign, when the quaestor of the sacred palace had taken over the duties of the new quaestor or quaesitor (ἐρευνητής) who had been created in 539 by Justinian.[29] Justin's law concerns the staff in the offices of the

---

[29] See *Novella* LXXX, ed. Schoell-Kroll, pp. 390–397 (περὶ τοῦ quaesitoros); XCIX, ed. Zach. von Lingenthal. Also Procopius, *Anecdota*, XX, 9: ὄνομα ταύτῃ ἐπιθεὶς κοιαισίτωρα (Dewing, VI, 236; Haury, III, 1, p. 125). Lydus, *De magistrati-*

quaestor sacri palatii, in his *scrinium* (office) *sacrae memoriae* and in his two other offices, *scrinia sacrarum epistularum sacrarumque libellorum*. Another undated law addressed to Tatianus *magister officiorum* deals with the procedure when the *adjutores* of the *quaestor sacri palatii* were accused of civil or criminal wrongdoings (XII, 19, 14; Krüeger, pp. 460–461). Finally, the rescript of 527, addressed by Justin and Justinian to the same *magister officiorum* Tatianus (XII, 19, 15; Krueger, p. 461) introduces some changes in the previous edict (XII, 19, 14) and in the edict addressed to the *quaestor sacri palatii*, Proculus, who we learn from the law of 527 had died before this time (*excelsae memoriae Proculo; magnificae memoriae Proculus*). The law deals with the filling of vacancies in the *scrinium sacrae memoriae* and in the two other *scrinia sacrarum epistularum* and *sacrorum libellorum*.[30]

A rather lengthy law in 524 was addressed to the *magister officiorum*, Licinius. It is incorporated in the *Code*, in the section entitled "No one can have two employments, or hold two dignities at once" (*ut nemo duplici militia vel dignitate et militia simul utatur*).[31] The opening lines of this rescript, which forbids one person to hold two or more offices or employments at the same time, clearly explain its real meaning. We read: "Those persons who, up to this time, have been invested with two, three, or more dignities (*cingulis*) which, according to former custom, are not compatible, but separate and distinct, shall be given the advice to retain whichever one they prefer, and reject the others; so that they may permanently hold the one which they have chosen, and may, undoubtedly, be excluded from those which they have rejected." But those who have two employments which are similar and can well be carried on together are excepted, and are not required to obey this law.[32]

---

bus, II, 29 (Wuensch, p. 85): τὸν λεγόμενον κυαισίτωρα, cf. III, 20 (Wuensch, p. 109): οἱ δὲ ἄμφω κυαίστορες. In the *Basilica*, VI, 6, 5 (ed. Heimbach, I, p. 176): τὸν τὴν ἀρχὴν τοῦ κοιαίστωρος ἤτοι ἐρευνητοῦ ἔχοντα (in Greek and Latin); ed. Zepos, I, 234 (in Greek only). See J. Bury, *The Imperial Administrative System in the Ninth Century*, pp. 73–74.

[30] English translation by Scott, XV, pp. 259–261.

[31] *Code* XII, 33 (34), 5; Krueger, p. 468; Engl. transl. by Scott, XV, 277.

[32] See *Basilica* LVII, 1, 45; ed. *Heimbach*, V, 185; ed. Zepos, V, 4194: ἡ διάταξις ἑλληνικὴ οὖσα βεβαιοῖ τὴν πρώτην διάταξιν τούτου τοῦ τίτλου τὴν λέγουσαν μηδένα κατὰ

JUSTIN THE FIRST

DECREE ON PRESCRIPTION

A very interesting law addressed to the Praetorian Prefect Archelaus was issued on the first of December, 525. In my opinion, it deserves a special study in connection with the history of Roman jurisprudence in general. The rather lengthy text is incorporated in the *Code*, under the title "Concerning the prescription of thirty or forty years" (*De praescriptione XXX vel XL annorum*) [33] and deals with the question of *hypothec*, a right or security given to a creditor over property of the debtor without transfer of possession or title to the creditor. After thirty years' prescription, the land which had been pledged by the debtor to the creditor might become full property of the latter. Justin extends the term to forty years in some cases (*non ultra quadraginta annos, ex quo competere coepit, prorogari*). After considering various questions pertaining to creditors and debtors the law turns to a certain form of land tenure known as *emphyteusis* (ἐμφύτευσις), a form of long-term or perpetual hereditary lease of land, a permanent tenure of land upon condition of cultivating it properly and making improvements. The word itself, *emphyteusis*, means "implanting" and comes from the idea of the cultivation of waste land by planting it with olives or vines or palms. The custom originated accordingly not in Roman but in Greek history and cases of *emphyteusis* had already been recorded in Egypt in the Papyri. The holder of this land (*emphyteutes*, ἐμφυτευτής) paid a fixed rent, and his tenure was perpetual and passed to his heirs, on condition that he fulfil his contract; but the proprietor had the right to take the land away from the holder in the case of default, or even of delay, in the payment of rent. In other words the proprietor continued to possess the land.[34] In the course of time, all

---

τὸν αὐτὸν καιρὸν δύο στρατείας ἔχειν, προστιθεῖσα, ὅτι οὐδεὶς ὀφείλει οὔτε στρατείας ἄλλας μετιέναι καὶ τοῖς τριβούνοις νοταρίοις ἐγκαταλέγεσθαι. . . . There is also the Latin translation of this text. The Greek text and Latin version are also reproduced by P. Krueger in his edition of the *Codex Iustinianus*, p. 468, n. 9.

[33] *Code* VII, 39, 7; Krueger, pp. 311-312; Engl. transl. by Scott, XIV, pp. 176-177.

[34] In Latin, the term *affictus* corresponds to that of *emphyteusis*. It is worth noting that in Old Russia an identical land lease system existed and was called "nasaždenie" (implanting), that is, had a name which is the exact translation of *emphyteusis*. On papyrologic material for emphyteusis see R. Taubenschlag, *The*

kinds of land, not only land under cultivation, might be held on the basis of emphyteutic tenure.

Evidently in the sixth century there were many cases when the holders of land by emphyteutic tenure, after holding it for forty years or some other considerable period, began to regard themselves as its true possessors. Justin's law emphatically points out that no matter how many years the lessee had held the land, he must return it to the proprietor if the latter, after the completion of the stipulated term, wanted to have it back.

The new term of forty years in this law is interesting. I wish more or less tentatively to connect the change in the number of years, from thirty to forty, with some legislative documents of a later period, the very end of the tenth century. In 996 the sternest foe of the large landowners, Basil II, abolished the forty years' prescription which protected the rights of the powerful who, "willing to satisfy their own desire have a reasonable pretext to use the forty years and who try to extend this term either by means of gifts, or by means of power, in order to acquire final ownership of that which they had acquired from the poor by wicked means." [35] Of this measure Zachariae von Lingenthal vaguely remarks that it seems the accepted view that a forty years' prescription guaranteed protection to the powerful; and then, without giving any evidence, he simply refers to the legislative text of the eleventh century, the *Peira* (Πεῖρα), and to the two *Novels* of Constantine Porphyrogenitus and Nicephorus Phocas.[36] Here is the text of these three documents, which deal with identical subject matter: In the *Peira* we read: "Soldiers who buy (land) from men in military service become its possessors if (the land) is not claimed during forty years." The *Novel* of Constantine Porphyrogenitus (between 945 and 959) says: "Those who have acquired military land in any way whatever take possession of it only if a period of forty years shall have elapsed without its being claimed." And finally, Nicephorus Phocas'

Law of Greco-Roman Egypt in the Light of the Papyri, § 31, pp. 199–204: "Long-Term Lease."

[35] A. Vasiliev, *History of the Byzantine Empire*, I, 422; French ed., I, 459; Spanish ed., I, 427. Zach. v. Ling., *Jus Gr.-Rom.*, III (1857), p. 308. Zepos, *Jus Graecoromanum*, I (Athens, 1931), p. 263.

[36] Zach. v. Lingenthal, *Geschichte des griechisch-römischen Rechts*, p. 268.

Novel of 967 proclaims: "If a period of forty years which had elapsed unchallenged and unclaimed granted the right of possession to those who had acquired (land) from the soldiers . . ." [37]

These three texts deal exclusively with military land; but the *Novel* of Basil II abolished the forty years' prescription for any land where the interests of peasants and small land tenants were involved. On the other hand, when scholars mention Basil's *Novel* of 996, they usually speak very vaguely without giving any exact information of the earlier rules or regulations stipulating the forty years' prescription.[38]

It seems to me that the vague regulation referring to the forty years' prescription, which was abolished by Basil II, may go back to Justin's law "*De prescriptione XXX vel XL annorum*," in which among other matters Justin on some occasions extended the term of prescription from thirty to forty years.[39] I think this law of Justin deserves further study, especially from this point of view.

DECREE ON THE VIOLATION OF SEPULCHRES

In 526 Justin issued a law addressed to the prefect of the city, Theodorus, which is incorporated in the Code in the section "Concerning the violation of sepulchres" (*De sepulchro violato*). It deals with a case when the creditor, after his debtor's death, alleging that the deceased person was still his debtor, and exacting the debt, inter-

---

[37] Πεῖρα, IX, 4: στρατιῶται μὲν παρὰ στρατούντων ὠνούμενοι διὰ τεσσαρακονταετίας ἀνεπιφωνήτως δεσπόζουσιν . . . Zach. v. Lingenthal, *Jus Graeco-Romanum*, I (1856), 30. Zepos, IV (Athens, 1931), p. 38. Const. Porphyrogenitus, *Nov.* VIII, 1: μὴ ἄλλως δὲ κυριεύεσθαι τὰ στρατιωτικὰ τοῖς ταῦτα οἰῳδήτινι τρόπῳ κτωμένοις, εἰ μὴ ὁ τῆς τεσσαρακονταετίας ἀνεπιφώνητος διαρρεύσει χρόνος. Zach. v. Ling., III (1857), p. 263. Zepos, I, p. 224. Nicephorus Phocas, *Nov.* XX, 2: ἐπειδὴ δὲ καὶ ἡ τῶν τεσσαράκοντα χρόνων παραδρομὴ ἀνέγκλητος μὲν καὶ ἀνεπιφώνητος παραρρέουσα τὸ δίκαιον ἐπεβράβευε τοῖς τὰ ἐκ τῶν στρατιωτῶν προσκτηθέντα κατέχουσι . . . Zach. v. Ling., III, p. 298. Zepos, I, p. 254.

[38] See among recent books G. Ostrogorsky, *Geschichte des byzantinischen Staates*, p. 217: "laut den früheren Regeln." Cf. also the same author, "Agrarian Conditions in the Byzantine Empire in the Middle Ages," in the *Cambridge Economic History of Europe from the Decline of the Roman Empire*, I (1941), p. 209. Here Ostrogorsky fails even to mention the forty years' prescription, saying only: "By his law of 996 Basil II repealed the legislation legalizing the purchase of land by the 'powerful' after a definite period of delay."

[39] See *Cod. Just.* VII, 39, 7, § 2: "sed locum esse quadraginta annorum praescriptioni. . . ."

fered with his burial. According to Justin's law, after the debtor's death, the case should be discussed again in its entirety, and all coercive steps on the part of the creditor should be prohibited. "Everything shall be restored to its former condition unaltered, and the principal matter, as it was in the beginning, shall be disposed of in court. Moreover, anyone who has been found guilty of a crime of this kind shall pay fifty pounds of gold, or, if he has not the means to do so, he shall suffer such corporeal punishment as may be inflicted by a competent judge." [40]

The undated rescript addressed to the prefect of the city Theodotus (or Theodorus) and incorporated in the *Code* in the section "Concerning money which is not counted out" (*De non numerata pecunia*) deals with securities which were given in writing for the payment of certain sums of money. This rescript may have some significance if studied in connection with the other laws included in this section of the *Code*.[41]

Justin's edict prescribing that all soldiers should adhere to the credo of the Synod of Chalcedon has been discussed above.

THE RESCRIPT OF 527

A very interesting rescript issued by the joint emperors, Justin and Justinian, in 527, has been preserved in an inscription discovered by G. Cousin in 1889 in Asia Minor, near the Turkish village Ali-faradin, in the district of Istanos, upon the confines of the ancient provinces of Pisidia and Cibyratis, somewhat north of Sögud-Göl, the ancient lake of Caralitis. The bilingual inscription in Latin and Greek was found upon a block of square stone and in spite of some mutilations has come down to us almost in its entirety. It was published and interpreted in 1893 by Charles Diehl.[42] The original text of the rescript was written in Latin; and its Greek translation made either in Constantinople or in Asia Minor does not represent an official version; it was rendered into Greek merely to be better understood in the region

[40] *Code* IX, 19, 6; Krueger, pp. 380–381; Engl. transl. by Scott, XV, 35.
[41] *Code* IV, 30, 13; Krueger, p. 170; Engl. transl. by Scott, XIII, pp. 72–73.
[42] Diehl, "Rescrit des empereurs Justin et Justinien, en date du 1er juin 527," *Bulletin de correspondance hellénique*, XVII, pp. 501–520.

for which it was intended. But since the Greek version is better preserved than the Latin original, it is of great value for the reconstruction of the original Latin document. The exact date of the rescript has been supplied not by the names of Justin and Justinian which originally appeared in the opening lines and have not come down to us, but by the name of the Consul Mavortius, sole consul in 527, whose name has been preserved at the end of the Latin text. Almost with certainty we may say that the rescript was addressed to Archelaus, who in 527 was the Praetorian Prefect of the Orient, and referred to the governor of the appropriate province and his staff (*rector provinciae una cum officio suo* [p. 504, 11. 17–18]).

Even if not all restorations and corrections proposed by Diehl are final, the general meaning of this important document is clear. In 527 the clergy of the oratory of the Apostle Saint John (*oratorium sancti Apostoli Johannis*, εὐκτήριον τοῦ ἁγίου ᾿Αποστόλου ᾿Ιωάννου),[43] situated in all probability in the province of Pamphylia, addressed a petition to Justin and Justinian for protection. The clergy possessed rather large tracts of land, which, with those who developed them, were exposed to continuous vexations from imperial officers, from passing soldiers, from police agents, and from the troops stationed in the neighborhood; some of their lands had already been taken over by violators. All their hope is only in the imperial justice and benevolence. And the imperial rescript satisfied their request. An inquiry was to be made and if the grievances presented were well founded, the governor of the province must assure imperial protection to the men and the land of the oratory of Saint John and return to the oratory all the portions of its property which had been usurped unduly. Severe penalties were to be inflicted upon the transgressors of this imperial ordinance.

In this rescript is a list of those connected with the development of the land of the oratory and molested by transgressors: these were *coloni* (γεωργοί), serfs (*adscripticii*, ἐναπόγραφοι), stewards (superintendents, *curatores*, φροντισταί) and tax farmers (*conductores*, μισθωταί).

The Latin text of the rescript ends with two words: *Rescripsi Recognovi*. In 1896, O. Karlowa wrote that the note *rescripsi recognovi* upon imperial documents occurred very rarely, up to the time of

[43] p. 504, 11. 4–5; p. 505, 11. 30–31.

writing only four times; and he refers, among others, to our rescript.[44] After several attempts to explain these terms scholars have now come to the conclusion that *rescripsi*, that is *m(anu) i(mperatoris) rescripsi*, means that the document was presented for signature to the emperor, and the latter signed it; and *recognovi* proves that the imperial document was taken to a suitable administrative office, examined, copied, and put in the archives.[45]

At first sight, the episode which occurred on the lands of the oratory of remote Pamphylia and which is told in our rescript has only local interest. But in reality this obscure episode reveals and illuminates the internal history and internual policy of Justinian's long reign. His novels give us a drastic picture of the desperate situation in the empire where large landowners, soldiers, police agents over all its vast territory were almost independent and lawless brigands whom the government was unable to control and who were a real scourge to the exhausted and defenseless population. Such an insignificant episode as that of the lands of the oratory of Saint John in Pamphylia fits into place in the general picture of the internal history of the empire in the sixth century.

JUSTIN AND THE *adjectio sterilium* (*epibole*)

In all probability, Justin's reign represents a new step in the general method of dealing with the very burdensome tax known as epibole (ἐπιβολή; in some sources περισσοπρακτία) in Greek and *adjectio sterilium* in Latin. The epibole (impost) was applied to the lands which had fallen out of cultivation and become unproductive or sterile. Someone, of course, was responsible for the taxes assessed on such lands. No doubt this tax was very ruinous for many, especially for

---

[44] O. Karlowa, "Ueber die in Briefform ergangenen Erlasse römischer Kaiser," *Neue Heidelberger Jahrbücher*, VI (1896), p. 213. See misleading reference *Heidelberger Jahrbücher*, VI, without indication of year, for *Neue Heidelberger Jahrbücher*, in E. Stein, "Justinus," *PW*, X, 1321. This misleading reference has passed into E. Kornemann, *Doppelprinzipat und Reichsteilung im Imperium Romanum* (Leipzig-Berlin, 1930), p. 159, n. 1 (section compiled by G. Ostrogorsky).

[45] Diehl, *op. cit.*, pp. 505–506. See the list of former opinions of Rescripsi and Recognovi in F. Preisigke, *Die Inschrift von Skaptoparene in ihrer Beziehung zur kaiserlichen Kanzlei in Rom* (Strassburg, 1917), pp. 4–11; on Diehl's inscription p. 7; 20, n. 1; 60, n. 1.

small landowners and farmers, upon whom it was imposed. The contemporary writer Procopius says that "the term epibole (impost) is used to describe a kind of unforeseen ruination that falls suddenly upon the owners of land and destroys root and branch their hope of a livelihood." [46]

Among the novels of Justinian is an edict of the Praetorian Prefect Demosthenes addressed to the governor of Lydia, Flavius Ortalinus, which has survived in the Greek and Latin languages, and which is entitled Περὶ ἀπόρων ἐπιβολῆς or De sterilium adjectione.[47]

Since Demosthenes was Praetorian Prefect twice, in 520–524 and 529–530, the question arises when he sent his edict to the governor of Lydia, whether during his first or second prefecture. I attribute the edict to the years 520–524 of his first prefecture, that is to the period of Justin, because in its address, which is accompanied with Demosthenes' honorific and brilliant titles,[48] there is no indication that he was holding the office of Praetorian Prefect for the second time (τὸ δεύτερον).[49]

Demosthenes' edict, which Monnier calls "a most important text" (p. 644) deals exclusively with the ἐπιβολὴ ὁμοδούλων.[50] This tax was imposed when one part of a large estate, which was not included in a commune, became unproductive, and the whole estate remained liable for the tax as originally estimated. The question arises why in this edict this particular epibolé only was discussed, and the other well

[46] Procopii, Anecdota XXIII, 15; Dewing, VI, 274.

[47] Novella 166; ed. R. Schoell-G. Kroll, pp. 753–754. Φλάβιος Θεόδωρος Πέτρος Δημοσθένης . . . Φλαβίῳ Ὠρταλίνῳ τῷ λαμπροτάτῳ ὑπατικῷ Λυδίας. Zachariae von Lingenthal omits this edict in his edition of the Novels. The tenor of this novel is not very adequately presented in English by Scott, XVII, pp. 201–202. He fails to give a full translation.

[48] ὁ μεγαλοπρεπέστατος ἔπαρχος τῶν ἱερῶν πραιτωρίων καὶ ἀπὸ ἐπάρχων τῆς βασιλίδος πόλεως καὶ ἀπὸ ὑπάτων; in Latin: "magnificentissimus praefectus sacrorum praetoriorum et expraefecto regiae urbis et ex consule." Novellae, ed. Schoell and Kroll, p. 753 (no. 166).

[49] See Schoell-Kroll, p. 754, note to line 12. H. Monnier, "Etudes de droit byzantin: L' ἐπιβολή," Nouvelle revue historique de droit français et étranger, XVI (1892), 644. Schoell and Kroll attribute Demosthenes' first prefecture to the years 521–523; Monnier (p. 644) and, following him Bury (I, 445) to the years 520–524.

[50] See the preamble to the edict: τῶν δὲ πρὸς τὰς ἀνωτέρω καὶ παλαιοτέρας ὁμοδούλους κτήσεις ἀναβαίνειν βιαζομένων; in the edict itself: τὸ βάρος τῆς τῶν ὁμοδούλων ἀπορίας (p. 573).

known ἐπιβολὴ ὁμοκήνσων was omitted. This second epibole was imposed when the small properties of the free farmers which were included in a commune were regarded as a fiscal unity liable for the total sum of the fiscal assessments of its members; so that if for any cause one property ceased to be solvent, the others were required to make good the deficiency.[51]

It is difficult to decide why Demosthenes failed to mention the ἐπιβολὴ ὁμοκήνσων. It does not seem likely that Demosthenes issued another edict dealing with it, which has not come down to us. The most plausible explanation of the omission may be found in the fact that the application of the epibole to the lands ὁμόκηνυα (*praedia contributaria*) was much simpler, and could be administered without detailed instructions.[52] With the ἐπιβολὴ ὁμοδούλων difficulties arose when parts of a larger estate, which was not included in a commune, were sold or when they were divided among several heirs. Demosthenes' edict tries to clarify this complicated question.

According to the preamble, the object of the edict is to make thoroughly clear to the citizens the ἐπιβολή-*epibole* (ἔν τε ταῖς τῶν ἀπόρων ἐπιβολαῖς) and to indicate definitely who in the case of the ἐπιβολὴ ὁμοδούλων should be liable for paying the tax as originally estimated. The rather complicated tenor of the edict has been well presented in French by Monnier (pp. 645–654) and from him in a succinct English form by Bury (I, p. 445, n. 2). If a farm or a whole complex of property is sold by its proprietor (A) or on his death passes either to outsiders (ἐξωτικούς, *ad extraneos*) or to his children (B); and if the purchasers or heirs should similarly alienate the land; and if the alienated land should become unproductive (εἰ . . . εἰς ἀπορίαν ἐλάσῃ; *si . . . ad sterilitatem delapsum sit*), then the epibole is to fall on the property of the last purchaser or inheritor (C), not on all those who formerly possessed it. But if the last acquirer (C) is insolvent, then the burden must fall on those from whom he immediately acquired it (B). If they are insolvent, then the epibole shall be imposed on the

---

[51] On the terms of ὁμόδουλα and ὁμόκηνσα see Zachariae von Lingenthal, *Geschichte des griechisch-römischen Rechts*, pp. 228–231. From Zachariae, in English, by Bury, I, 444.

[52] See Monnier, pp. 651–652.

original proprietor (A). Those on whom the epibole falls, whether few or many, shall bear it in proportion to the value of their fertile possessions.[53]

This edict shows that the liability for the burden of the *epibole* or ὁμόδουλα was determined not only by proximity but also by the history of the property, which in many cases created a very complicated problem for the decision of those officials who were in charge of fixing the amount of the tax itself and indicating those individuals who were to pay it. The edict closes with an epilogue in which Demosthenes sternly urges the governor to follow the instructions given in the edict and warns him and his staff that they will be fined ten pounds of gold and receive an even heavier punishment if the edict is not exactly executed.[54] Since Demosthenes' edict belongs to Justin's period, this very important fiscal institution of the empire marks Justin's reign as taking an essential step in the development of the general method of dealing with sterile lands.

The *Life* of Saint Sabas, who was Justin's contemporary, relates that owing to the intercession of Sabas and other Palestinian hermits, Justin to some extent relieved church lands from liability for the epibole, which is called in the text *perissopractia* (περισσοπραικτία).[55] I cannot flatly discard this information; but I think that Justin granted this relief only to some church lands situated in Palestine, whence Saint Sabas and his companions had come to Constantinople, not to all church property in the entire territory of the empire; the relief is

---

[53] ἀναλόγως τῆς οὔσης παρ' αὐτοῖς ἐκ τῆς αὐτῆς οὐσίας εὐπόρου κτήσεως; pro portione fertilis possessionis, quae qualibet ratione apud eos ex eadem substantia est. Cf. *Vita S. Sabae*: ἠναγκάσθησαν ἐπιρρῖψαι τὴν τούτων εἴσπραξιν . . . κατ' ἀναλογίαν τῆς ἑκάστου δυνάμεως. Cotelier, III, 304; Schwartz, p. 145; reproduced also by Monnier, *op. cit.*, p. 133.

[54] H. Monnier, *op. cit.*, pp. 644–654. See a brief and rather confusing remark by G. Bratianu, *Études byzantines d'histoire économique et sociale* (Paris, 1938), p. 200. Bratianu attributes the edict to the time of Justinian.

[55] καὶ οὕτως ἐκωλύθη ἐπὶ Ἀναστασίου ἡ ἐκ τῶν ἀπόρων περισσοπρακτία συγχωρηθῆναι. πλὴν ὅτι μέρος μὲν αὐτῆς συνεχωρήθη ἐπὶ τοῦ εὐσεβοῦς βασιλεύοντος Ἰουστίνου ἀναφορᾶς γενομένης ὑπό τε τοῦ πατρὸς ἡμῶν Σάβα καὶ τῶν λοιπῶν τῆς ἐρήμου ἡγουμένων. I. B. Cotelier, *Ecclesiae graecae monumenta*, III, p. 305; ed. I. Pomialovsky, p. 294 (Obščestvo Liubiteley Drevney Pismennosti, vol. 96); Schwartz, *Kyrillos von Skythopolis* pp. 146–147. In the same text, the *Life* of Saint Sabas states that the rest of the epibole was forgiven church lands by Justinian.

of only local interest for Palestine,[56] and may be explained by the emperor's regard for the heavy suffering Palestine had experienced from Persian devastations and natural disasters.

[56] Some scholars seem to hold different opinions and are inclined to regard this relief as a measure general in character. See B. Pančenko, "On the *Secret History* of Procopius," *Viz. Vremennik*, III, p. 500: The *Life* of Sabas reports that partly Justin and partly Justinian relieved this burden from the church. Therefore the whole burden of the epibole lay on private landownership (in Russian). Bury, II, p. 350, n. 2: Justin and Justinian relieved Church lands from liability to the epibole.

EPILOGUE

Justin's Death and Burial

In the spring of 527 Justin fell dangerously ill, and, as we know, yielding to the solicitations of the Senate, coöpted Justinian as his colleague on April 4. Justin's condition improved, but he survived only a few months. He died on August 1, 527, at the age of 75 or 77 years, from an old reopened wound in the foot, where he had been struck by an arrow in one of his old campaigns. His reign lasted from July 9, 518, to August 1, 527, or nine years and twenty-two days.[1]

The question of Justin's burial is rather complex, and, if I am not mistaken, has never been discussed in its entirety. The imperial sarcophagi were located in the mausolems connected with the Church

[1] Malalas, 424 (75 years of age). Malalas' Slavonic version, Istrin, p. 25; Spinka, p. 133 (at the age of seventy-seven). *Chron. Pasch.* 617 (died on Sunday, at the age of 77). Theodorus Lector, J. A. Cramer, *Anecdota Graeca*, II, p. 109. Procopius, *Anecdota*, IX, 54: ἐτελεύτησε νόσῳ, τῇ ἀρχῇ ἐπιβιοὺς ἔτη ἐννέα (Dewing, VI, 120). *Marcellini Comitis Chronicon*, s.a. 527: "vita decessit, anno imperii nono mense secundo" (ed. Mommsen, p. 102). Evagrius, IV, 9: ὑπελθὼν τὴν τέλειον ἡμέραν ἀνὰ τὴν πρώτην ἡμέραν τοῦ Λώου, τοῦ καὶ Αὐγούστου μηνὸς . . . τὰ ὅλα δὲ ἔτη τὴν αὐτοκράτορα διανύσας ἀρχὴν ἐννέα πρός τισιν ἡμέραις (ed. Bidez-Parmentier, pp. 159–160). *Iordanis De summa temporum . . . Romanorum*, 362; ed. Mommsen, p. 47. *Vita S. Sabae per Cyrillum Scythopolitanum*: ὁ τῆς εὐσεβοῦς μνήμης Ἰουστῖνος, χρόνους ἐννέα ἐν τῇ βασιλείᾳ διατελέσας, τέλει τοῦ βίου ἐχρήσατο (ed. Cotelier, III, 337; Pomialovsky, 386–389 (Greek and Slavonic version); E. Schwartz, p. 190. Theoph., s.a. 6019: τῷ δὲ Αὐγούστῳ μηνὶ τῆς αὐτῆς ε' ἰνδικτιῶνος ἐτελεύτησεν ὁ εὐσεβέστατος Ἰουστῖνος (de Boor, p. 173). Cedr., I, 642. Zonaras, XIV, 5, 42: βασιλεύσαντι ἔτη ἐννέα ἐφ' ἡμέραις εἴκοσι (CSHB, III, 151). *Nicephori Callisti Eccl. Hist.*, XVII, 7: τοῦ Λώου εἴτουν Αὐγούστου μηνὸς, τὴν τελείαν ὑπελθόντα ἡμέραν . . . τὰ ὅλα δὲ τῇ αὐτοκρατορικῇ ἀρχῇ ἔτη ἐννέα ἐκεῖνον πρὸς μησὶ τρισὶ διανύσαντα (Migne, PG, 147, 236). Zach. of Mityl., IX, 1: died at the end of July (Hamilton-Brooks, p. 221; Ahrens-Krüger, p. 168). *Chronicon Edessenum*, CI (XCVIII): died on the 10th of Nisan (August); ed. Hallier, p. 135 and his note; Guidi, p. 10; Cowper, p. 38 (§ 98). John of Nikiu, 47–48: he fell into a grievous illness, for he had a wound in his head (sic) which had been struck by an arrow in battle. The wound reopened and remained incurable for a long time . . . and thereupon he died (transl. Charles, p. 138). *Abulpharagii Gregorii sive Barhebraei Chronicon Syriacum*, ed. Bruns et Kirsch, II, 81. Michel le Syrien, IX, 20–21; Chabot, II, 189–190. Armenian version of Ischok, transl. by V. Langlois, p. 187 (confusion). Complete Collection of Russian Annals (PSRL) *Chronicle (Letopis) of Lvov*, XX, 32: Ustiyan died at the age of 77. XXII, 2, 108: Ustin (Yustin) lived seventy-seven years.

of the Holy Apostles, which was the burial place of the Byzantine emperors until the beginning of the eleventh century. A detailed although not absolutely complete list of the imperial sarcophagi has been preserved in the *Book of the Ceremonies* known under the name of the Emperor Constantine Porphyrogenitus, most of which was compiled in the tenth century. According to this work, in the mausoleum of the Holy and Great Constantine, among other imperial sarcophagi, was a sarcophagus of green Thessalian stone in which rests the Emperor Michael, son of Theophilus.[2] Then the text proceeds: "It is to be known, however, that this sarcophagus of the Emperor Michael is that of Justinian the Great ('Ιουστινιανοῦ ἐστιν τοῦ μεγάλου).[3] It (the sarcophagus) stood (formerly) in the monastery (nunnery) of the Augusta, below the church of the Holy Apostle Thomas, in which the garments of the Apostles were found. The Lord Leo the Emperor took it (the sarcophagus) and put it there (that is, in the Church of the Holy Apostles) in order to put into it the body of Michael."[4] The monastery or nunnery of the Augusta where Justin's sarcophagus stood had been built by him and by his wife Euphemia, who died before her husband and was buried there.[5] In the tenth century the chronicler Symeon Logothete, whose complete original Greek text has not yet been published, but whose complete Old Slavonic version

---

[2] This is Michael III (842–867). See *De cerimoniis aulae Byzantinae*, ch. 42; *CSHB*, pp. 642–643.

[3] This is a mistake; the text should read 'Ιουστίνου τοῦ μεγάλου, i.e., Justin the Elder. The sarcophagus of Justinian the Great is described a little later, and is placed in the mausoleum of the Great Justinian (p. 644).

[4] ἕτερος λάρναξ πρασίας λίθου Θετταλικῆς, ἐν ᾧ ἀπόκειται Μιχαὴλ ὁ βασιλεὺς, ὁ υἱὸς Θεοφίλου. Ἰστέον δὲ ὅτι ὁ τοιοῦτος λάρναξ Μιχαὴλ τοῦ βασιλέως 'Ιουστινιανοῦ ἐστιν τοῦ μεγάλου. Ἔκειτο δὲ ἐν τῷ μοναστηρίῳ τῆς Αὐγούστης . . . Ἔλαβεν δὲ αὐτὸν ὁ κῦρις Λέων ὁ βασιλεὺς καὶ κατέθετο αὐτὸν ἐνταῦθα εἰς ἀπόθεσιν τοῦ σώματος τοῦ αὐτοῦ Μιχαὴλ (p. 642–643). Leo is Leo VI the Wise or the Philosopher (886–912).

[5] Πάτρια, III, 183 (ed. Preger, p. 273): τὴν δὲ γυναικείαν μονὴν τὴν καλουμένην Αὐγούστης 'Ιουστῖνος ὁ Θρὰξ ὁ κράτιστος, ὁ θεῖος 'Ιουστινιανοῦ τοῦ μεγάλου, ἔκτισεν σὺν τῇ γυναικὶ αὐτοῦ Εὐφημίᾳ, ἐπεὶ καὶ τὸ σῶμα αὐτῆς ἐκεῖσε ἐτέθη. See also Πάτρια, II, 26 (Preger, p. 164). In his commentary to the *Ceremonies* Reiske used an old edition of Πάτρια in which the last words of the above passage read as follows: τεθὲν τὸ αὐτοῦ σῶμα πρότερον ἐκεῖσε. Reiske remarks: "extrema haec verba sunt perobscura. Suggerunt, ossa Iustini ex illo monasterio ablata fuisse." And then Reiske makes some surmises concerning this dark passage (*De Cerim.*, *CSHB*, II, 760–761), which now are of no value. On the Church of Saint Thomas see R. Janin, "Topographie de Constantinople byzantine: Le port Sophien et les quartiers environnants," *Etudes byzantines*, I (Bucarest, 1944), p. 144.

has been printed, states that Justin's body "was put in the Church of the Tsaritza (i.e. Empress, Augusta) in a sarcophagus of green marble together with that of his wife Euphemia."[6] Leo Grammaticus, one of the group of chroniclers of the tenth century who were not original writers but merely copyists, abbreviators, or revisers of Symeon Logothete, exactly reproduces his text.[7]

Thus we have two traditions: the first and older tradition which has been recorded in the Πάτρια, says that in the nunnery of the Augusta which had been built by Justin and his wife Euphemia the body of the Empress alone was buried. The second tradition reports that Justin was buried with his wife Euphemia in the nunnery of the Augusta.

In this connection the *Chronicle* of Theophanes Continuatus is extremely interesting. Here we read that immediately after the death of Basil I the Macedonian in 886 his son and successor Leo VI sent the commander (στρατηλάτην) Andreas and other high officials (συγκλητικούς) with clergy, candles, chariots, and horses to Chrysopolis. They removed Michael from his tomb, put him in a coffin of cypress and placed it on a couch; then with great veneration dressing the corpse in imperial robes, they brought it to the city, singing hymns, escorted the procession up to the Church of the Holy Apostles, and put (the corpse) into a sarcophagus; and Leo's brothers followed the procession.[8] According to this text the body of Michael III was brought to

[6] Simeon Metaphrastes, *Symeona Metafrasta i logotheta Spisaniye mira ot bytiya* . . . ed. by V. Sreznevsky (St. Petersburg, 1905), p. 56. This source has never before been used in this connection.

[7] Leo Grammaticus, *Chronographia*, p. 124: ἐτέθη δὲ τὸ σῶμα αὐτοῦ ἐν τῇ μονῇ Αὐγούστης, ἐν λάρνακι πρασίνῳ, μετὰ δὲ τῆς γυναικὸς αὐτοῦ Εὐφημίας. Another text, perhaps earlier than the tenth century, but absolutely identical with Leo Grammaticus, is found in J. A. Cramer, *Anecdota graeca* II, p. 319. The same text is also found in later sources. Cedr., I, 642. *Anonymi De antiquitatibus Constantinopolitanis.* Banduri, Imperium Orientale, I, reprinted in Migne, *P. G.*, CXXII, col. 1285.

[8] Theoph. Cont., VI, *CSHB* p. 353 (Par. 217): καὶ ἐξαγαγόντες τοῦ τάφου τὸν Μιχαὴλ ἐν γλωσσοκόμῳ κυπαρισσίνῳ κατέθεντο, καὶ ἐπὶ κραβάτου θέντες, ἐντίμως καὶ βασιλικῶς περιστείλαντες, ἐν τῇ πόλει εἰσήγαγον, καὶ μεθ' ὕμνων μέχρι τῶν ἁγίων ἀποστόλων προέπεμψαν, ἑπομένων ἐκεῖσε καὶ τῶν αὐτοῦ ἀδελφῶν, καὶ ἐν λάρνακι κατέθεντο. In curtailed form this story is narrated in Symeon Magister (p. 686; 700) and Georgius Monachus (p. 849). I refer here to the so-called Pseudo-Symeon Magister and the anonymous Continuator of George Hamartolus.

Constantinople from Chrysopolis (now Scutari) where Michael, after his assassination had been buried in the monastery Philippici.[9]

Apparently no specal imperial sarcophagus was made for Michael III, who had been treacherously murdered by Basil, and his body was inconspicuously and hurriedly buried in the vicinity of Chrysopolis, in a suburb of Constantinople. But in 886 after Leo VI had ascended the throne, one of his first acts was to honor the murdered emperor with an imperial burial and to place his body in the Church of the Holy Apostles with other members of the imperial families. But there was no sarcophagus vacant. Leo decided to use the sarcophagus of Justin I, which, according to the *Book of Ceremonies*, was in the nunnery of the Augusta. Apparently this sarcophagus was vacant. Probably before Justin's death a sarcophagus had been made in which to keep his body. But in accordance with his will, he was buried jointly with his wife in her sarcophagus, in the church which both of them had built. Otherwise we would have to deduce that three hundred and fifty-nine years after Justin's death, his body was removed from his own sarcophagus and put into the sarcophagus of his wife so that the other sarcophagus might be used for Michael's body. This seems to me very doubtful. Even if such a thing could have occurred, it would undoubtedly have been recorded in the sources; but we have no such evidence. It is absolutely clear, then, that Justin's body never had been in the Church of the Holy Apostles. In the thirteenth century Nicholas Mesarites as an eye-witness made a list of the imperial sarcophagi in the Church of the Holy Apostles; but he fails even to mention the sarcophagus of Michael III which had formerly belonged to Justin I.[10] The most plausible conclusion is that the body of Justin I rested in the nunnery of the Augusta, in the sarcophagus in which his wife Euphemia had earlier been buried. We know nothing of the final disposition of this sarcophagus.

[9] See Reiske, *Commentarii*, p. 760. See Φ. Ι. Κουκουλές, "Τὰ κατὰ τὴν ταφὴν τῶν Βυζαντινῶν βασιλέων," 'Επετηρὶς 'Εταιρείας Βυζαντινῶν Σπουδῶν, XV (1939), p. 64. Koukoules fails to mention Justin's sarcophagus.

[10] See A. Heisenberg, *Grabeskirche und Apostelkirche*, II: *Die Apostelkirche in Konstantinopel* (Leipsig, 1908), pp. 81–85; 108. Cf. H. Koethe, "Das Konstantins-mausoleum und verwandte Denkmäler," *Jahrbuch des deutschen archäologischen Instituts*, XLVIII (1933), 188–190; the whole article, 185–203.

The Archangel Ivory in the British Museum and the Coins of Justin the First

The British Museum possesses one of the most famous ivories: the leaf of a diptych with the standing figure of an archangel, which has been reproduced countless times and which has been studied, evaluated, and dated from various points of view and in various ways. According to Stuhlfauth, this piece is, in general, one of the finest early Christian ivories; according to Dalton, it is in some respects the noblest ivory in existence, or a work of singular grandeur and exceptional size; to Diehl, it is a masterpiece (*le chef-d'oeuvre*), and to Morey, one of the finest creations of late antiquity. More moderate in praising the ivory are Peirce and Tyler who write that for them this ivory shows considerable ability, but denotes a hybrid and anemic (*anémié*) style which has neither the qualities of antique sculpture nor those of Byzantine art.[1] The great majority of scholars and critics recognize, in the standing figure of the ivory, the archangel Michael or an angel in general.

Our ivory is the leaf of a diptych, whose second left leaf is lost. Here follows the description of this half of a diptych, given by O. Dalton: "The archangel Michael standing at the top of a flight of six steps under a round arch carved with acanthus ornament and supported by fluted columns. Within the arch is a scallop, before which is a wreath

---

[1] G. Stuhlfauth, *Die Engel in der altchristlichen Kunst* (Freiburg i. B. — Leipzig-Tübingen, 1897), p. 179. O. Dalton, *Byzantine Art and Archaeology* (Oxford, 1911), p. 200. *Idem, East Christian Art* (Oxford, 1925), p. 210. Charles Diehl, *Manuel d'art byzantin*, 2nd. ed., I (Paris, 1925), 296. Ch. R. Morey, *Early Christian Art* (Princeton, New Jersey, 1942), p. 90. H. Peirce and R. Tyler, *L'art byzantin*, II (Paris, 1934), 76.

bound with ribbons and containing a cross; in the spandrils are rosettes and acanthus leaves, and above these a tablet with the inscription + ΔΕΧΟΥ ΠΑΡΟΝΤΑ | ΚΑΙ ΜΑΘΩΝ ΤΗΝ ΑΙΤΙΑΝ. The archangel, wearing a tunic and mantle, with sandals on his feet, holds in his right hand an orb surmounted by a jewelled cross; in his left hand a staff with a ball at each end. He has no nimbus." [2]

The elaborate beauty of our ivory, its fine workmanship and exceptional size, as well as the attitude of the angel, who seems to offer the orb of imperial power, permit us to suppose that the diptych may well have been made for presentation to an emperor, and that the figure of the potential emperor may have been represented upon the second lost left leaf. But the latter point of view has not been shared by all critics. Stuhlfauth wrote that it is not only groundless but even unthinkable to imagine one or two emperors upon the lost leaf, and that the second leaf may have contained only the figure of the Virgin. For Stuhlfauth, the archangel Michael is represented as the lord of Paradise who, standing at its gates, grants or bars entrance into it to the faithful; so that the owner of the diptych invokes Michael to admit him among the inhabitants of Paradise through the intercession of the Holy Virgin, in spite of his sins. And in this connection, Stuhlfauth has suggested an alternative translation of the inscription upon our tablet, which I shall produce a little later.[3] Venturi wrote that the fragment of the ivory diptych of the British Museum represents a celestial minister, a beautiful and vigorous youth; he is a triumphal figure, to whom Victory has given the wings; a hero who appears to a prostrate crowd of worshippers and presents to them the fruit of the conquest *dall' alto del trono.*[4] Kondakov supposed the figure on our panel to represent the embodiment of Hagia Sophia, or the Holy Wisdom.[5] At present these opinions have only historical interest.

[2] O. Dalton, *Catalogue of Early Christian Antiquities and Objects from the Christian East in the British Museum* (London, 1901), p. 53. Also in his *Catalogue of the Ivory Carvings of the Christian Era in the British Museum* (London, 1909), p. 9.
[3] G. Stuhlfauth, *Die Engel*, pp. 180–181. *Idem, Die altchristliche Elfenbeinplastik* (Freiburg i. B. — Leipzig, 1896), p. 174.
[4] A. Venturi, *Storia dell'arte italiana*, I (Milan, 1901), 506.
[5] N. P. Kondakov, "The Byzantine Churches and Monuments of Constantinople," *The Works of the VIth Archaeological Congress at Odessa* [1884] (Odessa,

As I have noted above, at the top of the panel there is a Greek inscription which Dalton translates as, "Receive these gifts, and having learned the cause . . ." The beginning of this inscription was evidently carved on the second lost leaf. In connection with his fanciful interpretation of our ivory, which I have briefly summarized above, Stuhlfauth gives his own unacceptable translation: "Receive me, even if thou knowest my trespasses." [6] The translation of this fragmentary inscription, without the end, can only be tentative, so long as we are not aware of the exact meaning of the ivory itself. The word of the inscription παρόντα without the article may be read τὰ παρόντα or τὸν παρόντα, i.e., receive either the objects which the Archangel offers, or the Archangel himself. It is more natural to accept the first reading τὰ παρόντα, and to interpret this word as offerings, gifts, or certain emblems, symbols, which should have been explained in the second lost leaf. Of course, the correct meaning of the παρόντα in the inscription depends on the correct interpretation of our ivory as a whole, which in my opinion has not yet been made.

Almost all previous studies had dealt with two questions: either with the style and artistic beauty of our ivory, or with its dating. And in neither of these subjects have the scholars and critics come to a definite conclusion. As far as the style of the ivory and its origin are concerned, the ivory has been connected with the schools of Syria (Antioch), Alexandria, and Constantinople. As for the dating, numerous attempts of various scholars have clearly shown that it is not easy to determine its date with precision. It seems that before the years 1896–1897, when Stuhlfauth wrote his books, many scholars had attributed the ivory to the sixth century. After citing several names, Stuhlfauth stated: "now all the scholars agree that the British tablet with the archangel belongs to the first half of the sixth century." [7] A certain chronological vacillation is to be noticed in the twentieth century, when scholars have ascribed our ivory to the period from the fourth century to the begin-

---

1887), p. 116. E. Ryedin, His review of E. Molinier's book, in *Vizantisky Vremennik*, IV (1897), 212. Both in Russian.

[6] Dalton, *Catalogue of Early Christian Antiquities*, pp. 53–54. Stuhlfauth, *Die altchristliche Elfenbeinplastik*, p. 174.

[7] Stuhlfauth, *Die altchristliche Elfenbeinplastik*, p. 175. To the names mentioned by him I may add the name of N. P. Kondakov, *op. cit.*, p. 116.

Solidus of Justin I. Gold.

ning of the seventh, and there are various proponents of this view. In 1901, Dalton wrote that our ivory belongs to that early period of Byzantine art in which the reigns of Theodosius and Justinian stand out so conspicuously; in 1909, he said that the diptych may have been made perhaps as early as the fourth century, though to some critics the sixth century appears a more probable date; in 1911, he wrote: "It seems quite possible that this fine work may belong, as Graeven held, to about the time of Theodosius, though others assign it to the fifth, or even to the sixth century"; finally in 1925, he apparently modified his statements saying that it appears to date from the fifth century.[8] So during the twenty-four years since his above statements have come out, Dalton has not committed himself to any definite century; but we may say that he was in favor of the fourth or fifth century. In 1925, Diehl assigned the ivory to the sixth century. In 1929, Delbrueck gave "about 400"; but in 1930, the critic of his work, Weigand, rejecting his date, was in favor of attributing our ivory to the beginning of the sixth century. In 1934, Peirce and Tyler, basing their argument on the oral statements of Professors Morey and Friend, were inclined to ascribe the ivory to the sixth or even to the seventh century. In 1940, Kitzinger wrote that the Archangel relief is hardly earlier that A.D. 500. In 1942, Morey asserted a date at least as late as the fifth century and not far from the sixth. In 1947, Miss Loos-Dietz, dating our ivory from the sixth century, finds a certain analogy between the latter and the diptych of 525 of Philoxenus.[9]

Now, before turning to the ivory itself, I wish to indicate an essential change on the coinage of Justin I, which Professor A. M. Friend, Princeton University, has recently pointed out, revealing some connection between the new type inaugurated on Justin's coinage and the

[8] O. Dalton, *Catalogue of Early Christian Antiquities*, p. 53; *Catalogue of the Ivory Carvings*, p. 10; *Byzantine Art and Archaeology*, p. 202; *East Christian Art*, p. 210.

[9] Diehl, *Manuel*, I, 296. R. Delbrueck, *Die Consulardiptychen und verwandte Denkmäler*, p. 28. E. Weigand, "Zur spätantiken Elfenbeinskulptur," *Kritische Berichte zur Kunstgeschichtlichen Literatur*, 1930–31, 2 (Leipzig), p. 56. Peirce and Tyler, *L'art byzantin*, II, 75. E. Kitzinger, *Early Medieval Art in the British Museum* (London, 1940), p. 24. Morey, *Early Christian Art*, p. 90. Elizabeth Petronella de Loos-Dietz, *Vroeg-Christelijke Ivoren* (Assen, 1947), p. 161. I am greatly indebted to Professor Ernst Kitzinger, Dumbarton Oaks, Harvard University, who called my attention to this book as well as to Weigand's review.

archangel on our ivory. Friend's penetrating observation is of momentous significance for my study. According to him, during Justin's reign the Byzantine coinage passed through a very essential transformation.

It is on the reverse of the solidi of this period that the high-girdled standing female figure of Victory used in the preceding reigns is transformed into the frontal archangel clad in the usual male attire with the tunic and pallium. This new figure of the angel of Victory becomes the usual reverse of the coins of his nephew, Justinian. The type retains the old inscription VICTORIA AUG., appropriate for the female Victory, as well as the cross and staff held in the right hand (cf. W. Wroth, *The Catalogue of the Imperial Coins in the British Museum* [London, 1908], I, plates I, II, and IV; I. Tolstoy, *Byzantine Coins* [St. Petersburg, 1913], III, plates 16 and 18). The angel, however, also holds a globe surmounted by a cross. The famous and beautiful ivory in the British Museum which represents an archangel holding a staff in his left hand and a cross-surmounted globe in his right, and standing on the steps of an arched doorway under a panel with the Greek inscription + ΔΕΧΟΥ ΠΑΡΟΝΤΑ | ΚΑΙ ΜΑΘΩΝ ΤΗΝ ΑΙΤΙΑΝ (Receive these gifts and having learned the cause . . .) [10] should have some connection, according to Professor Friend, with the type inaugurated on Justin's coinage. Since the gift of the cross-surmounted globe and staff can most appropriately be made only to an emperor, the panel requires an ivory counterpart representing a standing portrait of an emperor to complete the diptych. The date of the ivories then, because of the iconography of the coin types mentioned above, would most reasonably be placed in the reign of Justin I or in that of his nephew, Justinian; so the imperial portrait depicted on the lost panel could have been either of these two emperors. The softness of the style would favor the earlier emperor Justin I, as Professor Friend believes.[11]

It is rather surprising that so far, if I am not mistaken, no one has yet attempted to find out the circumstances which may have suggested the idea of making our beautiful piece which, from the fineness of its

[10] See above, n. 6.
[11] See above, pp. 384–385.

style, as I have just pointed out, may be, with great probability, assigned to the reign of Justin I (518–527).

If we examine our panel attentively, we see at once that it is not a leaf of a diptych which announces a war victory, nor is it connected with the war in general. What is most noticeable is the peaceful atmosphere of the whole scenery. The two crosses — one within the scallop above the head of the archangel, the other upon the globe which he holds in the right hand — express clearly the idea of the domination of the Christian faith all over the world. Taking into consideration the religious character of the whole scene, we may conclude that the diptych in its entirety was made to glorify an event of momentous importance for the religious life of the empire. The unusual inscription which was to explain the cause (τὴν αἰτίαν) of making the diptych, the cause which was carved on the second lost leaf, also indicates that something new, unusual, and important, which needed to be explained, should be solemnly announced.

What was the central event of Justin's reign? It was, without any doubt, the union or reunion with Rome, which was signed in Constantinople, in the presence of the papal delegates, on Maundy Thursday in Holy Week, March 28, 519. Peaceful relations were reëstablished with Rome, and the break between the Eastern and Western Churches, dating back to the time of Zeno's *Henoticon* (482), came to an end. It was the moment when Easter Sunday, March 31, 519, and the holidays of the Easter Week took place in an atmosphere of religious elation and mutual satisfaction because the reunion between the two Romes had been achieved. It was the time when from the far West, the Bishop of Vienna on the Rhone, Avitus, sent the Patriarch of Constantinople his congratulations on the restoration of peace with the Roman bishop as a symbol of what the two Apostolic Princes should grant to the world. "Who among those who may be called catholics," Avitus continues, "would not rejoice at the peace between such great churches, at which the world looks as at a double star fixed in the heaven like a sign of faith." [12] The cause (ἡ αἰτία) of the appearance of the diptych was the solemn announcement of the fact that the

---

[12] *Aviti Viennensis Epistolae*, Migne, P.L., LIX, col. 228 (ep. VII); ed. R. Peiper (Berlin, 1883), ep. IX (7), p. 43. MGH, *Auctores antiquissimi*, VI.

unity of Christianity had been reëstablished all over the world, all over the universe. And the archangel on our tablet brings and proclaims this wonderful news to Justin, whose figure should have been represented on the second lost leaf of the diptych.

It is, of course, impossible to restore the exact beginning of the inscription which was carved on the lost left leaf. But without doubt, there was the address to an emperor, in our case, to Justin, who was probably qualified something like "restorer of the Christian faith in the world." The second part of the inscription which has been preserved, would be a perfectly fitting sequence to such a tentative text of the first part of the inscription. Only the conjunction καί and the participle μαθών, in the second part, seem to indicate that the sentence is not complete.

Our ivory, then, was a manifestation of the general exaltation and exuberant joy of the Christian world at the moment of, or shortly after the conclusion of the union, when difficulties and complications connected with putting into effect the provisions of the act of the union were not anticipated, or were minimized, or were not yet earnestly felt.

The union of 519 was established on condition of immediate and absolute recognition of the decrees of the Chalcedonian Council within the whole territory of the empire. In other words, Justin fundamentally changed the religious policy followed by his two predecessors, Zeno and Anastasius, who had been in favor of monophysitism. Justin's new policy alienated the eastern provinces of the empire, Syria and Egypt, which held on firmly to their monophysite doctrine; so that, a few years after 519, the empire was lacerated by religious difficulties, dissension, disputes, and persecutions against the monophysites and other dissidents. But in 519 and during a few following years, Justin's government made an attempt at religious leniency towards various dissidents, hoping in this way to reconcile them to the new trend. Our tablet must have been made in this period, at all events before the later years of Justin's reign, when the government, disappointed in its conciliatory trend, entered upon the policy of coercion and persecution which culminated in 527 in the issue of the famous edict against heretics. The turbulent period of Justin's last years could not be an appropriate moment for our panel, which is a symbol of peace and tranquillity.[13]

Referring to my statement that our panel represents the idea of an emperor as the Christian lord over the whole world, one may explain how he who strictly followed the Chalcedonian credo could at the same time be the lord of the countries lying outside the official boundaries of the empire which failed to accept the Council of Chalcedon. But it is not to be forgotten that outside the boundaries of his empire the Byzantine *basileus* was the protector of Christianity in general, no matter whether the neighboring countries subscribed to his religious dogma or not. In this way we must explain the friendly relations between Byzantium and Abyssinia under Justin, the one country orthodox (Chalcedonian) and frequently taking the offensive, the other monophysite.[14]

The same idea of the Byzantine emperor as the Christian lord over the world may be traced in the correspondence from Justin's period between Constantinople and Rome. Here are some examples. In his letter to Pope Hormisdas, April 22, 519, John, the Patriarch of Constantinople, points out among other things three achievements of Justin during the first year of his rule: "First he has manifestly displayed a brilliant victory in his struggle against the defeated enemy;[15] the second merit of his virtue: he has most wisely prepared the union of the holiest churches; the third blessing of his reign: he has joined what had been spread abroad, and has most wisely taken care of the peace of the world." [16]

In his congratulatory letter to the members of his legation in Constantinople, July 9, 519, Pope Hormisdas urges the legates with the help of Christ, of the most clement Emperor, and of his wife, the most pious Augusta, to act in such a way that all churches, no matter in

[13] On Justin's religious policy see above.

[14] See A. Vasiliev, "Justin I (518–527) and Abyssinia," *Byz. Zeitschrift*, XXXIII (1933), 72.

[15] Here the patriarch has in view the suppression of the plot just after Justin's elevation.

[16] *Epistulae imperatorum pontificum aliorum inde ab a. CCCLXVII usque ad a. DLIII datae Avellana quae dicitur collectio*, ed. O. Günther, II (Vienna, 1898), no. 161 (p. 612). *CSEL*, vol. XXXV. A. Thiel, *Epistolae romanorum pontificum genuinae*, I (Brunsbergae, 1868), no. 67 (pp. 862–864). Mansi, VIII, pp. 457–458. Baronius, *Annales*, year 519, pp. 60–62.

what part of the world they are located, may be recalled to communion with the Apostolic See.[17]

In addition, I wish to quote a passage from Pope Hormisdas' letter to Justin, dated March 25 or 26, 521. When we read this passage, the figure of the archangel on our panel comes immediately to our mind. But I must admit that it is quite possible that this is but a mere coincidence, preventing us from being certain about the connection between this passage and the ivory. The passage runs as follows: "The peace which Jesus Christ gave his disciples, the world has found through you. There is no doubt that the heavenly angels congratulate you." [18]

To sum up, our ivory could not be made before March 28, 519, when the union with Rome was signed. It had been made shortly after the union, when the feeling of joy and elation still prevailed. It may have been made before the death of Pope Hormisdas (August 6, 523), during whose pontificate the union had been signed. The ivory was made in Constantinople. The important change on Justin's coinage, which I have described above, was also due to the fact of the union. In this way, Byzantine art and Byzantine numismatics have jointly and beautifully recorded the central fact of the reign of Justin I, the reunion between Rome and Constantinople, between the Old and the New Romes.

[17] *Coll. Avellana*, no. 170 (p. 627). Thiel, no. 87 (pp. 884–885). Mansi, vol. VIII, p. 468. Baronius, *s.a.* 519, p. 77 (text itself not reproduced).
[18] "Nam pacem, quam ille discipulis dedit, per te mundus invenit. Non est dubium congratulari tibi angelos caeli." *Coll. Avell.*, no. 238 (p. 735, ll. 6–8). Thiel, no. 140 (p. 968). Mansi, vol. VIII, p. 518. Baronius, *s.a.* 521, pp. 7–14.

INDEX

ABBREVIATIONS FREQUENTLY USED

CIG	*Corpus inscriptionum Graecarum*, ed. August Boeckh
CIL	*Corpus inscriptionum Latinarum*
CSCO	*Corpus scriptorum christianorum orientalium*
CSEL	*Corpus scriptorum ecclesiasticorum Latinorum*
CSHB	*Corpus scriptorum historiae Byzantinae*
FHG	*Fragmenta historicorum Graecorum*, ed. C. Muller
Mansi	*Conciliorum Collectio*
MGH	*Monumenta Germaniae historica*
Migne PG or PL	*Patrologiae cursus completus*, ed. J. P. Migne: *Patrologia Latina*, 221 vols.; *Patrologia Graeca*, 161 vols.
PSRL	*Polnoe Sobranie Russkikh Letopisey* (*Complete Collection of Russian Annals*)
PW	Pauly-Wissowa, *Real-Encyclopädie*

INDEX OF NAMES AND SUBJECTS

429

INDEX

Arius, 155
Armenia, 3, 133, 231, 254, 301, 357
Artaxata, city, 357–359
Asclepius, Bishop of Edessa, 233, 236–238
Asia, province, 202
Asia Minor, 3, 203, 225, 254, 345, 358, 386
Assemani, 235, 278, 281, 285
Asterius, Patriarch of Alexandria (?), 285, 295, 298
Athalaric, Theodoric's grandson, 323, 325, 334–336
Athenaeus, writer, 357
Attila, 64, 286, 306
Augoflada, Theodoric's wife, 321
Aulona (Valona), 173, 215
Aurelian, emperor, 43
Avitus, bishop, 177–178, 197, 213, 342
Axiux (Vardar) River, 56, 64
Axum, city, 289, 292, 300, 370

Balami (Belami), Tabari's translator, 35
Balearic Isles, 3, 353
Balkan Peninsula, 3, 4, 43–44, 48, 50, 110, 173, 305–307, 309, 344–345, 349, 353, 355–356, 387
Bardenhewer, O., scholar, 17, 20, 66
Bardy, G., church historian, 295
Bar Hebraeus (see Abul Faradj)
Baronius, cardinal, 166–167, 248, 295
Barthold, W., scholar, 35
Basil I, emperor, 416–417
Basil II, emperor, 405–406
Basil of Seleucia, writer, 119
Baumstark, A., 23, 26, 28–30, 32, 37, 352
Baynes, N. H., scholar, 76, 132, 262
Bederiana, 53–59, 89
Beirut, 18
Beliaev, D. T., scholar, 73
Belisarius, general, 99, 127, 271–272
Beronice, town, 294–295, 367
Bessi, people, 48–49
Besta, E., historian, 337
Bezold, C., scholar, 33, 300–301
Bigleniza (Vigilantia), 59–63
Black Sea, 3, 254, 257–258, 307, 312, 357–358
Blandus, priest, papal legate, 170
Blemyes, African people, 41–42, 285–288, 295
Blemyomachia, 42, 285–286

Blues, the faction, 110–112; at Justin's elevation, 70–71, 76–77, 107; and Justin, 117–121
Boeckh, A., scholar, 41
Boethius, 325, 328, 333
Bolotov, V., church historian, 137, 177, 209–211
Boor, Carl de, scholar, 13–14
Borghesi, B., scholar, 126–128
Bosporus, 250, 270, 312–313, 356, 382
Bostra, city, 363
Bratianu, G., historian, 412
Bréhier, L., historian, 7, 19, 220, 331
Brockelmann, C., scholar, 35–36
Brooks, E. W., scholar, 23–27, 30, 32, 230
Brosset, M., scholar, 39, 257
Browne, E. G., scholar, 35
Brundisium, 173
Bryce, J., scholar, 22, 47, 61, 100
Buckler, F. W., scholar, 133–134
Budge, E. A. Wallis, 29, 31, 33, 300–301
Bulgaria, 387
Bulgarians, 306
Burckhardt, A., scholar, 39
Burgundians and Burgundian kingdom, 3, 41, 318, 341–343
Bury, J. B., historian, 7, 10, 17, 22, 47, 50, 65, 81–82, 86, 93, 95, 97, 103, 134, 216–217, 223, 248, 254, 259, 262, 279, 285–286, 295, 298, 306, 319, 321, 328–329, 331, 340, 375, 401–402, 411
Byzantium, 269, 272, 282, 298–299, 315–316, 322, 331, 341, 357, 362, 377

Caesarea (Palestinian), 149
Caesarius of Nazianzus, writer, 305–306
Callinicum, 31, 278, 359
Cappadocia, 226, 231, 316
Caracalla, emperor, 361
Caramallus, dancer, 111–112
Carinus, *comes*, 348–349
Carthage, 330, 339–340
Carus, emperor, 43
Caspar, E., church historian, 162, 189, 202, 208, 214, 220
Caspian Gates, 277, 316
Caspian Sea, 314
Cassiodorus, 20, 319–321, 323–325, 335
Caucasus, 250, 269
Cedrenus, chronicler, 15, 221

430

INDEX

INDEX

INDEX

INDEX

Jerusalem, in Kebra Nagast, 33, 201, 203–204, 301; Council at, 36; Synod at (518), 148–149

Jews, 246–247, 252, 301, 326, 371

Jireček, C., historian, 51, 59, 308–309, 311

John, bishop, papal legate, 170

John II, patriarch, 91, 145–146, 148, 150–151, 154, 156, 158–159, 163, 175, 177, 179, 188, 211, 218, 222; his death, 197; at Justin's elevation, 71, 79; letters to the Pope, 165; at the meeting of July 15, 135–140

John, Patriarch of Jerusalem, 148

John I, pope, 329–330, 334; his death, 219–220; voyage to Constantinople, 212–221

John Catholicos, Armenian historian, 39

John Chrysostom, 98

John Malalas, chronicler, 12–14, 33, 83, 103, 117, 123, 235, 255, 263, 363; on the earthquake at Antioch, 345–350; on Vitalian, 110–112

John Psaltes, hymn-writer, 30

John of Antioch, chronicler, 13, 67

John of Ephesus, 22–23, 30, 32, 161, 222, 230–231, 235–236, 238–239, 241–242, 315–316; and flood at Edessa, 350–351; on Theodora, 97–100

John of Nikiu, historian, 32–33, 83, 117, 240, 260, 265

John of Ptolemais, bishop, 156

John (Ioannes) of Tella, 31, 231

John the Khuzibites, bishop, 149

Jouguet, P., historian, 285

Jovian, emperor, 360

Jugie, M., church historian, 146, 208–209

Julian of Halicarnassus, 228

Justin II, emperor, 22, 62–63, 384

Justinian the Great, 71, 199f.; birthplace, 52–59; career, 91–96; coinage, 383; consulship, 344, 376; family, 59–63; legislation, 391–392; racial origin, 43–52; religious policy, 223; wedding gifts, 399; and adjectio sterilium, 410; and Amantius' plot, 102–108; and barbarian invasions, 354; and Greek sources, 9–18; and heretics, 241–250; and Hormisdas, 162–165, 168–171, 179, 183; and Justin, 3–6; and Latin

sources, 19–22; and monasticism, 252–253; and Rescript of 527, 407–408; and Scolarians, 401–402; and Scythian monks, 192–197; and Slavs, 309–311; and Syriac sources, 22f.; and Theodora, 98–101; and treaty with Persia, 272; and Vitalian, 108–113, 121, 135, 160

Justiniana Prima, 53, 59

Justiniana Secunda, 54

Justinopolis, 56, 351

Kaleb, King of Ethiopia, 33, 291, 294, 302

Kaoses, Persian prince, 265–266

Karlowa, jurist, 408–409

Kawad, King of Persia, 122, 255, 259, 269–270, 273, 277, 285, 315, 317, 359

Kebra Nagast (The Glory of the Kings), 33, 299–301

Khomyakov, A., 302

Kiracos of Gantzac, Armenian historian, 39

Kleyn, H. G., scholar, 31, 226, 231

Kondakov, N. P., scholar, 73, 89

Koukoules, P., scholar, 417

Kraeling, C., scholar, 361

Krüger, G., scholar, 24

Krueger (Krüger), Paul, scholar, 40, 390

Krumbacher, Karl, 10, 18

Kuban River, 314

Kugener, M.-A., scholar, 30, 227

Kulakovsky, J., historian, 7, 64, 91–92, 209, 257, 273, 312

Kunik, A., scholar, 44–45

Lakhmids, in Irak, 254, 274–275, 277, 290

Lamansky, V., scholar, 45, 304

Land, J. P. N., scholar, 23–24

Langlois, V., scholar, 28

Laurent, V., church historian, 146

Lazica, 251, 255–269, 315–316, 357

Lebeau, C., historian, 7, 257

Lebedev, A., church historian, 209–210

Lebon, J., church historian, 224, 241

Lefebvre, G., scholar, 41

Leo I, emperor, 63–64, 66, 79–80, 202, 261, 365–366, 401

Leo II, emperor, 80

Leo VI, emperor, 415–417

INDEX

INDEX

Nicaea, council, 142–144, 147, 155
Nicephorus Callistus Xanthopulos, historian, 12, 15
Nicephorus Phocas, emperor, 405
Nicholas Mesarites, writer, 417
Nicomedia, mint, 383, 388
Nicostratus, bishop, 188–189
Niederle, L., scholar, 49, 309, 311
Nika, riot, 60
Nisibis, 133, 267, 272, 359–360
Nobadae (Nubians), African people, 41, 285–289, 295
Nöldeke, T., scholar, 34, 268
Nonnosus, historian, 279
Noricum, 334
Notitia Dignitatum, 55, 275
Nubians (*see* Nobadae)

Odovacar, 318–320
Olybrius, consul, 345
Olympic games, 119–120, 382
Onogurs, Hunnic tribe, 313–314
Ortalinus, Flavius, Governor of Lydia, 410
Ostrogorsky, G., historian, 84
Ostrogoths and Ostrogothic kingdom, 3, 64, 318–337
Orontes, river, 273

Palace of Hormisdas, 377
Palestine, 3–4, 136, 158, 225, 247, 252, 360, 379, 385, 412–413
Palmyra, 41, 274–275, 363
Pamphylia, 408–409
Pančenko, B., 95, 101, 413
Pannonia, 334
Paternus, Bishop of Tomi, 190–191, 203
Patricius, senator, 106–107, 171, 174
Paul, Bishop of Edessa, 224, 233–234, 238
Paul of Antioch, bishop, 206, 235–236, 239
Paul of Samosata, 155
Paul of Sarug, 234
Paulus Diaconus, chronicler, 221
Peeters, P., scholar, 26, 30, 235
Peloponnesus, 338
Pereira, F. M. E., scholar, 301
Perozes (Firuz), Persian king, 317
Persarmenia, 271, 277, 357
Persia, 232, 254, 282, 290–291, 316, 357, 373; and Lazica, 255–268

Persian Gulf, 17, 361, 368–369
Peter, Bishop of Iotabe, 365
Peter, notary, papal legate, 170, 173
Peter of Apamea, bishop, 159–160, 229
Peter of Jerusalem, 250
Peter the Fuller, monophysite, 190
Peter the Patrician, historian, 11; on Justin's elevation, 69–75; on Justinian's elevation, 95–96
Peter Sabbatius (Justinian's name), 92–93
Petra, 230, 363
Pfeilschifter, G., historian, 208, 215, 218, 331, 341
Pharsan, islands, 367
Phasis River, 257–258
Philae, island, 287
Philippici, monastery, 417
Philippopolis, 228
Philoxenus, consul, 108; his diptych, 124–125
Philoxenus-Xenaia, bishop, 228–229
Phocas, emperor, 43
Phoenicia Maritima, 231
Photius, patriarch, 9, 197, 367
Phrygia, 248
Pigulevskaya, N., scholar, 23, 29, 281
Pillars of Hercules, 318
Pomialovsky, J., scholar, 15
Pompeius, nephew of Anastasius, 175, 180, 183
Pompioupolis, in Mysia, 349, 376
Pontus, 202
Porphyrius, charioteer, 111–112, 120–121
Possessor, African bishop, 195–196
Probus, Anastasius's nephew, 250, 270, 313, 315, 382
Probus, emperor, 43
Proclus (Proculus), quaestor, 82, 114, 121–122, 266–267, 391, 402–403
Procopius of Caesarea, 10–11, 44, 48, 75, 265–266, 268–269, 272, 275–276, 278, 288, 292, 297, 309–311, 352, 354, 356, 358, 364, 366, 372, 375, 382, 395, 410; on Amantius's plot, 102–103, 107–108; on the Arians, 326; on Bosporus, 312–313; on the Ephthalites, 314, 316–317; on the flood at Edessa, 351; on Iberia, 271; on Iotabe, 365; on Justin's age, 85; on Justin's birthplace, 52–55; on Justin's career, 66–67; on Justin's

INDEX

family, 60–62; on Justin's illiteracy,
82–84; on prediction of Justin's elevation, 88; on Lazica, 257–259; on the
Montanists, 248; on Philae, 287; on
Proclus, 122; on Theodora, 97–101;
on Theodoric, 213, 320, 328, 332, 336;
on the Vandals, 338–339; on Vitalian,
113
Pseudo-Dorotheus, of Tyre, 217
Pulcheria, wife of the emperor Marcian, 377
Pullio, imperial envoy to Rome, 181

Raetia, 334
Rambaud, A., historian, 46
Ramlah, 280, 282–283, 292, 297
Ranke, L., 47
Ravenna, 214, 219–220, 322–326, 328–333,
339
Red Sea, 295, 361–363, 367, 370–371
Reiske, J., scholar, 415
Rhine River, 318
Rhodes, 338
Roby, H. J., jurist, 46
Roesler, R., scholar, 49
Romano, G., historian, 327–328, 331
Romanus Melodus, 18
Rome, 132, 301; council in 518, 166–168;
Scythian monks in, 192–196
Romein, J., historian, 383
Rosen, V., baron, scholar, 35
Runciman, S., historian, 10, 81
Russia, 302, 304–305, 314, 356
Russian Chronicles, 37–38
Rusticus, Roman deacon, 249

Sabas, St., 15, 149, 252–253, 412–413
Sabatier, J., numismatist, 383
Sabbatius, Justinian's father, 44, 46, 60–
63
Saint-Martin, M. J., scholar, 39
Salvianus, writer, 337
Samaritans, 244, 247, 326
Sandars, T. C., translator, 40
Sapaudia (Savoy), 341
Saracens (Scenites), 360
Sapor III, king, 357
Sarapanis (Sarapa), fortress, 270
Sardica (now Sofia), 103
Sardinia, 3, 194, 337–338, 353
Sava River, 309, 312

Scampae (now Elbasan), city, 106, 173–
174
Schanz, M., scholar, 20
Scholarians, 401–402
Schröter, R., scholar, 25, 30
Schubert, H. von, church historian, 207
Schwartz, Eduard, scholar, 15, 191, 366
Sclavenes, 305–306, 309–312
Scupus (Scupi), 54–58
Scythia Minor (now Dobrudja), 108–
109, 190, 197
Scythian Monks, 190–197, 201, 203, 223
Scythians, 306, 308
Scythopolis (Palestine), 149, 379–380
Sea of Marmora, 307
Seeck, O., historian, 55, 64
Seleucia Pieria, 230, 349
Senate, 75, 79, 94, 252, 312, 414; at
Justin's elevation, 70ff.
Seoses, Persian official, 267–268
Sergius, archbishop, 65, 89
Sergius, Bishop of Resapha, 15, 279
Severus, Patriarch of Antioch, 109–110,
133–136, 138–141, 145, 147, 150, 153,
155, 158–159, 203, 226–228, 248
Seybold, C. F., scholar, 37
Shafarik (Šafarik), P. J., scholar, 44
Shakhmatov, A., scholar, 311
Shishmanov, historian, 305
Sicily, 3, 334, 337–338, 353
Sigismund, Burgundian king, 213, 321,
325, 342–343
Silko, "kinglet" of the Nubians, 41, 286
Simeon of Beth-Arsham, 17, 23, 31, 278,
280–282
Simeon of Gabbula, 23, 281–282
Sinai (Sinaitic Peninsula), 17, 364–365,
368
Singara, town, 360
Sirmium (Mitrovica), city, 43, 64
Sittas, commander, 271
Skanda (Skende), fortress, 270
Skok, P., scholar, 48, 57
Slavs, 4, 243, 302–312, 354
Solomon, 299–301
Sopatros, trader, 370–371
Sophia, wife of Justin II, 92
Spain, 334, 338
Spinka, M., historian, 13, 63
Sreznevsky, V., scholar, 14
Starr, J., historian, 41

INDEX

INDEX